Lecture Notes in Artificial Intelligence 599

Subseries of Lecture Notes in Computer Science
Edited by J. Siekmann

Lecture Notes in Computer Science
Edited by G. Goos and J. Hartmanis

Th. Wetter K.-D. Althoff J. Boose
B. R. Gaines M. Linster F. Schmalhofer (Eds.)

Current Developments in Knowledge Acquisition – EKAW '92

6th European Knowledge Acquisition Workshop
Heidelberg and Kaiserslautern, Germany,
May 18-22, 1992
Proceedings

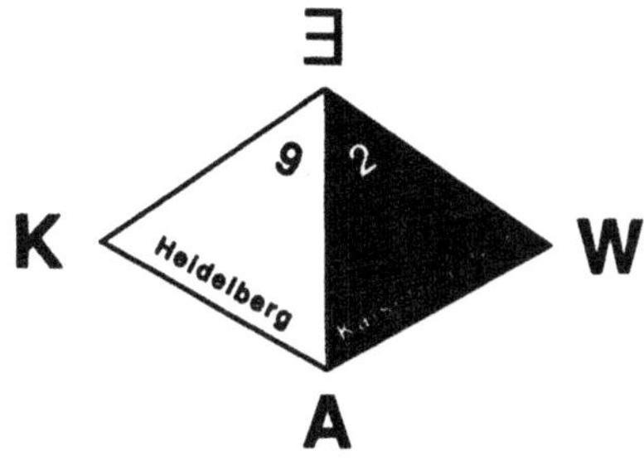

Springer-Verlag
Berlin Heidelberg New York
London Paris Tokyo
Hong Kong Barcelona
Budapest

Series Editor

Jörg Siekmann
University of Saarland
German Research Center for Artificial Intelligence (DFKI)
Stuhlsatzenhausweg 3, W-6600 Saarbrücken 11, FRG

Volume Editors

Thomas Wetter
IBM Germany, Scientific Center
Wilckensstraße 1a, W-6900 Heidelberg, FRG

Klaus-Dieter Althoff
University of Kaiserslautern, Dept. of Computer Science
P. O. Box 30 49, W-6750 Kaiserslautern, FRG

John Boose
Computer Science Organization, Boeing Computer Services
P. O. Box 24346, 7L-64, Seattle, WA 98124, USA

Brian R. Gaines
Knowledge Science Institute, University of Calgary
2500 University Dr. NW, Calgary, Alberta T2N 1 N4, Canada

Marc Linster
German National Research Center for Computer Science (GMD)
P. O. Box 13 16, W-5205 Sankt Augustin 1, FRG

Franz Schmalhofer
German Research Center for Artificial Intelligence
P. O. Box 20 80, W-6750 Kaiserslautern, FRG

CR Subject Classification (1991): I.2.4-6, I.2.8

ISBN 3-540-55546-3 Springer-Verlag Berlin Heidelberg New York
ISBN 0-387-55546-3 Springer-Verlag New York Berlin Heidelberg

Printed in Germany

Typesetting: Camera ready by author/editor
Printing and binding: Druckhaus Beltz, Hemsbach/Bergstr.
45/3140-543210 - Printed on acid-free paper

Preface

Methodological knowledge acquisition and knowledge engineering have achieved increasing attention over the last years due to both active research projects and successful practical applications. Both aspects have over the years been reflected in the structure of the ***European Knowledge Acquisition Workshops*** (EKAW), where a users' forum has always been combined with a scientific workshop.

Knowledge acquisition workshops also take place annually in North America (the "Banff" workshops) and Asia or Australia. Intense interaction between these communities, reflected in international conference attendance, shared authorship from different continents, and international program committees guarantees fast exchange and critical review of results, whereas the participation of practitioners in the scientific exchange and of scientists in practical projects enhances technology transfer.

All these elements can be found in this volume. Therefore it seems worthwhile not merely to distribute it as selected collection of isolated papers but to provide at least a rough and partly subjective map of the field as it can be presented in March 1992 on the basis of the texts included.

First of all we find a clear segmentation into extended abstracts of the invited speakers of the users' forum and into full papers to be presented at the scientific workshop. This distinction on the one hand reflects the "research notes" character of the Lecture Notes in Artificial Intelligence: the main purpose of fast communication of original research is captured by these full papers. On the other hand the strongly application oriented character of the field of knowledge acquisition qualifies short analyses about the need and impact of knowledge acquisition (KA) in high-tech industries (Allard[1]), project management for KA projects (Killin), the European marketplace for methodological KA (Georges), and an assessment of the industrial use of machine learning (Morik) as highly valuable supporting and directing evidence to be published together with front end research results.

As far as research contributions are concerned the European map is increasingly dotted with *general modelling approaches* which make up the second section of the book and to a considerable extent are also present in contributions in other sections (Jonker, Neubert, Dieng, Allemang, Porter). Their common underlying

---

[1] In the preface, contributions are indicated only by first author's name for the sake of readability.

principle is to be based on an explicit abstract humanly perceivable model of the expertise to be captured for a knowledge based system. The most influential modelling approach presently is KADS, which also plays a role in several of the papers included.

Eriksson generalizes Musen's work of generating domain-specific knowledge acquisition tools. Greboval presents a method of compiling efficient code from KADS conceptual models. Linster complements the KADS paradigm of starting analysis with the problem solving behavior by using tools that equally support the static relations of a domain as starting point for modelling. Gappa provides an in-depth comparison of two strategically different approaches to modelling that have both been pursued over the years: strong modelling approaches (such as her own expansions of Puppe's work) require close correspondence between a model of the domain and of the problem solving behavior and allow fast transition to operational representations whereas weak modelling (such as KADS) assumes the applicability of problem solving models to deliberate domain structures. In the latter case the type of connection has to be specified as part of the modelling process. The contributions of Schreiber and van Heijst specify two aspects within the KADS research program: Schreiber provides a detailed analysis of two similar diagnostic problem solving methods and how formal representation allows one to clearly identify distinctions. Van Heijst describes details and theory based tool support for the process of further specifying roughly specified models of problem solving ("interpretation models"). Finally, Geelen uses formal models as an objective basis for deriving problem solving models from expert protocols.

The section on *knowledge formalization and automated methods* starts with two of the three full papers in this book about machine learning. Tsujino has enhanced the mechanical induction of decision trees by methods of quality assessment of resulting trees. Nedellec has closely coupled manual acquisition with automated learning in such a way that the validation and maintenance activities based on new cases become a genuine part of the architecture. Schweiger presents a tool based on a logical theory of configuration which allows automated generation of knowledge based systems for the respective subclass of applications. Jonker and Neubert treat special aspects of KADS based modelling. Jonker's formal language for KADS conceptual models emphasizes the aspect of domain signatures that correspond to the models of problem solving and hence comes close to providing a bridge between the above weak and strong modelling approaches. Neubert provides a detailed specification of the activities required to achieve KADS conceptual models.

Elicitation and diagnosis of human knowledge ranges from foundations in theory of science to practical guidelines and tools for knowledge acquisition activities. Nwana provides a possible rationale for the stepwise justified transition from manifestations of expertise towards models in a wider sense than discussed above.

Portman demonstrates productive use of the metaphor of thinking for getting access to those facets of knowledge that are hard to elicit by methods that emphasize a question-response rather than a resolution of conflict view. Larichev differentiates among several settings in the process of eliciting expert classification knowledge. The next two approaches involve tools for elicitation activities. Dieng suggests an architecture where the so far neglected aspects of dealing with multiple experts and of laying the ground for explanation at the beginning of building a system are taken into account. Charlet introduces the additional guidance that can be made use of when a domain is known to be determined by causal relations.

Practice and experiences of knowledge acquisition starts with the subjects of knowledge base maintenance and consistency checking which form important requirements to be met by systems in practice. Accordingly, Maurer describes an extension of Althoff's MOLTKE workbench of which several aspects have already been introduced during the previous EKAWs. Allemang reports on an evaluatory study about how one of the early model based approaches – Chandrasekaran's generic tasks – is applied by practicing knowledge engineers. Porter reports practical experiences in applying KADS elements in similar large scale financial applications. Through his large-scale experiences with machine learning projects, Manago has arrived at the reported enhanced description of cases in order to improve the efficiency of inductive learning as well as to overcome some of its deficiencies by case based reasoning. Schmalhofer's hypermedia based support system unifies the two practical needs of providing easy access to existing industrial case bases and of using them in the development of knowledge based systems. Finally, Bradshaw contributes a large in-house application of modelling business processes for the purpose of better capture of the processes themselves and for computerized support of selected functions.

A total of 65 persons from around the world have done a great job in serving as the program committee. Their recommendations and partly very detailed comments have helped both workshop organizers and individual authors a great deal to achieve the quality that we hope the reader will notice. Their fast and reliable responses have allowed us to hold to the planned schedule in almost every detail. Therefore all the organizers of the conference would like to express their great gratitude to the colleagues listed below.

Tom Addis	University of Reading
Dean Allemang	Ist. Dalle Molle di Studi sull'Intell. Artific., Lugano
Klaus-Dieter Althoff	University of Kaiserlautern
Nathalie Aussenac	ARAMIIHS, Toulouse
John Boose	Boeing Computer Services, Seattle, WA
Guy Boy	ONERA-CERT, Toulouse
Jeff Bradshaw	Boeing Computer Services, Seattle, WA

Ivan Bratko	The Turing Institute, Glasgow
Joost Breuker	University of Amsterdam
Clifford A. Brunk	University of California, Irvine, CA
Steve M. Easterbrook	University of Sussex, Brighton
Henrik Eriksson	Stanford University School of Medicine
Rose Dieng	INRIA - CERMICS, Valbonne
Brian R. Gaines	University of Calgary
Jean Gabriel Ganascia	Institute Blaise Pascal, Université Paris VI
Ute Gappa	Karlsruhe University
Heiner Gertzen	Höchst AG, Frankfurt
Catherine Greboval	Université de Technologie de Compiègne
Thomas Gruber	Stanford University, Palo Alto, CA
Andreas Günter	University of Hamburg
Frank van Harmelen	University of Amsterdam
Koichi Hori	University of Tokyo
Willem Jonker	PTT Research, Groningen
Jonathan Killin	Touche Ross, KBSC, London
Georg Klinker	Digital Equipment Corp., Marlboro, MA
Yves Kodratoff	LRI, University of Paris-Sud and CNRS, Orsay
Jean-Paul Krivine	E.D.F. Direction des Etudes et Recherches, Clamart
Kevin Lano	Lloyd's Register of Shipping, Croydon
Hubert Lehmann	IBM Germany Scientific Center, Heidelberg
Marc Linster	Germ. Res. Inst. f. Math. and Data Proc., St. Augustin
Frank Maurer	University of Kaiserslautern
Riichiro Mizoguchi	Institute of Scientific and Ind. Res., Osaka University
Katharina Morik	University of Dortmund
Hiroshi Motoda	Hitachi Ltd., Hatoyama Saitama
Bernard Moulin	Université Laval, Ste-Foy, Québec
Shogo Nishida	Mitsubishi Electric Corporation, Hyogo
Susanne Neubert	University of Karlsruhe
Hyacinth S. Nwana	University of Keele
Ray Paton	University of Liverpool
Karsten Poeck	University of Karlsruhe
Bruce W. Porter	University of Texas at Austin
Angeliki Poulymenakou	The London School of Economics and Political Science
Frank Puppe	University of Karlsruhe
Thomas E. Rothenfluh	Ohio State University, Columbus, OH
Beate Schlenker	University of Freiburg
Franz Schmalhofer	University of Kaiserslautern
Gabriele Schmidt	University of Kaiserslautern
Guus Schreiber	University of Amsterdam
Johann Schweiger	Technical University of München
Joachim Selbig	Germ. Res. Inst. f. Math. and Data Proc., St. Augustin
Nigel R. Shadbolt	University of Nottingham

Mildred L. G. Shaw	University of Calgary
Ingeborg Sølvberg	Sintef DELAB, Trondheim
Maarten W. van Someren	University of Amsterdam
Marcus Spiess	IBM Germany Scientific Center, Heidelberg
Susan Spirgi	Swiss Bank Corporation, Basel
Werner Stephan	University of Karlsruhe
Hirokazu Taki	Mitsubishi Electric Corporation, Kanagawa
Wolfgang Tank	Technical University of Berlin
Bernd Welz	University of Karlsruhe
Dieter Wenger	Swiss Bank Corporation, Basel
Bob J. Wielinga	University of Amsterdam
J. Brian Woodward	University of Calgary
Nora Yue	University of London
Manuel Zacklad	ONERA, Groupe d'Intelligence Artificielle, Chatillon

Too many more persons and institutions have helped to make EKAW92 a success for all of them to be mentioned here. Nevertheless I cannot close without thanking IBM Germany and my manager Peter Greissl for providing me the liberty to put EKAW92 on top of my agenda whenever necessary. Furthermore I had highly efficient and continuous support from Christine Sperling and Mark Beers of IBM and from my students Simone Bürsner, Ralf Nüse, and Wolfram Schmidt, who never hesitated to assist me when things had to be ready yesterday.

Another special "thank you" goes to Christine Harms, whose experience in organizing conferences took considerable load from my shoulders and prevented me from overseeing important details.

Heidelberg
March 1992

Thomas Wetter
on behalf of the editors

Contents

Technology Transfer

General Modelling Approaches

Knowledge Formalization and Automated Methods

Elicitation and Diagnosis of Human Knowledge

A User's view of current practice and possibilities

Francois Allard

European Space Agency(ESA)
Keplerlaan 1
220 AG Noordwijk, NL

1.0 Introduction

ESA is funding currently a number of knowledge-based system (KBS) projects. All of them are confronted to the knowledge acquisition (KA) problem. The intention of this paper is to present current practice and possibilities as can be found in various projects and to highlight issues and unfulfilled needs. This report is broken down into four main parts:

- the practice of KA across the KBS Life-Cycle illustrated by various projects
- The particular role of technical documentation and its relation with knowledge acquisition
- The emergence of reusable conceptual models
- Issues and Needs

1.1 KBS Life-Cycle and KA

Knowledge Acquisition across the Life-Cycle will be decomposed in a set of tasks and viewed in the perspective of a particular project. These tasks are: knowledge identification, knowledge elicitation, knowledge editing, computer-supported knowledge acquisition.

1.2 EXACT and Knowledge Identification:

EXACT is a model-based diagnostic system meant to support the task of satellite diagnostic and planning. A long part of the project, which is still ongoing has been used to actually identify the knowledge required and adopt the correct representation format. It went from rule-based to model-based diagnostic through several steps. Once this was defined, the knowledge identification task could be performed much more easily. Although this is what should stay an atypical case, many lessons can be derived:

- starting with a pre-conceived idea of what the knowledge should look like creates many unnecessary problems.
- at the same time, predefined conceptual models do help in the identification task. Actually, one must remember that in the KA task one is looking for

knowledge that is useful, i.e. operating knowledge. There experience with many conceptual models helps considerably.

- no formal means of knowledge identification beyond test cases is used and could be useful.

1.3 The Battery Management System and knowledge elicitation

This system is one of the first developed at ESA. It concerns the support to the problem of managing batteries of in-orbit satellites, basically analyzing historical trends to predict battery output. The system was successfully developed to a level of prototype. Knowledge elicitation was used with interview techniques as they are in many of our projects. The questions raised were:

- how can the output from such sessions be maximized. No clear answers are available today. A complete interviewing methodology is still to be defined.
- how to qualify (or train) experts themselves for such tasks. They are not all adequate.

1.4 MARS and Knowledge editing

MARS is a scheduling tool. Its main KA module is composed of a sophisticated object editor. The MARS case is interesting because object editors are becoming standard features of KBSs. Using the tool, with certainly one of the best object editor available at ESA, has shown several aspects:

1. It is possible to standardize the characteristics of an object editor (context sensitive help, local verification, etc.) and that standardization should be pursued.
2. On the other hand Object editors impose an editing environment that is heavy. Users actually often bypass the object editor and write directly in KB files. Nor speed, nor lack of functionality can be here questioned. In this system for reason of coherence of attribute values, the knowledge editor is actually required. We have found that it is the format of the frame editor which seems to be undesired. What users wanted is actually that the KB page provides them with the same functionalities of the object editor while being able to scroll and have constantly at their disposal the detailed view of other objects.

This indeed requires very sophisticated functionalities. It could be argued that users should adapt and they do. But the lesson to us is that KA functions should always allow a very easy jump between the local view and the global view of a knowledge base, in a way mimicking the easiness with which persons actually do that mentally.

1.5 PREVISE and the development of knowledge acquisition module

PREVISE is a system under development meant to support the edition and checking of crew procedures and meant to support the evolution of the procedure concept and of the operations knowledge. Syntax, vocabulary, edition rules, operational knowledge, all is there represented as objects. It can be said that PREVISE knowledge acquisition features are the first example, at ESA, of full blown knowledge acquisition modules, except for machine learning which is not used at ESA for now.

1. The KA module is actually part of the functions of the system and is intended for supporting the evolution of concept and knowledge.
2. Test cases defined include evolution test cases.
3. The KA module does not rely on the shell's own (ProKappa) which is viewed as insufficient.
4. The procedure syntax is variable and since the KB on each procedure is built by "compiling" a procedure's text, it means that:
   a. Text (a very specialized one) is used here as a knowledge acquisition feature
   b. When the syntax is changed the compiler has to change which implies the user is given a means to change it (YACC).
5. there is a syntax editor, a vocabulary editor, a procedure editor as well as a general knowledge editor.
6. the HCI of the KA acquisition module was built using Open Interface, a HCI prototyping tool. It allowed to defined desirable features such as object filters, objects trees, template based editors, dictionaries, etc. We can say that this prototyping approach is here very beneficial because it allows experts and users to understand the KA process.

2.0 Technical Documentation

For an organization such as ESA, documentation is a way of life, not to say the main product. Tremendous quantities of knowledge are stored in documents in a very passive form. In order to exploit better this knowledge ESA has begun two parallel efforts:

1. the evaluation of text analysis tools such as K-Station, based on the KOD approach. K-Station is a very interesting tool. The first one really commercially available based on a solid methodology. Our evaluation concluded that:
   - it does support the task of text analysis whether it is used for interview transcripts or for existing documentation;
   - the concepts manipulated (actions, objects, etc.) are coherent and well-defined

- it allows to slowly accumulate knowledge which can easily transformed into a knowledge base
- it has a few technical drawbacks like the concept of multi-valued attributes is not supported and the notion of instances can only be awkwardly introduced; it does not support the analysis of graphics.
- its user interface suffers from the lack of hypertext capabilities
- the aggregation of different analysis versions (improvements) of the analysis of the same text is not really supported.
- Finally and mostly the process is heavy. It is felt that the cognitive process by which text is analyzed is only partially matched by K-Station. There is a very important work equivalent to understanding the structure of the document and the key concepts (building a semantic network) which is not supported by K-Station. Thus we think K-Station is a limited tool but which in some cases can really be of use. A consultancy study will later this year assess its use for requirements analysis purposes.

2. the development of a number of tools to support the life-cycle of systems and the support the slow gathering of formalized knowledge; these are:
   - PREVISE already mentioned, in which it is foreseen to slowly acquire the operational knowledge used in procedure writing and verification.
   - The RAMS (Reliability, Availability, Maintainability and Safety) initiative where in particular cases of problems and failures are being and will be stored for use in hazard analysis,
   - FSDKO where the transferred of satellite knowledge from development to operations is particularly considered and supported via a set of Hypertext-based tools.

   These are very important developments because they are the first explicit attempts to develop tools before the actual knowledge on new space systems (under development) is available and written in documents. Knowledge Acquisition is seen here as a way to support knowledge formalization (and reuse). These efforts still remain small and can only be considered as experimental.

3.0 Conceptual Models

The experience gathered at ESA allows to safely say that one of the very real way out of the KA bottleneck is the use of pre-defined conceptual models. The term is used here in a loose definition of a pre-defined model of task and domain description, possibly using a predefined knowledge representation.
For example, this is true of the Columbus FDIR (Failure Detection, Isolation and Recovery) which uses a pre-defined diagnostic conceptual model, simple and robust enough to be brought on-board. KA is then reduced to its simplest expression. The experience has been repeated successfully with COMPASS, a system for the diagnostic of payloads. Currently an effort is made to standardize the approach to knowledge-based scheduling tools in the same spirit of providing a reusable conceptual models

4.0 Conclusion: Issues and Needs

The experience so far of knowledge acquisition has shown that there are still many issues and needs not really solved or addressed. Many are mentioned above. The following is a complementary list which concludes this report:

1. This concerns the distance between the expert language and the knowledge engineering language. Although, conceptually, experts clearly manipulate classes, objects, attributes, instances, etc. they do not usually manipulate such abstract notions. We have found that abstraction, although necessary for KBS development, is not useful as a tool. This may seem a trivial problem but we think it is not. First it is a real one, and although it can be helped with some training of the expert or user, this training has to be done every time. But even more important is that knowledge representation (KR) should respect expert terminology and methods of representation. KA modules provide seldom to-day support for basic conceptual tools, used by experts such as decision trees, network diagrams, matrices and tables and general graphics not to mention text analysis support.
2. Experts and documentation use formalization as a tool not as an end, like in AI. This means that the flexibility with which they use conceptual tools such as types, classes, tables, graphs and text is much greater than the one offered by KA tools and KR in general. Moreover, the KA process increases formalization of knowledge beyond what experts and users are familiar with, find comfortable, useful, to the extent that they might oppose it. This was identified as one of the main problems and it is still not clear how it can be solved.
3. In order to greatly facilitate the knowledge acquisition process emphasis should be given to text analysis support, character recognition systems, the development of specific recognition tools for tables, drawings, etc. and the definition of a nomenclature in graphics. These may seem mundane problems but the goal is here to hide the internal representation layer that the machine uses. In the same spirit considerable efforts must be made so that KA modules are defined, labelled and coded in terms of the used knowledge.
4. Increasing the variety and availability of conceptual models at various levels is one way to solve the KA bottleneck: we have shown these are used for that purpose, sometimes inappropriately. Thus what is needed is the following:
   - define the criteria for matching conceptual models with problems
   - define a program of training on various conceptual models.
   - define a structure for managing these repositories.

   There might be considerable know-how in conceptual models and competition is never far away. The proposition is here to allow them to be public (for a fee). ESA is currently working on a plan to define a knowledge repository of knowledge on European satellite payloads. This program of work can only succeed if some of the issues addressed above are solved.

The management and maintenance of an operational KADS system development

Jonathan Killin

The Knowledge-Based Systems Centre, Touche Ross Management Consultants
London, U.K.

Abstract. The Barclaycard *Fraudwatch* knowledge-based system identifies potentially fraudulent transactions on Visa and Mastercard credit cards. It makes use of two generic tasks, *Select* and *Assess*. *Select* reduces the number of transactions to be considered from about one million to about fifty thousand. *Assess* further processes these fifty thousand to arrive at a set of about four hundred accounts, which are output to fraud operations staff for further action. Of these four hundred, about fifteen will eventually turn out to be fraudulent.

Fraudwatch was developed by Touche Ross and Barclays, using the KADS method for knowledge-based system development. It is fully embedded within the Barclaycard suite of business and cardholder programs running on IBM mainframes. *Select* is largely written in COBOL, *Assess* is written in KnowledgeTool™, and the peripherals and communications are written in JCL. Fraudwatch runs daily in batch mode. It saves about thirty percent of pre-status fraud losses on the products to which it is applied.

An initial implementation went live in November 1990. The system has undergone two cycles of knowledge maintenance, in order to adapt performance to organisational changes and changes in business objectives, and to enhance overall performance. Further systems and enhancements are planned during 1992 and 1993, which are intended to deploy Fraudwatch at earlier stages of transaction processing and to look at devolving processing.

creased expectations of a more informatics-mature market. It must be ***comprehensive***, addressing (i) ***V&V***: building the right product (***adequacy and appropriateness***) and building it right (***reliability***), (ii) ***evolution***: building for change, maintainability, (iii) ***interoperability***: with conventional software for ***hybrid system development***, (iv) ***life-cycle vision and control***: process modelling, project management and facilities for cooperative (team)work. It must offer ***computer-based tool support*** for handling knowledge complexity and volume, and for leading into implementation.

The offer around the method and supporting tools must also be complete, ranging from awareness 'campaigns' through seminars and training courses to technical consultancy.

The European Comission's ESPRIT programme has been and is funding various projects that address these KE issues, the most renowned KADS[1]. The industrial element of such a projects' consortia ***propel tangible results*** onto the market place: "original KADS" application have numbered over 30, approximately 20 of which have been carried out under the auspices of Cap Gemini Innovation. KADS industrial-quality ***competition*** in Europe is at the ***methodological level*** and is practically limited to SKE (Bolesian) and KOD (Cisi Ingénierie), while expert system shells are seen solely as upstream experimentation aids.

Nevertheless, it is clear that while the KADS methodology is the most advanced to date, it requires enhancement towards

- ***comprehensiveness***: this is the role of the KADS-II project[2].
- ***industrialization***: this is being addressed by members of the KADS-II consortium who are making available seminars and courses (Cap Gemini Innovation, Lloyd's Register, Touche Ross Management Consultants, ...), methodological guides (e.g. Cap Gemini Sogeti's "PERFORM-KBA"), and tool support (e.g. ILOG/Cap Gemini Innovation's "KADS-TOOL") for the present, operational version of KADS, responding to strong market demand.

---

[1] The partners of KADS project (ESPRIT P1098) were STC Tecnology Ltd. (UK), Cap Sesa Innovation (F), NTE Neutech GmbH (D), SD - SciCon Ltd. (UK), Touche Ross Management Consultants (UK), University of Amsterdam (NL).

[2] The partners of the KADS-II project (ESPRIT P5248) are STC Tecnology Ltd. (UK), Cap Sesa Innovation (F), NTE Neutech GmbH (D), SD - SciCon Ltd. (UK), Touche

Knowledge Engineering Trends in Europe

Mari Georges

Cap Gemini Innovation
118, rue de Tocqueville
75017 Paris
e-mail: mari@crp.capsogeti.fr

The industrial world is attracted by knowledge-based techniques. A certain number of increasingly pertinent and convincing experiments have been carried out. But for some reason, KBS technology just doesn't seem to take in commercial culture. What's wrong?

On the one hand, research has attacked and succeeded in controlling one of the principal technical issues: the so-called ***knowledge-acquisition bottleneck***. On the other hand, commercial software product developers have put a myriad of ***expert system generators*** at the market's disposal. But one can say that ***both approaches are incomplete.*** Schematizing:

- The former doesn't go far enough ***practically***: the KA methods are not comprehensive as (i) they don't cover the full ***application development life cycle***, (ii) they don't sufficiently address ***quality aspects***, (iii) there is not computer-based support in the form of ***integrated tools.***
- The other is ***superficial***: due to encouraging *ad hoc*, specificity-driven development, it does not go far enough in the ***generalization*** of basic methods and techniques permitting scale-up to production quality elements: it passes up opportunities both on ***reuse aspects*** and on exploiting ***the basic principles*** of the AI approach.

The latter approach may not appeal to the purists, but it certainly pleased (some of) the commercial world (for awhile). It offered fast, visual results. But taken in the long term, it broke down due both to its lack of generality and reusability, and to its unsatisfactory quality as a modern development approach. As a result, the European commercial world (and it appears, increasingly in the US) is shifting its interest towards ***methodologically-sound***, ***comprehensive approaches*** - something that makes the ***junction between the KA research results and the expert system shell.***

The European market is looking for a ***method***, ***supported by tools.*** The method must respond to all of the concerns of conventional software engineering, but even more rigourously due to the perceived complexity and nebulousness of KBS - and to their perturbation potential in the organizational fabric - and due to the in-

Applications of Machine Learning

Katharina Morik

University Dortmund,
Dept. Computer Science, LS VIII,
P.O.Box 500 500, 4600 Dortmund 50,
e-mail: morik@kilo.informatik.uni-dortmund.de

Abstract. During the last 10 years, machine learning has been successfully applied. Most often, the applications are confidential. Therefore, only few publications about real world applications exist. In this paper, an overview of machine learning applications is given with their scenarios. Some typical applications are described. Then, future directions of machine learning applications are proposed. It is argued that machine learning is now mature enough to be incorporated into standard systems as well as algorithms. The integration of learning modules into database and retrieval systems is one of the trends. Another trend is to automatically select an appropriate learning tool out of a toolbox. The third trend, which is even more challenging, no longer requires a distinguished learning module, but offers methods of machine learning to be applied by programmers in their regular system development. Software engineers of the future can use inductive techniques as they now use message passing, for instance. Then, any program can be enhanced by some learning ability.

1 Experience with Machine Learning

In the past 10 years, machine learning (ML) had several applications of two types of algorithms, namely

- top-down induction of decision trees,
  a family of algorithms from which ID3 [Quinlan, 1983] is the most famous one.
- conceptual clustering,
  a family of algorithms from which AQ [Michalski and Stepp, 1983] is the most famous one. The first break-through of applying machine learning was achieved by exploiting conceptual clustering for the building of a rule base on soy bean diseases [Michalski and Chilauski, 1980].

Both algorithms learn from examples which are represented by attribute values. Current research enhances the algorithms to deal with relations [Quinlan, 1990] and restricted first-order predicate logic [Michalski and Stepp, 1983]. Other, logic-oriented approaches have been developed, which use background knowledge for learning and even learn the background knowledge itself [Morik, 1987], [Morik, 1990], [Kietz and Wrobel, 1991], [Bisson, 1991], [Muggleton and Feng, 1990]. The new, more powerfull algorithms are not yet products on the market. So, the following description of applications refers to learning from attribute-value representations. A lot of knowledge processing can be performed using this representation [Morales, 1990].

There are two scenarios for applying ML:

- partially building up the rule base of an expert system:
  a software house applies ML in order to solve customers' problems more efficiently , or
  a company or public institution uses an expert system shell with an integrated ML tool;
- finding an optimal procedure:
  using ML technology, on the grounds of experience (either in the form of case data or in the form of interviews), a procedure for decision making or a plan for a working routine is developed which is then used by experts.

Several applications are of the first type. For instance, Donald Michie reports two applications of this type [Michie, 1989]. With the help of ExpertEase, a system with an integrated learning module, 3 000 rules which model the design of a gas-oil separator could be acquired for BP. Westinghouse, by using ExpertEase achieved increased throughput in an important factory to the extent of increasing business volume by more than ten million dollars per annum. In both applications, the gain was achieved by applying a knowledge-based technique which, in turn, was enabled and became appropriate with respect to the cost-benefit relation because of a learning module. Brainware GmbH, a German software house with a particular expertise in ML and neural networks, reports an application for Siemens [Brainware GmbH, 1990]. The expert system called BMT configures fire detection equipment. BMT drastically cuts administrative efforts thus reducing the time required for making quotations and processing orders. The large number of such applications can be seen from the fact that some companies make their living by ML technology. For instance, the company ISoft at Paris, funded in 1988, now already has a turn-over of 1 million Dollars.

However, ML cannot be reduced as a means to build-up rule bases. In many cases, the customers need a decision tree as a kind of a check list. Where it is known how to carefully analyze all features of a situation, under some circumstances the expert does not have the time to do so. A quick decision based on only a few features which are easy to determine, is necessary. An example is the immediate help needed by newborn children with a yellow skin colour. The unknown expertise is: which features correctly indicate a particular test to be necessary? In which order are which tests necessary? ML analysis of cases can provide a check list to be used by the doctor [1]. Another example of this type is reported by Donald Michie [Michie, 1989]. A pilot of a space shuttle has to decide whether to use the autolander or not. In some unobvious cases, many factors have to be taken into account. As the time for decision making is too short to do so, the few indicating factors have to be found out. These may then serve as a check list. If there are still too many factors, a system can propose the decision.

1 Of course, the doctor keeps in charge and the check list does not prescribe any procedure! However, doctors are often overloaded with work and cannot be specialists of all diseases. As the child dies if a particular diagnosis is missed, this diagnosis needs to be excluded immediately.

2 Future Directions of Machine Learning

2.1 Integrating Machine Learning into Standard Environments

For several years, ML programs suffered from their dependency of AI computer environments. ML tools were either stand-alone programs or integrated into expert systems without access to the companies' conventional programs. This was an obstacle preventing companies from applying ML. Current ML programs overcome this obstacle. For instance, the expert system shell TWAICE [2] has access to database systems. Also KET [3] has access to databases. The system analyzes databases and detects regularities which can be displayed as descision trees or If-Then-rules. This way of obtaining knowledge on the basis of given databases is also the success of RULEARN [4]. The concentration of acids could be determined successfully by this system inspecting an already existing database. Given the situation that many databases exist, which do no longer correspond to their documented data base schema, or which are not well documented at all, the analysis of databases becomes important. The term 'database mining' illustrates the situation. ML techniques are a suitable means to perform database mining. In particular, the understandability of the learning results helps database managers to determine what to do about the databases. They may even turn 'data mines' into effective knowledge bases. ML techniques can become the missing link between the conventional database technology and knowledge-based systems.

2.2 Multistrategy Learning

The use of just one learning module cannot cover all the applications. Instead of trying to find the one universal learning mechanism, the current trend is to develop specialized learning algorithms. Then, the user or even a system selects the appropriate algorithm for a particular problem. Founded by the European Community (ESPRIT P2154), the project "Machine Learning Toolbox" is currently developing such a system. In the United States of America, the first conference on multistrategy learning indicates a similar trend [Michalski, 1991]. This trend can already be observed in industry. For instance, a combination of neural network learning and inductive learning was applied by Brainware GmbH to classify 22 000 complex signals, each containing 8 192 numerical features. Applying just one algorithm to this huge amount of data is not feasible. However, seperating a preprocessing step which may exploit one strategy and then applying different learning strategies to the resulting compressed data allowed for cross-validating the results. The results were 20-25 percent better than those achieved by statistical techniques [Brainware GmbH, 1991].

2.3 Inductive Programming

Since learning in (restricted) predicate logic has been better understood, the possibility of inductive logic programming is now given. The first approach into that

2 registered trademark of Nixdorf Computer AG, now SNI

3 KET is a product of Brainware GmbH, running on PC and compatibles.

4 RULEARN is a product of Krupp Technologie-Transfer GmbH at Duisburg, Germany.

direction was Shapiro's debugging method for Prolog programs [Shapiro, 1983]. A programming environment can use inductive methods in order to support the Prolog programmer. Quicker program development and easier debugging becomes possible using inductive learning techniques.

However, the real challenge which is not yet realized is to teach software engineers such that they can exploit basic algorithms in whatever they program. In fact, any system incorporating conventional algorithms can be enhanced by introducing learning capabilities into these algorithms. A learning text editor, a learning database management system, a learning human-computer interface, a learning knowledge acquisition system, a learning scheduling program should be superior to any other system of the same type. This is the goal of introducing ML into everyday life of software industries. It is a far reaching goal, but it may guide our thinking about ML and current research.

References

[Bisson, 1991] Bisson, G. (1991). Learning of rule systems in a first order representation. Rapport de Recherche 628, LRI, University de Paris-Sud.

[Brainware GmbH, 1990] Brainware GmbH (1990). News from Companies - Germany. page 10.

[Brainware GmbH, 1991] Brainware GmbH (1991). Machine Induction on Complex Signals. *Pragmatica*, page 14.

[Kietz and Wrobel, 1991] Kietz, J.-U. and Wrobel, S. (1991). Controlling the Complexity of Learning in Logic through Syntactic and Task-Oriented Models. In Muggleton, S., editor, *Proc. of Int. Workshop on Inductive Logic Programming*, pages 107 – 126, Viana de Castelo, Portugal. Also available as Arbeitspapiere der GMD No. 503.

[Michalski, 1991] Michalski, R. (1991). Inferential Learning Theory as a Basis for Multistrategy Task-Adaptive Learning. In Michalski and Tecuci, editors, *Multistrategy Learning*. George Mason University, USA.

[Michalski and Chilauski, 1980] Michalski, R. and Chilauski, R. (1980). Learning by Being Told and Learning from Examples: An Experimental Comparison of the Two Methods of Knowledge Acquisition in the Context of Developing an Expert System for Soybean Disease Diagnosis. *Int. Journal of Policy Analysis and Information Systems*, 4(2):125 – 161.

[Michalski and Stepp, 1983] Michalski, R. S. and Stepp, R. E. (1983). Learning from Observation: Conceptual Clustering. In Michalski, R., Carbonell, J., and Mitchell, T., editors, *Machine Learning*, volume I, pages 331 – 363. Tioga, Palo Alto, CA.

[Michie, 1989] Michie, D. (1989). New Commercial Oppertunities Using Information Technology. In Brauer, F., editor, *Wissensbasierte Systeme*, number 227 in Informatik Fachberichte, pages 64–71, Berlin, Heidelberg, new York, Tokio. Springer.

[Morales, 1990] Morales, E. (1990). The Machine Learning Toolkit Database. Deliverable TI-MLT-5.5, The Turing Institute, Glasgow, UK.

[Morik, 1987] Morik, K. (1987). Acquiring Domain Models. *Intern. Journal of Man Machine Studies*, 26:93–104. also appeared in Knowledge Acquisition Tools for Expert Systems, volume 2, J. Boose, B. Gaines, eds., Academic Press, 1988.

[Morik, 1990] Morik, K. (1990). Integrating manual and automatic knowledge aquisition - BLIP. In McGraw, K. L. and Westphal, C. R., editors, *Readings in Knowledge Acquisition – Current Practices and Trends*, chapter 14, pages 213 – 232. Ellis Horwood, New York.

[Muggleton and Feng, 1990] Muggleton, S. and Feng, C. (1990). Efficient induction of logic programs. In *Proceedings of the 1th conference on Algorithmic Learning Theorie.*

[Quinlan, 1990] Quinlan, J. (1990). Learning Logical Definitions from Relations. *Machine Learning*, 5(3):239 - 266.

[Quinlan, 1983] Quinlan, J. R. (1983). Learning Efficient Classification Procedures and Their Application to Chess End Games. In Michalski, R., Carbonell, J., and Mitchell, T., editors, *Machine Learning - An Artificial Intelligence Approach*, pages 463 - 482. Tioga, Palo Alto, CA.

[Shapiro, 1983] Shapiro, E. Y. (1983). *Algorithmic Program Debugging.* ACM Distinguished Doctoral Dissertations. The MIT Press, Cambridge, Mass.

This article was processed using the LaTeX macro package with LLNCS style

Conceptual Models for Automatic Generation of Knowledge-Acquisition Tools

Henrik Eriksson* Mark A. Musen

Medical Computer Science Group
Knowledge Systems Laboratory
Stanford University School of Medicine
Stanford, CA 94305-5479, U.S.A.

Abstract. Interactive knowledge-acquisition (KA) programs allow users to enter relevant domain knowledge according to a model predefined by the tool developers. KA tools are designed to provide *conceptual models* of the knowledge to their users. Many different classes of models are possible, resulting in different categories of tools. Whenever it is possible to describe KA tools according to explicit conceptual models, it is also possible to edit the models and to instantiate new KA tools automatically for specialized purposes. Several *meta-tools* that address this task have been implemented. Meta-tools provide developers of domain-specific KA tools with generic design models, or *meta-views,* of the emerging KA tools. The same KA tool can be specified according to several alternative meta-views.

1 Introduction

Numerous knowledge-acquisition (KA) tools have been implemented in research laboratories. From a research point of view, implementations of tools provide the means to test KA models and methods in realistic situations. In many ways, the creation of these KA tools is still a research issue, and sometimes is an art. Nevertheless, it is desirable to classify and understand more clearly the principles behind various KA tools so that we can, for instance, outline new generations of tools.

One way of classifying KA tools is to group them according to the *conceptual model* that they present to their users [25]. A conceptual model, in this context, is the metaphor for the user interaction; for instance, it is the way in which knowledge is entered, edited, and presented. (We distinguish such conceptual models for KA tools from *conceptual domain models,* which describe the experts' view of the domain and the relevant domain knowledge.) Examples of conceptual models include *symbol-level, method-based,* and *task-based* conceptual models. KA tools supporting symbol-level conceptual models are concerned with rules, objects, and other symbol-level entities [28]. Tools adopting method-based conceptual models present a model of a particular problem-solving method—for example, methods for classification, planning,

*On leave from the Department of Computer and Information Science, Linköping University, S-581 83 Linköping, Sweden

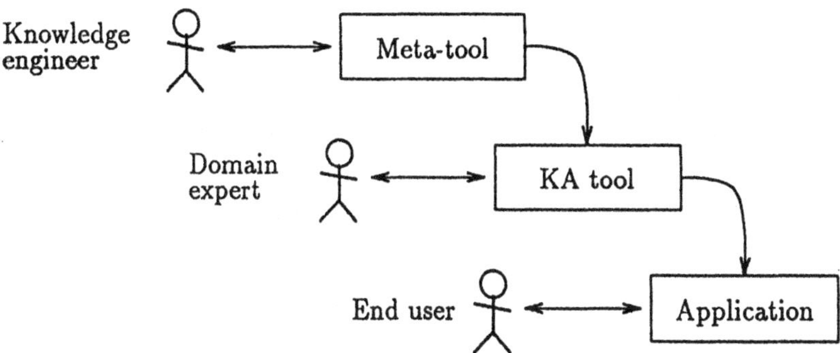

Figure 1: The fundamental basis of meta-tools. The knowledge engineer uses a meta-tool to develop a specialized KA tool that is used by a domain expert to enter knowledge for an application system.

or synthesis. Tools providing task-based conceptual models are tailored to a specific task in a particular domain.

The tradeoff between general tools that can be used in a broad variety of situations and highly supportive, specific tools is a classical software-engineering problem that applies to KA tools as well as to conventional computer programs. (In fact, this tradeoff is a general engineering problem, too.) Meta-tools are designed to provide the means to escape from this dilemma by making it easy to produce and custom-tailor new KA tools. As depicted in Figure 1, knowledge engineers can use meta-tools to create new KA tools suited to their particular needs; the KA tools in turn are used by experts to create knowledge bases. In particular, meta-tools are useful for development of domain-oriented KA tools that incorporate task-based conceptual models, since the range of domain-specific models is large.

As we shall see, the use of meta-tools uncovers a different set of problems at the metalevel, which is the tool-design and KA-model level, because the task of a KA tool quite different from the task of the application system. There are many ways in which a target KA tool can be described, and there also are many ways in which KA tools can be specified (i.e., described in such detail that they can be implemented automatically). This article discusses a number of such *meta-views* (or conceptual models for meta-tools), and describes the strengths and weaknesses of each. Different implementations of meta-tools are presented according to the meta-views that the meta-tools support, and the meta-tools are categorized according to their meta-views.

This article is structured as follows. Section 2 provides the background in terms of conceptual models of software. Section 3 describes several meta-views. Section 4 compares these meta-views and discusses approaches to combine and improve them. Finally, a summary and conclusions are given in Section 5.

2 Background

The purpose of this section is to provide the general ideas behind automated generation of KA tools and to summarize different conceptual models for KA tools.

2.1 Automatic Generation of KA Tools

The major impediment for designers of specialized KA tools, including those adopting task-based conceptual models, is the problem of implementing such tools for a broad variety of domains at a reasonable cost. In principal, the problem can be approached in several ways. One approach is to try to find the "right" level of generality for KA tools (i.e., to balance the cost of implementation and the level of support supplied by the tool). Note that it is not clear that such an optimal level exists. Even if such a level was proposed, it might be difficult for tool users—experts and knowledge engineers—to agree on it.

A second approach is to develop *generic* KA tools that can be configured for specific needs—for instance, for each domain. Examples of such configurations are specification of various tool properties in resource files, and wiring of subtools in the overall KA tool. These techniques form a knowledge-acquisition workbench. Simple configurations of generic KA tools can be performed by the domain expert (e.g., changing user preferences), whereas more sophisticated configurations can be performed by only the knowledge engineer (e.g., editing of resource databases).

A third approach, which is discussed in this article, is to introduce an additional layer of tool support that is used to build specialized KA tools. In this approach, knowledge engineers use supportive environments, or *meta-tools,* to develop the KA tools that are to be used by the domain experts. Meta-tools have the advantage of providing more generality than can generic KA tools, since knowledge engineers *specify* target KA tools, rather than merely *parameterize* generic tools. For instance, many conventional programs allow their users to custom-tailor certain predefined aspects of the program behavior. Resource editors can be used to custom-tailor forms, menus, accelerator keys, colors, and so on. Such resource editors, however, cannot make more radical changes to programs (e.g., they cannot turn a document editor into a spreadsheet program, or vice versa). Hence, the range of options for custom-tailoring is limited for conventional programs, as well as for KA tools. Sometimes, there is no clear distinction between generic KA tools and meta-tool systems. Indeed, a sophisticated generic KA tool could provide the same flexibility and support as do the KA tools produced by a meta-tool.

2.2 Conceptual Models of KA Tools

Interactive KA tools must adopt a conceptual model that allows their users to communicate with the tools and to provide the relevant domain knowledge. The conceptual model forms the language in which the tool and its users communicate. Following Musen [25], we identify three major conceptual model types for KA tools:

1. *Symbol-level conceptual models:* Symbol-level conceptual models comprise individual knowledge-base entities, such as rules, frames, and parameters. Thus,

this type of conceptual model addresses the most detailed level of the knowledge-base structure. Most commercial expert-system shells present the contents of the knowledge base in terms of such symbol-level entities [28]. Often, these shells provide editing facilities according to the same conceptual model. Certain KA tools allow their users to edit and debug knowledge bases at the symbol level—for example, in terms of individual rules. TEIRESIAS [6] was an early project to explore tool support for knowledge-base refinement at the symbol level.

The obvious drawback of symbol-level conceptual models is that tool users (e.g., domain experts) can be forced to think of their knowledge in a form that might be unnatural, since many symbol-level entities in reality are implementation details. For instance, although the medium of interaction in TEIRESIAS was a subset of natural language, users were restricted to think of their classification knowledge in terms of rule clauses and parameter values.

2. *Method-based conceptual models:* A more abstract way to view knowledge bases is to focus on the *behaviors* that are to be achieved by the target system. Method-based conceptual models attempt to describe particular problem-solving methods and classes of problem-solving methods.[2] For instance, Clancey [5] has described a model for heuristic classification where knowledge engineers can use terms and relationships of the model to describe the problem-solving behavior of the system.

   Models of problem-solving methods, such as heuristic classification, can be used as a basis for interactive KA tools. In such KA tools, the user dialog is not based on rules, frames, or other low-level entities in the knowledge base; instead, terms and relationships in the problem-solving method are used as a basis for communication. Examples of such KA tools include ROGET [1], MORE [14], MOLE [10], and SALT [19]. There are also tools that do not reveal the terms and relationships of problem-solving model to their users. Thus, users are not required to understand the model. Examples of KA tools that adopt an *implicit* model of problem solving are ETS [2] and its successor AQUINAS [3].

3. *Task-based conceptual models:* In addition to tools that adopt models of problem solving, there are also KA tools that attempt to incorporate models that reflect the *task* to be performed. (We use the term *task* to refer to the assignment and role of the application system in the organization. We use the term *domain,* to refer to a real-world discipline that several application systems can address.) Generally, these KA tools provide a conceptual model of a general task that can be instantiated to particular task instances, thus defining individual knowledge bases. Such KA tools are more or less domain-oriented and, hence, typically are restricted to a narrow class of similar applications.

   An example of such a task-based KA tool is OPAL [27]. OPAL is a graphical tool that allows cancer specialists to enter cancer-therapy plans for an expert system called ONCOCIN [29]. Unlike method-oriented KA tools, OPAL adopts a conceptual model that includes domain-specific concepts such as *chemotherapy,*

[2]Note that different terminology is used by different groups to denote problem-solving methods. Chandrasekaran [4] uses the term *generic tasks,* whereas the term *interpretation models* is used by the KADS group [30]. Karbach et al. [15] discuss this terminological problem.

drug, and *toxic reaction.* The problem-solving method of skeletal-plan refinement [29], which is the underlying reasoning mechanism in ONCOCIN, is transparent in OPAL. Physicians use this abstract task model of cancer therapy for entering and reviewing their knowledge in OPAL.

Another KA tool, P10, is designed for the same problem-solving method in the target expert system, but the domain task is different; in this case, it is planning of protein purification [9]. In spite of the similar problem-solving methods used by the expert systems generated, the domain terms and relationships used in the interaction differ substantially between the KA tools. Other examples of KA tools with task-based conceptual models are Student [12] and early versions of KNACK [17].

Note that these conceptual models are largely from the perspective of the tool user. As we shall see, there are other types of models of KA tools as well.

In addition to conceptual models for KA tools, a conceptual model for the *domain* can be defined. Such *conceptual domain models* describe the expert's view of the domain and the relevant domain knowledge, including the latter's structure, rather than describing the KA tools.

3 Meta-Views

The task of a meta-tool is to transform specifications provided by its users (typically knowledge engineers) into a target KA tool that can be used by domain experts. The conceptual model that a meta-tool presents to its users is the *meta-view* for the tool. Hence, meta-views are specification languages for KA tools. A second way of classifying meta-tools is to group them according to the type of target KA tools they produce. The knowledge-acquisition method supported by the target KA tools is an example of an aspect that is also relevant for meta-tool classification. A third way of classifying meta-tools is to describe various technical properties of the meta-tool implementations (e.g., the software environment required by the target KA tools, and incremental regeneration of target KA tools).

We shall present several meta-views and the meta-tools supporting them. Our reasons for focusing on meta-views, and for classifying meta-tools according to the meta-views that they support are that (1) meta-views represent models of how developers think of KA tools when developing those tools, (2) meta-views shape the interaction between knowledge engineers and meta-tools, (3) meta-views shows how target KA tools can be described at a level more abstract than program code, and (4) meta-views restrict the type of KA tools that can be developed with various meta-tools. From the perspective of the meta-tool user, it is important to be aware both of the meta-view supported and of that meta-view's limitations. The way in which KA tools are described and specified can differ substantially, depending on what aspects the meta-tool developer chooses to emphasize. In general, various approaches to meta-tool support can be distinguished by the meta-view adopted. Several prerequisites for meta-views can be identified. For instance, meta-views should be understandable, clearly defined, practicable, and easily maintained. Note, however, that requirements

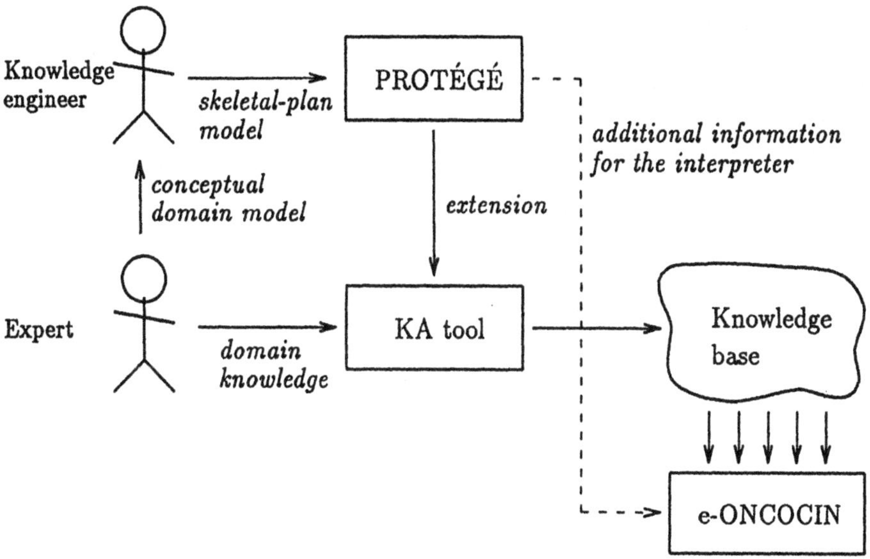

Figure 2: Generation of model-based KA tools from PROTÉGÉ. Knowledge engineers use PROTÉGÉ to instantiate model-based KA tools, which in turn are used to acquire knowledge from domain experts. The resulting knowledge bases are interpreted by e-ONCOCIN.

for meta-views are *not* the same as requirements for KA tools or for conceptual models for KA tools. Sections 3.1 through 3.6 describe several meta-views that have been implemented in meta-tools, as well as other potential meta-views.

3.1 The Method-Oriented View

The idea on which the *method-oriented* view is based is to use a high-level description of the domain knowledge required by the problem-solving method of the target expert system as a specification paradigm for generated KA tools. Target KA tools are assumed to be domain specific and to adopt a task-based conceptual model.

PROTÉGÉ. PROTÉGÉ [24, 26] is a meta-tool that adopts a method-oriented view. The tool presents an abstract model of skeletal planning—the framework for the specification—to its users. The knowledge engineers specify properties of various entities in the planning model. As depicted in Figure 2, PROTÉGÉ transforms these specifications into a target KA tool (and also into instructions needed by the inference mechanism, e-ONCOCIN). PROTÉGÉ has an a priori design for the target KA tools, which resemble OPAL [27].

PROTÉGÉ assumes *skeletal-plan refinement* [29] as the problem-solving method for the target KA tools and the target expert systems. Thus, PROTÉGÉ can be seen as an instantiation of a meta-tool for a single problem-solving method. Knowledge engineers who use PROTÉGÉ must learn the terms and relationships in the model of skeletal-plan refinement. PROTÉGÉ also assumes that the knowledge bases generated will be run by the e-ONCOCIN problem solver [26], a domain-independent version of ONCOCIN. Thus, the semantics of the resulting knowledge bases are defined by the e-ONCOCIN interpreter, which uses information both from PROTÉGÉ and from structures entered and subsequently generated by a target KA tool. We shall describe briefly the method-oriented view in PROTÉGÉ because it exemplifies a practical meta-view. The model of skeletal-plan refinement comprises four components:

- *Planning entities:* Planning entities are *processes* that take place over finite periods of time, such as drug treatment (as in ONCOCIN's domain). In the skeletal-planning model, the planning entities are structured hierarchically. In OPAL, for example, *chemotherapy* and *radiotherapy* are considered to be potential components of *protocol* (which is the entire plan). Knowledge engineers use PROTÉGÉ to define planning-entity *classes* and—in the generated KA tools—domain experts create and edit *instances* of such planning entities. The specification of planning entities also includes *attributes* of entities in a class and various *properties* of the attributes (e.g., data type, means for establishing values, and variations in values over time).

- *Task-level actions:* Task-level actions are unitary *operations* that control the planning entities. For example, in OPAL, task-level actions include delaying chemotherapy, attenuating the dose of a drug, and ordering a laboratory test. The actions modify the instantiation of the plan at run time (i.e., they can start and stop different components of the plan and change attribute values of planning entities). Each task-level action consists of an abstract series of operations, which must be instantiated before the action can take effect. These operations are defined according to a simple script language that allows definition of the semantics of each task-level action in a domain-independent manner.

- *Input data:* Input data can be divided into a number of user-specified data groups—for instance, data related to chemistry, to toxicity, and to disease status. The data groups make it easier to handle many data items in the target KA tool, and make it possible to display only the relevant data on the workstation screen. The model of the data items includes properties for each data item, such as what are the name, prompt message, upper and lower bounds if numerical, and whether the data item varies over time. In particular, every data item has associated with it a *data type* (discussed next). The target KA tool can take advantage of the type specification in creating graphical forms for data entry. For instance, if all data items in a data class have an enumerated type, the target KA tool can list in its graphical forms all the values possible.

- *Data types:* Every data item is associated with data type. Data types are also needed for planning-entity attributes and for action attributes. There are a few predefined data types—namely, *boolean, integer, real,* and *percent.* The knowledge engineer can introduce additional data types by specifying the input device and prompt message. For *enumerated* data types, the knowledge engineer can define *possible values* and *prompt texts* for each value.

In PROTÉGÉ, there also are facilities to enter additional low-level specifications, such as, *methods* and *rules*. The PROTÉGÉ model is an example of a meta-view based on a specific problem-solving method. Presumably, similar models—and meta-level tools—could be built for other problem-solving methods, such as diagnosis, troubleshooting, and configuration.

To build a KA tool using PROTÉGÉ, a knowledge engineer must (1) analyze the problem area with respect to the available problem-solving method (namely, skeletal-plan refinement); (2) identify relevant *planning entities* (processes) for the domain in question, and enter them into PROTÉGÉ; (3) identify planning operations, and describe them as *task-level actions* in PROTÉGÉ; and (4) determine the input data (available at run time) for the planning process, and define *input data* and *data types* in PROTÉGÉ. If necessary, this process can be iterated as experience with the generated KA tool allows developers to clarify deficiencies in their initial model of the problem area.

The Meta-View of PROTÉGÉ. In the method-oriented view, knowledge engineers instantiate an abstract model of the problem-solving method by specifying its properties. Through specification of particular properties of the problem-solving method, as well as of domain-related concepts used by the problem solver, the required knowledge-base structure is described sufficiently to allow generation of a KA tool for acquiring that knowledge. For example, a method-oriented view for a planning method could be instantiated by provision of domain-specific information about operations (e.g., name and ramifications), constraints, and parameters (i.e., data required for planning).

Further, knowledge engineers should be able to work at an abstract level in specifying the method—that is, they should *not* have to descend to symbol-level specifications and conventional programming. (However, they might have to do so anyway, whenever they must enter knowledge that is not definable in terms of the underlying problem-solving method. Indeed, PROTÉGÉ *requires* entry of symbol-level rules for domain-specific control knowledge.) It is the task of the meta-tool to transform these high-level specifications into a working KA tool. Typically, a method-oriented meta-tool uses an a priori design of the target KA tool intended in this transformation; thus, the general structure of the tool is predetermined by the meta-tool developer and by the knowledge engineer. The knowledge engineer can only extend the a priori design by specifying various domain properties.

Note that this specification style is dependent on the actual problem-solving method used to solve a particular problem in the domain. If the problem-solving method is changed, the meta-tool must be modified accordingly. Notably, the method-oriented view (1) can be made understandable if the method supported is understandable; (2) is clearly defined if the meta-view follows a well-defined method; (3) can be made practicable (as demonstrated by PROTÉGÉ), although there may be a large gap to bridge between the specification and the target KA tool; and (4) promotes specification and maintenance, provided that the method can be modularized and that the problem can be solved by the method supported. McDermott [22] argues that the use of explicit problem-solving methods makes expert systems easier to maintain in general.

In a way, the method-oriented view corresponds to the method-based conceptual model for KA tools (see also Section 2.2). The principal difference is that KA tools that adopt method-based conceptual models often are designed to interact with *experts* in terms of problem-solving methods, whereas meta-tools that adopt the method-oriented view are intended to interact with *knowledge engineers* in terms of problem-solving methods for the purpose of specifying KA tools. Thus, another way to view a method-oriented meta-tool and the KA tools that it generates is to see them as two-level KA systems with both method-based and task-based conceptual models.

3.2 The Abstract-Architecture View

A fundamentally different approach is to focus on the design of the target KA tools, instead of on properties of the problem-solving method. The general idea is to use the meta-level of knowledge-acquisition *tools*—rather than the meta-level of problem solving—for specification, since meta-tools produce KA tools, not expert systems for a domain. Thus, the *abstract-architecture* view involves a model of the desired KA tool architecture on an abstract level. Note that when we speak of *architectures* in this context, we mean architectures for KA tools, rather than architectures for knowledge bases or for target expert systems.

DOTS. DOTS [8] is an example of a meta-tool supporting the abstract-architecture view. The particular meta-view adopted by DOTS is intended to give knowledge engineers as much freedom as possible in the specification. At the same time, the meta-view is sufficiently restricted to allow fast and well-defined specification. DOTS is designed to support development of KA tools for a generic class of KA methods; that is, methods for knowledge acquisition via graphical knowledge editing by domain experts.

DOTS presents an abstract model of a KA tool. Knowledge engineers specify properties of components in the target KA tool. Such components include *knowledge editors* (which are targeted to specific knowledge chunks), *knowledge modules,* and *transformation rules* for knowledge-base generation. DOTS generates a KA tool from these specifications. The major components in the DOTS meta-view include the following (see also Figure 3):

- *Knowledge editors:* The knowledge editors are components of the user interface of the KA tool under specification. Each knowledge editor is intended to edit a particular chunk of knowledge in the conceptual domain model. In DOTS, the knowledge editors of the KA tool under construction are organized in a hierarchy with a number of intrinsic editor types at the top and user-defined specializations farther down. The notion of knowledge-editor types (classes) allows several instances of a knowledge-editor to be present on the screen in the target KA tool at run time. The knowledge engineer can specify properties—such as menu layouts, window size, screen positions, and icons—for each editor type and instance in the DOTS-generated tool.

- *Knowledge modules:* Knowledge modules are used to specify the internal knowledge representation within the target KA tool. Like the knowledge editors, the knowledge modules are organized in a hierarchy with intrinsic module classes at the top and user-defined specializations below them. The knowledge engineer can specify user-defined slots for storage of knowledge acquired and of intermediate results.

- *Update rules:* The purpose of the update rules is to define the relationships between the knowledge editors and the knowledge modules. The set of update rules can be seen as a definition of the internal logistics structure in the target KA tool. At run time, target KA tools use update rules to guide data transfer between instances of knowledge editors and knowledge modules.

- *Transformation rules:* A set of transformation rules is used describe the generation of knowledge bases from the internal structures (i.e., the knowledge modules) in the target KA tool. The preconditions of these rules are adapted to the contents of particular knowledge modules in the KA tool, whereas the conclusions describe knowledge-base structures to be generated. Knowledge-base generation through transformation rules is described in detail elsewhere [7].

Figure 3 shows what the relationships are among the architectural components in the abstract-architecture view, and how they form a model of the target KA tool. At the top, we find knowledge editors that handle interaction with the expert. The knowledge entered in these editors is communicated to the internal representation—the knowledge modules—through a set of update rules. Finally, a knowledge-base generator guided by transformation rules produces the knowledge base. Note that DOTS does not address the issue of providing problem-solving methods for the target expert systems. In other words, DOTS is unaware of the semantics of the target expert system—the transformation rules provide the necessary denotational semantics.

To construct a KA tool with DOTS, the knowledge engineer must (1) analyze the problem area and determine the KA tool support required, (2) define the surface structure of the KA tool in terms of knowledge editors in DOTS, (3) declare to DOTS the internal knowledge structure of the target KA tool in an object-oriented manner (i.e., as knowledge modules), (4) describe to DOTS the relationship between knowledge editors and knowledge modules in terms of update rules, and (5) define transformation rules for knowledge-base generation in DOTS. The tool-specification process does not necessarily have to proceed in this order. The ordering of steps 2 through 5 might be different; for instance, the internal knowledge structure of the KA tool might be defined before the user interface.

A salient aspect of DOTS is that the meta-view adopted can be modified or, if required, replaced completely. In fact, DOTS itself is implemented in DOTS according to the abstract-architecture view. Thus, DOTS is bootstrapped, which means that developers can use the system to modify and extend itself (e.g., to experiment with new meta-views).

SIS. Kawaguchi et al. [16] report on a Shell for Interview Systems (SIS) that can be used to create interview-oriented KA tools. SIS represents an instantiation of the abstract-architecture approach for another class of KA tools and for another generic KA method: interviews via textual question-and-answer dialogs. SIS serves as an interview skeleton-system that helps knowledge engineers to develop interview-based KA tools such as MORE [14], an interview-oriented KA tool for diagnostic expert systems. (Indeed, SIS has been used to recreate MORE.) Interview systems generated by SIS start by requesting initial information for the construction of a basic domain model in the form of a concept network. Sentences from the expert are parsed, and

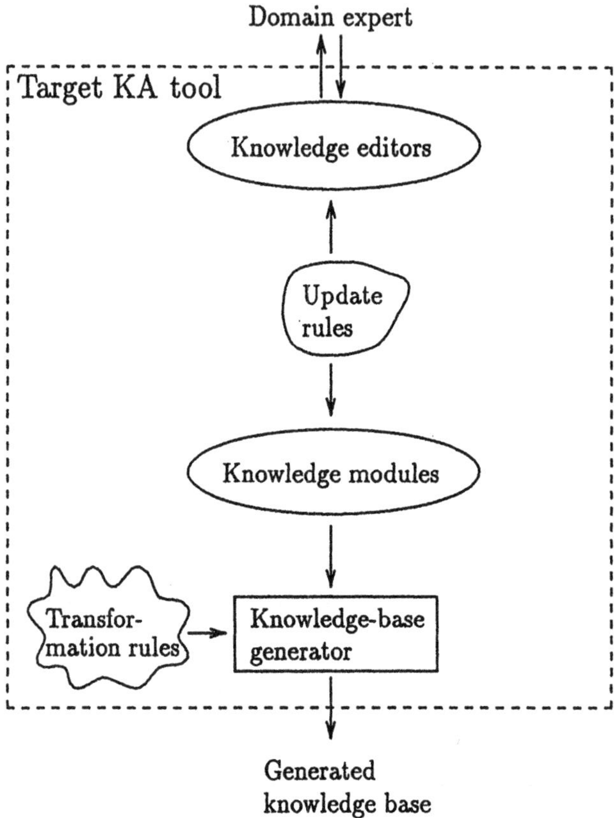

Figure 3: Components of the abstract-architecture meta-view in DOTS. The *knowledge editors* handle the interaction with the user (e.g., a domain expert), the *knowledge modules* represent the internal knowledge structures (e.g., knowledge acquired) within the KA tool, the *update rules* handle data transfer between knowledge editors and knowledge modules, and the *transformation rules* guide the knowledge-base generator in the transformation of the knowledge modules into a target knowledge base. (The dashed frame indicates the perimeter of the target KA tool.)

are used to generate a set of task-specific *attentions* that guides the questioning in the subsequent interview. The basic domain model is refined further throughout the interview.

The meta-view adopted by SIS is basically an abstract-architecture view. Because SIS is designed to generate interview-based KA tools, the particular architecture organization is different from meta-tools that generate graphical knowledge editors (such as DOTS). Nevertheless, the SIS model incorporates architectural components common to interview-oriented KA tools. In the SIS model, the architecture of the target KA tool is divided into three layers: (1) an *interview-system* layer that provides an overview of the system components, (2) an *internal-structure* layer that describes the system in terms of program modules, and (3) a *knowledge-layer* that describes the behavior of each module in the internal-structure layer. This hierarchical structure reflects the design of implemented KA tools. The most detailed specification level, the knowledge layer, comprises (1) a domain ontology, (2) a set of user-defined *generic attentions* (which can be composed from primitive attentions), (3) a specification on when to apply certain generic attentions, (4) a procedural description that controls the interview flow, and (5) a set of specific query texts. Generic attentions are a central part of the interview systems that SIS generates, since the questioning is driven by the generation and processing of attentions.

To create a KA tool with SIS, a knowledge engineer must analyze the interview situation, to model the target KA tool on each of the three abstraction layers, and to provide a detailed specification of the knowledge layer (including items 1 through 5). Although both SIS and DOTS adopt the abstract-architecture view, they are different meta-tools from the user's point-of-view. They use different sets of primitives for describing the architectures of the target KA tools. SIS and DOTS provide the architectural components required for developing interview systems and graphical knowledge editors, respectively. Further, these meta-tools cannot be used to generate target KA tools outside the scope of their toolboxes; for instance, DOTS cannot generate interview systems, and SIS cannot generate graphical knowledge editors. In fact, SIS has been used to regenerate MORE, and DOTS has the potential of generating KA tools such as OPAL. These facts illustrate that the abstract-architecture view is dependent on the class of target KA tools, and vice versa.

The Meta-View of DOTS and SIS. In the abstract-architecture approach, knowledge engineers specify target KA tools according to an abstract model of the latter's architecture: knowledge engineers specify properties of components and component behavior in the target KA tool architecture, rather than properties of the domain in question with respect to the problem-solving method. Hence, we use the term *abstract-architecture view* for this specification strategy.

The task of the meta-tool is to transform the abstract specification of the architecture into an efficient implementation of the target KA tool. Note that the KA tools generated do not necessarily have to be implemented according the architectural framework used for specification. (In principal, it is possible to conceive a meta-tool that produces target KA tools that are fundamentally different in their implementation from their abstract-architecture specification.) The abstract architecture is actually a *specification language* for KA tools. Unlike tools such as PROTÉGÉ, meta-tools supporting the abstract-architecture view have no a priori design for the target KA tools;

instead, it is the knowledge engineer's task (and freedom) to design an appropriate target KA tool. Through specification of KA tools according to the abstract-architecture view, developers can fashion meta-tools independent of the problem-solving method. (For example, transformation rules can be used to implement flexible knowledge-base generation for a variety of target environments.) However, meta-tools supporting the abstract-architecture view are restricted to the type of architecture supported.

Notably, the abstract-architecture view (1) requires training for knowledge engineers (but this training allows them to specify KA tools applicable to many problem-solving methods); (2) has a suitable scope, since the meta-view is not limited a particular method (it can be difficult, however, to anticipate the exact limitation profile); (3) is practicable (as demonstrated by DOTS and SIS), since there is a relatively small gap between the specification and the target KA tool; and (4) promotes specification and maintenance, since it can be modularized, and since it is not limited by a problem-solving method. The abstract-architecture view usually requires a thorough analysis of the KA tool support needed before specification of the KA tool is commenced. In this respect, the abstract-architecture view is similar to symbol-level conceptual models for KA tools. However, meta-tools are generally intended for knowledge engineers and not for experts.

Unlike the method-oriented view, the abstract-architecture view does not have a direct correspondence in a conceptual model for KA tools. The abstract-architecture view is an approach to configuring KA tools from a library of reusable components. Just as common modules can be used for compiler construction—for instance, scanners, parsers, symbol tables, and code generators—modules such as knowledge editors, various knowledge representations, and knowledge-base generators can be identified for KA tools.

3.3 The Organizational View

The idea behind the *organizational* view is to identify the role of the target expert system in an organization (e.g., a business organization) and to use this role as a starting point for specification of the problem solver and a corresponding KA tool [18]. The meta-tool is assumed to provide a library of typical organizational structures. Users (knowledge engineers or application experts) are asked to identify the relevant position and role in the organization.

Work at Digital Equipment Corporation has explored the organizational view. Klinker et al. [18] describe an architecture (Spark, Burn, and Firefighter) that adopts a role-limiting approach with respect to an organization. The Spark, Burn, and Firefighter model is actually a lifecycle view that takes into account the entire development process. One of the first phases of this development model is *task analysis,* in which the task of the application system is identified and described. The task analysis includes an organizational model for identifying the system's role in the organization. In other words, the organizational view is one of the models in the Spark, Burn, and Firefighter approach.

The Spark, Burn, and Firefighter approach emphasizes usable, as well as reusable, program components as an instrument for developing expert systems. Although the goal is to support configuration of a large class of software, domain-specific KA tool support also is an integral part of this approach. Spark provides the developer with a model of activities in an organization—the *enterprise model.* Spark asks the developer to identify the task in terms of the industry. The type of industry determines the vocabular of the subsequent dialog. The first step in developing a problem solver with Spark is to identify the type of organization (e.g., discrete manufacturing, process manufacturing, service industries, and government). The second step is to identify the specific type of industry (e.g., automotive, clothing, and electronics). Different activities within the specific type of organization are presented as *activity diagrams* to the developer. The activity diagrams can be seen as semantic networks that describe activities such as selling and distributing. The developer may specialize such activity diagrams for the domain in question. Spark uses activity diagrams to look up problem-solving methods (or mechanisms) that can automate various tasks in the organization. Often, there is more than one mechanism or combination of mechanisms that can be used to solve the problem. In such cases, Spark resolves the ambiguity by asking question to differentiate between candidate mechanisms. Spark also asks questions to ensure that the information required by the mechanisms is indeed available from either the developer (the expert) or the end user.

The task of Burn is to elicit task expertise from the developer. Burn uses a library of KA tools for acquiring the knowledge required by mechanisms that constitute the problem solver. Each KA tool in the library is associated with a mechanism. In fact, Burn can be seen as a form of scheduler, since it invokes appropriate KA tools for mechanisms configured by Spark. FireFighter debugs application programs developed by Spark and Burn. FireFighter addresses two basic types of failures in application programs: (1) insufficient or inaccurate expertise for the mechanisms and (2) inappropriate mechanisms for the task. FireFighter attempts to detect missing expertise and inappropriate mechanisms by invoking mechanism-specific diagnostic code.

The original role-limiting approach was modified subsequently in favor of smaller and decomposable mechanisms that define knowledge roles [20]. The reason for the change was mainly that the organizational perspective did not provide sufficient information for automatic program generation. Furthermore, the original role-limiting approach did suffer from a static model of the organization. The group at Digital Equipment Corporation is now considering a new model that will relax some of the assumptions by making task analysis an integral part of the overall framework. This approach allows for a dynamic model, but introduces the problem of how to map from a task analysis to mechanisms.

The KADS approach includes an organizational model that is used to identify the role of the expert system in order to state the requirements of the system [30]. This description includes functions, tasks, and bottlenecks in the organization, as well as a prediction of how the introduction of the system will influence the organization. Like the Spark, Burn, and Firefighter approach, KADS is really a lifecycle model for development of expert systems. The organizational model is only one of many models in KADS. KADS also includes *application models* that define the function of the system in an organization; *task models* that describe how the function of the system is achieved through a number of tasks the system will perform; *models of cooperation* that assign tasks to agents and specify cooperation among subtasks; *models of expertise* that describe the problem-solving expertise required to perform the problem-solving tasks; *conceptual models* that are abstract descriptions of objects and operations that the system should incorporate, expressed an implementation-independent way; and *design models* that reflect the actual system design. However, the models of KADS are primarily intended to form an overall development methodology; they are not intended as meta-views in meta-tools. The creation of domain-specific KA tools by meta-tools has never been an explicit goal of KADS.

3.4 The Ontology View

The *ontology* view is based on the idea that a description of concepts and their relationships in a domain (especially those that should be acquired by the target KA tool) can be used for specifying a KA tool that will be used to elicit detailed information about such concepts. The domain concepts used for specification are assumed to be relatively general; they are sufficiently specific to allow for automatic KA tool generation, but are sufficiently general to provide flexibility in the KA tool generated. For example, in the domain of troubleshooting automobile breakdowns, relatively general concepts—such as *electrical system, motor, spare part,* and *symptom*—can be used to describe what the KA tool should handle, whereas more specific concepts (and relationships)—such as *fan belt, low oil pressure,* and *broken fuse*—should be entered by domain experts in the KA tool generated.

This meta-view differs from those previously mentioned in that it focuses on the *declarative structures* required in the knowledge base, rather than on the instantiation of a problem-solving method, KA tool architecture, or organization. Ontologies in the ontology view are concerned with elements relevant for the target knowledge-base implementation, whereas ontologies in meta-tools such as PROTÉGÉ and DOTS address terms and relationships relevant to problem solving and KA tool architecture, respectively.

3.5 Programming Languages as Meta-Views

The simplest form of a meta-tool could be a general-purpose programming language (possibly augmented with a few suitable toolboxes). Many KA tools have been implemented successfully in Lisp, C, Prolog, and so on. In this case, the programming language itself is the meta-view; that is, it is the specification language for the KA tool. In fact, even tools such as PROTÉGÉ and DOTS require programming languages for entries outside their meta-views. In another sense, PROTÉGÉ and DOTS *are* high-level programming languages, although they are hardly Turing-complete. Some implementations of KA tools use special packages for user-interface management. HyperCard has been used in combination with programming languages—for instance, with Lisp. Evans [11] suggests the use of HyperCard as an environment for building expert systems. HyperCard stacks are used as the user interface, whereas modules implemented in Lisp are used to guide the acquisition process and to allow knowledge-base generation. Motta et al. [23] describe the use of domain-oriented *coding sheets* implemented in HyperCard for direct knowledge entry by domain experts.

Gappa [13] describes a toolbox for implementation of user interfaces for KA tools. This toolbox is essentially a program library that helps developers to create the KA tool's user interface—a laborious subtask in the implementation of graphical KA tools.

3.6 Composed Meta-Views

An obvious question is whether two or more meta-views can be merged to avoid some of the disadvantages in each of the original meta-views. For instance, a combination of a method-oriented view, such as the one implemented in PROTÉGÉ, and an abstract-architecture view, such as the one implemented in DOTS, would render a meta-view with the structure and guidance given by a problem-solving method as well as a high degree of flexibility in custom-tailoring of the target KA tool. Such combinations of meta-views should be regarded as *new* meta-views (rather than as simple combinations), since they represent distinct conceptual models for meta-tools. For example, a combination of the method-oriented and the abstract-architecture meta-views could require a user dialog in the meta-tool different from a straightforward merger of the user interfaces in PROTÉGÉ and DOTS, and possibly could require an alternative analysis of the domain, as well as a new way of working with the meta-tool.

There are, however, several theoretical and technical difficulties associated with implementing such a combined meta-view, since the meta-views in PROTÉGÉ and DOTS are partly incompatible. An example of a technical challenge is that changes to one part of the combined meta-view might affect other parts of the meta-view in a nontrivial way. Sometimes, this problem is not merely a technical one. For instance, it is sometimes possible to infer the structure of a form from an instantiation of a problem-solving method. The layout of forms generated can be custom-tailored later according to user preferences. Nevertheless, it is not clear what should be done if nontrivial modifications are made to the original instantiation of the problem-solving method. Pragmatic solutions might involve ignoring the changes in the method instantiation, discarding the custom-tailored layout, or applying heuristics to change the form layout.

There are many still issues to be resolved before composed meta-views can be implemented. A principal challenge for Spark (and for PROTÉGÉ II, the successor of PROTÉGÉ) is to generate KA tools that can seamlessly merge the knowledge requirements of all the components. Further, to achieve high-quality KA tools for composed problem solvers, the meta-tool must combine and structure a conglomeration of knowledge requirements into knowledge editors that are meaningful for experts.

4 Discussion

We divide our discussion into two parts: (1) a comparison between different approaches, and (2) an examination of implications for future meta-views and meta-tools.

4.1 Comparison of Meta-Views and Meta-Tools

At this stage, it is not possible to undertake a quantitative study comparing performance among various meta-views. We distinguish five criteria for comparing meta-views:

1. *Perspective:* The general perspective (paradigm) supported by the meta-view. This perspective includes what principal entities are used to specify target KA tools, and how those entities are viewed.

2. *Restrictions:* The scope, or limitations, of the meta-view. Every form of specification strategy will have boundaries in terms of the problem classes it addresses. (General programming languages are, for instance, restricted to computable problems.)

3. *Supportive power:* The degree of relevant modeling support provided by the meta-view (roughly corresponding to the level of abstraction). High supportive power usually entails use of a specialized specification strategy. Just as in any language, supportive power must be balanced against restrictions in meta-views.

4. *Practicability:* The degree of suitability for specification of real-world KA tools. A meta-view might be appealing from a theoretical or philosophical point of view, but still might be difficult to use for practical purposes by a majority of workers in knowledge engineering. Likewise, popular specification styles may have disputable theoretical bases.

5. *Meta-tool users:* The intended user category for the meta-tools supporting a meta-view. To create a meta-view (and thus meta-tool), we must know which members of the development team will use it.

6. *Training:* The training required to understand and use the meta-view for KA tool modeling. For instance, are general knowledge-engineering skills sufficient, or is additional training needed for a knowledge engineer to specify useful KA tools in a specific meta-view?

Table 1 summarizes these properties for four different meta-views: the method-oriented, abstract-architecture, organizational, and ontology meta-views. In addition, the corresponding properties for general programming languages are shown.

The method-oriented and abstract-architecture views have highly specialized perspectives. These meta-views are also intended for knowledge engineers trained in modeling according to the perspective adopted. To our knowledge, the ontology view has not been implemented in a meta-tool; consequently, no practical experience in this specification strategy has been reported. General programming languages provide indisputable generality, but much work is required to implement interactive KA tools in them. The developers must have programming skills and knowledge about the language, the environment, the window system, and so on.

Implementations of meta-tools can realize a meta-view in various ways. Designs (meta-views) are underspecified; therefore, examining implementations (meta-tools) makes comparisons more concrete. The same meta-view can be implemented in different manners, depending on considerations addressed by the meta-tool developer (e.g., dialog style, user community, and computing environment). At this time, only a few meta-tools—or tools exploiting meta-level structures—have been reported, so it is difficult to compare different meta-tools (and their underlying meta-views), especially by their strengths and weaknesses in practical use. Nevertheless, it is possible to make a rough classification of those available and to point out areas for development of new systems. We distinguish six criteria for meta-tools:

1. *Separate meta-tools and KA tools:* A distinction can be made between approaches that separate tool support into two or more levels (e.g., meta-tools and KA tools)

Aspect	Method-oriented	Abstract architecture	Organizational	Ontology	Programming language
Section	3.1	3.2	3.3	3.4	3.5
Perspective	Problem-solving method	KA tool architecture	roles & lifecycle	Concepts and relationships	Symbol-level expressions
Restricted to	problem class	KA tool architecture	predefined mechanisms & KA tools	domain description language	computable problems
Supportive power	High	High	High	N/A	Low
Practicable	Yes	Yes	Yes	Not tested	Yes
Meta-tool user(s)	KE	KE	KE & DE	KE & DE	Programmers
Training required	Yes, problem-solver modeling	Yes, KA tool design	Yes, domain modeling	N/A	Yes, programming

Table 1: A comparison of four different meta-views, as well as of conventional programming languages. The aspect "Section" refers to relevant sections in this article. (Abbreviations: KE = knowledge engineer, DE = domain expert, — = not available.)

and systems that maintain both levels in the same tool (e.g., KA workbenches). Integrated meta-tools and KA tools can potentially allow greater flexibility in terms of changes on the meta-level (e.g., faster update of the KA tool specification), whereas distinct meta-tools and KA tools can potentially run in different environments on different platforms.

2. *Meta-view:* The meta-view is the specification strategy (or model of the meta-level) for KA tools adopted (see Section 3).

3. *Specification model:* The specification model is the specific modeling framework used for specifying KA tools. For a method-oriented view, the specification model can be the particular model(s) supported; for the abstract-architecture view, the specification model would be the architectural framework and its components.

4. *Assumed domain class:* Meta-tools may assume a problem-solving method (e.g., classification and planning) for KA tools generated. The class of KA tools generated is also constrained by the meta-view. Generality in the domain class means that a meta-tool is useful in a broad variety of domains, whereas a restricted domain class could allow easier KA tool specifications since less definition information is required.

5. *Target KA tools family:* Target KA tools (or in the case of an integrated meta-level, the tool itself) might adopt different knowledge-acquisition strategies; for

Aspect	PROTÉGÉ	DOTS	SIS	Spark et al.	KNACK
Separate meta- and KA tools	Yes	Yes	Yes	Yes	No
Meta-view	Method-oriented	Abstract architecture	Abstract architecture	Organizational	N/A
Specification model	Skeletal-plan refinement	Editor-module architecture	Generic attentions	Tasks and mechanisms	N/A
Assumed domain class	Protocol management	None	None	Several domain classes	Reporting tasks
Target KA tool/method	Task-specific	Task-specific	Interview-oriented	Mechanism-specific	Interview-oriented
Target language	e-ONCOCIN	No assumptions	—	OPS5	OPS5

Table 2: A comparison of five tools that have meta-components. (KNACK is not a meta-tool, but rather is a KA tool that use meta-level representations of the domain to guide interrogation processes.)

example, they might use explicit knowledge editing, as in PROTÉGÉ and DOTS, and interview-based knowledge elicitation (i.e., KA tools oriented toward interrogation of domain experts in restricted natural language), as in SIS.

6. *Target language:* The target inference-engine or target knowledge-base format might vary. Meta-tools may or may not assume a particular inference engine or format for the resulting knowledge base.

Table 2 summarizes these properties for five systems: PROTÉGÉ [26]; DOTS [8]; SIS [16]; Spark, Burn, and Firefighter [18, 20]; and KNACK [17]. PROTÉGÉ, DOTS, and Spark are considered to be pure meta-tools in the sense that they separate the meta-level and KA level. Although KNACK features flexibility in adapting meta-level aspects of the KA tool, it was not originally intended as a meta-level tool for knowledge acquisition. As indicated in Table 2, the salient property that distinguishes the meta-tools PROTÉGÉ, DOTS, and Spark is the class of meta-view that they support. These tools also use specific models, which can be viewed as instances of meta-views; for example, PROTÉGÉ assumes skeletal-plan refinement as the method, DOTS assumes an architecture based on knowledge editors and modules, SIS relies heavily on attentions in its architectural model, and Spark is based on tasks and mechanisms for the method. PROTÉGÉ is tailored to a specific domain class (problems solvable by skeletal-plan refinement), whereas Spark supports several domain classes. Since the abstract-architecture view is independent of the domain, DOTS and SIS do not make assumptions about the domain class. In terms of target KA tool family, PROTÉGÉ, DOTS, and Spark all generate domain-oriented KA tools with graphical user interfaces for knowledge editing (the tools that Spark configures are mechanism specific, however), whereas SIS and KNACK assume an interview-oriented dialog with the expert. PROTÉGÉ is designed for e-ONCOCIN as the target language for knowledge bases produced by the KA tools. KNACK produces rule bases. DOTS does not assume a particular target language; transformation rules are used to ensure insulation from the target language in DOTS. The knowledge engineer, however, is assumed to know the target language and the transformation-rule format.

4.2 Examination of Implications of the Comparison for Meta-Views and Meta-Tools

An advantage of the method-oriented view is that it offers simplicity in the specification; that is, to specify KA tools, knowledge engineers need to be trained in only the problem-solving method. Another advantage is that an inference engine can be parameterized by largely the same specifications. The a priori design for target KA tools can be both a limitation and a strength. The abstract-architecture view is not limited to a single problem-solving method in the same way as is the method-oriented approach; its limitations can be found on the level of target KA tool architectures. However, the specification is more complex, and knowledge engineers need training in the abstract architecture supported. Since no a priori design for the target KA tools is presupposed, knowledge engineers are given extra freedom in custom-tailoring the tools generated.

Another important issue that concerns all types of meta-views is that of generality. Finding the "right" level of generality for meta-tools is primarily an empirical question. The implementations discussed in Section 3 are merely data points that can guide the development of the next generation of meta-tools. Meta-tools, and thus meta-views, need to be sufficiently general to be useful for a significantly large user community. Presumably, future generations of meta-tools must be generalized beyond current tools. In the method-oriented view, many different problem-solving methods can be supported by different meta-tools. Likewise, in the abstract-architecture view, many types of generic architectures can be supported. Tools such as PROTÉGÉ and DOTS adopt only specific *schemata* of the general meta-view. For instance, it is possible to conceive other method-oriented meta-tools for completely different classes of problem-solving methods.

5 Summary and Conclusions

Meta-level KA tools can be used to generate tailored KA tools automatically from a specification. Just as KA tools present different conceptual models to their users, meta-tools provide alternative meta-views to their users. Thus, a meta-view is the specification language used for describing the target KA tool.

This separation of KA-tool specification and implementation is analogous to the distinction between *epistemological* and *heuristic* adequacy for knowledge representation [21]. There are several epistemological problems at the level of meta-views for KA tools—for instance, how to view emerging target KA tools. The task of implementing a meta-tool includes solving the problem of establishing heuristic adequacy for the meta-view (i.e., ensuring the practicability of the meta-view). In fact, epistemological and heuristic adequacy must be ensured at every system level (i.e., expert system, KA tool, and meta-tool).

We have examined several different meta-views that can be used for KA tool specification. For instance, the method-oriented view adopts the metaphor of a problem-solving method, and the abstract-architecture view focuses on components of KA tools. Meta-views govern the design process of the target KA tools. Knowledge engineers might be encouraged to view the KA tool support in a certain manner, and to design their KA tools in certain ways. No meta-view (except perhaps a general programming language) is complete, in the sense that all conceivable KA tools can be specified in it. Although there are theoretical and practical difficulties in combining (sometimes partially incompatible) meta-views, doing so can remove certain biases introduced by a single meta-view in the knowledge-engineering process, improve the generality of the specification language, and provide more freedom for the knowledge engineer in designing KA tools.

Acknowledgments

This work has been supported in part by grants LM05157 and LM05208 from the National Library of Medicine, by a gift from Digital Equipment Corporation, and by scholarships from the Swedish Institute, from Fulbright Commission, and from Stanford University.

We are grateful to Lyn Dupré for providing editorial assistance. John Egar and Samson Tu commented on various draft versions of this article.

References

1. J. S. Bennett. ROGET: A knowledge-based system for acquiring the conceptual structure of a diagnostic expert system. *Journal of Automated Reasoning*, 1(1):49–74, 1985.

2. J. H. Boose. A knowledge acquisition program for expert systems based on personal construct psychology. *International Journal of Man–Machine Studies*, 23(5):495–525, 1985.

3. J. H. Boose and J. M. Bradshaw. Expertise transfer and complex problems: Using AQUINAS as a knowledge-acquisition workbench for knowledge-based systems. *International Journal of Man–Machine Studies*, 26(1):3–28, 1987.

4. B. Chandrasekaran. Generic tasks in knowledge-based reasoning: High-level building blocks for expert system design. *IEEE Expert*, 1(3):23–30, 1986.

5. W. J. Clancey. Heuristic classification. *Artificial Intelligence*, 27(3):289–350, 1985.

6. R. Davis. Interactive transfer of expertise: Acquisition of new inference rules. *Artificial Intelligence*, 12(2):121–157, 1979.

7. H. Eriksson. Architectural issues in KA tools: Towards structured transformation into knowledge-bases. In *Proceedings of the Fifth European Knowledge Acquisition for Knowledge-Based Systems Workshop, EKAW'91*, Crieff, Scotland, May 1991.

8. H. Eriksson. *Meta-Tool Support for Knowledge Acquisition.* PhD thesis 244, Linköping University, 1991.

9. H. Eriksson. Domain-oriented knowledge acquisition tool for protein purification planning. *Journal of Chemical Information and Computer Sciences*, 32(1):90–95, 1992.

10. L. Eshelman, D. Ehret, J. McDermott, and M. Tan. MOLE: A tenacious knowledge-acquisition tool. *International Journal of Man–Machine Studies*, 26(1):41–54, 1987.

11. R. Evans. Expert systems and HyperCard. *Byte*, 15(1):317–324, Jan. 1990.

12. W. A. Gale. Knowledge-based knowledge acquisition for a statistical consulting system. *International Journal of Man–Machine Studies*, 26(1):55–64, 1987.

13. U. Gappa. A tool-box for generating graphical knowledge acquisition environments. In *Proc. of the World Congress on Expert Systems*, Orlando, FL, Dec. 1991.

14. G. Kahn, S. Nowlan, and J. McDermott. Strategies for knowledge acquisition. *IEEE Transactions on Pattern Analysis and Machine Intelligence, PAMI*, 7(5):511–522, 1985.

15. W. Karbach, M. Linster, and A. Voß. Models, methods, roles and tasks: Many labels—one idea? *Knowledge Acquisition*, 2(4):279–299, 1990.

16. A. Kawaguchi, H. Motoda, and R. Mizoguchi. Interview-based knowledge acquisition using dynamic analysis. *IEEE Expert*, 6(5):47–60, Oct. 1991.

17. G. Klinker, J. Bentolila, S. Genetet, M. Grimes, and J. McDermott. KNACK: report-driven knowledge acquisition. *International Journal of Man–Machine Studies*, 26(1):65–79, 1987.

18. G. Klinker, C. Bhola, G. Dallemagne, D. Marques, and J. McDermott. Usable and reusable programming constructs. *Knowledge Acquisition*, 3(2):117–135, 1991.

19. S. Marcus and J. McDermott. SALT: a knowledge acquisition language for propose-and-revise systems. *Artificial Intelligence*, 39(1):1–37, 1989.

20. D. Marques, G. Klinker, G. Dallemagne, P. Gautier, J. McDermott, and D. Tung. More data on usable and reusable programming constructs. In J. H. Boose and B. R. Gaines, editors, *Proc. of the Sixth Banff Knowledge Acquisition for Knowledge-Based Systems Workshop*, pages 14.1–14.19, Banff, Canada, Oct. 1991.

21. J. McCarthy and P. J. Hayes. Some philosophical problems from the standpoint of artificial intelligence. *Machine Intelligence*, 4:463–502, 1969.

22. J. McDermott. Preliminary steps toward a taxonomy of problem-solving methods. In S. Marcus, editor, *Automating Knowledge Acquisition for Expert Systems*, chapter 8, pages 225–256. Kluwer Academic Publishers, Norwell, Massachusetts, 1988.

23. E. Motta, T. Rajan, and M. Eisenstadt. Knowledge acquisition as a process of model refinement. *Knowledge Acquisition*, 2(1):21–49, 1990.

24. M. A. Musen. *Automated Generation of Model-Based Knowledge-Acquisition Tools*. Morgan-Kaufmann, San Mateo, California, 1989.

25. M. A. Musen. Conceptual models of interactive knowledge acquisition tools. *Knowledge Acquisition*, 1(1):73–88, 1989.

26. M. A. Musen. An editor for the conceptual models of interactive knowledge-acquisition tools. *International Journal of Man–Machine Studies*, 31(6):673–698, 1989.

27. M. A. Musen, L. M. Fagan, D. M. Combs, and E. H. Shortliffe. Use of a domain model to drive an interactive knowledge-editing tool. *International Journal of Man–Machine Studies*, 26(1):105–121, 1987.

28. A. Newell. The knowledge level. *Artificial Intelligence*, 18(1):87–127, 1982.

29. S. W. Tu, M. G. Kahn, M. A. Musen, J. C. Ferguson, E. H. Shortliffe, and L. M. Fagan. Episodic skeletal-plan refinement based on temporal data. *Commun. ACM*, 32(12):1439–1455, 1989.

30. B. J. Wielinga, A. T. Schreiber, and J. A. Breuker. KADS: a modelling approach to knowledge engineering. *Knowledge Acquisition*, in press.

AN APPROACH TO OPERATIONALIZE CONCEPTUAL MODELS : THE SHELL AIDE

C. GREBOVAL, G. KASSEL *

URA CNRS 817 HEUDIASYC
Université de Technologie de Compiègne
Département de Génie Informatique
B.P. 649, 60206 - Compiègne Cedex
FRANCE
tel : (33) 44 23 44-23 poste 42 73
(33) 44 23 44 69
fax : 44 23 44 77
e-mail : cgrebo@hds.univ-compiegne.fr
gkassel@hds.univ-compiegne.fr

Abstract : In order to combine both the contribution of conceptual models to help knowledge acquisition and the contribution of second generation expert systems to build problem solvers that are less brittle and easier to explain, we propose an approach to operationalize conceptual models. This approach is based upon the shell AIDE which allows the knowledge engineer to model at a high level of abstraction. The shell is based upon a mechanism of translation to code automatically the completely formalized conceptual model, in a lower level model directly implemented. The link between the conceptual model and the KBS is thus preserved. In addition to the advantages bound to prototyping at the knowledge level, the AIDE's approach allows validation and explaination at this same high level of abstraction.

1. Introduction

Today, numerous research projects on the transfer and the modeling of knowledge propose different approaches and methods to construct Knowledge Based Systems (KBS). Among these approaches :

i) The "second generation expert systems" approach uses knowledge analysis tools, like the distinction between shallow and deep knowledge or the separation between domain knowledge and solving methods, to construct KBS in which these different types of knowledge are explicitely represented [31][32]. These KBS are generally based upon systems of representation which mix different formalisms. The systems NEOMYCIN [10] and CHECK [13] are characteristic of such an approach.

ii) The approach "model based development" proposes to use descriptions of solving processes at high levels of abstraction in order to elaborate, by refining of these intermediate models, the operational model that constitutes the KBS. Typical of such an approach is the method KADS [38].

---

* This research is partially supported by the French Ministry of Research and Technology under the PRC-IA project, and the French agency ANVAR under the programme "recherche exploratoire 90".

Each of these approaches has its own motivations : in the case of i) constructing KBS that are less brittle, easier to explain and validate; in the case of ii) helping in interpreting and acquiring knowledge, using descriptions nearer to the level at which the expert conceptualizes the domain and the task.

Because the advantages of these two kinds of approaches seek complementary, it seems interesting to try to combine them. The distinction of Newell [25] between *knowledge level* and *symbol level* illuminates the conditions that bring them closer together.

The motivation, emphasized by approaches of type ii), which consists in abstracting from implementation details, thus from the symbol level, is partly a consequence of the low level of current representation formalisms (rules, objects, logic).

Among the intermediate models, the *conceptual models* describe the desired behaviour of the KBS in terms of generic types of knowledge which take place in problem solving. These descriptions at the knowledge level are based upon *knowledge level architectures*[1]. By definition, they are not executable. The implementation of the conceptual model thus requires the construction of a *design model*, selecting a symbol level architecture. We find here the two characteristic steps of the method KADS[2].

The important point of that type of approach consists in going from the knowledge level to the symbol level, with the risk that the two models are distant (that the structure of the design model does not reflect the structure of the conceptual model) and that once the first prototype is elaborated, one cannot easily return to the conceptual model. In the case of the KADS method, as we are reminded in [28], the fact that the models are disconnected raises problems for validating and explaining the behaviour of the KBS.

An approach of the type second generation (i)) can be seen as an answer to these problems. Such an approach will consists in constructing jointly a design model at a high level of abstraction in which the different types of knowledge identified in the conceptual model will be explicitely represented. In bringing the design model nearer to the conceptual model, the objective is to make the latter operational.

The aim of remedying these problems, in trying to couple the two models, is at the core of numerous recent works [15] [22] [34] [37]. The method consists in bringing nearer the primitives at the knowledge level and the primitives at the symbol level. Nevertheless, in these works the two architectures do not completely coincide. Then, constructing a KBS always consists in elaborating the two models. As a consequence, the conceptual models are not really operational, because they are not directly executable.

We present, in this paper, an approach in which a perfect adequacy between the two models is realized, the conceptual model being really operational. The shell AIDE[3] which supports this approach is described in part 2. An example of KBS developed with this shell, the system of medical diagnosis SATIN, is presented in part 3. In part 4, we compare our approach with that of KADS and with works whose objectives are to operationalize conceptual models.

---

[1] This term is borrowed from [33]. It corresponds in KADS to the notion of *epistemological architecture*, i.e. a theory of knowledge identifying generic types of knowledge and specifying their role in the problem solving processes.

[2] The terms *conceptual model* and *design model* are used in the same sense as [28]. Note that in this last reference the conceptual model, renamed expertise model, effectively decribes (at the knowledge level) the KBS.

[3] This shell enters in a project of development of explicative systems and has recently been extended in a reflective framework (in french : Architecture Intégrant Déduction et Explication). The question of the production of explanation been not discussed in this paper, the interested reader can refer to [23] or [18].

2. The shell AIDE

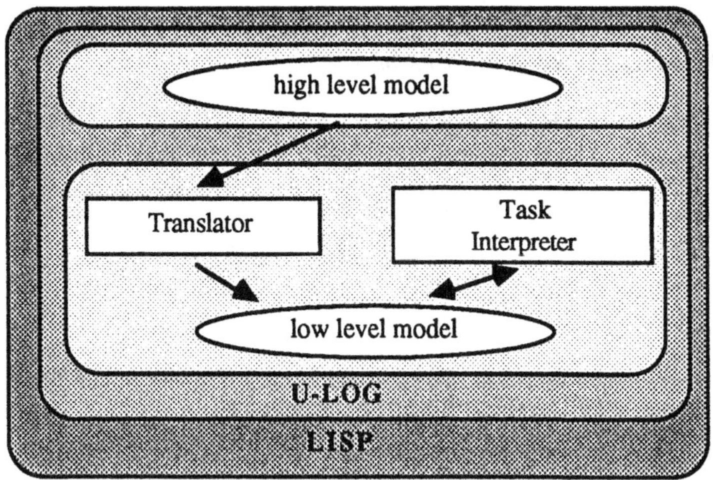

Figure 1 : Anatomy of the shell AIDE

The approach is based upon the computer framework which is sketched in the figure 1. The contribution of the shell AIDE is to allow modeling at the knowledge level without later needing to elaborate a design model, like in KADS. This is made possible thanks to a translation mechanism between two models of expertise specified at different levels of abstraction.

The adequation between the knowledge and symbol levels concerns the high level model of expertise, which is elaborated by the knowledge engineer. This adequation is based upon two points :

• A detailed knowledge level architecture that allows us to completely specify the conceptual model of the task to perform. This architecture distinguishes between the domain knowledge and the solving method, these two layers being detailed on the one hand in terms of *generic concepts, individual concepts, properties* and *relations* , and on the other in terms of *tasks and operators* .

• A symbol architecture, which is a strict reflection of the knowledge architecture. Each primitive at the knowledge level is associated to a symbol primitive.

Thus, at this level of abstraction, the conceptual model and the design model are just one model : the high level model of expertise. Nevertheless, this one is not directly executable.

The **Translator** implements, in AIDE, the high level model of expertise. This software module uses a transcription of the high level primitives (tasks, operators, concepts ...) into lower level primitives (objects, rules) in order to translate the high level model into a directly executable lower model. The low level model is represented in the primitives of U-LOG, a software integrating objects and logic programming, which has been developed in our laboratory [16][17].

The AIDE's knowledge level architecture is presented in **2.1** and illustrated in **2.2** with examples of knowledge extracted from the system of medical diagnosis SATIN. The symbol level architecture is presented in **2.3**. Then the works of the **Translator** and the **Tasks Intrepreter** are described in **2.4**.

2.1. The knowledge level architecture

The work of Clancey and his colleagues on the system NEOMYCIN [7][10] has widely inspired the knowledge level architecture of AIDE. The main point of this architecture is the distinction between the domain knowledge and the control knowledge, or the strategy. This distinction, which is present in many recent works in AI (in particular in KADS) is based upon three principles. We take them as hypotheses of work.

P1 It is possible and useful to identify, by its role, control knowledge which specifies when, how and what knowledge at an object level use.

P2 It is possible and useful to represent the control knowledge and the object level knowledge in two layers with limited interactions.

P3 It is possible and useful to represent abstractly the control knowledge, independently of a specific application.

These principles are based on stronger and stronger hypotheses and they have different advantages. Because the motivation of the project AIDE is the development of explicative systems [23], as in NEOMYCIN, we shall emphasize in the next paragraphs the advantages which concern more particularly the production of explanations.

Once the existence and the function of control knowledge are admitted, principle P2 raises the question of the declarative representation of the object level knowledge. If we admit this principle, this knowledge takes the statute of domain knowledge, being specified independently of its use, thus independently of a specific task.

One primary interest of P2 is that the domain knowledge can be used for different tasks. Another important interest concerns explanation : when the control knowledge is made explicit, it becomes possible to show the problem solving method which has been used [14][19][26].

Despite these advantages, principle P2 is not unanimously admitted, as proved by the position of Chandrasekaran and his colleagues in their approach to Generic Tasks[4]:

> [5, p. 1184] : «Our work is based an alternative view, viz., that knowledge representation and use cannot be separated.... That is, knowledge should be in different forms, depending upon the type of function for which it is used.»

In order to illustrate principle P3, we reproduce two examples of strategic knowledge presented in [8] :

S1 : To determine if the patient has an infection, ask if he has shivers.

S2 : To determine if the patient has a disease, verify if the findings associated with this disease are present.

---

[4] Related to that subject, the reader can read in the review 'Knowledge Engineering, 3(3), 1988' the presentation of Chandrasekaran [6] and the contradictory response of Iwasaki, Keller and Feigenbaum in favour of principle P2 [21].

This principle advocates to represent S2 rather than S1, S1 being just a particular case of the abstract strategy S2. The different advantages (also the limits) are described in [8]. P3 allows the presentation of the solving method either abstractly, or in concrete terms while instantiating the abstract principle with the concepts of the domain. This advantage has been exploited in the explanation module of NEOMYCIN [19].

The adoption of principles P1, P2 and P3 finally leads to consideration of two layers of knowledge : domain knowledge which is independent of the specific task and control knowledge independent of the domain[5].

The knowledge level architecture of AIDE, which is presented below, can be seen as a realization of these three principles.

In order to be complete in the description of the solving process, we have added a third layer of knowledge : the specific case knowledge. This latter concerns the knowledge which is related to the particular problem at hand. During the problem solving, reasoning objects are added to this layer which plays the role of working memory. Then the reasoning progresses by extensions of this knowledge layer.

2.2. Overview of the three layers

We now detail these three layers, noting in italic the primitives of the knowledge level architecture. Figure 2 illustrates graphically this presentation with examples of knowledge from the system SATIN, split according to the three layers. Some of these examples are reproduced in figure 3 which constitues a part of SATIN's high level model.

2.2.1. The strategic knowledge

This knowledge layer is organized around *tasks* whose function is to perform a solving method in order to realize an expected goal. The solving method is specified by a set of *operators* and an *indication of control* on these operators. When a task is called, it receives *data* as an input and tries to apply its operators with respect to the indication of control.

To apply an operator consists in testing the domain knowledge and the specific case knowledge in order to evoke other tasks. The tasks are thus useful in planning the extensions of the specific case knowledge, which are finally realized by terminal tasks.

This general conception of problem solving processes corresponds to that expressed in [11] [12][6] and implemented in NEOMYCIN. In the example of figures 2-3, the task "evocation-confirmation-hypotheses" comprises of three operators.

2.2.2. The domain knowledge

This layer is organized around *concepts*, characterized by *properties* and linked together by *relations*. The concepts are either *generic concepts* denoting a class of objects, or *individual concepts* denoting objects.

---

[5] The notion of independence is of course quite relative. One will consider, for example, that S2 is independent of the domain because it specifies a general strategy of medical diagnosis, that is not bound to a specific application.

[6][12, page 5] : The title of this paper reflects the idea that *control knowledge can be fruitfully described in terms of operators for constructing models, and this is something that all expert systems do.*

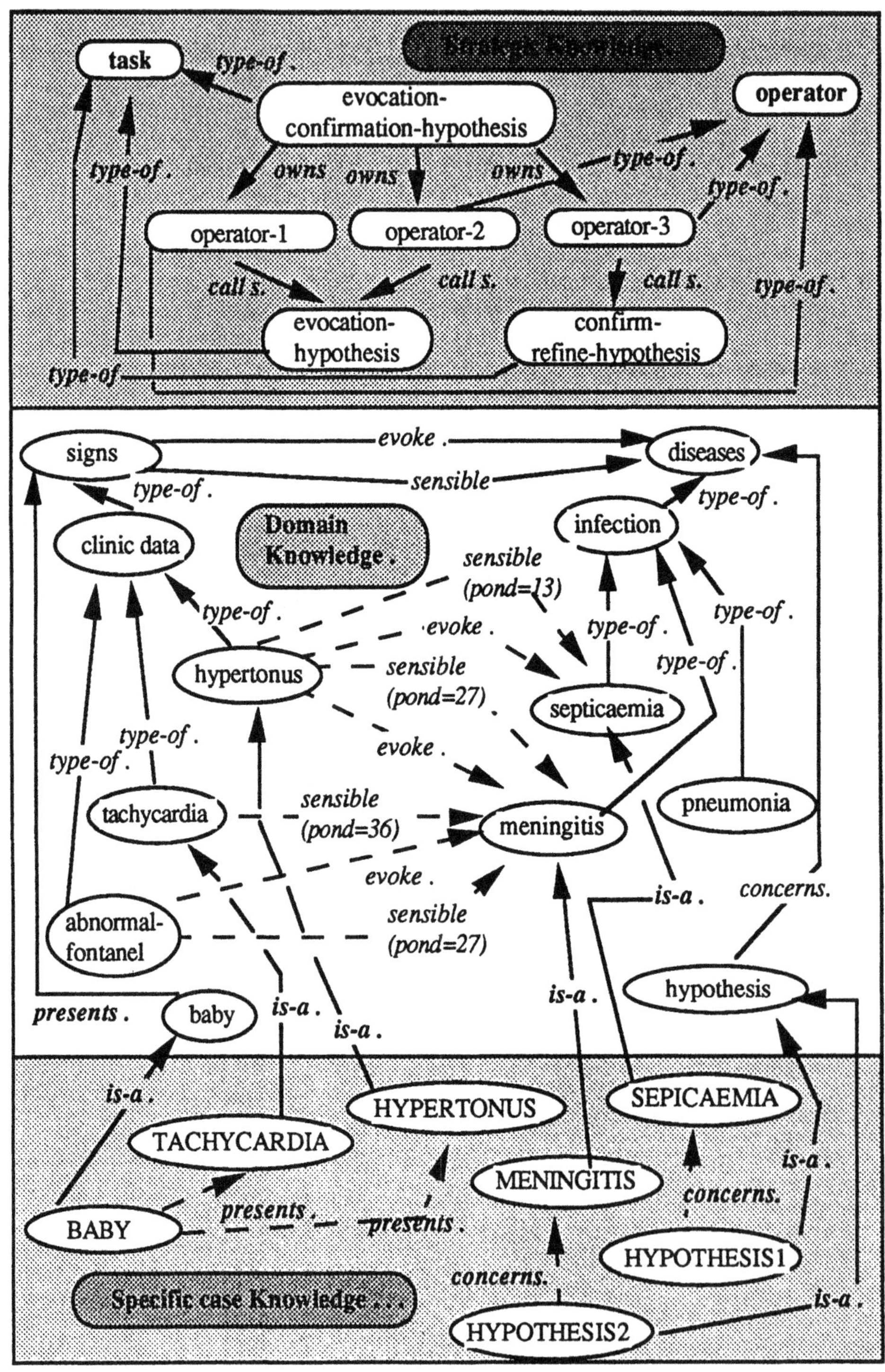

Figure 2 : Examples of knowledge shared out in the three layers.

This layer includes its own description. It is composed of descriptive knowledge, which corresponds to a declaration of the domain concepts: their name, the name of their properties and relations (see the definition of the relation "sensible" in figure 3), and assertional or factual knowledge (see the knowledge attached to the concept "hypertonus" in figure 3). The descriptive and assertional knowledge are respectively represented, in figure 2, by continuous and dotted arrows.

The descriptive knowledge consitutes a Conceptual Model (in the sense of Data Bases) of the assertional knowledge. This Conceptual Model (we note it with capital letters in order to differentiate it from the conceptual models of KADS) defines a relational language which is used by the operators of the strategic layer as a means of accessing the assertional and the specific case knowledge.

Above concepts, constraints between properties of concepts can be stated which increase the assertional knowledge. In SATIN, these constraints are used to represent the knowledge definition of concepts (see the rule defining the concept "abnormal-fibrinogene" in figure 3).

2.2.3. The specific case knowledge

At the begining of the solving process, this layer contains the initial data which characterize the problem to be solved. During solving process, it increases in size with objects of reasoning like (in the case of SATIN) the hypotheses of diagnosis, the final diagnosis and the proposed therapy.

This knowledge is specified by individual concepts, which are instances of generic domain concepts.

2.3. The symbol level architecture

Different to the conceptual models of KADS, which are only on paper, the three layers models of AIDE are formally described in a file, with a well defined syntax, in order to be automatically interpreted.

For the strategic knowledge, the syntax of tasks is the one presented in figure 3. Each task is thus characterized by its name, the name of the data it receives, an indication of control and the list of its operators. These operators are represented, as in HERACLES (the shell of NEOMYCIN), with a first order rule language[7].

The domain knowledge and the specific case knowledge are represented in the conceptual graph notation of Sowa [30], a choice that was motivated by the possibility of providing later on explanations in natural language [3]. For the purpose of this paper, we shall emphasize two main advantages of this notation :

- On the one hand, the Conceptual Model (the descriptive knowledge) is described using the same syntax as the assertional knowledge. The example of the relation “sensibility” in figure 3 illustrates this point.

---

[7] The terms preceded by an asterisk are variables which will be instantiated by the domain and specific case concepts (generic and individuals), during the session. The predicates used in condition correspond to the relations and properties of these concepts. A few pre-defined predicates such as "set", "for-each-element", extend the expressive language of the operators, providing primitives for elementary treatments on the concepts.

```
task = evocation-confirmation-hypothesis
control = and
operators
if [presents [mother *m] *q]
then execute evocation-hypothesis with finding = *q
if [presents [baby *x] *s]
then execute evocation-hypothese with finding = *s
if *ens = set [ *disease such-that [ concerns [hypothesis *h]
                                                    *disease ] ]
and *x = most-refined-instances [ *ens ]
and for-each-element [ *y *x ]
then execute confirm-refine-hypothesis with hypothesis = *y
```

STRATEGIC KNOWLEDGE

```
(defrelation "sensible" '(&x &y) '(*v f)
    "[sensible]-
        -> (link) -> [sign : &x]
        -> (link) -> [disease : &y]
        -> (specif) -> [pond],.")

(defconcept "hypertonus" '&g
  "[clinical data:&g]-
      -> (evoke) -> [septicaemia: *s]
      -> (link) -> [sensible] -
         -> (link) -> [septicaemia : *s]
         -> (specif) -> [pond : 13],
      -> (evoke) -> [meningitis : *m]
      -> (link) -> [sensible] -
         -> (link) -> [meningitis : *m]
         -> (specif) -> [pond : 27],,.")

(defconcept-ind
  "[regle_def_signs : sig1]-
    ->(defines)->[abnormal_fibrinogene]
    ->(specif)->[premise: [proposition:[baby:*x]->(specif)->[fibrinogene]-
                                 -> (inferior) -> [fibrinogene: 1.5],.]-
                     ->(or)->[baby:*x]->(specif)->[fibrinogene]-
                                 -> (superior)->[fibrinogene : 5],,.]
    -> (specif)->[action:[baby :*x]->(presents)->[abnormal_fibrinogene].],."
```

DOMAIN KNOWLEDGE

```
(defconcept-ind   "[baby: BABY]-
    -> (specif) -> [name : MARTIN]
    -> (specif) -> [first-name : Luc]
    -> (specif) -> [terme : 33]
    -> (presents) -> [tachycardia : TACHYCARDIA]
    -> (presents) -> [hypertonus : HYPERTONUS],.")
```

SPECIFIC CASE KNOWLEDGE

Figure 3 : Part of the high level model of SATIN

- On the other hand, it corresponds to each primitive at the knowledge level (generic concept, individual concept, property, relation) a representation primitive. Figure 3 shows a few examples of domain knowledge from SATIN, represented in the conceptual graph notation of Sowa.

The three layers of knowledge, represented each with its own syntax, constitute the high level model of expertise of AIDE, for which the two perspectives knowledge level / symbol level coincide. We describe in the next paragraph the computer framework which interprets these high level models.

2.4. Anatomy of the shell

This framework is written in U-LOG, a software integrating objects and logic programming : Prolog, in a Lisp environment, developed by Paul Gloess in our laboratory [16][17]. The system objects used are of the type semantic model, or "entities/relations" model. Prolog considers the object data base as a set of particular clauses which gives it the characteristics of a deductive data base.

The architecture of the shell AIDE, sketched graphically in figure 1, consists of two main programs : the **Translator** and the **Tasks Interpreter**.

2.4.1. The Translator

The function of this program is to translate a high level model in an U-LOG program, which constitutes an executable model. The power of representation of U-LOG, as well as its theory of interface between objects and logic programming, have allowed us to define a simple mechanism of translation between the high level primitives, presented in the former paragraphs, and the primitives of U-LOG.

- The tasks are represented by classes of objects (subtype of the class "task"), with a property whose value is a list of operators. Each operator is presented by a predicate.

- The descriptive knowledge (the Conceptual Model) is a declaration of the different classes with their properties. These classes code both the generic concepts and the relations, so there are in U-LOG "concept" classes and "relation" classes.

- The assertional domain knowledge and the specific case knowledge are represented according to the following correspondances : relations between generic concepts <-> instances of the classes "relation", individual concepts <-> instances of classes "concept", definition knowledge <-> instances of the class "definition rule".

Figure 4 presents a few examples of knowledge from figure 3 translated in U-LOG. This figure illustrates the simple isomorphism which exists between the high level primitives and the primitives U-LOG.

The fact that in U-LOG each instance must be described by a class is the reason why the Conceptual Model must be explicitely represented in the low level model. The Conceptual Model is thus translated before the assertional knowledge.

```
(DEFOBJ (|evocation--confirmation-hypothesis| TASK))
(DEFMESSAGE (|evocation-confirmation-hypothesis| :INIT) NIL
  (USLOT |evocation-confirmation-hypothesis| :CONTROLE USELF '|and|)
  (USLOT |evocation-confirmation-hypothesis| :OPERARORS USELF
                                         '(OP395 OP396 OP397)) USELF)
(DEFPREDICATE OP395
  ((OP395)
    (:= *395 (|mother| :ID *\m)) (|presents| :|predecessor| *395 :|successor| *\q)
    (& (PASSAGE-DATA '|evocation-hypothesis| '|findings| *\q))
    (& (EXECUTE-TASK '|evocation-hypothesis|))
    (& (DESTRUCTION-DATA '|evocation-hypothesis| '|findings|))))
```

```
((|rule_def_signs|
  :ID T173   :|reference| |sig1|
  :|action| ((:= *181 (|baby| *185 :|reference| *\x))
          (:= *182 (|abnormal_fibrinogene| *183 :|reference| *184))
          (|presents| :|predecessor| *181 :|successor| *182))
  :|premise| ((OR (AND (:= *175 (|baby| *177 :|reference| *\x :|fibrinogene| *176))
                        (|inferior| *176 1.5))
                   (AND (:= *178 (|baby| *180 :|reference| *\x :|fibrinogene| *179))
                        (|superior| *179 5.0))))))

 (defobj (|hypertonus| clinic_data|))

 (defobj (|sensible| relation)   (defpredicate |sensible|
   (|predecessor| |sign|)           ((|sensible| :|predecessor| |hypertonus|
   (|successor| |disease|)                       :|successor| |septiceamia|
    |pond|)                                      :|pond| 13)))
```

```
(defpredicate |baby|
   ((|baby| zz                     (defpredicate |presents|
       :|reference| |BABY|             ((|presents| :|predecessor| {|baby| zz}
       :|name| MARTIN                                :|successor| {tachycardiae ta})))
       :|first-name| Luc
       :|term|  33)))
```

Figure 4 : Part of the low level model of SATIN

2.4.2. The Task Interpreter

This program is a tasks manager developed as an extension of U-LOG. The mechanism of pattern-matching allowing operators to test the domain and specific case knowledge uses directly the mechanism of U-LOG which allows the extraction of couples of instances bound by a relation in the data base.

The shell AIDE, that we have defined so far, allows the development of arbitrary problem solvers because the **Translator**, the **Task Interpreter** and the knowledge level architecture are independent of a particular domain or task.

One of the first problem solvers, the system SATIN (in french : Système d'Aide au Traitement des Infections néonatales)[8], allowed us to validate the different modules of the shell and consitute a primary library of terminal tasks. Actually, this same shell is used to develop a new solver : an explanation module for the system SATIN [18].

Constructing a KBS with the shell AIDE consists in elaborating the high level model of expertise. Then the aim of the knowledge transfer is no longer to acquire rules, but to model domain knowledge and solving methods.

Founding upon our experience in the development of SATIN, we show in part 3 how, the fact of modeling at a high level of abstraction, radically modifies the approach of knowledge acquisition.

3. Modeling at the knowledge level : an example

The task realized by SATIN consists in establishing a first diagnosis (as soon as the children enters the pediatrics service) and in deciding of a line of conduct : simple surveillance or prescription of antibiotics. The diagnosis established by SATIN concerns more precisely the mother-foetal infections. In the present state of the project only the diagnosis task is modelled.

3.1. Selection of a generic method

The objective of knowledge acquisition is to specify domain knowledge and problem solving methods (independent of a specific application). Thus during our analysis of the task, we principally studied the different problem solving methods and their associated domain models.

Different "types" of methods, or generic methods, suited to diagnosis reasoning are described in the literature. For the three principal methods listed below, we have noted in parentheses the name of the diagnosis systems which use them :

- The "Hierarchical Classification" (CENTAUR [1], RED [29], DIVA [14], the "heuristic" component of CHECK : LITHO [13]).

- The "Heuristic Classification" (NEOMYCIN [7]).

- The "Causal Reasoning" (CASNET [36], the "deep" component of CHECK).

These methods distinguish themselves by the type of domain knowledge they manipulate. For instance, the causal reasoning necessitates the knowledge of a pathophysiological causal network.

In the domain of the mother-foetal infections, the pathophysiological processes being, still today, largely unknown, we have thus chosen a method of the type "classification". This type of solving method consists in comparing the characteristics of the case in hand (the findings presented by the child) to the characteristics of solutions or classes of solutions (the clinical board of diseases).

---

[8] A first prototype of this system, realized in collaboration with the pediatrics service of Professor Risbourg at the North Hospital of Amiens, is actually being validated [2]. Doctor G. Krim is the expert in this project.

Different ways of doing this comparison exist : [32, p. 40] lists six different methods of classification. Again, because these methods distinguish between themselves according to the type of domain knowledge they use, we have made our choice using the available knowledge.

The "heuristic classification" that we have finally chosen is in fact an optimization of the "hierarchical classification" : it supposes that we use heuristic association links between the data (the findings presented by the child) and the solutions (the diseases), avoiding the systematic examination in a top down fashion of the hierarchy of diseases.

3.2. Modeling the strategic knowledge : the role of the "Heuristic Classification".

This inference structure, presented graphically in figure 5, has shown its interest in describing the structure of control of many expert systems emphasizing a general common problem solving method [9].

Several tasks (abstraction, heuristic association, refinement) appear, linking together different models of the domain. This schema has guided us in the elaboration of the inference structure of our application. This latter is presented in figure 6. The tasks that we have defined are :

- The abstraction task is decomposed in two distinct tasks. The first one consists in establishing findings from the initial data (anamnestic and clinic data) by means of definition rules. The second one consists in establishing syndromes by means of regroupings the findings.

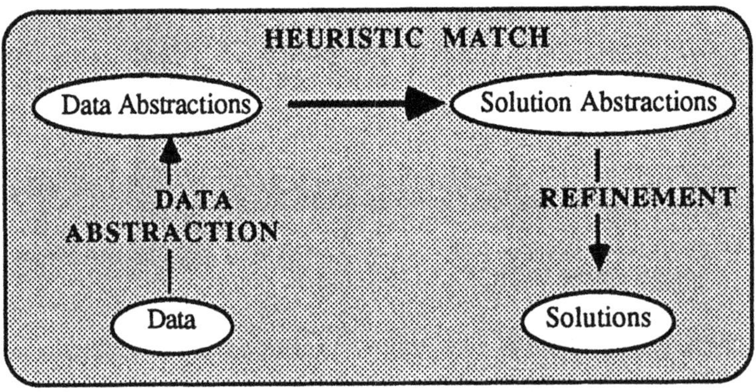

Figure 5 : The "Heuristic Classification" (from [9]).

- The evocation task is based upon association links between, on the one hand findings and syndromes, and on the other hand diseases (generic or specific). These links express that a finding, or a set of findings, is characteristic of a disease.

- The refinement task executes itself in two steps. First the confirmation/ infirmation task is performed. The evaluation of an hypothesis is based upon the specificity of the findings presented by the child, and the sensibility of findings the child does not present. When an hypothesis has been confirmed, the refinement task is then executed : more specific diseases are considered to be confirmed.

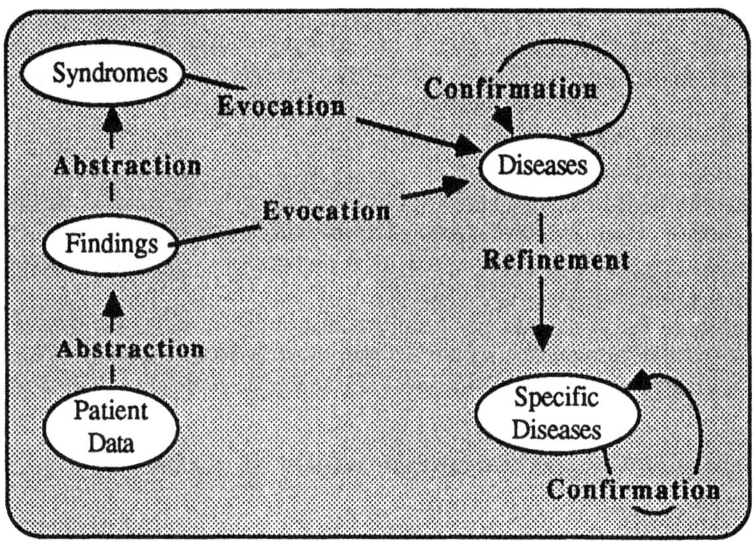

Figure 6 : Inference structure of the task "finding a diagnosis" of SATIN

The inference structure of the task "finding a diagnosis" of SATIN contains fifteen non terminal tasks and five terminal tasks. The role of terminal tasks is to apply a rule, create a concept, add a relation between concepts or modify the property of a concept.

3.3 Modeling the domain knowledge : the role of the Conceptual Model

The elaboration of these tasks lead us, at the same time, to refine the Conceptual Model of the domain knowledge. Thus, we defined with the expert the different taxonomies of concepts (findings, syndromes, diseases) and also the type of the links between these concepts : the relation of definition of findings, the relation of regrouping the findings in syndromes, a sensibility link between the findings and the diseases (in order to represent the different clinic, anamnestic, paraclinic boards of each disease) and an evocation link between findings and diseases. Once this Conceptual Model has been defined, it was given to the expert in order to acquire the assertional knowledge.

The approach that we have followed to elaborate the high level model of expertise of SATIN has been strongly imposed by the tool, the shell AIDE, and by the result we wanted to get. On that point, it is significant that in order to get models of expertise with near characteristics, approaches of the same type have been proposed in KADS [4] or by L. Steels in his "componential architecture" [32].

An important aspect of that type of approach is a good knowledge of the different solving methods. Thus, having in mind a taxonomy of such methods, we were able to reduce the combination of choices during acquisition and to orientate the interviews with the expert : after having chosen one type of method (the classification), we interested ourselves in its sub-types (the linear, hierachical, and heuristic classifications).

From the point of view of acquisition, we retrieve in AIDE the advantages bound to the conceptual models of KADS, mainly specicifications at a high level which help the communication between the expert and the knowledge engineer.

The contribution of the shell AIDE is precisely to render these specifications operational. We compare now in part 4 the approach AIDE to other works on the modeling at the knowledge level and on the operationalization of conceptual models.

4. Comparison with other works

We note that the high level models of AIDE are of the "same nature" as the KADS conceptual models, since they are expressed at the same level of abstraction. However, they are based upon a different knowledge level architecture. The two architectures are compared in **4.1**, refering for KADS to [28][9].

By contrast, as far as the passage from the knowledge level to the symbol level is concerned, the AIDE approach is nearer to work done in Steels' team [34], to Wetter's work [37] or to approaches like MODEL-K [22] or KARL [15]. This point is developed in **4.2**.

4.1. Comparison with the conceptual models of KADS

The high level models of AIDE are expressed at the same level of abstraction as the KADS conceptual models. However, they are based upon a different knowledge level architecture.

A first review shows that, beside the domain layers of KADS and AIDE which are exactly the same,.the AIDE's models have a supplementary layer : the specific case knowledge, but have "lost" two layers : the strategic level and the inference level. The strategic level is effectively not considered in AIDE, in return the loss of the inference layer is only apparent :

- The strategic layer has a role of control of the control, e.g the dynamic planning of the solving methods including the management of dead ends, a work realized by the control blackboard of BB1-ACCORD [18]. This knowledge level is actually not present in the models of AIDE. The meta control being a reflexive task, we propose for its management in [24] an extension of the shell AIDE in a reflexive architecture, following the works conducted in the project REFLECT [27]. This architecture is actually used by the explanation production task, another example of reflexive task.

- The KADS inference layer is divided into two parts. The meta-classes (which specify the role of the domain concepts during the problem solving) correspond to the AIDE problem solving concepts. Thus, the concept of "hypothesis" is distinct from the concept "disease".The knowledge sources are coded in the premisse of the operators whose role is to filter, arrange and assemble the domain knowledge.

This difference of description of the inference layer which allows in AIDE simplified models, has some important consequences for the implementation of the models.

[9] An operational comparison between the two approaches would be without foundation. first of al because we do not propose aid tools for the knowledge acquisition process like, for example, the KADS library of interpretation models. Further more because the two symbol level architectures can't be compared : in KADS, the design models can be based upon different AI paradigms.

4.2. Operationalization of conceptual models

The analysis of the works mentioned at the begining of this paragraph shows that the operationalization of a conceptual model requires the realization of two conditions :

i) The conceptual model must be represented in a formal language, in order to be completely specified.

ii) The design model must be elaborated at a high level of abstraction.

The main objective of Wetter [37] and the authors of KARL [15], by rendering executable specifications at a high level, is to validate these specifications before constructing the KBS : these two steps are clearly disconnected. They have in each case defined a formal language (around first order logic) in order to specify the KADS conceptual models. So the point i) is verified. But, since their objectives are not the realization of the final KBS, the elaboration of the design model is not tackled.

By contrast, for Steels' research team [34] and the authors of MODEL-K [22], the objective is to operationalize their conceptual models[10]. They elaborate to that effect design models based respectively on KRS [35] and BABYLON (two high level hybrid languages). The point ii) is then verified but not the first since their conceptual models are still based on semi-formal languages. Then, the operationalization of their conceptual models always necessitates two steps : the elaboration of the conceptual model and then the construction of the design model.

In the AIDE project, the conceptual models are totally operational. The development of a KBS necessitates only one step : the elaboration of the high level model of expertise.

For that, the knowledge engineer has at its disposal a library of terminal tasks and pre-defined predicates for the expression of operators, which allows him to ignore the details of the language U-LOG, thus to ignore the implementation details. A consequence of this approach is to warrant an effectice implementation of conceptual models. Indeed, the representation choices taken by the **Translator** have been studied in order to use the tool U-LOG to its full potential.

5. Conclusion and perspectives

We have presented the approach AIDE in which we try to combine both the advantages bound to high level specifications, to help in acquiring knowledge, and the contribution of the techniques of second generation expert systems (design models at a high level), to construct problem solvers that are less brittle, easier to validate and to explain.

The first point, the help in knowledge acquisition, has been illustrated in part 3. Modeling at a high level of abstraction induces a different approach in knowledge acquisition and radically modifies the respectives roles of the expert and the knowledge engineer. Of course, like in the method KADS, this approach has to be guided by tools. One of our objectives is to develop these kinds of tools around the shell AIDE.

Another direction of research, which concerns the second point, consists in using the shell AIDE for validation and explanation.

The consequences of this approach for the validation of KBS are important, as our experience in the development of SATIN has shown us [2]. On the one hand, the analysis

---

[10] The conceptual models of the Luc Steels' research team are based on the "componential framework" [32] and those of the MODEL-K approach are inspired from the KADS conceptual models.

at the knowledge level being more meticulous and more detailed, the question of the quality of knowledge is tackled as soon as the first prototype is constructed. The examination of the coherence and the completude of knowledge is treated earlier. On the other hand, the modifications to bring to the subsequent prototypes are facilitated. Since the conceptual models are operational, we can talk about *prototyping at the knowledge level.*

The principal motivation of the development of AIDE being the production of explanations, our present work is more particularly centred on that subject.

According to the constatation that explaining is a task in itself and that different explaining strategies must then be formalized, we have chosen the same shell in order to model the explaining reasoning. It corresponds then to the explaining task a high level model of expertise which bears the same characteristics than the model of the object task (to explain).

A reflective framework allowing the two models to interact is presented in [23]. The realization of a first prototype of an explicative system, around SATIN, has shown us how to take advantages from high level models for the production of explanations [18]. The development of this explicative system, with the refinement of explicative solving methods, is presently being carried out.

References

[1] Aikins, J.S. "Prototypical Knowledge for Expert Systems." In Artificial Intelligence, 20, (1983), pp. 163-210.

[2] Boulitreau-Lefèvre, P. "Validating at the knowledge level : an application to the project AIDE-SATIN." DEA report, University of Technology of Compiègne, September 1991 (in french).

[3] Bourcier, F. "An interface between the projects DOCAL and AIDE-SATIN using conceptual graphs." DEA report, University of Technology of Compiègne, Septembre 1991 (in french).

[4] Breuker, J. & Wielinga, B. "Models of Expertise in Knowledge Acquisition." In *Topics in Expert System Design, Methodologies and Tools*, North-Holland, Guida and al (Eds.), 1989, pp. 265-295.

[5] Chandrasekaran, B. "Towards a Functional Architecture for Intelligence Based on Generic Information Processing Tasks." In Proceedings of the IJCAI '87, pp. 1183-1192.

[6] Chandrasekaran, B. "Generic tasks as building blocks for knowledge-based systems : the diagnosis and routine design examples." In the Knowledge Engineering Review, 1988, 3(3), pp. 183 -210.

[7] Clancey, W.J. & Letsinger, R. "NEOMYCIN: Reconfiguring a Rule-Based Expert System for Application to Teaching." In Proceedings of the IJCAI '81, pp. 829-836.

[8] Clancey, W.J. "The Advantages of Abstract Control Knowledge." In Proceedings of the AAAI '83, pp. 74-78.

[9] Clancey, W.J. "Heuristic Classification." In Artificial Intelligence, 27, (1985), pp. 289-350.

[10] Clancey, W.J. "From GUIDON to NEOMYCIN and HERACLES in Twenty Short Lessons: ORN Final Report 1979-1985.", AI Magazine, 7 (3), (1986), pp. 40-60.

[11] Clancey, W.J. "Viewing Knowledge Bases as Qualitative Models." In IEEE Expert, summer 1989, pp. 9-23.

[12] Clancey, W.J. "Model construction operators." In Artificial Intelligence 53 (1992), pp 1-115.

[13] Console, L. & Torasso, P. "Heuristic and causal reasoning in check." In proceedings of the 12th world congress IMACS 88, Paris, july 1988, vol. 4, pp. 283-286.

[14] David, J.M. & Krivine, J.P. "Explaining Reasoning from Knowledge Level Models." In Proceedings of the ECAI '90, pp. 186-188.

[15] Fensel, D., Angele, J. & Landes, D. "KARL : a Knowledge Acquisition and Representation Language." In Proceedings of the Eleventh International Conference "Expert Systems and their Applications", Avignon, May 1991, pp. 513-525.

[16] Gloess, P. "Contribution to the optimization of mechanisms of reasoning in knowledge representation structures." Doctorat d'Etat Thesis, University of Technology of Compiègne, January 1990 (in french).

[17] Gloess, P. "U-LOG, an Ordered Sorted Logic with Typed Attributes." In Proceedings of the Third International Conference on Programming Language Implementation and Logic Programming, pp. 275-286; Lectures Notes in Computer Science n° 528, Springer Verlag, Passau, august 1991.

[18] Gréboval, M.H. "Modeling an explicative reasoning : an application to the projet AIDE-SATIN." DEA report, University of Technology of Compiègne, September 1991 (in french).

[19] Hasling, D.W., Clancey, W.J. & Rennels, G.R. "Strategic explanations for a diagnostic consultation system." In the International Journal of Man-Machine Studies 20(1), (1984), pp. 3-19.

[20] Hayes-Roth, B., Hewett, M., Vaughan Johnson, M. & Garvey, A. "ACCORD ; a framework for a class of design tasks." Report N° 88-19, Knowledge Systems Laboratory, Stanford University, Stanford, CA (1988)

[21] Iwasaki, Y., Keller, R. & Feigenbaum, Ed. "Generic Tasks or wide-ranging knowledge bases ?" In the Knowledge Engineering Review, 3(3), (1988), pp. 215-216.

[22] Karbach, W., Voß, A., Schuckey, R., & Drouven, U. "MODEL-K : Prototyping at the Knowledge Level." In Proceedings of the Eleventh International Conference "The Expert Systems and their Applications", Avignon, May 1991, pp. 501-511.

[23] Kassel, G. & Gréboval, C. "The project AIDE : first rapport." Report HEUDIASYC N° 91/46/DI, University of Technology of Compiègne, September 91 (in french).

[24] Kassel, G. "The principle of knowledge level reflection : a unifying principle in the project AIDE." Report HEUDIASYC, University of Technology of Compiègne. To appear in April 1992.

[25] Newell, A. "The Knowledge Level." In Artificial Intelligence 18 (1982), pp. 87-127.

[26] Nicaud, J.F. & Saïdi, M. "Explanation in the solving of algebraic exercises." In the french Review in Artificial Intelligence, Eds. Hermès, 4(2) (1990), pp. 125-148 (in french).

[27] Reinders, M., Vinkhuyzen, E., Voß, A., Akkermans, H., Balder, J., Bartsch-Spörl, B., Bredeweg, B., Drouven, U., Harmelen, F., Karbach, W., Karssen, Z., Schreiber, G. & B. Wielinga "A Conceptual Modelling Framework for Knowledge-Level Reflection." In AI Communications 4 (2/3) (1991), 49-128.

[28] Schreiber, A.Th., Wielinga, B.J. & Breuker, J.A. "The KADS Framework for Modelling Expertise." In Pre-Proceedings of the EKAW '91.

[29] Smith, J.W., Svirbely, J.R., Evans, C.A., Straum, P., Josephson, J.R. & Tanner, M.C. "RED : A red-cell antibody identification expert module." In the Journal of Medical Systems 9 (3), (1985), pp. 121-138.

[30] Sowa, J. "Conceptual structures : information processing in mind and machine." Addison wesley, Reading Mass.

[31] Steels, L. "The deepening of expert systems." In proceedings of the 12th world congress IMACS 88, Paris, july 1988, vol. 4, pp. 323-326.

[32] Steels, L. "Components of expertise." In the AI Magazine 11 (2), summer 1990, pp. 28-49.

[33] Sticklen, J. "Problem-solving architecture at the knowledge level." In the Journal of Experimental and Theoretical Artificial Intelligence, 1(4), (1989), pp. 233-247.

[34] Vanwelkenhuysen, J., Rademakers, P. "Mapping a Knowledge Level Analysis onto a Computational Framework." In Proceedings of the ECAI '90, London:Pitman, pp. 661-666.

[35] Van Marcke, K."KRS: an Object Oriented Representation Language." In the french Review in Artificial, Eds. Hermès,(4) (1987),.

[36] Weiss, M., Kulikowski, C.A., Amarel S. & Safir, A. "A Model-Based Method for Computer-Aided Medical decision-Making." In Artificial Intelligence, 11, (1978), pp. 145-172.

[37] Wetter, T. "First order logic foundations of the KADS conceptual model." In *Current Trends in Knowledge Acquisition*, B. Wielinga et al (eds.), IOS Press, Amsterdam, (1990), pp. 356-375.

[38] Wielinga, B.J. & Breuker, J.A. "Models of Expertise." In Proceedings of the ECAI '86, pp. 307-318.

Linking *modeling to make sense* and *modeling to implement systems* in an operational modeling environment

Marc Linster
AI Research Division, GMD
5205 St. Augustin 1, FRG

Abstract We argue that knowledge acquisition for knowledge-based systems is a constructive model-building process. We derive several requirements for modeling languages from this view on knowledge acquisition. We put a special focus on requirements that arise if one wants to support both *model building to make sense* and *modeling to implement systems* with one language. For example, among others such languages should support multi-faceted, bottom-up construing of behaviors, and they should have operational semantics.

We introduce the operational modeling language OMOS. OMOS is an experimental study that—in a KADS-like fashion—allows multi-faceted model building from a method and a domain point of view, but, unlike KADS conceptual models, results in directly operational systems.

Finally, we compare OMOS to other recent developments to put our work in context.

1 Moving From a Transfer View to a Constructive Modeling Point of View

Early work in knowledge acquisition for knowledge-based systems, for example work on ETS [Boose, 1985] or KRITON [Diederich *et al.*, 1987] emphasized a transfer view of knowledge acquisition. Knowledge was considered to be in an expert's head, and the knowledge engineer, using a tool, elicits the knowledge and represents it in a suitable operational formalism.

Today, we see knowledge acquisition as a constructive model-building process. The interaction between domain expert, knowledge engineer, and tool creates the knowledge. The description of the model is a structured understanding of a real-world task. The process of building such a description involves on the one hand side modeling to make sense of observed behavior and on the other side modeling to implement systems to re-construct comparable problem-solving actions. The implementation of the behavior cannot be separated from the model construction process, as models tend to become so complex, that their behavior can hardly be predicted on the basis of a document.

This paper analyzes how both modeling aspects can be supported. First, we detail requirements that a modeling language should fulfill to provide such support. The next section will give a brief description of the operational modeling language OMOS that we created to implement such support. To illustrate OMOS we describe aspects of a model of clamping-tool selection for lathe turning. Finally, we will compare OMOS to two other developments in knowledge acquisition—PROTEGE-II [Puerta *et al.*, 1991; Tu *et al.*, 1991] and SPARK, BURN, FIREFIGHTER [Klinker *et al.*, 1990; Marques *et al.*, 1991]—to explain the differences, and to discuss pros and cons of the approaches.

2 Some Requirements

This section describes several requirements for knowledge engineering environments that follow from our view on knowledge acquisition.

Remember that we see knowledge acquisition for knowledge-based systems as construction of operational models. We define a model as a structured understanding of the entities and processes that contribute to the solution of a real-world task.

On the basis of personal experience in the construction of knowledge-based systems, we define several kinds of support that we assume knowledge engineering environments must provide: (1) support for the model construction (Section 2.1); (2) support for the model implementation (Section 2.2); and (3) support for the closing of the gap between both aspects (Section 2.3).

These requirements, that will be detailed in the remainder of this section are our working hypotheses for the development of knowledge engineering environments.

2.1 Requirements for the Model Construction

Modeling to make sense is promoted by (1) explicit notations for different points of view in the modeling process; (2) a vocabulary that is used in a bottom-up fashion to construe aspects of the real-world task; (3) re-usable chunks, templates, or an ontology of generally accepted models.

2.1.1 Explicit Notations for Different Points of View in the Modeling Process

The development of a model can be seen as a discussion process between knowledge engineer and domain expert. The knowledge engineer proposes descriptions. Together with the application expert, he checks them against observed phenomena to validate their post-hoc rationalization capacity and tests their predictive power in novel situations.

To encourage discussion-like effects, the modeling language should provide primitives to express different points of view. For example one notation could represent a process-oriented point of view, another one a state-based stance, and a third one could be used to represent task-sharing aspects. These partial models are related to each other as they originate from the same real-world task. Switching between points of view helps in the incremental elaboration and refinement of an encompassing model. Ideally, the final model incorporates separate representations for these points of view, to allow for a multifaceted, congruent analysis that can start concurrently from many facets to acquire knowledge.

Multifaceted modeling is not new; it has been proposed in KADS [Wielinga *et al.*, 1992]. The development of a KADS conceptual model of the cancer chemotherapy-administration task of ONCOCIN [Linster and Musen, 1992] explains how the interaction between a method-oriented point of view and a domain-oriented one contributes to the elaboration of a model.

2.1.2 A Vocabulary to Construe Aspects of the Real-World Task

We consider knowledge acquisition to be a constructive modeling activity. Thus we need terms that serve as building blocks. As we do knowledge acquisition in situations that are ill-structured or largely not understood, these terms must support a bottom-up process of creating a an understanding, coined in terms of a modeling vocabulary. We refer to this as a bottom-up process of construing real-world tasks. As we want the modeling terms to be generally applicable and to have simple, well-defined semantics, they must be epistemological knowledge structuring primitives in the sense of Brachman [1985].

2.1.3 Re-Usable Templates or Chunks of Models

Parts of models re-appear in different situations, for example one finds *classification*-type processes in medicine, mechanical engineering, or office-space allocation. To make modeling more effective, we need re-usable generic parts of models. These can be a domain ontology, problem-solving methods, or interface components.

2.2 Requirements for the Model Implementation

To execute the model on a computer, it must be represented as code of some operational knowledge representation formalism. Two alternatives are possible here: (1) a manual re-coding phase, possibly going through several stages as it is done in KADS; or (2) the epistemological knowledge structuring primitives that are used for the model construction are operational constructs of a high-level knowledge representation formalism.

The next section will discuss this in more detail.

2.3 Closing the Gap between Both Aspects

To support model construction to make sense and to build systems, one must make sure that the requirements of the second aspect (e.g., unambiguity, formal representation, operationality, etc.) are ubiquitous during the initial model development. This can best be realized if the terms for the operational model are used in the making-sense phase too. Additionally, this gives the terms operational semantics.

Furthermore, an operational model provides important feedback for the model-construction process, as complex interactions can become transparent and the computer can be used to find ambiguous parts or loop holes in the model.

A manual re-implementation phase that transforms an informal model into a running system cannot provide this kind of feedback for two reasons: (1) implementation happens after the modeling process has been completed; and (2) feedback from the operational code cannot necessarily be traced back unambiguously to parts of the informal model.

This means that to make good use of the *system*-building aspect of knowledge engineering when building a model to understand a phenomenon, the modeling primitives must directly be operational.

3 The Operational Modeling Language OMOS

This section describes the operational modeling language OMOS. It is an experimental language to test whether an approach that fulfills the requirements of Section 2 is feasible, and whether such an approach facilitates the knowledge engineering process. OMOS and MODEL-K [Karbach *et al.*, 1991] are part of a larger venture exploring the use of explicit problem solving methods in the construction of knowledge-based systems.

OMOS has been used to implement a KADS conceptual model of the cancer-chemotherapy administration task of ONCOCIN [Linster and Musen, 1992], a model of clamping-tool selection for lathe turning [Kühn *et al.*, 1991], and it has been used to develop a system for office allocation [Linster, 1991]. We will use the clamping-tool selection example to illustrate OMOS in this paper.

Section 3.1 gives a short description of the task of selecting clamping tools. Section 3.2 introduces the modeling language, and illustrates its primitives with features of the application example. Section 3.3 recapitulates how OMOS meets the requirements delineated in Section 2.

3.1 The Application Example

Clamping-tool selection for lathe turning is one ingredient of a larger task of generating production plans for the manufacturing of rotational parts [Bernardi *et al.*, 1991].

Figure 1 shows a rotational part (a drive shaft) overlaid with the mold from which it is to be manufactured. The numbers indicate the sequence of cuts by which the material is removed.

A clamping tool centers a workpiece in the lathe and transmits the rotational forces. In Figure 1 the left fixture, which transmits the rotation, is a lathe dog and the right fixture is a lathe center. Other clamping tools are clamping jaws, collet chucks, etc.

Clamping tools are, among others, characterized by the ways they fasten the workpiece in the lathe, and the types of access that they allow the cutting tools. Lathe dogs hold the workpiece from the side and allow free access to all surfaces except the left and the right vertical planes. Clamping jaws and collet chucks, on the other hand, do not use the vertical planes to fix the workpiece but use parts of the outside plane. Besides the accessibility of different sections of the workpiece surface there are other criteria that are relevant for the selection of a clamping tool. In our application we will only consider the set-up time, that is, the time that is needed to mount the clamping tool on the lathe, and the clamping time, that is, the time that it takes to

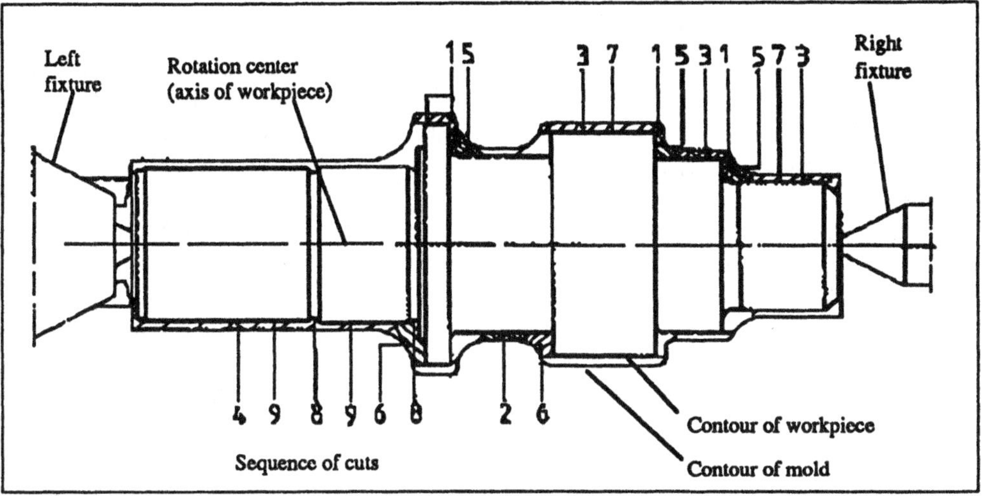

Fig. 1: A rotational part, with the clamping tools (left fixture and right fixture) and the cuts that must be executed to turn the mold into the desired shape (adapted from [Kühn *et al.*, 1991]).

close the clamping tool when a new mold is inserted into the lathe. Other criteria, not considered here are the geometry of the workpiece, its technological requirements, the available production environment (machines and already mounted tools), and the customer's requirements (lot size and delivery deadlines).

The analysis of the clamping-tool–selection task and the development of a model are explained in detail in [Kühn *et al.*, 1991].

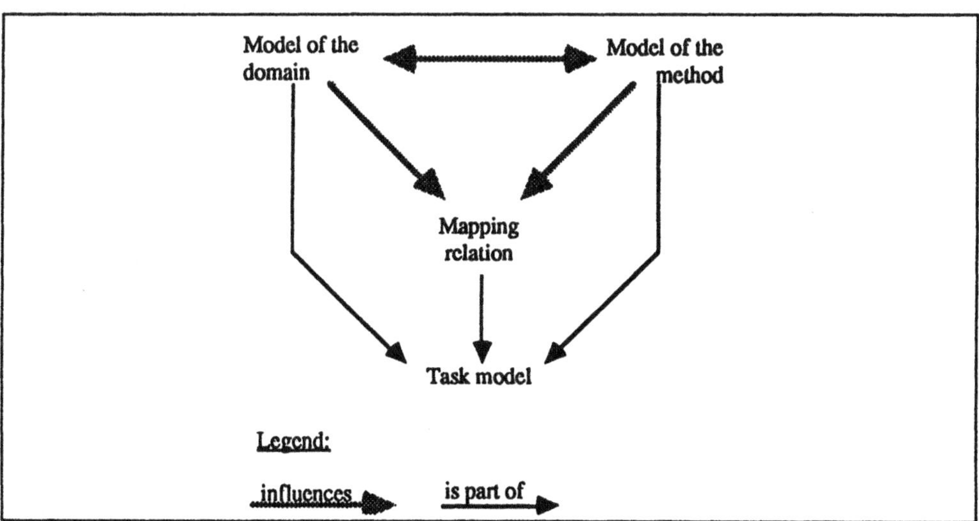

Fig. 2: The interaction of the model of the method, the model of the domain, and the model of the task in OMOS.

3.2 The Modeling Language

In the model-building process, OMOS allows the description of observed phenomena from a problem-solving–method oriented point of view and from a domain-structure oriented point of view. The first one is described in the *model of the method*, the second one in the *model of the domain*. Other points of view, such as as task-sharing are not considered in OMOS.

Both models combine into the *model of the task* (see Figure 2), which is directly operational. The model of the task can be executed, tested, and analyzed to provide feedback for the actual model-building process.

Section 3.2.1 introduces OMOS' constructs for the domain model, and illustrates them with features from the clamping tool application. Section 3.2.2 explains the modeling primitives for the method. Section 3.2.3 describes the task model.

3.2.1 The Model of the Domain

The model of the domain is a structure-oriented view on the real-world phenomenon to be modeled, i.e., a view that looks for an infrastructure of types, their entities, and the relations among the entities.

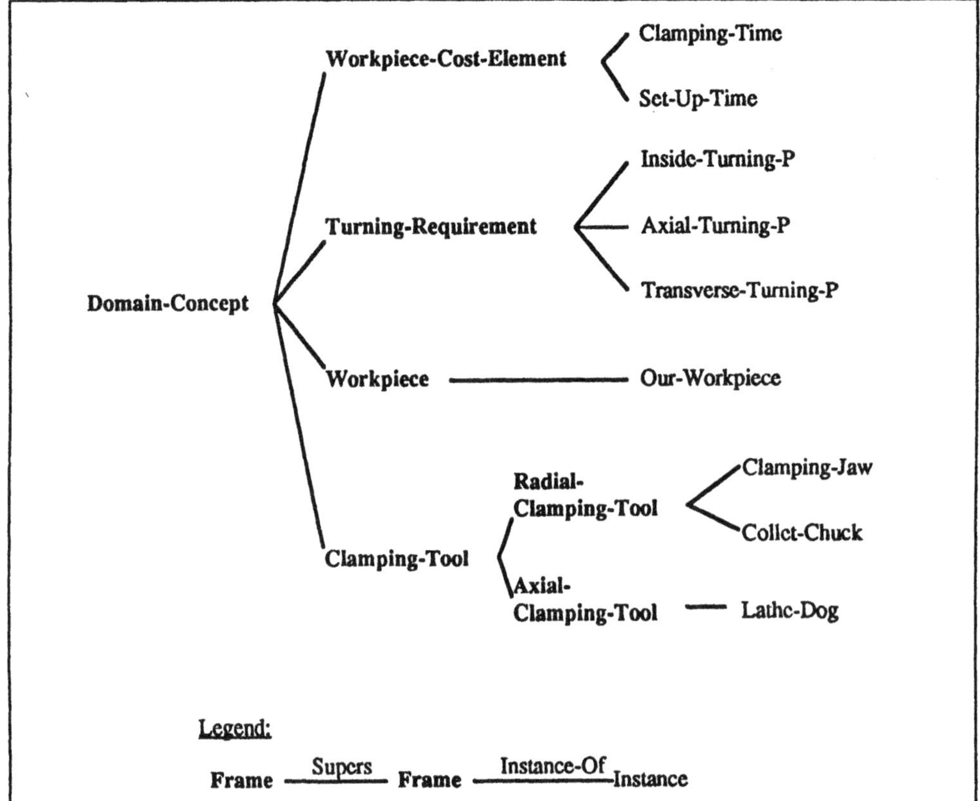

Fig. 3: The hierarchical definition of frames and instances for the clamping-tool selection task.

Tab. 1: The declaration of the domain relation **optimal-clamping-tool** with two of its tuples.

```
(DEFINE-DOMAIN-RELATION Optimal-Clamping-Tool
 WITH ARITY = 2
      TYPE-SEQUENCE = (((INSTANCE Clamping-Tool)
                        (EXTENSION-* Turning-Requirement)))
      ARGUMENT-SEQUENCE =
                       ((Clamping-Tool Important-Turning-Requirements))
      TUPLES = ((
               ((Optimal-Clamping-Tool
                   Collet-Chuck
                    ((Transverse-Turning-P Required-Value = Yes)
                    (Inside-Turning-P Required-Value = No))))

               ((Optimal-Clamping-Tool
                   Lathe-Dog
                   ((Axial-Turning-p Required-Value = Yes)
                    (Inside-Turning-P Required-Value = No))))
               ...
```

Frames and Instances To define the structures of the domain, we use an object-oriented approach, consisting of hierarchically defined classes—called *frames* in OMOS, with attributes—called *slots*, an inheritance relation, and instances of frames. In OMOS, we assume that classes—represented by frames—are used only to provide structured definitions. They are not modified in the reasoning process. Only instances are handled during problem-solving.

Figure 3 shows the hierarchical definition of frames and instances for the domain of clamping-tool selection.

Relations and Tuples To express relationships among instances of different classes, OMOS provides relations. Relations consist of a declaration and of tuples. The declaration part of the relation describes the data-types of the arguments of the tuples. Tuples can link instances and instance-attribute-value triplets.

The relation **optimal-clamping-tool**[1] describes the ideal clamping tool for certain turning requirements (see Table 1). For example, the first tuple states that *collet chuck* is an ideal choice if transverse turning is required and inside turning is not considered.

3.2.2 The Model of the Problem-Solving Method

The model of the problem-solving method represents a process view on the real-world phenomenon, i.e., a view documenting changes and (intermediary) states. To be able to compare methods of problem solving, to reuse them, and maybe develop a catalog

[1]To improve readability, we use special typesetting conventions for *domain concepts*, **domain relations**, roles, and INFERENCE ACTIONS.

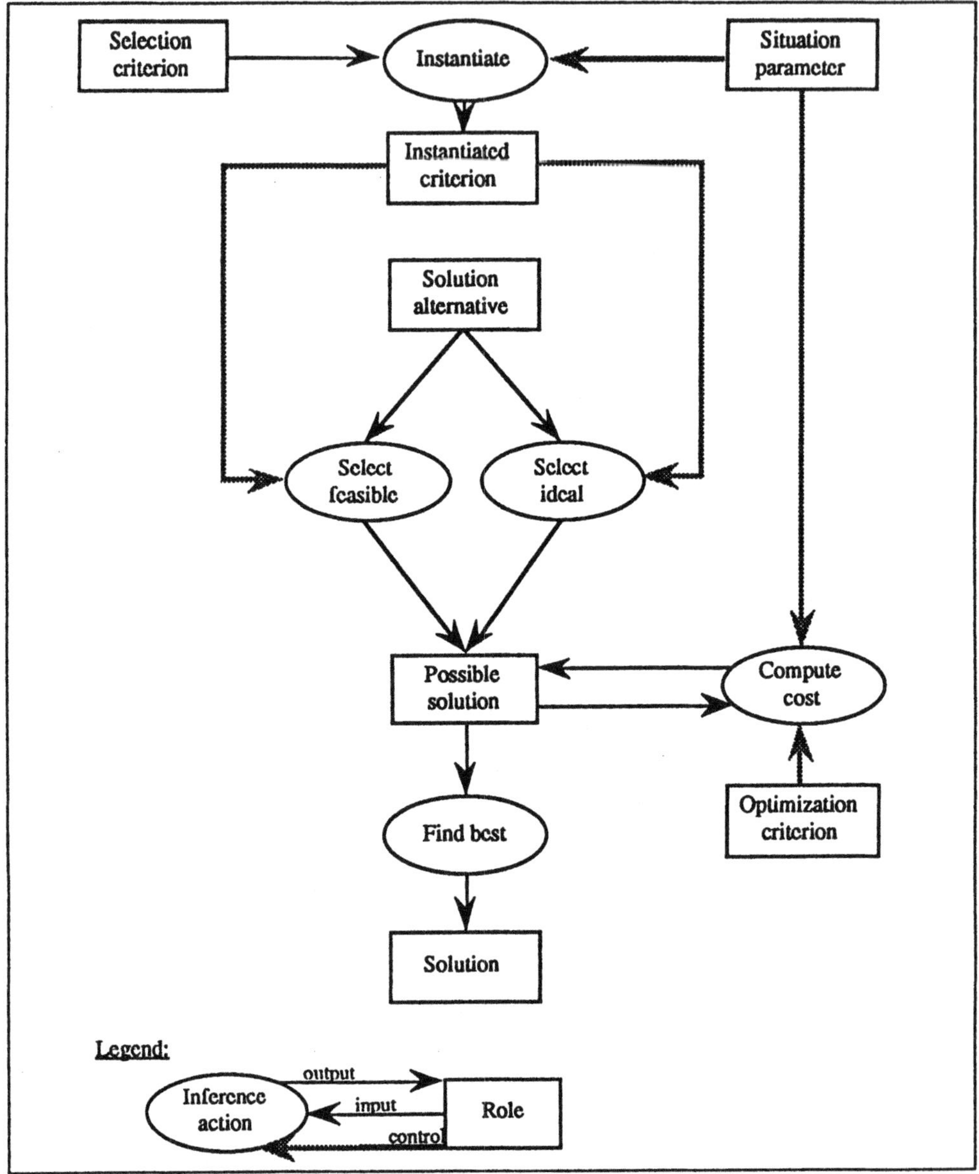

Fig. 4: The inference structure for the problem-solving method *selection by elimination and optimization* (adapted from [Kühn *et al.*, 1991].

of methods, the methods must be phrased independently from the domain that they are currently being applied to. To support the constructive, bottom-up process, the models of methods are built from primitive elements.

The primitives that OMOS uses for the description of the method are KADS [Wielinga *et al.*, 1992] oriented. A method consists of a set of INFERENCE ACTIONS—comparable to KADS knowledge sources, a set of roles—quite like KADS meta-classes, and a *control structure*, which is somewhat comparable to KADS task structures. The abstract data dependency between roles and inference actions is expressed in the *inference structure*.

We will first give a high-level description of the problem-solving method. We will then use it to illustrate OMOS' method building blocks—inference action, role, inference structure, and control structure.

An Abstract Description of the Problem-Solving Method The choice of a good clamping tool to turn a workpiece is a selection process that observes (1) discrete criteria that eliminate unsuitable alternatives from the set of possible clamping tools (e.g., inside turning is a knock-out criterion for collet chucks); and (2) optimization criteria that are used to single out a best choice on the basis of numerical ratings (e.g., best set-up time).

The use of the discrete criteria happens in two ways: (1) criteria can be used rigorously to select an ideal clamping tool; or (2) criteria can be relaxed somewhat to make a less than optimal choice, which is called a feasible choice. The second alternative is used if the first one does not result in a solution.

This problem-solving method is called *selection by elimination and optimization.*

Informally, but using the terms of the inference structure of Figure 4, the method proceeds as follows:

- In the first step, the description of the workpiece to be turned (i.e., the situation parameter in generic method terms) is used to instantiate a set of criteria, which will be the basis for the selection of the clamping tool.

- In the next step, one tries to make an ideal choice of those clamping tools (i.e., the solution alternatives) that totally fulfill the instantiated criteria.

- If this fails to produce possible solutions, a less than optimal choice is made through the inference action SELECT FEASIBLE.

- On the basis of the workpiece description (i.e., the situation parameters in the abstract method terms), numerical costs are computed for all the possible solutions. This involves factors such as set-up time, clamping time, etc.

- The inference action FIND BEST selects the clamping tool with the lowest costs.

The remainder of this section takes elements of the method definition and discusses their representation in OMOS.

Tab. 2: The definition of the inference action SELECT-IDEAL with its corresponding roles, the value- and role-assignment descriptions, the domain relation and the mapping of the roles onto the arguments of the domain relation.

```
     (DEFINE-INFERENCE-ACTION Select-Ideal
 (1)   WITH INPUT-ROLE = Solution-Alternative
 (2)        OUTPUT-ROLE = Possible-Solution
 (3)        CONTROL-ROLES = ((Instantiated-Criterion))
 (4)        VALUE-ASSIGNMENT = FALSE
 (5)        ROLE-ASSIGNMENT = TRANSFER
 (6)        DOMAIN-RELATION = Optimal-Clamping-Tool
 (7)        REL-ARG-TYPE = (((0 . INSTANCE)
                             (1 . EXTENSION-*)))
 (8)        PROJ-ROLES-REL-ARGS = (((INPUT-ROLE . 0)
 (9)                               (OUTPUT-ROLE . 0)
(10)                              ((CONTROL-ROLES . 0) . 1))))
```

Inference Actions An inference action is a generic description of elementary change occurring during problem-solving.

In the context of OMOS, change is limited to value assignments and role assignments. In the case of value assignment, the value of an attribute of a domain instance is modified. If an inference action modifies a role assignment, then it assigns a new role (see description below) to a domain instance.

An inference action operates on domain instances, and it uses domain relations. The specification of the inference action describes the nature of the change to be inflicted in terms of value or role assignments. The domain relation contains the detailed information about instances, attributes, and values needed to implement the change. The description of the actions in terms of changes in role or value is generic. If it is combined with the domain knowledge, it becomes task-specific.

Table 2 renders the definition of the inference action SELECT-IDEAL. Lines 1–3 state the input, output and control roles. *Input* roles are consumed when read; *output* roles are written by the inference action; *control* roles are read without modification. Line 4 declares that the inference action does not assign values to attributes of domain instances. The fifth statement says that domain instances are transferred from the input role to the output role, if the inference action fires. Line 6 indicates the domain relation that is used to provide the detailed knowledge that the inference action needs to implement the kind of change declared in Lines 4 and 5. Lines 8–10 map the roles of the inference action onto the arguments of the domain relation (see Table 1).

Lines 1–5 are the generic description of this building block of the method. Lines 6–10 describe the connection of the method model with the domain model.

When the model is executed, inference actions compile into forward-chaining rule schemata. These rule schemata are instantiated with the detailed information of the tuples of the domain relations. Table 3 renders the instantiated forward-chaining rule schema for the inference action SOLUTION ALTERNATIVE, instantiated with the domain knowledge described in the first tuple of the domain relation `optimal-clamping-tool`.

Tab. 3: The forward-chaining rule-schema that implements the inference action SELECT IDEAL (see Table 2), after it has been instantiated with the first tuple of the relation `optimal-clamping-tool` (see Table 1).

```
IF (CURRENT-ROLE Solution-Alternative Collet-Chuck)
   (CURRENT-ROLE Instantiated-Criterion Transverse-Turning-P)
   (CURRENT-ROLE Instantiated-Criterion Inside-Turning-P)
   (Transverse-Turning-P Required-Value = Yes)
   (Inside-Turning-P Required-Value = No)
THEN
   (TRANSFER-ROLE Solution-Alternative Possible-Solution Collet-Chuck)
```

Roles During a problem-solving process, domain elements play varying roles. In our example, this is illustrated best through the different roles that a clamping tool can play. Looking at the inference structure in Figure 4, initially all clamping tools play the role solution alternative. If they fit the current turning requirements, then they change role to become a possible solution. The one that has lowest set-up time and clamping time becomes the solution of choice.

Roles are assigned dynamically, and are part of the current state of the problem solver.

The problem-solving method *select by elimination and optimization* knows, among others, the following roles:

Solution alternative: this role describes all those clamping tools that are part of the model.

Possible solution: denotes all those tools that fulfill the criteria that are imposed by the cutting sequence.

Solution: describes the optimum choice, selected on the basis of the optimization criteria (e.g., set-up time).

Roles are implemented as dynamic predicates. Some roles are initialized, for example solution alternative is initialized with all the clamping tools that are part of the domain knowledge of the model. Other roles are computed dynamically, for example possible solution is the result of the inference actions SELECT IDEAL and SELECT FEASIBLE.

The declaration of the role is part of the generic problem-solving method. The initialization describes part of the link of the model of the method with the model of the domain.

The Control Structure The control structure is a generic procedure that decides which inference action will be executed next. It calls inference actions, tests whether they did inflict any change (i.e., change a role assignment of a domain instance, or assign a value to an attribute of a domain instance), or verifies whether a role currently describes domain instances.

Tab. 4: The OMOS control structure for the method *selection by elimination and optimization.*

```
 (DEFINE-CONTROL-STRUCTURE Select-by-Elimination-and-Optimization
       CALL-SEQUENCE =
(1)                  (((CALL-IA Instantiate)
(2)                    (CALL-IA Select-Ideal)
(3)                    (WHEN (NOT (ROLE-P Possible-Solution))
(4)                             (CALL-IA Select-Feasible))
(5)                    (CALL-IA Compute-Cost)
(6)                    (CALL-IA Find-Best))))
```

The control structure for the method *selection by elimination and optimization*, rendered in Table 4 calls the inference action INSTANTIATE first, to define the turning requirements for the current workpiece. Line 2 calls the inference action SELECT IDEAL to make a rigorous choice of tools. If this fails to produce any possible solutions (Line 3), an inference action for suboptimal choices is triggered (Line 4). Lines 5 and 6 select the best solution on the basis of optimization criteria, such as *set-up time.*

3.2.3 The Model of the Task

The model of the task results from the combination of the model of the method with the model of the domain (see Figure 2). The model of the task is not defined explicitly, it results from the definition of the mapping of the method elements onto the elements of the domain model. The inference actions are mapped onto the domain relations, the roles are mapped onto domain frames and their instances. Figure 5 shows how the clamping-tool task model is combined from the method model (see the inference structure in Figure 4) and the domain model (see Figure 3 for the definition of the frames and instances), by establishing a mapping relation between roles and frames, and between inference actions and domain relations.

The following roles of the problem-solving method are initialized with elements of the domain (see the gray links between subframes of the frame *domain-concept* in Figure 5):

1. Optimization criterion is initialized with all instances of the frame *workpiece cost element.* If the domain model corresponds to Figure 3, then the instances *clamping-time* and *set-up-time* play this role initially.

2. Situation parameter is initialized with the description of the workpiece to be turned.

3. Selection criterion denotes the turning requirements, that is, *inside turning, axial turning,* and *transverse turning.*

4. Solution alternative is the role that all the instances of the frame *clamping tool* play initially.

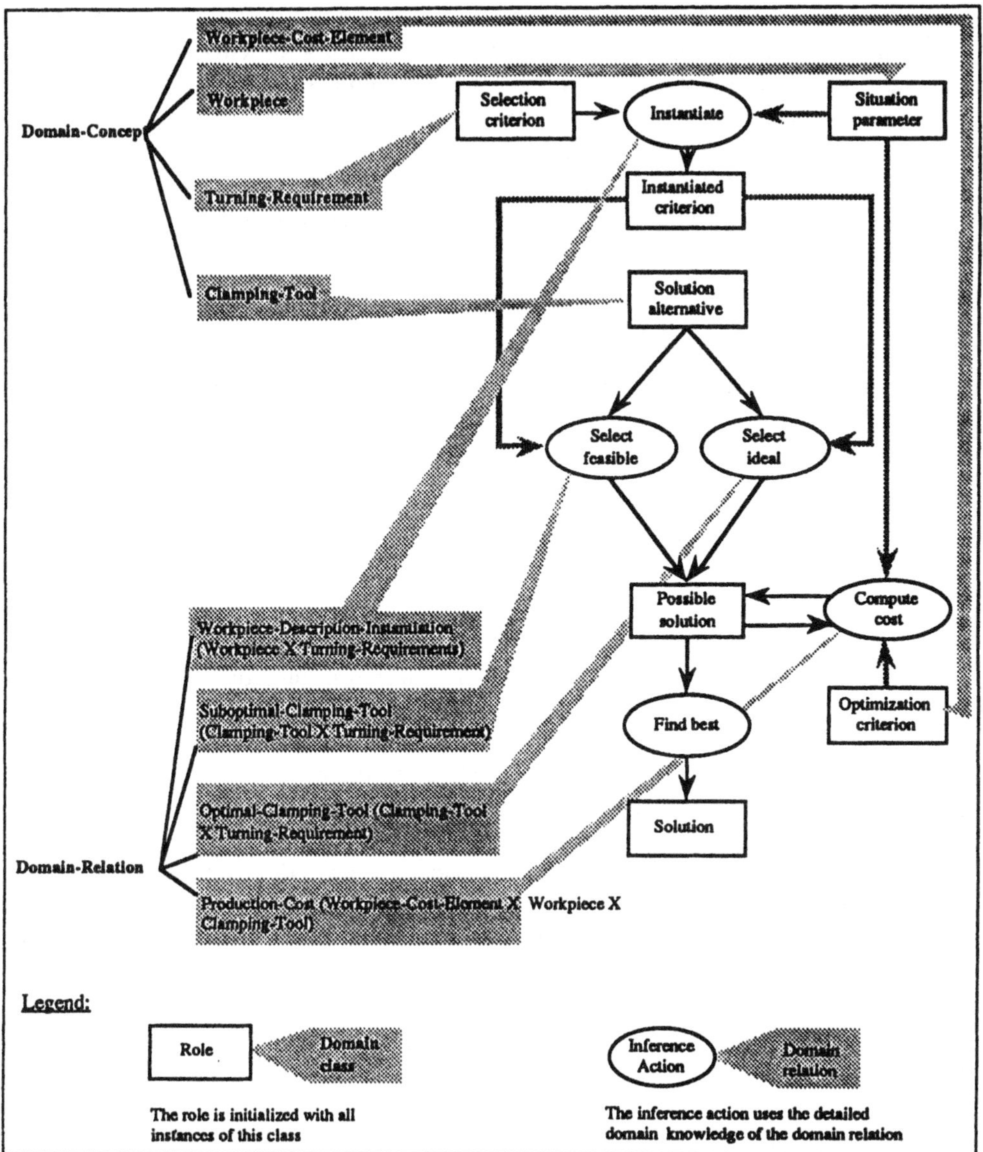

Fig. 5: The domain model (left side), with the frames and relations, combines with the method model (right side) to form the task model. The links between both models represent the mapping relation.

Instantiated criterion, possible solution and solution are not initialized.

The inference actions of the method get their detailed knowledge from the tuples of domain relations (see the gray links between the domain relations of the domain model and the inference actions of the method model.

It is important to remember that both partial models (i.e., method and domain) are developed in parallel and in relative independence. However, the fact that they must combine into a coherent model of the task makes sure that they converge. One might argue that a more powerful, or more flexible mapping between both models would allow the combination of heterogeneous partial models into a task model. But this would not be helpful from a model-construction point of view, as the domain provides those distinctions that the method uses, and vice versa, the method indicates distinctions that the domain must provide. For example, a hierarchical classification problem-solving method makes sense only if the domain provides a natural hierarchy, which the method can use

Minimal and Full-Blown Task Models In OMOS one can distinguish between minimal and full-blown task models. In a minimal task model, the domain model contains only those frames and relations that are used directly in the mapping from the method to the domain. Tuples or relations, instances or sub-frames can be added gradually to the minimal model, to turn it into a full-blown model.

By comparing the domain model of Figure 5 with the one in Figure 3, the distinction between a minimal model and a full-blown one becomes obvious. For example, in the full-blown model the domain frame *clamping tool* has subframes *axial clamping tool* and *radial clamping tool.* They have been defined to impose more structure onto the domain model. However, they do not introduce distinctions that the method uses. That way, they are not part of the minimal task model.

This distinction is important for two reasons. First, the minimal task model contains those domain distinctions that are accessed directly by the problem-solving method. This makes it an abstract re-usable framework that can be used if a similar problem is to be solved again in the same domain.

Second, the minimal task model provides a framework in which one can analyze the use of domain knowledge elements by the problem-solving method. Thus, whereas the minimal task model must be developed manually, the extension of the minimal task model into a full-blown task model is supported by automated analysis tools.

OMOS provides several tools to analyze the use of the domain knowledge in the framework of the problem-solving method. The *dead-end analysis* looks for intermediary role-assignments that are not used by any of the subsequent inferences. For example, the concept *clamping jaw* can play the role solution-alternative (see Figure 4), but neither SELECT-FEASIBLE nor SELECT-IDEAL can access it, as they do not have the necessary detailed knowledge in their domain relations. Table 5 renders the result of an analysis of the role solution alternative. Other tools focus on the definition of domain relations (coverage analysis) and inference actions (loop-hole analysis).

3.3 OMOS and the Requirements

As mentioned earlier, we developed OMOS as an experimental language to analyze whether it is possible to fulfill the requirements listed in Section 2. In this section, we

Tab. 5: The result of a dead-end analysis for the role solution alternative.

```
The domain concept CLAMPING-JAW can be assigned to the role
SOLUTION-ALTERNATIVE, but it is not used by any of the inference
actions SELECT-IDEAL, SELECT-FEASIBLE that use
SOLUTION-ALTERNATIVE as control- or as input-role.

To change this do AT LEAST ONE of the following:

    Add a tuple to the relation OPTIMAL-CLAMPING-TOOL, which is used
    by the inference action SELECT-IDEAL. CLAMPING-JAW must be
    mentioned in the 0. argument of the tuple, which is of type
    (INSTANCE CLAMPING-TOOL) and is called CLAMPING-TOOL.

    Add a tuple to the relation SUBOPTIMAL-CLAMPING-TOOL, which is
    used by the inference action SELECT-FEASIBLE. CLAMPING-JAW must be
    mentioned in the 0. argument of the tuple, which is of type
    (INSTANCE CLAMPING-TOOL) and is called CLAMPING-TOOL.
```

point out the features of OMOS that are meant to satisfy certain requirements.

For the model construction OMOS provides two points of view: (1) the method view, emphasizing a procedural perspective; and (2) the domain view, which focusses on the structures, entities, and relations. Both points of view result in independently phrased partial models. [Linster and Musen, 1992] analyze the interaction of the different modeling views of KADS—which are comparable to those that OMOS provides—and show that multiple points of view enhance the modeling process.

Each modeling view has its own knowledge structuring primitives: (1) inference actions, roles, and procedural control statements for the method model; and (2) frames, instances, relations, and tuples for the domain model.

Parts of both models can be re-used. Theoretically this should be possible for the domain, method and minimal task models. It has only been done for the method model, though. For example the core of the method *selection by elimination and optimization* has been re-used in the *straightforward-assignment method* of the office allocation task [Linster, 1991]. Figure 6 shows the core of the method for the office allocation task. The inference action SELECT-&-SPECIFY FEASIBLE implements the same changes as SELECT IDEAL in the current example, that is, it uses discrete criteria—denoted by the roles assigned element, unassigned element, open slot, and filled slot—to make a good selection. In both models FIND BEST makes a slection on the basis of optimization criteria. Thus, even though the terms changed, the concept of first selecting on the basis of discrete criteria before optimizing this choice, can be expressed and reused in OMOS.

The combined partial models are directly operational. OMOS does not require a separate implementation phase.

To link closely both modeling to make sense and modeling to implement systems, OMOS modeling primitives combine directly into operational task models, and these task models are accessible to formal analysis tools. The results of the analysis tools

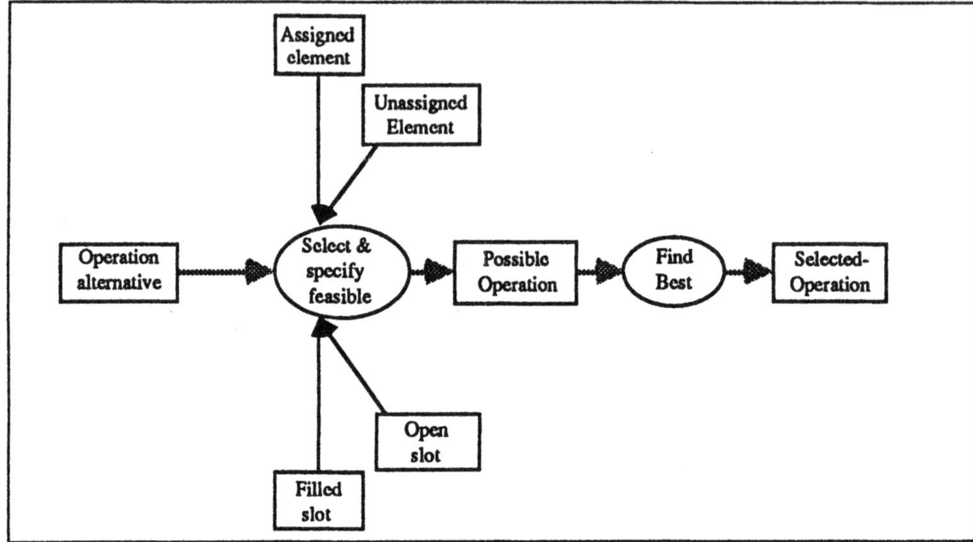

Fig. 6: The core of the problem-solving method ***straightforward assignment*** that was used for the office allocation task (see [Linster, 1991]). This is a reuse of parts of the problem-solving method described in this paper.

provide precise indications for the agenda of the ongoing knowledge acquisition process. For example, the analysis of Table 5 puts clamping jaw on the agenda of the next focussed interview, with the goal to determine those turning operations that use clamping jaws.

4 Discussion

We will compare our work to two other approaches that are currently being developed and that have similar goals: analysis of flexible problem-solving methods and their exploitation in automated knowledge acquisition. The PROTEGE-II approach continues the work on PROTEGE. SPARK, BURN, and FIREFIGHTER (SBF) have been developed on the basis of experiences with the Role-Limiting-Method approach.

This section highlights differences between the approaches, and puts our work into a broader context.

4.1 PROTEGE-II

PROTEGE-II [Puerta *et al.*, 1991; Tu *et al.*, 1991] has been developed to overcome two deficiencies of PROTEGE: (1) application-specific attributes, such as *dose of a drug* did not have a role in the problem-solving process that was defined by the underlying problem-solving method; and (2) the problem-solving method was limited to episodic skeletal-plan refinement.

At the same time, one wanted to maintain the major characteristic of PROTEGE in PROTEGE-II, that is, the separation between a special tool for the knowledge engineer to define a task-model—PROTEGE did this in the old approach, and a task-model–driven tool for the domain expert to extend the task model into an application model—p-OPAL realized this formerly.

In PROTEGE-II the task model, consisting of a problem-solving method and of domain-specific data-structures, is configured from *mechanisms* and their *generic* data-structures, that are refined in an object-oriented fashion to suit the domain.

A mechanism is a *primitive* problem-solving method working on object-oriented data-structures. These data-structures can be refined, so that they carry domain-dependent labels. The method combines with the refined data-structures due to the object-oriented approach, and forms a *primitive* task. The original, generic data-structures define the *knowledge-needs* of the mechanism. They can be fulfilled with the help of special editors. Again, these properties are inherited, when the mechanism is transformed into a primitive task.

Mechanisms can be combined, by linking their data-structures. A special grammar has been developed for this, so that the dovetailing of data-structures of different mechanisms can be controlled, and that the knowledge-needs of combined mechanisms can be defined automatically.

PROTEGE-II can be used from two ends: (1) the user selects a problem-solving method, with its input and output data-structures. The method is then decomposed—manually or in a semi-automatic heuristic mode—into communicating mechanisms. Their data-structures will be refined to the terms of the domain. From this task model, consisting of the combination of the mechanisms and their domain-dependent data-structures, the knowledge-needs of the method can be derived, that guide the p-OPAL–like tool in the acquisition of the detailed knowledge in the framework of the task model; and (2) on the basis of mechanisms, each corresponding to observed problem-solving steps, the user configures a task-model. First he refines individual mechanisms into primitive tasks. These are then combined into a global, compound task with the help of the mechanisms-configuration grammar.

4.2 SPARK, BURN, and FIREFIGHTER

The SBF approach [Klinker *et al.*, 1990; Marques *et al.*, 1991] provides a framework in which application specialists can develop knowledge-based applications, without being confined by the pre-defined problem-solving method of a tool, for example SALT. SBF is similar in many ways to PROTEGE-II.

To this purpose, SBF contains two sub-systems: SPARK and BURN. SPARK helps the user decompose his real-world task into a combination of pre-defined tasks, presented in an encompassing industry model. For each pre-defined task, SPARK provides a combination of mechanisms, that can fulfill the task. Interactively, a mechanism is chosen for every selected task, and combined into a method that fulfills the needs of the real-world task. BURN is then used to flesh out the detailed knowledge that the combined mechanisms need to perform properly.

In the SBF approach, two major characteristics of the RLM-approach have been maintained: (1) the support of SPARK and BURN aims at the application expert, who is not necessarily an expert programmer; and (2) the knowledge-needs of the combined mechanisms, expressed through BURN, are phrased in method-oriented terms.

4.3 Comparing OMOS, PROTEGE-II, and SBF

PROTEGE-II and SBF concentrate on a method-oriented view onto a real-world task. The knowledge of the task is coerced into pre-defined data structures, which are part of the mechanism definitions. In both approaches this means that a method must be built from mechanisms (or selected from a library) before the knowledge engineer can start with an analysis of the domain elements in the framework of the approach.

This dependence between method and domain-knowledge representation has three implications. First, an analysis of initial protocols, texts, or interview data must be done outside the framework of the tool's knowledge structuring primitives, as a minimal amount of knowledge must be acquired about the real-world task before a method of problem solving can be phrased.

Second, the creative interaction between varying points of view, such as method and domain, is not supported.

Third, the domain knowledge appears to be represented as object-oriented refinement, respectively instantiation of method-depending building blocks. This may imply that a change in the method definition requires a re-coding of the domain knowledge.

However, the fact that PROTEGE-II and SBF view the knowledge of a real-world task solely in the light of the method does have considerable advantages, too.

In OMOS, the connection between method knowledge and domain knowledge is established *after* the definition of both partial models. The connection is defined as a mapping relation between structures (e.g., between inference actions and domain relations). In PROTEGE-II and SBF it is a refinement, respectively instantiation relation. This is much *stronger* in McDermott's [1988] terms. It defines precisely the structure and the kind of domain knowledge needed by the method. p-OPAL-like editors can then be used to acquire it. A mapping relation—as OMOS provides—is much weaker. It can only be used to point out that the domain model must provide certain distinctions for the method (e.g., the domain must provide a relation that can be used by an abstraction inference). A mapping relation does not define the format for the representation of these distinctions.

Another difference lies in the ways mechanisms (or inference actions) are phrased. In PROTEGE-II and in SBF, mechanisms are black boxes. In OMOS we defined simple knowledge structuring primitives. All actions are phrased uniformly in terms of value assignments and role assignments. We assume that such uniform representation makes it easier to derive coherent knowledge needs from a complex method. This will prevent redundant acquisition or representation of domain knowledge. For example, in OMOS we expect to use the same domain knowledge for abstraction and for differentiation inferences in diagnosis problems.

5 Conclusions

We developed OMOS as an experimental modeling language, to show that the requirements of Section 2 can be fulfilled, and that this leads to good knowledge engineering support. This means that the goal of OMOS is different from the goals of the PROTEGE-II and SBF projects, which aim at the large-scale development of broadly usable tools. In the latter projects much effort has been invested into interface development and usability of the tools. OMOS, however is a programming environment that we have only used internally for experimental purposes.

Furthermore, OMOS is limited. It represents inference actions as value assignments and role assignments. Even though it has been used for the modeling of several applications, we know that additional primitives are needed, such as structure manipulation or instance creation.

Nonetheless, we claim that in the discussion about the role of explicit models of problem-solving methods in knowledge acquisition, we have shown that:

1. One can combine multifaceted modeling to make sense—as it is done in the KADS conceptual models, which are not operational—with directly operational systems and knowledgeable tool support for the acquisition of the detailed knowledge—as it is done in PROTEGE or SALT.
2. It is not absolutely necessary to structure the knowledge of a real-world task only along pre-defined structures of a problem-solving method if one wants to obtain operational models. A parallel modeling of the domain and the method is possible, provided that both models converge.

Thus, we have shown one way of closing the gap in knowledge acquisition between modeling to make sense and modeling to build operational systems.

Acknowledgements

Gabi Schmidt and Otto Kühn helped me develop the clamping tool example. The members of the knowledge-modeling team at GMD's AI Research Division contributed significantly to many of the ideas presented in this paper. Angi Voß, Gabi Schmidt, Otto Kühn and three anonymous reviewers provided very useful comments on earlier versions of this paper.

References

[Bernardi *et al.*, 1991] Ansgar Bernardi, Harold Boley, Christoph Klauck, Philip Hanschke, Knut Hinkelmann, Ralf Legleitner, Otto Kühn, Manfred Mayer, Michael Richter, Franz Schmalhofer, Gabi Schmidt, and Walter Sommer. Arc-tec: Acquisition, representation and compilation of technical knowledge. In Jean-Paul Haton and Jean-Claude Rault, editors, *Proceedings of Avignon 91*, volume 1, pages 133 – 145, Avignon, France, 1991. EC2.

[Boose, 1985] John H. Boose. A knowledge acquisition program for expert systems based on personal construct psychology. *International Journal of Man-Machine Studies*, 23:495 – 525, 1985.

[Brachman and Schmolze, 1985] R. Brachman and G.J. Schmolze. An overwiev of the KL-ONE knowledge representation system. *Cognitive Science*, 9(11):216–260, 1985.

[Diederich *et al.*, 1987] Joachim Diederich, Ingo Ruhmann, and Mark May. KRITON: A knowledge acquisition tool for expert systems. *International Journal of Man-Machine Studies*, 26:29 – 40, 1987.

[Karbach *et al.*, 1991] Werner Karbach, Angi Voß, Ralf Schukey, and Uwe Drouven. MODEL-K: Prototyping at the knowledge level. In *Proceedings of the First International Conference on Knowledge Modeling and Expertise Transfer*, Sophia Antipolis, France, 1991.

[Klinker *et al.*, 1990] Georg Klinker, Carlos Bhola, Geoffroy Dallemange, David Marques, and John McDermott. Usable and reusable programming constructs. In John H. Boose and Brian R. Gaines, editors, *Proceedings of KAW90*, pages 14–1 – 14–20, Calgary, 1990. AAAI, University of Calgary.

[Kühn *et al.*, 1991] Otto Kühn, Marc Linster, and Gabi Schmidt. Clamping, COKAM, KADS and OMOS. In Duncan Smeed, Marc Linster, John H. Boose, and Brian R. Gaines, editors, *Proceedings of EKAW91*. University of Strathclyde, 1991.

[Linster and Musen, 1992] Marc Linster and Mark Musen. Use of KADS to create a conceptual model of the ONCOCIN task. *Knowledge Acquisition*, Special Issue on KADS, 1992.

[Linster, 1991] Marc Linster. Tackling the office-planning problem with OMOS. In Duncan Smeed, Marc Linster, John H. Boose, and Brian R. Gaines, editors, *Proceedings of EKAW91*, Glasgow, 1991. University of Strathclyde.

[Marques *et al.*, 1991] David Marques, Georg Klinker, Geoffroy Dallemange, Patrice Gautier, John McDermott, and David Tung. More data on reusable programming constructs. In John Boose and Mark Musen, editors, *Proceedings of the 6th Banff Knowledge Acquisition Workshop*, pages 14/1 – 14/19, University of Calgary, 1991. AAAI, University of Calgary.

[McDermott, 1988] John McDermott. Preliminary steps toward a taxonomy of problem-solving methods. In Sandra Marcus, editor, *Automating Knowledge Acquisition for Expert Systems*, pages 225 – 256. Kluwer Academic, Boston, 1988.

[Puerta *et al.*, 1991] Angel Puerta, John Edgar, Samson Tu, and Mark Musen. A multiple-method knowledge-acquisition shell for the automatic generation of knowledge-acquisition tools. In John Boose and Brian Gaines, editors, *Proceedings of the 6th Banff Knowledge Acquisition Workshop*, pages 20/1 – 20/19, University of Calgary, 1991. AAAI, University of Calgary.

[Tu *et al.*, 1991] Samson Tu, Yuval Shahar, John Dawes, James Winkles, Angel Puerta, and Mark Musen. A problem-solving model for episodic skeletal-plan refinement. In John Boose and Mark Musen, editors, *Proceedings of the 6th Banff Knowledge Acquisition Workshop*, pages 34/1 – 34/20, University of Calgary, 1991. AAAI, University of Calgary.

[Wielinga *et al.*, 1992] Bob Wielinga, Guus Schreiber, and Jost Breuker. KADS: A modelling approach to knowledge engineering. *Knowledge Acquisition*, Special Issue on KADS, 1992.

Common Ground and Differences of the KADS and Strong-Problem-Solving-Shell Approach

Ute Gappa, Karsten Poeck

Karlsruhe University, Institute of Logic
P.O. Box 6980, D-7500 Karlsruhe
Germany

Abstract. Model-based knowledge acquisition seems to be one obvious way to make the development of expert systems more effective and in particular helps to overcome the knowledge acquisition bottleneck. In this paper two approaches for model-based knowledge acquisition are compared: 1) the KADS approach offering generic conceptual models (Interpretation Models) as well as a language to describe, adapt and construct conceptual models and 2) the shell approach providing predefined and operationalized models of problem solving methods combined with a computer environment to acquire the domain knowledge, desirably with graphical knowledge editors, to apply it to a case and to explain the problem solving behavior. To get a better insight to KADS, the cognitive model of a well-established shell for heuristic classification is studied and expressed in terms of KADS. Strengths and weaknesses of the both approaches are pointed out as well as hints given for their mutual fertilization.

1 Introduction

Experiences from the development of expert systems have shown that expert systems with a high degree of competence can in principle be realized but their development still requires an enormous amount of time and effort. Unsolved problems in knowledge acquisition and maintenance in many projects indicate that an overall methodology of a systematic procedure for modeling new domain tasks is still be missing. Almost all solutions to overcome the knowledge acquisition problem focus on the development of conceptual models which serve as an intermediate step in the development abstracting from the details of knowledge implementation [Musen 89a]. The striking advantage of models at the knowledge level [Newell 82] is that they can be exploited to structure and guide the knowledge acquisition process because of the fact that they determine the roles knowledge plays in the problem solving process.

Concerning conceptual models, there are two main favorite approaches in current research. One of them is to provide knowledge engineers and/or experts with predefined models of problem solving, so-called *role-limiting or strong problem solving methods* [McDermott 88, Puppe 90] or even models of a specific domain task [Musen et al. 87]. Most of those models are rather sophisticated, however their application requires a pre-phase of task analysis to find out which of the available models might fit – and in quite a few cases there might not any be available. The alternative to this analytic approach is the synthesis one providing some kinds of building blocks, *generic tasks, mechanisms* in order to allow the construction of new models for a given task [Chandrasekaran 87, 90; Klinker et al. 90; Marques et al. 91; Puerta et al. 91].

The European KADS-project [Breuker et al. 87, Wielinga et al. 88, 91] is one of the first more comprehensive approaches, which both tries to provide predefined models – by its library of semi-formalized *Interpretation Models* – and facilitates the construction of new models either from scratch or by adapting given ones. The language for KADS models is about to become formally specified [Akkermanns et al. 90]. Probably because KADS is an overall methodology trying to integrate well-established models in a uniform language, it has gained great popularity in recent years, at least in the European area. We omit a detailed introduction to KADS as we assume that the reader is already familiar with it or may look it up in the literature. As we, the authors of the paper, usually work on strong problem solving methods and build shells with graphical interfaces for them, we have been interested to find out the similarities and differences of the KADS and the strong-problem-solving-shell approach.

Besides the incorporation of a specific problem solving method, expert system shells provide facilities to build up a knowledge base (knowledge acquisition system), to run the knowledge-base (problem solver) and to give explanations of the steps taken for problem solving (explanation component). Examples of shells or knowledge acquisition systems based on predefined problem solving methods are

- OPAL [Musen et al. 87] for skeletal plan refinement in the domain of cancer therapy
- PROTÉGÉ [Musen 89b] for a specific kind of skeletal plan pursuance and refinement
- SALT [Marcus 88a] for configuration with a propose-and-revise strategy
- COKE [Poeck 91a, b] for assignment with a propose-and-exchange strategy
- MORE [Kahn 88], MOLE [Eshelman 88], TDE/TEST [Kahn 87], AQUINAS [Boose et al. 89], KSS0 [Shaw et Gaines 89] and MED2/CLASSIKA [see below] for various types of classification problem solving.

The underlaying model of an expert system shell can be regarded as its predefined types of its internal knowledge representation together with all abstractions from it. We call a problem solving method *strong*, when the roles of the knowledge pieces are fixed by predefined object and relation types so that a knowledge base only contains instances and relations between instances [Puppe 90]. The more a knowledge representation is typed, the better the knowledge acquisition process can be supported, for example by sophisticated graphical knowledge editors which can even enable experts to build expert systems by themselves. When we refer to the term *shell* throughout the paper, we always mean shells based on a strong problem solving method, not general expert system tools like Nexpert Object, KEE, KAPPA, GoldWorks, etc.

Figure 1 shall help us to clarify the relation between shells and KADS. In KADS the development of an expert system is divided into a sequence of phases each ending up with a model at a different degree of abstraction and system realization. The first main step, which requires the most amount of abstraction, is the construction of the Conceptual Model M1 described at the four layers domain, inference, task and strategy layer. To support this conceptualization, Interpretation Models are provided, that already owe the inference, task and strategy layer and allow model-based knowledge acquisition.

The knowledge models of shells based on strong problem solving methods are on the same abstraction level as the Interpretation Models in KADS, since a shell is an implementation of one specific Interpretation Model. In addition to KADS Interpretation Models, shells predefine the generic concepts and relations of the domain layer, so that their descriptions contain "3 1/2" of the four layers. This is because one part of the domain layer describes the concept and relation types incorporated in the shell, while the other part contains the instances of those concept and relation types corresponding to the objects of any of the shell's knowledge bases. Different to the Conceptual Models in KADS, the models of shells are operationalized and the expert system can be executed as soon as a knowledge base is supplied.

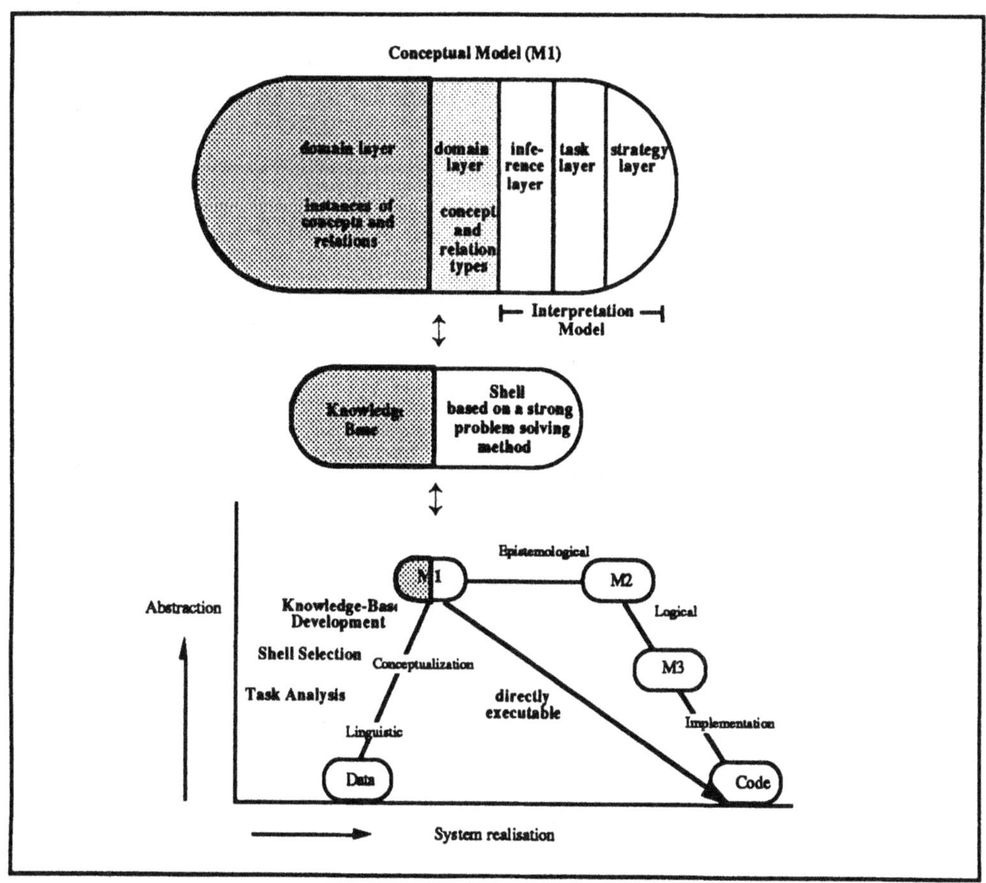

Fig. 1. Embedding the shell approach in the KADS system realization diagram (extended from [Gappa 88])

In the following main part of the paper, we study the conceptual model of the expert system shell MED2/CLASSIKA*. We first give a short overview of the knowledge model (section 2), before we describe it in more detail on one hand in terms of KADS (section 3) and in comparison on the other hand in terms of the graphical representations (section 4) used by the knowledge acquisition user-interface CLASSIKA. In the last section of the paper we report on our experiences with KADS and try to summarize strengths and weaknesses of the KADS and the strong-problem solving-shell approach.

---

* The original MED2 was developed at the University of Kaiserslautern mainly by Frank Puppe. The research group, now at the University of Karlsruhe, continued to develop sophisticated graphical user interfaces for it, especially CLASSIKA for knowledge acquisition, and extents it to further types of classification problem solvers and further types of use (hypertext, tutoring).

2 Overview of the Knowledge Model of the Expert System Shell MED2/CLASSIKA

The application tasks of the classification shell MED2/CLASSIKA [Puppe 87ab, Gappa 89, D3 91, Puppe & Gappa 92] are those of *heuristic classification*, in which *diagnoses* (solutions) are identified because of *symptoms* (data) observed. The problem solving method is based on a hypothesize-and-test strategy: Starting with the initially given data, the system generates *hypotheses* and pursues them by asking for additional data. When new data is obtained, the *working memory* containing the actual hypotheses is updated again and a new set of data is requested.

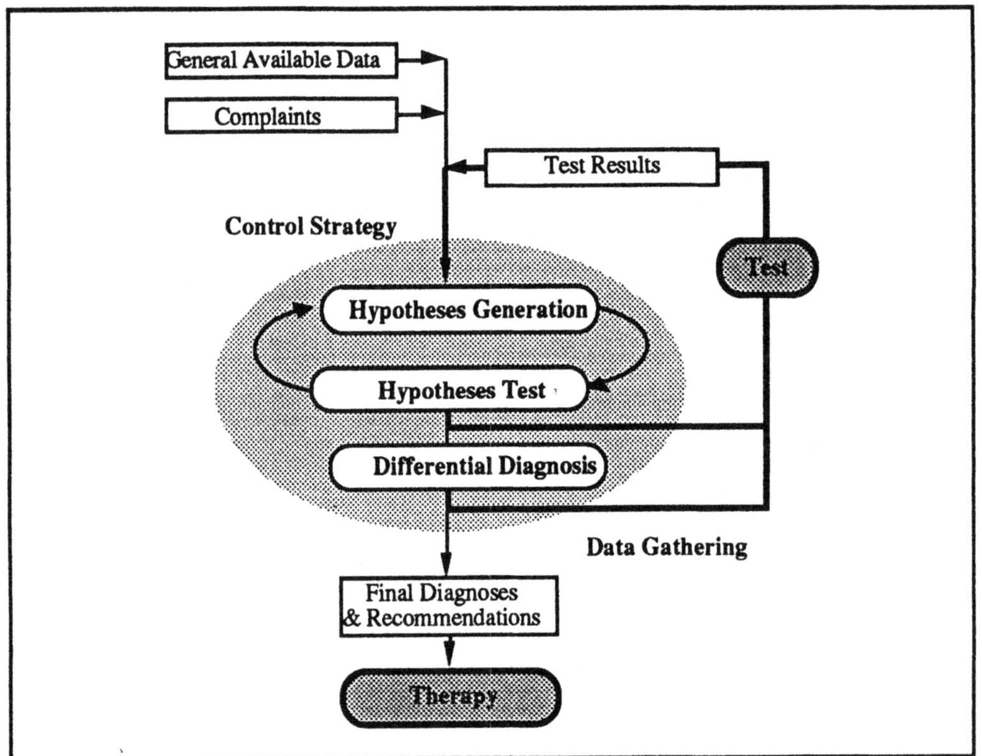

Fig. 2. Overview of MED2/CLASSIKA´s problem solving method

For the purpose of data gathering, questions are grouped into questionsets corresponding to *general information*, various *leading symptoms* (complaints) or results of *manual* or *technical examinations* (tests). Once a questionset has been selected either by the user or the system, a questionnaire with standard questions and - depending on the given answers - follow-up questions are displayed on the screen and filled out by the user. The data might also be automatically transfered from external data bases or technical sensors.

In order to evaluate the current hypotheses, the system has to decide, which questionset is most useful to be obtained. Priority is given to dialogue guiding rules categorically indicating questionsets, e.g. routine tests, and to further questionsets selected by the user. If there is no certain questionset, a *cost-benefit-analysis* is performed, which takes into account the benefits of questionsets for the evaluation of the currently suspected diagnoses and apriori and case-dependent costs of the questionsets´ gathering. When the new questionset is completed, the data interpretation and question asking cycle starts anew until final diagnoses and recommendations (suggestions) are selected.

So, the main object types are Symptoms (data), Diagnoses (solutions), Questionsets (symptom classes, tests, questionnaires), Suggestions (therapies, recommendations) and Rules. Symptoms represent both the Questions asked to the user and Symptom Abstractions (data abstractions), which can be infered from the questions by simple database reasoning [Chandrasekaran 83]. Both diagnosis categories (solution abstractions) and final diagnoses from Clancey´s scheme for heuristic classification (fig. 3) are represented by Diagnoses. For data abstraction as well as for the heuristic match and the refinement of diagnosis categories there are predefined types of rules.

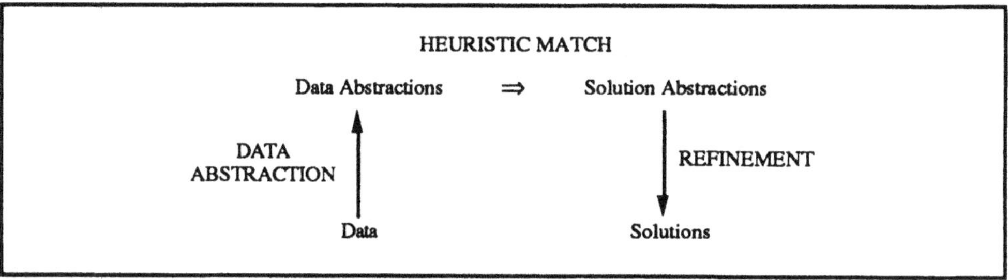

Fig. 3. Classification problem solving inference structure (from [Clancey 85])

Rules are typed according their type of action. There are types of rules that draw conclusions from the obtained data, namely infering data abstractions, adding positive or negative evidence to diagnoses and selecting suggestions (therapies). Other important types of rules concern the dialogue guidance: There are rules for asking follow-up questions, indicating or contraindicating questionsets, assessing the benefits and costs of questionsets, suppressing answer alternatives because of given answers and checking the user input for plausibility. The rules´ conditions are structured into the main condition, secondary conditions, contexts and exceptions. The knowledge representation for object and rule types will be taken up again when describing the domain layer types in the next section.

For the purpose of this paper, we concentrate on the kernel mechanisms of MED2. Further knowledge types concern for example the interpretation of time-concerning symptoms, of the histories of symptom values in follow-up sessions, the belief revision algorithm for efficient conclusion retractions, pointers to picture windows of the hypertext system and a case-comparison problem solver using additional knowledge about similarities, weights and abnormalities of symptoms. Details on the heuristic and case-comparison knowledge model can be found in [D3 91], [Puppe & Goos 91].

3 The Knowledge Model in Terms of KADS

As MED2 is an implemented expert system shell, its conceptual model of knowledge is already given by its predefined types of knowledge representation and their abstractions. So we use KADS not to construct a new model, but to describe the pre-existing model of MED2 (reverse engineering). This work is similar to the re-modeling of parts of ONCOCIN in KADS by [Linster & Musen 91].

3.1 The Domain Layer

The instances of the knowledge representation are domain specific and belong to the knowledge base of the expert system shell. But the shell predefines the types of concepts and relations of the domain layer. Figure 4 shows the types of concepts of the domain layer of MED2 and those of their attributes (designed in circles), that do not represent relations. Most of the object types in the figure are already known from the introduction. We shortly describe the purpose of the additional objects and the semantics of only some of the attributes.

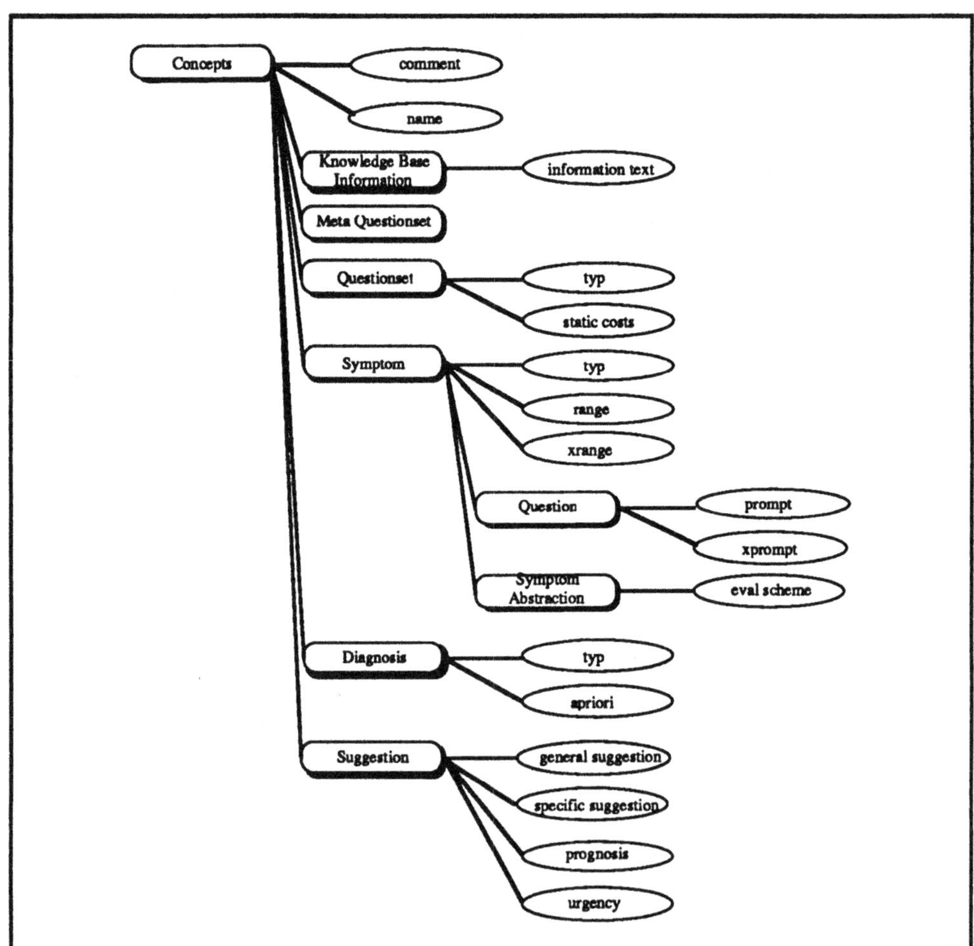

Fig. 4. Concept types and their attributes of the domain layer

The concept Knowledge Base Information may contain an `information text` about the domain and scope of the expert system. It is a special concept only to be instantiated once. Meta Questionsets are used for a hierarchical structuring of the questionsets which eases the survey and user selection of questionsets. An attribute more important for the problem solver is `static costs` of a Questionset which gives a measure for the expenses of the questionset`s gathering, e.g. performing a test. The attribute `eval scheme` of Symptom Abstractions with `answertype` "one choice" controls the mapping of a computed numerical score of the symptom abstraction to one of its answer alternatives.

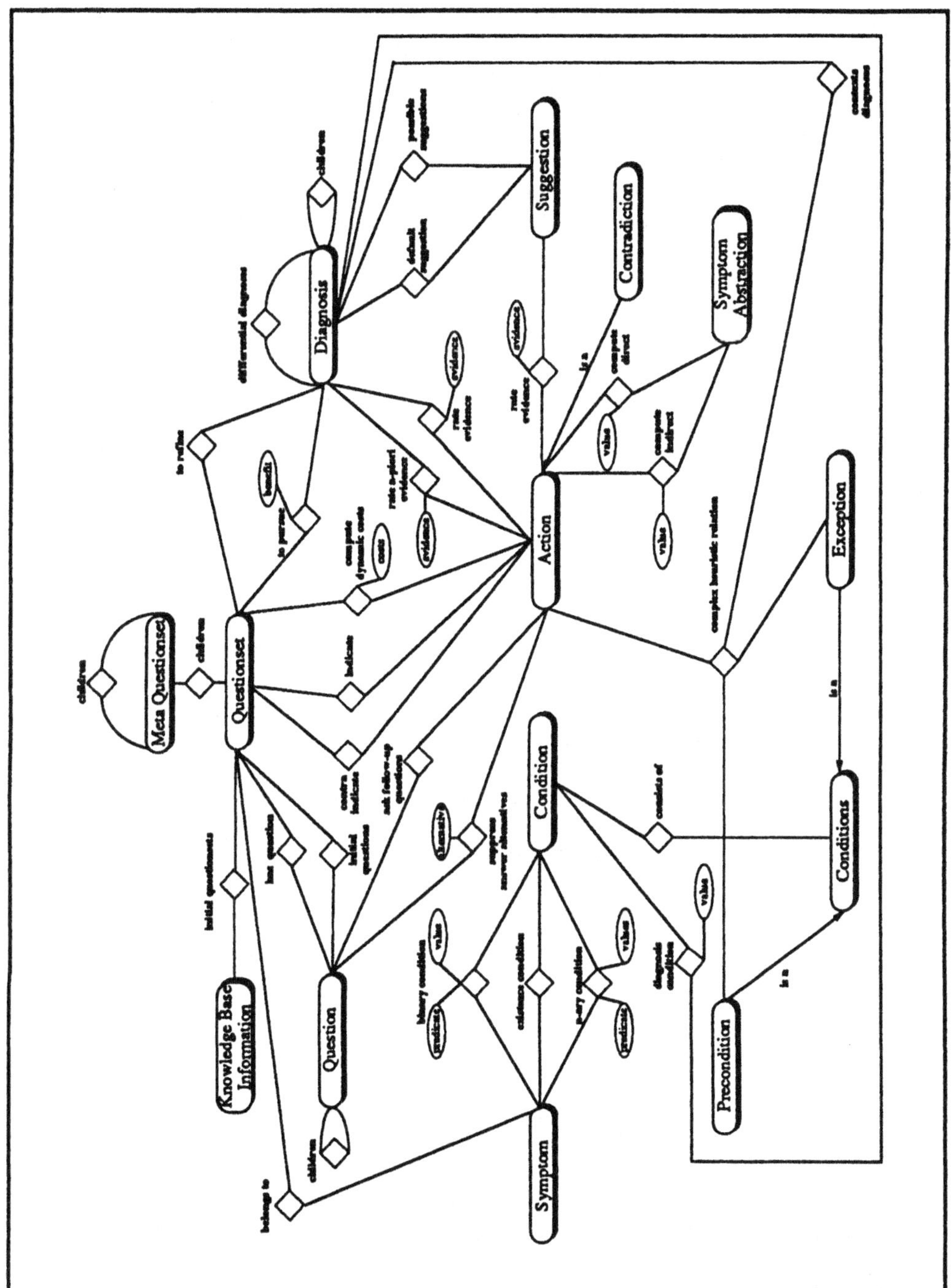

Fig. 5. Relation types of the domain layer (cardinalities omitted)

For each attribute, the type of possible values is predefined. Possible value types are boolean, number, text, choice from a predefined set or some other composed syntax.

Examples for text attributes are • `name` used for the identification of a concept, • `comment` for notes of the expert, • `information text` of the concept Knowledge Base Information, • `prompt`, `xprompt` and `xrange` which provide further text and explanations used for asking a Question, • `range` with the possible answer alternatives for one and multiple choice symptoms (list of texts), • `general` and `specific text` and `prognosis` for Suggestions.

Examples of attributes with a fixed set of values are: • The attribute `answertype` of symptoms which may be "yes/no", "one choice", "multiple choice", "numeric", "time", "duration", "frequency" or "text", • the `type` of a questionset, which may be either "general data", "leading symptom", "physical examination", "test", "data from a data base" or other "automatically tranfered data", • `a-priori`-probability of diagnoses with the categories "extremely often", "often", ..., "extremely seldom".

The relations between the concepts are described in the entity relationship diagram of figure 5. Some of these relations are only used to structure the instances of a concept in hierarchies or heterarchies (e.g. `children` of diagnoses, `children` of Meta Questionsets; see fig. 10, 11 for examples); others define simple inferences like: questionsets to be obtained in order to pursue a hypothesized diagnosis specified by a weight of the benefit (`to pursue`; see fig 15 for examples) or which competitors of a diagnosis must be evaluated before the diagnosis could be established (`differential diagnosis`).

The most difficult relations are represented by rules. They connect e.g. Symptoms and Diagnoses by the intermediate concepts Condition and Action. Rules consist of a main precondition, further preconditions, a number of context diagnoses, which must be established before the rule is evaluated, an action of several action types and eventually exceptions. The preconditions interpret the value of a symptom using predefined operators for the different symptom´s type of answer; for example "equal", "not equal", "one of", "and" for one or multiple choice symptoms and number comparing operators like "less equal" etc. for numerical symptoms. In addition it is possible to check the status of a diagnosis, if it is "excluded" or "established". The actions of rules correspond to the already mentioned rule types like: adding positive or negative evidence to a diagnosis (`rate evidence`), indicate or contra-indicate a questionset and so on.

The use of all these relations is further described by figure 8 which specifies for which purpose (knowledge source) the diverse elements of the knowledge representation are used.

3.2 The Inference Layer

The inference layer of MED2´s problem solving is described in figure 6. The upper part of this figure reflects the dialog guidance of MED2.

- *Receive Questionsets* allows the user to select Questionsets to describe his problem.
- *Select Questionsets to be Gathered* collects all currently activated Questionsets. Active Questionsets are initial Questionsets given in the knowledge base, those selected by the user, indicated by given answers, to pursue a hypothesized diagnosis, or to refine an established diagnosis.
- *Select Current Questionset* selects the at the moment most useful Questionset.
- *Select Questions* determines the current questions to be presented to the user. First are the initial questions, then possibly follow up questions depending on the given answers, and so on. The answering is represented via the knowledge source *Obtain Answers*.
- *Detect Contradictions* and *Present Contradictions* perform plausibility checks on the given

answers and eventually inform the user of the detected inconsistencies.

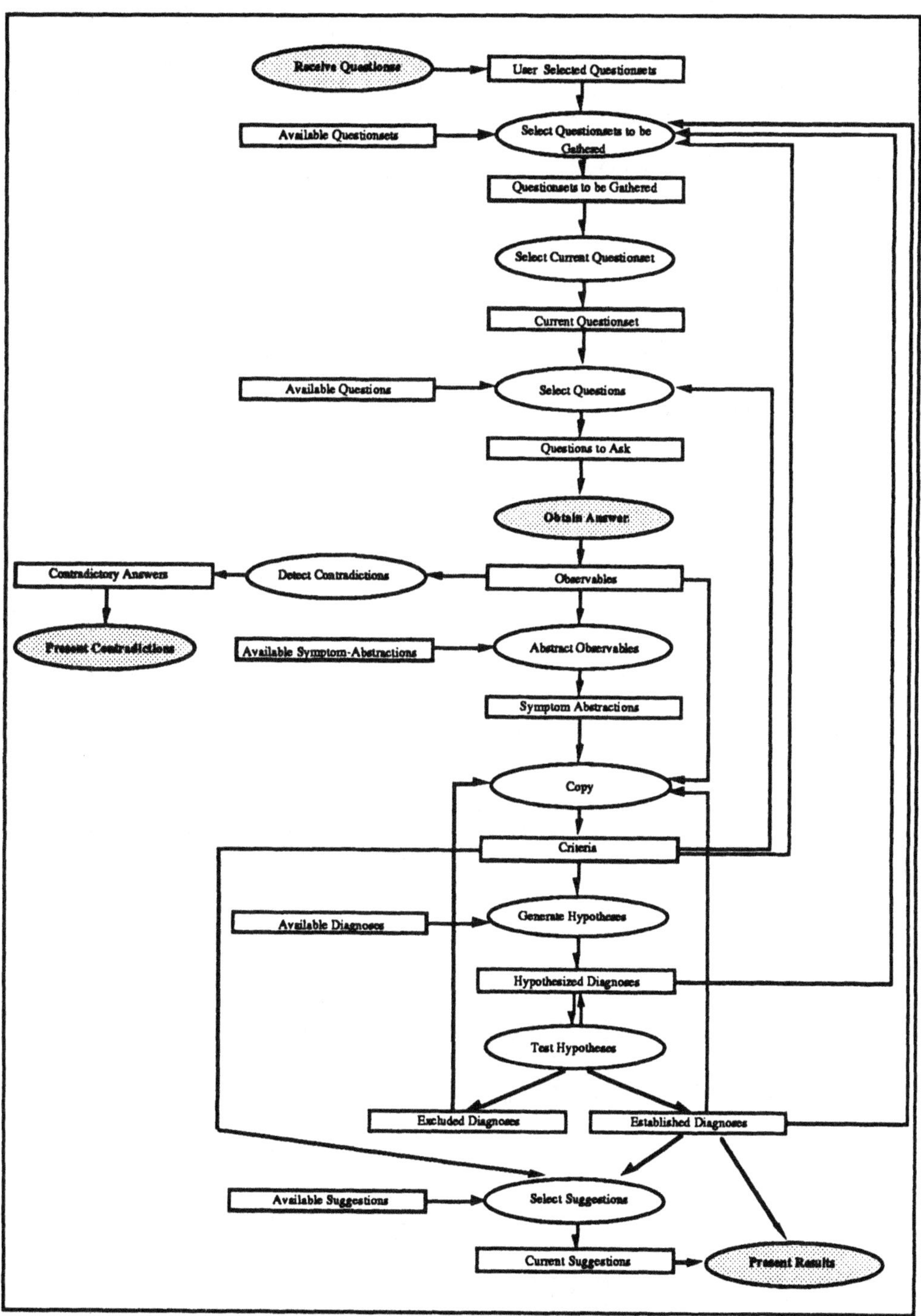

Fig. 6. The inference layer of MED2

From the observables entered more useful Symptom Abstractions are derived in the knowledge source *Abstract Observables*. The heuristic match between symptoms and diagnoses is carried out by the following knowledge sources:

- *Generate Hypotheses* as well as *Test Hypotheses* add positive or negative evidence to the diagnoses depending on the Criteria. The evidence mechanism is similar to the scheme used in INTERNIST [Miller et al. 82].
- *Specify Diagnosis Status* classifies the evaluated Diagnoses to one of "excluded", "hypothesized" or "established". The status of a diagnosis may be used for further conclusions.

The last knowledge source *Select Suggestions* derives recommendations for the set of established diagnoses.

Meta classes	**Knowledge Types of Domain Layer**
Available Questionsets	All instances of concept Questionset
Initial Questionsets	Set of Questionsets
User Selected Questionsets	Set of Questionsets
Questionsets to be Gathered	Set of Questionsets
Current Questionset	A Questionset
Available Questions	All instances of concept Question
Questions to Ask	List of Questions
Contradictory Answers	Set of set of pairs of Questions and their `values` (a dynamic attribute)
Observables	Set of Questions with `values` (a dynamic attribute)
Available Symptom-Abstractions	All instances of concept Symptom Abstraction
Symptom Abstractions	Set of pairs of Symptom Abstractions and `values` (a dynamic attribute)
Criteria	Set of pairs of either Symptom Abstractions or Questions and `values`, and Diagnoses with `status` (a dynamic attribute) established or excluded
Available Diagnoses	All instances of concept Diagnosis
Status of Diagnoses	Table of Diagnoses with their `ratings` (a dynamic attribute)
Hypothesized Diagnoses	Set of Diagnoses
Established Diagnoses	Set of Diagnoses
Excluded Diagnoses	Set of Diagnoses
Available Suggestions	All instances of concept Suggestion
Current Suggestions	Set of Suggestions

Fig. 7. Correspondence between the inference layer meta classes and domain layer

Knowledge Sources	**Knowledge Types of Domain Layer**
Receive Questionsets	Transfer task: Questionset Hierarchy (relation `children` of Meta Questionsets and Questionsets)
Select Questionsets to be Gathered	Categorical indication: • `initial questionsets` (a relation) • `indicate` and `contra-indicate` (relations) • `to refine` (a relation) Cost/benefit-analysis: • `static costs` of concept Questionset (a attribute) • `compute dynamic costs` (a relation) • `to pursue` (a relation)
Select Current Questionset	Static priorities: at first `initial`, user selected and `indicated` Questionsets, then cost/benefit-analysis

Select Questions	• `initial question` of the Current Questionset (a relation) • `standard questions` of the Current Questionset (a relation) • `follow-up questions` (a relation)
Obtain Answers	Transfer task: • `question text`, explanation (`xprompt`), answer alternatives (`range`) etc. (attributes) • `suppress answer alternatives` (a relation)
Detect Contradictions	• `contradiction` (a relation)
Present Contradictions	• Transfer task
Abstract Observables	• `compute direct`, `compute indirect` (relations)
Copy	
Generate Hypotheses and Test Hypotheses	• `rate a-priori evidence` and `rate evidence` (relations)
Select Suggestions	• `rate evidence` (a relation)
Present Results	Transfer Task

Fig. 8. Mapping between the inference layer knowledge sources and domain layer

3.3 The Task Layer

While the inference layer defines all possible inferences, the task layer specifies the control, *when* which of the inferences is performed. The task layer structure of MED2 is quite obvious (fig. 9).

```
Select Questionsets to be Gathered
WHILE NOT EMPTY Questionsets to be Gathered
        Select Current Questionset
        Select Questions
        WHILE NOT EMPTY Questions to Ask
                Obtain Answers
                Detect Contradictions
                IF NOT EMPTY Contradictory Answers THEN Present Contradictions
                Abstract Observables
                Copy
                WHILE new Criteria become known
                        Generate Hypotheses
                        Test Hypotheses
                        Copy
                END WHILE
                Select Questions
        END WHILE
        Select Questionsets to be Gathered
END WHILE
IF NOT EMPTY Established Diagnoses THEN Select Suggestions
Present Results
```

Fig. 9. The task layer of MED2

4 The Knowledge Model in Terms of Graphical Representations

MED2's knowledge acquisition environment CLASSIKA (*k*nowledge *a*cquisition for *classi*fication) facilitates human experts to represent their knowledge graphically by

- entering their domain vocabulary of symptom names and diagnosis names into hierarchies,
- specifying mainly local information to those terms by filling-in forms and
- establishing their relations by arranging and filling-in tables or rule forms.

The predefined graphical knowledge editors are the intermediating representations used both for communicating the underlaying knowledge model of the expert system shell and to acquire the domain and relation instances from the expert. By arranging and filling in the given types of knowledge editors, the expert instantiates the predefined concept and relation types of the internal knowledge representation. Each knowledge editor window summarizes a couple of attribute and/or relation types and therefore represents a view or abstraction of the knowledge model. In this chapter we analyze the most important types of graphical representations used in CLASSIKA and specify their mapping to the concept and relation types of the internal knowledge representation or types of inference (knowledge sources).

The diagnoses of the domain are entered into a graphical *Diagnosis Hierarchy* (fig. 10) represents the `children` relation. In another setting of the hierarchy additional lines of another line type are pointed out to indicate the refinement relation of diagnoses

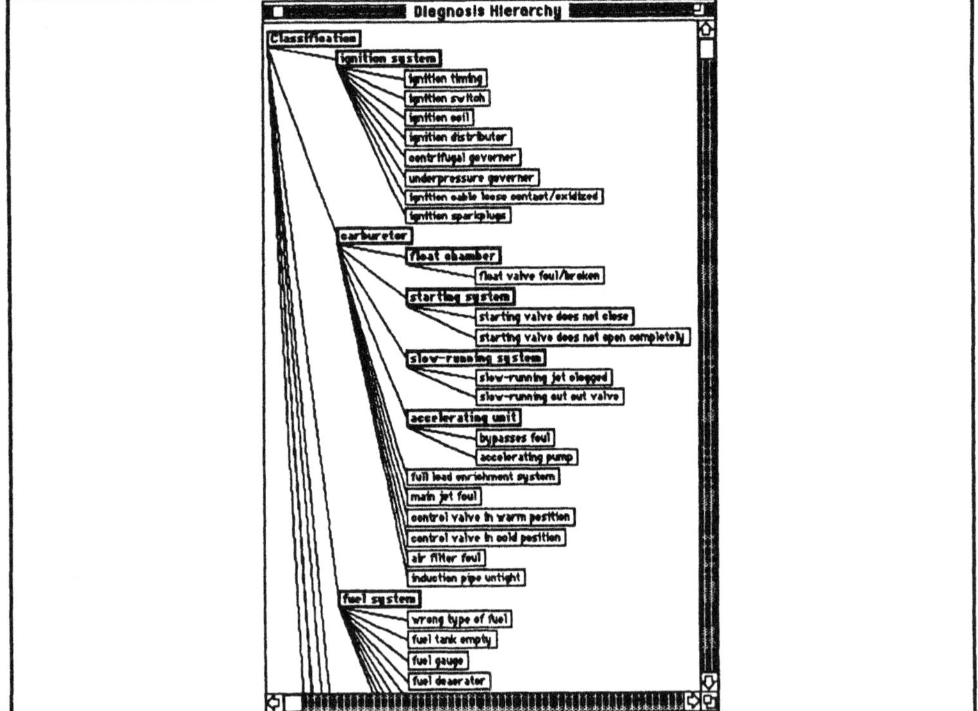

Fig. 10. The Diagnosis Hierarchy

Meta-Questionsets, Questionsets, Questions and Symptom Abstractions are all summarized

in the *Symptom Hierarchy* (fig. 11), which can be viewed at different layers of abstractions by restricting the object types to be displayed.

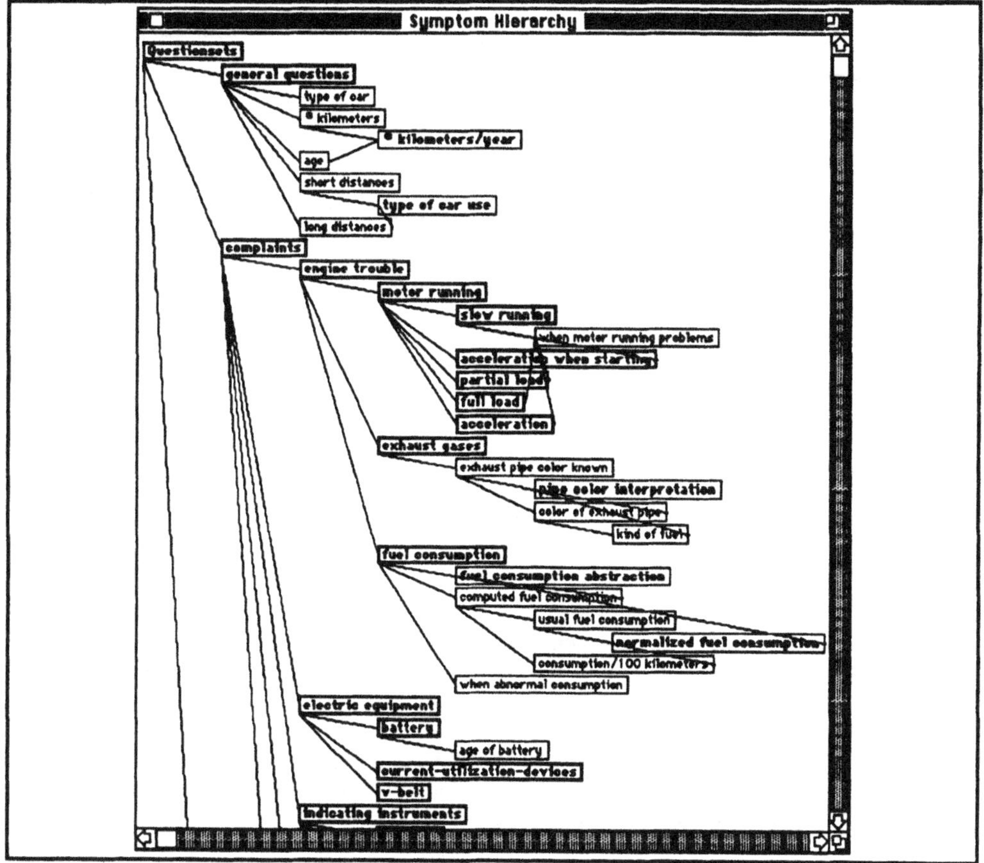

Fig. 11. The Questionset/Symptom Hierarchy

The Symptom Hierarchy starts with the hierarchical structure of the Meta Questionsets and Questionsets in bold letters and bold boxes (relation `children`). Each questionset gathers a couple of Questions displayed in plain letters and boxes, some of them asked always when the questionset is obtained (relation `initial questions`) and some depending on the user's answers (follow-up questions, relation `children`). Observables may also be preprocessed to Symptom Abstractions appearing in bold letters and plain boxes. At this level of abstraction the detailed preconditions for asking follow up questions (relation `ask follow up questions`) and for deriving symptom abstractions (inference *Abstract Observables*) are hidden. They can be inspected by a double-click onto the connecting line.

Forms are used to acquire the local information and a few relations of a concept. In the form for Questions (fig. 12) for example, the expert may specify the name, text and further explanations of the question presented in the dialog (`name`, `prompt`, `xprompt`, `xrange`), the `answertype` and depending on the answertype, the `range` of the symptom and an optional `comment`. Further entries specify if the symptom is a Question or Symptom Abstraction and the questionset the symptom belongs to (relation `qmember`).

Question "exhaust pipe color known"

Name: exhaust pipe color known — Delete — OK — Cancel

Answer Type: ○ yes/no ○ numerical ○ frequency ◉ one-choice ○ point of time ○ multiple-choice ○ duration

Question Text: Did you pay attention to the color of the end piece of the exhaust pipe?

Explanation

Value Range: yes, color is known
no, I didnot pay attention

Value: ◉ to be asked ○ to be derived

Question Sets: exhaust pipes

Comment

Explanations for Value Range

Fig. 12. A form for a symptom

The predefined syntax of the attribute values are find again in their graphical representations for acquiring them. Attributes with predefined value alternatives are represented and acquired by radio boxes or pop-up menus, texts by editable text boxes etc.

The classical phases of *data abstraction*, *heuristic match* and *refinement* of heuristic classification problem solving is captured in the following graphical representations:

- the data abstraction of the raw data within the Symptom Hierarchy,
- the heuristic match between data and solution categories (N:M-relationships) by types of *Symptom-Diagnoses-Tables* and
- the refinement of solution categories by the *Diagnosis Hierarchy* (heterarchy).

Figure 13 summarizes the knowledge to derive a set of diagnoses (labeled the columns) used in the knowledge sources *Generate Hypotheses* and *Test Hypotheses* Each table entry represents a relation for rating a diagnosis (`rate apriori-evidence`, `rate evidence`). The selected entry means for example: "*If* the fuel consumption interpretation is slightly too high, *then* rate the diagnosis air filter foul with evidence 60 %". Relations with more complex conditions, which cannot be represented in this table, are indicated by a preceding "+" in the table cell. They may be inspected individually by rule forms which can be opened by a double-click onto the table's cell, or by tables for individual diagnoses listing each of its derivation rules in a column of the table.

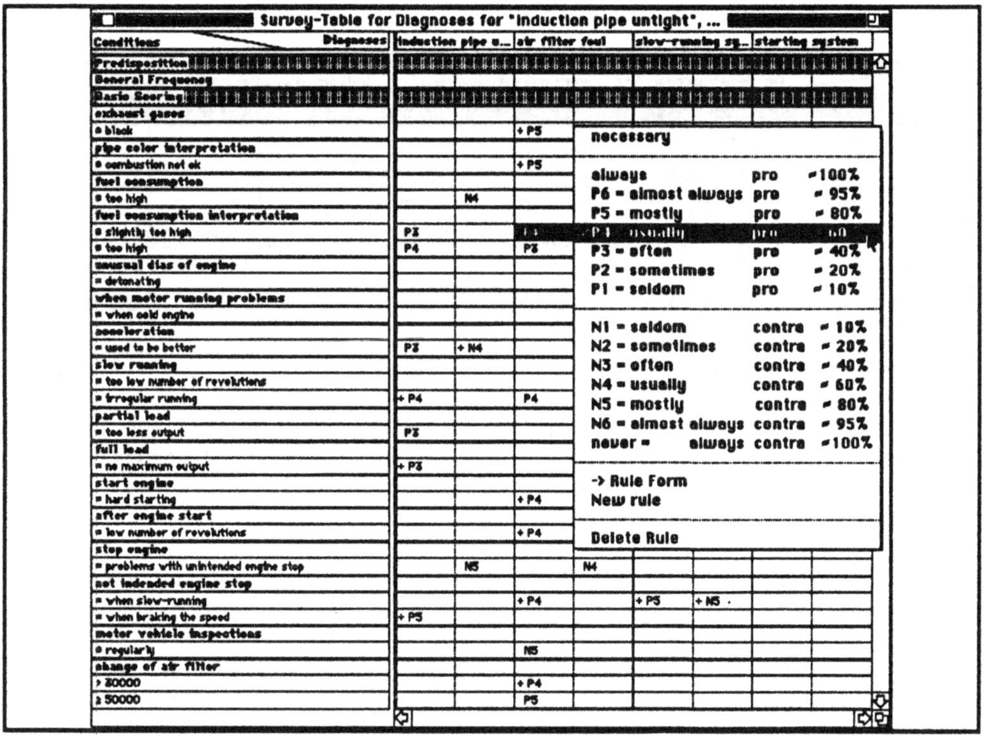

Fig. 13. N:M-relations between Criteria and Diagnoses (*Generate* and *Test Hypotheses*)

Figure 14 shows such a detailed table for the derivation of a Symptom Abstraction. The highlighted entry means "*If* the color_of_exhaust_pipe is black sooty *and* the type of gasoline contains lead, *then* the combustion is not ok".

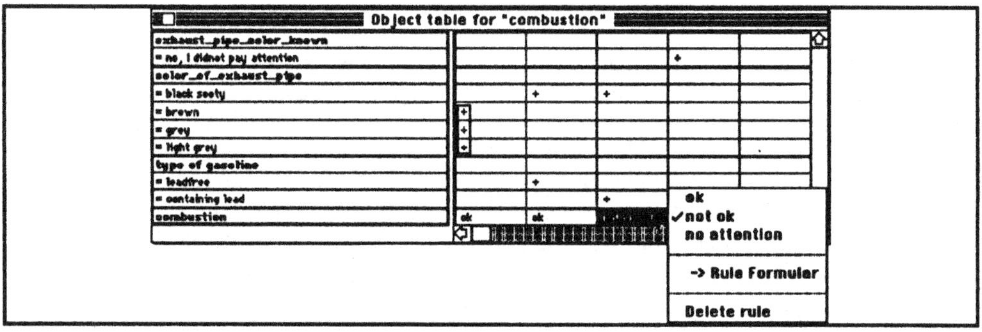

Fig. 14. Rules to derive a Symptom Abstraction

Another type of table represents all knowledge for the global dialog guidance of MED2, used in the knowledge sources *Select Questionsets to be Gathered* and *Select Current Questionset*. The relations to categorically `indicate` or `contra-indicate` a questionset are be specified in the first and third section of the table. The knowledge used for the cost/benefit-analysis, namely how useful a questionset is for the evaluation of a hypothesized diagnosis (relation `to pursue`), what the costs are to obtain a questionset (attribute `static costs` and relation dynamic costs) is represented in the second and fourth section of the table.

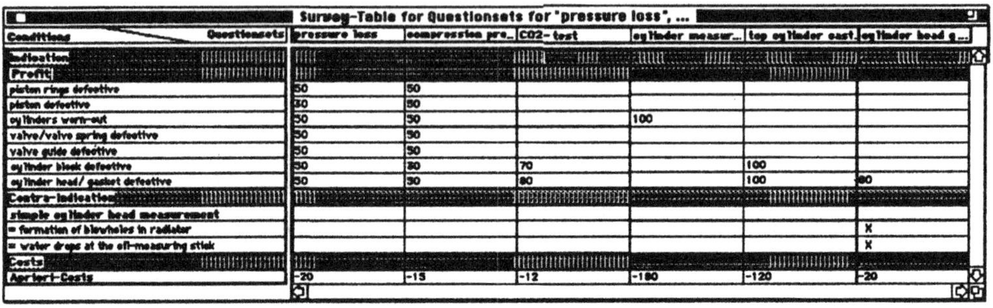

Survey-Table for Questionsets for "pressure loss", ...

Conditions \ Questionsets	pressure loss	compression pre...	CO2-test	cylinder measur...	top cylinder cast.	cylinder head g...
Indication						
Profit						
piston rings defective	50	50				
piston defective	30	50				
cylinders worn-out	50	30		100		
valve/valve spring defective	50	50				
valve guide defective	50	50				
cylinder block defective	50	30	70		100	
cylinder head/ gasket defective	50	30	80		100	80
Contra-Indication						
simple cylinder head measurement						
= formation of blowholes in radiator						X
= water drops at the oil-measuring stick						X
Costs						
Apriori-Costs	-20	-15	-12	-180	-120	-20

Fig. 15. Knowledge for determining the most useful Questionset

The knowledge editors of CLASSIKA include a direct mapping from the graphical to the internal (symbol level) knowledge representation and vice versa, such that the expert is able to describe his knowledge in the graphical terms and can test his knowledge base without a further compilation step.

MED2/CLASSIKA is in use in about half a dozen serious projects and quite a few users experiment with it or use it for educational purposes. Examples of applications concern fault finding in technical devices (automatic transition control unit [Puppe et al. 91], paper machines), fault finding in the production of elastomers [Plog 90], hot-line support for a computer center and medical diagnosis (rheumatology). In most of the cases the domain expert themselves are the users of the system developing large knowledge bases with no or limited help from the developers of the shell or local knowledge engineers.

5 Experiences and Discussion

First of all we want to summarize our experiences made with the representation of the knowledge model of MED2 in KADS. The task of re-modeling has proven to be feasible and not very expensive.

- For the specification of the domain layer, we only had to write down the given knowledge representation of the shell in KADS terms of concepts, attributes and relations. The only problem was to represent the rules of MED2, which are rather complex relations between concepts. Therefore we introduced the auxiliary concepts Condition, Precondition and Exception for the entity relationship diagram. Also we abstracted from some details of the knowledge representation, which would have complicated the diagram but had not improved the comprehension, e.g. the matching predicates to evaluate diagnoses and symptoms of different answer types as well as other attribute dependencies.
- The description of the inference layer was more difficult. We started to develop it by identifying the *roles* our concepts can play, like hypotheses (Hypothesized Diagnoses) and final diagnoses (Established Diagnoses) of Diagnosis and indicated questionsets (Questionsets to be Gathered) of the concept Questionset. Those sets of entities are also displayed in the system's consultation session. Another motivation was to include the diagrams we usually use for explaining the knowledge model to users (fig. 2 and 3 are examples) and we summarized similar relation types for knowledge sources. There seem to be a lot of possible descriptions of the inference layer and ours is just one. So we suspect that it is not possible to decide whether two given inference structures are the same.

- There is little help in the KADS approach to find out how to choose the right granularity. Figure 16 contains a legal Interpretation Model, but is certainly not at the right level of abstraction. Concerning the granularity we oriented ourselves about the formalization of other Interpretation Models, but it would have been desirable to have a better library of predefined knowledge sources than the existing ones.

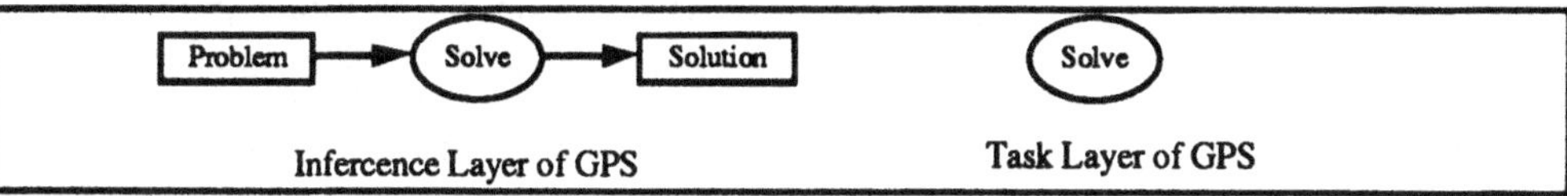

Fig. 16. Interpretation Model for the General Problem Solver

- Another problematic aspect is the lack of hierarchical description elements. Some knowledge sources like *Select Questionset to be Gathered* and *Generate Hypotheses* could be described in greater detail, but this would further enlarge the inference structure and make it unreadable. The possibility of hierarchical descriptions, like in other languages, e.g. SADT, or KARL [see below], a KADS derivative, would be a great help.
- The support of views which comprise certain parts of the model in a new constellation would also be a great advantage. Both figure 2 and 3 are good abstractions which help to clarify different aspects of the model of heuristic classification, but we had to decide on one of them for the design of the inference layer. Although the knowledge model is a concrete refinement of Clancey´s scheme, it can not be directly recognized in the structure.
- The mapping from the meta classes and knowledge sources of the inference layer to the concept and relation types of the domain layer has been unambiguous because we know very well for which inferences the types of knowledge are needed. But with this description of the inference layer and its mapping it is not expressed how the domain knowledge is interpreted to perform the knowledge sources.
- The description of the task layer was rather simple. We only had to reformulate an existing description of MED2's control structure (algorithm) in terms of calls to knowledge sources and comparisons of meta classes for the branching conditions.

The problem that the KADS language does not have an unambiguous semantics is well-known and there is also a great demand for a direct execution of the KADS model descriptions. Recently there are a number of research projects to develop a formal specification of the KADS models, like ML^2 [Akkermanns et al. 90], or to operationalize them, like MODEL-K [Karbach et al. 91], OMOS [Linster 90] or to unify both like restricted ML^2 , KARL [Fensel et. al. 91], FORKADS [Wetter 90]. Nevertheless the usage of the proposed formal languages with a well defined semantics to describe conceptual models seems to be hard work. We guess that a convenient and wide usage of them will not happen before reusable primitives are identified and a library of predefined knowledge sources and Interpretation Models is offered.

One of the most important deficiencies in KADS is that Interpretation Models do not include a definition of the knowledge types from the domain layer together with their mapping to the inference layer. Since shells already include a fixing of the knowledge representation they are more powerful in supporting developers of expert systems. Knowledge acquisition is reduced to instantiating the predefined generic structures. On the other hand shells usually lack a reasonable language to describe their predefined problem solving strategy. So if Interpretation Models could be described at "3 1/2 layers", it would allow the construction of a public available library of problem solving methods, which include the models of successful implemented shells like the ones mentioned in the introduction. A new, improved library of Interpretation Models, describing in a uniform language most known problem solving methods, together with pointers to public available implementations, could reduce drastically the development time and costs for new applications.

Another perspective becoming realistic because of fixed concept and relation types is the definition of a graphical user interface for knowledge acquisition and the mapping of the knowledge editors to the knowledge types of the domain layer (or inferences). We demonstrated the principle and feasibility of such an extension to KADS with the CLASSIKA example in the last section.

One of the goals of KADS' conceptual models is to support the communication between the knowledge engineer and the expert. So it seems reasonable to compare them with model based graphical knowledge acquisition of shells, implementing a role limiting or strong problem solving method. OPAL and CLASSIKA have proven, that it is possible for domain experts with little background in computer science to enter their knowledge via graphical knowledge editors by themselves, without the help of a knowledge engineer. Since their graphical input is directly executable by the underlying problem solver, they are able to maintain their knowledge base themselves, without knowing the implementation details of the problem solver.

One problem with this graphical knowledge acquisition approach is the enormous development amount for depicted graphical interfaces. The first implementation of CLASSIKA contained about 1.5 MB of compiled LISP code compared to 140 KB of the problem solver. To facilitate the development of knowledge editors for further problem solving methods, we identified reusable graphical structures [Gappa 91a] and developed a library of generic graphical primitives [Gappa 91a, b]. The main objects of this library are knowledge editors like hierarchies, graphs, tables and forms. Using these primitives we reimplemented and extended CLASSIKA and developed other knowledge acquisition environments with drastically reduced development times.

Since the usage of these general user-interface primitives for knowledge acquisition still requires the realization of the mapping between the graphical and internal representation, we currently develop a language for the generation of knowledge editors and the mapping onto the internal formalism needed from the problem solver. Like in DOTS [Ericsson 91] the approach operates directly on the knowledge representation (but is bidirectional) and not on problem solver building blocks.

The main problem with the shell approach is the missing flexibility of the hard wired knowledge model of the shell. This may lead to a shoehorn problem, where the expert's knowledge does not directly fit into the shell model but must be adapted. Contrary, KADS allows an easy adaptation of the inference model through adding or changing the knowledge sources or meta classes. The obvious solution for this problem is to build a meta system to generate or configure shells from predefined building blocks, which is attempted in the PROTÉGÉ II [Puerta et al. 91] and Spark, Burn and Fire Fighter [Klinker et al. 90, 91] approaches also including the generation of graphical knowledge editors.

It seems, that both approaches are converging: KADS becomes more and more operational, while shells become more and more configurable.

Acknowledgements

We thank Dieter Fensel and Frank Puppe for their helpful comments on an earlier draft of the paper and all who have encouraged us to write it.

References

Akkermanns, H., van Harmelen, F., Schreiber, G., Wielinga, B. (1990). A formalization of knowledge-level models for knowledge acquisition. International Journal of Intelligent Systems.

Boose, J. H., Shema, D. B., Bradshaw, J.M. (1989). Recent progress in AQUINAS: A knowledge acquisition workbench. Knowledge Acquisition 1 (2), pp. 185–214.

Breuker, J., Wielinga, B., van Someren, M., de Hoog, R., Schreiber, G., de Greef, P., Bredeweg, B., Wielemaker, J., Billaut, J. P., Davoodi, M., Hayward, S. (1987). Model-driven knowledge acquisition: Interpretation models. KADS Technical Report, ESPRIT Project P1098, University of Amsterdam.

Chandrasekaran, B. (1987). Towards a Functional Architecture for Intelligence Based on Generic Information Processing Tasks. IJCAI-87, pp. 1183–1192.

Chandrasekaran, B. (1990). Design problem solving: A task analysis. Artificial Intelligence Magazine, 11 (4), pp. 59–71.

Clancey, W. (1985). Heuristic classification. Artificial Intelligence Journal, 27, pp. 289–350.

Eriksson, H. (1991). Meta-tool support for knowledge acquisition. Dissertation. Linköping University.

Eshelman, L. (1988). MOLE: A knowledge acquisition tool for cover-and-differentiate systems. [Marcus Ed. 88], pp. 37–80.

Fensel, D., Angele, J., Landes, D. (1991). KARL: A Knowledge Acquisition and Representation Language. Proceedings of expert systems and their applications, 11th International Workshop, Conference "Tools, Techniques & Methods", May 27-31th, Avignon, pp. 513-525

Gappa, U. (1988). Knowledge acquisition for expert systems and design of the acquisition system CLASSIKA for heuristic classification. Diploma Thesis, University of Kaiserslautern, Germany.

Gappa, U. (1989). CLASSIKA: A knowledge acquisition tool for use by experts. Proceedings of the Fourth Knowledge Acquisition for Knowledge-Based Systems Workshop, Banff, Canada.

Gappa, U. (1991a). Graphical knowledge representations (in German). Proceedings of the German Workshop of Artificial Intelligence, Springer, Informatik Fachberichte 285, pp. 221–230.

Gappa, U. (1991b). A toolbox for generating graphical knowledge acquisition environments. Proceedings of the first World Congress on Expert Systems, Orlando, Ed.: Liebowitz, J., Vol 2, Pergamon Press, pp. 787-810.

Kahn, G. (1987). TEST: A model-driven application shell. Proceedings of the Seventh Annual National Conference on Artificial Intelligence (AAAI).

Kahn, G. (1988). MORE: From observing knowledge engineers to automating knowledge acquisition. [Marcus Ed. 88], pp. 7–35.

Karbach, W., Voß, A., Schukey, R., Drouven, U. (1991). Model-K: Prototyping at the knowledge level. Proceedings of the 11th International Conference on Expert Systems and their Applications, Avignon, France.

Klinker, G., Bhola, C., Dallemagne, G., Marques, D., McDermott, J. (1990). Usable and reusable programming constructs. Proceedings of the Fifth Knowledge Acquisition for Knowledge-Based Systems Workshop, Banff, Canada.

Linster, M. (1990). Declarative problem-solving procedures as a basis for knowledge acquisition: a first proposal. Arbeitspapiere der GMD, no. 448.

Linster, M., Musen, M.A. (1991). Use of KADS to create a conceptual model of the ONCOCIN task. Proceedings of the Fifth European Knowledge Acquisition for Knowledge-Based Systems Workshop, Strathclyde University, Scotland.

Marcus, S. (1988a). SALT: A knowledge acquisition tool for propose-and-revise systems. [Marcus Ed. 88], pp. 81–123.

Marcus, S. (Ed.) (1988b). Automating knowledge acquisition for expert systems. Kluwer Academic Publishers, Boston.

Marques, D., Klinker, D., Dallemagne, G., Gauthier, P., McDermott, J , Tung, D. (1991). More data on usable and reusable programming constructs. Proceedings of the Sixth Knowledge Acquisition for Knowledge-Based Systems Workshop, Banff, Canada.

McDermott, J. (1988). Preliminary steps toward a taxonomy of problem-solving methods. [Marcus Ed. 88], pp. 225–256.

Miller, R., Pople, H., Myers, J. (1982). INTERNIST1: An experimental computer-based diagnostic consultant for general internal medicine. New England Journal of Medicine 307, No. 8, pp. 468–476.

Musen, M. A. (1989a). Conceptual models of interactive knowledge acquisition tools. Knowledge Acquisition, 1 (1), pp. 73–88.

Musen, M. A. (1989b). Automated generation of model-based knowledge acquisition tools. Morgan Kaufmann Publishers, Pitman, London.

Musen, M. A., Fagan, L., Combs, D., Shortliffe, E. (1987). Use of a domain model to drive an interactive knowledge-editing tool. International Journal of Man-Machine Studies, 26, pp. 105–121.

Newell, A. (1982). The Knowledge Level. Artificial Intelligence, 18, pp. 87–127.

Plog, J. (1990) Quality insurance in the production of elastomers using an expert system (in German). Forschrittsberichte VDI, Reihe 2: Fertigungstechnik, Nr. 200, VDI-Verlag

Poeck, K. (1991a). COKE: An expert system shell for assignment problems. Proceedings of the Sixth Planning and Configuration Workshop, Hamburg, Germany.

Poeck, K. (1991b). Modeling the YQT-office-planning-problem with COKE. Proceedings of the SISYPHUS-Workshop at EKAW-91 (to appear).

Puerta, A., Egar, J., Tu, S., Musen, M. A. (1991). A multiple-method knowledge-acquisition shell for the automatic generation of knowledge-acquisition tools. Report KSL-91-24, Stanford University.

Puppe, F. (1987a). Diagnostic problem solving with expert systems (in German). Informatik Fachberichte 148, Springer.

Puppe, F. (1987b). Requirements for a classification expert system shell and their realization in MED2. Applied Artificial Intelligence, 1, 1987.

Puppe, F. (1990). Problem solving methods in expert systems (in German, translation to English in preparation), Springer.

Puppe, F., Gappa, U. (1992). Towards knowledge acquisition by experts, The fifth International Conference on Industrial & Engineering Applications of Artificial Intelligence and Expert Systems, Paderborn (to appear).

Puppe, F., Goos, K. (1991). Improving case based classification with expert knowledge. Proceedings of the German Workshop of Artificial Intelligence. Springer, pp. 196-205.

Puppe, F., Legleitner, T., Huber, K. (1991). DAX/MED2: A diagnostic expert system for quality assurance of an automatic transmission control unit. G.P. Zarri (Ed.), Operational Expert Systems in Europe, Pergamon Press.

Shaw, M., Gaines, B. (1989). Comparing conceptual structures: Consensus, conflict, correspondence and contrast. Knowledge Acquisition 1, No 4, pp. 341–363.

Wetter, T. (1990) First order logic foundation of the KADS conceptual model. Current Trends in Knowledge Acquisition, IOS Press, Amsterdam.

Wielinga, B., Bredeweg, B. Breuker, J. (1988). Knowledge Acquisition for Expert Systems. Proceedings of ACAI-88.

Wielinga, B. J., Schreiber, A. Th., Breuker, J. A. (1991). KADS: A modelling approach to knowledge engineering. KADS-II Technical Report, ESPRIT Project P5248, University of Amsterdam.

[D3]. Bamberger, S., Gappa, U., Goos, K., Meinl., A., Poeck, K., Puppe, F. (1991). The classification expert system shell D3 (in German, translation to English in preparation). Manual. Karlsruhe University.

Differentiating Problem Solving Methods*

Guus Schreiber † Bob Wielinga † Hans Akkermans ‡

Abstract

Problem solving methods (PSM's) are important in constructing modular and reusable knowledge-based systems, as they specify the different types of knowledge used in knowledge-based reasoning, as well as under what circumstances what knowledge is to be applied. We argue that the formal modeling of PSM's is a useful means for clarifying, communicating and comparing problem-solving knowledge. This paper shows how such PSM's can be formally defined. We illustrate this by developing a formal model for the Cover-and-Differentiate method for diagnosis, and comparing this to Heuristic Classification.

1 Introduction

A generally accepted principle underlying Knowledge-Based Systems (KBS) is that they solve problems through the application of domain specific knowledge. On the basis of this principle many useful systems have been developed [McDermott, 1988], some of which are in operational use. However, the principle of *problem solving power through application of domain knowledge* does not specify what the *nature* of the knowledge is that these systems use and *under what circumstances what* knowledge should be applied, i.e. the *method* of solving a particular problem through

*The research reported here was carried out in the course of the REFLECT (P 3178) and the KADS-II (P 5248) projects. These projects are partially funded by the ESPRIT Basic Research resp. ESPRIT-II Programmes of the Commission of the European Communities. The partners in the REFLECT project are the University of Amsterdam (Amsterdam, The Netherlands), the Netherlands Energy Research Foundation ECN (Petten, The Netherlands), the National German Research Centre for Computer Science GMD (St. Augustin, Germany) and BSR Consulting (Munich, West-Germany). The partners in the KADS-II project are Cap Gemini Innovation (Paris, France), Cap Gemini Logic (Stockholm, Sweden), the Netherlands Energy Research Foundation ECN (Petten, The Netherlands), Entel (Madrid, Spain), IBM France (Paris, France), Lloyds' Register (Croydon, United Kingdom), the Swedish Institute of Computer Science (Stockholm, Sweden), Siemens AG (Munich, Germany), Touche Ross MC (London, UK), the University of Amsterdam (Amsterdam, The Netherlands) and the Free University of Brussels (Brussels, Belgium). This paper reflects the opinions of the authors and not necessarily those of the consortia.

†Affiliation: University of Amsterdam, Department of Social Science Informatics, Roetersstraat 15, NL-1018 WB Amsterdam, The Netherlands. Electronic mail: schreiber/wielinga@swi.psy.uva.nl

‡Affiliation: Software Engineering & Research Department, Netherlands Energy Research Foundation ECN. P.O. Box 1, NL-1755 ZG Petten, The Netherlands. Electronic mail: akkermans@ecn.nl

application of knowledge still needs to be explicated. In recent work [McDermott, 1988; Clancey, 1983] several of such Problem Solving Methods (PSM's) have been described, but so far no comprehensive theory of PSM's has emerged. The goal of this paper is to show that a PSM can be formally defined. The example PSM that this paper focuses on is the Cover-and-Differentiate method [Eshelman *et al.*, 1988; Eshelman, 1988]. We also illustrate how several methods, which are seemingly alike at the level of informal description, can be rigorously compared, and can be shown to be formally different.

What constitutes a PSM? It is progressively becoming clear [Clancey, 1985; Wielinga & Breuker, 1986; Wielinga *et al.*, 1992; Steels, 1990] that there are a number of basic ingredients that are needed in order to specify a problem solving method. These ingredients are *types* of knowledge which would be instantiated for each specific method. There are at least the following types of knowledge required in the specification of a PSM.

1. Knowledge describing which *inferences* are needed in an application. Inferences (in KADS: "knowledge sources" [Wielinga *et al.*, 1992]) describe the elementary reasoning steps that one wants to make in some domain and the *roles* that pieces of domain knowledge that are manipulated by the inferences play in the overall reasoning process (e.g. *finding* or *hypothesis*; , in KADS these are called "meta classes"). The set of inferences is often graphically represented in a diagram showing the input-output dependencies between inferences: the so-called "inference structure".

2. Knowledge about the *structure of the domain-specific knowledge* required to perform inferences. For example, an inference in which quantitative *data* are abstracted into qualitative *findings* requires domain knowledge which relates pieces of domain knowledge that play the role of data and findings (e.g. definitions, generalisations or qualitative abstraction relations [Clancey, 1985]). This type of knowledge corresponds to the notion of *domain view* in KADS [Wielinga *et al.*, 1992].

3. *Control knowledge* which is used to determine how inferences are sequenced in a particular situation. The notion of a *task* is used to structure this control knowledge. A task defines a typical decomposition into inferences and/or subtasks together with internal sequencing information.

The different types of knowledge can be viewed as located in layers which have a object-meta-like relation. An inference *applies* domain knowledge with a particular structure; control knowledge *invokes* inferences.

Generally speaking, there are two ways in which PSM's are described in the literature: the *informal* description using either natural language or an informally defined graphical notation [Breuker *et al.*, 1987; Wielinga *et al.*, 1992], and a *computational* description, which is formal and unambiguous, but difficult to interpret and not independent of implementation details. Both ways of describing PSM's make it hard to compare methods, let alone to develop a theory of problem solving in KBS.

There is a clear need for an intermediate, formal but implementation-independent, description of PSM's.

In this paper we show how formal methods can be used to define the different knowledge types required for specification of PSM's. There are several reasons why a formal account of PSM's is important. First, formal models are a means for concise and precise communication of PSM's. Second, formal models allow us to identify distinguishing properties of different PSM's. and thus to compare them. A third reason is ***re-usability***. When we specify different knowledge types in a modular way, modules can be re-used over different PSM's. Such re-usability is of great practical importance for building KBS's. Last but not least, formal approaches to modelling PSM's can provide first steps towards a theory of automated problem solving.

2 Framework for Formal Modelling

In a recent paper [Akkermans *et al.*, 1991] we have proposed a logic-based language called ML^2 for the formal description of PSM's. As pointed out in the previous section, a PSM is defined in terms of different types of knowledge. Accordingly, our formal modelling language has been designed such that the various knowledge types can be expressed by means of different formal constructs. The main ingredients of ML^2 are briefly described below.

An ML^2 description is basically a structure of logical theories. Each theory consists of a signature and a set of axioms. The logical language is usually first-order order-sorted, but it can be extended to include, for example, modal operators. ML^2 allows for the specification of knowledge modules of PSM's as separate theories. These theories can be combined by means of simple meta-theoretic operators, such as the *import* operator which generates the union of two theories. In this respect ML^2 is the KBS equivalent of algebraic specification languages for conventional software [Bergstra *et al.*, 1990]. In addition to these more or less standard facilities, ML^2 offers a number of primitives which facilitate the description of links between the various types of knowledge used in a PSM:

Meta-level organisation
The three different types of knowledge are defined in ML^2 as three layers, each layer consisting of a set of modules of a certain knowledge structure. The modules in different layers have an object-meta relation: knowledge structures in one layer can be viewed as meta-level objects in another layer. These meta-level objects can be reasoned about and can be applied in order to derive new information.

Meaningful naming: the lift operation
In ML^2 the so-called *lift* operation defines the connection between domain (object-level) structures and their corresponding meta-objects by establishing a naming relation. This mapping is achieved via sets of rewrite rules. A particular feature is that we do not use the conventional quotation or structural-

descriptive names, but instead employ a *definable* naming. This type of naming relation makes it possible to give names to knowledge elements that express the role that these elements play in the reasoning process. Inferences usually require a certain structure of the domain knowledge in order to be effective. This structure is provided in an ML^2 description by meaningful naming. For example, it is possible to give names to indicate that certain domain statements are to be interpreted as definitions and can thus be used in an abstraction inference step.

Reflection rules
Names only are not sufficient to establish the link between object- and meta-theories. It is also desirable, like in control types of knowledge, to be able to influence inferences in a theory at one level from theories at another level. This is realised in ML^2 by reflection rules. The most important reflective predicates are $ask_{\vdash}$, related to the standard upward reflection rule stating that $ask_{\vdash}(\lceil \mathcal{O} \rceil, \lceil P \rceil)$[1] is true if the assertion P is derivable in object-theory $\mathcal{O}$, and $tell_{\in}$, whose behaviour is defined by the downward reflection rule:

$$\frac{\vdash_{\mathcal{M}} tell_{\in}((\lceil \mathcal{O} \rceil, \lceil P \rceil, \lceil \mathcal{O}' \rceil)}{Q \in \mathcal{O}' \textit{ iff } Q \in \mathcal{O} \textit{ or } Q = P} \tag{1}$$

saying that $\mathcal{O}'$ is a theory with the same axioms as O plus P. For an extensive description of reflective rules in ML^2, see [van Harmelen *et al.*, 1990].

In short, our formal modelling language has a multi-level and multi-language structure (hence the name ML^2). As such, it has some features in common with systems like Socrates [Jackson *et al.*, 1989], REFLOG [Lavrač & Vassilev, 1989] and FOL [Weyhrauch, 1980].

3 A Model of Cover-and-Differentiate

In this section parts of a formal description in ML^2 of the problem-solving method *cover-and-differentiate* (C&D) are presented. The full formal description can be found in [van Harmelen *et al.*, 1990]. The information sources for this description [Eshelman *et al.*, 1988; Eshelman, 1988] do not supply a complete description of all the details of C&D. Parts of the underlying specification are thus a more or less "educated guess" about the workings of C&D. The idea behind this description is to create a platform to discuss what PSM's like C&D actually do and to be able to compare them.

Note All free variables in the theories given below are implicitly assumed to be universally quantified.

[1] The notation $\lceil P \rceil$ should be read as "the name of P".

3.1 Conceptual Description of C&D

Cover-and-differentiate [Eshelman, 1988] is a problem solving method for diagnostic tasks. The main knowledge structure on which C&D operates is a causal network. The nodes in this network are expressions about the state of the system being diagnosed. Reasoning basically comprises two types of inferences: *cover* inference steps in which the causal network is used in an abductive manner to generate potential explanations for nodes that need to be explained, and *differentiate* inference steps in which these potential explanations are confirmed or disconfirmed by applying additional knowledge in the network. C&D uses in its reasoning two general principles: *exhaustivity* (every symptom should be explained), and *exclusivity* (a form of Occam's razor: all things being equal, parsimonious explanations are preferred). The solution that C&D comes up with is an explanation path from symptoms to (potentially multiple) causes. The solution can be a partial one.

One of the points that triggered the work presented in this paper is the following quote from [Eshelman, 1988; page 37]:

> "MOLE is an expert system shell that can be used in building systems that use a specialised form of heuristic classification to solve diagnostic problems."

In the comparison between Cover-and-Differentiate and Heuristic Classification in Section 4 we will come back to this statement and show that there are a number of fundamental differences between these two problem solving methods.

3.2 Structure of Domain-Specific Knowledge in C&D

Concepts Two types of concepts are distinguished: *states* and *qualifiers*. States are the nodes in the causal network. Fig. 1 shows the example causal network defined in this section. The start-nodes in the causal network are the initial causes, the end-nodes are the complaints or symptoms. and the intermediate ones are internal states. Qualifiers are observations, that do not play the role of symptoms. These are used to qualify (or disqualify) the ' 'truth" of a state or of a causal relation between states.

Relations In C&D, six types of relations are distinguished between states and/or qualifiers:

S1 covers S2

S1 is a potential cause of S2. Cover relations define a causal network from causes to symptoms, potentially via intermediate states.

The theory *potential-causes* shows some axioms representing causal relations in a domain of ischaemic heart diseases[2]. The axioms can be read as "some

[2] To save space, we have left out the declaration of the signature (sorts, constants, functions, and predicates) and also unessential module connectors like some import operations. For more details

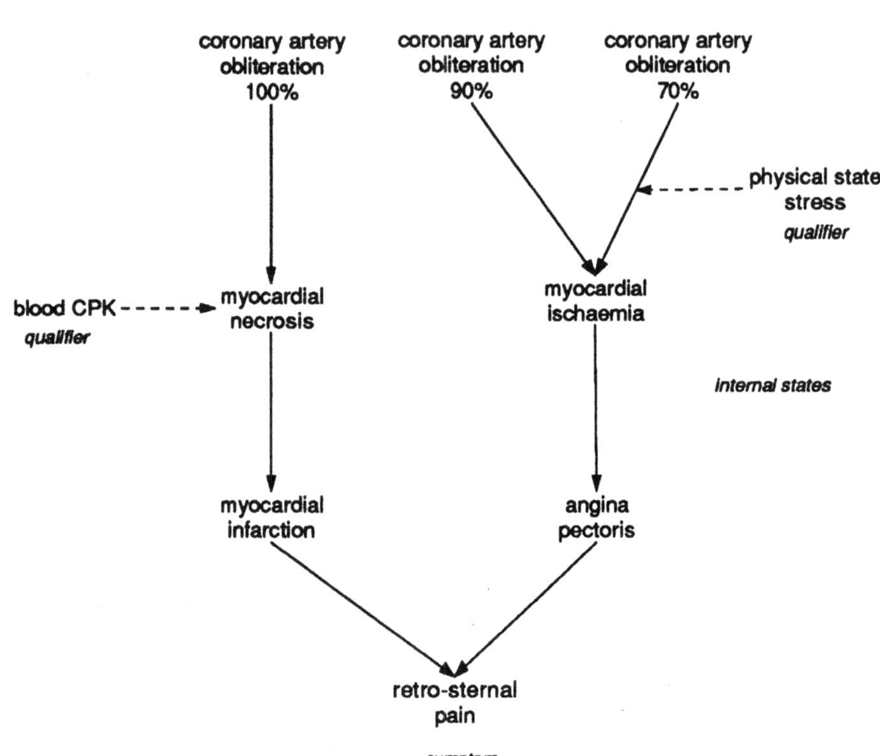

Figure 1: Example causal network for Cover-and-Differentiate

state may cause some other state". We use a modal operator ◇ ("it is possible that") to stress the fact that we are specifying potential cause-effect relations[3].

theory *potential-causes*
axioms
◇ (coronary-artery-obliteration(70-percent)
→ myocardial-ischaemia(present)) ;
◇ (coronary-artery-obliteration(90-percent)
→ myocardial-ischaemia(present)) ;
◇ (myocardial-ischaemia(present)
→ angina-pectoris(present)) ;
◇ (angina-pectoris(present)
→ retro-sternal-pain(present)) ;
◇ (coronary-artery-obliteration(100-percent)
→ myocardial-necrosis(present)) ;
◇ (myocardial-necrosis(present)

on these issues, please refer to [Akkermans *et al.*, 1991]

[3]This presents no problems, as we do not deduce new theorems in this theory, See also section 3.3

```
    → myocardial-infarction(present)) ;
  ◇ (myocardial-infarction(present)
    → retro-sternal-pain(present)) ;
```

S1 anticipates S2

S1 always causes S2. These relations are thus necessary causal relations, The axioms can be read as "some state always causes some other state".

```
theory necessary-causes
  axioms
      coronary-artery-obliteration(100-percent)
        → myocardial-necrosis(present) ;
```

A "necessary causal" relation is viewed a stronger variant of the "potential causal" relation. Every axiom in this theory appears thus also (in a modal form) in the previous theory.

If Q, prefer/rule-out S

States can be qualified through certain observations. The effect of such a qualifier can be positive (a state becomes more likely) or negative (a state becomes less likely).

```
theory state-indicators
  axioms
      blood-CPK(high)
        → myocardial-necrosis(present) ;
```

If Q, prefer/rule-out S1 as explanation of S2

In a similar spirit, causal relations between states can be qualified through certain observations. The effect of such a qualifier can be positive (a causal relation becomes more likely) or negative (a causal relation becomes less likely).

```
theory connection-indicators
  axioms
      physical-state(stress)
      → ◇ (coronary-artery-obliteration(70-percent)
          → myocardial-ischaemia(present)) ;
```

Due to space limitations we will only treat in this paper axioms defining a preference for either a state or a connection.

Lift operation The required domain structure for C&D is specified by providing *meaningful names* (see Sec. 2) for the domain specific axioms shown above. This is done in a so-called *lift operator*. The connection between axioms and their names is realised through a set of rewrite rules, that specify the relation between object-level (= domain-specific) and meta-level (= PSM-specific) knowledge structures.

In the lift-operator *domain-schemata* below we show how the axioms of the theories presented above can be mapped onto names on a meta-level. The names are in this case uninterpreted function terms such as *cover-relation(S1, S2)* and correspond to what we call a meaningful name. The first argument of the mapping function *lift* in the rewrite rules is the name of some object-level theory; the second argument specifies an axiom schema in this theory. The right-hand side of the rewrite rule maps instances of such a schema onto names in the meta-theory, such as a complex term of type *cover-relation*.

```
lift-operator domain-schemata
  from potential-causes, necessary-causes, state-indicators, ...
  to cover-theory, anticipate-theory, prefer-theory, ...
  signature
    sorts:
      % event has two sub-sorts
      (event (state qualifier))
    functions:
      cover-relation: state × state → ...
      anticipate-relation: state × state → ..
      prefer-state: qualifier × state → ..
      prefer-connection: qualifier × state × state → ..
      ...
  meta-variables: P1, P2, P3: atom
  mapping
      lift(potential-causes, ◇ (P1 → P2) )
        ↦ cover-relation(⌈P1⌉:state, ⌈P2⌉:state) ;
      lift(necessary-causes, P1 → P2)
        ↦ anticipate-relation(⌈P1⌉:state, ⌈P2⌉:state) ;
      lift(state-indicators, P1 → P2)
        ↦ prefer-state(⌈P1⌉:qualifier, ⌈P2⌉:state) ;
      lift(connection-indicators, P1 → (P2 → P3))
        ↦ prefer-connection(⌈P1⌉:qualifier, ⌈P2⌉:state, ⌈P2⌉:state) ;
      ...
```

The approach of separating the two views of knowledge structures (domain-specific and PSM-specific) has important advantages. Domain-specific theories could be re-used in other PSM's. Multiple mappings can facilitate multiple use of essentially the same knowledge. In C&D , this separation also keeps intact two distinct views on nodes in the causal network, namely the node as an expression about a value of an attribute of the system (at the object level) and the node as an object in its own right (at the meta level).

3.3 Inference knowledge in C&D

Roles in inferences

Cover-and-differentiate operates on a causal network of states. This network is actually present in two forms:

1. The *causal network* itself as defined by the *cover* relations. These relations describe possible explanations.
2. The *explanation network* that is built during problem solving. The explanation network is a subset of the causal network and can be viewed as its instantiation for a particular problem.

The explanation network consists of three subsets, namely considered explanations, preferred explanations and rejected explanations.

The inference theories operate on the following data elements:

1. Element of the three subsets of the explanation network: (i) considered explanations, (ii) preferred explanations, or (iii) rejected explanations.
2. A focus: a state in the considered or preferred explanation network that is not explained by a another state.

These data elements correspond to what were called *roles* earlier.

```
theory role-defs
  use domain-schemata
  signature
    predicates
      considered-explanation: state × state
      preferred-explanation: state × state
      rejected-explanation: state × state
      focus: state
```

The phrase "explanation network" as used in the rest of this text refers to the considered solutions. Note that inference theories specify elementary inference steps. Updates of the sets of considered, preferred and rejected explanations are handled in the control knowledge (see further). Through the **use** clause one declares that the theory needs access to the object-level terms provided by the lift-operator *domain-schemata*.

Inference theories

The elementary inference steps are described as a set of first-order theories, that use the domain schemata described in Sec. 3.2. Fig. 2 depicts the inference steps (the ovals) we have specified for C&D and their input-output (the boxes).[4] The inferences can be divided in two groups:

1. Inferences that use the domain knowledge defined by the lift operator *domain-schemata*. Examples of these inferences are *cover*, *anticipate*, *prefer* and *rule-out*.

2. Inferences that reason only about the current state of working memory, e.g. the current contents of the explanation network. Examples of these inferences are *occams-razor* and *establish-focus*

Due to space consideration we omit a full description of the inferences *rule-out* and *establish-focus*. These can be found in [van Harmelen *et al.*, 1990; Chapter 5]

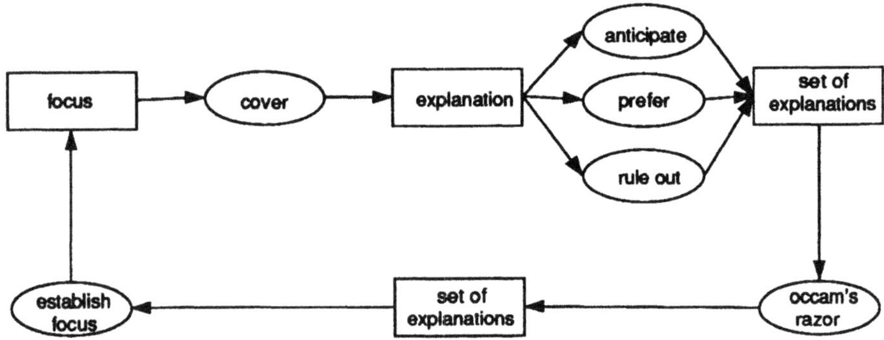

Figure 2: Inferences in Cover-and-Differentiate: their input-output dependencies.

Cover Inference The *cover* inference generates considered explanations. It uses the *cover-relation* to find a potential explanation of a state that is not yet explained (the focus). The cover inference step builds the explanation network by going backwards through the causal network. *Cover* models the *exhaustivity* principle of C&D: all symptoms should be explained, whenever possible.

theory *cover-theory*
  use domain-schemata
  import role-defs
  axioms

$$\mathsf{focus}(S_1) \land ask_{\in}(\mathsf{potential\text{-}causes},\ \mathsf{cover\text{-}relation}(S_2, S_1)) \rightarrow \mathsf{considered\text{-}explanation}(S_2, S_1)$$

$Ask_{\in}$ is one of the reflective predicates. It requests the lift operator *domain-schemata* to find out whether the complex *cover-relation* term can be mapped onto an axiom of the "potential-causes" theory. Note that the predicate *considered-explanation* is

[4] Note that this diagram does not prescribe a particular order in which the actual problem-solving should be carried out. This is specified as separate control knowledge.

an example of a description of the *role* that an object (or in this case, a tuple of objects) plays in the inference process. These role predicates are defined in the *role-defs* theory specified earlier. This theory is *imported* into the inference theory.

The structure of the defining axiom of inferences that make use of domain knowledge is typically:

$$< inputs > \wedge\ ask_{\in}(domain\ knowledge) \rightarrow < output >$$

where the inputs and outputs are role-names of objects in the reasoning process.

Anticipate Inference The differentiation part of C&D is more complicated than covering and consists of a number of elementary inferences (see also below). The *anticipate* inference is part of this differentiation process, in which the considered explanations generated by *cover* are pruned. The *anticipate* theory defines that if a state S1, that is considered as an explanation for a state S2, should always cause some other state S3, then S3 should be true. If this is not the case, then S1 should be rejected as an explanation of S2.

theory *anticipate-theory*
  use domain-schemata
  import role-defs
  axioms
    considered-explanation(S_1, S_2)
    $\wedge$ $ask_{\in}$(necessary-causes, anticipate-relation(S_1, S_3))
      $\rightarrow$ ((fact(S_3) $\wedge$ considered-explanation(S_1, S_3)) $\vee$
        ($\neg$ fact(S_3) $\wedge$ rejected-explanation(S_1, S_2))) ;

We do not define *fact* here. It is assumed to find out whether a state is part of the explanation network or to query the user for a value, whatever is appropriate.

Prefer Inference *Prefer* is also part of the differentiation step of C&D. The *prefer* theory uses two prefer relations (*prefer-state* and *prefer-connection*) to prefer a particular state as the explanation of a state over other states that are not explicitly preferred. The preference is established by the presence of qualifiers for this state or causal relation. E.g., in the example causal network of Figure 1 the finding that a patient is physically stressed would give rise to a preference for the state with a smaller degree of coronary artery obliteration as the explanation of myocardial ischaemia (i.e. oxygen shortage in the heart muscle).

theory *prefer-theory*
  use domain-schemata
  import role-defs
  axioms
    considered-explanation(S_1, S_2)

$\wedge$ *ask*$_\in$(state-indicators, prefer-state(S_1, Q))
$\wedge$ fact(Q) $\rightarrow$
preferred-explanation(S_1, S_2)) ;

considered-explanation(S_1, S_2)
$\wedge$ *ask*$_\vdash$(connection-indicators, prefer-connection(S_1, S_2, Q))
$\wedge$ fact(Q) $\rightarrow$
preferred-explanation(S_1, S_2) ;

Occam's Razor *Occam's razor* models the *exclusivity* principle of cover-and-differentiate. Exclusivity is a form of Occam's razor. All things being equal, parsimonious explanations are preferred.

The axiom below says that if a state S_1 explains a state S_3 and also some other state S_4, then this explanation should be preferred above a competing explanation S2 for S_3 where the explaining state explains only S_2.

theory *occams-razor-theory*
axioms
considered-explanation(S_1, S_3) $\wedge$ considered-explanation(S_2, S_3)
$\wedge$ ($\exists$ S_4 considered-explanation(S_1, S_4) $\wedge$ $S_3 \neq S_4$)
$\wedge$ $\neg$ ($\exists$ S_5 considered-explanation(S_2, S_5) $\wedge$ $S_3 \neq S_5$)
$\rightarrow$ rejected-explanation(S_2, S_3)

An interesting feature of this inference theory is that, unlike the other theories, it does not make use of domain knowledge (i.e. there is no *ask* statement). This is fully in accordance with the generality of this principle. To re-use this theory in another PSM it would be sufficient to rename the predicate-symbols[5].

3.4 Control Knowledge in C&D

The central object in control knowledge is the notion of a *task*. A task specifies how elementary inference steps can be combined to achieve a particular goal. We distinguish two types of tasks: (i) *primitive* tasks and (ii) *complex* tasks.

Primitive tasks Primitive tasks specify how inference theories can be applied during actual problem solving. This task-view of inference theories is achieved through the meta-level operations of ML^2. The axioms below show how the reflective predicates are used to specify the cover *task*[6]. Other primitive tasks are specified in a similar fashion.

cover-task(Foci, New) $\leftarrow$ New =

[5] In ML^2 this theory can be specified PSM-independent as a parameterised theory.

[6] Due to space considerations the specification of the corresponding lift operator is left out.

$\{ < S_1, S_2 > \mid S_2 \in \text{Foci} \land$
$tell_{\in}(\text{cover-theory, focus}(S_2)) \land$
$ask_{\vdash}(\text{cover-theory, considered-explanation}(S_1, S_2)) \}$;

The axioms in this section can be read as logic programs. The cover task takes as an input the set of states that need to be explained (Foci) and produces all considered explanations (the set of two-tuples $< S_1, S_2 >$) for all states in Foci. $Tell_{\in}$ generates a new cover theory with an additional *focus* axiom. $Ask_{\vdash}$ infers new *considered-explanation* terms in the cover theory.

Complex Tasks Complex tasks specify the dependencies between sub-tasks, that can be either primitive or complex. The *differentiate* part of C&D is such a complex task. It consists of four primitive tasks. The primitive tasks differentiate the network of explanations. Three sub-sets of explanations are distinguished: considered explanations ($Cset$), preferred explanations ($Pset$) and rejected explanations ($Rset$). The inferences operate on elements of these sets. These elements are two-tuples of state terms. The *anticipate-task* extends the set of considered explanations on the basis of anticipatory relations that are satisfied and puts explantions whose anticipations are not fulfilled in a set of rejected explanations. The *prefer-task* operates on the set of considered explantions with the rejected ones removed and builds a set of preferred explanations. The *rule-out* and *occams-razor* tasks detect rejections in the remaining set of considered explanations. Finally, one set results from the removal of all rejected and preferred explanations from the set of considered ones and a second set is constructed that contains all preferred explanations sofar.

differentiate-task(CsetIn, PsetIn, CsetOut, PsetOut) $\leftarrow$
anticipate-task(CsetIn, Cset', Rset)
prefer-task(Cset' $\setminus$ Rset, Pset') $\land$
rule-out-task(Cset' $\setminus$ (Pset' $\cup$ Rset), Rset') $\land$
occams-razor-task(Cset' $\setminus$ (Pset' $\cup$ Rset $\cup$ Rset'), Rset") $\land$
CsetOut = Cset' $\setminus$ (Pset' $\cup$ Rset $\cup$ Rset' $\cup$ Rset") $\land$
PsetOut = PsetIn $\cup$ Pset';

The two axioms below specify the top-level task *cover-and-differentiate*. It is an iterative task, alternating between the *cover-task* and *differentiate-task* and an additional task *establish-focus*. This last task calls the corresponding inference to find those states in the current explanation network that are not themselves explained by another state. The top-level task terminates when no new states are generated by the *cover-task* that need to be explained.

cover-and-differentiate-task(CsetIn, PsetIn, Solution) $\leftarrow$
establish-focus-task(CsetIn $\cup$ PsetIn, Foci) $\land$
cover-task(Foci, NewC) $\land$ NewC $\neq \emptyset$ $\land$
differentiate-task(CsetIn $\cup$ NewC, PsetIn, Cset', Pset') $\land$
cover-and-differentiate-task(Cset', Pset', Solution) ;

```
cover-and-differentiate-task( CsetIn, PsetIn, Solution ) ←
    establish-focus-task(CsetIn ∪ PsetIn, Foci) ∧
    cover-task(Foci, ∅) ∧
    Solution = CsetIn ∪ PsetIn ;
```

4 Analysing Cover-and-Differentiate

Given a formal account of cover-and-differentiate as a problem solving method for a diagnosis task, we are now in a position to use the formalisation for analysing the relation of C&D to other methods for diagnosis. Eshelman [Eshelman, 1988] states that C&D is a form of heuristic classification (HC) [Clancey, 1985]. A formal description of parts of HC is presented in [Akkermans *et al.*, 1991]. When we compare C&D and HC there appear to be a number of fundamental differences.

1. A crucial elementary inference step in HC is the *abstraction* inference: the left leg of the Clancey's "horseshoe" [Clancey, 1985]. This abstraction step in the HC problem solving method is used to abstract specific findings (e.g. patient is alcoholic) to more general ones such as "compromised host". These general findings are then used in an *association* step to generate hypotheses. It is clear from the formal definition of C&D that there is no equivalent of such abstraction steps in the C&D method. Findings are either symptoms or qualifiers and are directly associated with hypotheses (states that explain other states). Of course abstraction could be added to C&D, but this would require an additional domain theory describing the relations to be used in the abstraction inferences. In addition it would require the definition of an *abstract* problem solving step, changes to the cover-theory would be needed and a new role would have to be defined: *abstracted-data*. Although these changes are not very difficult to make in the formal model, they would yield a different structure of the knowledge at several levels.

2. A second difference concerns the way in which hypotheses (*considered-explanations*) are generated. In the *cover-theory* these hypotheses are generated through a query of the potential-causes theory concerning cover-relations. This means that only those hypotheses are generated which are directly linked to the symptom being focussed on. In HC hypotheses can be generated from an etiological hierarchy through trigger relations. A trigger relation can relate one or more symptoms to a hypothesis anywhere in the hierarchy. So, the method for generating hypotheses in HC is more flexible and more of a heuristic nature than the one in C&D. Changing the C&D model to incorporate such heuristic associations would require significant changes. In order to maintain the exhaustivity principle (all symptoms are explained) a new inference would be needed. This inference would establish an explanation path between hypotheses somewhere in the causal network and the symptoms. Moreover the simple control structure of C&D would need to be replaced by a more complex one, since the set of covered symptoms would have to be derived.

3. A third difference between C&D and HC concerns the way in which the differential is reduced. In C&D the set of hypotheses is reduced by applying rule-out anticipation and preference inferences. Each of these inferences applies to a *single hypothesis*. The HC method differentiates *between* competing hypotheses by searching for discriminating evidence. For example, the equivalent in HC of the *anticipate* inference would look like the theory below.

   theory *hc-anticipate*
   axioms
   considered-explanation(S1, S3) ∧ considered-explanation(S2, S3) ∧
   ask_{ϵ}(necessary-causes, anticipate-relation(S1, S4)) ∧
   ask_{ϵ}(necessary-causes, anticipate-relation(S2, ¬ S4))
   →
   (fact(S4) ∧ rejected-explanation(S2, S3)) ∨
   (¬ fact(S4) ∧ rejected-explanation(S1, S3))

   The premise of the theory mentions two *considered-explanation* atoms. The reason why in C&D differentiation can be performed on single hypotheses is that the exhaustivity principle allows C&D to prefer hypotheses by ruling out alternatives. There are thus essential differences between what is called *differentiation* in C&D and HC.

4. In HC hypotheses (internal states) are structured in a hierarchy which is used to generalise or specialise a hypothesis. No such hierarchical relations are present in the C&D domain theories, nor are they used in the inferences. Again such knowledge could be incorporated in a new domain theory and inferences and tasks could be updated accordingly.

In fact, there are many more differences. The solution in HC is in principle one cause; in C&D the solution can be multiple causes and includes the causal pathway's to these causes.

If we step back and take a global view on both C&D and HC, we observe some similarities. Both PSM's are specialisations of a general *generate and test* schema. In C&D the generate process is simply represented by the cover-theory. In HC this process is represented by a more complex combination of abstraction and heuristic association. The test process in C&D is realised by the differentiate task, which in turn applies the rule-out, prefer and anticipate inferences. In HC the test is performed through a different *differentiate* task using the hierarchy of hypotheses. Concerning the principles that underlie HC and C&D we see that both PSM's are based on abductive generation of hypotheses, but that C&D requires the symptoms to be fully explained by the solution, and that HC only requires that a solution is consistent with the symptoms.

All in all, we can conclude that C&D and HC have some similarities when viewed at a sufficiently high level of abstraction, but that the differences at a more detailed level turn out to be considerable. The given formal account has thus shown that is not warranted to view C&D as a special form of HC. In addition we can see how new PSM's can be constructed by combining the ingredients of both models.

5 Conclusions

We have sketched in this paper a framework for the formal modeling of problem solving methods. This has been illustrated by constructing a formal definition of the Cover-and-Differentiate method that can be used for certain types of diagnosis tasks. On the basis of this formal definition, we have brought to light considerable differences with the heuristic classification method. Different formalisations of the Cover-and-Differentiate method are conceivable. We are not claiming that our formal model is the only correct one, nor that it fully reflects the actual implementation in MOLE. However, the formal account given in this paper can be a starting point for a precise definition of what Cover-and-Differentiate is.

The main conclusion of this paper is that formal modeling of problem solving methods, which underly reasoning in knowledge-based systems, is a useful means for clarifying and communicating the precise nature of problem-solving knowledge. We have shown that informal statements in the literature about methods such as Cover-and-Differentiate are often imprecise, and sometimes misguided, if not incorrect. Formal models allow a much more detailed definition and comparison of different problem solving methods. One could argue that the differences that we have discussed could have been found by using other means of analysis. At hindsight this is plausible, given the thorough understanding that we now have of the two problem solving methods. However, we doubt whether such an understanding is easily achieved without some form of formal analysis.

In the context of the practice of knowledge acquisition, formal models can serve as a means for specifying the knowledge required for a particular application, and they can support re-use of knowledge through modularisation of the different types of knowledge occurring in a problem solving method.

References

Akkermans, H., van Harmelen, F., Schreiber, G., & Wielinga, B. (1991). A formalisation of knowledge-level models for knowledge acquistion. *International Journal of Intelligent Systems*. forthcoming.

Bergstra, J., Heering, J., & Klint, P. (1990). Module algebra. *Journal of the ACM*, 37(2):335–372.

Breuker, J., Wielinga, B., van Someren, M., de Hoog, R., Schreiber, G., de Greef, P., Bredeweg, B., Wielemaker, J., Billault, J.-P., Davoodi, M., & Hayward, S. (1987). Model Driven Knowledge Acquisition: Interpretation Models. ESPRIT Project P1098 Deliverable D1 (task A1), University of Amsterdam and STL Ltd.

Clancey, W. (1983). The epistemology of a rule based system -a framework for explanation. *Artificial Intelligence*, 20:215–251. Also: Stanford Heuristic Programming Project, Memo HPP-81-17, November 1981, also numbered STAN-CS-81-896.

Clancey, W. (1985). Heuristic classification. *Artificial Intelligence*, 27:289–350.

Eshelman, L. (1988). MOLE: A knowledge-acquisition tool for cover-and-differentiate systems. In Marcus, S., editor, *Automating Knowledge Acquisition for Expert Systems*, pages 37–80. Kluwer Academic Publishers, The Netherlands.

Eshelman, L., Ehret, D., McDermott, J., & Tan, M. (1988). MOLE: a tenacious knowledge acquisition tool. In Boose, J. & Gaines, B., editors, *Knowledge Based Systems, Volume 2: Knowledge Acquisition Tools for Expert Systems*, pages 95–108, London. Academic Press.

Jackson, P., Reichgelt, H., & van Harmelen, F. (1989). *Logic-Based Knowledge Representation*. The MIT Press, Cambridge, MA.

Lavrač, N. & Vassilev, H. (1989). Meta-level architecture of a second-generation knowledge acquisition system. In Morik, K., editor, *Proceedings EWSL-89*, pages 99–109, London. Pitman.

McDermott, J. (1988). Preliminary steps towards a taxonomy of problem-solving methods. In Marcus, S., editor, *Automating Knowledge Acquisition for Expert Systems*, pages 225–255. Kluwer Academic Publishers, The Netherlands.

Steels, L. (1990). Components of expertise. *AI Magazine*. Also as: AI Memo 88-16, AI Lab, Free University of Brussels.

van Harmelen, F., Akkermans, H., Balder, J., Schreiber, G., & Wielinga, B. (1990). Formal specifications of knowledge models. ESPRIT Basic Research Action P3178 REFLECT, Technical Report RFL/ECN/I.4/1, Netherlands Energy Research Foundation ECN.

Weyhrauch, R. (1980). Prolegomena to a theory of mechanized formal reasoning. *Artificial Intelligence*, 13. Also in: *Readings in Artificial Intelligence*, Webber, B.L. and Nilsson, N.J. (eds.), Tioga publishing, Palo Alto, CA, 1981, pp. 173-191. Also in: *Readings in Knowledge Representation*, Brachman, R.J. and Levesque, H.J. (eds.), Morgan Kaufman, California, 1985, pp. 309-328.

Wielinga, B. & Breuker, J. (1986). Models of expertise. In *Proceedings ECAI-86*, pages 306–318.

Wielinga, B. J., Schreiber, A. T., & Breuker, J. A. (1992). KADS: A modelling approach to knowledge engineering. *Knowledge Acquisition*, 4(1). Special issue "The KADS approach to knowledge engineering".

Using Generalised Directive Models in Knowledge Acquisition*

Gertjan van Heijst[1], Peter Terpstra[1], Bob Wielinga[1], Nigel Shadbolt[2]

[1] Social Science Informatics, Department of Psychology, University of Amsterdam, Roeterstraat 15, 1018 WB Amsterdam, The Netherlands

[2] AI Group, Department of Psychology, Nottingham University, University Park, Nottingham NG7 2RD, United Kingdom

Abstract. In this paper we describe Generalised Directive Models and their instantiation in the ACKnowledge Knowledge Engineering Workbench. We have developed a context sensitive rewrite grammar that allows us to capture a large class of inference layer models. We use the grammar to progressively refine the model of problem solving for an application. It is also used as the basis of the scheduling of KA activities and the selection of KA tools.

1 Introduction

As part of the ACKnowledge ESPRIT II Project (P2576) we have been designing and building an integrated knowledge engineering workbench (KEW). KEW provides the knowledge engineer with operational support for knowledge acquisition in the development of knowledge-based systems. KEW is an integrated environment that allows the combination of a variety of knowledge acquisition tools and techniques, ranging from interactive elicitation techniques to machine learning. The knowledge engineer can take advantage of the differential efficacy of the various tools and techniques for acquiring different kinds of knowledge.

KEW allows to progressively formalise knowledge. The KEW elicitation techniques use intermediate representations that are supportive of human ways of describing knowledge. The acquired informal descriptions are gradually reformulated and refined into the standard AI formalisms of frames and first order logic. KEW facilitates the integration of the results of several acquisition techniques. Thus KEW provides support for merging partial knowledge bases into a consistent knowledge base.

KEW embodies a variety of types of knowledge about knowledge engineering: knowledge about the knowledge acquisition process, knowledge about the effective use of

* The research reported here was carried out in the course of the ACKnowledge project partially funded by the ESPRIT Programme of the Commission of the European Communities as project number 2567. The Partners in this project are GEC-Marconi, University of Nottingham (both UK), Cap Gemini Innovation (F), Sintef, Computas Expert Systems (both N), Telefonica (ES), and the University of Amsterdam (NL).

particular acquisition tools and techniques, knowledge about how to integrate knowledge from different tools, knowledge about how to validate the results of acquisition, and knowledge about the types of the components of expertise (for example, what is involved in a typical diagnostic application).

The description above illustrates that KEW is a complicated system, both technically and conceptually. To effectively manage the combination of functionality, KEW provides the knowledge engineer with active advice for constructing a model of the expert task, for selecting appropriate techniques, for planning of his/her knowledge acquisition (KA) work and for organising the final knowledge base (KB). It is this directive and active component of KEW which we will discuss in this paper.

KEW views knowledge acquisition as a model driven activity. It uses models of the knowledge acquisition process and the task of the target system to suggest what to do next in the KA process. In the sequel we will call these models *directive models.*

These directive models contain information about typical inferences steps that are used in a particular task, information about the type of domain knowledge that is required to make these inferences, information about the way this domain knowledge can be elicited and information about alternatives for particular subtasks.

KEW uses these directive models for the following purposes:

- To figure out how to discover the nature of the task that the target system has to perform.
- To decide which domain knowledge is required to perform that task.
- To structure the target knowledge base in a way that mimics the inference structure of the task at hand. This aids partial evaluation of the knowledge base and it also aids maintenance once the system has been delivered.

In section 2 we will discuss in detail how directive models can guide the knowledge acquisition process and we will introduce the notion of *generalised directive models.* Section 3 is about the top level control loop that drives the KEW's advice and guidance module and about the tools that realise this loop. In section 4 we will illustrate by means of a scenario how our models can direct and organise the KA process. In section 5 we will relate out work to other approaches and draw some conclusions.

2 Model Driven Approaches to Knowledge Acquisition

Currently the main theories of knowledge acquisition are all model based to a certain extent. The model based approach to knowledge acquisition covers the idea that abstract models of the tasks that expert systems have to perform can highly facilitate knowledge acquisition. These abstract models have taken the form of interpretation models [22], generic tasks [4] and task specific shells and tools [15,14,13].

Abstract models can be used as high level templates that put constraints on the required domain knowledge. They direct knowledge acquisition because they make explicit what kind of knowledge is used in the problem solving process and they structure the knowledge base. This is exactly what is needed in an environment like KEW. In ACKnowledge we have chosen the KADS type of abstract models as a starting point for our exercise. These seemed a good candidate because KADS provides a semi formal language for the description of arbitrary models [9]. However, the approach that has evolved could be adapted to model types, that reflect other theories about knowledge acquisition.

According to KADS, the construction of a KBS goes through a fixed set of stages. Each of these stages results in a particular model. KADS discerns the following milestones in the KA process: First there is the *task model.* This is a high level description of the task that the system has to perform. The next important milestone in the KA process is a construction of the reasoning to be done by the system — this is the construction of a *model of expertise*. This describes the reasoning of a human expert at the conceptual level. The *conceptual model* is then produced through a transformation and synthesis of the model of human expertise and the model of cooperation. The conceptual model is real-world oriented in that it describes the competence in expert problem solving. The next model in the process, the *design model*, is a model at the same level of abstraction as the conceptual model, but is a model of the artifact, not of the real world. The design model is undertaken from two viewpoints: the functional viewpoint, whereby the functions to be performed by the system are discussed; and the physical viewpoint, where discussion focuses on the realisation of those functions in the physical system to be built.

KADS supplies a library of interpretation models that can be used to bridge the gap between the task model and the model of expertise. These interpretation models describe the inference structures of prototypical tasks. Interpretation models are abstract in the sense that they do not contain domain knowledge. They consist of knowledge sources, representing "primitive" inference steps, and meta classes, which index domain knowledge according to its role in the problem solving process. A conceptual model is an instantiation and adaptation of an interpretation model for a particular domain.

In ACKnowledge we have limited our scope to the first three stages of the KADS view on KBS construction. That is, the output of KEW is a conceptual model. Moreover, in KEW we have taken the view that the conceptual model should be executable.

2.1 Task Identification and Model Selection

The first step in the knowledge acquisition process in KADS is the identification of the task that the target system should perform. Since the task description will be used to select an interpretation model from the library this library is indexed on features that discriminate between tasks. Figure 1 (taken from [22]) shows a part of the decision tree that is used to select an interpretation model. The interpretation models are associated with the leafs of this tree.

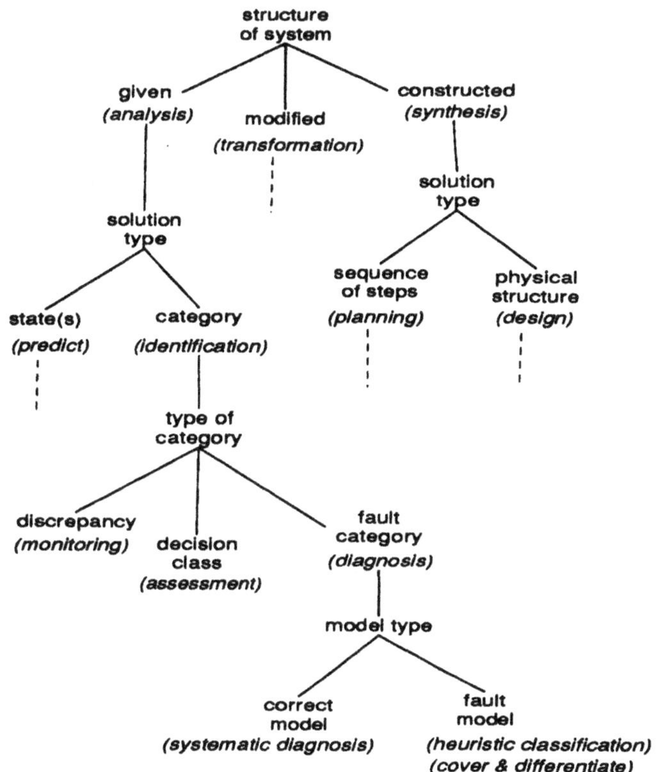

Fig. 1. Partial decision tree for interpretation models

In the upper part of the decision tree the task features are very general and they are used to discriminate between different types of tasks, (e.g. analysis versus synthesis). Features like these are usually easy to establish without actual elicitation of domain knowledge. In the lower parts of the decision tree the discriminating features are more specific. These features are used to discriminate between models that realise the same type of task but use have different task decompositions and control regimes. Features like these are usually closely related to characteristics of the domain knowledge that realises the inferences of the directive model. Here issues like the structure of the domain concepts, the use of uncertain information, the number of components etc.

are relevant. Unfortunately it is difficult to answer questions like this without actual elicitation of domain knowledge.

We can conclude from the foregoing discussion that, although it is certainly possible to elicit relevant features of the task that the system should perform, in general it will not be possible to select a single model without eliciting domain knowledge.

2.2 Model Driven Knowledge Elicitation

When a directive model is selected the "semantics" of this model put constraints on the knowledge that is to be elicited. These constraints can be exploited to guide the acquisition process in two ways.

The first constraint is related to the structure of the directive model. This structure can be used to define a structure on the target knowledge base that mimics the structure of the directive model. That is, for every knowledge source and for every metaclass in the directive model there is a partition in KEW's *Core Knowledge Base* (CKB from now on). The interdependencies in the directive model can then be used to suggest an optimal time sequence for the elicitation of the domain knowledge in the different partitions. Several "optimality principles" have been identified to guide this operation. These will be described in section 3.2.

The second way the directive model can be exploited has to do with the semantics of the primitive knowledge sources. Every primitive knowledge source puts constraints on the structure of its input and output metaclasses and on the syntactic structure of its domain rules. For example, if there is a knowledge source *taxonomic abstraction* in a directive model, the domain knowledge for the input metaclass of that knowledge source must have a hierarchical structure.

2.3 Generalised Directive Models

In model driven knowledge acquisition directive models are used to advice the knowledge engineer about usage of tools for eliciting domain knowledge. If there is no directive model only limited advice is possible. However, in subsection 2.1 we pointed out that usually domain knowledge is needed to select an appropriate model. This is recognised as a dilemma in ACKnowledge. If there is no directive model, there can only be limited advice; on the other hand, selecting the most appropriate directive model requires some knowledge of the domain. Eliciting domain knowledge to select the model will be difficult if there is no model to direct its selection! ACKnowledge has attempted to resolve this dilemma by the use of what have been called *generalised directive models* (GDM's). These are directive models, but they leave parts of the problem-solving process underspecified. These underspecified parts are represented by *generalised knowledge sources*, which describe non-primitive problem-solving steps. The idea is that these can then be used to describe problem-solving processes which we understand at only a coarse-grained level. However, there will still be enough structure to guide elicitation of domain knowledge sufficient to reveal new information about the domain which will then be used to "fill in" the underspecified portions of the model.

Another way of saying this is that a generalised knowledge source describes a set of similar extensions. These extensions could be primitive knowledge sources but they could also be partial models that consist of multiple generalised and primitive knowledge sources and intermediate meta classes. However, these extensions do have in common that they describe the same relation between the input and the output of the generalised knowledge source.

The use of GDM's is based on three related principles:

- *knowledge acquisition is a cyclic process*
  We view knowledge engineering as an iterative process of elicitation of domain knowledge, integration of the elicited knowledge with previously acquired knowledge and evaluation of the acquired knowledge to assess the current state of the acquisition process [18]. Model construction is an integral part of this cycle.
- *compositionality*
  A directive model describes a relation between inputs and outputs. With the extension of a (partial) model we mean the set of input /output combinations for which that relation holds. The compositionality principle states that the extension of a model only depends on the extensions of its parts and the way they are related. This implies that model parts with equal extensions can be exchanged, leaving the extension of the model as a whole unaffected.
- *a delayed commitment strategy*
  The third principle states that the knowledge engineer should only commit himself to a particular model if there is sufficient evidence that it is the "right" model. This reflects the idea that backtracking on abstract model construction is difficult and should be avoided.

The GDM's enable us to interleave model selection and knowledge elicitation. Although it is still required that there is an abstract model of the problem solving process before the domain knowledge is elicited, this initial GDM may be very general, leaving all parts that depend on properties of the domain knowledge unspecified. This initial model can then be used to direct acquisition of domain knowledge. Formally a GDM could be described in the following way:

```
GDM --> {input-metaclass}+ GKS output-metaclass
GKS --> {knowledge-source}+ {{meta-class}+ knowledge-source}*
```

In KEW the library of GDM's is represented as a generative grammar, where the final directive models are sentences, the generalised knowledge sources are non terminal symbols and the knowledge sources and meta classes are terminal symbols. The model construction steps in each acquisition cycle correspond to the application of rewrite rules. Each of the rewrite rules has associated conditions that have to be true before the rule may be applied. These conditions are the link between the abstract model and the features of the domain knowledge. In section 4 we give some examples of grammar rules that we used.

In summary, in this section we have argued that an abstract model of the problem solving task can highly facilitate knowledge acquisition. We have also argued that such a model can only be selected after a certain amount of domain knowledge has been elicited. Finally, we have suggested a way out of this dilemma based on the observations that on the micro level knowledge elicitation is a cyclic process and that model construction should be a stepwise process that is part of this cycle. In the next section we will show how these ideas are realised in KEW.

3 KEW Top Level Control Loop

In the previous section we described the theory of knowledge acquisition that KEW exploits to give active support for the KA process. In this section we will show how this theory is supported by the different subtools of KEW's advice and guidance module.

The KEW advice and guidance module is implemented as a top level control loop on the workbench. This loop can be viewed as an instantiation of the knowledge acquisition cycle as described in [18] an shown in figure 2. The cycle occurs throughout the life cycle, and so forms part of most KA activities. However, the emphasis will vary depending on the KA context. The cyclic nature of the KA process can be captured by a number of basic processes, which we can now briefly discuss:

- *Planning* takes into account the current activity in which KEW is engaged, available information about the task or domain, and possibly an assessment of the current state of the KB. Output of the planning process is a goal.
- Usually, a goal may be achieved in any one of a number of different ways. Hence many factors (e.g. the availability of an expert, the nature of the task and domain, the state of the KB) are relevant to *selection* of an operation.
- KEW can *apply* the selected operation.
- KEW then *stores* and *assimilates* the results into an information repository.
- Finally in the cycle, the resulting state of the KB is *evaluated* in terms of consistency, completeness, correctness, etc.. When problems emerge during evaluation, those problems are communicated to the planning component, which attempts to set up remedial goals.

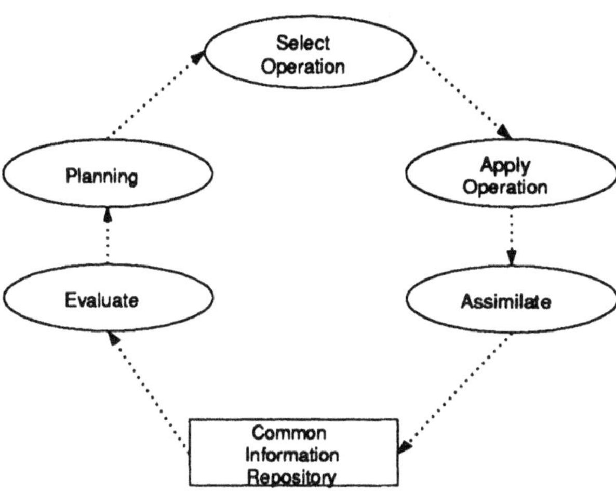

Fig. 2. The Generic KA Cycle

Figure 3 gives an overview of the different steps in the KEW top level control loop. In the remainder of this section we will describe each of the steps in this control loop. Some of these steps are done automatically but others have to be done by the knowledge engineer. For each of the steps in the loop KEW delegates control to a tool of the advice and guidance module.

3.1 Select Initial GDM

The first step in the acquisition process is the selection of an initial GDM. As described in section 2 we assume that we can select an initial GDM without eliciting domain knowledge. To select this initial GDM KEW contains an interview facility that asks multiple choice questions to establish features of the task that the target system has to perform. The interview is structured in a way that mimics the decision tree in figure 1. Every node in the decision tree has an associated interview question and a generalised directive model. For example, one of the questions in the interview is "What is the task of the System?", and a possible answer to this question is "Analytic (i.e. diagnosis or classification)". Associated with this answer are the GDM *diagnosis* and another interview question. If the interviewee is able to answer this next interview question the interview proceeds, but if the interviewee is unable or unwilling to answer this new question, the interview finishes and the GDM diagnosis is selected as the initial GDM.

3.2 Generate a Task Schedule

In section 2.2 we pointed out that the partition structure of the CKB should mimic the form of the directive model. So the next step in the KA process is to generate

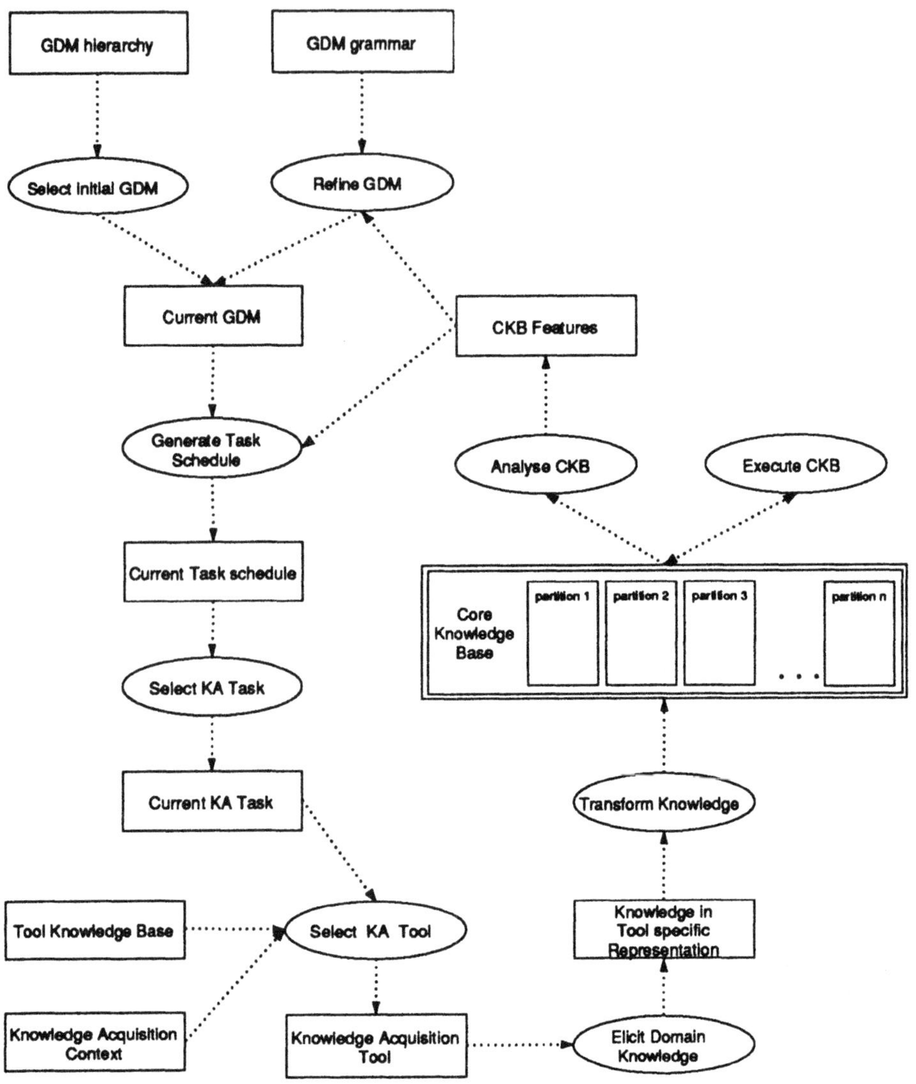

Fig. 3. KEW's Top Level Control Loop

a sequence of KA tasks that must be performed to build the CKB that corresponds to the current GDM. For this purpose KEW contains a scheduling tool. The KA task scheduler analyses the current GDM and suggests a task break down for the knowledge acquisition process, the *task schedule*.

When using GDM's there are two types of knowledge acquisition tasks: tasks to acquire domain knowledge that is used in the problem solving process, and tasks to acquire domain knowledge for GDM refinement. The function of the task scheduler is to identify these tasks and to suggest a temporal ordering. In order to do this the scheduler has to know about the constraints that are imposed on the acquisition process, and about the guiding principles that can be exploited to choose between legal alternatives. We will now describe some assumptions and heuristics used by the scheduler.

- *Work on one CKB partition only at each cycle.*
  This assumption allows KEW to associate one task with every component of the directive model.
- *Focus acquisition around primitive knowledge sources.*
  The directive model can be broken up in partial models that consist of a knowledge source and its related input and output meta classes. Since the domain knowledge for a partition is constrained by the role that the knowledge fulfills in the problem solving process, that is, by the semantics of the associated knowledge sources, it makes sense to start with partial models whose knowledge source is primitive. Moreover, if the knowledge source is primitive, and all the components of such a partial directive model have been filled in, the submodel can be evaluated on consistency and completeness. That is, it can be checked whether the knowledge source supplies a complete mapping of its inputs on its output.
- *Start with partial directive models whose inputs/output are known.*
  The second principle is concerned with the order in which the partial directive models are filled with domain knowledge. If a partial directive model has been marked as complete there are two ways to undo this fact. Either an input or an output meta class can be modified. Both types of modifications imply that the partial directive model is not longer complete so the primitive inference action has to be adapted and evaluated again. It is clear that this implies a lot of extra work that should be avoided when possible. However, knowledge acquisition is a difficult process so every once in a while a situation like this will occur. The only way to ease the pain is to work systematically, and to start with the partial directive models that depend least on the contents of other partial directive models. These are the partial directive models that require user input or generate system output. The next partial directive model would be the one whose inputs/outputs are the inputs/outputs of partial directive models that already have been filled in, and so on.

Based on the above principles the task scheduler generates a diagram of tasks with their interdependencies. Each task corresponds either to a knowledge source or to a meta class. The dependencies can be exploited to check whether a partial directive model is still complete, when another part of the directive model has been modified. At the same time, the dependencies can be considered as a suggested time schedule.

3.3 Select a Knowledge Acquisition Task

The output of the scheduling tool is a set of tasks that must be performed to build the executable knowledge base, and a suggested time schedule for these tasks. The next step in the top level control loop is the selection of one of these tasks to work on. In KEW this decision is made by the knowledge engineer. The task scheduler visualises the current schedule as a PERT diagram. The user can select one of the tasks in the diagram ad tell KEW to analyse the task. The analysis in the task will reveal the constraints that the GDM puts on the domain knowledge for the corresponding domain partitions. For example, if the CKB partition that corresponds to the selected task is the input partition for the knowledge source partition for *taxonomic abstraction*, the analysis will reveal that the required knowledge should be organised in a taxonomy. The results of this analysis are put in a temporary knowledge base that contains all the information that is available about the selected task. This knowledge base is then handed over to the tool selector.

3.4 Select a Knowledge Acquisition Tool

The next step is the selection of a knowledge acquisition tool (or a sequence of tools) to perform the selected KA task. In order to do this the selected KA task is passed to the tool selector of KEW. This tool selector exploits three types of information to suggest an appropriate KA tool.

The first type of information are the constraints that the semantics of the directive model put on the knowledge that is to be elicited. This is the knowledge that resulted from the analysis in the previous step. secondly, there is contextual information about the knowledge acquisition situation. This type of information refers to things as "the availability of experts", "the time constraints" and so on. The third type of information is knowledge about the tools that are available in KEW and about their functionality and requirements.

Based on this information the tool selector will come up with a set of appropriate tool configurations to elicit the knowledge for the partition that we are currently working on. We speak of tool configurations instead of tools because the tool selector does also suggest the transformation and integration operations that are needed to merge the new knowledge in the CKB.

3.5 Elicitation, Transformation and Integration

After a tool configuration has been selected KEW hands over control to the selected KA tools. KEW's knowledge acquisition tools are not the subject of this paper. For the reader who is interested in this subject we refer to [8]. Here we just remark that the elicited knowledge is will be put in the appropriate CKB partition.

3.6 Execute the CKB

In section 2 we mentioned that we considered KEW's CKB as an executable conceptual model. In this section we will say a bit more about the internal organisation of the CKB and the way it is executable. A conceptual model contains three types of knowledge: domain knowledge, inference knowledge and control knowledge. In KEW's CKB domain knowledge can be represented in two languages: a frame language (SFL, [1]) and first order predicate logic (NTP, [17]). We have explained already that the partition structure of the CKB corresponds to the structure of the directive model, that is, the inference structure of the system task. We have used ideas from the $(ML)^2$ language [20] to specify how domain knowledge is used by the inference knowledge and how to use the partition structure of the CKB.

To be executable, the CKB does also require *control* knowledge: when to make which inference. In the KADS four layer model [22] this kind of of knowledge resides at the *task layer*. KEW contains a control knowledge editor that supports the elicitation of this control knowledge. Control knowledge is specified by means of a mixture of dataflow between knowledge sources, constraints between these dataflows and execution modes for knowledge sources. The tool has a facility to transform the inference model corresponding to a GDM automatically into a data flow model. The user only has to specify the constraints between different dataflows and the type of computations within a knowledge source to specify the task layer control. This knowledge can be entered using a simple graphical (boxes and arrows) language. Once the control knowledge is specified, the user can execute the CKB to test if the combination of task-layer control, the specification of the inference layer and the contents of the domain layer partitions works as intended.

Although the issue of control knowledge is related to the use of directive models, the elicitation of the control knowledge itself is not model driven at the moment. The GDM grammars that we have at the moment do not specify "typical" control structures that can be associated with the right hand sides of rewrite rules.

3.7 Analyse CKB

When the CKB is modified, it is analysed and evaluated. The results of this evaluation are expressed as *CKB features*. These features are used to plan the next cycle of the top level control loop. We distinguish three types of CKB features:

- *GDM independent features.*
  With this we mean features like the completeness of the partitions. They are called "GDM independent" because these features are not used to evaluate or refine the current GDM. Knowledge source partitions can be evaluated on the criterion that they realise a complete mapping of the input partitions on the output partition. That is, for every input there is an output and for every output

there is an input. This type of evaluation is only meaningful when all the related meta class partitions are "filled" with domain knowledge.

- *Features that are characteristic for the current (G)DM.*
  These are the features that are mentioned in the conditions of the rewrite rules of the GDM grammar. A rewrite rule is only applied when its conditions are true. After the application of the rule the Model Selection Tool continues to check whether the conditions remain true. If this is no longer the case this might imply that the current GDM is wrong after all.
- *Features that are useful for GDM refinement.*
  The features are similar to the features of the type mentioned above, but they have another function. If there are some rewrite rules available to refine the current GDM, these features are used to decide which rewrite rule is applicable. If there is a rewrite rule applicable the GDM will be refined and the update will be forwarded to the KA-Task Scheduler. The scheduler makes a new decomposition of the input and output dependencies and constructs a new agenda of KA-tasks. When this is all done the knowledge engineer can select the next task in the updated KA-task schedule.

3.8 Refine GDM

When the CKB has been analysed, the next step in the top level control loop is GDM refinement. If the GDM contains non primitive components (generalised knowledge sources), it is usually the case that there were multiple applicable rewrite rules in the GDM grammar. The reason that there were more rules applicable was that there was not enough domain knowledge (or more precisely, meta knowledge about the domain knowledge) available to rule out some of these rewrite rules. It might be that this is not longer the case, since the most recent knowledge acquisition cycle might have revealed new CKB features. Because the conditions on the rewrite rules in the GDM grammar are formulated in terms of CKB features this has a direct impact on the applicability of the rules. If there is only one rule applicable for a certain generalised knowledge source in the GDM, this must be the correct refinement. In this situation the knowledge engineer is expected to apply the rewrite rule and start with the next knowledge acquisition cycle. Refining the GDM will automatically cause an update of the task schedule.

4 A Scenario

In this section we will illustrate the way KEW exploits GDM's to direct the knowledge acquisition process. The example is derived from a knowledge acquisition scenario for a system that is able to establish the edibility of mushrooms. This domain is rather small and we use only three grammar rules in the example. We think however that the scenario gives a good idea of the way KEW supports knowledge acquisition.

```
----------------------------------------------------------------------------
?Input1, NT-Classify, ?Output --> ?Input1, T-Classify, ?Output.          [1]

    Conditions: - Size of ?Input1 is less than 10.
                - Size of ?Output is less than 10.

?Input1, NT-Classify, ?Output --> ?Input1,                               [2]
                                  T-Abstract,
                                  Findings,
                                  NT-Classify,
                                  ?Output.

    Conditions: - Size of ?Input1 is more than 10.
                - Structure of ?Input1 is hierarchical.

?Input1, NT-Classify, ?Output --> ?Input1,                               [3]
                                  NT-Classify,
                                  Abstract-Solutions,
                                  T-Refine,
                                  ?Output.

    Conditions: - Size of ?Output is more than 10.
                - Structure of ?Output is hierarchical.
----------------------------------------------------------------------------
```

Fig. 4. A Fragment of a GDM Grammar

The grammar fragment that we used is shown in figure 4. We will explain the notation of the rules using the second rule in the figure. The left hand side (*LHS*) of the rule contains three symbols: The meta class variables **?input1** and **?output** and the non terminal symbol **NT-Classify**. The metaclass variables are used for two reasons. The first reason is that the *RHS* of a rewrite rule does not necessarily have a strict linear internal structure. A meta class associated with the non terminal in the *LHS* of the rule can be associated with more than one knowledge source and non terminal in the *RHS* of the rule. To express such facts in the rewrite rules we need labels for these meta classes. The variables are a way of labeling the meta classes. The second reason for the introduction of input and output variables is that we need the ability to refer to the input and output meta classes in the conditions.

When the conditions that are associated with rule 2 are true, that is, when the partition that corresponds to the output partition of **NT-Classify** contains more than 10 expressions and these expressions are hierarchically organised, **NT-Classify** can be replaced by rule 2's *RHS*, which contains one generalised knowledge source (**NT-Classify**), one primitive knowledge source (**T-Abstract**), and three meta classes (**?input1**, **?output** and **Findings**).

Rule 2 reflects the following intuition: If some kind of classification takes place in a problem solving process, and there is a large set of potentially classifiable objects, and we know that these objects are organised hierarchically, then it is likely that some kind of abstraction takes place before the actual classification rules are applied.

At a particular moment in the scenario we have identified the task of the mushroom KBS as some kind of classification. This enables KEW to select the initial GDM illustrated in figure 5.

Fig. 5. The Initial GDM

From the GDM we know that we need at least an **`observables`** partition and a **`solutions`** partition. Since we do not know the size and the structure of the observable space or the solution space so all the rules in figure 4 are in principle applicable. The least commitment principle forces KEW in this situation to continue with the initial **`NT-Classify`** GDM. The Task Scheduler uses this GDM to generate the task schedule shown in figure 6.

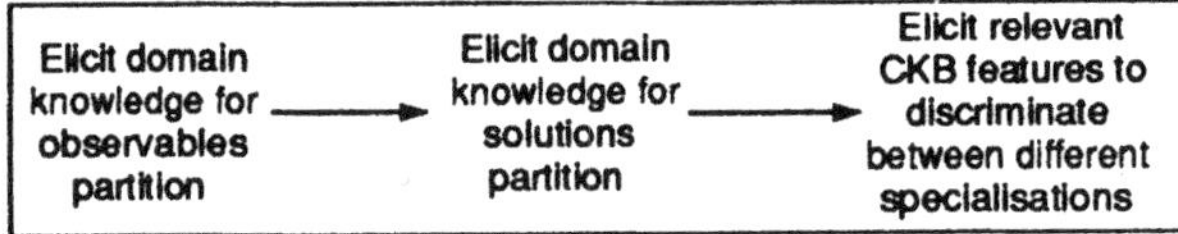

Fig. 6. The Initial Task Schedule

The knowledge engineer decides to start working on the first task in the task schedule: elicitation of domain knowledge for the **`observables`** partition. Analysis of the GDM reveals that the **`observables`** partition is the input for the generalised knowledge source **`NT-Classify`**. KEW compares the conditions of the two applicable rules[3] (rule 1 and 2) to find features that discriminate between these rules and finds two:

- **`(:hierarchical-structure observables-partition :no)`**
  If there is no hierarchical structure in the knowledge that is elicited only rule 1 is applicable.
- **`(:partition-size observables-partition)`**
  If the number of possible observables is known KEW knows which of the two rewrite rules is applicable.

[3] Technically rule 3 is applicable as well, but this rule is not taken into consideration because application of that rule would not reveal new knowledge about the role of the observables meta class in the problem solving process.

Note that these features do **not** reflect properties of KEW's current CKB. They are features that would be informative for GDM refinement if they were known. The analysis above is done automatically by KEW when the user decides to work on a particular partition.

In the next step KEW's Activity Selector searches the tool knowledge base to find a knowledge acquisition tool that can reveal the size and the structure of the observables partition and that is applicable in the current context. It is decided that a laddering tool [10] is the best candidate. Laddering reveals both the size and the amount of structure of the observables space. If the resulting ladders would be very flat it would be evident that not much abstraction is possible in this domain. To make sure that the laddering tool is applicable in the current KA context the knowledge engineer is asked if there is an expert available. Fortunately this is the case in the mushroom scenario. The next step is the application of the laddering tool. The elicited knowledge is transformed into the appropriate representation language and put in the right CKB partition. Subsequent analysis of the CKB shows that there is indeed a hierarchical structure in the observables space, and that there are more than 10 observables. In the next step in the top level control loop, GDM refinement, these facts are used to decide that rule 2 is the correct rule and the rule is applied. This results in the GDM that is shown in figure 7.

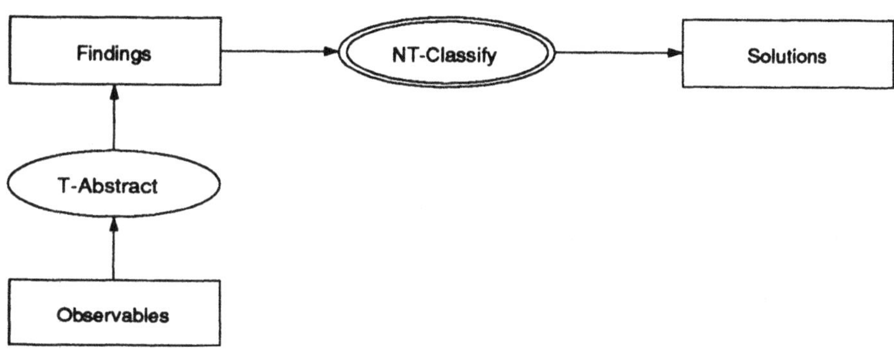

Fig. 7. The Refined GDM

Refining the GDM was the last step of the first cycle of the top level control loop. The second cycle starts with an update of the task schedule: KEW has to make sure that there is still a one to one mapping between the task schedule and the directive model. The task scheduler comes up with the task schedule shown in figure 8.

In this section we have given a detailed description of the way GDM's guide the knowledge acquisition process. The complete mushroom scenario consists of three cycles of the top level control loop, but many aspects of the GDM approach where already illustrated in the first cycle. In the second cycle of the scenario the knowledge engineer concentrated on the `solutions` meta class. Analysis of the corresponding partition revealed that there where less than 10 solution classes. This made rule 1

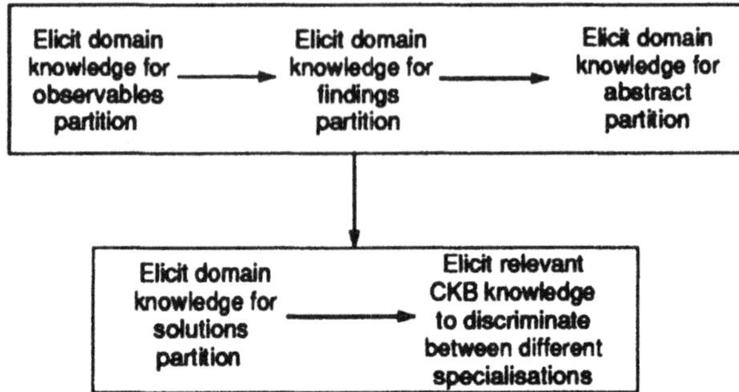

Fig. 8. The Updated Task Schedule

the only applicable rule. So the generalised knowledge source `NT-Classify` in figure 7 was replaced with the primitive knowledge source `T-Classify`.

5 Conclusions

In this paper we have described a method and a set tools that differ from earlier approaches in two ways. First, the development of the model and the acquisition of static domain knowledge are interwoven. Initially a highly abstract model of the reasoning task is used to acquire some basic domain knowledge. Subsequently the model is refined using properties of the already acquired domain knowledge. This approach allows a much more flexible and iterative knowledge acquisition process than the two-stage process used in other approaches. Second, knowledge about the use of knowledge acquisition methods and tools is coupled to specific transitions in the model search space. When a specific refinement of a model is required, the nature of the required domain knowledge is used to select a particular knowledge acquisition tool. Thus, the model is not just a guide to the acquisition of the domain knowledge, but also supports the choices that a knowledge engineer has with respect to methods and tools. The scenario that we have presented clearly shows how a system like KEW can actively support the knowledge acquisition process without making strong concessions to the flexibility and task specificity.

5.1 relation to other approaches

The approach taken by Musen in OPAL and PROTEGE [14] starts from the view that a task-specific model of the domain knowledge that is to be acquired is necessary to support the acquisition of the static domain knowledge. In PROTEGE such models are derived from a template (skeletal plan refinement) through interaction with the knowledge engineer, while the acquisition of the static domain knowledge is done in interaction with the domain expert. McDermott and co-workers [13,11,7] also developed knowledge acquisition tools based on models for specific tasks. The MOLE system for example [7] uses a model of the Cover-and-Differentiate method for diagnostic reasoning to acquire domain knowledge from an expert. Compared with KEW these approaches are powerful in the sense that knowledge acquisition with the expert is strongly focussed, but suffer from the severe limitation that the approach and the supporting tools are entirely task specific and thus limited in scope. Moreover, the task specificity puts a strong emphasis on task identification at an early stage in the acquisition process.

The use of KADS interpretation models [22] is more flexible. Models can be selected for a wide variety of tasks. However, the models in KADS are less explicit with respect to the required domain knowledge than the models in OPAL. Moreover, KADS interpretation models generally require substantial modification for a specific application and this in turn requires information about the nature of the static domain knowledge. KADS does not offer any support for model modification.

In PROTEGE-II [16] the limitation of using a fixed template is removed. In this system the knowledge engineer can create his own template. However, the system does not actively support model construction or model editing. The functionality of PROTEGE-II resembles that of the Inference Structure Editor in the SHELLEY workbench [2].

The GDM approach combines the advantages of the approaches mentioned above. Because of the dynamic model construction process the GDM approach offers the strong guidance of task specific models while it still covers a wide range of tasks. Moreover, the delayed commitment strategy allows incremental task identification.

More recent developments based on KADS and the "Components of Expertise" approach [19,21] introduce the notion of *problem solving methods* [3] as a way of generating task-specific models. A problem solving method describes how a particular goal can be decomposed in primitive and/or non-primitive subgoals. Application of one or more methods to a goal results in a full model of the task. In addition to the knowledge about goals and how to decompose them, requirements for the domain knowledge are associated with each method. While these requirements are in general used for determining the applicability of methods, they could also be used for knowledge acquisition. Methods can thus be viewed as similar to the rewrite rules in a GDM grammar.

The idea of using a grammar to represent abstract models of problem solving fits quite well with the recent work of Chandrasekaran [5]. The task analysis for design that he presents can easily be reformulated as a GDM grammar. The work on advice and guidance in KEW is also quite similar to the approach recently presented by [12]. Their workbench consists of three tools: SPARK, which is intended for model selection, BURN which selects the appropriate KA tools, and FireFighter, which functions as an application debugger. The SPARK/BURN approach is similar to ours in the sense that an abstract task model is used to select appropriate knowledge acquisition tools. However, this work is also based on the two stage assumption mentioned before. Moreover, tool selection is a very simple process in BURN: there is a more or less one to one mapping between the inference steps in the model (mechanisms, as they call it) and knowledge acquisition tools. KEW takes also into account information about the knowledge acquisition context. The Advice and guidance model in KEW does not have a debugging tool comparable with FireFighter.

5.2 General Conclusions

Because the tools presented in this paper are implemented a short while ago, the KEW advice and guidance module has only been used in two experiments: a small scale experiment in the mushroom domain and a moderately large experiment in the field of respiratory medicine. Although we think that our result are promising the real test of the approach lies in it's future application of course.

For these experiments we have implemented a grammar for diagnostic problem solving. Although this grammar is rather small and implementing a grammar that can handle a wider range of problem types remains a major enterprise the idea appears quite powerful. The rules in our grammar are intuitively sensible and they seem to produce correct models. The grammar is able to generate the "classical" models for heuristic classification [6] and systematic diagnosis [22], together with a wide range of less well known models that make sense though.

We have not been very specific about the nature of the conditions on the rewrite rules. The conditions in the example where rather simplified for the sake of clarity. The conditions used in the respiratory medicine application where more elaborate, but still tentative. We think that, in general, the nature of the conditions can only be established empirically, through a thorough analysis of knowledge acquisition scenarios.

Acknowledgements

The research reported here was performed in cooperation with Han Reichgelt, Fano Ramparany and Inge Nordbo. We also want to thank Anjo Anjewierden and Jan Wielemaker for their implementation assistance and Manfred Aben and four anonymous reviewers for their useful comments.

References

1. G. Aakvik, A. Aamodt, and I. Norbo. A knowledge representation framework supporting knowledge modelling. In *Proceedings of the fifth EKAW*, University of Strathclyde, 1991. Not Published.
2. A. Anjewierden, J. Wielemaker, and C. Toussaint. Shelley - computer aided knowledge engineering. In B. Wielinga, J. Boose, B. Gaines, G. Schreiber, and M. van Someren,

editors, *Current Trends in Knowledge Acquisition*, pages 173–189. IOS Press, Amsterdam, 1990.

3. V.R. Benjamins, A. Abu-Hanna, and Wouter Jansweijer. Dynamic method selection in diagnostic reasoning. In *submitted to the 12th Int. conf. on Artificial Intelligence, Expert Systems, Natural Language, Avignon'92*, Avignon, 1992. EC2. SKBS/A2/92-1.
4. B. Chandrasekaran. Towards a functional architecture for intelligence based on generic information processing tasks. In *Proceedings of the 10th IJCAI*, pages 1183–1192, Milano, 1987.
5. B. Chandrasekaran. Design problem solving: a task analysis. *AI Magazine*, Winter:59–71, 1990.
6. W.J. Clancey. Heuristic classification. *Artificial Intelligence*, 27:289–350, 1985.
7. L. Eshelman. MOLE: A knowledge-acquisition tool for cover-and-differentiate systems. In S. Marcus, editor, *Automating Knowledge Acquisition for Expert Systems*, pages 37–80. Kluwer Academic Publishers, The Netherlands, 1988.
8. C. Jullien et al. Acknowledge final report. Technical Report ACK-CSI-WM-DL-007-A-pre4, Cap Gemini Innovation, 1992. Final report of ESPRIT Project 2567.
9. W. Karbach, M. Linster, and A. Voß. Model-based approaches: One label - one idea? In B. Wielinga, J. Boose, B. Gaines, G. Schreiber, and M. van Someren, editors, *Current Trends in Knowledge Acquisition*, pages 173–189. IOS Press, Amsterdam, 1990.
10. N. Major and H. Reichgelt. Alto: an automated laddering tool. In B. Wielinga, J. Boose, B. Gaines, G. Schreiber, and M. van Someren, editors, *Current trends in knowledge acquisition*, pages 222 – 236, Amsterdam, May 1990. IOS Press.
11. S. Marcus and J. McDermott. SALT: A knowledge acquisition language for propose-and-revise systems. *Artificial Intelligence*, 39(1):1–38, 1989.
12. D. Marques, G. Dallemagne, G. Klinker, J. McDermott, and D. Tung. Easy programming: Empowering people to build their own applications. Technical report, Digital Equipment Corporation, 1991. submitted to the IEEE Expert.
13. J. McDermott. Preliminary steps towards a taxonomy of problem-solving methods. In S. Marcus, editor, *Automating Knowledge Acquisition for Expert Systems*, pages 225–255. Kluwer Academic Publishers, The Netherlands, 1989.
14. M.A. Musen. *Automated Generation of Model-Based Knowledge-Acquisition Tools.* Pitman, London, 1989. Research Notes in Artificial Intelligence.
15. M.A. Musen, L.M. Fagan, D.M. Combs, and E.H. Shortliffe. Use of a domain model to drive an interactive knowledge editing tool. In J. Boose and B. Gaines, editors, *Knowledge-Based Systems, Volume 2: Knowledge Acquisition Tools for Expert Systems*, pages 257–273, London, 1988. Academic Press.
16. A. Puerta, J. Egar, S. Tu, and M. Musen. A multiple-method knowledge acquisition shell for the automatic generation of knowledge acquisition tools. Technical Report KSL-91-24, Stanford University, Knowledge Systems Laboratory, Medical Computer Science, Stanford University, Stanford, California, 94305-5479, May 1991.
17. H. Reichgelt. *Logic-Based Knowledge Representation*, chapter Assertion Time Inference. The MIT Press, Cambridge, MA, 1989.
18. N. Shadbolt and B.J. Wielinga. Knowledge based knowledge acquisition: the next generation of support tools. In B. J. Wielinga, J. Boose, B. Gaines, G. Schreiber, and M.W. van Someren, editors, *Current Trends in Knowledge Acquisition*, pages 313–338, Amsterdam, 1990. IOS Press.
19. L. Steels. Components of expertise. *AI Magazine*, Summer 1990. Also as: AI Memo 88-16, AI Lab, Free University of Brussels.
20. F. van Harmelen and J. Balder. $(ML)^2$: A formal language for kads models of expertise. Technical Report ESPRIT Project P5248 KADS-II/T1.2/PP/UvA/017/1.0, University

of Amsterdam & Netherlands Energy Research Foundation ECN, 1991. This paper is published in *Knowledge Acquisition Journal*, 1992.

21. J. Vanwelkenhuysen and P. Rademakers. Mapping knowledge-level analysis onto a computational framework. In L. Aiello, editor, *Proceedings ECAI-90, Stockholm*, pages 681–686, London, 1990. Pitman.
22. B. J. Wielinga, A. Th. Schreiber, and J. A. Breuker. KADS: A modelling approach to knowledge engineering. *Knowledge Acquisition*, 1992. Special issue on KADS, forthcoming. Also as: Technical Report ESPRIT Project P5248 KADS-II/T1.1/PP/UvA/008/2.0, University of Amsterdam.

Towards a Formal Framework to Compare Protocol Interpretations and Task Specifications

Pieter Geelen
Zsófia Ruttkay
Jan Treur

Vrije Universiteit Amsterdam
Department of Mathematics and Computer Science
Artificial Intelligence Group
De Boelelaan 1081a, 1081HV Amsterdam The Netherlands
email: geelen@cs.vu.nl, zsofi@cs.vu.nl, treur@cs.vu.nl

Abstract. In this paper we discuss a formal framework that can be used to relate and compare different possible interpretations and formal task specifications of a given (verbal) expert protocol. Notions are defined that can be used to describe the differences and relations between these task specifications. The framework is used to structure the analysis of an example protocol dealing with an office assignment task. We give examples of different task specifications based on alternative interpretations of this protocol.

1 Introduction

It is well-recognized that a subject performing protocol analysis is making his or her own interpretation of the protocol [1, 3, 8, 13]. Therefore the model or task specification resulting from a protocol analysis is essentially subjective and may be biased by the mental background of the one who was doing the analysis. During the modelling process various (often unconscious) choices are made. To be able to compare different task specifications that are made on the basis of one given protocol (e.g. by different persons) it would be helpful to have an overview or taxonomy of the types of choices that are possible in principle. Such an overview can be thought of as a kind of *map* (i.e., a picture or graph) of all possibilities in the search space of interpretations and task specifications. By positioning interpretations and task specifications on such a map and defining different branching points, the process of adopting one of the interpretations and creating one of the task specifications can be made more concrete and visible.

In practice a complete map as discussed is not always needed and feasible; in general such a complete map may be infinite. One depends on the possible interpretations and task specifications that one is able to identify. Therefore in practice only a *partial map* will be considered. And even if this happens to be a complete map (which is very unlikely), it will not be easy to conclude that one has been exhaustive. But also a partial map might increase one's insight in the task behind the protocol and its possible specifications.

From a theoretical viewpoint one may give an *abstract definitional framework*, independent of the question whether in practice one is able to consider a complete map, or only a partial map. To design such a framework in a well-defined manner it will be helpful if the task specifications that are considered are well-defined, i.e., can be given in a formal format [9]. A possible approach to formal task specifications is offered by the formal specification framework DESIRE (framework for DEsign and Specification of Interacting REasoning modules; see [7, 10]). We have this type of formalisation in mind, but since the description we will give in this paper is at a more abstract level, other approaches may fit in as well. What is important though is that a task specification takes into account both static and dynamic aspects of the task. The behaviour of the task (the order of the steps in the problem solving process) should be determined completely by the specification: given such a specification it should be possible to create unambiguously a related reasoning trace.

In order to illustrate the abstract definitional framework we give possible different interpretations of a sample protocol, provided by Marc Linster as a test problem in the Sisyphus project. Originally, participants of this international project were asked to provide a model of the problem solving process reported in the protocol (for the solutions, see [11, 12]). When building our model (fully discussed in [5]) we identified a lot of possible choices for the interpretation of the protocol. The analysis of the given protocol raised most of the issues which will be discussed in an abstract way in this paper.

In Section 2 we give the content of a formal framework that can be used to compare formal protocol interpretations and formal task specifications and define the basis notions underlying this framework. In Section 3 the example protocol is presented. Section 4 gives an overview according to our framework of different protocol interpretations and task specifications that can be made for the example protocol. Finally, in section 5 we draw some conclusions about our approach.

2 The Content of the Framework

We assume that the protocol to be interpreted states the problem to be solved and gives an account of the solution process. The latter is given in the form of steps taken by the expert, with some explanations. However, the explanations usually do not fully reflect all details of the problem solving process. Very likely not everything that was taking place in the expert's head was registered. On the other hand, some irrelevant statements may also have been included, which the expert did not really use. Our aim with interpreting a protocol is to reconstruct the expert's model for problem solving.

Of course, usually there is a pragmatic aim too, namely to build a system which is capable to replace an expert's problem solving activity. The idea is to build a system based on the expert's problem solving model. Although we assume this model may be present in the expert's head, it is not directly available to us. The only thing we can do is to use information available in the protocol (or several sample protocols) and make an interpretation of it. This protocol interpretation can be used as a basis for a task specification that specifies an executable problem solving model for the task that may or may not be the same as the expert's model. Notice that we require that a task specification determines unambiguously the dynamic aspects of the task behaviour (the order of the process steps). This is an important difference with a protocol interpretation: this is related to the given protocol only and a complete specification of the process is not required. For shortness, sometimes we will use the word "model" to refer to either a protocol interpretation, or to a task specification.

2.1 Basic Elements of the Framework

Usually, the reasoning process as expressed in a protocol is underspecified. It gives only fragments of the real expert's problem solving model, and maybe even these fragments are not expressed sincerely. Therefore several interpretations can be given for one single protocol. If a task specification has been created then some of its parts may relate to parts of the given protocol. But often not all parts of the protocol are covered. Some protocol fragments may contain irrelevant information or may be found so unclear that one is not able to determine whether they are relevant and what they should mean. Conversely, and

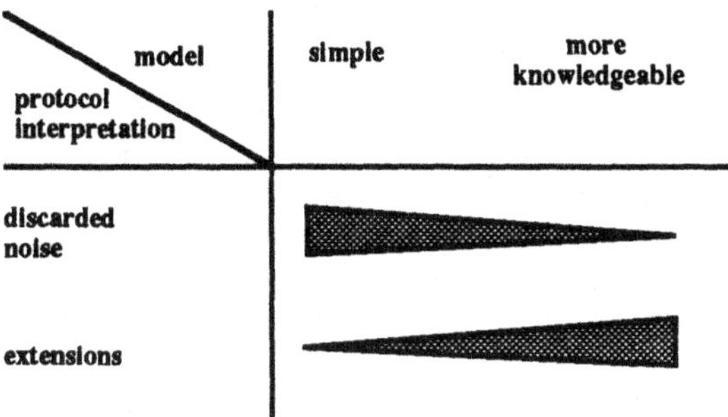

Fig. 1. Discarded noise versus additional assumptions

partly related to this phenomenon, the task specification will contain parts that do not relate directly to parts of the protocol. These were the missing links in the protocol interpretation; the modeller has used her or his own creativity and fantasy to fill these gaps. They may have some unknown relation to obscure parts of the protocol but equally well that may not be the case.

Note that a modeller is not necessarily aimed at interpretations which maximally cover the given protocol. First of all because the amount of knowledge to be included in the task specification does depend on how abstract, general and powerful model we are aiming at. The more text one interprets, the more ambiguities and gaps in the reasoning process as reported in the protocol need to be bridged. Roughly speaking, the fewer items one considers as noise, the more extensions in the form of assumptions and additions one has to make, and the more knowledgeable model one can build (see Fig. 1.). However, a highly knowledgeable model necessarily cannot be unambiguously related to the protocol, due to the number of assumptions that have to be made.

The fact that a protocol usually gives an underspecified and sometimes obscure account of the expert's reasoning process has essential implications. Only a part of the protocol can be interpreted sincerely, and due to the missing links in this partial protocol interpretation no unique extension can be found that gives a complete specification of the task as performed by the expert. One is forced to choose one of the possible extensions to obtain a complete (executable) task specification, and there is no guarantee that this chosen task specification coincides with the specification of the task as actually performed by the expert. So, the problem is not to simply avoid a possible impact of the modeller's fantasy or bias, but is more essential. No absolute solution can be established: the modeller *has* to use fantasy to make a choice that cannot be motivated by the protocol itself. Between a constructed task specification and the expert's model no over-all relation can be established; only the parts of both models (the expert's model and the constructed model) that correspond to the (partial) protocol interpretation can be related. To clarify this issue we analyse in more detail what choices often are made during the protocol interpretation and the design of a task specification. Sometimes these choices are made unconsciously, but at other times the modeller may be completely aware of this. We distinguish the following types of choices, not necessarily done in this order (see Fig. 2.):

Selecting a relevant part of the protocol. This concerns the choice to focus on a part of the protocol that is considered to provide relevant information and to ignore the other parts as being noise. Sometimes this choice will mainly be a negative one: just leaving out things that cause too much trouble. By taking the explicit decision to leave out these undefinable statements the remaining protocol-part can be interpreted with more confidence.

Interpretation of the selected protocol text. The concepts and relations in the selected part of the protocol are specified by introducing some (formal) concept-names and relation-names, and the knowledge that can be acquired from the protocol is expressed. This gives a protocol interpretation that in fact is only a partial task specification. In general it does not contain enough knowledge to really specify the task: concepts and knowledge that were not mentioned explicitly in the protocol are still missing; in particular the arguments behind the order of steps taken in the problem solving process (i.e., knowledge concerning the dynamics of the task) often are missing.

Extending the protocol interpretation to a task specification. To obtain a (complete) task specification one has to add concepts and knowledge from one's own ideas and fantasy about the task. The requirement that a task specification should determine uniquely the behaviour of the problem solving process makes it necessary to take some hypothetical steps to determine how the complete process specification could be constructed (the dynamics of the task). The additional requirement is that the process as simulated by executing the task specification should show the same problem solving steps and in the same order as can be seen in the protocol.

Notice that the three main concepts used here can be given a formal definition. A *protocol text* can be viewed as a text string, and a *task specification* can be expressed as a specification document using a formal specification language, for instance as given by DESIRE (see [7, 10]). A *protocol interpretation* can be expressed as a partial (i.e., a subset of) formal specification document. So the space of all protocol interpretations and task specifications can be defined formally by the *set of all (partial) formal specification documents*. In this space we can use the extension relation denoted by $\leq_E$. A partial specification document $\mathcal{T}$ *extends* a partial specification document $\mathcal{S}$, if all parts of $\mathcal{S}$ occur in $\mathcal{T}$. In Fig. 2 the lines between the protocol interpretations and the task specifications denote extension relations. For instance the following relations hold: $\mathcal{P} \leq_E \mathcal{P}_1$, $\mathcal{Q} \leq_E \mathcal{Q}_2$, $\mathcal{R} \leq_E \mathcal{Q}_3$. This extension relation is a partial ordering on the space of partial task specifications.

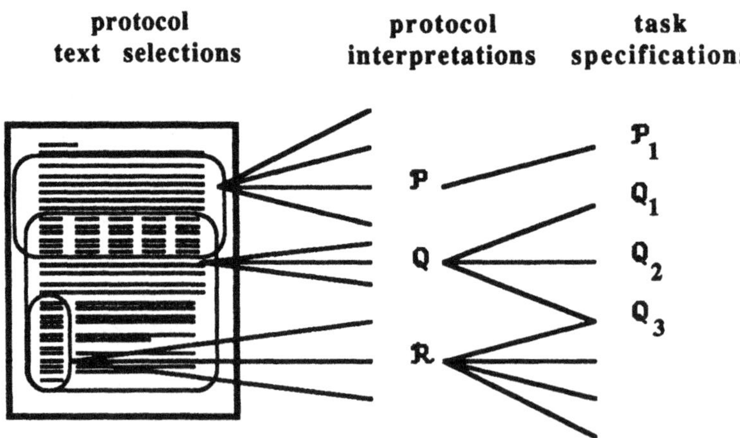

Fig. 2. Overview of the protocol interpretations and task specifications

2.2 Protocol Interpretations

A protocol interpretation reflects a selected protocol text, if all the statements given in this selected text are related to expressions in the protocol interpretation. Here we do not discuss the linguistic details of the mapping from a given protocol text to a protocol interpretation. What is important, is that there is a relation between the expressions in a certain subset $\mathfrak{K}$ of the protocol and the constructs of a protocol interpretation $\mathfrak{P}$ of $\mathfrak{K}$. A protocol interpretation $\mathfrak{P}$ *interprets* the subset $\mathfrak{K}$ of the entire protocol $\mathfrak{T}$. We call $\mathfrak{P}$ a *partial interpretation*; if $\mathfrak{K} = \mathfrak{T}$ we call it a *full interpretation* of the protocol $\mathfrak{T}$. Note that in a protocol interpretation there can be constructs which do not have a corresponding textual form in the protocol. These construct are in the model due to some assumptions by the knowledge acquisitor or to some other sources of information than the given protocol (e.g., the expert himself). The protocol interpretation $\mathfrak{P}$ *mirrors* $\mathfrak{K}$ if all constructs in the protocol interpretation correspond to some text fragment in the protocol part $\mathfrak{K}$.

Obviously, there are several possible partial interpretations of a given protocol $\mathfrak{T}$. Some of these can be compared, by comparing the part of the protocol they fully interpret: $\mathfrak{P}_2$ *interprets more than* $\mathfrak{P}_1$, if $\mathfrak{K}_1 \subseteq \mathfrak{K}_2$. This partial ordering is denoted by $\leq_I$. For example, in Fig. 1. it holds $\mathfrak{R} \leq_I \mathfrak{Q}$. As this relation is based on the subset relation between text strings, it can easily be defined formally.

2.3 From Protocol Interpretations to (Complete) Task Specifications

A usual problem with interpretations mirroring a given protocol is that they are not complete. A non-complete protocol interpretation does not capture all details of the entire problem solving process, and cannot serve as a formal definition for some process simulation. Hence, we are interested in complete extensions of a protocol interpretation in the sense that they specify a reasoning trace. Note that in Fig. 2 we have $\mathfrak{R} \leq_I \mathfrak{Q}$, the interpretation $\mathfrak{P}$ is a complete interpretation but does not mirror the entire protocol, $\mathfrak{R}$ and $\mathfrak{Q}$ have a common complete extension, $\mathfrak{Q}_3$.

We expect that a task specification should exhibit the same behaviour as registered in the protocol. Namely, not only the same solution as reported in the protocol is finally found, but also along the same steps. If the process steps that are generated by the task specification correspond to the steps reported in the protocol, then the task specification *reproduces* the solution of the problem, and is called *reproductive*.

Notice that the main goal of the knowledge acquisition is to come up with a reproductive task specification related to the protocol. The usual first attempt is to give a completion of a maximal mirroring protocol interpretation (maximal in the sense of the ordering $\leq_I$), hoping that it will be also a reproductive interpretation. However, this is not necessarily the case. Usually the completion requires the extension of the knowledge directly reported in the protocol, so it is not mirroring the protocol any more and, moreover, the added knowledge can specify a dynamics of the task that is different from the dynamics as shown in the protocol.

On the other hand, there is a straightforward and trivial way to give a complete and reproductive task specification for a given protocol: a task specification that contains knowledge directly specifying the steps in turn, as reported in the protocol. However, this trivial completion will not take into account explanations the expert gives on the steps that are taken. This means that this trivial solution only applies to a very restricted protocol text selection where all explanations have been left out. This is not satisfactory. A more realistic minimal reproductive task specification will take into account at least a part of the explanations given by the expert.

2.4 Criteria for Comparing Task Specifications

Applicability and Genericity of a Task Specification. A given protocol accounts on the solution process of a given problem. However, the expert solves a given problem on the basis of experience gained by previous experience with other problems of the same type. Moreover, the system to be built on the basis of the task specification is going to be used in the future to solve other problems as well. One would like to have a task specification related to a given protocol which will not only reproduce the reported solution process of the given problem, but also will (re)produce the solution process of several other problems.

What sets of problems can be identified ? It is very common that problems only differ in the initially given input facts. If we know that the initial situations that really occur can differ only in certain facts, then the possible input facts can be divided into two disjoint sets, namely the fixed ones which may not change (these may be viewed generic) and the ones which may change. Similarly fixed (stable) and specific (changeable) entities or objects, and goals can be defined. Hence for each task specification $\mathfrak{P}$ one can define a set of problems $s(\mathfrak{P})$, the ones which can be modelled by changing specific components of the problem description of the protocol.

Further on we will refer to a set of problems $\mathcal{A}$ which the task specification should be able to cope with, and a subset $\mathfrak{B}$ of $\mathcal{A}$ for which a protocol was given. One can think of the analogy of approximating an unknown function: the elements of $\mathfrak{B}$ correspond to basis points where the value of the unknown function is given, and the elements of $\mathcal{A}$ as those points where the approximating function should have the same value as the unknown function. Where the analogy breaks down is the lack of a distance measure for problems and task specifications. For the time being we assume that $\mathfrak{B}$ has one element. Informally, a task specification $\mathfrak{P}$ is more *generic* than $\mathbf{Q}$, if $\mathfrak{P}$ provides an interpretation of all protocols for which $\mathbf{Q}$ is an interpretation. This partial ordering is denoted by $\leq_G$.

One would like to elucidate the 'right' generic theory for the problems to be solved. Of course it cannot be assured in any way that an expert will solve all the problems just in the way as a task specification would do. Note, that for the elements in $\mathcal{A}\backslash\mathfrak{B}$ the problem solving process is unknown. In principle the expert could use different strategies for all problem instances. All the same, we can declare some necessary conditions.

A task specification is *stable* with respect to certain facts, entities or goals of the problem statement if by changing the appropriate components of the problem description only, we gain a complete and reproductive task specification related to the protocol of the altered problem. A necessary condition for stability is that *generic knowledge* has been found: knowledge that does not refer to specific facts, entities and goals, only to generic ones. Note that from a given task specification one can identify the specific initial facts, objects and goals. We do not elaborate the formal definition of stability here.

The generality of a task specification cannot be decided unless we have a protocol for the solution of all the relevant problems. Obviously, this never happens. However, bearing in mind the intended scope of problems the system has to cope with, certain task specifications are better than others. Roughly speaking, the fewer number of 'unstable' facts are referred to, the more stable the task specification is.

Problem-solving Power of a Task Specification. Another aspect of problems is their difficulty. Namely, how many solutions to the problem exist. The expected difficulty of situations to cope with should be considered. The task specification $\mathfrak{P}$ is more *powerful* than $\mathbf{Q}$, if all the problems that can be solved by $\mathbf{Q}$ can also be solved by $\mathfrak{P}$.

The partial ordering induced by the comparison of the set of problems the task specifications can cope with is denoted by $\leq_P$.

It is hard to predict if a task specification is powerful enough to cope with another problem. If not, then the problem solving model should be extended with strategic knowledge to be able to cope with situations which have not been reported in the available protocols, but are likely to occur.

Abstraction Ability. Whenever a new problem will be solved, the user of the knowledge-based system will have to provide the initial facts describing the input information. If a system is built on the basis of protocols given by an expert, then many facts given by him could not have been given by a less experienced person. For instance a less experienced person cannot tell that a patient has fever, given he has a temperature of 39°C, whereas an expert can derive that by means of a reasoning process called *data abstraction* (for instance, see [2]). The less experienced person needs the fact "fever" as an input: he lacks the knowledge to be able perform the data-abstraction himself.

The *ability to abstract* of a task specification can be defined in terms of the concepts used in the inputs. Informally, the *abstraction ability* of a task specification $\mathcal{P}$ is higher than the one of $\mathbf{Q}$, if some concepts required to give the input facts for $\mathbf{Q}$ can be determined using other (more primitive) concepts by means of knowledge in $\mathcal{P}$. The partial ordering induced by the comparison of abstraction level of the protocols is denoted by $\leq_A$. Note that at a task specification with a lower abstraction level is more knowledgeable, that is its knowledge about the world is richer.

2.5 Overview of the Comparison Primitives

Different interpretations and task specifications related to the same protocol can be compared from different points of view, expressed by the following partial orderings:

$\leq_E$ *extension*
Does one specification contain the other.

$\leq_I$ *mirroring*
How much of what has been said in the protocol is modelled.

$\leq_G$ *genericity*
How big is the set of those other protocols for which the given task specification is reproductive.

$\leq_P$ *powerfulness*
How difficult problems (with different initial facts) can be solved.

$\leq_A$ *abstraction ability*
How difficult it is to give the initial world situation by the user.

As all the orderings above are partial, not all alternatives can be compared from all points of view. Moreover, the different partial orderings are not in some sense dependent on each other. For instance, there can be task specifications, $\mathcal{P}_1, ..., \mathcal{P}_4$ for which

$$\mathcal{P}_1 \leq_R \mathcal{P}_2 \text{ and } \mathcal{P}_3 \leq_R \mathcal{P}_4 \quad \text{but } \mathcal{P}_1 \leq_A \mathcal{P}_2 \text{ and } \mathcal{P}_3 \geq_A \mathcal{P}_4$$

In principle, the ideal task specification related to a protocol would be a most general, most powerful and most knowledgeable one, which maximally mirrors the given protocol. However, such an ideal task specification usually does not exit. Earlier we pointed out that the maximal mirroring interpretation of a protocol is usually not complete and not reproductive.

To sum up: protocol interpretations and related task specifications can be compared from different points of view. The objectives of the knowledge acquisition - that is, what interpretation are we aiming at - can be thought of as points in the 5-dimensional space of evaluating protocol interpretations and task specifications. The criteria of optimality could be formulated as a pareto-optimum by ranking the different aspects of evaluation.

3 An Example Protocol

The text included in this section is a shortened version of the Sisyphus sample protocol, offered by Marc Linster ([12]).

The task is to assign offices to members of a research group. They get a very limited number of offices indicated in Fig. 3. Some will have to share an office. The protocol to be analysed has been produced by the expert Siggi D., who managed to solve the problem.

3.1 Some Information

Within the subset of members of YQT we have the following organizational structure: Thomas D. is the head of the group YQT; Eva I. manages YQT; Monika X. and Ulrike U. are the secretaries; Werner L. and Angi W. work together in the RESPECT project; Harry C., Jürgen L. and Thomas D. work in the EULISP project; Michael M. and Hans W. work in the Babylon Product project; Hans W. is the head of this large project, Marc M., Uwe T. and Andy L. pursue individual projects; Katharina N. and Joachim I. are heads of larger projects that are not considered in this problem. More information can be found in

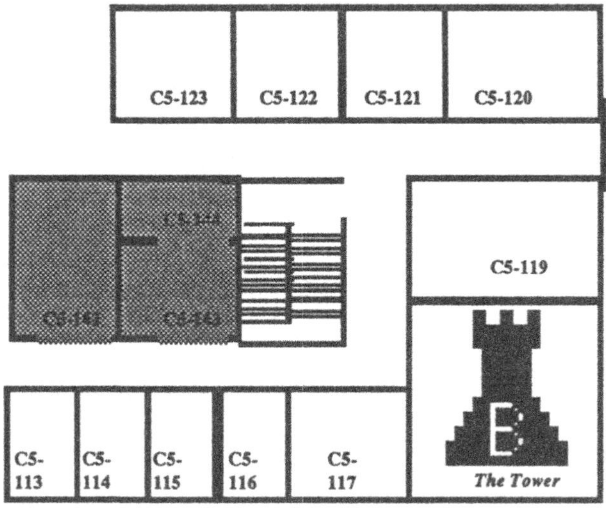

Fig. 3. The part of the floor-plan of the château that we will consider

the protocol itself. The rooms C5-123, C5-122, C5-121, C5-120, C5-119 and C5-117 are large rooms that can host two researchers. Large rooms can be assigned to heads of groups too. The rooms C5-113, C5-114, C5-115 and C5-116 are single rooms.

3.2 The Sample Protocol

The words of the expert		Comments, questions and annotations	
1	Put Thomas D. into office C5-117	1 a	The head of group needs a central office, so that he/she is as close to all the members of the group as possible. This should be a large office.
		1 b	This assignment is defined first, as the location of the office of the head of group restricts the possibilities of the subsequent assignments.
2	Monika X. and Ulrike U. into office C5-119	2 a	The secretaries' office should be located close to the office of the head of group. Both secretaries should work together in one large office.
		2 b	This assignment is executed as soon as possible, as its possible choices are extremely constrained.
3	Eva I. into C5-116	3 a	The manager must have maximum access to the head of group and to the secretariat. At the same time he/she should have a centrally located office. A small office will do.
		3 b	This is the earliest point where this decision can be taken.
4	Joachim I. into C5-115	4 a	The heads of large projects should be close to the head of group and the secretariat.
		4 b	There really is no reason for the sequence of the assignments of Joachim, Hans and Katharina.
5	Hans W. into C5-114	5 a	The heads of large projects should be close to the head of group and the secretariat.
6	Katharina N. into C5-113	6 a	The heads of large projects should be close to the head of group and the secretariat.
7	Andy K. and Uwe T. into C5-120	7 a	Both smoke. To avoid conflicts with non-smokers they share an office. Neither of them is eligible for a single office.
		7 b	This is the first twin-room assignment, as the smoker/non-smoker conflict is a severe one.
8	Werner L. and Jürgen L into C5-123	8 a	They are both implementing systems, both non-smokers. They do not work in the same project, but they work on related subjects. Members of the same project should not share offices. Sharing with members of other projects enhances synergy effects within the research group.
		8 b	There really are no criteria of the sequence of these twin room assignments.
9	Marc M. and Angi W. into C5-122	9 a	Marc is implementing systems, Angi isn't. This should not be a problem. Putting them together would ensure good cooperation between the RESPECT and the KRITON projects.
10	Harry C. and Michael T. into C5-121	10 a	They are both implementing systems. Harry develops object systems, Michael uses them. This creates synergy.

4 Comparing Different Models of the Example Protocol

4.1 A Generic Task Model and a Minimal Model

Reading sections 3.1 and the right hand side of 3.2, we encounter a number of quite unambiguous statements about the world the expert is reasoning about. For example, it is said that there is a room C5-117 which is large, and that there is a person Andy K. who smokes. We consider these as parts of the domain- or world knowledge. The description of the world consists of facts (describing the world situation) that may be true, false or (as yet) unknown. For this particular problem, the world situation is described by facts about the offices, the persons, and also about which person is in which office (although of course these 'facts' are as yet unknown). The facts can be considered as a picture of the world situation that should be created.

Since not all facts are known from the beginning of the problem solving process, the initial description of the world situation is always partial. In this case, the truth values of the facts about the world situation that describe which person is in which office are initially undefined. The aim is to get these truth values defined during the problem solving in such a way that certain logical relations (requirements) between the facts are satisfied. Such logical relations (the 'world theory') also belong to the world knowledge. It may be possible to reason with this knowledge and conclude new facts about the world situation.

Since the world knowledge only specifies the facts and relations that (should) hold, separate *strategic* knowledge is needed and used to generate such a solution. This is crucial, especially if the problem is difficult in the sense that only a few of the possible instantiations of the undefined truth values provide a solution. Therefore, in addition to the world knowledge, *knowledge on the problem solving process* is involved. This knowledge refers to the current state of the reasoning process itself and to (strategic) decisions that could be taken to continue the process. We call it process- or *meta-level* knowledge.

Separating this knowledge from world knowledge is a basic modelling decision. Certain statements in the protocol section 3.2 justify this decision: we encounter statements such as "This assignment is defined first, as ..." [3.2.1b], "There really is no reason for the sequence of the assignment of ..." [3.2.4b]. Such statements refer to the process of problem solving (e.g. what step is possible or required, which order of steps is useful) and not directly to the world.

We will first consider the protocol as a whole (constructing a generic task model), distinguishing different reasoning tasks that are involved and the relation between them, and then determine which of the expert's statements belong to which reasoning task.

The statements just mentioned ("This assignment is defined first..." etc.) also justify *interpretations* according to which the expert constructs the solution to the problem in small steps, by solving a number of *subproblems* (i.e. assuming the expert does not perform parallel processing, nor jump to a complete solution at once). From statements such as "This is the earliest point where this decision can be taken" [3.2.3b], we can furthermore assume that the steps mentioned in the protocol are represented in chronological order. We may thus model his reasoning process as a cyclic process of determining a subproblem to be solved, and then solving it. Note that in order to do so, the expert must have some way of decomposing the problem into subproblems. For the moment, we consider a subproblem as being the problem of "finding a room for a certain person, and determining a room-mate if necessary".

Solving such a subproblem also seems to involve several reasoning subtasks. The proliferation of statements about which assignments are *possible* ("person X should be (assigned to a room) near person Y", "person X is (not) eligible for a single office", "person X must have a large room", etc.) indicate that the expert first determines certain (all?) *possible* assignments that would solve the subproblem, and then chooses one. Other statements ([3.2.8a/9a/10a] in particular) seem to indicate that the expert chooses *optimal* or *advantageous* assignments. Note that in principle this selection process has a defeasible nature: a solution to the current subproblem is proposed, but it might turn out that with such a partial solution no satisfactory total solution can be found. In that case, one could revise this partial solution (using belief revision or backtracking): we consider the partial solutions essentially as *assumptions*. However, note that the given protocol does not show any revision actions. Probably this is the case since the expert's strategic knowledge is rich compared to the complexity of the problem.

Description of a Generic Task Model. We are now ready to describe a generic task model. We discern five major subtasks:

world
Reasoning with world knowledge
problem decomposition
Decomposing the problem into sub-problems
problem selection
Selecting a subproblem to solve
assumption generation
Determining possible solutions for this subproblem
assumption selection
Selecting one of these possibilities

The reasoning process starts with the world module (an object level task; the other four subtasks are reasoning about the problem solving process; we view them as meta-level subtasks). The problem decomposition task reasons about the (meta-)information about (the partial description of) the world state in order to determine which subproblems are yet to be solved (see Fig. 4). It will pass the subproblems to the problem selection task, which will select one and pass it on. The assumption generation task is one of determining a set of possible assignments that would solve the selected subproblem. These are passed on to the assumption selection task, which selects one. The selected assumption will be 'effected' as a new fact in the world module. We thus consider the expert to 'cycle' through these five modules until there are no subproblems left to solve (see Fig. 4.).

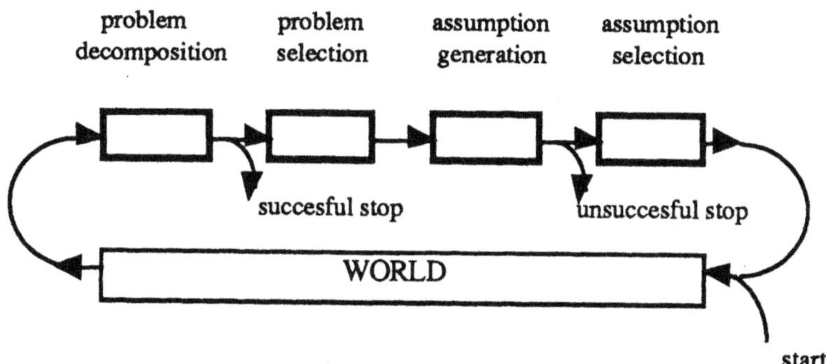

Fig. 4. Schematic picture of the generic task model's control flow

Description of a Minimal Model. In this section we will discuss a *minimal* instantiation $\mathcal{M}$ of the generic task model (a *minimal task specification* or *minimal model*, related to the protocol). A minimal model is an instantiation of the generic task model mirroring as much of the protocol text as possible by making the 'most natural' assumptions possible whenever we have to make an assumption. However, 'natural' is a matter of taste. One could wonder, for instance, how one is to check wether a room is centrally located or not. The protocol says nothing about this. Are we therefor to assume that the expert provides us with a set of facts "C5_117 is centrally located", "C5_115 is not centrally located", etc.? Intuitively, we may consider this less far-reaching than assuming that the expert uses, let's say, the average bird-flight distance-function from doorknob to doorknob or some such. However, this intuition is hard to generalize. Consider a similar statement: "This assignment is executed as soon as possible, as its possible choices are extremely constrained" [3.2.2b]. Somehow, intuitively, we can *not* imagine that we will have a list of facts beforehand stating how constrained the possible choices are for each assignment. On the other hand, there is *nothing* in the protocol stating whether this is so or not, let alone an indication of the techniquc the expert used to determine these facts. How could we best capture the interpretation *meant* by the expert (aside from asking him, which we can not do in this case).

As far as the purpose of the minimal model *discussed here* is concerned: it suffices to say that all alternative instantiations that will be discussed later on are less minimal (i.e. more far-reaching assumptions are involved).

We will first discuss the instantiations of each reasoning task, and explain what kind of knowledge will be needed to perform the reasoning. Then we will mention which choices we made with respect to the protocol text.

Problem Decomposition

We will consider the basic subproblems to be of the form "find a room for a person X, and determine a room-mate if necessary". The knowledge needed for this task is straightforward - but not mentioned explicitly anywhere in the protocol: we have a basic subproblem for every person X that has not yet been assigned to a room. The part "determine a room-mate if necessary" can be justified when one considers that the expert never places a person in a room leaving an empty seat to be filled up later (left hand side of 3.2). That we find a room for a person (and not vice versa) can be justified by [3.2.4b] in particular: "There really is no reason for the sequence of assignments of Joachim, Hans and Katherina". Some of these subproblems, and the researchers-subproblem can be decomposed further according to individual persons or pairs of persons.

Problem Selection

Looking *only* at the left hand side of 3.2, one might conclude that Siggi D. works in the sequence "head of office", "secretaries", "managers", "heads of projects", "researchers". The expert may have discovered this sequence as successful by experience.

Assumption Generation

We assume the expert to determine one or more possibilities to solve a basic subproblem. No information is available to see how many possibilities the expert produces. In this minimal model we consider *all* possibilities. Knowledge that plays a role are statements such as "The head of group needs a central office." [3.2.1a], "The manager (...) should have a centrally located office." [3.2.3a] (i.e. non-central offices are not possible for managers); "Members of the same project should not share offices." [3.2.8a] etc.

Assumption Selection
One could argue that there is *no* statements at all in the protocol about any possibility being preferred above another (only that possibilities are preferred over non-possibilities). As a minimal interpretation we could therefore select any possibility at random.

World
Here we will find all facts about the world situation (e.g. "Andy K smokes"), and rules to derive new facts from given facts (e.g. "if person X is a researcher, and room R is a single room, then person X is NOT eligible for room R").

Most of the statements in the protocol [3.1 to 3.2] are unambiguous and could easily be fitted into the generic task model. Some sentences we considered ambiguous, however, and some sentences we decided to ignore as 'noise'.

As far as ambiguities are concerned: "the smoker/non-smoker conflict is a severe one" [3.2.7b] we assume to mean that smokers and non-smokers may *never* share an office. "Neither is eligible for single office" [3.2.7a] we assume to mean that researchers are *never* eligible for single office (as opposed to "*at the moment no single offices are left*").
We also ignored the statements below that we considered as *redundant explanatory statements* (statements that in our opinion explains how the expert acquired his own knowledge, i.e. we do not think the expert *used* that knowledge to derive anything):

- "so that he/she is as close to all the members of the group as possible" [3.2.1a];
- "as the location of the office of the head of group restricts the possibilities of the subsequent assignments" [3.2.1b] ;
- "This is the earliest point where this decision can be taken" [3.2.3b] ;
- We do not consider the advantages mentioned about the assignments [3.2.8 - 3.2.10] to have played any part in the reasoning process.

Finally, we ignore the statement "Members of the same project should not share offices." [3.2.8a],(since the expert *does* put two members of the same project together in [3.2.10a]. We have also chosen to ignore the statement "This assignment is executed as soon as possible, as its possible choices are extremely constrained" [3.2.2b] since the protocol gives absolutely no indication of how one could determine how "constrained the choices of an assignment" are.

4.2 An Overview of Alternative Interpretations and Task Specifications

In this section we analyse the given protocol especially with respect to possible different interpretations of certain statements by Siggi D. and to extensions that are inevitable in order to be able to give more sophisticated interpretations. We will give examples for various kinds of refinements of the minimal task specification. Refinement is meant in the sense that in the refined task specification some more subtle theory replaces certain knowledge (simple theory or facts) of the minimal task specification. From the technical point of view of model building, a refinement can be achieved by:

- refining the world knowledge;
- refining the strategic knowledge concerning subproblem generation and selection;
- refining the strategic knowledge concerning the solution of subproblems.

The refined theory to be included is either gained by mirroring some parts of the protocol which were considered as 'noise' by the minimal interpretation, or by understanding in a different way certain parts of the text also mirrored by the minimal interpretation, or by adding knowledge which does not mirror any text in the given protocol. Only in the first and the last cases a refinement necessarily is an extension as well. In the first case the refinement interprets more of the protocol. We will point out what sentence is mirrored additionally or in a different way in the alternative refined interpretations. In this entire chapter the numbers will refer to protocol sections of the problem description.

The refinements require the modification of the knowledge in certain modules of the minimal model and/or the insertion of new modules or replacement of a module by new ones, as well as the modification the control rules.

Refinements of the World Theory. Reading the explanations under points a. in the right hand side of [3.2], a number of new notions occur: "... needs a *central* office" [3.2.1a], "... they work on *related subjects*" [3.2.8a]. The expert refers to the newly introduced relations as known facts. There are two alternatives to interpret such a reference:

- We accept that the the truth or falsity of certain facts (e.g. room C5-117 is central) should be given in advance, as part of the problem specification, by the user. The facts that are not explicitly given are unknown (e.g. we do not assume that e.g. room C5-120 is *not* central, we simply do not know).
- We assume the expert having some theory on how to derive the truth of the referredfact from the initially given facts. E.g. he has derived the centrality of the rooms by looking at the layout. We include into our model knowledge declaring the truth or falsity of the referred fact with respect to the truth or falsity of certain, initially given facts. If there is nothing said explicitly about the theory used then one has to guess it.

In the minimal model we took the first approach. Below we extend the world model with different theories on how to derive centrality from some other facts of the world.

Model $\mathcal{C}_1$: common sense theory for centrality

The first emerging idea is to interpret "centrality" in the ordinary sense, by analysing only the layout of the rooms. However, a task model based on this interpretation does not reproduce the given protocol: obviously, in such interpretation C5-119 would be the most central room. Hence one should be careful not to include too general common sense knowledge.

Model $\mathcal{C}_2$: domain dependent theory for centrality

The world theory is refined with knowledge to derive centrality of a room from its position and size (for details, see [5]). The centrality of a room is computed by taking a weighted sum of the Manhattan distance of the selected room from the rest of the rooms. (The Manhattan distance is chosen to model that walls of the rooms cannot be crossed.) This domain dependent weight selection is meant to express that the centrality of a room is defined with respect to the role of the people in the rest of the rooms and to their relative position. Small rooms count more as they are to be assigned to heads of projects, and it is emphasized that the heads of projects should be close to the head of the group. Note that the user is expected to describe the initial situation in less abstract terms than in $\mathcal{M}$: instead of centrality, only the position of the distinct rooms should be given.

Model $\mathcal{C}_3$: domain independent theory for centrality

For the sake of simplicity we explain the definition of centrality for the room of the head of the group only. Centrality can be understood as an aggregate measure of how well the requirements on closeness to the rooms of staff members can be met by a distinct room. In order to model this interpretation one has to refine further the theory given above. Instead of giving the relevance of the rooms by their size, we give a more elaborate evaluation on the basis of the structure of the problem. When selecting a room for the head of the group, one would like to select the one which will make it possible to place the staff members in such a way that they are the closest to the room selected for the head. This means that the room of the head of the group should be selected in such a way that it will lead to a solution of the entire problem where certain relations - in our case, those on closeness - are satisfied the best.

We estimate how well the closeness requirement can be satisfied for each possible room assignment by using more elaborate weights: for each room we take the ratio of the a staff members and the number of all persons who can be assigned to the room (for details, see [5]). This estimate neither leads necessarily in all situations to the selection of the best room, however, it is superior to the previous one. All the staff members are taken into account, and it is not misleading in situations where not only small rooms will be assigned to the heads of groups (e.g. not enough small rooms, or the only smoker non staff member should be assigned to a single room). Note that in order to be able to compute the weight of a room, the problem should be analysed by calculating all the possible assignments in advance.

Refinements for Problem Decomposition and Subproblem Selection. The statement "There really are no criteria of the sequence of these twin room assignments" [3.2.8b] may suggest that Siggi D. realizes that the remaining problem is to make pairs of the unassigned people, while assigning them to rooms is not relevant (any assignment of the remaining rooms will be equally well). Our minimal model could be refined in a straightforward way, by 'duplicating' our minimal model, but with different kinds of assignments and problems: the assignment of one person to a room and the subproblems of finding the room for a person for the staff assignment problem, and the assignment of a person to another one and the subproblems of finding the room-mate of a person for the researchers assignment problem.

The order of dealing with the subproblems has strategic importance. Some meta-statements on the possible solutions relate solutions of different subproblems (e.g. "The manager must have maximum access to the head of the group and to the secretariat" [3.2.3a]). Hence, whenever a subproblem is to be solved, the solution of the already solved subproblems may restrict the possible solutions of the current subproblem, even to the extent that the current subproblem has no solution at all compatible with the given solutions of the previously solved subproblems. Hence it is useful to analyse how strongly the different subproblems are interrelated. A widely used general problem solving strategy is to solve the most constrained subproblem first. It also makes sense to select the one with the fewest solutions to be solved first. The protocol does give the hint that Siggi D. did apply both problem selection criteria.

Model V: room-view theory for problem decomposition and selection

In our minimal model the problem decomposition and selection were driven by the role of the unassigned people. We emphasized that the 'macro actions' at the left hand side of [3.2] could be generated in different ways, depending on if first a room or room-mate was assigned to a selected person. Moreover, Siggi D. used a different criterion for subproblem selection if an unassigned room was a bottle-neck (e.g. only one set of persons can be assigned to it) in the problem yet to be solved. In order to be able to exploit such situations, we refine the knowledge of subproblem generation and selection by adding some theory (not corresponding to any text in the protocol) on how the certain macro steps were generated. We extend the notion of subproblems: a room to be filled up is also considered to be a subproblem. We allow to switch from the persons' view to rooms' view in looking at and selecting from subproblems. Before examining the subproblems from the persons' view, as done in the minimal model, now we check if there is a room to which only one set of persons can be assigned. If so, this subproblem is selected as the next one to be solved. This task can be performed by introducing a separate module, with knowledge for analysing subproblems from the rooms' view (for the specific rules, see [5]). The rooms' view is used only to perform unique assignments opportunistically. Such opportunistic detection of critical views and assignments would help to avoid dead-ends. See proving experiments with Fox's opportunistic scheduling system (see [4]).

In a further refinement of the minimal model, the same result (a room filled up) could be generated via several steps, e.g. select a person, select his roommate, select a room for them.

Model $\mathcal{P}_1$: select the most critical subproblem

The explanations for the strategy followed give evidence for a more general, domain-independent subproblem selection criteria: *selection of the most critical subproblem.* Explanation for selecting the assignment of the head of the group as the first subproblem refers to restrictions on the remaining subproblems: "... the location of the office of the head of group restricts the possibilities of the subsequent assignments" [3.2.1b]. Indeed, the location of the head of the group constrains all the remaining subproblems, as all the staff members should be close to him, [3.2.2a, 3.2.6a] and he has to be "as close to all members of the group as possible" [3.2.1a].

Note, that the *selection by role* can be considered as the domain-dependent version of the *selection by criticality*: in this domain, usually if a person has a higher role than another, then he is more critical too, in the above sense. Note, that in the given case this did not apply for the secretaries and the manager. However, if the prescription of the world changes, the selection by criticality will work, while the selection by role not necessarily.

Model $\mathcal{P}_2$: select subproblem with the least solution

Occasionally, Siggi D. applied another criterion, that is *selection of the subproblem with the least solutions.* In [3.2.2b], the secretaries are assigned "... as soon as possible, as its possible choices are extremely constrained". We take Siggi D. to mean that there are very few possibilities. (Indeed, a secretary has only one possibility: C5-119 is the only large room close to the head of group, and her room-mate must be the other secretary). This can also explain why [3.2.7] was done before [3.2.8-3.2.10]: the smokers are assigned first of all researchers "... as the smoker/non-smoker conflict is a severe one" [3.2.7b]. That is, Andy K and Uwe T. are unique room-mates of for each other.

Model $\mathcal{P}_3$: select from subproblems with equal solutions randomly

The statement "There are really no criteria of the sequence of these twin room assignments" [3.2.8b] can be understood in a different way as was done in the task specification $\mathcal{P}_1$ above. It also can be the case that this statement emphasizes that random selection should be used when the subproblems are equally constrained in the above sense. Note that from a modelling point of view there is much difference if random selection in a complete task model mirrors the protocol, or if there is a non complete interpretation available, and random selection is assumed and used as a necessary extension of the incomplete interpretation.

Refinements for Solving Subproblems. In [3.1] we encounter statements like "... large rooms ... *can* host two researchers", "large rooms *can* be assigned to heads of groups". On the right hand side of [3.2] there are several similar statements, e.g. "The head of group *needs* a central office" [3.2.1a], "Both secretaries *should* work together in a large office" [3.2.2a]", "The heads of large projects *should* be close to the head of group and the secretariat" [3.2.4a]. These are normative statements, which prescribe which evaluations of the goal facts in the world situation are *possible* ("can" statements) and *acceptable* as a solution ("should" and "need" statements). This type of statements are heavily used on the meta-level, in the process of constructing the solution. In the minimal model we considered only the statements directly stating what is a possible evaluation of the goal facts, and what is required to accept them as a solution.

Usually there are many solutions of a subproblem. From the protocol we could not definitely decide if the proposed solution was selected from all the possible solutions, or only some or even only one was considered. Hence in the minimal model we did not make any arbitrary restrictions on the set of possible solution to be generated. However, the explanations gave the impression that Siggi D. has considered only such solutions of a subproblem which, in combination with the assignments that already had been made, do not violate the prescriptions for the solution.

Model $\mathcal{S}_1$: reflecting time-dependent goal reconsideration

The somewhat shocking explanation [3.2.10a] gives rise to a more subtle interpretation. Here Siggi D. uses just the opposite of the argument in [3.2.8a] about the synergy of assignment. Is it because of BABYLON is a Product, not a Project? Or BABYLON is an exception? If so, then our problem description should be reconsidered. Or it would be better not to have Harry C. and Michael T. in the same room, but instead of trying to improve the pairing of the people by backtracking, Siggi D. convinces us and himself that after all the current assignment is not too bad. This question is a central one as there are 10(!) other assignments where a synergy conflict does not occur at all, and the hacker constraint is violated similarly only for one pair.

One may assume that Siggi D. has come up with a specific solution because of his limitations. Obviously, we do not want to mimic errors due to limitations of human experts. Here we do not dwell further on the reliability/trustability of the protocol. But we note that even the second interpretation could be captured by a more sophisticated model. As time proceeds (or the yet unsolved part of the entire problem shrinks), the criteria of solution of the subproblems can be relaxed. Note that the relaxation of the criteria of solution has as a significant positive effect: the time spent on finding a solution decreases.

Model $\mathcal{S}_2$: to differentiate hard and soft requirements

A more careful look at the first subproblem with several possible solutions — that is, the subproblem solved in step [3.2.8] — raises questions. This is the first time, that a pair is preferred to some other, equally feasible ones. Is there really no basis for preferring a pair (more precisely, a division of the remaining 6 people) over another? In that case, the chosen room-mate is due to random selection. Or, did Siggi D. compare the possible room-mates and selected the best one in some sense? If so, on what basis?

The explanation for forming the pairs in steps [3.2.9-3.2.10] can serve as a basis for comparing the different solutions of a subproblem. This suggests that not all the prescriptions for the world are equally severe ones. There are ones which should be met anyway, but certain others can be violated. The statement "...the smoker/non-smoker conflict is a severe one" [3.2.7b] suggests that not all the prescriptions for the possible assignments are equally 'hard': if there is no solution, certain requirements can be sacrificed. E.g. a smoker/non-smoker conflict is never allowed, while an implementor/non-implementor conflict may occur. (Note that in the task specification $\mathcal{P}_2$ we interpreted this sentence in a very different way.) We refine the prescriptions when two people can share a room in the world model: certain prescriptions are 'hard' ones, others are 'soft' ones. Only the hard prescriptions should be fulfilled by a solution, the soft ones are taken into account when selecting a best solution from the ones fulfilling the soft prescriptions. If a best assignment does not exist, that is, the soft requirements cannot be fulfilled, then any of the possible assignments should be selected (see [5]).

4.3 Comparison of the Alternative Interpretations

Not all the refinements we have discussed can be compared in all respects. Moreover, usually one refinement is superior to another one in one respect, and inferior in some other respect. The map of the above models of the same protocol is illustrated in Fig. 5. It shows task specifications corresponding to different interpretations of the example protocol, indicating the text they mirror and the extensions relation. All the refinements mirror at least as much of the given protocol as the minimal model. There are task models which interpret the same part of the protocol, though in a different way. Obviously, $\mathcal{C}_1 =_I \mathcal{C}_2 =_I \mathcal{C}_3$. Moreover, $\mathcal{P}_1 =_I \mathcal{P}_2$. Other models which can be compared with respect to the text interpreted: $\mathcal{P}_2 \leq_I \mathcal{P}_3$ and $\mathcal{P}_1 \leq_E \mathcal{P}_3$. For all refinements considering centrality the initial world situation is described in less abstract terms, hence $\mathcal{M} \leq_A \mathcal{C}_1$, $\mathcal{M} \leq_A \mathcal{C}_2$, $\mathcal{M} \leq_A \mathcal{C}_3$. It is also true that $\mathcal{C}_2 \leq_A \mathcal{C}_3$, as for model $\mathcal{C}_3$ weights are derived from less abstract data. As we explained, $\mathcal{C}_1$ does not reproduce the

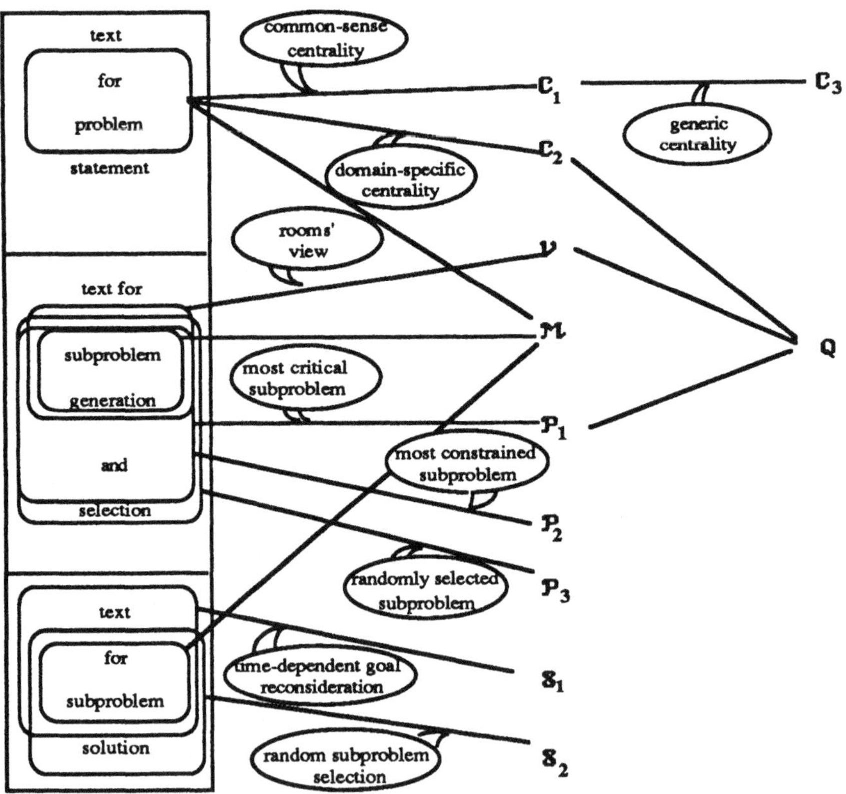

Fig. 5. Map of different models related to the example protocol

given protocol. But $\mathcal{M} \leq_G \mathcal{C}_3$, as it derives centrality by analysing the structure of the problem in a general way. All models which contain refined strategic knowledge are more powerful and general than $\mathcal{M}$. Moreover, $\mathcal{P}_2 \leq_P \mathcal{P}_3$ and $\mathcal{P}_2 \leq_G \mathcal{P}_3$. Note that in our examples we refined only one type of knowledge (world-, problem decomposition and solution generation) at a time. You could gain more complex refinements by refining both world and strategic knowledge. An obvious way is to 'unify' some specific refinements. Such a possible $\mathcal{Q}$ refinement is also indicated on the map, for which $\mathcal{Q} =_A \mathcal{C}_2$, $\mathcal{P}_1 \leq_P \mathcal{Q}$, $\mathcal{V} \leq_P \mathcal{Q}$, $\mathcal{P}_1 \leq_A \mathcal{Q}$, $\mathcal{V} \leq_A \mathcal{Q}$.

5 Conclusions

The assumption that a protocol usually gives an underspecified account of the expert's reasoning process implies that the problem is not to find the one and only right interpretation of the protocol. Essentially different interpretations and models are equally well possible since one has to use fantasy to find any complete task specification: the modeller has to make a choice that cannot be motivated by the protocol itself. Only parts of the expert's model and the constructed task specification correspond. The framework we discussed is intended to clarify the range of possible task specifications related to a given protocol. It can be used to analyse in more detail what choices often are made during the protocol interpretation and the design of a task specification.

By means of the criteria we introduced protocol interpretations and related task specifications can be compared from different points of view. The possible outcomes of the analysis of a given protocol can be described as points in a 5-dimensional space of models. Given one's objectives one may optimize one or more of the dimensions. We think the criteria that we discussed are relevant, but there may be others as well.

The framework as discussed has not been finished yet. We have given different items that could be covered. We are aware of the fact that there is much to be done in order to gain a really usable, sound framework. In the future we wish to refine the issues by:

- relying on experience with more sample protocols;
- giving more in-depth and thoroughly formal definition of the introduced concepts.

Moreover, our list of evaluation criteria very likely could be and needs to be augmented. It is a challenging task to compile a full list of evaluation criteria. Moreover, some criteria very well can be structured: some basic ones always need to be considered, while some (groups of) others only in the case of specific domains and/or knowledge acquisition and modelling objectives.

We also need to justify our approach, by proving that different interpretations and models of the same protocol can be compared along the suggested dimensions in practice.

We have left open what type of formal specification language is used for the models. In fact the framework can abstract from the precise specification language that is used. However, to give more detailed definitions one will have to make use of certain characteristics of the specification language: one expects at least certain aspects to be expressible. The formal specification framework DESIRE we have developed gives a possibility for this, but also other specification languages may be used.

Acknowledgements

We thank Marc Linster for his suggestion to use the material that was obtained in the context of the Sisyphus project to describe a framework as presented here (see [11, 12]). Parts of this research were supported by SKBS and NWO.

References

1. J. A. Breuker, B. J. Wielinga: Interpretation of verbal data for knowledge acquisition. In: O'Shea T. (ed) Advances in Artificial Intelligence, Amsterdam:Elsevier Science Publishers, 1985
2. W. J. Clancey: Heuristic classification. Artificial Intelligence 27 (1985), pp. 289-350
3. K. A. Ericsson, H. A. Simon: Protocol analysis, Cambridge, MA:M.I.T. Press, 1984
4. M. S. Fox: Constraint guided scheduling: A short history of scheduling research at CMU, Computers in Industry 14 (1990) pp.79-88
5. P. A. Geelen, Zs. Ruttkay, J. Treur: Logical analysis and specification of an office assignment task. Rapport IR-283, Dept. of Mathematics and Computer Science, Vrije Universiteit Amsterdam, 1991, shorter version in [11, 12]
6. P. E. Johnson, I. Zualkerman, S. Garber: Specification of Expertise. International Journal of Man-machine studies, 26, (1987) pp. 161-181.
7. W. Kowalczyk, J. Treur, On the use of a formalized generic task model in knowledge acquisition. Proc. European Knowledge Acquisition Workshop, EKAW-90. In: B. J. Wielinga, J. Boose, B. Gaines, G. Schreiber, M. van Someren, M. (eds.), Current trends in knowledge acquisition, Amsterdam:IOS Press, 1990, pp. 198-221
8. B. Kuipers, J. P. Kassirer: Knowledge acquisition by analysis of verbatim protocols. In: Kidd, A.L. (ed) Knowledge Acquisition for Expert Systems: a Practical Handbook, New York:Plenum Press, 1987 pp. 45-71.
9. I. A. van Langevelde, J. Treur: Logical methods in protocol analysis. Proc. European Knowledge Acquisition Workshop, EKAW-91, 1991, Berlin:Springer Verlag
10. I. A. van Langevelde, A. W. Philipsen, J. Treur: Formal specification of compositional architectures. Report IR-282. Department of Mathematics and Computer Science, Vrije Universiteit Amsterdam, 1991
11. Linster , M. (ed.), Sisyphus Working Papers, University of Strathclyde, 1991
12. Linster, M. (ed.), Sisyphus-1 yearbook 1991, To appear
13. N. Shadbolt, A. M. Burton, Knowledge elicitation. In: Wilson, J., Corlett, N. (eds). Evaluation of Human Work: Practical Ergonomics Methodology. London:Taylor and Francis, 1989
14. J. Treur: On the use of reflection principles in modelling complex reasoning. International Journal of Intelligent Systems 6 (1991), pp. 277-294
15. J. Treur: Declarative functionality descriptions of interactive reasoning modules. in: H. Boley, M. M. Richter (eds.), Processing Declarative Knowledge, Proc. of the International Workshop PDK-91, Lecture Notes in AI, vol. 567, Springer Verlag, 1991, pp. 221-236

Knowledge Acquisition Driven by Constructive and Interactive Induction

Katsuhiko TSUJINO tsujino@sys.crl.melco.co.jp
Vlad G. DABIJA vlad@cs.stanford.edu
Shogo NISHIDA nishida@sys.crl.melco.co.jp

System 4G, Central Research Laboratory, MITSUBISHI Electric corp., 8-1-1, Tsukaguchi-Honmach, Amagasaki, Hyogo 661 JAPAN

Abstract. This paper describes the basic framework and the latest configuration of a knowledge acquisition system named KAISER. This system inductively learns classification knowledge in the form of a decision tree, and analyzes the results and the processes with domain and task specific knowledge to detect improper states. Then it asks suggestive questions to eliminate the improprieties and acquires new domain knowledge for the next induction cycle. One of the final objectives of this research is to frame a unified theory in the classification trees' paradigm arguing: (1) what means to have a good/bad tree; (2) why it is good/bad; and (3) how to obtain a better one. To achieve this goal, KAISER has been enhanced with a meta-learner named Meta-KAISER to accumulate the meta-knowledge by keeping track of the experts' response of domain level interaction.

1 Introduction

Inductive learning is one of the most powerful techniques for constructing knowledge-based systems. It enables systematic and full (or semi) automatic construction of knowledge bases. However, the learned results are sometimes not developed enough from the expert's point of view. When an expert inspects such a tentative result, he can easily point out some improper conditions (which we call *improprieties* in this paper) that are neither errors nor faults statistically, but something that seems unsatisfactory to an expert. By interpreting the reason of their occurrence, the expert can recommend corrective knowledge such as new examples and constraints according to his experience. Nevertheless, this knowledge is difficult to acquire beforehand by top-down reflection. This fact suggests that inductive learning can be an efficient mental stimulus for knowledge acquisition as well as a powerful method to get reasonable knowledge automatically.

This paper discusses the latest version of a knowledge acquisition system named KAISER [8,11] (Knowledge Acquisition Inductive System driven by Explanatory Reasoning). KAI-

SER learns decision trees inductively, evaluates the trees to detect improprieties and asks appropriate questions to eliminate the improprieties. The key idea of this process is that (i) improprieties constitute a qualitative measure of the goodness and badness of a decision tree, and therefore (ii) by defining an appropriate set of improprieties, their explanations and elimination actions, we can conduct an intelligent knowledge acquisition process through interactive and constructive induction of decision trees.

By investigating improprieties, we believe we can make a pragmatic approach to frame a unified theory in the classification trees' paradigm for issues like pruning, integration of induction and deduction, constructive induction and interview strategies.

2 Basic Framework

Figure 1 presents the working diagram of KAISER. It adopts an ID3 [3] like algorithm to learn decision trees from examples. Examples are represented as *class-attribute-value* vectors (i.e., a name of class which an example belongs to, a feature vector which an example has and corresponding values that an example satisfies). The domain knowledge base includes (possible incomplete/incorrect) knowledge about (i) the relation between classes and the attribute values, (ii) ordinal relationships among attribute values, and (iii) derivation knowledge of an attribute value from other attribute values.

By referring this domain knowledge and general statistic knowledge stored in the impropriety knowledge base, the impropriety detector detects various improprieties. An impropriety represents anything that the expert believes is not right about a decision tree. It may be something definitely wrong about it (like a node which has examples belonging to conflict-

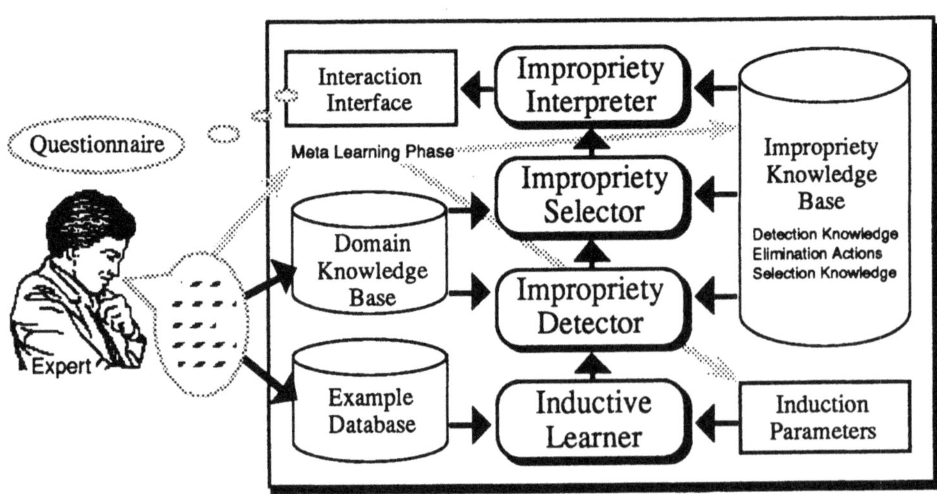

Fig.1.Architecture of KAISER

ing classes), or something that the expert finds strange (like a path which appears to lack some essential condition), or even something that may be fine in general, but in this particular case the expert would prefer it otherwise (like two sibling subtrees which are not identical but consist of similar conditions). The impropriety selector chooses the most important node to be treated next. The impropriety interpreter generates a questionnaire with adequate explanation and elimination actions for the selected node according to the detected improprieties. The questionnaire is presented to prompt the expert for new examples and domain knowledge.

Through the iteration of this *induce-eval-ask* cycle, a human expert can refine the tree incrementally by updating both domain and example databases. KAISER also allows the expert to edit the trees directly by aborting the session. When the expert wants to be assisted again, he/she can just re-invoke it. Although KAISER provides helpful suggestions, the final judgment is due to the expert. Therefore, KAISER is assumed as a sophisticated workbench for revising and improving decision trees with intelligent decision support which helps an expert to elicit his/her own knowledge by introspecting through trial and error.

3 Related Work

The most important part of KAISER is the impropriety knowledge, which is meta-level knowledge representing: (k1) what means to have a good/bad decision tree; (k2) why it is good/bad; and (k3) how to obtain a better one. Similar knowledge is issued in the field of constructive induction [4,6,10]. Matheus [10] pointed out three primary questions: (m1) When should new features be constructed?; (m2) What constructive operator should be used and to which existing features should it be applied?; and (m3) which features should be discarded? KAISER's knowledge (k1) and (k3) will directly correspond to Matheus' questions (m1) and (m2) respectively. Some of the restriction knowledge in (k3) may correspond to (m3).

However, the main difference between them is that KAISER aims at interactive knowledge acquisition while constructive induction aims at automatic feature generation. Therefore, KAISER furnishes explanation knowledge (k2) to help human experts understand the current problem, and it offers a larger variety of elimination actions (k3) in addition to constructing new features, such as pruning, asking for new examples and domain knowledge or redefining the probμlem (i.e., class and attribute) definition.

The impropriety knowledge also plays an essential role in combining machine learning (inductive and deductive) and knowledge acquisition. In order to achieve reliable induction and efficient deduction, this is one of the reasonable ways to combine induction and deduction to control each other. Pazzani proposed an induction system named FOCL [7], which accepts deductive relationships between classes and attributes in the form of Horn clauses and evaluates and refines them by induction. Although KAISER is mainly based on induction, it also provides deductive explanation-based optimization of induced knowledge by using domain knowledge. Instead of refining all this knowledge automatically, KAISER tries to conduct a dialogue with the expert and obtain new knowledge based on the heuristic knowledge expressed as improprieties. Pazzani also suggests using such heuristics to achieve interactive knowledge acquisition in his article on KR-FOCL [9].

The idea of acquiring knowledge by integrating knowledge from different sources or methods is one of the hot issues in knowledge acquisition [5]. Obviously, learning efficiency is one of the most important merits of integrating induction and deduction. Furthermore, we have to notice that we can derive more reliable knowledge if we can get initial knowledge from multiple sources, and even if these are inconsistent with each other, we can obtain very important clues for acquiring new knowledge for eliminating the inconsistency.

4 Impropriety-based Processing

The process of decision tree evaluation is divided into three steps: (i) detection of three types of improprieties, i.e., structural, semantic and global improprieties; (ii) selection of the next node to ask; and (iii) generation of appropriate questionnaires to acquire new knowledge. This section gives a brief description of the impropriety knowledge needed for these steps.

4.1 Structural Improprieties

Improprieties of this type are task-specific and domain-independent, meaning that they are not dependent on the target knowledge to be acquired but that they are specific to the classification task or the learning algorithm employed. They are detected as some generalization failures or some unreliable conditions, e.g., affected by the noisy examples. These improprieties give many kinds of clues for reasonable generalization according to the common knowledge about the classification task. Typical structural improprieties are described as follows:

(ST1) *Noisy node impropriety:* A node has few examples, e.g., less than half of the average leaf size. This is a typical clue for pruning.

(ST2) *NIL leaf impropriety:* The class of a leaf cannot be determined by induction because of the lack of examples. This often arises when we use multiple valued (not binary) attributes.

(ST3) *Inseparable examples impropriety:* Some examples can not be separated only with given attributes. This impropriety possesses features of both ST1 and ST2.

(ST4) *Similar node impropriety:* Two brother nodes refer the same attribute, their entropies are near, and they consist of similar component classes. This is a structural clue to generalize the attribute of their father by merging the links to them.

(ST5) *Similar class impropriety:* More than one node tries to separate the same set of classes at different places in a decision tree. This is a primitive clue for a new attribute for separating the conflicting classes, which is represented by a subtree induced from the subset of examples that belong to the conflicting classes.

4.2 Semantic Improprieties

Ideally, all the conditions in a decision tree can be explained by domain theory, however, this matching practically fails because of a lack of or fault in examples and domain knowledge. This mismatching and other characteristic problems are detected as semantic improprieties, and are indispensable in generating intelligent and efficient questionnaires. Although semantic improprieties signify domain dependent problems, the detection knowledge itself is domain independent, because it represents general matching knowledge between decision trees and domain knowledge.

KAISER accepts three types of domain knowledge: (i) explanation knowledge (*Eknow*) which is the relation between classes and the attribute values (e.g., the value of attribute *number-of-legs* will be *six* if the class is *insect*), (ii) derivation knowledge (*Dknow*) of an attribute value from other attribute values (e.g., the value of attribute *weight* can be calculated from the values of *mass* and *density* by multiplying them together), and (iii) attribute knowledge (*Aknow*) which is the ordinal relationship among attribute values (e.g., the value *yellow* of attribute *color-of-warning-lamp* is between the values *red* and *green*). *Eknow* is further specified by three conditions: *Econd* (essential conditions, which typical examples will satisfy), *Dcond* (desirable conditions, which ideal examples can satisfy), and *Pcond* (permissible conditions, which exceptional examples may require).

By explaining the conditions in a decision tree by *Eknow* using *Dknow*, KAISER tries to estimate matching factors (called *support factors* in this paper) for each node and *Eknow* by the following algorithm:

For all domain knowledge and paths in a decision tree:

(1) if a path includes all of the Econd of a domain knowledge, then set the support factor of the path by the knowledge to 1.0;

(2) if a path does not satisfy (1) but includes the conditions generalized by replacing some conditions in the Econd by Pcond, then set the support factor by the knowledge to 0.8^n, where n is the number of replaced conditions; and

(3) if a path satisfies (1) or (2), and it also includes some conditions in Dcond, then multiply the support factor by 1.2^n, where n is the number of matched Dcond's.

Semantic improprieties are detected based on this factor. Typical semantic improprieties are described as follows:

(SE1) *Contradictory explanation impropriety:* The conditions to a leaf are explicable by domain knowledge that belongs to a different class. A primitive elimination action of this impropriety is to specialize the Econd or Pcond of the miss-matched domain knowledge, and/or to generalize the Econd or Dcond of the domain knowledge that should match and get higher support factors.

(SE2) *Multiple explanation impropriety:* More than one explanation is suggested by domain knowledge. This impropriety is a clue to change an Econd to a Dcond to lessen the support factor of a piece of knowledge that is not so important, and/or add some conditions to Dcond to strengthen the factor of a preferable piece of knowledge.

(SE3) *Near-miss explanation impropriety:* One and only one condition in Econd is missing to explain a leaf. This impropriety is a strong clue for over-fitting. A primitive elimination action is to add the missing condition and expand the tree.

(SE4) *Twin immediate siblings impropriety:* The immediate siblings of a node belong to the same class. This impropriety is a clue for noisy examples. A primitive elimination action is to change the node between the siblings into a leaf of the siblings' class.

(SE5) *No explanation impropriety:* No explanation is given. It is a clue to generalize the Econd and Pcond of a piece of knowledge that should match, and/or ask for a new piece of domain knowledge for the leaf.

4.3 Global Improprieties

While the previous two improprieties detect rather "local" features of decision trees to suggest mainly minor revisions of the decision trees (e.g., pruning, merging or reconstruction of subtrees), global improprieties aim at detecting global and macro features of decision trees to suggest major changes of the problem definition (i.e., class and attribute definitions). Such a re-organization is necessary to improve the performance and reliability of the knowledge base.

KAISER adopts the non-metric multidimensional scaling (MDS) method [1,2] to detect global features of decision trees. To apply MDS, we have to extract a rank ordered (dis-)

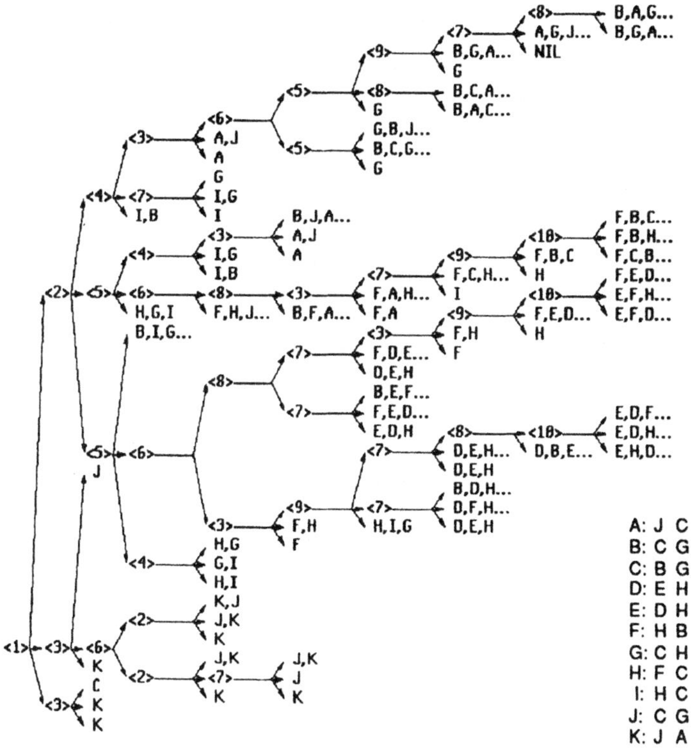

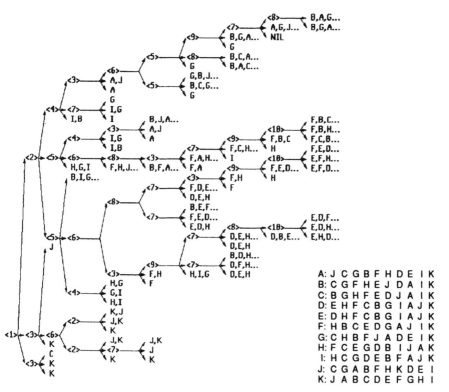

A:	J	C	G	B	F	H	D	E	I	K
B:	C	G	F	H	E	J	D	A	I	K
C:	B	G	H	F	E	D	J	A	I	K
D:	E	H	F	C	B	G	I	A	J	K
E:	D	H	F	C	B	G	I	A	J	K
F:	H	B	C	E	D	G	A	J	I	K
G:	C	H	B	F	J	A	D	E	I	K
H:	F	C	E	G	D	B	I	J	A	K
I:	H	C	G	D	E	B	F	A	J	K
J:	C	G	A	B	F	H	K	D	E	I
K:	J	A	B	C	D	E	F	G	H	I

(a) An example of a complex decision tree. (b) The class similarity matrix for the tree.

Fig.2. A decision tree and the class similarity matrix.

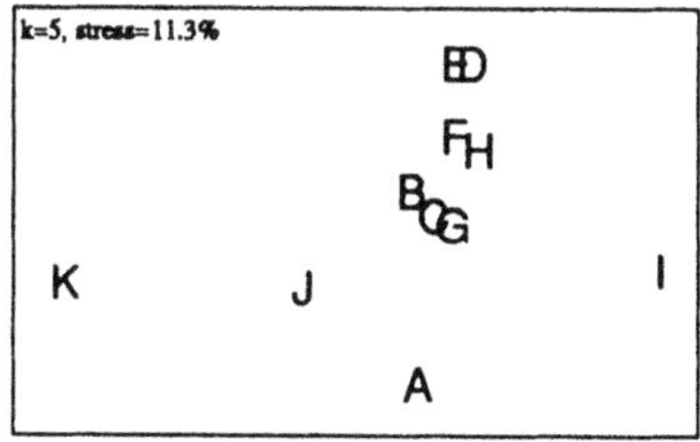

Fig. 3. The two-dimentional class space extracted from Fig.2(b).

similarity of some feature on decision trees. Currently, KAISER extracts a mutual similarity of classes, by counting and sorting the nodes which contain every pair of classes, assuming that similar classes should appear in similar places in a decision tree. Figure 2 shows an example of a decision tree and the class similarity matrix extracted from the tree. The first row of this matrix means that class "A" appears together with class "J" most frequently. By applying MDS to this matrix, we can get a two-dimensional space as shown in Figure 3. If we look into this chart, we can get several intuitions, e.g., classes "B, C, G" seem to belong to the same cluster, there seems to exist two axes from "K" to "I" and from "E, D" to "A".

Although I haven't yet implemented the code to detect the global improprieties representing these intuitions from this chart, some domain experts stated that this chart itself is sometimes very implicative and effective to remind them new attributes and class hierarchies.

4.4 Selection of the Next Point to Ask

The next step is to determine which node should be asked next by taking into consideration the position of the node in the decision tree and the combination of improprieties. Although this knowledge is actually realized by arithmetic operations over gravities of each impropriety and support factors in case of semantic improprieties, the main policy of this step will be summarized as follows:

(1) Semantic improprieties take precedence over structural ones.

(2) An impropriety that recommends a modification of the tree takes precedence over those that require refinement of domain knowledge.

(3) An impropriety that recommends structural reconstruction of the tree takes precedence over those that only prune or change the labels of nodes.

(4) An impropriety related with an upper node (i.e., near to the root) takes precedence.

4.5 Questionnaire Generation

If it is possible to offer the best recommendation based on the detected impropriety itself, we don't need this step to generate the questionnaire. With some simple improprieties this will be possible, but not with most. Therefore, combinations of improprieties, especially combinations of structural and semantic ones, are important clues for identifying underlying fundamental improprieties. Figure 4 illustrates the role of the questionnaire generation knowl-

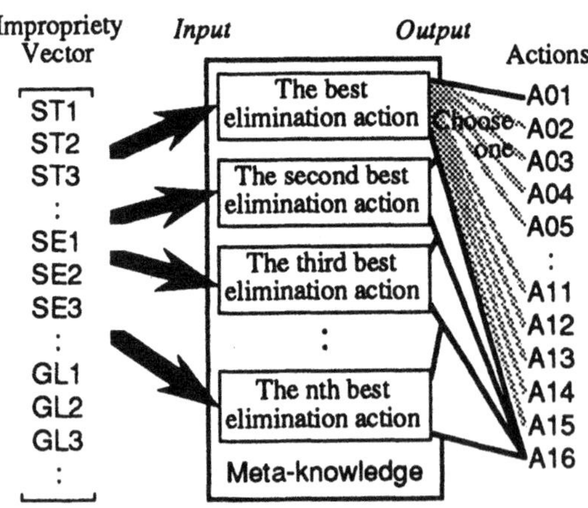

Fig. 4. Questionnaire generation as classification.

edge. The input to the questionnaire generation module is a (possibly null) list of improprieties, and the output is an ordered list of explanation and elimination actions. Current elementary actions are described as follows:

(A01) Name the class of a leaf.

(A02) Give new examples that will arrive to the current node.

(A03) Give the domain knowledge that will explain the current node (or one of its predecessors).

(A04) Merge current node with one of its siblings.

(A05) Change the node into a leaf of its major class.

(A06) Remove the examples of the minor class.

(A07) Further separate the class of a node.

(A08) Give new attributes to separate the class of a node.

(A09) Merge two siblings and generate a subtree from the union of their examples

(A10) Merge two siblings and ignore the examples of one of them.

(A11) Generate automatically a new attribute to discriminate a pair of classes by generating a separate tree for the examples belonging only to this pair of classes.

(A12) Merge two classes into a single one and rebuild the tree.

(A13) Refine domain knowledge.

(A14) Graft a condition to node and expand the tree.

(A15) Accept the suggestion of class for node.

(A16) No action (cancel the impropriety).

This is what we want to do in this last step of questionnaire generation; however, because of the wide variety of combinations and weak theoretical aspects in the impropriety (i.e., meta) domain, it's quite difficult to prepare these heuristics. The first version of KAISER [8,11] employed hand coded heuristics, which soon turned to be unsatisfactory. The second (and latest) version of KAISER adopts a recursive learning architecture named Meta-KAISER [12] to acquire the meta-heuristics as well while KAISER is learning the experts' domain.

5 Meta-knowledge Acquisition

As shown in the previous section, given a decision tree, KAISER uses its impropriety detection knowledge to generate a (possibly null) list of improprieties for a selected node in the tree. When working together with Meta-KAISER, this list is then applied by the system to the decision trees representing the impropriety meta-domain, obtaining as a result a questionnaire presented to the expert to help him by suggesting different actions to take to resolve the improprieties.

From the expert's reaction to the way KAISER treats improprieties in the expert domain's decision tree, Meta-KAISER collects new positive and negative examples for the impropriety domain in the background and uses these examples to refine its impropriety domain decision tree when the expert makes a claim for changing the recommendation of KAISER and agrees to invoke Meta-KAISER.

It is already known that the performance of a knowledge-based system is heavily dependent on knowledge representation. In representing the impropriety knowledge (for instance, to determine an elementary action) of Meta-KAISER, we investigated two kinds of representations that determine: (1) the position in questionnaire for each elementary action; (2) and the elementary action for each position in questionnaire. Eventually, we decided to employ the latter, because (i) when we define a new action, we usually have to wait for a long time to get enough examples for generating a reliable tree for the action if we use the former, while we can incorporate even one example if we use the latter; and (ii) it's usually quite difficult to acquire examples for subordinate positions for each action for the former, whereas we can prepare significant number of trees (i.e., number of elimination actions whose order is significant) as many as we need if we use the latter.

Figure 5 shows a tentative decision tree for the elimination actions on the first position. When an expert chooses another action during the session of KAISER, Meta-KAISER stores the choice for future revisions of the meta-knowledge. Currently Meta-KAISER pro-

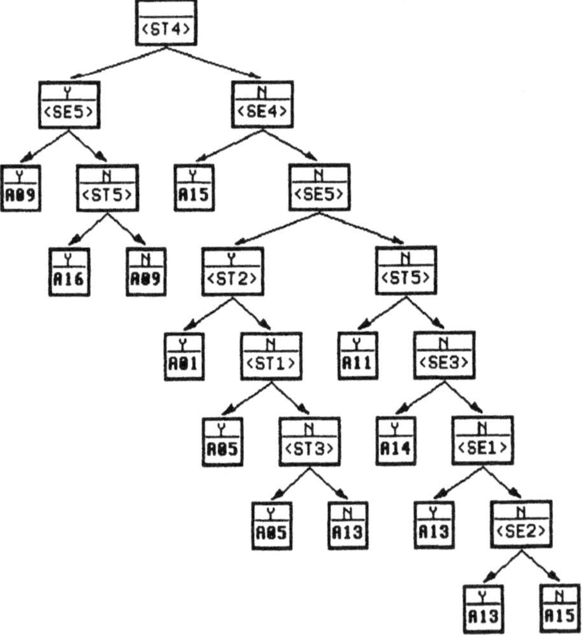

Fig. 5. An example of an impropriety domain decision tree.

poses only the first position, and all other possible actions (resp. explanations) are added by applying action (resp. explanation) generation functions which spontaneously generate their own actions (resp. explanations) if possible.

When defining new improprieties or actions (resp. explanations), a domain expert has to ask a system developer of KAISER to describe impropriety detection functions or action/explanation generation functions. Although this step is difficult to automate, we hope this need will be eventually diminished as we accumulate most functions by using Meta-KAISER for several domains.

6 Implementation

The current version of KAISER is implemented on Symbolics' LISP machine using Common-Lisp and OPS5 (expanded to deal with Lisp data structures and unification functions, e.g., LIST and MEMBER). The inductive learner and user interface including the questionnaire generation and interaction driver module are written in Common-Lisp. The impropriety detector, selector and interpreter were originally using OPS5. They are currently being replaced by Lisp functions with the development of the meta-knowledge generated by Meta-KAISER.

The initial decision tree is learned as a Lisp expression, and converted into OPS5 working memory as shown in Figure 6(a). Each node in the tree is represented as a working memory element with statistical information about the node, such as the number of samples in the node and the information gain of the attribute used at the node. The impropriety knowledge is represented in OPS5 rules as shown in Figure 6(b). The impropriety detection rules are applied to the node elements, and detect improprieties that are also represented by the working memory elements associated to the tree by indexing the node elements. The impropriety selection and interpretation rules work together to combine the improprieties and pick up the most important one to ask next. When all of these rules are fired, the questionnaire is generated by applying the action and explanation generation functions, and presented to the expert. According to the response of the expert, the node elements are reconstructed, and the above process is repeated until all the improprieties are eliminated. Finally, KAISER converts the elements back into the same expression as the initial tree. This internal expression is easily converted into Lisp functions, C functions or OPS5 rules according to the specific necessities.

When the meta-knowledge is acquired by Meta-KAISER, the detected improprieties are directly mapped to the actions and explanations without the interpretation rules. The detection and selection rules can be used as they are, or can be replaced by Lisp functions when their specifications are fixed.

Currently, a subset kernel of KAISER is also being implemented in C on UNIX workstation, which can be installed with the meta-knowledge developed by the fullset Lisp version KAISER and will be distributed to the domain experts.

```
(node ^no 1 ^type COND ^attr C2H4_C2H2 ^gain 1.3774192 ^nsamp 42 ^consists_of (OH PD AC) ^depth 0)
(link ^from 1 ^to 2 ^val (LEFT))
(node ^no 2 ^type COND ^attr C2H6 ^gain 0.49123737 ^nsamp 28 ^consists_of (AC OH) ^depth 1 ^parent 1)
(link ^from 2 ^to 5 ^val (M))
(node ^no 5 ^type LEAF ^nsamp 1 ^consists_of (AC) ^depth 3 ^parent 2)
                                    :
(stab ^attr C2H6 ^val M ^siblings (L S))
                                    :
(support ^of 5 ^by OH-0 ^class OH ^factor 1.0)
                                    :
(impropriety ^id G0234 ^at 5 ^type STRUCTURAL  name NOISY-LEAF ^ask G0523 ^recommends ASK)
(impropriety ^id G0339 ^at 5 ^type SEMANTIC ^name CONTRADICTORY ^will_be OH ^ask G0523 ^recommends MODIFY)
(impropriety ^id G0437 ^at 5 ^type SEMANTIC ^name TWIN-IMMEDIATE-SIBLINGS ^related_to (4 6) ^will_be OH ^ask G0523
        ^recommends MODIFY)
(impropriety ^id G0523 ^at 5 ^type DERIVED ^name COMBINE-SAME-SUPPORT ^derived_from (G0234 G0339 G0437)
        ^will_be OH ^ask SELF ^recommends MODIFY)
```

(a) Representation of a decision tree and improprieties in the working memory.

```
(defp NOISY-LEAF
  (detect)
  (thresholds ^noisy-leaf <nn>)
  (node ^no <no> ^nsamp < <nn>)
  -->
  (make impropriety ^id (lisp (get-ID)) ^at <no> ^type STRUCTURAL ^name NOISY-LEAF ^ask SELF ^recommends ASK))

(defp TWIN-IMMEDIATE-SIBLINGS
  (detect)
  (node ^no <pa> ^attr <aa>)
  (link ^from <pa> ^to <t1> ^val <v1>)
  (link ^from <pa> ^to { <t2> > <t1> } ^val <v2>)
  (link ^from <pa> ^to { <t3> > <t2> } ^val <v3>)
  (stab ^attr <aa> ^val @in <v2> ^siblings { @has <v1> @has <v2> })
  (node ^no <t1> ^type LEAF ^class <cc>)
  (node ^no <t3> ^type LEAF ^class <cc>)
  -->
  (make impropriety ^id (lisp (get-ID)) ^at <t2> ^type SEMANTIC ^name TWIN-IMMEDIATE-SIBLINGS
                  ^related_to (lisp (list <t1> <t3>)) ^will_be <cc> ^ask SELF ^recommends MODIFY))

(defp COMBINE-SAME-SUPPORT
  (derive)
  (impropriety ^at <at> ^id <id1> ^will_be <cc> ^ask SELF)
  (impropriety ^at <at> ^id <id2> ^will_be <cc> ^ask SELF)
 -(impropriety ^at <at> ^name COMBINE-SAME-SUPPORT)
  -->
  (bind <id0> (lisp (get-ID)))
  (modify 2 ^ask <id0>)
  (modify 3 ^ask <id0>)
  (make impropriety ^id <id0> ^at <at> ^type DERIVED ^name COMBINE-SAME-SUPPORT
                  ^derived_from (lisp (list <id1> <id2>)) ^will_be <cc> ^ask SELF))

(defp SELECT-SEMANTIC
  (select)
  (impropriety ^at <aa> ^type SEMANTIC ^ask SELF ^id <id>)
  (impropriety ^at <aa> ^type STRUCTURAL ^ask SELF)
  -->
  (modify 3 ^ask <id>))
```

(b) Rule representation of impropriety knowledge.

Fig.6. Knowledge representation in KAISER using OPS5.

7 An Example

This section illustrates the knowledge acquisition process by a small example of gas analysis of oil insulated electric transformers. When some problems occur in the electric transformer, the insulation oil is dissolved and several kinds of characteristic gas arise. By inspecting the gas composition chart as shown in Figure 7, a human expert can guess the kind of problem occurred in the transformer. To realize this behavior, the chart is represented by sixteen attributes as shown in Figure 8. Forty two charts are prepared for learning examples. Each of the examples belongs to a class either AC (ArC discharge), PD (Partial Discharge) or OH (Over Heat). Initial domain knowledge is shown in Figure 9. For example, AC-1 rep-

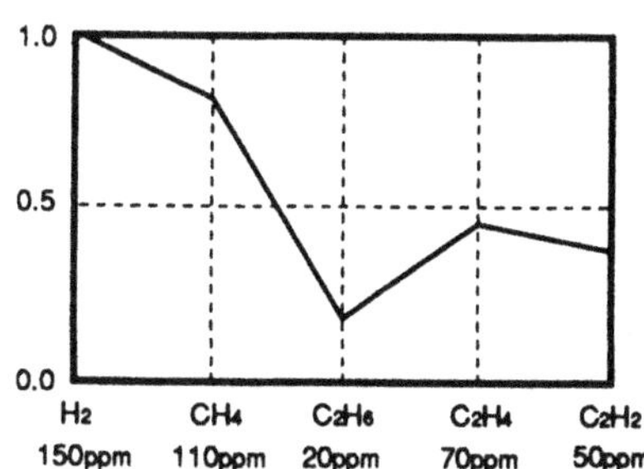

Fig. 7. An example of the gas composition chart.

H2, CH4, C2H6, C2H4 and C2H2:
Normalized contents of disolved gas. (Range: LL,L,M,S,SS)

H2_CH4, H2_C2H6, H2_C2H4, H2_C2H2, CH4_C2H6, CH4_C2H4, CH4_C2H2, C2H6_C2H4, C2H6_C2H2 and C2H4_C2H2:
Relative comparisons of contents. (Range: LEFT, EVEN, RIGHT)

DOMINANT:
Dominant gas. (Range: H2, CH4, C2H2, C2H4, C2H6)

Fig. 8. Attributes used for the gas chart analysis.

```
;;; Explanation knowledge
(define-Eknow AC-1 AC
   (Econd (H2_C2H6 LEFT) (H2_CH4 LEFT)) (Dcond) (Pcond))
(define-Eknow AC-2 AC
   (Econd (C2H6 LL) (C2H4_C2H2 LEFT))
   (Dcond) (Pcond (C2H6 L)))
(define-Eknow OH-0 OH
   (Econd (C2H4_C2H2 LEFT)) (Dcond) (Pcond))
(define-Eknow PD-0 PD
   (Econd (H2_CH4 LEFT) (CH4_C2H2 RIGHT))
   (Dcond) (Pcond))

;;; Derivation knowledge (Three out of thirty)
(define-Dknow H2_CH4
   (get-AB-AXBX H2_C2H6 CH4_C2H6))
(define-Dknow H2_CH4
   (get-AB-AXBX H2_C2H4 CH4_C2H4))
(define-Dknow H2_CH4
   (get-AB-AXBX H2_C2H2 CH4_C2H2))

;;; Attribute knowledge (One out of fifteen)
(define-Aknow H2_CH4 (LEFT EVEN RIGHT)
   (Merge (LEFT EVEN) (EVEN LEFT RIGHT) (RIGHT EVEN)))
```

Fig. 9. Domain knowledge for the gas chart analysis.

resents that the content of small gas like H2 is usually bigger than larger gas like C2H6 or C2H4 when the arc discharge occurs (because of the high dissolving power of arc). Figure 10 shows the initial decision tree generated from the forty two examples. Figure 11 shows the final decision tree acquired through eighteen questions and answers, which are generated out of thirty-two structural and eleven semantic improprieties. A human expert accepted eight recommendations out of the eighteen, selected four alternative choices and ignored the other six. The following shows three characteristic questionnaires:

Q01> There is no domain knowledge that explains the class **AC** of leaf 5. **OH-0** insists that the class will be **OH**. The classes of the siblings are also **OH**s. Leaf 5 has only one example.

Recommendation: Change the class of this leaf to **OH** according to **OH-0** and the siblings.

Choices 0) Accept the recommendation.
1) Describe/Edit domain knowledge to satisfy this leaf/node.
2) Leave it as is.
3) Invoke Meta-KAISER.

Choose [default 0]: **0**

(Three questionnaires are omitted.)

Q05> There is no domain knowledge that explains the class **AC** of leaf 25. **AC-1** insists that it will lack the condition on **H2_C2H6** to be **AC**. **PD-0** insists that the class will be **PD**.

Recommendation: Satisfy the Econds of **AC-1** (class **AC**) by changing this leaf to a node of attribute **H2_C2H6**.

Choices 0) Accept the recommendation.
1) Change the class of this leaf to **PD** according to **PD-0**.
2) Describe/Edit domain knowledge to satisfy this leaf/node.
3) Leave it as is.
4) Invoke Meta-KAISER.

Choose [default 0]: **0**

(Two questionnaires are omitted.)

Q08> According to the derivation knowledge, the conditions to this leaf 20 are inconsistent. There must be conflicts among the facts that **C2H4_C2H2** is **RIGHT**, **CH4_C2H4** is **EVEN** and **CH4_C2H2** is **LEFT**.

Recommendation: Change the class to **ERROR**.

Choices 0) Accept the recommendation.
1) Describe/Edit domain knowledge to satisfy this leaf/node.
2) Leave it as is.
3) Invoke Meta-KAISER.

Choose [default 0]: **3**

***** Enter Meta-KAISER *****

Twenty-seven examples have been stored since the last update of meta-knowledge. In total, ninety-two examples are available.
Shall we generate new meta-knowledge from them? (Yes, No, Edit or Save) **Yes**.
Learning meta-knowledge.... Done.

MQ01> Leaf 5 consists of two different classes, **A04** and **A06**. There is no domain knowledge that explains the class **A04** nor **A06** of leaf 5. Leaf 5 has only three examples.

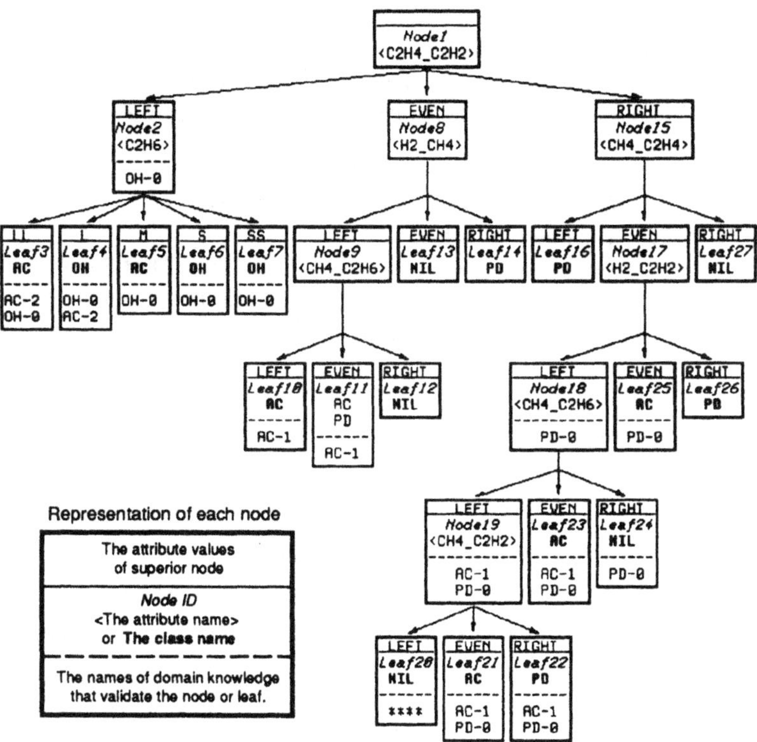

Fig. 10. The initial decision tree for the gas chart analysis.

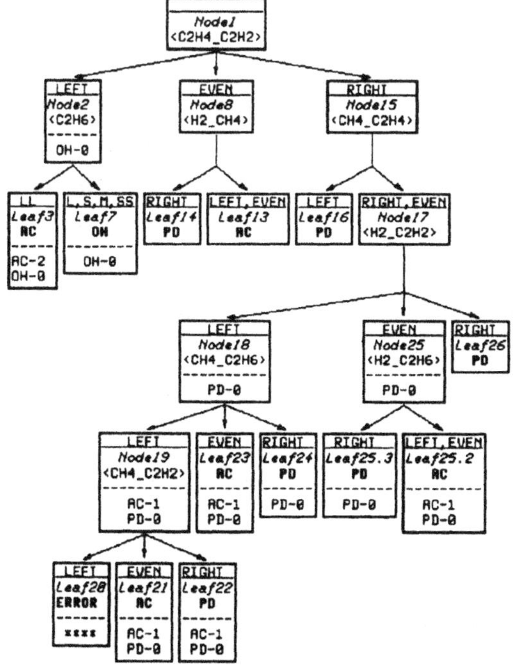

Fig. 11. The final decision tree for the gas chart analysis.

Recommendation: Change the class of this leaf to the major class **A04**.
Choices 0) Accept the recommendation.
1) Describe/Edit domain knowledge to satisfy this leaf/node.
2) Add new attributes to separate the conflicting classes **A04** and **A06**.
3) Leave it as is.
Choose [default 0]: **0**

(The rest of meta-level questionnaires are omitted.)

All of the improprieties have been eliminated.
Do you want to use this new knowledge from now on? (Yes, No, Edit or Save) **Yes**.
Meta-knowledge was updated. Return to the questionnaire **Q08** of domain level session...

(The rest of questionnaires are omitted.)

Q01 was generated from one structural impropriety, ST1 (noisy node) and two semantic improprieties, SE1 (contradictory explanation) and SE4 (Twin immediate siblings). The system recommended to change the class of this small leaf 5 from AC to OH, because a piece of domain knowledge OH-0 insists that the class will be OH and because the immediate siblings of leaf 5 belong to the same class OH. Q05 recommends to expand a path by grafting a condition H2_C2H6 based on the semantic impropriety SE3 (near-miss explanation), which insists that the path may (must) miss the condition H2_C2H6 to be the class AC. Such a problem (i.e., over-fitting) often arises, because of the lack of the counter examples that may (must) exist when we can prepare enough examples. Q08 insists that the combination of conditions to the leaf 20 is inconsistent according to the derivation knowledge, although the paths to the siblings (leaf 21 and leaf 22) are consistent. It recommends to change the class to a special label ERROR.

Here, the expert selected the choice No. 3 to invoke Meta-KAISER and refine the meta-knowledge. Meta-KAISER has stored twenty-seven examples since the last update. Meta-KAISER conducts (meta-) knowledge acquisition based on structural improprieties since the meta-level domain knowledge is not yet prepared. After eliminating all of the improprieties, Meta-KAISER asks if the new knowledge should be used immediately or saved for future use, and resumes domain KAISER to continue the domain level session.

Other major revisions of the domain level are: (1) Generalizing leaf 11 that originally consists of inseparable examples of classes AC and PD into a leaf of class AC; (2) Merging leaves 12 and 13 into leaf 9 to make a generalized leaf 13 in final tree; (3) Merging NIL leaf 27 into the sibling node 17 according to the attribute knowledge on CH4_C2H4; and (4) Changing the class of NIL leaf 24 to PD according to the domain knowledge PD-0.

8 Evaluation

Table 1 shows the comparison of the initial and the final decision trees in two experimental domains. In both cases, the size of the final tree is smaller than the initial one, while the number of explained nodes of the final tree is larger than that of the initial tree. They respec-

Table 1. Comparison of the initial and final decision trees in two domains.

Domain The number of attributes / classes / examples	**Gas analysis** 16 / 3 / 42		**Electric switchgeer** 6 / 4 / 96	
	Initial	Final	Initial	Final
Number of conditions	8	8	20	20
Number of leaves	19	13	41	33
Total number of nodes	27	21	61	53
Depth	5	5	3	4
Number of explained nodes	15 (56%)	13 (62%)	28 (46%)	32 (60%)
Classification accuracy	95%*	95%	92%*	90%
Number of Eknows	4	4	8	10
Number of revisions	12		15	

* The examples in the jumble leaves are assumed to be miss-classified.

tively suggest that the final trees are more generalized and understandable for the experts. Since the expert decided to ignore some noisy examples in the electric switchgeer subject, the classification accuracy of the final tree for this subject is worse than the initial one. Although there is no appropriate way to figure out the efficiency of KAISER, the effect is validated by the experts' assertion that it would have been impossible to construct the diagnosis knowledge for the electric switchgeer domain because the knowledge was too extensive and complicated for them to refine it without the systematic support of KAISER.

9 Conclusion

Inductive learning is a powerful technique not only for constructing knowledge bases but also for giving an expert various mental stimuli to make him/her recognizes missing knowledge. To enhance this process, KAISER conducts a dialogue arguing over various kinds of improprieties arisen while iterating induction and explanation on tentative examples and domain knowledge. The major objective of this research is to establish the (meta-) knowledge base for detecting, interpreting and eliminating the improprieties and achieve intelligent knowledge acquisition. Since it is quite difficult to describe such knowledge, KAISER has been enhanced with Meta-KAISER, a meta-knowledge learner which watches the domain level interaction and refines the meta-knowledge for itself. Currently, KAISER is being applied to several diagnosis problems, such as electric motors, tap-changers in electric transformers and gas insulated switchgears. In parallel, Meta-KAISER is being used to incorporate the global improprieties and new elimination actions through these subjects. The authors hope we can eventually refine the meta-knowledge base when it will be applied to and evaluated through these problems.

References

1. J. B. Kruskal: Multidimensional Scaling by Optimizing Goodness of Fit to a Non-metric Hypothesis. Psychometrika 29, 1964
2. O. Kakusho and R. Mizoguchi: A New Algorithm for Non-Linear Mapping with Applications to Dimension and Cluster Analyses. Pattern Recognition 1, 1983
3. J. R. Quinlan: Induction of Decision Trees. Machine Learning 1, 1986
4. C. J. Matheus and L. A. Rendell: Constructive Induction On Decision Trees. Proc. of IJCAI'89, 1989
5. P. B. Brazdil and L. Torgo: Knowledge Acquisition via Knowledge Integration. Current Trends in Knowledge Acquisition, B. Wielinga, J. Boose et al. (Eds.), 1990
6. G. Pagallo and D. Haussler: Boolean Feature Discovery in Empirical Learning. Machine Learning 5, 1990
7. M. J. Pazzani and D. Kibler: The Utility of Knowledge in Inductive Learning. UCI Tech. Rep., TR-90-18, 1990
8. K. Tsujino, M. Takegaki and S. Nishida: A Knowledge Acquisition System That Aims as Integrating Inductive Learning and Explanation-based Reasoning. Proc. of JKAW'90, 1990
9. M. J. Pazzani and C. A. Brunk: Detecting and Correcting Errors in Rule-Based Expert Systems: An Integration of Empirical and Explanation-based Learning. Knowledge Acquisition 3, 1991
10. C. J. Matheus: The Need for Constructive Induction. Proc. of ML'91, 1991
11. K. Tsujino and S. Nishida: A Knowledge Acquisition System driven by Inductive Learning and Deductive Explanation: KAISER. (In Japanese.) Journal of Japanese Society for Artificial Intelligence 7, 1992
12. V. G. Dabija, K. Tsujino and S. Nishida: Theory Formation in the Decision Trees Domain. (In English.) Journal of Japanese Society for Artificial Intelligence 7, 1992

KNOWLEDGE REFINEMENT USING KNOWLEDGE ACQUISITION AND MACHINE LEARNING METHODS

Claire Nedellec and Karine Causse

CNRS & Laboratoire de Recherche en Informatique
Equipe Inférence et Apprentissage
Université Paris-Sud, Bt. 490
F-95405 Orsay Cédex France
email : cn@lri.lri.fr
causse@lri.lri.fr

ISoft
Chemin du Moulon
F-91190 Gif sur Yvette, France
email : cn@isoft.fr

Abstract

APT system integrates Machine Learning (ML) and Knowledge Acquisition (KA) methods in the same framework. Both kinds of methods closely cooperate to concur in the same purpose : the acquisition, validation and maintenance of problem-solving knowledge. The methods are based on the same assumption : knowledge acquisition and learning are done through experimentation, classification and comparison of concrete cases. This paper details APT's mechanisms and shows through examples and applications how APT underlying principles allow various methods to fruitfully collaborate.

1 Introduction

We present APT: A system that integrates machine learning and knowledge acquisition methods to acquire, validate and maintain problem-solving knowledge in the same framework. We will first present this framework, then detail APT's mechanisms and show how their underlying principles can in general be put into practice. Finally, we show the generality of this approach through its use for various problem-solving tasks.

1.1 The Knowledge Acquisition Framework

The Life Cycle of a KBS can be organized into four fundamental phases: acquisition, implementation, validation and maintenance.

In the *acquisition* phase, expert and knowledge engineer try to elicit all the elements of the expertise (the problem solving methods and all the objects concerned) and to structure all this knowledge in an organized model of how to solve the problem. In the *implementation* phase, the system defined by the preceding model is built into a working computer system. In the *validation* phase, the system is tested in its environment to verify that it follows the specifications, and finally, in the *maintenance* phase, the system must be adapted to the evolutions of its environment.

Our framework encompasses those four phases into one integrated knowledge acquisition and learning system. Indeed, this separation in four phases of the life cycle of a KBS is actually an *idealization* of the real evolution of a system. Actually, the phases overlap one over the other. For instance, validation is necessary at each phase of the life cycle, and after validation of the final system or during its maintenance, it might be necessary to re-construct part of the model of the system and to re-implement it, because of insufficiencies in the initial implementation, or simply because the requirements on the system have evolved. Eliciting knowledge, structuring it into a model, validating it on examples and maintaining the KBS are closely mingled activities.Therefore, we present a framework for integrating learning and knowledge acquisition in a system able to help a user not only in the acquisition phase but also in the validation and maintenance phases of a KBS.

To be able to cover the different phases of the life cycle, our framework is based on a system that learns to solve problems with the help of the expert: a learning apprentice. Through *experimentation* guided by the expert, the system can acquire reasoning and domain knowledge, validate this knowledge on new problems and if needed, extend, refine and revise its knowledge to cope with new problems and increase its performances.The integration of knowledge acquisition and learning techniques enables the system to correctly learn how to solve problems from *real concrete examples*. In this learning process, the system can diagnose deficiencies in the domain theory, and with, the help of the expert revise the theory according to the preceding findings. This knowledge acquisition process can be compared to a computer assisted *protocol analysis*.

[Aussenac 90], [Mitchell et al., 89], [Carbonell et al., 90] and [Morik, 89] explains that the best way to acquire knowledge in the perspective of problem solving is to use experience in problem-solving. The objects of expertise are not objects of the world, but a subjective view on those objects that are directly implied in the process of problem solving. Therefore, it is by analyzing and explaining expert's behavior while solving problems through protocol analysis that those objects of expertise can be accessed and acquired. In our framework, after a first manual phase for acquiring an initial domain theory (that might be incomplete and incorrect, and probably is), the system will refine the domain knowledge and acquire a pertinent view on the objects of the world, through their use in problem solving. The difference with Aussenac's approach is that instead of building a sophisticated model that the expert must validate, we have a system capable as LEAP, PRODIGY and MOBAL of using knowledge directly to solve problems. Therefore, we do not ask of the expert to validate the system's model, but its behavior.

Since the system is able to use the rules it learned to solve new cases of the problem, it can be used not only for acquisition, but also for *validation and maintenance*. When an error is discovered in the system's reasoning, it can be immediately repaired with the help of the expert, and as in the acquisition phase, the domain theory may be revised in consequence. In addition, the system may be used for *maintenance*, since it is quite easy to adapt the system to new requirements that stem from an evolution in the domain, whether this evolution concerns the theory of the domain or the methods for solving the problem.

1.2 The means for this framework

An important part of the framework we propose is the capability of the system for immediate *validation*, since what is learned can be immediately tested. In the domain of validation, two options exist [Lopez & al. 90]. The first option, structural validation, consists in a systematic search of inconsistencies (redundancies, etc.) in the domain, based on some syntactic criteria of consistency. The only way the expert may be involved in this validation phase is by giving some constraints of the domain that will be syntactically verified.

The second option is a functional validation of knowledge based on the resolution of concrete cases of the domain. If the learning tool behind the knowledge acquisition is a "black box," then only the results of the system can be tested. But when the learning tool is an interactive open learner, then this type of validation takes into account the *behavior* of the system and has a semantic character. The comparison of the behavior of the system with that of the expert on concrete cases not only validates the result given by the system but also the adequacy of the system's representation of the problem to the expert's representation. It is therefore possible to approach the expert's cognitive model with the system. Furthermore, the expert is not asked to evaluate an abstract model of the problem that the system possesses, but only to evaluate the system in the context of solving real, concrete cases that the expert knows perfectly how to solve.

This approach is not only well-suited for validation, but also allows the system to be corrected as soon as an error is detected (whether the error is relative to the final result or to a reasoning step of the system). Reasoning on concrete cases will then be an important asset for acquiring and refining knowledge, because the case establishes a context for learning and the right level of interaction between the system and the expert. This point is illustrated by APT's Problem Solver in section 2.2.

In this perspective, the second important part of our framework is the process of correcting errors as soon as a problem is detected, using this problem to point to an insufficiency in the knowledge. Two different cases can then appear: either the causes of the error are quite easy to identify in the context, or not. In the first case the expert can easily correct the cause of the failure, or an automatic learning process can be used to change automatically the knowledge bases of the system by adding new terms. This kind of automatic modification is limited to "simple" modifications such as the definition of a new general concept as a conjunction of more specific concepts and the expert's evaluation is generally needed. A semantic knowledge revision is not automatically feasible without the expert.

In the second case, the cause of the problem is quite hard to identify. Both the expert and the system together have to try to identify the cause of the failure and correct it. Indeed, the expert can not be asked directly to correct the systems knowledge without any more information when the error has been detected. Not only is it very difficult to locate the origin of the error simply on one case of failure, but also, the expert does not always understand perfectly the consequences of his modifications on the behavior of the system. Therefore, the system must help the expert to correctly identify the cause of the problem in the knowledge base, and then propose modifications by using the context of the problem, showing to the expert all the consequences of the proposed modifications to the behavior of the system. Finally, the system must make sure that the new knowledge and the modifications are correctly integrated into the knowledge base as it is illustrated by APT's refinement methodology in section 4.3. To insure a good interaction with the expert, the strategy we followed is to:

* use concrete cases as much as possible that are easier for the expert to evaluate,
* ask the expert only to evaluate and compare cases, not general knowledge,
* formulate all propositions of modifications on concrete cases and generalize them after they are accepted.

Finally, our framework allows to cover all phases of the life-cycle of the target KBS through experimentation of problem-solving on concrete cases with the help of the expert.

2 APT

2.1 APT's Architecture

These principles have been implemented in the APT system. APT's architecture is based on that of DISCIPLE, [Tecuci, Kodratoff, 90]. The following sections show how APT illustrates the general framework presented above. Our purpose is not to formally describe the Machine Learning and Knowledge Acquisition algorithms used. APT's algorithms are detailed in [Nedellec, 1991a]. The purpose is to describe the general features of the algorithms to show how it has been possible to fruitfully integrate them in the same system.

We will now present APT's knowledge bases, making a parallel with KADS' four layer model of expertise[1] [Wielienga & al 91]. The knowledge of the domain layer is represented in the Domain Theory, which describes the concepts of the domain and their possible relationships. The Domain Theory is represented by a semantic network where the relation IS-A is the transitive generality relation. So the concepts are hicrarchically organized and linked. This description of the knowledge of the domain is clearly separated from the description of the way it may be used to solve problems, allowing to control easily the consequences of the modifications of the knowledge bases.

The equivalent of the inference and task layers[2] are represented through a problem-solving rule base. APT will dynamically construct an instantiated task structure from these elementary rules to solve a given problem. Each rule is defined by the type of the problem that it solves, by the input data called pre-conditions and the output data called post-conditions. The pre-conditions of a rule contain the classes of objects of the domain theory to which the rule may be applied (the context) and the role that they play in the problem solving process of the rule. The post-conditions contain the classcs of the domain theory resulting from the application of the rule to the input classes. New classes may be introduced, old classes may be deleted and the state of the current classes may be changed by the execution of the rule, as it is done by STRIPS' operators [Fikes & al. 1971]. Input and output data are described at the same level of generality. Usually, APT's rules are rules that decompose a problem into more specific problems, called sub-problems. The sub-problems of a rule can either be decomposed again, and then they can be compared to a task in KADS, or be primitive actions (of a granularity equivalent to or smaller than KADS' primitive inferences). The fact that a sub-problem is primitive does not have to be predetermined, but only decided when constructing a specific task structure for a problem. It is therefore always possible to refine the primitive inferences by defining new problem-solving rules.

2.2 APT's Problem Solver

2.2.1 General principles

APT's Problem Solver constructs task structures to achieve particular goals by dynamically combining the rules defined in the rule base. As the rules are decomposition rules, the task structures take the form of decomposition trees where each node is a

---

[1] We do not claim that APT is an acquisition system for a KADS model of expertise, but simply that the knowledge acquired by APT can be well described within this framework.

[2] APT has simple tasks that are decomposed into sub-tasks to be executed sequentially, without tests nor iterations.

problem-solving rule provided by the rule base.

A task is described by the problem that it solves and its input and output. The *task* input/output are described by conjunctions of specific concepts of the Domain Theory. That means that these concepts are leaves of the hierarchies of concepts. But, the input/output of the *problem-solving rules* are defined by conjunctions of general concepts of the Domain Theory. Therefore, the generality level of the rule input/output is higher than those of the tasks, according to the generality relation IS-A defined in the Domain theory on the concepts.

At each step of the decomposition of the task into a task structure, the Problem Solver looks for all the rules of the base that may be applied to solve the current problem. The candidate rule must satisfy two conditions to be retained :

- the type of the problem of the candidate rule must be the same as the current problem.
- the description of the input/output classes of the rule must be more general than or equal to the context of the current problem according to the Domain Theory.

The selected rule completes the task structure and the sub-problems of the selected rule replace the current problem in the list of the problems to solve. The problem decomposition ends when all the problems to solve are elementary ones that cannot be decomposed further. The resulting task structure describes the elementary actions to execute to solve the task problem. These actions are the leaves of the decomposition tree.

2.2.2 Example

Let us give an example. Suppose that the aim of the Problem Solver is to build the task structure of a task T (Figure 1).

Task T	
Pre-conditions	Location of Box is the assembly line
	Location of Robot is the warehouse
Problem	Moving
Post-conditions	Location of Box and Robot is the warehouse

Figure 1 : Example of rule used by APT

We suppose that the Domain Theory describes all the concepts that may be involved in the move such as machines, robots, boxes, locations and so on.

In this example and in the following ones, we have simplified the representation language to improve the readability of the paper. In fact, the language used to represent the Domain Theory and the input and output of the rules is a restriction of First Order Logic without negation and functional terms [Nedellec, 91b]. So, the pre-conditions of task T are expressed by APT by the formulae :

Box(x) & location(x,y) & Assembly-Line(y) & Robot(z) & location(z,t) & Warehouse(t)

Using variables allows, for instance, to distinguish objects of the same class and their relations, represented in the same context. [Kodratoff & al., 91a], [Bisson, 92] study the expressive power of FOL compared with other representation languages.

The current problem that must be solved to decompose the task T is "*moving*". Rule R1 in Figure 2 may be applied as first rule. First, the current problem of the task and the problem of R1 are the same. Next, we suppose that the Domain Theory says that the concept of *object* is more general that the concept of *box*, (for instance, "*box IS-A object*") and that *line* is more general than *assembly line*. The pre-conditions (input) and post-conditions (output) of the candidate rule R1 are then more general than those of the task problem. Therefore rule R1 is applicable.

Rule R1	
Pre-conditions	Location of the Object is a line
	Location of the Robot is the warehouse
Problem	Moving
Sub-problems	Robot moves to the line
	Robot takes the object
	Robot moves to the warehouse
Post-conditions	Location of Object and Robot is the warehouse

Figure 2 : Example of rule used by APT

Once rule R1 is selected to accomplish a part of task T, the input and output descriptors of rule R1 are specialized into rule R1' (figure 3). Then rule R1' is integrated into the task structure of T. The specialization is done by replacing rule R1 descriptors by the corresponding descriptors of the current problem. In our example, *Object* is replaced by *Box* and *Line* by *Assembly Line.*

Once the specialized rule is integrated into the task structure, the problem of *Moving* which was the current problem is replaced by the sub-problems of *Robot moves to the assembly line*, *Robot takes the box* and *Robot moves to the warehouse*, in the list of the problems to solve.

Rule R1'	
Pre-conditions	Location of the *Box* is the assembly line
	Location of the Robot is the warehouse
Problem	Moving
Sub-problems	....

Figure 3 : A specific rule applicable to decompose T

2.2.3 Validation

These functionalities would be sufficient to decompose tasks using knowledge represented in the Domain Theory and the rule base if there would be one and only one way to decompose a task into rules. As we make the assumption that the knowledge description of the different bases may be incomplete and even incorrect, it is not certain that a task decomposition exists and that will be unique.

Therefore, as long as APT needs to acquire and revise knowledge, APT's Problem Solver needs the intervention of the expert to validate the task decomposition. Therefore, at each step of the task decomposition, APT asks the expert to evaluate the candidate rules that it has selected from the rule base and specialized as described above. For instance, APT's Problem Solver would propose to the expert the rule R1' (specialization of the rule R1) to build the first step of the task structure of T.

As the task decomposition is specific in the sense that it achieves a given goal in a *specific* context, the expert is not asked to reason about abstractions. The expert is confronted with a concrete solution to the problem, proposed by the system. This way of validating the behavior of the Problem Solver through experimentation allows the expert to use his own skill in solving problems to decide the validity of the system's proposition. By not asking general information of the expert, APT only asks him what he knows how to do best.

Whenever a rule misapplication is detected by the expert or whenever APT has no rule to propose, the expert is asked to give his own solution rule to build the current resolution step, according to the specific resolution context. APT's Problem Solver could be satisfied simply by recording the expert's specific solution. But before continuing the decomposition phase, APT's Problem Solver hands over the deal to APT's Learner. the role of APT's Learner is to exploit as much as possible the expert's solution by generalizing it to all cases where it could be applicable, and by revising the knowledge description of the Domain Theory if necessary through interaction with the expert. As APT knows the specific context of its failure, it is able to communicate with the expert in a concrete and efficient way by using the information related to the current resolution experimentation.

In that sense, APT has some common points with PROTOS [Bareiss 89]: it learns as a consequence of problem-solving, the system engaging in learning only when it fails to solve correctly a problem. In addition, APT, as PROTOS, learns from only few examples, being able, by using explanations and by generating its own examples, to generalize and learn correct rules from only one original expert-provided example. Therefore, APT, like PROTOS, is able to offer a wide range of assistance in the acquisition of domain knowledge and its refinement during problem solving. However, they differ in their learning mechanisms and the type of tasks solved. PROTOS' learning is case-based and instead of being based on generalization from examples, and APT is concerned with learning the decomposition of problem-solving rules and general heuristic rules, while PROTOS is specialized for classification tasks.

3 APT's Learner

APT's Learner uses methods of knowledge acquisition and of machine learning from examples [Kodratoff & Ganascia, 1986] to complete the expert's rule and then to generalize it at the best level of generality it can reach. Then for APT, this means that the learned rule must be applicable to as many cases as possible, different from the specific case for which the rule has been initially built by the expert, and must not be applicable in any wrong case. The generalization takes effect on the description of the input and of the output of the expert's rule. The description of the problem and its decomposition remains unchanged since the role of the generalization phase is only to extend the application scope of the rule.

The first stage consists in completing the expert's rule with explanations deduced from the Domain Theory. This rule will be further genralized. As the Domain Theory may be incorrect, the Learner uses a prudent generalization strategy called "smallest generalization steps strategy" detailed in [Nedellec, 1991a]. But this strategy is not always sufficient and the generalized rule may be nevertheless too general. It is then specialized by using some of the information acquired by applying the smallest generalization steps strategy.

The intervention of the expert is necessary if the over-generalization of the learned rule is caused by an insufficiently constrained description of its application scope or more seriously if the over-generalization is an indication that the Domain Theory must be revised. In both cases, examples are used by the generalization method to help the expert in the location of and the recovery from the errors of the description of the rule and the errors of the Domain Theory, so that the cause of the over-generalization disappears.

3.1 Completing the expert's solution

APT uses explanations to elicit and acquire the application conditions of reasoning rules. Although the expert's rule is specific, since it is proposed in the frame of a specific resolution, the application condition of the rule may be incomplete and subsequently too general because the expert forgets to mention concepts or needed relations between concepts. Some of them may be still only implicit. If the preconditions are not correctly elicited from the expert the learned rule will be overgeneralized and applicable to irrelevant situations. Therefore to complete the expert's rule, APT uses at the same time, a method issued from the Machine Learning field to automatically generate explanations and knowledge acquisition methods to obtain other explanations through an interaction with the expert.

APT's Learner builds explanations of the expert's rule, by looking in the Domain Theory for relations between the concepts of the rule conditions, (see saturation in [Rouveirol, 91]). These explanations justify the fact that the rule is applicable by showing how concepts occurring together in the same rule are semantically related in the Domain Theory. Therefore, the explanations allow to constrain the application scope of the expert's rule.

For example, if APT has no rule to solve the problem of *Moving* described above, the expert gives its own solution which may be something like rule R1'. Suppose that the expert forgets to specify in the pre-conditions the initial location of the *robot* in the *warehouse*. This might result in the application of the learned rule in wrong cases where the *robot* and the *box* are at the same place. Therefore, APT will propose to explain the initial location of the *robot* by searching in the Domain Theory for the various possible locations for a robot, such as "*Location of the Robot is the warehouse*".

Next, the expert is asked to select among the generated explanations those that he thinks to be the most relevant. These explanations use the expert's terminology since they are expressed by using the vocabulary of the Domain Theory, defined by the expert.

The expert has also the possibility to express the explanations that he may think of by studying the system's ones. In this case, the expert may use new concepts or relations not yet defined in the Domain Theory. This new vocabulary and its semantics are then integrated to the Domain Theory by APT, in an interactive process that will be described in section 4.3. APT's explanation language is the same as the rule condition language [Nedellec, 91b].

Thus, the explanation capability of APT not only allows to efficiently constrain the expert's example through an interaction between the expert and the system, but also allows to acquire new knowledge about the concepts of the domain and their interrelations.

The explanation capability of APT is not as sophisticated as the one found in PROTOS, for instance, because its explanation language is not as powerful as the PROTOS language. APT does not allow for example to express the idea of conditional explanation. However, APT has the capability to autonomously look in the Domain Theory for explanations of reasoning steps, linking automatically the two layers of knowledge, and symmetrically, it can use the expert's explanations at the reasoning level to enhance the domain layer. This capability of using a specific and concrete reasoning step to improve the Domain knowledge allows APT to fruitfully acquire Domain knowledge from the expert.

Next, the explanations are added as constraints to the expert's rule. The completed rule may then be used for the generalization process. This explanation phase is very important because if relevant explanations are missing, this will lead to the over-generalization of the learned rules as it will be shown below.

3.2 Generalizing the expert's rule

The aim of the generalization method is to find general rules in the search space, which are as less numerous as possible and as general as possible, without being applicable to wrong cases. They are called *target rules*. They are constructed by incrementally generalizing the expert's rule using automatically generated examples.

As the Domain Theory may be erroneous, the Learner uses a cautious generalization method applying the "smallest generalization step strategy" that first consists in building a lattice that represent the initial search space. The nodes of the lattice represent all the possible rule hypotheses among which the Learner searches for the target rules. The expert's rule is represented by the root of the lattice. The rule hypotheses are ordered in the lattice depending on their degree of generality. The generality relation between two rule hypothesis is determined by the generality relations in the Domain Theory between the concepts they use (see section 2.1). Two successive rule hypothesis in the lattice differ only in one concept changed on only one degree of generality in the corresponding hierarchy of the Domain Theory. To generalize from a node to a next one no dropping rule is applied, but only climbing in the hierarchies of concepts and properties. Therefore there is no possible intermediate hypothesis between two successive nodes. This allows to control the risk of over-generalization due to insufficiencies of the Domain Theory such as cautious generalization in MARVIN [Sammut and Banerji 86].

To validate general hypothesis, APT's generalization method uses examples which are specific rules automatically generated by analogy with the expert's rule. Building these rule examples consists in replacing the descriptors of the conditions of the expert's rule by other specific descriptors that belong to the same hierarchies in the domain theory and that are leaves of these hierarchies. The method for building examples is detailed in [Nedellec, 1991a].

Thus, the rule hypothesis lattice partitions the set of all the possible examples (all the automatically generated specific rules) in small independent example sets. Each small example set is labeled by the most specific rule hypothesis of the lattice, by which it is covered.

At the beginning of the generalization phase, the expert's rule is the only valid rule hypothesis in the lattice. APT tries to validate one of the closest rule hypothesis of the lattice, by submitting to the expert one example labeled by this closest rule hypothesis. If the example is accepted (it is called positive), the corresponding rule hypothesis is validated, otherwise (it is called negative), the corresponding rule hypothesis is definitively rejected (it is similar to [Smith & Rosenbloom, 90] who use near misses to prune the search space).

More generally, any candidate rule hypothesis is considered to be valid by APT's Learner, if all the less general hypothesis in the lattice are valid and if the expert validates one example from the example set which is labeled by this candidate rule hypothesis (as in the version space algorithm [Mitchell, 1978]). The validation of the rule hypothesis is then propagated in a breadth first way along the lattice by the acceptation of submitted examples, until it is stopped in all the directions, by the rejection of submitted examples. An example of this propagation in the generalization lattice is given in section 4.1.

This way of interacting with the expert by using examples is much more helpful than directly asking him which degree of generalization is acceptable, since it is generally much easier for an expert to reason about concrete examples. Moreover, the examples submitted to the expert are ordered in such a way that two successive examples are as semantically close as possible since they are attached to the closest hypotheses. In this way, the successive questions asked to the expert are less likely to appear irrelevant or surprising and as the examples are automatically generated, the expert is not asked to provide examples.

By doing more than controlling the generalization and interacting in a user friendly way with the expert, by partitioning the search space, this method also helps in the detection and the correction of errors in the learned rules and in the Domain Theory.

3.3 Evaluating the learned rules

At the end of the generalization phase, the most general valid hypothesis are considered as the target rules that the system was looking for. This is true only if the expert has forgotten no explanations for his initial rule solution and if the Domain Theory that determined the generality relation between concepts is complete and correct.

If neither of the assumptions are verified, the Learner has no means of detecting the problem, since the learned concept is consistent with everything the Learner knows (e.g. the examples and the concept description language). This classical problem in knowledge refinement accepts three types of solutions. First, other strategic information about what is a good degree of generality may be used, but they are difficult to acquire. Second, what is learned may be tested and improved through many examples as with learning in the limit methods such as CLINT [De Raedt, 91]. Third, an expert of the domain may be directly asked to validate the learned concepts [Sammut & Banerji 86], [Benbasat & Dhaliwal 89]. In this paper we are interested in the latter approach. On the one hand, the use of knowledge acquisition techniques allows to reduce the number of examples required compared with learning in the limit methods. But on the other hand, the expert is asked to evaluate learned rules and this evaluation may be less reliable than the example evaluation, depending on the domain and the task.

If the expert accepts the learned rules, they are added to the rule base and they are not only applicable to the initial specific problem, but also to many other problems. If the expert does not validate one of the learned rules because it is too general and is applicable on negative cases, he has the possibility to definitively reject it or to ask APT's Learner to analyze it, in order to find the causes of the over-generalization. This is done by specializing the over-generalized rule, backtracking node by node through the lattice and submitting to the expert the intermediate rule hypothesis corresponding to these nodes that had been validated during the generalization phase. The backtrack stops when the expert accepts a rule hypothesis. But this accepted hypothesis is also not satisfactory, because it is too specific. It does not cover the positive examples that had lead to the over-generalized learned rule.

APT cannot find on its own a good degree of generalization; it needs additional knowledge from the expert to express a rule that is neither too specific nor too general, a rule that would be just between the accepted hypothesis and the overgeneralized hypothesis produced by the next generalization step. This new rule must no longer cover negative examples. This task would also be difficult for the expert if no further information was provided by APT. But by having applied its smallest generalization step strategy, APT is able to help the expert.

Due to the fact that the generalization lattice partitions the example set in small independent sets, all the negative examples that must be excluded from the application scope of the new rule belong to the same small example set. This particular inconsistent set is labeled by the over-generalized hypothesis produced by the next generalization step. This means that the new rule must divide in two parts the inconsistent set, so that it covers all the positive examples and no negative ones.

In addition, as a consequence of the lattice properties, this inconsistent set is *as small as possible* because two successive nodes differ only by one concept generalized on one degree. Consequently, the examples of the same set are semantically close because they use concepts that are close in the hierarchies of the Domain Theory. They are then easier to compare, and the concepts concerned with the problem of over-generalization, much easier to identify. The problem of finding the right rule is then reduced to the more simple one of acquiring knowledge to distinguish the positive examples of a small example set from the negative ones. In this way, APT is able to provide means to detect the cause of the problem and correct it as it is shown by the following example.

4 Example

We will illustrate the method with the classical arch problem. This toy example is not representative of all the capabilities of the system, but it allows to explain in a simple manner how the algorithm works and, although it seems to be very simple, it points at some interesting problems. The concepts and the properties used in the rule base are defined in the Domain Theory, a part of which is described in Figure 4.

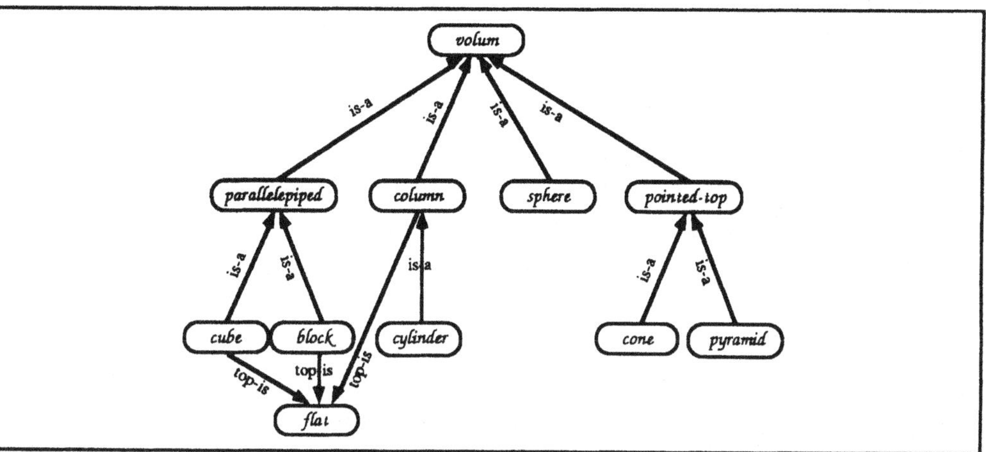

Figure 4: A part of the domain theory

4.1 Generalization

Let us suppose APT's Problem Solver was decomposing the task of building a bridge and it has no rules to describe how to build the arches of the bridge by using blocks of concrete. Then the expert gives his own rule solution. Rule R_e in Figure 5 is the expert's rule completed by explanations.

R_e :	IF there are three blocks x, y and z made of concrete		
	THEN solve the problem of	building an arch	
	by solving the subproblems	FIRST,	ERECT the block x
		NEXT,	ERECT the block y
		FINALLY,	LAY the block z

Figure 5 : An expert's example of rule

A part of the generalization lattice corresponding to the generalization of the three *blocks* is represented by Figure 6. The generalization of the concepts *made-of* and *concrete* are not represented in order to simplify the example. Consequently, the dimension of the represented lattice is three. The expert's rule is represented by the node at the root, labeled R_{000}. To validate nodes R_{001} and R_{100}, APT proposes examples where the bases of the arch are *cubes* (which are not *blocks* but *parallelepipeds*). To validate R_{010}, APT proposes an examples where the top of the arch is a *cube* .

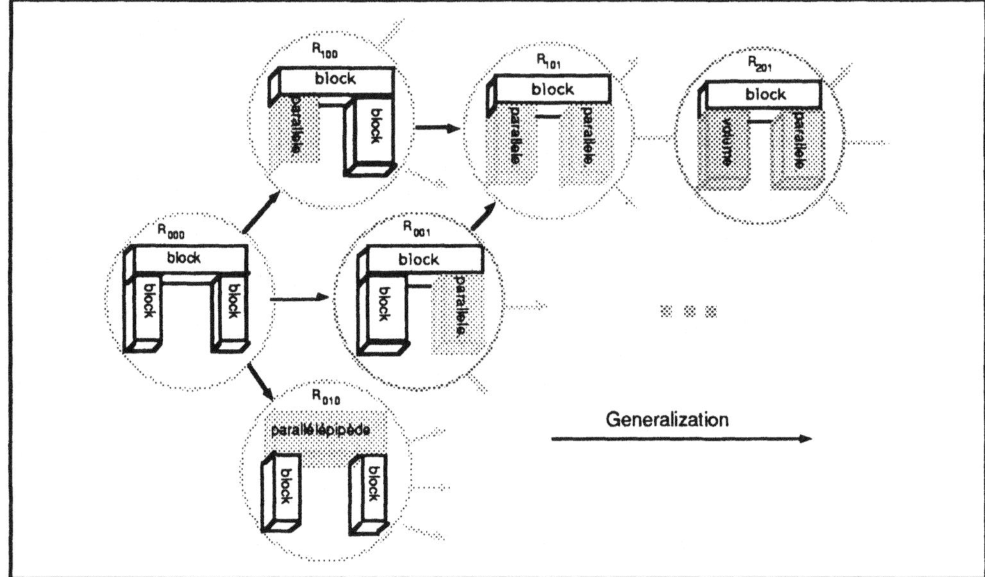

Figure 6: A part of the generalization lattice

Suppose that these three examples have been accepted, APT continues to progress through the lattice by proposing examples where the bases of the arch are *columns*, that are accepted by the expert and it is finally stopped by the rejection of the other examples such as an arch with a *sphere* top.

4.2 Specialization

Then, APT learns rule Rl (Figure 7) which says that it is possible to build the bases of an arch with any kind of *volume* and the top with a *parallelepiped*. This learned rule is submitted to the expert who asks APT to specialize it. As the Domain Theory is incomplete, the learned rule Rl is too general because it covers also negative cases where the bases of the arch are *spheres* or *pyramids*. This is due to the fact that the Domain Theory defines not only *columns* but also *spheres* or *pyramids* as *volumes*. The expert has the possibility to select the direction of specialization to restrict the range of the search by pointing out the too general concepts of the learned rule. In our example, *volume* should be pointed out.

R_l :	IF there are two **volumes** x, y and a parallelepiped z made of concrete		
	THEN solve the problem	of building an arch	
	by solving the subproblems	FIRST,	...

Figure 7 : The learned rule.

The rule R_S in Figure 8 is the rule hypothesis accepted by the expert after backtracking along the lattice. This rule R_S is obviously too specific since it does not cover the acceptable cases where the bases of the arch are *columns* or *cylinders*: because the Domain Theory does not define *columns* and *cylinders* as *parallelepipeds*.

R_S :	IF there are three **parallelepipeds** x, y and z made of concrete	
	THEN solve the problem	of building an arch
	by solving the subproblems	FIRST, ...

Figure 8 : The rule accepted by the expert

As there is no possible intermediate concept between *parallelepiped* and *volume* in the Domain Theory, the only way to express a rule consistent with all the examples is to constrain the over-generalized rule R_l by adding concept descriptions. The expert has to be guided to do this correctly.

In this example, the different possibilities are quite obvious but this will not be the case if the rule is more complex and the Domain Theory broader. However, the properties of the lattice stemming from the way it is built, are independent of the domain. Whatever the complexity of the domain is, the rule accepted by the expert after backtrack along the lattice can be nothing but over-specialized and all the more general rules, even the nearest ones are over-generalized. Consequently, the negative examples that must be excluded from the learned rule scope are always easy to locate, because they belong to the small set of the examples not covered by the accepted rule and covered by the overgeneralized rule produced by the next generalization step.

At this stage in our example, APT knows that the inconsistent example set that must be cut into two parts is the set labeled by the rule R_l of the examples that are not covered by R_S. It contains all the examples where the bases of the arch are *volumes* without being *parallelepipeds*, therefore it contains the examples of rules where the bases of the arch are *columns*, *spheres*, and *pointed-top* .

4.3 Refinement

When the inconsistent example set is identified, the next stage consists in asking the expert to identify some negative examples and to compare them with the positive examples from the same set that he has accepted during the generalization. The aim of this process is to lead him to use knowledge that allows to describe separately good and bad examples at a high degree of generality.

4.3.1 Comparing examples

Firstly, the expert is asked to identify negative examples in the examples selected by APT from the inconsistent example set. To avoid having to study all the examples, which may be too numerous, the expert has the possibility to choose an example subset by selecting concepts in the list of concepts that APT proposes. These concepts are the concepts known by APT as concepts involved in the over-generalization problem. In our example, these concepts are *parallelepipeds*, *columns*, *pointed-top* and so on. If the expert has an intuitive idea of the causes of the problem, he will choose to examine the examples of rules where the arch bases are *pointed-top* and *spheres*. If not, he will probably examine more examples before identifying negative ones.

When negative examples have been identified, APT asks the expert to compare the positive example he has previously accepted with the negative examples that he has just identified. These examples are all semantically close since their concepts have the same parents in the Domain Theory due to the properties of the generalization lattice and it is then much easier to find what knowledge description would allow to distinguish them.

If for instance, the example in Figure 9 is identified as a negative example and the example in Figure 10 was the positive example that had led to learn the rule R_1 during the generalization phase, the expert may think that the knowledge that allows to distinguish a *sphere* from a *cylinder*, when building an arch, is the shape of the top or the stability.

IF there are a **sphere** x, a **block** y and a parallelepiped z made of concrete,		
THEN solve the problem	of building an arch	
by solving the subproblems	FIRST,	...

Figure 9: A negative example

IF there are a **block** x, a **cylinder** y and a parallelepiped z made of concrete,		
THEN solve the problem	of building an arch	
by solving the subproblems	FIRST,	...

Figure 10: A positive example

The over-generalized rule R_1 has now to be constrained by using this new knowledge elicited through the comparison of the examples. The expert has the possibility, if it is sufficient, to add directly new constraints or to modify the Domain Theory without necessarily adding constraints. APT reacts to each modification by indicating if the modifications are sufficient to exclude the negative examples from the scope of the over-generalized rule.

4.3.2 Adding new constraints to the rule

The expert may add a constraint such as in Figure 11 which is sufficient to exclude the negative examples where the base of the arch is a *sphere* or a *pyramid.*

IF there are two volumes x and y **with a flat top** and a parallelepiped z made of concrete		
THEN solve the problem	of building an arch	
by solving the subproblems	FIRST,	...

Figure 11: The overgeneralized rule constrained by the expert

If the constraints that the expert adds to the rule contain concepts or properties that are unknown in the Domain Theory, they are integrated in the Domain Theory. APT uses the learning context of the rule to modify, to make easier the improvement of the Domain Theory by proposing probable modifications.

If the expert adds a new concept, the father and the sons of the concept must be chosen in the Domain Theory. In our example, x was defined as a *volume* in the rule and the expert adds that "x is a *flat-top*", APT does not know this concept *flat-top* and proposes to integrate it in the hierarchy of *volume*, as a son of *something*, of *volume*, of *parallelepiped* or of *block*. When the father of the new concept is chosen, such as *volume*, APT asks which sons of the father *volume* must become sons of the new concept. In our example, APT would ask which concepts among *parallelepiped*, *columns*, *sphere* and *pointed-top* must become the sons of *flat-top*. The expert will select *parallelepiped*, and *column* without having to look in the Domain Theory how to make the right modification in the hierarchies at the right level of generality.

If the expert adds a new property such as "*the color of volume x is red*", APT proposes to the expert to select which concepts, sons of *volume*, this property has to be added to: *parallelepiped*, *columns*, or sphere. Except for the case where all the sons are chosen by the expert, the rule will become more selective because applicable to the selected concepts only.

These examples shows how APT guides the expert in the improvement of the over-generalized rule and the Domain Theory by proposing modifications inspired by the learning context and how APT proposes to propagate the expert's modifications in the Domain Theory to other concepts that those which are involved in the modified rule. These modifications are oriented by the erroneous rule, but the expert has also the possibility to perform modifications on the Domain theory that are directly oriented by the specific concepts occurring in the positive and negative examples from the inconsistent set.

4.3.3 Modifying the domain theory

The cause of the overgeneralization may not be not only the definition of the rule as it is shown above, but incorrect or incomplete definitions in the Domain Theory. APT then provides three means to directly improve the Domain Theory without necessarily modifying the rule. In this case, the modifications are not guided by the rule concepts but by the positive and negative example concepts. The aim is then to acquire new knowledge so that positive examples from the inconsistent set may be described separately from negative ones. Figure 12 shows in grey, some of the possibilities for the arch domain.

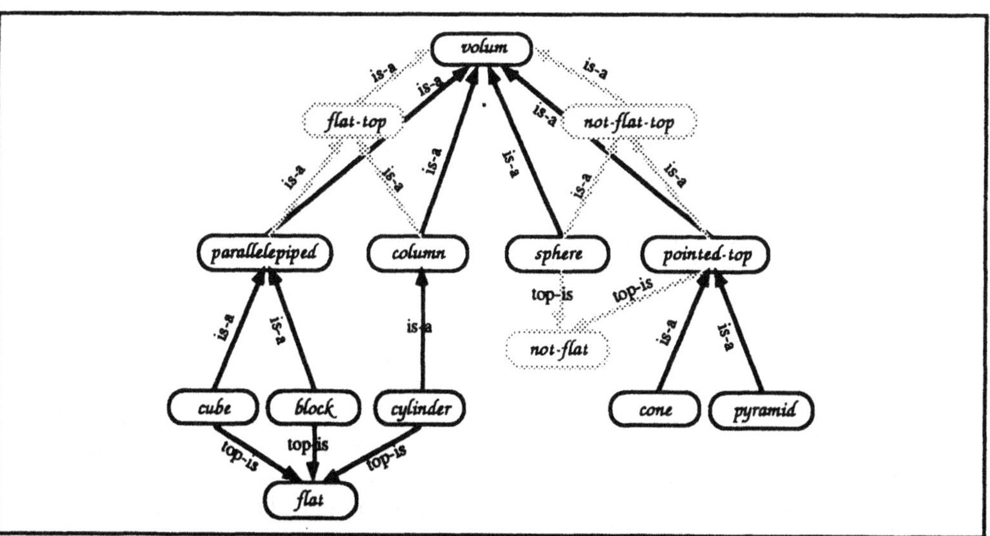

Figure 12 : a part of the modified theory

• First, APT proposes to add intermediate predicates in the hierarchies, to gather in two different clusters "positive" concepts occuring in positive examples (such as *parallelepiped* and *cylinder* in our example), and "negative" concepts occuring in negative examples (such as *pointed-top* and *sphere*). To make easy the expert's task, APT displays separately the list of "positive" concepts and "negative" ones. For instance, the expert may ask APT to integrate in the Domain Theory the new concept *flat-top* as father of *parallelepiped* and *cylinder* and the new concept *not-flat-top* as father of *pointed-top* and *sphere*. APT proposes different solutions to place the new concepts in the corresponding hierarchies. The expert has also the possibility to choose the roots of both clusters among the existing concepts and to easily move them in the corresponding hierarchies.

• Second, APT proposes to add new properties to distinguish "positive" concepts from "negative ones". If the values for the property given by the expert are unknown in the Domain Theory, APT proposes to integrate them at the right level in the hierarchy as described above. In our example, if the property *top-is* is given by the expert, with the values *flat* for the "positive" concepts and *not-flat* for the negative concepts, APT will automatically link the "positive" concepts *parallelepiped* and *cylinder* to the concept *flat* by the property *top-is* and the "negative" concepts *spheres* and *pointed-top* to the concept *not-flat* by the property *top-is*. Generally, it is much better to add properties instead of intermediate concepts. Indeed, the features to be added generally concern only one aspect of the concepts and not really new concepts. Moreover, new properties allow APT to constrain the over-generalized rules in the same way as new concepts.

• Third, the system also proposes to rename some occurrences of already existing properties. If they are polysemic, it may be necessary to distinguish some occurrences from the other ones. To make easier the expert's task, APT displays the list of the properties that link the "positive" concepts and the "negative" ones in the examples. The expert has the possibility to rename those that he wants and the corresponding modifications are propagated.

The localization of the part of the Domain Theory to improve and the identification of the smallest inconsistent set of examples has allowed APT to propose relevant modifications of the over-generalized rule and of the Domain Theory, and to automatically execute the main part of these modifications without help from the expert.

5 APT in real applications

APT has been used in three main applications in different domains, inindustry, medecine and finance and on different tasks. In the industrial domain, an application involving the design of loudspeakers has used APT to acquire design decomposition rules as described in [Tecuci & Kodratoff 90]. This application pointed to the importance of having a problem-solver and a learner closely integrated together. But APT can be used for tasks other than design or construction such as medical diagnosis or financial decision making.

The medical application consisted in diagnosing and treating hyper-tension [Bento & al 91a]. It was developed by a medical expert with the support of the University of Coimbra (Portugal). This application illustrates that APT can be used for classification tasks, and in this case to learn good rules for a heuristic match. The problem consisted first in diagnosing the type of hypertension of a patient and second in deciding a good therapy for the patient to follow. The domain of hyper-tension therapy is a difficult one, because hypertension is a very common disease, and you must take into consideration when prescribing a therapy that the patient may suffer from secondary diseases.

In this application, the acquisition problem was difficult because only few examples were available, and the expert did not have a complete theory for the domain. APT was therefore used to generalize interactively the examples provided by the expert, and to elicit and correct the missing domain knowledge. APT proved to be very efficient in both those tasks, allowing for good general rules to be learned and a correct and complete theory to be built. The knowledge acquisition principles of APT indeed helped the expert to identify missing or incorrect knowledge and to integrate the modifications in an efficient way. Figure 13 shows a rule describing a case and the associated prescription.

IF the patient C suffers from a depression and from essential-hypertension. mao_inhibitor and thiazide have been administred

THEN solve the problem of curing essential hypertension
where the secondary disease is a depression
the other medication is mao inhibitor
the other failed prescription is thiazyde

by solving the subproblemsof prescribing nifedipine
used in treatment of essential hypertension
used on failure of thiazide

Figure 13 : An example of rule for hyper-tension therapy

From such a specific example of a prescribed therapy, APT has learned general rules by using its smallest generalization step strategy and proposing other similar cases to the expert that APT has automatically generated. The expert could easily evaluate the cases proposed by APT, and could understand when APT pointed to a deficiency in the domain theory. The knowledge acquisition principles of APT help the expert to identify missing or incorrect knowledge and to integrate the modifications in an efficient way. As the development of this application is continuing, it has not been yet operational in a medical environment.

In the financial application, APT was used to refine an already existing knowledge base. The task consisted in deciding whether financial aid could be offered or not. An expert system called SPAC had been previously built to solve this problem, using conventional, "manual" knowledge acquisition techniques such as unsupervised and supervised interviews, repertory grids and readings loan guide books. APT was used to evaluate its capabilities as a knowledge acquisition tool, using SPAC as a comparison [Bento & al 91b].

The application consisted of two parts, first evaluating the economical and financial feasibility of a project based on the company's lifetime, its economical and financial covering, its historic and provisional analysis; second deciding a loan considering this first evaluation in combination with the quality of the project and the promoter's profile. APT started with the already existing domain theory of SPAC, and was used by an expert to learn new feasibility evaluation and decision rules. The set of rules learned by APT proved to be more general than SPAC's. This set of rules was five times smaller than the SPAC set of rules, and performed better. Not only were the rules more efficient but they had been acquired in far less time then when developing SPAC. Of course, the fact that using APT resulted in a shorter development time must be nuanced, since a significant part of the knowledge acquisition process came from the SPAC's application. Comparison tables are provided in [Bento & al 91b].

APT can be used for a varied number of tasks. It has proved to be a useful knowledge acquisition tool, enhanced by its machine learning capabilitities as well as by the problem solving context in which it functions.

6 Discussion

We have described in this paper how APT learns and revises knowledge by using specific rules given by an expert in problem solving failures. Both the rule base and Domain Theory may be refined by APT's learner but only Domain Theory (semantic network) can be revised. However, the rule base may need to be corrected, this is why our future research will concern the way the over-generalized rules that are proposed by APT's Problem Solver in a failure case, and should not have been proposed, could be corrected. This can be simply done by cautiously specializing the misapplied rule until it does no longer cover the current wrong case. The smallest generalization step strategy could be symetrically used as a smallest specialization step strategy by generating and inversely ordering examples in the same way as described above.

We have not raised here the problem of over-specialization of the rule learned by APT. The choice of treating the problem of over-generalized rules rather than the one of over-specialized rules is due to the historic choice of applications for the system (section 5). Some application domains such as medical applications, for instance, must not accept over-generalized rules; it may be too dangerous for the patient ! Thus, it is better for APT not to be applicable to some cases than to be mis-applicable.

One crucial point for KA and interactive ML systems is the number of questions required to converge. APT is concerned with this problem since it uses a cautious generalization strategy so that an example is proposed to the expert for each generalization step such as in MARVIN and CLINT. But APT uses negative examples in the course of the generalization process in order to stop the search in the corresponding direction as soon as possible, avoiding to propose too many examples. In addition, the number of examples required is proportional to the number of concepts in the initial rule which is generally small, because only the relevant concepts which are kept are those occurring in the relevant explanations deduced from the Theory. The number of examples required is also proportional to the height of the hierarchies, which is never very large. However, it should be necessary to restrict the range of the search by using preference criterion to choose the best generalization direction and then to reduce the number of the examples required and to increase the relevancy of the examples proposed.

Using the negative examples during the generalization allows APT not to use the dropping rule generalization operator that consists in dropping terms to generalize. If APT can generate a sufficient number of examples (one by generalization step) to converge on a disjunction of rules, no term can be dropped from a learned rule without this rule covering a negative example because of the density of the generalization lattice. If the learning does not converge, a lower bound and an upper bound are learned for each rule, as in DISCIPLE.

APT's rule refinement differs from the way [Shapiro, 83], MARVIN [Sammut & Banerji, 86], CLINT [De Raedt, 91] or BLIP [Wrobel, 89] process negative examples. APT maximally generalizes from examples but it does not specialize from examples. Instead of waiting to derive contradictions from what the oracle says and what it has learned and instead of generating examples covered by the concepts learned that may be rejected by the oracle, APT directly asks the expert to validate the learned rules. This allows to reduce the number of examples required before an error is found because by rejecting learned rules the expert allows APT to identify the erroneous knowledge. One negative example is required when the wrong generalization step is identified so that the oracle can compare it to a semantically close positive example in order to elicit the missing knowledge. APT does not only validate its learned rules through experimentation by the Problem Solver which could be very long, but also tries to actively locate exceptions with the help of the expert, as soon as a rule is learned. This evaluation may be less reliable than example evaluation because if the domain and the task are complex, the expert may forget exceptions and accept an over-generalized rule. This is why APT's Problem Solver behavior must be also validated through experimentations.

7 Conclusion: on the integration of Machine Learning and Knowledge Acquisition methods

It has been possible to integrate in the same framework the Knowledge Acquisition (KA) and Machine Learning methods (ML) used by APT because they are based on the same assumption: the evaluation and the comparison of automatically generated examples of rules. Using examples has been recognized by both communities as a very interesting way to acquire new knowledge descriptions. As they are based on the same framework, the integration of both methods renders them able to fill each other respective lacks.

In the acquisition phase, KA methods elicit the expert 's knowledge and insert it in the KBS. These methods are not only able to transfer shallow knowledge but also to modelize the expert's problem solving model in interaction with the knowledge engineer. This elicitation is difficult since the expert may be not conscious of the reasons for his behavior.

ML methods are not able to acquire the Domain knowledge by themselves, but they are able to compute *basic expert cases* to extract, compact and generalize the relevant information that *determines* the expert's behavior and to automatically represent this information in a usable way. ML technics are then able to induce general knowledge from basic knowledge and to explore systematically all the consequences of the addition of the expert's knowledge. In that sense they complete the role of the knowledge engineer.

In the validation phase, some ML methods are able to detect erroneous knowledge and to automatically revise it in simple cases. During the maintenance phase, using ML methods may also allow to extend the application scope of a KBS by just introducing new examples which are automatically computed without the knowledge engineer.

Nevertheless, ML methods generally need KA techniques. If they use a Domain Theory, this theory has to be built with the expert. If they complete or correct the theory, the expert is needed to evaluate the modifications. If they generalize examples, the degree of generality must be evaluated by the expert and if they use semantic criteria to restrein the search space of the learned concept, they need an expert to give them these criteria. These Human Machine interactions are based on KA techniques.

Integrating KA and ML methods in the same system increases at the same time its flexibility, its capabilities of reasoning about and revising what it acquires. But the necessary condition for a good integration of these technics is that the ML module is open and is able to explain its behavior so that experts and users can trust it. The conception of a ML system as a black box which never needs to be repaired is an idealistic view. Machine Learning methods need Knowledge Acquisition methods to acquire a part of their knowledge, to evaluate and to maintain what is learned. That means that the expert must understand the system's behavior to add or revise its knowledge.APT system is an illustration of how Machine Learning and Knowledge Acquisition methods may cooperate in a common open system to improve the system's performance.

Acknowledgements

The author would like to thank Yves Kodratoff for the support he has provided to this work, Ernesto Costa, Jose Ferreira for their work on APT's applications and the reviewers for their useful comments. This work is partially supported by CEC, through the ESPRIT-2 contract MLT (n°2154) and CNRS through PRC-IA.

References

AUSSENAC N., "Conception d'une méthodologie et d'un outil d'acquisition de connaissances expertes", Thèse d'Informatique, Université Paul Sabatier de Toulouse, 1989.

BAREISS R., *"Exemplar-Based Knowledge Acquisition"*, Academic Press Inc, San Diego, 1989.

BENTO C., COSTA E., FEREIRA J.L., *"APT as a knowledge elicitation tool in the domain of hypertension therapy "*, MLT Esprit Project report, January 1991.

BENTO C., COSTA E., FEREIRA J.L., *"APT as a knowledge acquisition tool in the domain of Analysis "*, MLT Esprit Project report, October 1991.

BISSON G.,"Learning in FOL with a similarity measure", *Proceedings of AAAI* , eds AAAI press, (to appear), July 1992.

CARBONELL J. G., KNOBLOCK C. A., MINTON S., "PRODIGY: An integraated Architecture for Planning and Learning,", in *Architectures for Intelligence* , K. VanLehn (Ed), 1990.

DE RAEDT L., *"Interactive Concept-Learning"*, Ph.D. diss. Katholieke Universiteit Leuven,1991.

FIKES, R. E. AND NILSSON N. J., "STRIPS : A new approach to the application of theorem proving to problem solving. *Artificial Intelligence 2* pp. 198-208, 1971

KODRATOFF Y., ADDIS T., MANTARAS R.L, MORIK K., PLAZA E. "Four Stances on Knowledge Acquisition and Machine Learning", *Proceeding EWSL 91*, Springer-Verlag, Porto, 1991.

KODRATOFF Y. AND GANASCIA, J. G., "Improving the generalization step in Learning", in *Machine Learning II : An Artificial Intelligence Approach*, RR.S. Michalski J.G. Carbonell and T.M. Mitchell (Eds) Morgan Kaufmann, 1986.

LOPEZ B., MESEGUER P. and PLAZA E., "Knowledge Based Systems Validation: A State of the Art", in *AICOM* Vol. 3, June 1990.

MITCHELL, T. M., *"Version Spaces : An Approach to Concept Learning"*, Ph.D. diss. Standford University, 1978.

MITCHELL, T. M., MAHADEVAN S., STEINBERG L. I. *"LEAP : A Learning Apprentice for VLSI Design "*, in *Machine Learning III : An Artificial Intelligence Approach*, pp 271-289, Kodratoff Y. & Michalski R. (eds), Morgan Kaufmann, 1989.

MORIK K. "Underlying Assumptions of Knowledge Acquisition and Machine Learning", in *Knowledge Acquisition*, Vol. 3, No. 2, pp. 137-156, 1991.

MORIK K. "Sloppy modeling", in *Knowldge Representation and Organisation in Machine Learning*, Morik K. (ed), 1989..

NEDELLEC C. "A smallest generalization steps strategy" in *the proceedings of the International Workshop on Machine Learning, IWML-91* Chicago, 1991

NEDELLEC C. *"APT User's Guide"*, MLT Esprit Project Deliverable 4.2, 1991.

ROUVEIROL C., "Semantic Model for induction of First Order Theories", Proceeding of 12th IJCAI, pp 685-690 Sydney, 1991.

SAMMUT, C.A AND BANERJI, R.B., "Learning Concepts by asking Questions", in *Machine Learning II : An Artificial Intelligence Approach*, pp 167-192, R.S. Michalski J.G. Carbonell and T.M. Mitchell (Eds) Morgan Kaufmann, 1986.

SHAPIRO, E. Y. *"Algorithmic program debugging"*, MIT press, Cambridge, MA, 1983.

SMITH B. D. AND ROSENBLOOM P. S., "Incremental Non-Backtracking Focusing: A Polynomially Bounded Generalization Algorithm for Version Space.", in proceedings of AAAI-90.

TECUCI G. & KODRATOFF Y., "Apprenticeship Learning in Nonhomogeneous Domain Theories", in *Machine Learning III : An Artificial Intelligence Approach*, Kodratoff Y. & Michalski R. (eds), Morgan Kaufmann, 1989.

WIELIENGA B.J., SHREIBER A. TH., BREUKER J.A., "KADS: A Modelling Approach to Knowledge Engineering", Submitted to Knowledge Acquisition, May 8 1991.

WROBEL S., "Demand-Driven Concept Formation", in *Knowldge Representation and Organisation in Machine Learning*, Morik K. (ed), 1989.

Generating Configuration Expert Systems from Conceptual Specifications of the Expert Knowledge

J. Schweiger

Real-Time Systems and Robotics Group
Institut für Informatik, Technische Universität München

Abstract. The manual formalization and implementation of the expert knowledge about a class of configuration problems by the knowledge engineer is a rather time-consuming and labour-intensive job. I have therefore developed concepts for a special knowledge acquisition tool called KONFGEN-II for the domain of configuration tasks. KONFGEN-II gets as input a high-level description of the expert knowledge in a conceptual specification language tailored to configuration tasks. From a given specification, KONFGEN-II automatically generates the internal knowledge representation of production rules and constraints and compiles it into an executable expert system which can immediately be evaluated and used. KONFGEN-II is currently being implemented on the basis of the distributed production system MAGSY [10] and the constraint satisfaction system YACSS [5].

1 Introduction

For several years there has been a trend of consumers buying individual rather than standard goods. Therefore, producers are forced to offer customized products which can be configured according to the demands of the consumers. As a result of this, sales engineers and product managers are faced with many complex configuration tasks to be solved in a short time. As a supporting facility, domain-specific configuration expert systems are often used. Because configuration tasks are not yet well understood, configuration expert systems are mostly developed in cooperation by the configuration expert and a knowledge engineer. The bottleneck in the development of an expert system is knowledge acquisition. Following [1] and [6], knowledge acquisition can be divided into the phases elicitation, interpretation, formalization, implementation and evaluation. In the phase of formalization the knowledge engineer maps the interpreted expert knowledge into an internal knowledge representation of production rules, constraints, frames etc., which are programmed during the implementation phase.

As there is a great discrepancy between the terminology of the expert and the interpretation model of the knowledge engineer on the one side, and the internal knowledge representation on the other, the formalization and implementation of the interpreted expert knowledge by the knowledge engineer is a time-consuming and labour-intensive job. Furthermore, the manual transformation of the interpreted expert knowledge into internal knowledge representations carries the risk of errors. Finally, the maintenance of the expert system is also time-consuming and labour-intensive, because every change in the interpreted expert knowledge leads to a partial

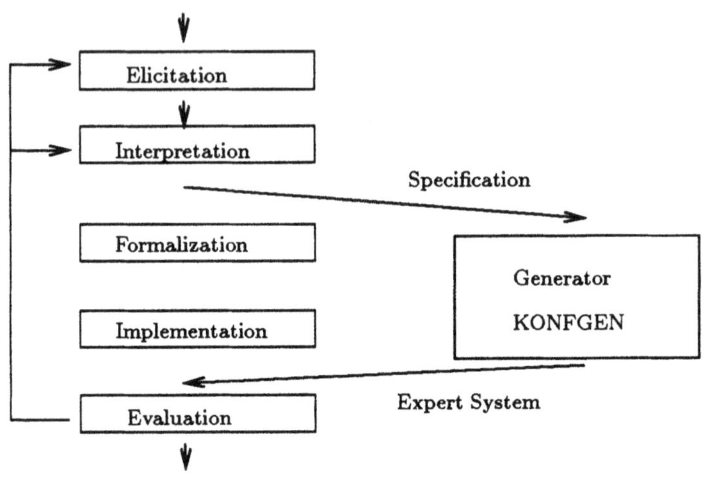

Figure 1: Principle of KONFGEN

reformalization and a partial reimplementation of the expert system. This means that, for every change, the knowledge engineer has to become familiar again with the details of the particular program. The existing tools for the development of configuration expert systems support the knowledge engineer only partly when formalizing and implementing the interpreted expert knowledge. More or less large parts of the interpreted expert knowledge have to be formalized and implemented by the knowledge engineer manually - they must be programmed in the form of production rules, facts, constraints, etc. Thus, the need arises for a special tool which automatically formalizes and implements interpreted knowledge of a configuration expert.

One possible tool is the generator KONFGEN as shown in figure 1. The generator receives a conceptual specification of the interpreted expert knowledge (built in cooperation by the configuration expert and the knowledge engineer). The generator automatically transforms this specification into an internal knowledge representation (production rules, facts, constraints, etc.) and compiles it into an executable expert system which can immediately be evaluated and used. Having a generator like this, the knowledge engineer avoids the problems mentioned above. First concepts for the generator were developed, fully implemented and validated in the generator KONFGEN-I [3, 8]. KONFGEN-I provides a language to specify the interpreted knowledge of a configuration expert. The specification language is based on a 'box of bricks' attributed with sets of high-level constraints. From a given specification, KONFGEN-I generates VAX-OPS5 source code with external Pascal functions. This first prototype was tested by reimplementing KONFIGULA [2], an expert system for the configuration of gantry robots of the company Liebherr Anlagenbau, Kempten (Germany).

The validation of KONFGEN-I proved that the concepts of the specification language are not adequate for specifying every configuration task. First, external functions

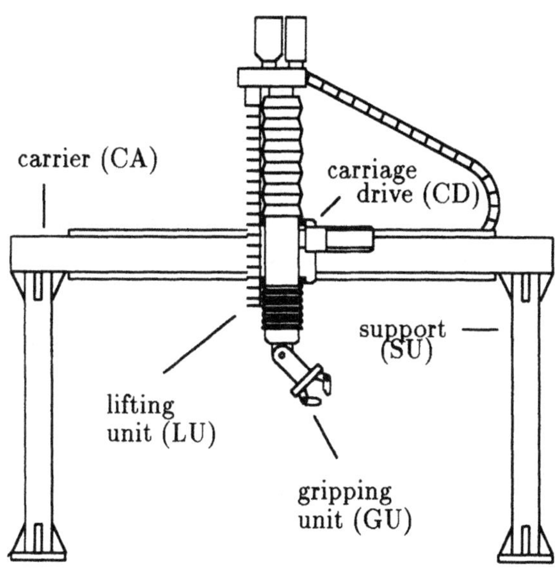

Figure 2: Parts of a gantry robot

were necessary to specify weak restrictions. Second, the hierarchy of a configuration task has to be transformed into a flat structure. Third, the specification concepts for control knowledge, like the sequence in which the particular components were treated, were too inflexible. I therefore extended the concepts of that generator to KONFGEN-II. This paper presents the results of this extension. The following section 2 gives a formal definition of configuration tasks, which is necessary to define exactly the kind of tasks the generator can handle. Section 3 introduces the specification language of KONFGEN-II. Section 4 shows the principle of the generation process, and section 5 concludes with a discussion and an outlook.

2 Configuration Tasks

In this section a formal definition of configuration tasks is given. This formal definition is necessary to determine exactly the field of application of the special tool KONFGEN-II. All definitions are additionally explained by an example from the domain of configuring gantry robots. A gantry robot is part of a manufacturing cell that serves the machines of the cell with tools and workpieces. The parts of a gantry robot are shown in figure 2. For a further explanation of gantry robots see [2, 8].

Definition:

A **part** is an object which can be characterized by a set of properties.

Example:

Given: Carriage drives CDa_1, CDa_2 of a gantry robot, both having the properties: price = 12500 DM, speed = 50 cm/s, mass limit = 80 kg, cable length = cardinal number between 6 and 15 meters.
Carriage drives CDb_1, CDb_2, CDb_3 of a gantry robot, all having the properties: price = 9500 DM, speed = 30 cm/s, mass limit = 50 kg, cable length = cardinal number between 4 and 10 meters.

Then: The carriage drives CDa_1, CDa_2 and CDb_1, CDb_2, CDb_3 are parts.

Definition:

A **variant V** of a set of parts P is a subset of P which fulfills

$$\forall x, y \in V : \text{x has the same properties as y}$$

Example:

Given: The set of parts PG of a gantry robot as shown in figure 2 with
PG := $\{CDa_1, CDa_2, CDb_1, CDb_2, CDb_3, \ldots, CAb_1, CAb_2\}$
VG:= $\{CDa_1, CDa_2\}$

Then: VG is a variant of PG.

Definition:

The **set of variants SV** of a set of parts P is defined as:

$$SV := \{ V: V \text{ is a variant of } P \}$$

Example:

Given: The set of parts PG
SVG := Power($\{CDa_1, CDa_2\}$) $\cup$ Power($\{CDb_1, CDb_2, CDb_3\}$) $\cup \ldots$
$\cup$ Power($\{CAb_1, CAb_2\}$)
Power (X) := set of all subsets of the set X

Then: SVG is the set of variants of PG.

Definition:

A **restriction** of a set of parts P is a dependence between the properties of the parts of P.

Example:

Given: The set of parts PG and the following statements:

R1: 'The *sum SU* of the mass of the gripping unit, of the maximal mass of the workpiece and of the mass of the lifting unit is approximately 80% of the mass limit of the carriage drive and does not exceed the mass limit of the carriage drive.'

R2: 'Use supports which are as short as possible.'

Then: R1 and R2 are restrictions for PG.

Definition:

A **quality function Q** for a set of restrictions R for a set of parts P is a mapping:

$$Q : \begin{cases} Power(P) & \longrightarrow & M \\ S & \longmapsto & m \end{cases}$$

and fulfills: $Q(S_1) \sqsubseteq Q(S_2) \Leftrightarrow$
S_1 fulfills the restrictions of R more than or equal to S_2

with: P: set of parts, S: S $\in$ Power(P), R: set of restrictions for P,
M: set with a total ordering relation $\sqsubseteq$, m: m = Q(S) $\in$ M

Informally, the result of a quality function is a value which shows *how much* a set of parts fulfills a set of restrictions.

Example:
Given: set of parts PG, set of restrictions RG := {R1, R2, ..., Rn}
set of values MG := { good, acceptable, not_acceptable } with total ordering relation $\sqsubseteq_G$ and good $\sqsubseteq_G$ acceptable $\sqsubseteq_G$ not_acceptable

$$QG : \begin{cases} Power(PG) & \longrightarrow & MG \\ SG & \longmapsto & \begin{cases} good & if & CON1 \\ acceptable & if & CON2 \\ not\_acceptable & else & \end{cases} \end{cases}$$

CON1: 'The sum SU of restriction R1 when using the parts of SG is between 75% and 85% of the mass limit of the carriage drive, and SG contains supports which are as short as possible and some other conditions which are not explained here.'
CON2: 'The sum SU of restriction R1 when using the parts of SG is between 60% and 75% or between 85% and 100% of the mass limit of the carriage drive, and SG contains supports which are as short as possible and some other conditions which are not explained here.'
Then: QG is a quality function for RG for PG.

Definition:
A composition C of parts of P to parts of O is a partial mapping of the form:

$$C : \begin{cases} Power(P) & \longrightarrow & SV & & \\ S & \longmapsto & V & if & CPR(R, S) \end{cases}$$

with: P,O: set of parts SV: set of variants of O
R: set of restrictions for P CPR: Predicate on R and S

The composition C simulates the joining of the parts of S to a variant of the set of parts O. Thereby, the properties of the single parts of S are mapped into the properties of the variant V. The predicate CPR determines the scope in which the partial mapping C is defined. Therefore, the predicate CPR describes by means of the restrictions R these subsets of parts S which can also be joined in reality.

Example:
Given: set of parts PG, set of restrictions RG,
set of parts OG with OG := { parts w with properties:
height of w $\in$ [1..8], price of w $\in$ [0..1000000] }

set of variants SVOG of OG

$$CG:\begin{cases} Power(PG) & \longrightarrow & SVOG \\ SG & \longmapsto & \begin{cases} \text{V with } |V| = 1, & if \quad CPRG(RG,SG) \\ \text{height of V} := \text{HEI}, & \\ \text{price of V} := \text{PRI} & \end{cases} \end{cases}$$

HEI: 'Sum of the length of a support of SG and the upper length of the lifting unit of SG.'

PRI: 'The sum of the prices of all parts of SG.'

CPRG: 'CPRG(RG,SG) is *true*, if the sum SU of R1 of RG does not exceed the mass limit of the carriage drive and some other conditions which are not explained here.'

Then: CG is a composition which simulates the joining of the single parts of a gantry robots to a complete gantry robot with its particular properties.

Definition:

A **demand D** for a set of parts O is a tuple of the form:

$$D := (\, R_D,\, G_D,\, H_D,\, H)$$

with:

R_D: set of restrictions for O

G_D: quality function for R_D with G_D: Power(O) $\rightarrow$ M and M: set of values with $\sqsubseteq$

H_D, H: $H_D, H \in$ M (lower quality bounds for G_D and G as shown later)

Example:

Given: set of parts OG

set of restrictions RG_D for OG with $RG_D := \{$ RD1, RD2 $\}$ and

RD1: 'The height should be lower than $X_1 := 5$ m and may not exceed $X_2 := 6$ meters.'

RD2: 'The price should be approximately $X_3 := 85000$ DM.'

set of values MG with total ordering relation $\sqsubseteq_G$

quality function QG_D with

$$QG_D:\begin{cases} Power(OG) & \longrightarrow & MG \\ SDG & \longmapsto & \begin{cases} good & if \quad CON3 \\ acceptable & if \quad CON4 \\ not\_acceptable & else \end{cases} \end{cases}$$

CON3: 'The height of the parts of SDG is lower than $X_1 = 5$ m and the price of every part in SDG is between $X_4 = 70000$ DM and $X_5 = 90000$ DM.'

CON4: 'The height of the parts of SDG is between $X_1 = 5$ m and $X_2 = 6$ m and the price of every part in SDG is between $X_4 = 70000$ DM and $X_5 = 90000$ DM.'

lower quality bounds $HG_D := HG :=$ good

DG := (RG_D, QG_D, HG_D, HG)

Then: DG is a demand for OG.

Definition:

A **configuration problem CP** is a tuple of the form:

CP := (P,R,Q,C,D)

with:
P: set of parts
R: set of restrictions for P
Q: quality function for R with Q: Power(P) $\rightarrow M$
C: composition of parts of P to parts of O with predicate CPR
D: demand for O with D:=(R_D, Q_D, H_D,H) and
R_D: set of restrictions for O and
Q_D: quality function for R_D with Q_D: Power(O) $\rightarrow$ M
H_D: lower quality bound for Q_D with $H_D \in M$
H: lower quality bound for Q with H $\in M$

The parts of P are the resources of the configuration problem with which the requested objects are built. The composition C maps a selected subset of P to the configured objects of O with their particular properties. Whether a selected subset of P can be composed is determined by the predicate CPR of the composition C, which refers to the restrictions of R. The predicate CPR guarantees that the composed objects work. The restrictions R_D of the demand D refer to the properties of the configurable objects of O. That is why, for instance, a customer of a gantry robot only knows the properties of the whole gantry robot like the *height* or the *price*, but does not know anything about the *mass limit* of a carriage drive or other internal properties of a gantry robot. The lower quality bounds H_D and H are limits for the quality of the configured objects which are determined by Q_D and Q.

Example:

Given: set of parts PG, set of restrictions RG, quality function QG,
composition CG, demand DG,
CPG := (PG, RG, QG, CG, DG)
Then: CPG is a configuration problem.

Definition:

A **solution S** of a configuration problem CP := (P,R,Q,C,D) is a subset of P which fulfills:

$$CPR(S) \wedge Q(S) \sqsubseteq H \wedge Q_D(C(S)) \sqsubseteq H_D)$$

C(S) is called **composed solution.**

Informally, the solution S of a configuration problem CP is a subset of parts of P which fulfills three conditions: first, it can be joined to functioning objects (CPR(S) is *true*). Second, the parts of S work and harmonize according to the internal quality of the demand ($Q(S) \sqsubseteq H$). Third, the composed objects satisfy the quality criterion of the demand to the corresponding degree ($Q_D(C(S)) \sqsubseteq H_D$).

Example:
Given: configuration problem CPG
$SG := \{CDa_1, LUa_1, GUb_1, SUa_1, SUa_2, CAb_1\}$
Then: SG is a solution for CPG if considering all restrictions for gantry robots.

Definition:
A **class of configuration problems CLCP** is a tuple of the form:

CLCP := (P,R,Q,C,$D^\star$)

with: P,R,Q,C: as in a single configuration problem CP
$D^\star$: set of demands for O

The set $D^\star$ of a class of configuration problems CLCP contains all possible demands for the class. Choosing an individual demand of $D^\star$ provides a single configuration problem of the class.

Example:
Given: set of parts PG, set of restrictions RG, quality function QG,
composition CG,
$DG^\star$:= {DG=(RG_D, QG_D, HG_D, HG) with
$X_1, \ldots, X_5 \in$ cardinal numbers}
CLCPG := (PG, RG, QG, CG, $DG^\star$)
Then: CLCPG is a class of configuration problems.

Definition:
A **configuration task** is finding the solution and the composed solution for a given configuration problem of a certain class of configuration problems.

Every composed solution of a configuration problem can be an element of another configuration problem. This means that every configuration task is recursively divisible into a hierarchy of configuration tasks. For instance, the configuration task of gantry robots can be divided into the task of configuring the *transport unit* and of configuring the *support unit*. The formal definition of a configuration task is necessary in order to fix exactly the area of application of KONFGEN-II. Without this formal definition, critics would consider KONFGEN-II a general expert system generator similar to a general problem solver, which is not true.

3 The Specification Language

Moreover, the formal definition of configuration tasks given in section 2 is also the basis for the specification language of KONFGEN-II. This section introduces the general structure of the specification language and gives an example from the domain of gantry robots. The specification language provides a model to the knowledge engineer with which he can describe the knowledge of one or more configuration experts about their class of configuration problems, for instance the class of gantry robots. According to the definitions in section 2, every configuration task can be recursively divided into a hierarchy of configuration tasks. Therefore, the specification of the expert knowledge consists of a list of hierarchically connected specifications of classes of configuration problems as follows:

class: <cl_name_1>; ...
...
class: <cl_name_i>;
  superclasses: <cl_name_o>,...,<cl_name_p>;
  subclasses: <cl_name_r>,...,<cl_name_s>;
  problem_definition: **set_of_parts:** ...
    set_of_restrictions: ...
    quality_function: ...
    composition: ...
    set_of_demands: ...
  problem_solving: ...
...
class: <cl_name_n1>; ...

Every class of the list has a unique name <cl_name_i> and contains a list of the names of the corresponding superclasses and subclasses. In the domain of gantry robots, for example, a usual class name is *transport_unit*. The specification of one class of the hierarchy is further structured into a problem definition part and a problem solving part. The problem definition part contains the expert knowledge about the kind of configuration tasks the expert can solve. The problem solving part contains the expert knowledge of how the configuration expert solves a given configuration problem of the class. According to the definition of a class of configuration problems in section 2, the problem solving part includes specifications of the given set of parts, the set of restrictions, the quality function, the composition and the possible demands which the user of the generated expert system can state. The general structure of the specification of the set of parts is as follows:

set_of_parts:
  component: <co_name_1>; ...
  ...
  component: <co_name_i>;
    declarations:
      constant_attributes: <ca_name_1_1>,...,<ca_name_1_p> : <type_c_1>;
        ...
        <ca_name_o_1>,...,<ca_name_o_p> : <type_c_o>;
      variable_attributes: <va_name_1_1>,...,<va_name_1_t> : <type_v_1>;
        ...
        <va_name_s_1>,...,<va_name_s_t> : <type_v_s>;
    parts:
      variant: <v_name_1>; ...
      ...
      variant: <v_name_i>; <ca_name_1> := <value_1>;
        ...;
        <ca_name_v> := <value_v>;
      ...

```
      variant: <v_name_j>; result (<cl_name_k>);
      ...
      variant: <v_name_n2>; ...
  ...
  component: <co_name_n3> ...;
```

The set of parts is specified as being structured into so-called components, which are arbitrary subsets of the set of variants. Every component has a unique identifier <co_name_i> and consists of a declaration of the kind of properties present in that component and of a specification of the parts involved. The possible kinds of properties are declared as constant or variable attributes of a certain type. Constant attributes contain fixed properties of the parts which do not change during the configuration process. The values of variable attributes are flexible and are calculated during the configuration process according to the restrictions. <ca_name_i> and <va_name_i> are unique identifiers. <type_i> is one of the possible types including strings, cardinals, integers, reals and their ranges and lists. The parts of a component are specified as being clustered into variants. Every variant has a unique name <v_name_i>. A variant can be specified in two ways. First, it can be specified by an assignment of the fixed property values of the variant's parts to the corresponding constant attributes as declared in the declaration part of that component (<ca_name_i> := <value_i>). Second, it can be specified by a reference to the result of a configuration task of a subclass of configuration problems in the hierarchy (result (<cl_name_k>)). <value_i> can also be a *copy* or *link* reference. The *copy* reference copies the value of its parameter into its destination when generating the expert system. The *link* reference is a pointer to its parameter, which is evaluated when accessing the variant during the configuration process. The parameter of *copy* and *link* is normally an external function. By means of this mechanism, it is possible to include data from other programs, like facts from databases or CAD systems, into a specification. For example, the component *carriage_drive* of the class *transport_unit* including the carriage drives mentioned in section 2 is specified as follows:

```
component: carriage_drive;
  declarations:
    constant_attributes: price, speed, mass_limit: cardinal;
    variable_attributes: cable_length: [6..15] of cardinal;
  parts:
    variant: CDa;
      speed:= 50; mass_limit:= 80; price:= copy(dblookup(CDa,price));
    variant: CDb;
      speed:= 50; mass_limit:= 80; price:= copy(dblookup(CDb,price));
    variant: CDs; result (special_carriage_drives);
```

The set of restrictions of a class of configuration problems as introduced in section 2 is specified as a list of single restriction specifications of the form:

set_of_restrictions:

restriction: <r_name_1>; ...

...

restriction: <r_name_i>;

validity: <r_predicate_i>;

expression: <r_expression_i>;

operator: <r_operator_i>;

...

restriction: <r_name_n4>; ...

Every restriction of the list has a unique identifier <r_name_i>. The predicate <r_predicate_i> determines the cases in which the restriction <r_name_i> is valid. The dependence that the restriction <r_name_i> describes is specified by the expression <r_expression_i> and the operator <r_operator_i> The expression leads to a certain result based on the values of the attributes of the components and on external functions. The operator maps the results of the expression in the range of real numbers [0..1]. The result of the operator indicates the grade of how well the dependence of the restriction is fulfilled. The more the restriction is relaxed, the lower the result of the operator. As the operator can be a continuous function as well as a list of reference points with an interpolation rule, so case-based and model-based specification of the restrictions are possible. The following example shows the specification of the restriction R1 of section 2 tailored to the special case of using a gripper with shape gripping:

restriction: mass_limit_shape;

validity: gripping_unit.kind = "shape_gripping";

expression: gripping_unit.mass + workpiece_mass + lifting_unit.mass ;

operator: interpolation ((0.8 × carriage_drive.mass_limit, 1.0), (0.7 × carriage_drive.mass_limit, 0.7), (0.0,0.1), (carriage_drive.mass_limit, 0.0));

The specification of the quality function of a class of configuration problems as introduced in section 2 has the following form:

quality_function:

weights: <r_name_1> : <r_factor_1>;

...

<r_name_n4> : <r_factor_n4>;

operator: <q_operator>;

The quality function is specified by an operator <q_operator> which integrates the results of the restrictions <r_name_1>, ..., <r_name_n4> to a real number of [0..1]. The result of the operator indicates the degree of how much the solution found for the given configuration task fulfills the internal restrictions. Factors <r_factor_1>, ..., <r_factor_n4> can be specified to give the results the of the restrictions a particular weight in the operator <q_operator>. An example for an operator is a *FUZZY-AND*. The specification of the composition as introduced in section 2 has the following structure:

composition:

range: <sa_name_1_1>,...,<sa_name_1_f> : <type_s_1>;

...

<sa_name_e_1>,...,<sa_name_e_f> : <type_s_e>;

domain: <co_name_1> : <co_predicate_1>;

...

<co_name_n3> : <co_predicate_n3>;

regulation:

partial_regulation: <sr_name_1>; ...

...

partial_regulation: <sr_name_i>;

validity: <sr_predicate_i>;

mapping: <sa_name_1> := <expression_1>;

...

<sa_name_m> := <expression_m>;

...

partial_regulation: <sr_name_n5>; ...

As the composition is a partial mapping, the specification of the composition is structured into a description of the range, the domain and the regulation. The range is specified by declaring the attributes <sa_name_i> of the configurable objects with their type <type_s_i>. Analogous to the definition of the composition in section 2, the domain is described by a predicate on the results of the restrictions. To reduce complexity, the predicate is specified by a list of single predicates, one for each component (<co_predicate_i> for <co_name_i>). The composition is only defined if all component-specific predicates are *true*. The regulation is specified by a list of partial regulations <sr_name_i> whose validity is defined by a predicate <sr_predicate_i>. The mapping of a regulation is a list of assignments of expressions to the corresponding attributes declared in the solution declaration of the composition (<sa_name_i> := <expression_i>). For example, the predicate of component *carriage_drive* of gantry robots and the regulation to calculate the ***height*** of the configured gantry robot is specified as follows in the composition of gantry robots:

composition:

range: height: real; ...

domain:

carriage_drive : (mass_limit_shape > 0.0) ∧ (speed_limit > 0.2) ∧ ...

...

regulation:

partial_regulation: height_calculation;

validity: true;

mapping: height := support.length + lifting_unit.upper_length;

...

The possible demands of a class of configuration problems as introduced in section 2 are specified by a single incomplete demand. The user of the generated expert system defines his individual demand out of the set of possible demands by filling the incomplete demand with his input. Therefore, the input of the user of the generated expert system, for instance a customer of a gantry robot, determines the configuration task which has to be solved. Because of this, the specification of the set of demands of a class of configuration problems has the following structure:

```
set_of_demands:
  demand_restrictions:
    restriction: <dr_name_1>; ...
        ...
    restriction: <dr_name_i>;
      interactions:
        ...
        output: <dr_output_i>;
        input:  <in_name_1> : <type_in_1> : <in_default_1>;
                ...
                <in_name_n6> : <type_in_n6> : <in_default_n6>;
        ...
      expression: <dr_expression_i>; ...
      operator: <dr_operator_i>;
    ...
    restriction: <dr_name_n7>; ...
  demand_quality_function:
    interactions: ...
    weights:    <dr_name_1> : <dr_factor_1>;
                ...
                <dr_name_n7> : <dr_factor_n7>;
    operator: <dq_operator>;
  demand_quality_bound: <dqb_output> : <dqb_default>;
  quality_bound: <qb_output> : <qb_default>;
```

The restrictions of the specified incomplete demand are listed with their identifier <dr_name_i>. The dependence of a demand restriction <dr_name_i> contains an interaction whose inputs <in_name_h> or defaults <in_default_h> of type <type_in_h> complete the expression <dr_expression_i> and the operator <dr_operator_i>. Filling the expression and the operator of a specified restriction pattern leads to a complete, executable restriction for the composed object as introduced in section 2. In the same way, the weights <dr_factor_i> and the operator <dq_operator> of the user-defined quality function of the demand is completed. As the lower quality bounds of a demand are single values of the real range [0..1], the bounds are prompted directly by the output <dqb_output> and <qb_output>. All output of the specified set of demands, for instance <dqb_output>, can be of formated text with external function calls. For example, the demand restriction RD1 of section 2 for the height of the configured gantry robot can be specified as follows:

demand_restrictions:
restriction: height_limit;
interactions:
output: "The full height of the gantry robot should be lower than?";
input: in_1 : real : 6.0;
output: "The full height of the gantry robot must be lower than?";
input: in_2 : real : 10.0;
expression: height;
operator: interpolation ((in_1,1.0),(in_2,0.0));

By means of the language concepts for the problem definition part, the knowledge engineer can describe the kind of configuration tasks the configuration expert is able to solve. The problem solving part of a specification contains a description of how the configuration expert solves a given configuration task of the class defined in the problem definition part. The problem solving knowledge can be divided into modularization knowledge and strategic knowledge. With his modularization knowledge, the configuration expert divides a complex configuration problem into small subproblems with lower complexity. Then, the solution of the complex configuration problem can be found by solving all subproblems and integrating the partial solutions. The specification language provides two modularization concepts. First, every class of configuration problems can be divided into a hierarchy of classes of configuration problems. Second, components can be defined so that every configuration task of a class can be considered as a set of connected component-specific subtasks which can be solved instead of the given configuration task. Solving a component-specific subtask means selecting (under consideration of the relevant restrictions) a subset of the variants of the component and inserting a subset of parts from every selected variant into the solution. The specification language provides no special facilities for the specification of the modularization knowledge because the problem definition part can be specified according to the modularization knowledge.
With his strategic knowledge, the configuration expert knows an adequate sequence for solving the component-specific subtasks of a class. Additionally, he knows which configuration tasks of which classes of the hierarchy can be treated in parallel and which must be treated sequentially. By means of his strategic knowledge he also knows the heuristics of how many parts of which variants of a component are best-suited if there are alternatives. Finally, he knows with his strategic knowledge which solutions of which component-specific subtasks have to be revised if there are inconsistencies. In the specification language the determination of the sequence in which the component-specific subtasks are solved is considered a special kind of configuration task. All components of a class are redundantly clustered into subproblems just as variants are clustered into components. According to a given set of restrictions, in every problem solving step a subset of components is selected from a particular subproblem, whose component-specific subtasks are solved next. How a component-specific subtask is to be solved can be specified at each subproblem. Therefore, the problem solving part of a specification is structured into a specification of the various subproblems, a specification of the problem solving restrictions and a specification of the single problem solving steps as follows:

```
problem_solving:
  subproblems:
    subproblem: <sp_name_1>; ...
    ...
    subproblem: <sp_name_i>;
      component: <co_name_a>; ...
      ...
      component: <co_name_j>;
        demand_restrictions: <dr_name_x>,...,<dr_name_y>;
        subclass_configuration: <sc_predicate_j>;
        selection_heuristic: <s_heuristic_j>;
        consistency_checking: <c_strategy_j>;
        solution_presentation:
                successful: <e_presentation_j>;
                not_successful: <n_presentation_j>;
      ...
      component: <co_name_b>; ...
    ...
    subproblem: <sp_name_n8>; ...
  set_of_restrictions:
    restriction: <psr_name_1>; ...
      ...
    restriction: <psr_name_n9>; ...
  steps:
    step: <st_name_1>; ...
    ...
    step: <st_name_i>;
      subproblem: <sp_name_i>;
      predicate: <st_predicate_i>;
      heuristic: <st_heuristic_i>;
    ...
    step: <st_name_n10>; ...
```

The subproblems are specified in the form of a list of single subproblems with a unique identifier <sp_name_i>. Every subproblem consists of a list of components specified in the problem definition part of that class referred by their name <co_name_j>. For every component mentioned, knowledge is specified as how to solve the corresponding component-specific subtask. First, a list of names of restriction patterns <dr_name_x>,...,<dr_name_y> of the class is specified, which must be filled with input of the user of the generated expert system before treating the component <co_name_j>. Second, a predicate <sc_predicate_j> is specified which defines whether configuration tasks of the subclasses, referred in <co_name_j>, are solved in general or solely if there is no solution when considering only the explicitly specified variants of <co_name_j>. The explicitly specified variants of a component can be seen as standard solutions for the subclasses of configuration problems of the component. Third, a heuristic <st_heuristic_i> is specified which determines a quality function selecting the best possible parts of the component <co_name_j>.

Beside the quality functions already specified, one's own definitions of a quality function by using the language concepts mentioned above are possible. Fourth, a strategy <c_strategy_j> is specified which determines a sequence in which the consistency of the other component-specific subtasks have to be checked after inserting the parts of the selected variants of the <co_name_j> into the solution. Fifth, one can specify how to present the result of the component-specific subtask to the user of the generated expert system. If the problem solving was successful, the solution of the component-specific subtask is presented in the form of <e_presentation_j>. If the problem solving was not successful, a certain message is given according to <n_presentation_j>. Beside some standard presentations, it is possible to specify external functions, for instance special graphics interfaces.
The problem solving restrictions <psr_name_i> are specified similar to the restrictions <r_name_i> of the problem definition part. But instead of expressing a dependence between the attributes of the components, a problem solving restriction describes a relation between the components for the sequence in which the components are configured. The single problem solving steps are specified in the sequence in which they are executed in the generated expert system. Every step has a unique identifier <st_name_i> and refers to one of the specified subproblems <sp_name_i> of the class. <st_predicate_i> is a predicate on the problem solving restrictions. It is *true* only for such subsets of the components of the subproblem <sp_name_i> which can be treated in step <st_name_i>. The heuristic <st_heuristic_i> is, like the selection heuristic <st_heuristic_i>, a quality function which selects the best alternative of the treatable components. The following example shows the subproblem of configuring the units for moving the workpieces and tools gripped. Depending on the kind of the configured gripping unit, it is better to configure either the carriage drive or the lifting unit first. The subproblem is treated in the first step of the gripper integration.

```
problem_solving:
  subproblems:
    subproblem: motion_unit_1;
      component: carriage_drive;
        demand_inputs: height;
        subclass_configuration: true;
        selection_heuristic: least_commitment;
        consistency_checking: configuration_sequence;
        solution_presentation:
            successful: simulation (); not_successful: standard;
      component: lifting_unit; ...
      ...
  set_of_restrictions:
    restriction: carriage_drive_before_lifting_unit;
      validity: gripping_unit.kind = "shape_gripping";
      expression: before (carriage_drive,lifting_unit);
      operator: case ((true,1.0),(false,0.0));
    restriction: carriage_drive_after_lifting_unit; ...
    ...
```

steps:
  step: gripper_integration_1;
    subproblem: motion_unit_1;
    predicate: (carriage_drive_before_lifting_unit +
        carriage_drive_after_lifting_unit) $\geq$ 1.0;
    heuristic: most_incomplete_demand_restrictions;
  step: gripper_integration_2; ...
  ...

The operational semantics of the specification language is defined by mapping into the internal knowledge representation as shown in the following section.

4 The Process of Generation

The generator KONFGEN-II parses the specification language and maps it into an internal knowledge representation. In contrast to the mapping of the specification language of KONFGEN-I, which only produces production rules [3], the mapping of the specification language of KONFGEN-II generates a hybrid knowledge representation. As shown in figure 3, the hybrid knowledge representation generated consists of a control component in the form of production rules which create small constraint problems during their execution. A constraint satisfaction component solves these small constraint problems and returns the result to the production rules of the control component. The basis for this mapping is, on the one hand, a distributed production system called MAGSY [10]. MAGSY uses the syntax and inference mechanism of OPS5 and, as it is a tool for the development of multi-agent systems, it has special concepts for interchanging facts asynchronously between parallel MAGSY processes. MAGSY is implemented in C and runs on UNIX machines. On the other hand, the mapping is based on the constraint system YACSS [5], which is implemented in CommonLISP and which provides a well-defined language interface for the dynamic formulation of constraint problems. Therefore, the generator KONFGEN-II creates from the specification language MAGSY source code which is afterwards compiled by the MAGSY compiler into an executable program. During the program execution, the rules of the various MAGSY processes formulate constraint problems in YACSS syntax, call YACSS for solving them, and integrate the results into their further program execution.
The generated rules and constraint problems operationalize the specification of a class of configuration problems according to the following abstract inference mechanism:

1. Initialization:
   Set the results of all unexecutable validity predicates to *false* and of all invalid or unexecutable operators to *1.0*. Prompt for the demand quality function and the quality bounds.

2. Select components treated next:
   Treat the steps in sequence in which they are written. Select in each step components according to the predicate and the heuristic of the step.

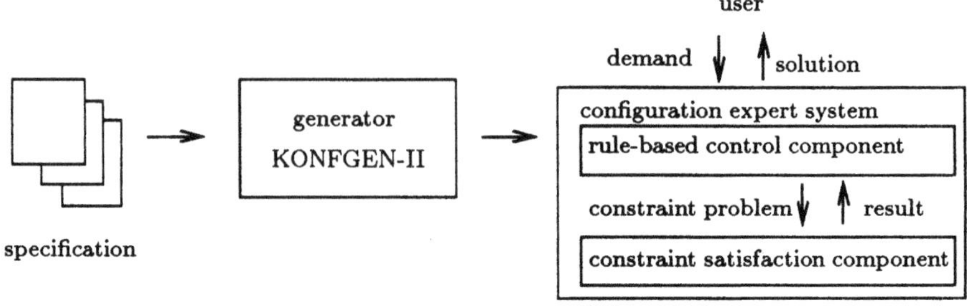

Figure 3: Principle of the generation process

3. Check consistency for selected components:
   In the sequence in which the steps are specified, check whether the predicate of every step is still *true*. If the predicate of a step is false, do backtracking to this step and select other components by means of the heuristic.

4. Treat components:
   Treat the selected components as follows. Complete the demand restrictions of the component and, according to the subclass predicate, configure the subclasses of the component. Select parts of the variants of the component in such a way that the domain of the composition is not left, that the internal and the demand quality function reach their lower quality bounds and that the selection heuristic of the component is maximized. If parts can be selected, display them according to the solution presentation. If no parts can be selected, try to configure the subclasses in case not already done, or advise the user to revise his input.

5. Check consistency for selected parts:
   In the sequence of the specified consistency strategy, check for all components already treated as to whether the domain of the composition is still kept to. If in a component the domain is left, backtrack to this component and select another alternative of parts in this component by means of the selection heuristic.

5 Discussion and Outlook

The main advantage of the generator KONFGEN is that the knowledge engineer can describe the knowledge of the configuration expert on a high, problem-oriented level and can automatically formalize and implement this high-level description simply by calling the generator program. As the size of the specification is approximately only 1/5 of the source code of the corresponding manual implementation [8], the development of a configuration expert system is shortened when using KONFGEN. Also the maintenance of the configuration expert is simplified, because the knowledge engineer can alter the specification instead of the code and generate a new expert system. Thus, he needs not be familiar with the details of the internal knowledge representation, for instance the complex precondition of a certain production rule in the large rule set. As the internal knowledge representation is automatically generated, the risk of errors is lower than with manual formalization and implementation. The specification language being a well-defined interface, it is possible to connect other knowledge acquisition systems to KONFGEN-II. These can be special knowledge elicitation tools or special learning systems. Because the interface to the generated configuration expert system can be specified by the knowledge engineer, it is possible to integrate the generated expert system into other programs, for instance support programs for salesmen. Furthermore, the well-defined user interfaces allow the use of KONFGEN-II in generic problem solvers [4], since all tasks which are intended to solve a configuration problem can be implemented and integrated using KONFGEN-II. In the same way, it can be applied to operationalize particular parts of a KADS model [9].

Currently I am implementing KONFGEN-II in C and UNIX using MAGSY and YACSS. First tests showed that generating a configuration expert system with a complexity similar to KONFIGULA will only take a few minutes. After finishing the implementation, I want to develop a graphics knowledge elicitation system for the specification language similar to that for KONFGEN-I [7]. Besides, I am planning the validation of the specification language by building some configuration expert systems from different domains.

References

[1] Buchanan B., Barstow D., Bechtal R.: Constructing an Expert System. In: Hayes- Roth F., Waterman D., Lenat D.: Building Expert Systems. Addison-Wesley, 1983

[2] Buchka P.: Entwurf und Implementierung eines regelbasierten Expertensystems zur Konfigurierung von Ladeportalen. Technische Universität München, Diplomarbeit, November 1987

[3] Bocionek S., Buchka P., Schweiger J.: Generating Expert Systems for Configuration Tasks. IEEE International Conference on Robotics and Automation. Cincinnati. May 1990

[4] Chandrasekaran B.: Towards a Functional Architecture for Intelligence Based on Generic Information Processing Tasks. Proceedings of the IJCAI-87, Milan, August 1987

[5] Hahndel S.: Vergleich verschiedener Constrainttechniken bezüglich des darstellbaren Wissens und der Inferenzstrategie, sowie Entwurf und Implementierung eines Constraint Satisfaction Systems am Beispiel einer Verkehrssituation. Technische Universität München, Diplomarbeit, May, 1991

[6] Karbach W., Linster M.: Wissensakquisition für Expertensysteme: Techniken, Modelle und Softwarewerkzeuge. Hanser Verlag, München, 1990

[7] Lichtenfeld R.: Entwurf und Implementierung einer Wissensakquisitionskomponente für einen Konfigurierer-Generator. Technische Universität München, Diplomarbeit, March, 1991

[8] Schweiger J.: Reimplementierung eines Expertensystems zur Konfigurierung von Ladeportalen mit Hilfe des Konfigurierer-Generators KONFGEN. In: Günter A., Cunis R.: Beiträge zum 5. Workshop "Planen und Konfigurieren". Hamburg, April 1991

[9] Wielinga B., Breuker J.: Models of Expertise. Proceedings of the ECAI, 1986

[10] Windisch H.: Entwurf und Implementierung eines Regelinterpreters für Echtzeitplanungsaufgaben. Technische Universität München, Diplomarbeit, November 1990

Yet another formalisation of KADS Conceptual Models

Willem Jonker and Jan Willem Spee
PTT Research
P.O. Box 15000
Groningen
The Netherlands

Abstract
This paper presents the use of the VITAL conceptual modeling language to formalise KADS conceptual models. This language is a formal language based on algebraic specification and order sorted predicate logic.
The formalisation distinguishes itself from previous formalisations through the use of signature types parameterised by sorts and predicates for the specification of domain independent interpretation models. The approach will be compared to the $(ML)^2$ and FORKADS formalisations. The comparison will especially focus on the representation of interpretation models and the link between the domain and inference layer. This paper will show that the use of parameterised signature types is a very natural way of binding domain layers to interpretation models.

1. Introduction

The KADS approach ([Wielinga, 1991]) to knowledge engineering has gained much influence. One of the major activities in this approach is the construction of a conceptual model. In KADS, conceptual models are described in an informal language. The lack of preciseness of these descriptions turned out to be a serious problem ([Wielinga, 1989]) and therefore currently efforts are undertaken to develop a formal representation of the models, called $(ML)^2$ ([Akkermans, 1990], [Harmelen, 1992]) and FORKADS [Wetter, 1990]. The reasons presented for formalising are well known from software engineering ([Meyer, 1985]): clarity, unambiguity, precision and verification.
This paper will present a formalisation of KADS conceptual models using the VITAL conceptual modelling language. This language has been developed within ESPRIT-II project 5365 VITAL[1] and is based on formal specification techniques from software engineering ([Jonker, 1991]). This formalisation will be compared to the $(ML)^2$ and

[1]The research described here was partly funded by the CEC under ESPRIT-II project 5365 VITAL *A methodology-based workbench for KBS life-cycle support*. Partners are SYSECA (Coordinator), ANDERSEN CONSULTING, BULL CEDIAG, NOKIA RESEARCH CENTER, ONERA, ROYAL PTT NEDERLAND NV, THE OPEN UNIVERSITY, UNIVERSITY OF NOTTINGHAM. This paper reflects the opinions of the authors and not necessarily those of the consortium.

FORKADS formalisations. The comparison will especially focus on the representation of interpretation models and the link between the domain and inference layer.
The next section contains a brief description of the VITAL conceptual modelling language. Section 3 describes the formalisation of KADS conceptual models using the VITAL conceptual modelling language. Section 4 contains a comparison between this formalisation, $(ML)^2$ and FORKADS. Section 5 contains conclusions and prospects.

2. The VITAL Conceptual Modelling Language

The aim of the VITAL project is to produce a methodology together with a workbench, which is an integrated set of tools to support the development of knowledge-based systems (KBS). The VITAL project started in 1990 and will last until 1995. The project aims at using existing methodologies and tools from Software Engineering (SE) and Artificial Intelligence (AI).
The VITAL methodology is centred around a number of intermediate models (e.g. conceptual model, design model, executable KBS). The development of these models will be supported by an integrated set of languages and tools. The languages are used to represent the intermediate models in the KBS development. Tools assist the knowledge engineer when building the models using these languages. In addition, tools support the transformations between the models.

2.1. VITAL Conceptual Models

In VITAL, a conceptual model is the model of the expertise needed in the KBS under development. A conceptual model is constructed during the knowledge acquisition activity and is represented using the VITAL conceptual modelling language. The conceptual model serves as an input for the system specification and the system design activities.
This section contains a brief outline of the elements of a conceptual model: domain data, domain knowledge and problem solving behaviour. A more detailed description is given in [Spee, 1991].

Domain Data
Domain data describe the domain concepts, objects and their properties, they define *what it is all about*. Both abstract ('a chair') and physical objects ('the chair you are sitting on') are modelled by the domain data.

Domain Knowledge

The domain knowledge describes *what is known about* domain objects. It has to capture the statements that can be made about domain objects ('that chair is never used') and relationships between these statements ('if this chair is never used it can be put aside').

Problem Solving Behaviour

The problem solving behaviour describes *which* tasks are carried out and *how* these tasks are carried out in the domain. It is described in terms of manipulating domain data and applying and manipulating domain knowledge ('to sit on a chair, first move it from under the table; then sit on it and move it a bit forward').

2.2. The VITAL CML[1]

The VITAL Conceptual Modelling Language is used to represent conceptual models. It contains constructs to represent the elements of conceptual models presented above. The following sections contain brief descriptions of these language constructs.

Domain Data

Domain data is specified by means of Abstract Data Types (ADT) based on the algebraic specification technique ACT-ONE ([Ehrig, 1985]), extended with subtyping. An algebraic specification of an ADT consists of a *signature* and a set of *equations*. The signature contains the names of the *sorts* and *functions* of the ADT. The signature is used to represent the elements of the sorts by terms constructed from the functions.

For example the following signature can be used to specify natural numbers:

```
sorts Nat
functions
    0   : -> Nat
    succ: Nat -> Nat
    add : Nat, Nat -> Nat
```

Terms that can be constructed from this signature are for example:

```
succ(succ(0)); add(succ(0),add(0,succ(0)))
```

Equations are equivalence relations between terms and can be used to determine whether two terms are equal and thus represent the same element of the sort. For example the following equations can be used to infer that the terms above represent the same natural number.

---

[1] The VITAL CML also has a graphical informal counterpart, however this paper focuses on the formal part only.

```
equations
  var X, Y: Nat
    add(0, X) = X
    add(succ(X), Y) = succ(add(X,Y))
```

As underlying semantics *initial algebra semantics* is taken. This means that terms of a sort are equal only if they can be proven equal by the equations. The equivalence sets of terms can be used to represent the elements of the sort. Furthermore, a sort contains exactly those elements represented by the equivalence sets. The user interested in algebraic specification is referred to [Bergstra, 1989].

Domain Knowledge

Domain knowledge is specified by means of order sorted predicate logic. A domain knowledge specification consists of a domain data specification extended with *predicate names*, *signature types* and *theories*. The predicate names become part of the signature of a domain knowledge specification. Signature types are tuples of sort names and predicate names and define signatures of theories. Theories are sets of first order logic expressions. Take for example the following predicate, signature type and theory definitions:

```
predicates
    small: Nat
    larger_than: Nat, Nat

sigtypes
    T1 = [sorts Nat predicates larger_than]
    T2 = T1 ∪ [predicates small]

theories
    T1_theory = { larger_than(succ(x), x),
                  larger_than(succ(x), succ(y)) <- larger_than(x,y),
                  larger_than(x,z) <- larger_than(x,y) & larger_than(y,z)
                }
    T2_theory = { small(y) <- small(x) & larger_than(x,y) }
```

The signature type T1 allows theories in terms of the predicate 'larger_than' over the sort Nat, while the signature type T2 allows the predicate 'small' as well. The theory T2_theory has signature type T2.
As underlying semantics of theory expressions the well known Tarski semantics are used ([Dalen, 1980]).

Problem solving behaviour

Problem solving behaviour is specified by means of *tasks*. A task specification consists of a task name, a specification of the input and output parameters, a set of local variable declarations and a behaviour description. The type of the parameters and variables are signature types. The behaviour description is given in terms of a control oriented specification language. It consists of a list of statements. Examples of statements are:

- assignment
```
<variable> := <expression>
```

- task call
```
<taskname>(<expression_1>, ... , <expression_n>)
```

- generalised if
```
choice
  <condition_1> -> <statement-list_1>
  []
  ...
  []
  <condition_n> -> <statement-list_n>
end
```

- endless loop
```
do <statement-list> od
```

The language used is a high level imperative language including guarded commands ([Dijkstra, 1976]).

Structuring

Conceptual models can be structured by decomposing them into modules. The VITAL CML has two kinds of modules: data/knowledge modules (*Dmodules*) and behaviour modules (*Bmodules*). A specification of a conceptual model in the VITAL CML consists of a collection of Dmodules and Bmodules.

A Dmodule consists of a collection of sort, function, predicate and signature type definitions together with a collection of equations and theories (all these elements are optional). A Bmodule consists of a collection of signature definitions together with a collection of tasks. Modules can use elements from other modules by importing these modules; Dmodules can import Dmodules, Bmodules can import both Dmodules and Bmodules.

```
Dmodule NatQueues is Nats
    sorts Natqueue
    functions
      ins: Nat, Natqueue -> Natqueue
      ...
    equations ...
End NatQueues
```

In the above example the Dmodule Nats, which specifies the natural numbers, is imported by the Dmodule NatQueues.

In order to be able to specify generic modules, that is, modules that can be applied to a number of domains, Dmodules can be *parameterised* with sorts, functions and predicates. In such a parameterised module *formal sorts*, *formal functions*, and *formal predicates* are given. In this way, besides the well known parameterised data types it is also possible to specify *parameterised theories.*

As an example consider the following generic queue specification.

```
Dmodule GenericQueues
    formal sorts Element
    sorts        Genericqueue
    functions
        create: -> Genericqueue
        ins   : Element, Genericqueue -> Genericqueue
        ...
    equations
        ...
End GenericQueues
```

A parameterised module can be *actualised* by binding the formal sorts, functions and predicates to actual sorts, functions and predicates. The generic queue module of the example above can be used to specify a queue of natural numbers by binding the formal sort Element to the actual sort Nat from the Dmodule Nats.

```
Dmodule NatQueues is GeneralQueues
    actualised by Nats using Nat for Element
End NatQueues
```

To fully actualise a module the parameterised elements from the module itself and those of the imported modules have to be bound.

3. Using the VITAL CML to formalise KADS conceptual models

3.1. KADS conceptual models

A KADS conceptual model consists of four different layers. The first layer, the domain layer, is used to model *static domain dependent knowledge*. Within the second layer, the inference layer, canonical inference steps and the information exchanged between these steps is modelled. The canonical inferences are called *knowledge sources*, and the type of the information exchanged between them *meta-classes*. The third layer, the task layer, models how the canonical inferences can be combined in a *task* to reach a certain goal. The fourth layer models strategic knowledge. This layer contains *plans* or *metarules* that describe how tasks can be combined to achieve goals. Each layer interprets or manipulates the description at the lower layer. One of the major modelling paradigms in KADS is the existence of *interpretation models*. These are conceptual models with an empty domain layer, that can be applied to or instantiated for a number of domains.

3.2. Representing a KADS CM in VITAL CML

This section demonstrates how a KADS conceptual model is specified using the VITAL CML. The formalisation is presented by formalising an example conceptual model given in [Hickman, 1989]. This leading example is an application of the heuristic classification interpretation model applied in a medical domain: medical observations of a patient are transformed into symptoms of diseases. These symptoms are matched against probable diseases. These probable diseases are further specified into actual diseases.

Formalisation of the domain layer

The domain layer is domain dependent and contains concepts, objects, relations between concepts and objects, and structures built from relations. This layer is task neutral, which means that, in principal, the knowledge specified at this level may be used for a variety of tasks.

The formalisation of the domain layer in VITAL CML is straightforward by using Dmodules; concepts are modelled by ADTs and knowledge is modelled by theories. The formalisation of the domain layer of the medical example in Hickman is given below.

```
Dmodule CharacteristicToSymptomDefinition is RealNumbers
    sorts characteristics, symptoms
    predicates
        value      : characteristics, reals
        indication: symptoms
End CharacteristicToSymptomDefinition

Dmodule CharacteristicToSymptomInstantiation
is CharacteristicToSymptomDefinition
    functions
        age, temperature, pressure, food_intake         : -> characteristics
        fever, spots, headache, hypertension, mouth_pain: -> symptoms
    theories
        values_to_indications =
          { value(temperature,X) & X > 38.0 -> indication(fever),
            value(pressure,Y) & Y > 100 -> indication(hypertension) }
End CharacteristicToSymptomInstantiation

Dmodule SymptomsToDiseasesDefinition is CharacteristicToSymptomDefinition
    sorts probable_diseases
    predicates
        is_caused_by    : symptoms, probable_diseases
        general_disease: probable_diseases
End SymptomsToDiseasesDefinition

Dmodule SymptomsToDiseasesInstantiation is SymptomsToDiseasesDefinition
    functions
        measles, liver_sclerosis, indigestion,
        bacterial_infection: -> probable_diseases
    theories
        causal_net =
          { is_caused_by(headache,liver_sclerosis),
            is_caused_by(mouth_pain,indigestion)      }
End SymptomsToDiseasesInstantiation

Dmodule DiseaseHierarchyDefinition is SymptomsToDiseasesDefinition
    sorts actual_diseases < probable_diseases      %% subsort specification
    predicates
        specialization_of: actual_diseases, probable_diseases
        disease          : actual_diseases
End DiseaseHierarchyDefinition
```

```
Dmodule DiseaseHierarchyInstantiation
is DiseaseHierarchyDefinition, SymptomsToDiseasesInstantiation
    functions
        pneumococcea, pneumonia_caused_by_pneumococcea: -> actual_diseases
    theories
        disease_hierarchy =
        { specialization_of(pneumococcea, bacterial_infection) }
End DiseaseHierarchyInstantiation
```

In this example there are three pairs of Dmodules. The definition modules contain sort and predicate definitions, corresponding to concepts and relations. The instantiation modules contain functions corresponding to values (instances of concepts), and theories that represent the actual knowledge and correspond to structures (instances of relations).

Formalisation of the inference and task layers

The inference layer consists of meta-classes and knowledge sources. Meta-classes describe the role that domain concepts play in the problem solving process. Knowledge sources describe what types of inferences can be made on the basis of the relations in the domain layer. The meta-classes and knowledge sources are organised in an inference structure, which specifies what meta-classes are related to what knowledge sources.

Objects at the task layer are goals and tasks. Tasks describe in what way knowledge sources an be combined to reach a certain goal ([Hickman,1989]). A complete description of a task consists of a goal and a method or operation how to achieve this goal.

The inference and task layer in KADS are closely related and the knowledge sources can be considered as primitive tasks. In our formalisation we model both knowledge sources and KADS tasks by VITAL CML tasks. The advantage of this approach is that knowledge sources and tasks can be combined in arbitrary ways and no explicit binding between inference and task layer is needed.

The formalisation of meta-classes is done by parameterised signature types. These types describe the role of the concepts (sorts) and relations (predicates) that exist in the domain layer.

The formalisation is illustrated by the interpretation model for heuristic classification. The inference layer is given below.

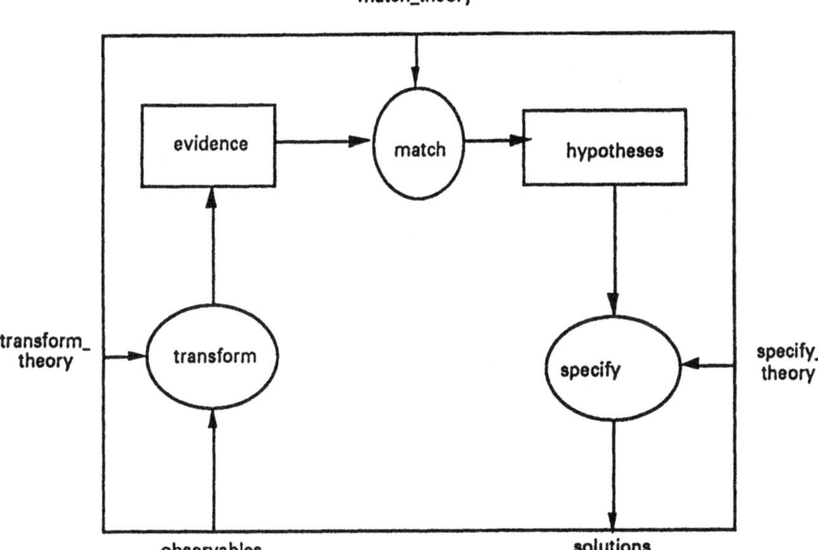

Three knowledge sources are used: a knowledge source transform, that transforms elements from meta-class observables into a elements of the meta-class evidence, using a theory 'transform_theory'. The evidence is matched against hypotheses, and these are further specified into solutions.

Note that inference structures are domain independent, i.e. the meta-classes are generic and must be bound to domain concepts to get a complete conceptual model. This means that we have to use formal sorts to model the role of the concepts and formal predicates to model the role of the predicates.

So, the four meta-classes are modelled by the signature types of four Dmodules parameterised by formal sorts and formal predicates.

```
Dmodule ObservablesRole is
  formal sorts attributes, values
  formal predicates observ: attributes, values
  sigtypes observables = [sorts attributes, values predicates observ]
End ObservablesRole

Dmodule EvidenceRole is
  formal sorts associations
  formal predicates evid: associations
  sigtypes evidence = [sorts associations predicates evid]
End EvidenceRole

Dmodule HypothesisRole is
  formal sorts findings
  formal predicates hypot: findings
  sigtypes hypotheses = [sorts findings predicates hypot]
End HypothesisRole

Dmodule SolutionsRole is HypothesisRole
  formal sorts most_specific_findings < findings
  formal predicates solut: most_specific_findings
  sigtypes solutions = [sorts most_specific_findings predicates solut]
End SolutionsRole
```

The meta-class observables is modelled by the signature type observables. Observables are modelled as attribute-value pairs (e.g. the value of the attribute temperature is 40 will be modelled as observ(temperature,40)). So the meta-class observables consists of theories of the form {observ(Att_1,Val_1),...,observ(Att_n,Val_n)}.
So, the four meta-classes are modelled by the signature types of four Dmodules parameterised by formal sorts and formal predicates.
In a domain, knowledge sources apply not only knowledge specified in meta-classes, but also specific knowledge from that domain. For example the knowledge source transform needs specific knowledge about how to perform transformations in a certain domain. In the KADS description of inference structures these parameters of the knowledge sources are omitted, which we think is wrong. Therefore, we added them explicitly and they are given below. These parameters again are modelled by parameterised signature types and must be bound to actual domain theories to complete the conceptual model.

```
Dmodule TransformSource is ObservablesRole, EvidenceRole
  sigtypes transform_theory = observables ∪ evidence
End TransformSource

Dmodule MatchSource is EvidenceRole, HypothesisRole
  formal predicates caused_by: associations, findings
  sigtypes match_theory = evidence ∪ hypotheses ∪
                          [sorts associations,findings predicates caused_by]
  theories cause_theory = { hypot(y) <- evid(x) & caused_by(x,y) }
End MatchSource

Dmodule SpecifySource is HypothesisRole, SolutionsRole
  formal predicates is_a: most_specific_findings, findings
  predicates chain: findings, most_specific_findings
  sigtypes specify_theory = hypotheses ∪ solutions ∪
                          [sorts  findings  predicates  is_a]
  theories descend_is_a_hierarchy =
              { solut(x) <-  hypot(y) & chain(y,x),
                chain(y,x) <- ( is_a(x,z) & chain(y,z) ) | is_a(x,y) }
End SpecifySource
```

For example the Dmodule MatchSource specifies predicates used in the knowledge source 'match' shown below. The signature type 'match_theory' describes the type of the theory match takes as a parameter. The theory 'cause_theory' is a domain independent theory about how to relate evidence to hypothesis.
The knowledge sources are described below. A knowledge source is described by a task. The input and output parameter types indicate the meta-classes and are signature types. As said before, apart from the meta-classes the knowledge source can take specific theories as inputs.

```
Bmodule Transform use TransformSource
  task transform
    input ob: observables
          th: transform_theory
    output ev: evidence
    { th := union( th, ob, |-, [all])1;
      ev := intersection(th, { evid(x) }, |-, [all]);
      return(ev);
    }
End Transform

Bmodule Match use MatchSource
  task match
    input ev: evidence
          th: match_theory
    output hyp: hypotheses
    {  th := union(th, ev, |-, [all]);
       th := union(th, cause_theory, |-, [all]);
       hyp := intersection(th, { hypot(x) }, |-, [all]);
       return(hyp);
    }
End Match

Bmodule Specify use SpecifySource
  task specify
    input hyp: hypotheses
          th: specify_theory
    output sol: solutions
    { th := union(th, hyp, |-, [all]);
      th := union(th, descend_is_a_hierarchy, |-, [all]);
      sol := intersection(th, { solut(x) }, |-, [all]);
      return(sol);
    }
End Specify
```

For example the specification of the knowledge source 'specify'states that in order to find solutions, one first needs to take the union of the input hypothesis and the theory of specify, that is, an isa-hierarchy. Then one has to add general knowledge about how to descend an isa-hierarchy and finally one has to filter the terms of the form 'solut(x)' that denote solutions.

The task layer contains only one KADS task, modelled by the VITAL CML task 'classify' that describes how to use the knowledge sources described above.

---

[1] The operator ***union (<expression_1>, <expression_2>, <inference operator>, <mode>)*** is a predefined operation, it generates the sentences that can be derived from the union of expression_1 and expression_2. An *inference operator* is specified to support derivations using different types of logics. A *mode* is a control oriented parameter that specifies the type of inference algorithm to use, [all] means derive all sentences. Besides the *union* also other inference operators have been defined: *intersection*, *difference* and *one_of*. The *intersection* operator computes the intersection of the closure of two theories, the *difference* operator computes the difference of the closure of two theories, and *one_of* takes an arbitrary sentence from a theory.

```
Bmodule HeuristicClassification is Transform, Match, Specify
  task classify
    input obs: observables
          tk : transform_theory
          mk: match_theory
          sk: specify_theory
    output sol: solutions
    var ev: evidence
        hyp: hypotheses
        one_obs: observables
    {   one_obs := {};
        do one_obs := one_of(difference(obs, one_obs, |-, [all]));
            ev := transform(one_obs, tk);
            hyp := match(ev, mk);
            sol := specify(hyp, sk);
             choice
              sol != {} -> exit
             end;
        od;
     return(sol);
    }
End HeuristicClassification
```

The specification of the task classify states that in order to find the solutions by means of heuristic classification one takes an observable, transforms this into evidence, matches this evidence to create a hypothesis and finally tries to specify a solution. This process is repeated until a solution is found.

Linking the domain layer and the inference layer

In KADS, a conceptual model is an instantiation of an interpretation model, that is, the interpretation model, consisting of an inference, task and strategy layer, is applied to a certain domain modelled by a domain layer. This means that a binding mechanism is needed to bind an interpretation model to the actual domain. This calls for a binding of the domain layer to the lowest layer of the interpretation model: the inference layer.

As has been shown above, the inference layer is specified by generic signature types and generic tasks. The signature types contain formal sorts and formal predicates. Linking the domain layer to the inference layer in our formalisation is simply a binding of the formal sorts and predicates in the signature types of the inference layer to actual sorts and predicates in the domain layer.

The example below shows how the interpretation model HeuristicClassification is bound to the domain model.

```
Bmodule MedicalDiagnosis is HeuristicClassification
actualised by CharacteristicToSymptomDefinition, SymptomsToDiseasesDefinition,
              DiseaseHierarchyDefinition
  using
    characteristics for attributes
    reals for values
    symptoms for associations
    probable_diseases for findings
    actual_diseases for most_specific_findings
    value for observ
    indication for evid
    general_disease for hypot
    specialization_of for is_a
    disease for solut
```

```
    is_caused_by for caused_by
End MedicalDiagnosis
```

The formal sorts attributes, values, associations etc. are bound to the actual sorts characteristics, reals, symptoms etc. The formal predicates observ, evid etc. are bound to the actual predicates value, indication etc.

The result of this actualisation is a domain specific task classify that can for example be used to give medical advise, as is shown in the example below.

```
Bmodule MedicalAdvise is MedicalDiagnosis
  use  CharacteristicToSymptomInstantiation, SymptomsToDiseasesInstantiation
       DiseaseHierarchyInstantiation

       %% the Dmodules containing the actual domain theories (e.g. 'causal_net')
       %% are imported with the use statement.

  types ...

  task advise
    var patient_data: data_transform_type
        possible_diseases: specialization_type

   { environment(patient_data, input);
     possible_diseases := classify(patient_data, values_to_indications,
                                   causal_net, disease_hierarchy);
     %% the actual domain theories are passed as parameter to the 'classify' task

     environment(possible_diseases, output);
     %% the 'possible_diseases' theory is directed to output.
   }

End MedicalAdvise
```

Formalisation of the strategy layer

The strategic layer should contain control knowledge. The knowledge in the strategic layer allows a system to make plans and control and monitor the execution of tasks. The strategic layer generates a task structure, which represents the order in which goals are pursued. A task structure can be represented in a goal tree and a corresponding task decomposition. Such a goal tree can be fixed or it can dynamically be generated.

Formalisation of the strategy layer using the current version of the VITAL CML is not possible, since a formalism to represent strategy or meta reasoning is currently missing. However we will sketch how the language needs to be extended to allow formalisation of the strategic layer.

To represent meta reasoning in the VITAL CML, there needs to be a representation for goals and how goals can be reached by executing tasks. This calls for a link between tasks and goals: a goal will have one (or a number of tasks) that can achieve it. The global idea is to associate pre- and post-conditions with tasks formulated in first order logic. Goals also need to be represented in first order logic. Now a task can satisfy a goal when its post-condition implies that goal. A task can only be performed if its precondition is satisfied, so this becomes a subgoal.

We need to register which beliefs hold in order to be able to determine whether a goal is already satisfied. This set of beliefs can be represented by a theory.
The outline of the strategic reasoning is: determine a goal, see if the goal can be inferred from the current beliefs, if not determine the tasks, the post-conditions of which imply the goal. The preconditions of these tasks are the subgoals.

4. Comparison with other formalisations

This section contains a comparison of our formalisation with $(ML)^2$ ([Akkermans, 1990], [Harmelen, 1992]) and FORKADS ([Wetter, 1990], [Wetter, 1991]). The comparison will focus on two important aspects of the formalisations: the representation of interpretation models and the binding of domain layers to these interpretation models.

4.1. General approach

As has been outlined above, our general approach is based on the use of algebraic specification for data modelling, order sorted predicate logic for knowledge modelling and an imperative language for task specification.

The framework developed by $(ML)^2$ is also based on order-sorted logic to represent theories of knowledge. These theories are used at the domain and inference layer, in the way that a theory at the inference layer is regarded as the meta-level theory of the object-level theory at the domain layer. That is, the meta-level theory *interprets* the object-level theory.
The link between object-level and meta-level consists of a binding between elements of the object-level theory and elements of the meta-level theory, and a mechanism to affect a theory at the object-level by inference at the meta-level of reasoning at the meta-level, or vice versa.
The binding between meta-level and object-level elements is done by means of a *lift operator*, which is a mapping from terms from the object level theory to ground terms in the meta-level theory. Example (taken from [Akkermans, 1990]):

```
lift-operator findings from definitions to confirm-hypothesis
   signature
    sorts hypothesis
    constants [fever], [adult] : hypothesis
    predicates possible-hypothesis: hypothesis
   end-signature
   mapping
    lift(definitions, fever) -> possible_hypothesis([fever])
    lift(definitions, adult) -> possible_hypothesis([adult])
   end-mapping
end-lift-operator
```

To affect a theory at one level by inference in a theory at one level lower or higher *reflective rules* are used. These are combinations of special predicates and inference rules, that define what can be derived at one level if a theorem at another level is proven *true*.

$$\frac{|-_M \ \mathrm{ask}_{\in} \ (O, \ [P] \ )}{O \ |- \ P}$$

As basic language concept for constructing conceptual models, modules are used, consisting of a signature and a set of axioms. Modules can be imported into another module. Lift operators are stored in separate modules, in which the names of the object-level theories from which elements are taken, and the meta-level theories onto which they are mapped, must be specified. No parameterisation is introduced in the language.

FORKADS is also based on order sorted logic, but instead of introducing theories at different levels, the approach aims at a representation of conceptual models in first order logic. Domain layer knowledge is represented by first order theories. At the inference and task layer goal statements can be specified, consisting of first order logical expressions. Within goal statements so-called attached procedure predicates can be used. These are predicates to which a procedure can be attached. The arguments of such a predicate are seen as the input or output parameters of the attached procedure. These procedures themselves also consists of goal statements. No modularisation mechanism is available.
Example of a goal statement (from [Wetter, 1991]):

```
judge(Subindex, Difference, Chosen_reference)
<-    a_select_target_value(in: Subindex, out: Target_value)
   & a_select_reference_value(in: Subindex, Chosen_reference,
                               out: Reference_value)
   & a_compute_difference(in: Target_value, Reference_value,
                           out: Difference)
```

In this example we see a goal statement consisting of three attached procedure predicates. The arguments of the predicates do not represent variables, but sorts in the sort model. When applying this goal to some application domain, the sort indications are replaced by variables.

Comparing the approaches we see that all approaches use order sorted predicate logic to specify the domain layer. Our approach uses an imperative language to model both inference and task layer. Binding the domain layer to the inference layer is done by actualising formal sorts and predicates. The inference layer in $(ML)^2$ is specified by an order sorted predicate logic as a meta-layer of the domain layer and connected by lift-operators. The task layer is defined as a super-theory of the inference layer, in which a more expressive logic (dynamic logic) can be used. FORKADS uses order sorted predicate logic for the inference and task layer; here the domain and inference layer are bound via the sort model.

None of the approaches has a worked out specification of the strategy layer.

The specification of interpretation models (inference and task layer) and linking of domain and inference layer will be discussed in more detail below.

4.2. The representation of interpretation models

In KADS, interpretation models are used to specify generic problem solving knowledge in a domain independent way. A language to represent conceptual models should support such an approach. As has been illustrated above our approach uses parameterised signature types and task descriptions by means of an imperative language to represent interpretation models. In VITAL CML, interpretation models can be specified in a domain independent way: formal sorts and formal predicates allow a domain independent representation of interpretation models.

In $(ML)^2$, this is not the case. Akkermans admits this deficiency [Akkermans, 1990, p.29] and suggests alternatives by defining the lift-operators in the domain. This will however not solve the problem, since it is more fundamental: in $(ML)^2$ meta-classes are specified within lift-operators, which gives lift-operators a dual role: on the one hand they specify the inference layer and on the other hand they are a linking mechanism between the domain and the inference layer. Mixing up these roles causes the problem.

There is another problem representing domain independent interpretation models, again due to the nature of the lift operators: at the inference level, it has to be specified explicitly which lift-operators are used. However, the lift-operators are domain dependent (since they map domain elements to inference elements) and introduced during the binding of a domain to an interpretation model. As a result inference layer modules have to be adapted each time an interpretation model is instantiated for some application domain.

FORKADS is able to represent interpretation models domain independently, however at the cost of introducing a new layer: the sort model. Interpretation models can be specified domain independently: goal statements, consisting of logical sentences, are specified in terms of the sort model, which is domain independent.

Applying an interpretation model to a certain domain is realised by expanding the goal statements with role-of predicates, and substituting sorts for variables in all predicates of the expanded goal statement:

```
judge(SI, Difference, Chosen_reference)
<-   role_of(SI; S_index)
   & role_of(Actual_value; S_target_value)
   & a_select_target_value(in: S_index, out: S_target_value)
   & role_of(SI, Chosen_reference; S_index, S_reference)
   & role_of(Standard_reference_value; S_reference_value)
   & a_select_reference_value(in: S_index, S_reference,
                              out: S_reference_value)
   & role_of(Actual_value, Standard_reference_value;
             S_target_value, S_reference_value)
   & role_of(Difference, S_value)
   &  a_compute_difference(in: S_target_value, S_reference_value,
                           out: S_value)
```

So a domain independent task description has to be expanded by adding predicates and changing parameter names in order to apply it to a certain domain. It is clear that also with this approach each time a generic task description is applied to a certain domain, it needs to be revised by adding role_of predicates.

In our approach, no modification of generic modules that specify the interpretation model is needed during actualisation.

4.3. Linking domain layers and interpretation models

In our approach, interpretation modules are parameterised with sorts and predicates. The linking of a domain layer to an interpretation model is done by actualising a generic module. The actualisation consist of a mapping of domain sorts and predicates onto formal ones.

$(ML)^2$ uses lift-operators to bind a domain layer to an interpretation model. Apart from the problems of the lift-operator discussed above, the lift-operator itself also gives rise to many questions. We agree with Wetter [Wetter, 1990, p. 373] that the semantics of the operator is not entirely clear (see the worked out example in [Akkermans, 1990]). Another disadvantage of the lift operator is that it is based on term-mapping, instead of the more general principle of sort and predicate mapping (mapping all terms of a large domain specification is a tedious job).

Summarizing, the lift operator is a source of confusion, and as a result the mapping between different layers is unclear at several points.

The binding mechanism introduced by FORKADS is a sort model. This is an order sorted signature, consisting of sorts, functions and predicates and has a close correspondence to our formal sorts and predicates. The sorts in this signature are meant to represent the KADS meta-classes. To such meta-classes a domain sort can be bound a role-of (domain sort; sort-name) predicate, that maps domain sorts onto the sort model. We do not understand why the role-of predicate is limited to sorts, because this implies that at the inference level only domain *data* can be manipulated.

We feel that our approach solves the linking problem in a more convenient way. First, we do not need to introduce an extra layer (lift-operators as $(ML)^2$ does or a sort model as FORKADS does), and second, our approach using parameters is closer to intuition.

5. Conclusions and Prospects

In this paper we have shown how the VITAL CML can be used to formalise KADS conceptual models, although the language was not specially developed for this purpose. We also showed that a number of issues raised by the other formalisations can be overcome by the use of signature types parameterised by formal sorts and predicates.
As far as the VITAL CML is concerned,we are currently working on the representation of meta-reasoning and we also adopt the language to use it for KBS design in addition to conceptual modelling.

6. Acknowledgements

We would like to thank our colleagues Marion Koopman and Linda in 't Veld at PTT Research for their fruitful cooperation during the development of the VITAL CML. In addition, we like to thank Kieron O'Hara, Mandy Mepham and Nigel Shadbolt from Nottingham University, Luis Montero from Andersen Consulting and Enrico Motta from the Open University for their useful comments on the VITAL CML.

7. References

[Akkermans, 1990] Akkermans, H., Harmelen, F. van, Schreiber, G., Wielinga, B., *A formalisation of Knowledge-Level Models for Knowledge Acquisition*, Department of Social Science Informatics, University of Amsterdam

[Bergstra, 1989] Bergstra J.A., Heering J., Klint P., Algebraic Specification, Addison-Wesley, 1989.

[Dalen, 1980] Dalen, D. van, *Logic and Strucuture*, Springer Verlag, 1980.

[Dijkstra, 1976] Dijkstra, E.W., *A Discipline of Programming*, Englewood Cliffs, N.J., Prentice-Hall, 1976.

[Ehrig, 1985] Ehrig, H., Mahr, B., Fundamentals of Algebraic Specification 1, Springer Verlag, 1985.

[Harmelen, 1992] Harmelen, F. van, Balder, J., *$(ML)^2$: A formal language for KADS models of expertise*, The Knowledge Acquisition Journal, March 1992.

[Hickman, 1989] Hickman, F.R. *Analysis for Knowledge-based Systems: A Practicle Guide to the KADS Methodology*, Ellis Horwood Limited, 1989

[Jonker, 1991] Jonker, W., Spee, J.W., In 't Veld, L.J., Koopman, M.R.J., *Formal Approaches towards Software Engineering and their role in KBS Design*, Proc. IJCAI Workshop on Software Engineering for Knowledge Based Systems, Sydney, Australia, 1991.

[Meyer, 1985] Meyer, B., *On Formalisms in Specifications*, IEEE Software, January 1985, pp. 7-26.

[Spee, 1991] Spee, J.W., Koopman, M.R.J., Jonker, W., Veld, L.J. in 't, *The VITAL Conceptual Modelling and Design Approach*, SGES91.

[Wetter, 1990] Wetter, Th., *First Order Logic Foundation of the KADS Conceptual Model*, EKAW90.

[Wetter, 1991] Wetter, Th., Schmidt, W., *Formalization of the KADS Interpretation Models*, AISB91.

[Wielinga, 1989] Wielinga, B.J, Akkermans, H., A.Th. Schreiber, Balder, J, *A Knowledge Acquisition Perspective on Knowledge Level Models*, Proc. 4th Knowledge Acquisition for Knowledge Based Systems Workshop, Banff, 1989.

[Wielinga, 1991] Wielinga, B.J, A.Th. Schreiber, J.A. Breuker, *KADS: A modelling Approach to Knowledge Engineering*, KADS-II/T1.1/PP/UvA/008/1.0, May 8, 1991.

The *KEEP* Model,

a *K*nowledge *E*ngin*E*ering *P*rocess Model

Susanne Neubert and Rudi Studer

Institut für Angewandte Informatik und Formale Beschreibungsverfahren, Universität Karlsruhe (TH)
P.O. Box 6980
7500 Karlsruhe 1
Germany
email: neubert@aifb.uni-karlsruhe.de, studer@aifb.uni-karlsruhe.de

Abstract

The idea of building a specification in the first phase of modeling a system, a principle known from Software Engineering, has been transferred to the area of knowledge engineering. In the context of the so-called model-based knowledge engineering, KADS is a very popular methodology ([BWS87], [WSB91], [WSG89], [HKL89], [KLV89]). However, KADS only provides some basic principles but no complete method how the knowledge engineer should perform his tasks. Therefore, the knowledge engineering process model - the so-called KEEP model - was developed as a guideline for the process of model-based knowledge engineering in the sense of KADS.

The KEEP model resulted from some experience in using the KADS methodology and an assessment of the life-cycle model of Hickman et. al. [HKL89]. The KEEP model is described at different layers of abstraction with the help of a dataflow diagram to give a detailed and structured description of the knowledge engineer's tasks and its results. Furthermore, the KEEP model includes a specification of the control flow for determining the order in which the different activities have to be carried out.

Keywords: KEEP model, conceptual model, knowledge acquisition, knowledge elicitation, knowledge collection, knowledge interpretation

1 Introduction

A central problem in building knowledge based systems (KBSs) is still the knowledge acquisition phase. In the last years, different methods and tools have been developed that shall support this phase. A very promising proposal is the model-based knowledge engineering approach. The aim of this approach is to build an abstract description of the knowledge base similar to the specification known from Software Engineering.

KADS ([BWS87], [WSB91], [WSG89], [HKL89], [KLV89]) - falling into that group - is a methodology that insists in developing an abstract model of expertise, the so-called conceptual model, before constructing the knowledge base. Introducing this intermediate model is a means to cope with the complex knowledge engineering process [WSB91]. Another aid for simplifying this process is a library of domain-independent templates which are reusable for classes of problems and can be used for top-down knowledge acquisition by filling out the missing parts according to the application. The templates can also be combined to describe a complex problem.

In spite of having such a promising methodology for developing the knowledge based system, the knowledge engineer has some problems in applying the basic principles. The fundamental difficulty is that the knowledge engineer does not have any guideline how to start and how to proceed in building a knowledge base according to the principles of KADS described above. KADS-I[1] itself gives only a rough description of the knowledge engineering subtasks.

This paper introduces a guideline for the knowledge engineer to construct the KBS where the development of the conceptual model is of central interest. In analogy to the life-cycle models

1. The ideas for supporting the knowledge engineer developed in the KADS-II project are described in chapter 4.1.

known from Software Engineering like the Spiral model [Boe86][2] etc., a control flow is given describing the ordering of activities in the knowledge engineering process. Moreover, the data flow is described, since this knowledge engineering process (KEEP) model is specified as a data flow diagram (DFD) for describing the relation between activities of the knowledge engineer and their results. This model distinguishes several levels of abstraction in order to describe the complex knowledge engineering process.

The second chapter of this paper shortly discusses the basic principles of the KADS methodology as well as it provides an assessment of KADS. A collection of problems and questions is given resulting from attempts to build a conceptual model on the basis of the KADS methodology for a concrete application. Moreover, the formalism of data flow diagrams (DFDs) is shortly described.

Chapter three presents the KEEP model in detail.

In chapter four, the KEEP model is assessed by comparing it to other approaches describing the process of constructing the conceptual model or the knowledge base. The proposals of the KADS group [WSB91] to develop a KBS as well as the life-cycle model of Hickman et. al. [HKL89] and the principles of EMA [SpW91] are introduced. A comparison between the KEEP model and the existing approaches is given. Finally, first results of using the KEEP model in modeling a formal conceptual model are provided. The chapter ends with discussing the open problems of the existing KEEP model and the required improvements that are done in the current and the future work.

2.0 Overview of Basic Principles

In this chapter, a short overview of the KADS methodology, its basic principles and its present stage is given. Problems with KADS that lead to the development of the KEEP model are described, too.

2.1 Basic Principles of the KADS Methodology

The central approach of model-based knowledge engineering is the KADS methodology which is the foundation for the KEEP model. Therefore, some basic principles of KADS are shortly described. Further information can be found in [BWS87], [WSB91], [HKL89], [WSG89], [KLV90].

Life-cycle orientation

One principle of KADS is to distinguish different phases of developing a knowledge based system, the life-cycle known from Software Engineering. KADS separates the phases *knowledge gathering, analysis, design,* and *implementation.* In the phase of knowledge gathering, information about the expertise is acquired. This information is collected in so-called knowledge protocols. In the analysis phase, the expertise is analysed and structured. The result is the so-called conceptual model. In the design phase, the specified expertise is transformed into a first description of the expert system, the so-called design model. In the implementation phase, this design model is transformed in the knowledge-based system.

2. The spiral model [Boe86] evolved from various refinements of the waterfall model [Roy70] in order to avoid its disadvantages.

The knowledge level - symbol level distinction

At the knowledge level (see [New82]), the specification generally describes what the final system should do. The symbol or program level represents the concrete design and implementation of the knowledge base.

The four layer model

KADS separates different kinds of knowledge categories [WiS90], [WSB91], [HKL89], [Fen91]. Therefore, the conceptual model consists of four different layers[3]:

- The *domain layer* contains the domain specific knowledge about concepts, their features, and their relationships. At this layer, the objects of the domain are described.
- The *inference layer* consists of knowledge about the used problem-solving method. The inference layer includes two kinds of elements: meta classes and knowledge sources. The knowledge sources are active elements and specify the relationships at the domain layer. They perform an action that operates at some input and can produce new information, the output. These data elements are the meta classes which are data containers or placeholders for domain objects at the domain layer. Meta classes describe the role of these concepts in the problem-solving process. A whole inference structure is a network which shows the dependencies between meta classes and knowledge sources.
- The *task layer* describes the control flow[4] of a problem-solving method, i.e. it specifies *when* inferences are made.
- The *strategic layer* is not exactly defined yet. It contains meta knowledge about combination and selection of different possible tasks in order to solve a problem adequately.

Reusability

The four layer model (see 2.1.3) is the foundation for the reusability of program constructs. Separating the generic layers[5], a library of generic problem-solving methods called interpretation models is proposed. The construction of the conceptual model is simplified by these interpretation models. A selected interpretation model is a template for the conceptual model and has to be adapted to the problem at hand by modifying the three layers and by supplementing the domain specific knowledge, the domain layer.

Guide for the Knowledge Acquisition Process

The existing library of interpretation models is also helpful for the knowledge acquisition process itself. A selected interpretation model can serve as a template for the expertise. In this way, the knowledge engineer has some indications from the abstract interpretation model which information he still has to collect.

2.2 An Assessment of KADS

In the following, the advantages and the problems arised when using KADS as a knowledge engineering method are discussed.

---

3. Each successive level interprets the description at the lower level [WSB91].
4. Note, that "control flow" has two meanings: a) the ordering of activities and b) the controlling of the execution of activities. Here, we mean the ordering of activities.
5. Generic means domain independent: the inference layer, the task layer and the strategic layer.

Different advantages result from the structuring principles of KADS. At the one hand, the knowledge engineering process has been structured in different phases, on the other hand, the knowledge itself is structured separating different kinds of knowledge categories. Thus, the knowledge engineer need not care about the implementation formalism in the first knowledge acquisition phase and the development of the knowledge base becomes much easier for him. The expert is able to understand a model of knowledge better that is structured like the conceptual model. If a comprehensive representation of that model is given, the expert can support the knowledge engineer constructively, e.g. with the help of a tool, in constructing, interpreting and checking the conceptual model developed by the knowledge engineer.

Another central point in the area of knowledge engineering can be improved by having a structured specification: the conceptual model can be used for documentation, being abstract and more comprehensive than the knowledge base. The aspect of documentation has still been neglected in most of the existing KBS development approaches. Basing on a good documentation the maintenance of KBS is also improved. The parts of the knowledge base that have to be modified can be found more quickly.

Another principle of KADS provides further improvement: with the library of interpretation models the knowledge engineer gets templates which he can use in order to acquire knowledge.

The principles of KADS mostly seem to be plausible and useful for the process of knowledge engineering. Nevertheless, some problems and questions arise in developing a concrete knowledge base on the foundation of KADS. Mainly, these problems result from trying to use the KADS methodology as a knowledge engineering method. KADS certainly provides a good framework for model-based knowledge engineering, but a guideline how to use it does not exist. For using KADS, some modifications, improvements, and updates have to be done which have already been started in the KADS-II project.

Some of the questions for which some answers will be given with the KEEP model are listed here:

- → How does the knowledge engineer start his work?
- → How is the knowledge engineer able to identify the fitting interpretation models?
- → How can the knowledge engineer assess an interpretation model or when does an interpretation model match (a part of) the problem?
- → In how many cases does the model library contain adequate models? How often a new model has to be created?
- → Is the knowledge engineer able to adapt the selected interpretation model to his problem?
- → Is it easy to combine the appropriate modified interpretation models?
- → How has the domain layer to be built and how has the mapping between domain layer and inference layer to be defined?
- → How can the knowledge engineer decide which task structure is the best one?

All the questions are related with the problem of supporting the knowledge engineer in developing the conceptual model and the knowledge base i.e. in applying the basic principles of KADS.

2.3 Data Flow Diagrams (DFDs)

For formally illustrating the tasks of the knowledge engineer the KEEP model is specified as a dataflow diagram (DFD) [You89]. This formalism known from Software Engineering is shortly described here.

In a DFD, there exist *processes* which are graphically represented as a ellipse. Furthermore, there are *stores* (of data) for which the notation of two parallel lines is used. *Terminators*, representing external entities with which the system communicates, are represented as a rectangle. The processes, stores and terminators are numbered[6]. The flows between all these elements are represented as arrows. You can distinguish between data flow and control flow[7], where the latter is represented as a non-continuous arrow. Data flow arrows have to be signed with the data that flow to the according process. The control flow arrows have to be marked with the numbers of the stores or the terminators where they come from (in front of a separating point) and the processes where they go to (after the point).

The DFDs may be *levelled* so that each level provides successively more detail than the one above it. The number of a level element always starts with the number of the process which is refined. The arity of a number shows the refined level of this diagram section. The diagram at the highest level of abstraction that also shows the relation to the environment is called context diagram.

3.0 The KEEP Model

Figure 1 illustrates the global structure (the so-called context diagram) of the model-based and incremental[8] knowledge engineering process in DFD notation.

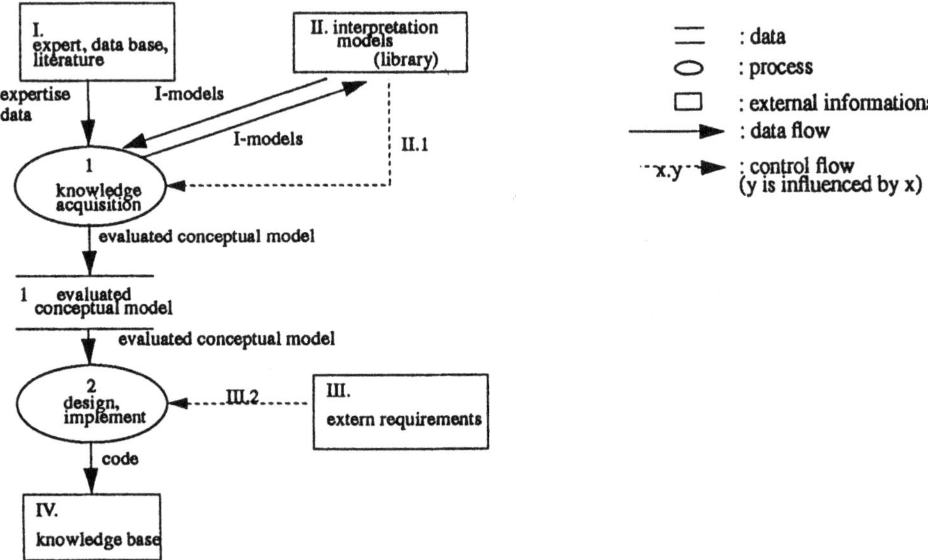

FIGURE 1: DFD (context diagram) for the global, model-based development of KBS

In analogy to the life-cycle models known from Software Engineering like the Spiral model [Boe86], the control flow describes the ordering of activities within the knowledge engineering process. Moreover, the data flow is given for describing the relationship between activities of the

6. The reason becomes clear in the following section.

7. Here, 'control flow' means the influence of data on processes.

8. The incremental nature of the process becomes clearer in the control flow diagram (figure 7).

knowledge engineer and their results as it is known from so-called process models in the area of Software Engineering [DoT90]. The KEEP Model distinguishes several levels of abstraction in order to describe the complex knowledge engineering process. We start with describing the data flow in detail, before a control flow diagram is given at the end of chapter three.

The overall task of the knowledge engineer, the development of a knowledge base, is split into two so-called subtasks (or subactivities): *knowledge acquisition* (1)[9] and *design and implementation* (2). The result of the *knowledge acquisition* (1) is the *evaluated conceptual model* (1), the final specification of the knowledge base. Process 1 is based on expertise data acquired from an *expert,* from *a data base* or from *literature* (I)[10]. The existing *interpretation models* from the library (II) are also used as an input for *knowledge acquisition* (see chapter 2.1.4). The library can be expanded during the knowledge acquisition process by new interpretation models. Additionally, the *interpretation model library* influences some subtasks (II.1) of *knowledge acquisition.*

In the *design and implementation* phase (2), the *knowledge base* (IV) is developed, influenced by *external requirements* (III) and originating from the *evaluated conceptual model* (1)[11].

Because the phase of modeling the *conceptual model* (1) is of central interest, the process of *knowledge acquisition* (1) will be further differentiated now (see figure 2).

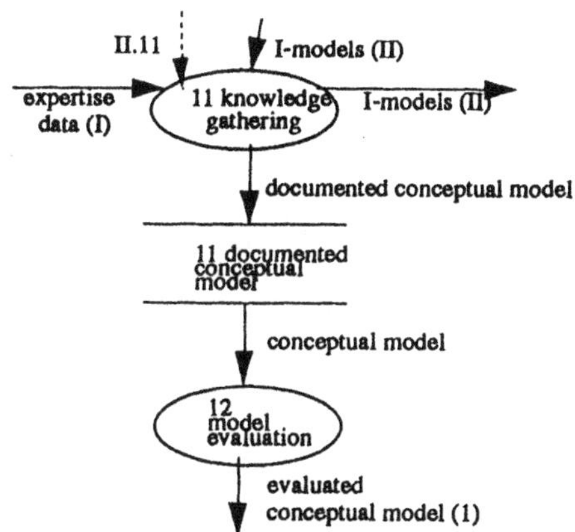

FIGURE 2: Refinement of *knowledge acquisition* (1)

In the *knowledge gathering* process (11) the knowledge engineer collects, structures and formalizes *the expertise data.* The input of *knowledge gathering* (11) is known from figure 1. The resulting *conceptual model* (11) has to be *evaluated* (12). Having a *conceptual model* (11) that is operational, e.g. in the formal specification language KARL [AFL91a], the realization of the requirements can be checked with the help of the results of the execution of the *conceptual model.* The output of the *knowledge evaluation* phase is the *evaluated conceptual model*[12] which may

9. Note, that terms used in the KEEP model like *knowledge acquisition* are printed in italic letters.

10. In the following the source of knowledge, an expert, a data base or a book, will be addressed as "expert".

11. Note, that the maintenance of the knowledge base is not included in the DFD. Modifications should be carried out in the *conceptual model* since this model represents the specification of the knowledge base. Then, the knowledge base has to be adapted according to these modifications. Otherwise, inconsistencies may arise. Thus, a tool which supports the transformation of the conceptual model into the final knowledge base is needed in order to make maintenance more manageable.

eventually have been modified according to results found when checking the model. The refinement of *knowledge gathering* is shown in figure 3.

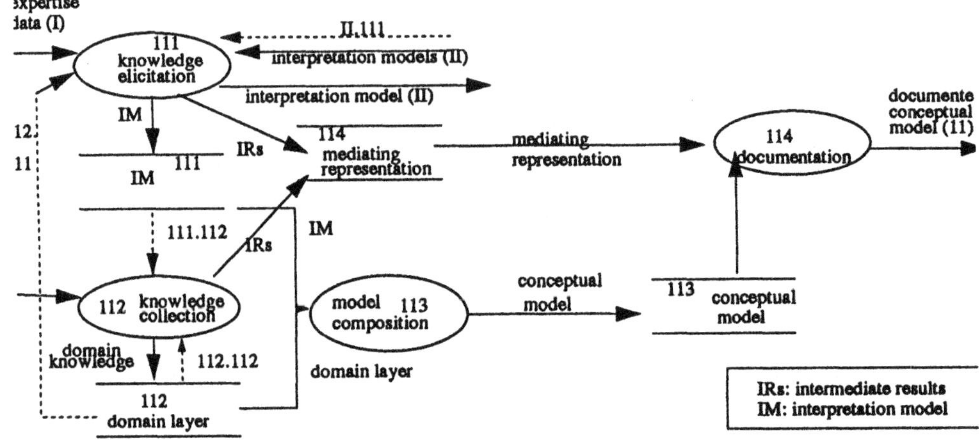

FIGURE 3: Refinement of *knowledge gathering* (11)

In the *knowledge elicitation* phase (111) the knowledge engineer gets *expertise data* about the problem-solving method. Existing *interpretation models* of the library may influence this phase (II.111) by being a guideline for top-down knowledge acquisition. Moreover, the *interpretation model library* is an input, since these partial models are used as a template for the *conceptual model*. The result of the *knowledge elicitation* phase (111) is an *interpretation model* (111) that describes the problem-solving method used for the given task. This may be a rough description, but also an already modified, complex interpretation model since the phase of *knowledge elicitation* can be passed several times in the cycle of *knowledge elicitation* (111) and *knowledge collection* (112)[13]. The phase of *knowledge elicitation* will be described later in more detail. The resulting *interpretation model* describing the complex problem solving process can be stored in the model library[14], but also subparts of it can be included in the library. Thus, *interpretation models* are an output of *knowledge elicitation* (and of the whole *knowledge gathering*). The complex *interpretation model* (111) influences (111.112) the *knowledge collection* process (112) as it is used as a guideline to get static domain knowledge which is gathered, interpreted i.e. structured, and formalized in process 112 (see below). The already existing *domain layer* (112) also influences this process (112.112) in order to avoid asking things twice. The resulting formalized *domain layer* (112) is combined with the *interpretation model* (111), that describes the complex problem-solving method of the whole given problem, in the *model composition* phase (113) which provides the *conceptual model* as a result (113). In this phase, the relations between *domain layer* and inference layer of the *interpretation model* have to be determined. Important results of the two processes *knowledge elicitation* and *knowledge collection* are *intermediate results* that together form a so-called *mediating representation* (114)[15] which informally or semiformally describes the structure

12. The conceptual model can be improved by starting an additional knowledge gathering phase. The ordering of activities is described later.

13. Note, that the ordering of activities is not described here, this is done later on in figure 7.

14. This is useful, if the new interpretation model can be used for a set of other problems similar to the current one.

of the expertise. Therefore, it is a good foundation for the *documentation* of the *conceptual model* (114). *Documentation* will not be further described here.

In the following, the processes of *knowledge elicitation* (111) and *knowledge collection* (112) will be further refined. The subprocesses of *knowledge elicitation* are illustrated in figure 4.

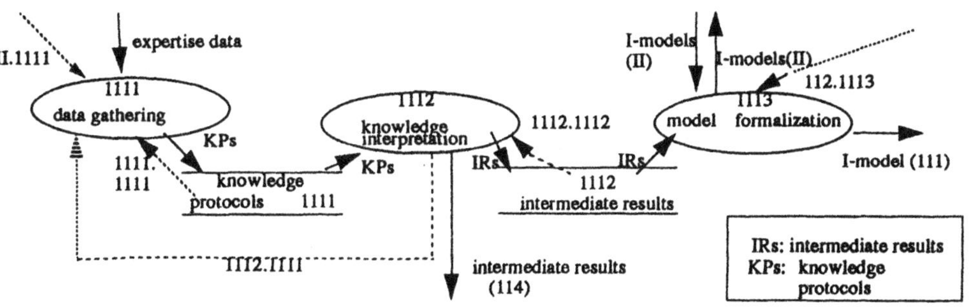

FIGURE 4: Refinement of *knowledge elicitation (111)*

The knowledge engineer starts to get the *expertise data* in the *data gathering* phase (1111), e.g. by interviewing an expert[16]. This phase is influenced by the *interpretation model library* (II.1111). If another phase of *knowledge elicitation* precedes, already existing *knowledge protocols* also have some influence (1111.1111) on avoiding to ask for an information twice. The expert's answers are recorded in *knowledge protocols* (1111). *Knowledge protocols* are the basic data for *knowledge interpretation* (1112). Here, the expertise stored in *knowledge protocols* is informally structured into *intermediate results* (1112)[17]. *Interpretation of knowledge* is done according to the already structured expertise, i.e. the existing *intermediate results* (1112.1112). These *intermediate results* are an output of the whole *knowledge elicitation* process and together with the *interpretation models* from the library, they are the basis for *model formalization* (1113). Here, the generic parts of the *conceptual model* are formally specified. For this, an adequate interpretation model has to be selected from the model library (or several models), which eventually have to be modified and combined to one complex model of the given problem. This means that those parts of the selected interpretation model that are not already formalized have to be formulated in a formal specification language (see e.g. [AFL91a], [AFL91b], [KVS91], [WeS91], [AHS90]). The formalization of generic knowledge is influenced by the already formalized domain layer describing static knowledge (1122.1113, data 1122 is coming from *knowledge collection* described in figure 6).

The result is a completely defined i.e. formalized *interpretation model* for the problem.

Refining the phase of *formalization* (1113) leads to figure 5.

15. A representation which has the function to promote understanding of two existing representations is called mediating representation.

16. Note, that data gathering means only getting data from the expert. The phase of knowledge gathering (11) (see fig. 2) is more global and means gathering of data and structuring and formalizing it to a conceptual model.

17. The proposal is to get an informal structure of the expertise with support of the expert before constructing a formal specification model.

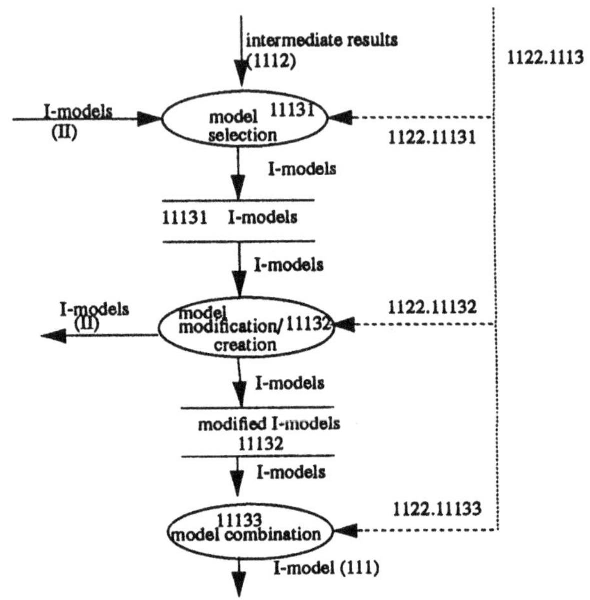

FIGURE 5: model formalization (1113)

On the basis of *intermediate results* and the set of given *interpretation models* the knowledge engineer has to *select* (11131) some appropriate *interpretation models*, a combination of which describes the problem-solving methods for the given problem. The selected *I-models* (11131) are the input for the *model modification/creation* phase (11132)[18]. As the *interpretation models* embody only global inferences, they must be *modified* (11132) according to the characteristics of the application domain. The easiest case is renaming some elements. But mostly the refinement of the abstract knowledge sources and the deletion and extension of some elements of the model is necessary. *Model modification* also includes *model creation*: if existing models of the library are inadequate to model the given problem or parts of it, a new model has to be developed for this part.

In the *model combination* phase (11133) the resulting *modified or created interpretation models* (11132) will be combined to make up the *interpretation model* describing the whole problem.

Every subprocess of *knowledge interpretation* is influenced by relevant *domain knowledge* (1122.11131, 1122.11132, 1122.11133), if *knowledge collection* has already been done[19].

Looking at figure 3, so far only the process of *knowledge elicitation* (111) has been described, i.e. developing an generic *interpretation model* (111) for the problem-solving method of the whole problem. This *interpretation model* (111) influences the *knowledge collection* process (112) where the static domain knowledge is gathered, structured and formalized. The refinement of the *knowledge collection* phase (112) is shown in figure 6.

18. The KADS group calls this process knowledge differentiation [WSB91].

19. Remember the cycle of *knowledge elicitation* and *knowledge collection* which will be described in detail in figure 7 (control flow diagram).

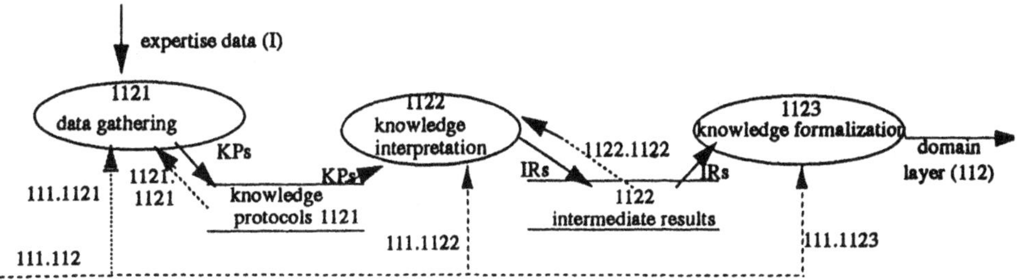

FIGURE 6: Refinement of *knowledge collection* (112)

Expertise data about the static elements of the domain has to be acquired in the *data gathering* phase (1121). Here, the *interpretation model* - selected, modified and combined in the *knowledge elicitation* phase - is used as a guideline by the knowledge engineer[20] (111.1121). The *gathering of data* is done according to the already existing *knowledge protocols* in order to avoid to acquire some information twice (1121.1121). *Knowledge interpretation* (1122) includes selection and structuring of relevant knowledge. This is done by analysing the *knowledge protocols* with regard to already structured parts of *domain knowledge* (1122.1122). The *domain knowledge* is specified in the *knowledge formalization* phase (1123) by defining concepts and relationships between these concepts in a formal specification language[21].

The result of *knowledge specification* is a formalized *domain layer*. All processes of *knowledge collection* are influenced by the *interpretation model* already found (111.1121, 111.1122 and 111.1123).

Looking at the description of the processes and data stores of the KEEP model above, one can see that no ordering of processes is given explicitly. This is done in an explicit control flow diagram giving a rough framework of the ordering of phases. The control flow of the KEEP model is shown in figure 7 and can be compared with life-cycle models known from Software Engineering like the Waterfall Model [Roy70] or the Spiral Model [Boe86].

The knowledge engineer starts with *gathering data* about the problem-solving method (1111). His goal is to get knowledge which allows to roughly classify the problem, i.e. to select an interpretation model two phases later. After having informally structured the knowledge protocols in the phase of *knowledge interpretation* (1112) the knowledge engineer has laid grounds for formalizing the knowledge: therefore, he *selects* interpretation models (11131) that are sufficiently close to the problem-solving method of the expert. The selected interpretation models are *modified* (11132) and *combined* (11133) according to the current problem solving method. If none of the existing models is adequate, new models have to be *created* (11132). Note, that additional knowledge can be acquired after every subphase of knowledge elicitation . If knowledge is missing, the phase 1111 can restart. These cycles inside the whole knowledge acquisition phase show that it is an incremental process.

20. Note, that also an interpretation model that has not already been modified or combined can be the basis for the acquiring of knowledge (1121), e.g. in the first phase of acquiring static domain knowledge.

21. In the same sense as gathering, interpretation and formalization of knowledge (see figure 4 and 6) the KADS group [WSB91] distinguish the phases: eliciting, interpreting and formalizing knowledge.

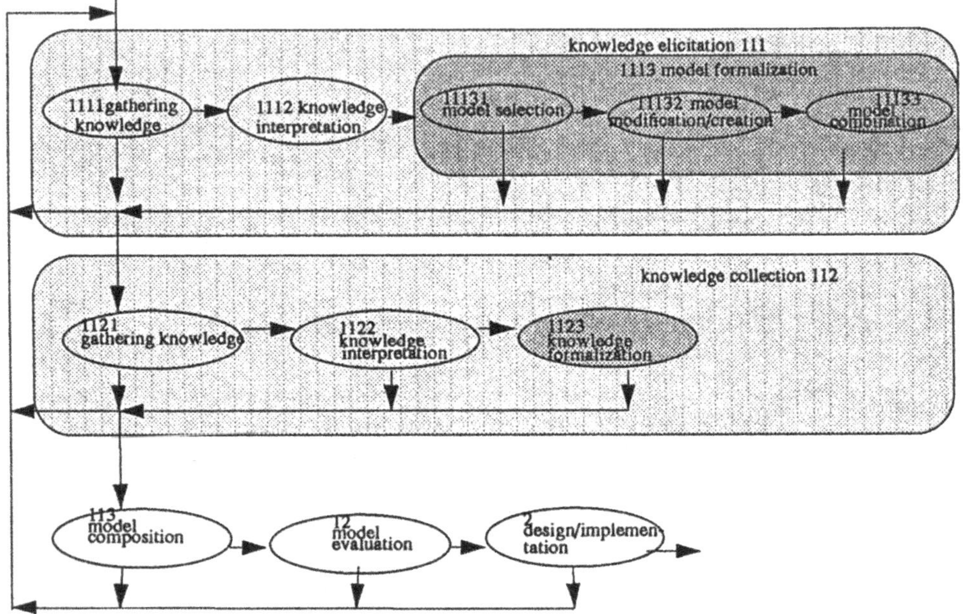

FIGURE 7: The control flow of the knowledge engineering process

Having found a model (or different models) of the current problem-solving method (which may already be modified and combined), it (they) can be used for *knowledge collection* (112). Static data is *gathered* (1121), and then, *interpreted* (1122) and *formalized* (1123). It is also possible to acquire new knowledge, i.e. to restart the cycle of *knowledge collection* before finishing the *formalization* of the complex knowledge. During the phase of *knowledge collection*, the cycle of *knowledge elicitation* can also begin once again[22].

Note, that it is possible to *gather* static data as well as process knowledge in parallel[23]. Having selected an *interpretation model* (11131) that guides the knowledge collection process, both processes, 1121, i.e. getting static knowledge, and 1111, i.e. getting more detailed process knowledge, will follow in one gathering phase.

If parts of the domain layer and of the *interpretation model* have been *formalized* (1113 and 1123 must have been done at least once), the *composition* (113) of the resulting layers can begin. Here, the relations between static domain knowledge and process knowledge are defined. In case of missing knowledge, *knowledge elicitation* (111) or *knowledge collection* (112) will continue. Otherwise, the resulting *conceptual model* can be documented (114) and evaluated (12). Both phases may require an improvement of the mediating representation or the conceptual model so that *knowledge elicitation* (111) or/and *knowledge collection* (112) will continue.

Finally, a *design model* will be constructed on the basis of the *conceptual model* and in the last step, the *design model* will be *implemented* (2).

---

22. E.g. if the domain dependent knowledge gives some indication that the interpretation model is incomplete or wrong.

23. Practically, e.g. in interviewing the expert, it is nearly impossible to separate the two types of knowledge.

4.0 An Assessment of the KEEP Model and Related Work

In this chapter, the KEEP model introduced in this paper is compared with three other proposals to support the knowledge engineer in constructing a knowledge base. First of all, the proposal of the KADS group [WBS91] itself is described. Moreover, the life-cycle model given by Hickman et. al.[24] [HKL89] is introduced which was the basis for the development of the KEEP model. A new model-based approach of developing a knowledge base together with a guideline for the knowledge engineer is given with EMA [SpW91].

In the fourth section of this chapter, results from applying the KEEP model are given. The last section describes open problems with the current version of the KEEP model and outlines some improvements.

4.1 Proposals of the KADS Group for Constructing a KBS

Central Principles

Concerning the complex process of KBS development, the KADS group proposes a decomposition of the knowledge engineering task by providing different intermediate models [WSB91]: the organisational model, the application model, the task model, the model of cooperation, the model of expertise, the conceptual model and the design model. The organisational model provides an analysis of the environment in which the KBS will work, the application model defines the function of the KBS and the external constraints. The task model consists of a decomposition of the complex task into a number of primitive tasks. The model of cooperation gives a further description of these subtasks e.g. the assignment of the tasks to the user or the system. The model of expertise represents the knowledge level [New82] i.e. the functional specification of the problem. The conceptual model is the combination of the model of expertise and model of cooperation, the design model includes design decisions i.e. computational and representational aspects. Each of these intermediate representation models represent a particular view on the KBS.

The intermediate models which are described in detail in [WSB91] provide a decomposition of the knowledge engineer's task. A diagram is given which shows the ordering of the model construction process. But a guideline how to construct the intermediate models is missing.

For developing the model of expertise, KADS currently provides two kinds of support: On the one hand, KADS describes the phases, activities and techniques for knowledge engineering, on the other hand, KADS provides implemented support tools. The activities to build a first model of expertise are called *knowledge identification* and *knowledge modelling*. *Knowledge identification* means collecting data, task analysis, task feature analysis, lexicon construction, glossary construction, concept identification and relation identification, i.e. the preparation phase before constructing the conceptual model. The *knowledge modeling* phase include knowledge collection, interpretation model selection, domain schema definition, building domain structures, model assembly, model validation, model differentiation and bottom-up model construction. For all these activities, techniques and resulting products are given [WSB91]. But the activities are not further described. Only the crucial activity of selecting an interpretation model is guided by a decision tree. This decision tree bases on a taxonomy of task types. The decision points concern e.g. the structure of the system, the type of solution, the nature of the domain knowledge, etc.

24. In the following, this life-cycle model of Hickman et. al. will be called 'Hickman model'.

The second kind of support for the knowledge engineer in constructing a model of expertise is the tool Shelley which contains an integrated set of computerised support tools like a domain text editor, a concept editor, the interpretation model library and an interpretation model editor.

"KADS gives you a vocabulary, but it provides little support for the current knowledge engineering process." [WSB91].

Comparing the Proposals of the KADS Group and the KEEP Model

The global aspect, the development of intermediate models to represent different views on the problem, is a good idea but it has to be described how to develop these models.

The KEEP model concentrates on describing the development of the *conceptual model* which is currently the most interesting model in the sense of the life-cycle model of KADS. For this phase, KADS also provides some helpful steps:

With the separation of the phases *knowledge identification* and *knowledge modelling* the KADS group has done a first step in the direction of structuring the knowledge engineering process. Different subactivities described in section 4.1.1. can also be found in the KEEP model, e.g. the *model selection*, the model assembly (*model composition*), the model differentiation (*model modification*) or the model construction (*model creation*). The subactivities of the *knowledge identification* [: the task analysis with the decomposition of tasks, the lexicon construction and the glossary construction, the concept identification and the relation identification, can be found in the activity of *structuring the knowledge protocols* in the KEEP model.

But one central point is missing: The phases of knowledge engineering are not formally and thus not precisely described for the knowledge engineer. Moreover, a guideline of an ordering of activities and a detailed description of activities is not provided by the KADS group. Therefore, the KEEP model contains a control flow diagram (figure 7) specifying the order of activities. Moreover, the control flow diagram shows possible cycles in the incremental development process. Starting new cycles of acquiring and formalizing knowledge after having evaluated a first operational conceptual model integrates also prototyping (see [AFL91a]).

The implemented tool Shelley is very useful for the technical support of the knowledge engineer. But Shelley does not guide the knowledge engineer in developing the knowledge base.

4.2 The Hickman's Life-cycle Model

Central Principles of the Life-cycle Model of Hickman

The Hickman model is a guideline for the knowledge engineer for the analysis phase of the development of a KBS with KADS. The Hickman's model describes in a SADT formalism the knowledge engineer's tasks. The basic principles and problems of the life-cycle model of Hickman are shortly discussed in the following sections.

The life-cycle model developed by Hickman et. al. [HKL89] is shown as a SADT diagram that describes the individual activities within KBS analysis. The model is illustrated in figure 8, for a description of the figure and detailed information look at [HKL89]. A central principle of Hickman et. al. is constructing some documents as intermediate results. Moreover, Hickman et. al. separates an *external stream* and an *internal stream*, which clearly distinguishes between several requirements that have to be asked for and the phase of understanding which means the analysis of knowledge and the construction of the conceptual model.

Comparing the Hickman Model and the KEEP Model

Experiences with the Hickman model as a help to develop a KBS [Web91] showed us that the model is not easy to use, because the activities are not described in enough detail and no ordering is given. Insufficiencies of the Hickman model were a motivation for developing the KEEP model.

Looking at the Hickman model, with the external stream one main point is given by reviewing the feasibility continuously throughout the analysis phase. After every step of the internal stream, output documents are taken as indicators. In the KEEP model, the aspect of feasibility assessment is integrated in one activity, the *model evaluation* (12). This evaluation can be done at different stages of knowledge acquisition (see figure 7) so that in the same way as in the Hickman model different aspects can be evaluated. They are not described in detail in the KEEP model, yet. It seems to be more important to refine the processes of the internal stream.

The claim of the KEEP model was to get a detailed description of the activities the knowledge engineer has to do to construct the conceptual model and to give him a guideline how and when to execute the activities.

Looking at the *internal stream* of the Hickman model (the phase of understanding), only three activities are distinguished and these activities are described very roughly. Comparing the KEEP model with the Hickman model the three activities of the *internal stream* can completely be found in the KEEP model: *Analysis of static knowledge* corresponds to the *knowledge collection* (112) phase (see figure 3 and 6). The process of *analysing the expert tasks* of Hickman et. al. can be identified with the *knowledge elicitation* (111) phase (see figure 3 and 4). A crucial difference is the ordering of these two activities that is implicitly given in the Hickman model. Hickman et. al. start the *internal stream* with the *analysis of static knowledge*. This process is not influenced by the interpretation model library. The fifth principle of KADS - having a guideline for the knowledge acquisition process - is neglected. Just for the *analysis of the expert and users tasks* the interpretation model library is used. The KEEP model starts with analysing the task that results in finding fitting interpretation models that guide the knowledge engineer in the *knowledge collection* phase, where static knowledge is acquired. Finally, the *construction of the conceptual model* corresponds to the *model composition* (figure 3, 113) of the KEEP model where the complete *conceptual model* is defined.

Using the Hickman model, the knowledge engineer has hardly any help to get familiar with e.g. the *construction of conceptual model*. He needs a detailed model or description of what he has to do in such a process. For example, a knowledge engineer who has to *collect static knowledge* (which is the first activity of the *internal stream*) may have severe problems to do so. On the one hand, he has to follow the KADS principle of using a given guideline, on the other hand, the knowledge engineer has to get static knowledge in a very early phase. The process of finding such a plausible guideline - an interpretation model of the library - is neglected in the Hickman model. The model includes the interpretation model library only in the process of *analysing the task*. The top-down approach is not realized i.e. to use given interpretation models for getting static knowledge in the sense of KADS.

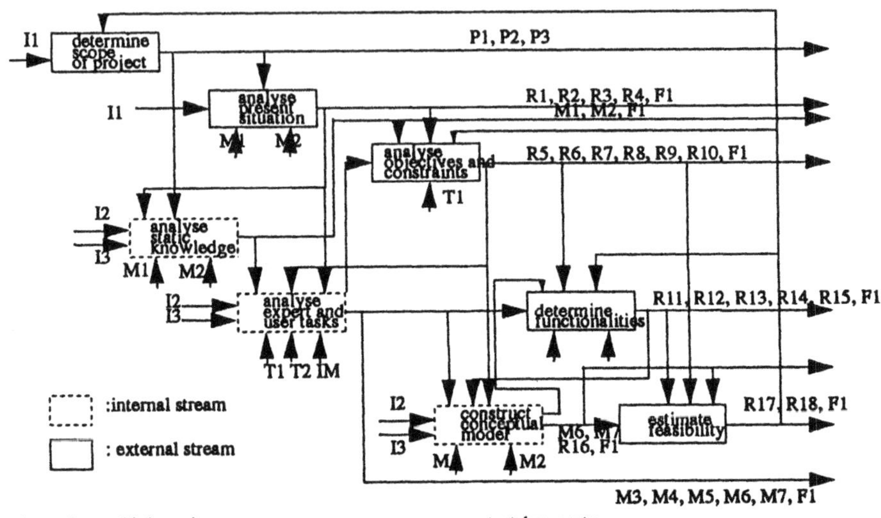

input data and control informations:

I1: present system
I2: expertise
I3: writen data
IM: interpretation model library
T1: elicitation techniques
T2: analysis techniques and tools

M1: Lexicon
M2: Static structure
M3: Interpretation model
M4: Inference structure
M5: Task structure
M6: Strategies
M7: User models

output documents:

P1: Background and prerequisities
P2: Project terms and directive
P3: Project life-cycle model, plans and organisation
R1: Model of present situation
R2: Functioning objectives of management
R3: Functioning problems of management
R4: Task orientation
R5: Objectives of prosepctive system
R6: Compatibility requirements
R7: Human factors of the user interface
R8: Development and operational envirement
R9: Control and security constraints
R10: Organisational model
R11: Functional requirements
R12: System structure
R13: Information requirements
R14: Expected future requirements
R15: Consequences
R16: Knowledge Base Requirements
R17: Development Requirements
R18: Validation Procedures

FIGURE 8: The life-cycle model of Hickman et. al. [HKL89]

To some extent the KEEP model is similar to the Hickman model. The main difference is the omission of control flow[25] in the Hickman model, that is given only implicitly. So, the knowledge engineer has no suitable guideline. Moreover, nothing is said about cycles of activities. But this is important, because most of the knowledge engineering processes will alternate between activities.

Another difference is the detailed *external stream* of the Hickman model, whereas the KEEP model concentrates on a detailed and more refined description of the *internal stream* which is described too short in the Hickman model.

The principle of a top-down development is neglected by Hickman whereas in the KEEP model, we integrate a detailed description of how to work with the *interpretation model library.*

---

25. Here, 'control flow' means the ordering of activities.

4.3 Support of the Model-based Knowledge Acquisition with EMA

With the last two sections of this chapter, two principles of structuring the modeling process of KBS development in the sense of KADS were given. EMA is another methodology for the development of knowledge base applications [SpW91]. EMA is an active partner for the developer. The information of the whole development cycle is kept and managed by EMA and "it supports the developer from the first to the last step in application development" [SWP91]. In EMA, generic techniques (G-TECs) which solve a certain kind of problem are instantiated for an application.

Central Principles

In this section, a natural language description of the process of model-based knowledge acquisition with the help of generic techniques (G-TECs) is given [SpW91], [SWP91]:

1. Result-oriented knowledge acquisition

   A required result is identified. A central principle of EMA is to classify a problem according to the kind of produced result. The result is classified e.g. as evaluation, as planning, as classification information etc. with the following criterion: "What is the produced result used for and interpreted as by the user?"

2. Model-based knowledge acquisition

   There exist different criteria to apply a G-TEC. They are classified according to the kind of produced result[26] i.e. whether the produced result is an evaluation, a planning, a classification information etc. Therefore, the type of the required result is defined in this step. The solution-info can be expressed formally with the help of so-called info-sets[27].

3. Meta-model knowledge acquisition

   If a G-TEC exists, knowledge acquisition driven by the G-TEC and supported by EMA is carried out. The decision whether a G-TEC can be selected depends on the availability of the acquired information of the domain. A successful process of knowledge acquisition leads to a model of a G-TEC instantiating which is integrated in the knowledge model, see [SpW91]. EMA asks for input information and context information.

4. User interaction

   The selected G-TEC implies different info-sets. The user interaction is driven by the info-sets. The info-sets become required results. For getting a required result go to 1.

If no G-TEC exists for a required result, this part of the knowledge model has to be built from scratch with the help of other kinds of knowledge acquisition techniques provided by EMA.

All these steps are supported by EMA.

Comparing the Modeling Principles of EMA and the KEEP Model

Looking at the four points of modeling described in 4.3.1, it is obvious that only a very rough description of the modeling process is given. Nothing is said about how the G-TECs are instantiated or how a new G-TEC is constructed with EMA. The support offered by EMA isn't described in detail so that it is difficult to decide about the helpfulness of EMA.

---

26. Because the solution type and the problem are related by one to one, but the solution information is easier to express than the model of problem description.

27. An info-set is a meta-concept of EMA and is a set of info-units, atomic pieces of information in EMA. These info-units are in a is-a or instance-of relation and have the same attribute. A so-called agent manipulates the info-units of an info-set.

4.4 Results of Using the KEEP Model

The KEEP model has already been used at our institute to construct conceptual models for different applications in KARL, the formal specification language for the conceptual model [AFL91a].

In the application of emission control measure [Sch91], of insurance configuration [Ohl92], and of selecting operations research methods the KEEP model provided a good guideline. The problem of emission control measure is a configuration problem for which an interpretation model is missing in the model library so that a new interpretation model had to be created. Experience showed that different activities in the knowledge engineering process have to be formulated in more detail in the KEEP model. These deficiencies and some proposals for the refinement of the KEEP model are described in the next section.

4.5 Problems and Current Work

Although the KEEP model is a more detailed guideline for the development of a KBS compared e.g. with the Hickman model, different questions are not answered, yet:

How has the acquired knowledge to be structured so that the subsequent phases of the knowledge engineering process are simplified? How do you select, modify and combine interpretation models? How is an interpretation model created? How is the domain layer constructed?

These questions will be answered in the current work by refining activities of the KEEP model. The basis for all subsequent activities is a good *structuring of the gathered knowledge protocols* which has to be described by a refinement of process 1112 (see figure 5). The resulting mediating representation (see figure 3). A mediating representation involves improving the knowledge engineering process in different ways [FCA91], [Neu92]:

- ◆ With a mediating representation the gap between the natural language knowledge protocols and the formal conceptual model is diminished.
- ◆ The mediating representations help the knowledge engineer during the modeling process by improving his understanding of the given domain.
- ◆ The mediating representations support the cooperation between the expert and the knowledge engineer. Having a comprehensive formalism the expert is able to provide help in building the conceptual model. He supports the structuring of the knowledge protocols as well as he can analyse and check the already structured documents. Faults can be found and modified in an early modeling phase.
- ◆ A mediating representation improve the model-based knowledge engineering process: the structured intermediate results support the selection, the modification and the combination of models.
- ◆ The decisions about the formalisation of knowledge elements have only to be made, if the knowledge is completely analysed and structured.
- ◆ Mediating representations are able to facilitate documentation, maintenance, and explanation of the system.

The proposal is to use hypermedia (see [ShK89], [Nie90],[DeS87]) for representing these informal intermediate results. Hypermedia is a good means to get informal and semiformal structures of the expertise on the way to a formal specification. Hypermedia is usually defined as an nonlinear representation of information [ShK89]. There is no single order like in traditional text like books, newspapers etc. that determines the sequence in which the text is to be read [Nie90].

For using hypermedia as a representation formalism for the mediating representation, a knowledge model, the so-called hyper model, has been developed in [Neu92].

Looking at the last point of the advantages of mediating representations above, the model-based knowledge engineering is supported by the hyper model as follows:

- The model selection phase becomes easier, because the informal structures of the hyper model are similar to the structures of the inference layer and the task layer of the interpretation models. Therefore, the hyper model or parts of the hyper model can be compared to the interpretation models to find an adequate one. This process is supported by making a result oriented comparison of interpretation models. Moreover, central concepts of the hyper models, represented in informal documents, are compared with attributes related to the existing interpretation models.
- The model modification phase can be supported by the refined hyper model with the help of which the selected abstract interpretation model(s) can be adapted to the domain.
- The model combination phase can be improved by using the hyper model since it describes the complex structure of the whole problem solving process.
- If no appropriate interpretation model could be selected, the model creation is done by using generic parts of the hyper model or by abstracting the domain dependent ones.
- A part of documentation may be achieved e.g. by relating the informal hyper model with the formal conceptual model, such that an informal description is provided for every formal concept, relationship, and fact.

The described steps of central activities of the knowledge engineer are integrated into the KEEP model at present.

5.0 Conclusion

Developing a KBS with a model-based methodology like KADS, the knowledge engineer needs a guideline. Insufficiencies of the Hickman model [HKL89] resulted in developing the KEEP model. With the KEEP model an approach is provided that integrates useful principles of existing proposals ([WSB91], [HKL89]) of using the KADS methodology and principles known from process models of Software Engineering [Tul89].

The KADS group [WSB91], Hickman [HKL89] and EMA [SpW91] give interesting proposals to construct the conceptual model. But this is done too abstract in EMA [SpW91] and in the life-cycle model of Hickman [HKL89] or without providing an ordering of activities [WSB91], [HKL89]. Without a formalism ([SpW91]. [WSB91]) it is not possible to describe the complex control flow of the model-based and incremental knowledge engineering process with its cycles of KBS development.

The formal KEEP model, a DFD providing a data flow and a control flow description, is a good basis for describing all the activities of the knowledge engineer. Especially the ordering of activities by the control flow diagram (see figure 7) was necessary for the knowledge engineer to know how to proceed. There exists a detailed description about the global activities and cycles of activities are described. Moreover, the top-down directed development of the KBS is supported which has been neglected in the Hickman model [HKL89].

Currently, several activities of the KEEP model are refined for covering the hyper model approach having been outlined in chapter 4.5.

6.0 Acknowledgement

We gratefully thank Jürgen Angele, Dieter Fensel, Dieter Landes and Barbara Messing for supporting the development of the KEEP model, Dieter Landes and Rainer Rauleder for correcting the manuscript.

7.0 Bibliography

[AFL91a] Angele, J.; Fensel, D.; Landes, D.; and Studer, R: KARL: An Executable Language for the Conceptual Model. In: Proceedings of the Knowledge Acquisition Workshop AKW'91, October 6-11, Banff, Canada, 1991

[AFL91b] Angele, J.; Fensel, D.; Landes, D.; and Studer, R: Sisyphus - No Problem with KARL. In Proceedings of the 5th European Knowledge Acquisition Workshop EKAW'91, Crieff, Scotland, May 20 - 24, 1991

[AHS90] Akkermans, H.; Harmelen, van F.; Schreiber, G.; Wielinga, B.: A Formalisation of Knowledge-Level Models for Knowledge Acquisition. Submitted to the International Journal of Intelligent Systems, 1990

[AnW90] Anjewierden, A.; Wielemaker, J.: Shelley - Computer Aided Knowledge Engineering. In: Current Trends in KA, IOS 1990

[Boe86] Boehm, B.W.: A Spiral Model of Software Development and Enhancement, ACM SIGSOFT Software Engineering Notes, vol.11, no 4, p. 14-24, 8/1986

[BRW89] Breuker, J.; and Wielinga, B.: Models of Expertise in Knowledge Acquisition. In Topics in Expert Systems Design, G. Guida and C. Tasso (eds.), Elsevier Science Publisher B. V., North-Holland, 1989

[BWS87] Breuker, J.; Wielinga, B.; Someren, M.v.; de Hoog, R.; Schreiber, G.; de Greef, P.; Bredeweg, B.; Wielemaker, J.; and Billault, J.-P.: Model-Driven Knowledge Acquisition: Interpretation Models. Esprit Project P1098, University of Amsterdam (The Netherlands), 1987

[CLA85] Clancey, W.J.: Heuristic classification. In Artificial Intelligence 27, 1985, 289-350.

[DeS87] Delisle, N.; Schwartz, M.: Neptune: A hypertext system for CAD applications. In: Proceedings ACM SIGMOD'86, Washington, DC, May, 28-30 1986, pp 132-142

[DoT90] Dorfman, M.; Thayer, R.: Standards, Guidelines, and Examples on System and Software Requirements Engineering. IEEE Computer Society Press, Los Alamitos, California, 1990

[dGB85] de Greef, P.; Breuker, J.: A case study in structured knowledge acquisition. In Proceedings of the 9th IJCAI, Los Angeles, 1985, pp 390-392

[Fen91] Fensel, D.: An Introduction into KADS. Research Report no. 226, Institut für Angewandte Informatik und Formale Beschreibungsverfahren, University of Karlsruhe, 1991

[FCA91] Ford, K.; Canas, A.; Adams-Webber, J.: Explanation as a Knowledge Acquisition Issue. In: Proceedings of the 8th National Conference on Artificial Intelligence AAAI'91, Workshop Knowledge Acquisition, Anaheim, California, July 14-19, 1991

[HKL89] Hickman, F.R.; Killin, J.L.; Land, L.; Mulhall, T.; Porter, D.; and Taylor, R.M., Analysis for Knowledge-Based Systems: a practical guide to the KADS methodology, Ellis Horwood Limited, Chichester, GB, 1989

[KLV89] Karbach, W., Linster, M., Voss, A.: Model-based approaches: One label - one idea? In Wielinga, B.; Boose, J.; gaines, B.; Schreiber, G.; & van Someren, M., editors: Current trends in Knowledge Acquisition, pp 173-189. IOS Press, Amsterdam, 1989

[KVS91] Karbach, W.; Voß, A.; Schuckey, R.; Drouven, U.: MODEL-K: Prototyping at the Knowledge Level. Proceedings of the 11th International Workshop Expert Systems & Their Applications, Avignon, 1991

[MGH89] McGraw, K.L.; and Harbison-Briggs, K.: Knowledge Acquisition - Principles and Guidelines, Prentice-Hall International, Inc., Englewood Cliffs, NJ, 1989

[Mus89] Musen, M.: Automated Generation of Model-Based Knowledge-Acquisition Tools, Research Notes in Artificial Intelligence, Pitman Publishing, London, 1989

[MYL89] Malone, T.; Yu, K.; Lee, J.: What Good are Semistructured Objects? Adding Semiformal Structure to Hypertext. Research Report of Massachusetts Institute of Technology, CCSTR #102, SSM WP #3064-89-MS, 1989

[New82] Newell, A.: The knowledge level, Artificial Intelligence, Vol. 18, 1982, pp 87-127

[Neu92] Neubert, S.: Einsatz von Hypermedia im Bereich der Modellbasierten Wissensakquisition. To appear in: Expertensysteme in der Wirtschaft 1992 - Anwendungen und Integration mit Hypermedia. Herausgeber: Biethahn, J.; Bogaschewsky, R.; Hoppe, U., Gabler Verlag, 1992 (in German)

[Nie90] Nielsen, J.: Hypertext & hypermedia. Academic press, San Diego, London, 1990

[Ohl92] Ohlgart, C.: Spezifikation eines Wissensbasierten Systems zur Konfiguration eines Versicherungsschutzes für Privatkunden. Diploma Theses at the University of Karlsruhe, Institut für Angewandte Informatik und Formale Beschreibungsverfahren, 1992 (in German)

[Roy70] Royce, W. W.: Managing the Development of Large Software Systems: Concepts and Techniques. In: Proceedings WESCON, August 1970

[Sch91] Schweier, T.: Modellierung von Expertenwissen über Maßnahmen zur Emissionsminderung. Diploma Theses at the University of Karlsruhe, Institut für Angewandte Informatik und Formale Beschreibungsverfahren, 1991 (in German)

[ShS90] Schütt, H.; Streitz, N.: HyperBase: A Hypermedia Engine based on a Relational Database Management System. Working papers of GMD no. 469, St. Augustin, 1990

[ShK89] Shneiderman, B.; Kearsley, G.: Hypertext Hands-on!. An Introduction to a New Way of Organizing and Accessing Information. Addision-Wesley Publishing Company, Massachusetts, 1989

[SpW91] Springi, S.; Wenger, D.: Generic Techniques in EMA: A Model-based Approach for Knowledge Acquisition. In: Proceedings of the Knowledge Acquisition Workshop AKW'91, October 6-11, Banff, 1991

[Ste90] Sten, K.: Einsatzmöglichkeiten von Hypertext in Wissensbasierten Systemen.Diploma Theses at the University of Karlsruhe, Institut für Angewandte Informatik und Formale Beschreibungsverfahren, 1990 (in German)

[SWP91] Springi, S.; Wenger D.; Probst, A.: Project Sisyphus, EMA Approach. In Proceedings of the 5th European Knowledge Acquisition Workshop EKAW'91, Crieff, Scotland, May 20 - 24, 1991

[Tul89] Tully, C.: Representing and Enacting the Software Process. Proceedings of the 4th International Software Process Workshop, Devon, UK, 1988. ACM Sigsoft Software Engineering Notes, Volume 14, nr. 4, June 1989

[Wet90] Wetter, T.: First Order Logic Foundation of the KADS Conceptual Model. In: Current Trends in Knowledge Acquisition, Wielinga et. al. (eds.), IOS Press, Amsterdam, 1990, pp 356-375.

[WSB91] Wielinga, B.J.; Schreiber, A.Th.; Breuker, J.A.: KADS: A Modelling Approach to Knowledge Engineering. ESPRIT Project P5248 KADS-II, An advanced and Comprehensive Methodology for Integrated KBS Development, Amsterdam, 1991

[WiS90] Wielinga, B.; and Schreiber, G.: KADS: model based KBS development. In Proceedings of the 14th German Workshop on Artificial Intelligence GWAI-90 (Eringerfeld, September 1o-14), 1990, pp 322-333

[WSG89] Wielinga, B.; Schreiber, G.; and de Greef, P.: Synthesis Report. Esprit Project P1098, UvA-Y3-PR-001, University of Amsterdam (The Netherlands), 1989

[You89] Yourdon, E.: Modern Structured Analysis. Prentice-Hall International Editions, Englewood Cliffs, NJ07632

Domain-Driven Knowledge Modelling: Mediating & Intermediate Representations for Knowledge Acquisition

Hyacinth S. Nwana*, Ray C. Paton+,
Michael J. R. Shave+ & Trevor J. M. Bench-Capon+

* Department of Computer Science
University of Keele
Keele, Staffordshire
ST5, 5BG, U.K.
email: nwanahs@cs.keele.ac.uk

\+ Department of Computer Science
University of Liverpool
Liverpool, L69 3BX
U.K.

Abstract. Knowledge modelling, despite the existence of numerous techniques and tools, still remain an *ad hoc* process which is still more of an art than a science. This is due to the fact that there is as yet no systematic or formal theory for it. Naturally, it is a central goal of the Knowledge Acquisition community to make this process more principled. This paper presents a theoretical framework which is an extension of some of the current thinking about knowledge modelling, with hopefully some clarifications. It draws heavily from the knowledge acquisition literature; its key contribution is a novel combination of known techniques into some (hopefully) coherent framework, rather than a radical new philosophy for knowledge modelling. This framework has been used for several projects we have carried out for industrial partners; it is also the basis of a hybrid tool we intend to develop.

1 Introduction

It is certainly now more in vogue to talk of knowledge being modelled than it being transferred or captured [2, 5, 9, 16, 17, 29] as it certainly "is not a substance that can be stored" [7]. Nwana [22] examines some of the central metaphors in knowledge acquisition and suggest it is time to replace them and amend the research agenda accordingly. Perhaps, it is prudent at this stage to take a stance on what knowledge is.

We agree with Clancey that knowledge is something an observer ascribes to a human agent in order to describe and explain recurrent interactions the agent has with its environment or the real world [7]. He notes that knowledge can be represented but you can never have it in hand; the representations only exist physically in an observers statements, drawings, computer programs, silent speech, visualizations, etc.; otherwise, no observation has occurred. It is also important to note a very important point highlighted by Clancey in an interview with Sandberg [26]: most researchers would say this/that is the knowledge, in so doing claiming the representations are isomorphic to what is in the expert's head and that they are functionally identical. Clancey correctly notes that they are not. They are just models open to interpretation. He also points out that researchers have confused representations (models) with the phenomenon we are modelling: "the map is not the territory". This cogent argument goes to further clarify the shift away in talking from knowledge being transferred or captured to it being *modelled.*

In knowledge acquisition, the resulting representations of knowledge fall under two categories: mediating and intermediate representations. Both furnish the *knowledge model* for the domain in question. Knowledge modelling is seen as a necessary activity in knowledge acquisition: this process culminates in an intermediate model which reflects (or is intended to reflect) the various types of knowledge which characterise the domain independently of eventual implementation considerations. It should also serve as a basis for making decisions about the target system representations and reasoning strategies [1]. However, successful knowledge modelling is complex and fraught with difficulties: it typically suffers from some major shortcomings including:

- The process tends to be driven by the intended final form of the knowledge base. As argued in [22], this backwards approach puts "the cart before the horse". It is the nature of the *domain* that should guide the knowledge modelling process [23]; the final form of the knowledge base should emerge from a characterisation of the domain.
- It is unprincipled: there is as yet no theory of how to acquire human knowledge. The epistemological, cognitive and conceptual foundations of knowledge modelling leave much to be desired [4].
- An unfortunate result of current unstructured approaches is that knowledge models are *ad hoc* as knowledge engineers often move too quickly through some of the cognitive definition and organisation work to enter the later phases of acquisition and implementation without an adequate *modelling* the domain. Again, this is partly due to the fact that the designs and functions of many available knowledge acquisition tools were driven by implementation rather than cognitive concerns [27]. This creates problems for neglected area of knowledge base maintenance which is a real issue for practical systems

The motivation of this paper is to provide or work towards a more principled approach to knowledge modelling which is totally domain-driven. It draws heavily from our work on MEKAS [22, 24] but also from the work of many other researchers in knowledge acquisition. Since it is much based on other researchers' work, we seek to provide some clarification and extension to the theoretical framework. We strive to achieve a principled (not formal) basis to our mediating/intermediate representations by postulating a hypothesis of knowledge modelling. In so doing, we hope to make the process less a matter of inspiration than of technique.

2 What is Knowledge Modelling?

It is important to start by answering this question because as [17] points out, the terms "knowledge" and "modelling" are used with different meanings in the literature corresponding to different views of knowledge acquisition. Figure 1 serves to illustrate what knowledge modelling entails. Knowledge modelling or analysis, in our view, really concerns the characterisation and acquisition of the knowledge in some domain. It is the first phase activity in the construction on knowledge based systems. As Figure 1 shows, it involves the iteration of the key sub-activities of elicitation, analysis and synthesis culminating in some intermediate representation models for the domain. The elicitation-analysis-feedback loop serves to emphasise the new cooperative or constructivist view of knowledge modelling [16, 17].

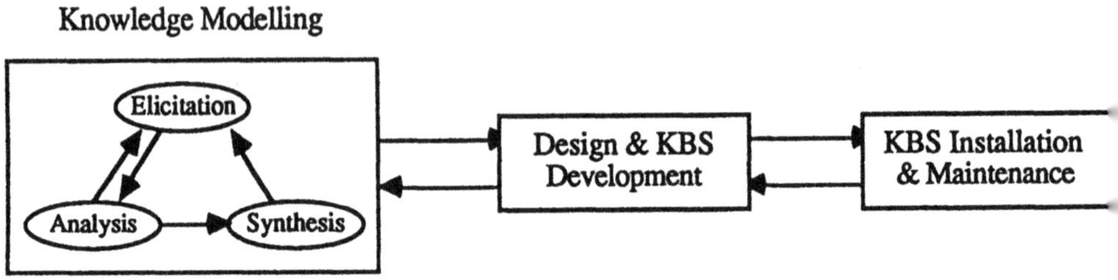

Knowledge Modelling

Figure 1 - Phases in KBS Development

It should only be after such a modelling phase that later phases of KBS development and implementation should proceed. However, this paper focuses on the mediating and intermediate representations which emerge independently of these later stages, i.e. domain-driven knowledge modelling.

3 Mediating & Intermediate Representations

There are two kinds of representations in knowledge acquisition and they are mentioned in the title of this paper: mediating and intermediate representations. Sometimes the terms have various interpretations in the literature [2, 9]. However, though it is the case that they are sometimes used interchangeably in knowledge acquisition parlance, there is a difference between the two; they also play different roles in the knowledge modelling process. Since the distinction is useful, we will draw it in some detail here.

3.1 Mediating Representations

A mediating representation is the major tool in constructing a machine-independent statement of the knowledge and associated background information which we call a competence model [13]. Put more simply, it aims to provide a medium of communication between the knowledge engineer(s) and a 'grammar' of the expert's task ([12], page 184). It strives at conveying the sense of synthesis and coming to share a similar perspective with the expert of the domain through representations. Repertory grids which have been extensively used in knowledge acquisition (e.g. [28]) are a good example of a mediating representation. Another example is the concept map which also promotes communication and understanding via easily-learned generic knowledge representation forms. Hence, any representation which enhances communication amongst participants in the knowledge acquisition/modelling process and improves their understanding of evolving a conceptual domain model will pass as a mediating representation. The criteria for mediating representations are [12]:

- They should be sufficiently expressive.
- They should be economical.
- They should aid communication between all members of the team, i.e. help bridge the gap between the human participants (domain expert, knowledge engineer and users) and provide a means by which they can communicate independent of lower-level machine-oriented representations.
- They should guide the knowledge modelling process in a significant way.

In addition to Johnson's list are the following further attributes we consider important of mediating representations:

- They should help harmonise the knowledge engineer's view of the given domain with the expert's perspective, i.e. harmonising their mental models as they can not just be merged together [25]; this also supports Morik's [16] constructivist view of knowledge.
- The should be "easily readable by those not involved in the original development programme" ([8], page 34). This is crucial since executable knowledge bases "are seldom organised from the perspective of humans, but rather for the convenience of representation and reasoning mechanisms of performance environments: hence, the design of mediating representations is optimised for human insight rather than machine efficiency" [3]. In this way, they could facilitate maintenance and explanation by enabling the system's eventual users to explore the conceptual or abstract domain structure without resorting to any low-level representations, eg C or Lisp code [10].
- They should have the potential to evolve/transform to (or map to) intermediate representations.
- They should be domain-driven: there must be a rationale for their use and they should definitely not driven by lower-level implementation concerns.
- Graphical mediating representations should possibly be preferred to, say, text if they could be made less ambiguous: a picture is sometimes worth a thousand words. However, though the claim that graphical representations are more comprehensible have been made by several people in knowledge acquisition (egs [18, 30]) there is still not as yet an adequate psychological basis for this. However, we have a hunch that they are.

Further examples includes Ford *et al.* 's ICONKAT [9] which exploits repertory grids and concept maps in a synergistic fashion. Johnson's [12] personal preference which she has used extensively in her interviews are for systemic grammar networks (SGNs).

3.2 Intermediate Representations

An intermediate representation is a representation "which only exists between flanking representations and is bound to them by clearly defined projection rules which map one representation to the next" ([12], page 184). They are necessary because of the following:

- The gap between mediating representations and code is so wide that it needs to be bridged.
- They facilitate the integration of knowledge acquisition and performance systems as well as allow rapid feedback, dynamic analysis and verification throughout the development process [15]. Figure 2 adapted from [3] elucidates the essential difference between intermediate and mediating representations.

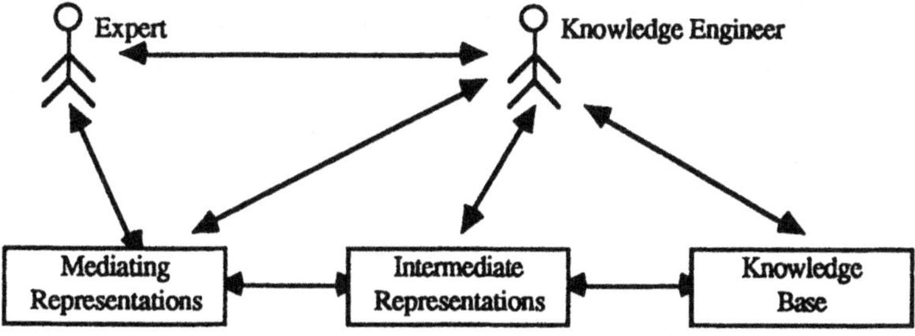

Figure 2 - Mediating & Intermediate Representations

- Intermediate representations need to be capable of integrating the diverse perspectives of the variety of mediating representations and help bridge the gap between the human participants and the implementation formalism required of the performance environment.

The intermediate representation would usually contain an integrated view of different knowledge types: concepts and concept definitions, causal relationships, functional dependencies, causal models, heuristics, list of previous cases, etc. These may/may not be at different levels of abstraction.

4 A Hypothesis/Framework for Knowledge Modelling

Figure 3 is a detailed elaboration of the first phase of Figure 1 which attempts to structure the notoriously difficult and *ad hoc* domain modelling phase of knowledge based systems development.

In so doing, it is an attempt to provide a hypothesis of knowledge modelling as well as a principled basis for constructing more structured domain modelling/characterisation tools. This hypothesis draws mainly from experiences of knowledge modelling exercises we have carried out ourselves, but also from work of other researchers referenced in this paper. The lack of a systematic or more formal theory of knowledge modelling makes such an exercise even more crucial to do. Knowledge modelling is being done daily by knowledge engineers; hence, there is a pragmatic need for systemising the process. This paper could be seen as proposing preliminary heuristics to facilitate the analysis of a domain and later synthesis of intermediate representations to provide the knowledge model for the domain. Of course, this proposal is open to debate.

Essentially, a knowledge engineer is given a domain to model (normally, though not always with the assistance of some expert) with a view of yielding a set of intermediate representations which together comprise the domain model. The knowledge engineer interviews the expert and they communicate and come to share a similar perspective [25] via suitable mediating representations such as concept maps, hierarchies, etc. However, as any knowledge engineer will tell you the elicitation (interviewing) and analysis processes are closely intertwined. For completeness sake, we define elicitation to be the process of obtaining knowledge from an expert to produce what may be called the 'raw data'; these can exhibit a high or low degree of organisation depending on the technique used [6]. Analysis refers to the process of organising this raw data gained from experts (but also from literature, manuals, journals, video tapes and other sources, eg examples) into a coherent unambiguous structure for the domain.

As Figure 3 illustrates, there are several elicitation techniques in the literature which the knowledge engineer can use. Similarly, there are also domain analysis techniques. For the latter, we have proposed some basic facets that we believe characterise most domains including: it has a lexicon/glossary, a history, a theory, a metatheory, some basic metaphors, relations to other domains, a structure and purpose [24]. We would use these in this paper, as we have done several projects for industrial partners, as top-level analytical primitives which help knowledge engineers to analyse a domain.

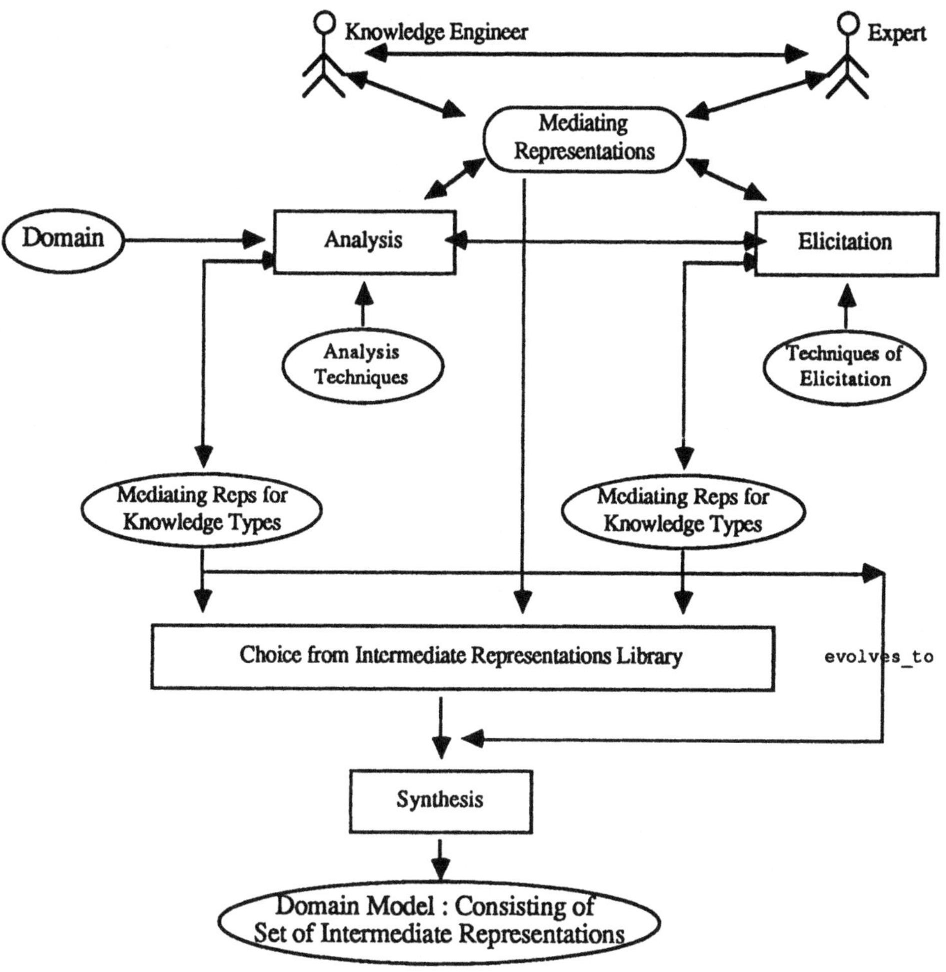

Figure 3 - Structuring the Knowledge Modelling Process

A key point to note is that both the analysis and elicitation processes yield different knowledge types, i.e. knowledge represented in different forms. These knowledge types are mediating representations until they are transformed (or evolved) to intermediate representations. Clearly, depending on the knowledge elicitation technique one uses, one gets a different knowledge type. For example, laddering will yield hierarchies (trees) while repertory grids yield facts and heuristics. However, analysis should have revealed *a priori* that the domain is hierarchical in nature before laddering is used; the idea here being there must be rationale for choosing the elicitation technique in the first place. Analysis, similarly, will yield different knowledge types depending on the top-level analytical primitive being considered. For example, the lexicon/glossary is just a list, while structure will yield diagrams, pictures, etc. The key point to emphasise here is all the representations being generated are **domain-driven**, *evolving either from considerations of the analysis and/or elicitation processes.*

Often these various mediating representation knowledge types evolve/transform naturally to intermediate representations. However, sometimes they can map to several intermediate knowledge representations: hence the library from which a choice of intermediate representations can be made. The set of resulting intermediate representations are *synthesised* at possibly different levels of abstraction to provide the domain model. Clearly, a hypertext-based tool will be invaluable here.

Culling from our experiences and from the literature, mediating representations (which subsume all the knowledge types) include concept maps, repertory grids, systemic grammar networks (SGNs), annotations, partially complete flow charts & diagrams, partially complete attribute & a-kind-of (AKO) lists, (concept) hierarchies, incomplete lists & tables, partial causal networks, equations, incomplete procedures and so forth.

Intermediate representations which we have produced have included structured english (evolved from annotations), heuristics (elicited or evolved from repertory grids), flow charts, diagrams, task decomposition trees (evolved from hierarchies or repertory grids), domain/sub-domain perspective diagrams showing the boundaries of the domain (evolved from concept maps), lists, tables, equations, pictures, glossary, event diagrams/charts, concept attribute lists, AKO lists, causal networks, annotations, etc. The domain models consists of these.

There are thus a plethora of mediating and intermediate knowledge representations. Clearly what is now missing is some information of ***when*** and ***where*** to use the various representations; Nwana *et al.* (1991) identified this as one of the problems with knowledge modelling. In the absence of a good and formal theory to knowledge acquisition, we can only provide some heuristics gleaned from our experiences or from the literature. These follow.

4.1 Mediating Representations for Analysis Techniques

It has been mentioned that Paton *et al.* [24] have proposed some top-level characteristics (knowledge types) to look for in domains; their bases is explained in the paper. Table 1 attempts to highlight suggested/associated mediating representations. Whether or not one agrees with our proposal here is less relevant than the central idea that analysis/elicitation suggests 'natural' mediating representations to use.

Knowledge Type	**Mediating Representation(s)**
STRUCTURE:	Concept maps
[Parts	SGNs
Relations	Diagrams/Pictures
Organisation]	Partial attribute lists
	Partial AKO lists
PURPOSE:	
[Goals (objectives)	Goal hierarchies
Tasks (to meet objectives)	Task hierarchies
Inference Knowledge	Partial goal/task annotations
Strategic Knowledge]	Partial Causal Networks
	Partial flow charts
	Incomplete procedures
THEORY:	Annotations
[Sub Theories]	Equations
	Formulae

HISTORY:	Annotations
METAPHORS/ANALOGIES: [Global and main ones including: Ontological metaphors Functional metaphors Structural metaphors]	 Annotations Tables
RELATION TO OTHER DOMAINS:	Partial Lists Concept maps
LEXICON/GLOSSARY	Incomplete Lists Incomplete Tables

Table 1 - Mediating Representations for Analysis Process

4.2 Mediating Representations for Elicitation Techniques

Table 2 similarly attempts to capture mediating representations which result 'naturally' through the use of various knowledge elicitation techniques. This section draws mostly from the literature [6, 11, 14, 21, 30]. Of course, we do not claim to have used all these techniques in our work: for example, we have never found the need to use twenty questions or multi-dimensional scaling.

Elic. Tech.	Knowledge Types	Use When	Med.Representation/s
INTERVIEW			
Unstructured	Generally high-level Stories highlighting e.g. history, metaphors theories, layouts related other domains (R.o.d)	Early sessions	History: annotations Metaphors: lists/tables Theories: annotations R.o.d: concept maps Pictures/diagrams
Structured	Conceptual-factual yielding parts, relations, tasks strategy, inference, organisation, goals heuristics	Middle sessions, Seeking advice, Determining interconnections	Concept maps, SGNs Part diagrams/pictures Task hierarchies Goal hierarchies Part goal/task annotation Partial AKO lists Partial attribute lists Partial causal networks Partial flow charts Incomplete procedures
Focussed	Factual-low grain size	Middle sessions	Similar to Structured interview
Teachback	N/A	Verifying stage Final session	N/A

TASK EXECUTION			
Protocol Analysis	Factual/declarative procedural/script Strategic/heuristic Inference	Procedural, Non-verbalisable knowledge	Incomplete procedures Flow charts Also as in Structured interviewing above
Induction	Rules of thumb Facts	Significant amount of case histories/ records	Rules of thumb Inference rules
FORMALISED			
Laddering	Hierarchies	Hierarchy 'seen' Cataloguing categories	Concepts hierarchy Task decomposition hierarchy Goals hierarchy
Repertory Grids	Relational, factual	Domains with small number of facts Ascertain attributes of concepts	Un-verified Heuristics Partial attributes lists
Card Sort	Conceptual structure	Early sessions Determining interconnections	Concept maps Partial attribute lists
Twenty Questions	Factual, procedural Heuristic, strategic inference	Procedural, factual strategic Knowledge	?
Multi-dimensional Scaling	Conceptual Structure	Similarity of concepts needed	Concept maps ?
Prototype Review	N/A	Prototype available	N/A

Table 2 - Mediating Representations for Elicitation Techniques

4.3 From Mediating Representations to Intermediate Representations

One of our criteria for mediating representations is that they should have the potential to evolve/transform to (or map to) intermediate representations. Often, the mediating representation evolves naturally into an intermediate representation as we cycle through the iterations of knowledge modelling. However, there are cases when this is not the case and there are several possible choices of intermediate representations. Culling from our experience, Table 3 illustrates the evolutions/mappings that exist between mediating and intermediate representations. This is by no means ideal, but it however captures our view of the sometimes subtle distinction between mediating and intermediate representations; it is no wonder that the two terms are used interchangeably in knowledge acquisition parlance. Some may consider this too vague to be convincing, but it does provide a starting point for debate which may further clarify it.

Mediating Representation **Representation(s)**	**Intermediate**
Concept maps	Expert's perspective diagrams of domain showing bounds Concept-relationship diagrams Event diagrams
Repertory grids	Rules/Heuristics Structured english Facts
Systemic grammar networks Incomplete Annotations	Hierarchies Complete Annotations Structured English
Partially complete flow charts	Complete Flowcharts
Partially complete diagrams	Complete diagrams
Incomplete lists	Complete lists
Incomplete tables	Complete tables
Incomplete attribute lists	Complete concept attribute lists
Incomplete AKO lists	Complete concept AKO lists
Incomplete causal networks	Complete causal networks
Equations	Equations
Formulae	Formulae
Incomplete task hierarchies	Complete task hierarchies
Incomplete goal hierarchies	Complete goal hierarchies
Un-verified Heuristics	Verified heuristics
Incomplete/Unverified procedures	Complete/verified procedures Structured English
Partially complete lexicon	Full lexicon
Incomplete glossary	Full glossary

Table 3 - Evolving/Transforming Mediating Representations to Intermediate Representations

Naturally, the word 'complete' which occurs many times in Table 3 is relative.

5 Conclusions: Towards a Tool for Domain Modelling

Section 4 has presented a hypothesis for domain modelling. Some of the latter section's contents may look trivial because it is what knowledge engineers do every day. However, this is the whole point. If it is not, then how comes we keep on hearing/reading about the knowledge acquisition "bottleneck" (we will prefer to refer to it as the knowledge modelling problem)? The lack of a more formal theory to knowledge modelling leaves us in a situation where all we have is a bag of elicitation techniques and tools and with little guidance of their usage. The fact is knowledge acquisition still remains much of an *art* which comes naturally to the gifted knowledge engineers. To be engineering, it needs to become more disciplined - less an art than a science, akin to the development of conventional software engineering techniques. This is necessary in order to train new knowledge engineers, to construct more maintainable knowledge based systems (KBSs), to facilitate their routine development, to improve their quality, etc. That is our key motivation for trying to structure the unstructured, ie. striving to articulate what we believe comprises successful knowledge modelling which so far is undeniably an intractable problem despite the existence of numerous tools and techniques. We have also attempted to pull together the efforts of many researchers into what we believe is a plausible framework for knowledge modelling. For lack of space, we could not include conclusive examples of our usage of this framework with so far encouraging results. We would appreciate the comments of other researchers who find it useful.

We also believe our proposal/hypothesis forms the basis for a hybrid tool for knowledge modelling. So far, we envisage a hypertext-based and/or CASE tool which would capture all aspects of our hypothesis of Figure 3. However, the tool would also consists of various diagrammatic aids, facilities for structuring text, annotating and so forth. It will enable knowledge engineers to keep track of their actions when carrying out knowledge modelling, to document all that goes on at this vital phase of KBS development. We envisage the tool being used in both off-line and online mode depending on what cycle the knowledge engineer has reached in his iterative cycle. For example, initially, the early unstructured interviews may could be modelled using the tool off-line (i.e. expert not present in this context), while later structured sessions could use the tool online (i.e. expert present).

We also strive to keep our intermediate representations totally independent of all implementation concerns. In this way, we hope to avoid *shoe-horning* a domain into some (set of) representations. We believe this to be the one of the central problems in knowledge modelling [22]: the fact that most knowledge acquisition tools/techniques are driven by implementation concerns rather than by the nature of the domain [27, 32]. The fact that we have carried out several domain modelling exercises *without* a view to developing KBSs did help us in this goal. It actually emerged that some of the industrial domains we modelled were not feasible/suitable for KBS development thereby saving the costs of a possible failed project.

In addition, a domain model could be relatively easily transformed into designs/implementation. The reader is also referred at this juncture to Wetter's interesting work [31] which attempts to directly identify intermediate representations by formalising KADS's conceptual models. In fact, one of the anonymous reviewers for this paper points out that KADS's view of modelling [5] can be mapped onto Figure 3: the conceptual model (for interaction between knowledge engineer and expert) using the mediating representations and the KADS design models using the intermediate models. We are pleased with this comment because we have stated before in [22] that our approach largely complements KADS. However, from our experience, there exists a continuum of representations ranging from mediating representations at one end via intermediate representations in the middle to machine representations at the other end. For example consider the following:

```
concept maps -> perspective diagrams ->  semantic networks -> conceptual graphs ->
   predicate calculus -> PROLOG
concept maps -> concept-relationship diagrams -> semantic networks -> conceptual
   graphs -> predicate calculus
concept maps -> event diagrams -> temporal semantic nets/objects
Incomplete flow charts -> Complete flow charts -> Procedures (Algorithms)
repertory grids -> facts -> knowledge base facts
repertory grids -> heuristics -> knowledge base rules
Incomplete attribute lists -> Concept attribute lists -> Objects/Frames
Incomplete AKO lists -> Concept AKO lists -> Objects/Instances/Inheritance hierarchies
concept maps -> causal networks -> inference networks
Incomplete task hierarchies -> Complete task hierarchies -> generic tasks models
   (KADS)
```

In summary, we envisage the proposed tool to characterise/model domains will go some way in addressing some of the key problems with knowledge modelling which we highlighted in [22]. They included:

- Developing techniques to enable the expert(s) and the knowledge engineer(s) to harmonise their mental models as suggested by Recogzei & Plantinga [25]. (The recognition that this is even desirable is important).
- Providing techniques of analysing a problem domain so as to reveal *what* elicitation techniques/tools to use *when* so as to address the mismatch problem.
- Develop techniques to navigate and make sense of the sheer mass of information involved in knowledge acquisition.
- Letting the nature of the *domain* guide the knowledge acquisition process [3]; the final form of the knowledge base should emerge from the model of the domain. This is possible since our framework is principally analysis, and hence domain-driven: all mediating representations result from considerations of analysis/elicitation decisions.
- Structured the knowledge modelling process so that knowledge engineers do not move too quickly through some of the cognitive definition and organisation work to enter the later phases of acquisition and implementation without an adequate *specification/model* of the domain. This has partly been due to the fact that the designs and functions of many available knowledge acquisition tools were driven by implementation rather than cognitive concerns [27]. This creates problems for neglected area of knowledge base maintenance which is a real issue for practical systems.
- Evolving a pragmatic theory of knowledge modelling as the epistemological, cognitive and conceptual foundations of knowledge acquisition leave much to be desired [2].

Acknowledgements

This research is sponsored by Shell Research UK (Thornton) and Unilever Research (Port Sunlight). We acknowledge especially the encouragements from Drs Ken Lunn, Keith McFarlane and Hugh Dorans of Shell Research UK. The comments of the four anonymous referees are also acknowledged.

References

1. Aakvik, G., AAmodt, A. & Nordbo, I. (1991), "A Knowledge Representation Framework Supporting Knowledge Modelling", Proceedings of the *5th European Knowledge Acquisition Workshop (EKAW-91)*, Crieff, Scotland, May.
2. Bradshaw, J. M. & Boose, J. H. (1989), "Knowledge Acquisition as CASE for Knowledge Based Systems", *Paper presented at the 3rd International Workshop on Computer-Aided Software Engineering (CASE-89)*, London, England, July.
3. Bradshaw, J. M. & Boose, J. H. (1991), "Mediating Representations for Knowledge Acquisiton", *Proceedings of the AAAI-91 Workshop on Knowledge Acquisition: From Theory to Techniques to Tools*, Anaheim, California, July.
4. Bradshaw, J. & Woodward, B (1989), "Knowledge Acquisition Tools" (Panel Discussion Summary of IJCAI-89 Knowledge Acquisition Workshop), In Boose, J. & Gaines, B. (eds), *Knowledge Acquisition for KBS Newsletter* **1** (3), 12.
5. Breuker, J. A., Wielinga, B. J., van Someren, M., de Hoog, R., Schreiber, G., de Greef, P., Bredeweg, B., Wielemaker, J., Billeaut, J. P., Davoodi, M. & Hayward, S. (1987), *Model-Driven Knowledge Acquisition Interpretation Models*, Deliverable Task A1, ESPRIT Project 1098, Commission of the European Community.
6. Burton, A. M., Shadbolt, N. R., Hedgecock, A. P., & Rugg, G. (1987) "A formal evaluation of elicitation techniques for expert systems: domain 1", In Moralee, D. S. (ed), *Research and Developments in Expert Systems*, Cambridge University Press.
7. Clancey, W. J (1989), "The Knowledge Level Reinterpreted: Modeling How Systems Interact", *Machine Learning* **4**, 285-291.
8. Diaper, D. (ed.) (1989), "Designing Expert Systems - from Dan to Beersheba", In *Knowledge Elicitation: Principles, Techniques and Applications*, London: Wiley.
9. Ford, K., Stahl, H., Adams-Webber, J., Novak, J. & Jones, J. C. (1990), "ICONKAT: An integrated constructivist knowledge acquisition tool", *Proceedings of AAAI-90 Workshop on Knowledge Acquisition: Practical Tools and Techniques*, Boston, Mass., July.
10. Ford, K. M. & Canas, A. J. (1991), "Explanation as a Knowledge Acquisition Issue", *Proceedings of the AAAI-91 Workshop on Knowledge Acquisition: from Theory to Technique to Tools*, Anaheim, California, July.
11. Grover, M. D. (1983), "A Pragmatic Knowledge Acquisition Methodology", *Proceedings of IJCAI* **8**, 436-438.
12. Johnson, N. E. (1989), "Mediating representations in knowledge elicitation", In Diaper, D. (ed), *Knowledge Elicitation: Principles, Techniques and Applications*, Chichester: Ellis Horwood, 179-194.
13. Keravnou, E. & Johnson, L. (1986), *Competent Expert System*, London: Kogan Page.
14. LaFrance, M. (1987), "The Knowledge Acquisition Grid: a method for training knowledge engineers", *International Journal on Man-Machine Studies* **26**, 245-255.
15. Linster, M. & Gaines, B. (1990), "Supporting Acquisition and Performance in a Hypermedia Environment", *Paper Presented at Terminology and Knowledge Engineering Workshop*, Germany.
16. Morik, K. (1989), "Sloppy Modelling", In Morik, K. (ed), *Knowledge Representation and Organisation in Machine Learning: Lecture Notes in Artificial Intelligence* **347**, London: Springer Verlag, 107-134.
17. Morik, K. (1991), "Underlying Assumptions of Knowledge Acquisition and Machine Learning", *Knowledge Acquisition* **3**, 137-156.
18. Motta, E., Eisenstadt, M., Pitman, K. & West, M. (1988), "Knowledge acquisition in KEATS: The knowledge engineer's assistant", *Expert Systems* **5**(2).
19. Motta, E., Rajan, T. & Eisenstadt, M. (1990), "Knowledge Acquisition as a process of model refinement", *Knowledge Acquisition* **2**, 21-49.
20. Musen, M. A. (1989), "Conceptual models of interactive knowledge acquisition tools", *Knowledge Acquisition* **1**, 73-88.

21. Neale, I. M. (1988), "First generation expert systems: a review of knowledge acquisition methdologies", *The Knowledge Engineering Review* 3(2), 105-145.
22. Nwana, H. S., Paton, R. C., Bench-Capon, T. J. M. & Shave, M. J. R. (1991), "Facilitating the Development of Knowledge Based Systems: A Critical Review of Acquisition Tools and Techniques", *AI Communications*4(2/3), 60-73.
23. Paton, R. C. & Nwana, H. S. (1990), "Domain Characterisation through Knowledge Analysis", *Proceedings of AAAI-90 Workshop on Knowledge Acquisition: Practical Tools and Techniques*, Boston, Mass., July.
24. Paton, R. C., Nwana, H. S., Shave, M. J. R., Bench-Capon, T. J. M. (1991), "From Real World Problems to Domain Chracterisations", Proceedings of the *5th European Knowledge Acquisition Workshop (EKAW-91)*, Crieff, Scotland, May.
25. Recogzei, S. & Plantinga, E. P. O. (1987), "Creating the domain of discourse: ontology and inventory, *International Journal of Man-Machine Studies* 27, 235-251.
26. Sandberg, J. (1991), Interview with Bill Clancey, *AI Communications*.
27. Shaw, M. L. G. (1989), "A Grid-Based Tool for Knowledge Acquisition", *Proceedings of IJCAI-1989 Workshop on Knowledge Acquisition*, Detroit, Michigan, 19-22.
28. Shaw, M. L. G. & Gaines, B. R. (1987), "Techniques for knowledge acquisition and transfer", *International Journal of Man-Machine Studies* 27, 251-280.
29. Steels, L. (1990), "Components of Expertise", *AI Magazine*, Summer 1990, 20-49.
30. Welbank, M. (1990), "An overview of knowledge acquisition methods", *Interacting with Computers* 2(1), 83-91.
31. Wetter, T. (1990), "First Order Logic Foundation of the KADS Conceptual Model", In Wielinga, B., Boose, J., Gaines, B., Schriber, G. & Van Someren, M. (eds), Current Trends in Knowledge Acquisition, Amsterdam: IOS, 356-375.
32. Woodward, B. (1990), "Knowledge acquisition at the front end: defining the domain", *Knowledge Acquisition* 2, 73-94.

PMI: Knowledge Elicitation and De Bono's Thinking Tools

M.-M. Portmann and S.M. Easterbrook

School of Cognitive and Computing Sciences, University of Sussex
Falmer, Brighton, BN1 9QH. <mariap@cogs.susx.ac.uk>

Abstract. Much attention in knowledge acquisition has been directed at the question "What is Knowledge?". In this paper, we discuss a related question, which we consider to be of equal importance, namely "What is Thinking?". We present a definition of thinking that emphasizes the importance of arriving at new arrangements of knowledge, and discuss how having knowledge about something can be used to avoid thinking. Given this view, it is clear that stimulating an expert to *think* about the domain can provide more detailed knowledge about both the domain and about the expert himself. We have taken one of De Bono's thinking tools, the PMI (plus - minus - interesting) and built a knowledge elicitation tool for use in a domain where the expert's responses are likely to be based on unquestioned judgements. The tool requires the expert to think about the domain in ways that he is perhaps not used to, and the information elicited from this exercise gives an insight into the judgement policies of the expert. This, in turn, is of use when applying the knowledge, particularly where the resolution of conflicts becomes necessary.

1 Introduction

The problems of engineering knowledge-based systems inevitably beg the question "What is knowledge?". Many approaches to knowledge acquisition have arisen based on various perspectives on the nature of knowledge (see Boose 1989 for a survey), and experience with these has lead to a growing realisation that knowledge is not some objective essence to be mined and refined. Rather, knowledge seems to change its shape depending both on the task to which it is applied and the social setting. An extreme version of this view is expounded by Winograd & Flores (1986), who suggest that knowledge is socially constructed, and that it is in the act of communication that knowledge gets formulated.

The task of knowledge engineering then is to construct plausible domain models with the help of the expert. This involves stimulating the expert's thinking in order to discover how the knowledge is used. In this paper we examine the hypothesis that the use of de Bono's thinking tools in knowledge elicitation should prove advantageous in two main ways: they should allow a finer granularity of knowledge to be elicited; and they should help to characterise an expert, enabling better comparison between experts.

2 Background Work

Knowledge elicitation and knowledge representation have long been regarded as the bottleneck in building intelligent systems. The human expert cannot be treated as part of a machine, which means that psychological and sociological factors must be taken into consideration. This makes knowledge elicitation difficult and time-consuming. Three interconnected problems are involved:

1. The nature of the knowledge elicited: it has long been recognised that expert behaviour is not necessarily open to introspection, and that the knowledge used by the expert is compiled, and cannot be broken down into consecutive, neatly fitting chunks (du Boulay & Ross 1991).
2. The method of eliciting the knowledge: the type and quality of the knowledge acquired varies according to the elicitation technique, so that the availability of a range of techniques is desirable.
3. Conflict resolution: one cannot overlook the fact that the information an expert gives is coloured by his special interests in a domain, hence that knowledge needs to be elicited from more than one expert in order to cover the domain evenly. This in turn generates its own problems.

Similar problems also apply to users of a knowledge-based system: introspecting their requirements might be as difficult for the users as introspection of knowledge is for the experts, for very much the same reasons. Users of the system will also have special interests in the domain which might be different from the ones embodied in the system. In fact we are concerned with domains where there is no real distinction between experts and users. If the domain involves questions of subjective judgement, then the user might have just as much claim to "knowledge" as the expert.

2.1 Knowledge and the Interview

The most general elicitation technique is the interview. However, interviews are by no means trivial to conduct, nor is the data gathered from an interview always easy to analyse. The interview is made up of many different – possibly interfering – relationships:

- between expert and question: the expert might find the question threatening because it concerns an area of the domain in which he is not so hot;
- between interviewer and question: the interviewer might be personally interested in this;
- between interviewer and expert: differences of race, sex, class and age all might matter here;
- between interviewer and answer: does the interviewer understand the answer? Is it a matter of the interviewer being satisfied with the answer or not?;
- between expert and answer: where 'answer' needs to be read as 'knowledge'.

LaFrance (1988) addresses the issue of knowledge being multi-modal, and makes use of the fact that different types of question elicit different *forms* of knowledge. Her *knowledge acquisition grid* organises knowledge and questions as "separate but interacting dimensions" (La France 1988, p.85). The "Types of Question"-dimension ranges from the open-ended to increasingly more specific and directed questions; the "Forms of Knowledge"-dimension ranges from more declarative ("what") to more procedural ("how") types of knowledge.

Gammack & Young (1985) justify the need for the "deeper" knowledge of the expert (beyond empirical rules) and hence of a more complex knowledge structure for expert systems, and also focus on a variety of methods for the elicitation of the different *kinds* of expert knowledge, but they admit that identifying some broad categories of knowledge can be done only for restricted domains.

There is merit in having a number of different question types, but it is hard to see how, in the process of an interview, the engineer can decide on the question type, as "...questions cannot only extract content but can follow it as well" (La France 1988, p.

89). A certain type of question does not necessarily guarantee a certain form of knowledge as a response, hence the information elicited by a question would need to be analysed before deciding on the type of the next question. The Grid may have its passive use, for decoding transcripts of interviews.

Whilst traversal of the Grid might be interesting for the expert, it is extremely demanding on the engineer. Further, it has been found that the relationship between question to be asked and question asked is not straightforward. Greenwell (1990) refers to Brenner (1982) as reporting that interviewers altered one third of the questions during the interview. This throws doubt on the usefulness of linear traversal of the grid.

LaFrance does admit that how the Grid is used (linear fashion or cyclical fashion) depends on the needs of different expert system teams, and that the use of the grid is a skill which engineers need to be trained for. However, DeLamater (1982) has found that "Using well trained interviewers ... [is] ...not related to responses they obtain" (DeLamater 1982, p. 37). He found that characteristics of respondents generate a greater difference of responses than question types.

2.2 Knowledge and Conflict

Shaw (1980; 1981) is concerned with conflicts not just between two or more experts, but within a single expert. Her work is based on Kelly's Personal Construct Theory (Kelly 1955) which holds that a person is made up of several sub-personalities, and that at any one moment, we might be operating with one of those sub-personalities. Furthermore, any communication act might be addressed not to another person, but to some sub-personality of this other person.

As a consequence of this Shaw identifies three aspects of conversation:

1. between sub-personalities of one person
2. between two sub-personalities, each of a different person
3. in a group of persons, which constitutes one or more sub-personalities.

Hence "adequate communion is dependent on the recognition and acceptance of difference both within and between people" (Shaw 1981, p. 132).

In Personal Construct Theory, a role, or sub-personality "implies a particular way of construing" (Shaw 1981, p. 129). This amounts to a particular conceptual system, and knowledge is treated as a widely shared and particularly significant conceptual system, seemingly "having an existence virtually independent of their carriers". This makes repertory grid methodologies based on personal construct psychology ideal for the elicitation and analysis of information from experts. The repertory grid is used as a conversational tool, or feedback device, relating to all aspects of conversation identified above. The tool takes over the tedious parts of the task of elicitation – hence the programs embody "content-free conversational algorithms" (Shaw 1980, p. 148). Shaw's tools do not force an analysis, and feedback facilities enable the user to change or eliminate constructs at any stage in the elicitation process.

In addition to eliciting the constructs and building the repertory grids, Shaw & Gaines (1988) compare and match grids, extract equivalences, measure similarities and highlight differences between grids to promote understanding between people and within individuals themselves. The tool SOCIO extends personal construct theory to knowledge acquisition. It uses the repertory grid not only for deriving conceptual systems but also for deriving relations between conceptual systems, of which four are identified:

consensus - between experts' views as a basis for communication.

correspondence - different terminology for shared concepts; a basis for mutual understanding.

conflict - same terminology for different concepts.
contrast - different terminology for different concepts; highlights difficulties for understanding.

SOCIO analyses and classifies the differences between conceptual systems. The derivation is entirely algorithmic, and there is no pressure on experts to reach consensus.

Critics of personal construct theory claim that it is very time-consuming, that it might intimidate the expert, and that Shaw & Gaines have not made it clear how the data is going to be used as the basis of a knowledge base. Greenwell (1990) concludes that "repertory grids have their place in knowledge engineering when the need arises in domains in which the conceptual structure is complex, limited in scope and without a clear nomenclature" (p. 55).

Certainly, personal construct theory is more appropriate and yields more useful information in some specific situations than others, i.e. in clinical psychology where the client voluntarily takes part in construct derivation as s/he has a vested interest to get to know their own various perspectives on the world. However, in knowledge acquisition, it is the knowledge engineer first and foremost who is interested in the expert's constructs, not the expert, and it is not certain whether experts are likely to be convinced of the usefulness of opening up the cabaret of their sub-personalities to the engineer. But without the co-operation of the expert, nothing would be gained, as Shaw & Gaines restrict themselves to the personal construct theory.

2.3 Conflict Resolution

Whilst Shaw & Gaines emphasise identification of conflict, Easterbrook (1991) focuses on encouraging conflict and the provision of productive resolution methods. By emphasizing collaborative resolution methods, such as education and negotiation, conflict is harnessed to explore the issues and assumptions underlying the experts' contributions. In this approach, a conflict is simply a "difference that matters". All different viewpoints are elicited, modelled and compared enabling differences to be captured and correspondences to be established. The comparison is intended to be exploratory, although it might offer some conflict resolution which might or might not be used. The support tool, Synoptic, provides mainly guidance through exploration of conflict, identification of conflict issues, generation of conflict resolution and evaluation of resolutions. Thus the final decision on the choice of a resolution happens in the final phase of the process.

The model described in Easterbrook (1991) relates mainly to requirements specification in systems analysis, where inevitably, information has to be gained from more than one person, and where each person's views might offer a different perspective of the function of the system to be built. It is an area where clashes occur between the needs of different groups of people within the organisation and where it is essential that none of the most important needs of any group should be compromised. While this requirement may be more acute in requirements specification, it is in essence the same requirement which has to be met in knowledge elicitation.

2.4 Summary

LaFrance's method treats the expert as a reactive system which can be prompted with questions and will come out with answers, and in this spirit she assumes that feeding it different question types will make it come out with different types of knowledge. This puts the emphasis on the external process, on what goes into the system (the questions), and what comes out of it; what goes on between the expert and the knowledge engineer, but not what goes on within the expert himself. Whilst Shaw and Gaines do take into account the psychological make-up of the expert, they employ a method which is primarily designed to get information about the expert himself, not about a domain.

The notion of encouraging conflict and then providing co-operative conflict resolution methods is a positive step forward. If knowledge is a social construct then the social context needs to be explored. Instead of maintaining a consensus, the different perspectives of various experts need to be captured and explored. The process of comparing conflicting perspectives then provides a productive focus for the exploration of the finer details of the expert's thinking. The comparisons reveal important information about the perspectives each expert takes, including hidden assumptions, and the relative importance attached to various issues.

Although various limited conflict resolution techniques have been proposed, these have yet to be integrated into knowledge acquisition methodologies. The model described in Easterbrook (1991) is limited in the sense that it leaves many questions still unanswered. In particular, it shares a fundamental flaw with all the techniques we have described: although it is assumed that the expert is a thinking being, there has been little consideration of what exactly this means - that is, the models take thinking for granted. We suggest that a fourth problem needs to be added to the list given at the beginning of this section, namely, "thinking".

3 What is "Thinking"?

If we are to define knowledge elicitation as getting information from a thinking subject, then the two crucial terms in this domain are knowledge and thinking. We shall attempt to define these terms:

Firstly, we will adopt a Wittgensteinian definition of knowledge, which amounts to knowledge being a matter of making a judgement about the truth of something. Any such judgement needs to be backed up by evidence, where such evidence is objective and publicly examinable. However, the judgement itself is subjective and does not say anything about the fact judged - it is merely "a characteristic of the manner in which I make judgements" (Wittgenstein 1984, para 149, page 47 - our translation). This means that the judgement says something about the person who is making it - a fact which this project exploits.

Definitions of thinking are harder to come by, as it is thinking behaviour, rather than the thinking process itself which has received the attention. De Bono regards thinking as a skill which can be learned, and hence can be done proficiently or badly, and that some ways of thinking are more profitable than others. We regard thinking as a kind of mental orienteering, which is best done with the help of tools. De Bono claims that traditional tools have led our thinking into rigid patterns and recommends attention directing tools to break those habitual and restricting patterns.

Our assumption is that the application of de Bono's thinking tools have a place here, and our enquiry starts with two hypotheses:

1. The application of different thinking patterns by the expert should in some way affect the information given by him. What exactly is to be expected has not been defined a priori, but we anticipate that the information should be of a finer grain than it would otherwise be, as the application of different thinking patterns should encourage the expert to consider different aspects of the subject.
2. The information gathered would not only say something about the domain, but about the expert, too - a fact which can be exploited in knowledge acquisition.

3.1 De Bono on Thinking and Conflict

In his Letters to Thinkers de Bono writes: "Thinking is our way of moving from one arrangement of knowledge to a better one." (De Bono 1988, p26). Taking this definition literally means that "if we had complete information in a situation then we would not have to think" (*ibid.* p26). A corollary of the definition is the paradox that "we might make better use of (the) information by not knowing about it" (*ibid.* p28). Knowing about something means having a specific arrangement of knowledge about something. Thinking about something is arranging the knowledge about that something in a specific way. Looking at all the information is looking at the domain via that specific arrangement.

This view of knowledge and thinking has some interesting implications. For example, if the knowledge claims authority in the domain, then we will not try to move to a better arrangement of knowledge, or to our own - we will not have to *think*. This corresponds to Heidegger's notion of *blindness* (Winograd & Flores 1986): the patterns of knowledge and the abstractions that we use to get by in everyday life blind us to other possibilities. De Bono suggests that it is better to have just enough information to be able to develop our own ideas about something, and then to look at the information in our own way. This gives thinking a chance to find new ways before being forced or tempted into the old concepts.

Conflicts between people often arise because people insist on their own arrangement of knowledge about something. This is the thinking style de Bono calls "small circle rightness" (De Bono 1988, p22) which only leads to further entrenchment of the conflicting parties within their position. de Bono has long been the advocate for a different style of thinking - lateral thinking - which is creative, as opposed to analytic thinking which is rigid and uses logic as its only resource, resulting in "small circle rightness". The tools of lateral thinking are of a quite different nature: provocation - mostly random, observation, exploration and intuition. The major difference between the two styles is this: Lateral thinking simply takes an *interest* in the topic, whilst analytic thinking is interested in the correctness of one's own argument or the fallacy of someone else's argument.

Analytic thinking has produced conflict resolution methods more appropriate to conflict perpetuation than conflict resolution - it merely changes the *shape* of the conflict: Instead of open warfare, there is a cold war - but still a war. In contrast, de Bono suggests a design approach to conflict. Traditionally, a conflict is a state of affairs in which the conflicting parties not so much try to win over one another, but in which both parties are trying to prolong their "state of victory": both sides are winning, because neither side is giving in to the other. Whilst both parties may wish for the end of the conflict, victory, in effect, consists of the prolongation of the dispute.

For de Bono, a conflict "is a situation with different perception, principles, needs and emotions" (*ibid.* p234). The conflict resolution task is "to design an outcome". This approach concentrates on a possible state of affairs *without* conflict, instead of "trying to reduce the concept to its basic confrontation simplicity" (*ibid.* p234-5) - in other words, concentrating on the clash of fundamental principles. Paradoxically, this simplification results the conflict becoming even more irresolvable. The design stance, by doing the opposite, achieves the opposite: by complicating the concept or conflict situation, it "enrich[es] the situation so that a design can be made" (*ibid.* p236). This process of complication is a creative process. It relies on observation, not evaluation: new perspectives are added, new comparisons made, different scenarios thought of. This involves both parties in an exercise of exploration, not of confrontation.

This may even result in a re-definition of the conflict which might lead to the perception of different approaches to solving the conflict. Thus the design stance sets out to achieve a desired situation (instead of trying to eliminate an undesired problem). This turns the eyes of both parties in the same direction - i.e. of a common future.

3.2 PMI - the Thinking Tool

The idea of enrichment through exploration, as opposed to restriction through judgement, is inherent in PMI, one of de Bono's most powerful thinking tools "that is so simple that it is almost unlearnable" (De Bono 1985, p19). P stands for Plus or good points, M stands for Minus or bad points, I stands for Interesting or interesting points. The tool "should most especially be used when we have no doubt about the situation" (*ibid.* p23), in other words, when we are tempted to refuse to explore a situation further, as our judgement has been firmly made.

The PMI is intended to direct the attention of the thinker to those aspects which might otherwise be ignored. It would be wrong to think that doing a PMI consists of simply listing all the points we can think of concerning a situation, and then ordering them into plus, minus and interesting points. This would be a classification exercise, not an exploratory one. Doing a PMI consists of looking into the direction of Plus, Minus and Interesting, and giving roughly equal time to the exploration of each of these directions. The PMI "is always from the point of view of the thinker doing the PMI" (De Bono 1988, p85): the thinker is not required to list everything that is generally known about a situation, but to list the points he finds when looking at the situation through the channels of Plus, Minus and Interesting - but always from where he happens to be. Again, it is not a matter of finding out what is right, or correct: "No point of itself is Plus or Minus. Those are just directions in which the thinker looks" (*ibid.* p85).

At the same time, the PMI serves to by-pass our - in de Bono's view - naturally reactive and emotional judgements, by allowing a situation to be explored, whether it is liked or not. In the judgemental stance, any points listed would only ever be the points which back up the judgement already made. What is gained by the PMI - especially by looking through the channel Interesting - is the exploration of what is beyond acceptance (making a positive judgement) or rejection (making a negative judgement). To list points found in the direction of Interesting - though not necessarily leading to a reversal of one's opinion - might well lead to just that. Further, in situations of disagreement, I-points might allow a re-definition of the situation and to the perception of alternatives not previously observed. "'Interesting' is a signpost to nowhere and yet a signpost to everywhere" (*ibid.* p170). Again, Interesting points are not found to be interesting *after* they have been observed, but are *found* via the stance of the observer: "the sense of 'Interest' which leads the creative thinker to dwell on a point or an observation and then to look around that point to see what can be found." (*ibid.* p171).

4 Using PMI as a Knowledge Elicitation Tool

Using de Bono's tool, we have developed a program, also called PMI, which gives assistance to a knowledge engineer in the first stage of knowledge acquisition for an advice giving system. For this type of system the task of the knowledge engineer is not to get the *correct* information from an expert, but to get as finely grained information as possible from a variety of experts. Facts and goals are less well defined in advice-giving than in fault-finding or diagnosis - it is therefore harder to know what constitutes success. The one certain criterion for success is in fact the client's satisfaction with the advice given by the system. Such a system will need to satisfy a variety of clients from different economic and cultural backgrounds.

We take as an example of this kind of problem the domain of choosing a restaurant. We treat the problem as one of matching a client to a restaurant, and hypothesize that it should be possible to achieve this by matching a client with an expert. The problem of knowledge elicitation for such a system, then, is one of extracting the criteria which are responsible for the match between an expert and the restaurant s/he is giving information about. What emerges is that the task for an advice giving system in this domain - though not typically a diagnostic one - could be seen as just that: a client's requests concerning eating out are matched against the requests of a 'known case' - one of the experts - which then leads to the 'prescription' of a specific restaurant intended to satisfy the client's requests.

The system must be able to satisfy not only individual clients, but should be able to resolve the conflict between individuals within a group of clients with possibly differing motivations for eating out, and it is in this sense that the system goes beyond case-based reasoning. Traditional conflict resolution methods such as persuasion or negotiation leading to compromise are inadequate, and de Bono's thinking tools provide a framework for respecting the differences between people with clashing interests. Paradoxically, this is achieved by not focussing on them: Instead of the focus being on the conflict or the reasons for the conflict - that is the present, or past - it is directed towards finding a jointly acceptable way ahead, a future.

The program PMI elicits information from a variety of experts on a variety of restaurants, building up different perspectives of a restaurant and stereotypes of experts - to be matched with prospective clients for the restaurant. This is done by finding out not only what motivated the expert's choice, but which of his needs the choice is supposed to meet. The latter obviously determines the former, and it is a matter of working backwards from the information received to the original need to be satisfied, the purpose served by eating out. Though the basic requirement in the domain *is* eating out and the entity needed to meet this requirement is a restaurant, eating out is not necessarily motivated by the need to be fed. The purpose to be served by eating out *could* of course be to be fed, but it could also be to avoid having to cook, to enjoy the setting, to get away from home, to eat a speciality, and so on.

What might happen is that an individual expert, or client, could be at odds, not only with other experts, or fellow clients, but also with himself. For example, a person's judgement on a particular restaurant may change depending on the context in which that restaurant is being discussed. The rationale behind using de Bono's thinking tools for knowledge elicitation is that the system it belongs to should be able to offer more imaginative alternatives to the solution of conflicts than negotiation or compromise. When selecting a restaurant, compromise is usually a disappointment, whereas the alternative could be an adventure.

4.1 Characteristics of Test Domain

The utility of the PMI needs to be tested in a situation especially suited to it. Because the PMI is supposed to counteract reactive and emotional judgements, we have used a domain in which experts are required to express personal opinions rather than textbook knowledge. As the purpose of doing a PMI is not to get the correct information but to extract viewpoints, the domain needs to be one in which there are no canonical criteria for judging something right or wrong, yet one in which the expert has no doubt in the situation. In the restaurant domain, just about everyone has an opinion on at least one restaurant and feels himself expert enough to hold that opinion as any client to a restaurant is of course expert in judging his satisfaction with the restaurant. But what might be good for one expert (a steak eater) might be bad for another (a vegetarian). 'Noisy' is a Minus point only for someone who likes restaurants to be intimate and quiet. The same applies to the clients which an advice giving system would have to satisfy: Every client wants the restaurant to be 'good' - but what constitutes 'good' for one client is quite different from what constitutes 'good' for another.

There is bound to be disagreement between experts or clients, and the exploration of the 'Interesting' direction might help to find a jointly acceptable alternative for a group of disagreeing clients. The idea is not to get them to agree on points previously disagreed, but to find a way out of the deadlock by changing their motivation: instead of going to eat to satisfy the hunger, they might be persuaded to go to a restaurant to look at its decor, to enjoy the music, or to observe the weird clientele. This basically means that the clients are able to see the occasion of eating out in a different light.

4.2 Elicitation Method

Care has to be taken that knowledge elicitation does not become an exercise in classification or judgement for the expert. At the same time, it is obviously desirable that the information elicited covers as many aspects of the domain as possible. To present the expert with a questionnaire containing three columns - Plus, Minus and Interesting - forces him to concentrate on all three directions at once, which is not in the spirit of PMI.

As a pilot study for the project, two questionnaires were circulated to a test group. Both asked for information on two restaurants most of the subjects had been to. The first contained only the three columns in which to list Plus, Minus and Interesting points, together with a like / dislike box for each restaurant. The second had a list of numbered aspects pertaining to restaurants and eaters attached to it, with the intention that this would be used to number the points in the P, M and I columns *after* filling them in. We found that on the second questionnaire, people simply went down the list of aspects, writing their opinion next to the aspect, and then transferring it to either the P, M or I column. This is counteractive to the exercise of focussed exploration.

Clearly, listing all the aspects that ought to be covered on the questionnaire does, on the one hand, ascertain that no aspect gets overlooked for consideration. On the other hand, attention gets focussed on each aspect in turn, requiring a judgement, rather than an exploration. This defeats that aim of observing which aspects present themselves when focussing on one particular direction - P, M or I - in turn.

There is a trade off between closed questions and open questions: it has been found that certain aspects of, say, a job are mentioned 13 per cent less often in the open questions than with the closed questions, in which that aspect was one of the answer choices. Items that are self evident are more often forgotten in open questions (Molenaar, 1982). Closed questions, however, go against the spirit of the PMI.

Consequently, passive knowledge elicitation methods are less well suited to the use of the PMI. Directed questions (requiring yes/no answers) too are to be avoided as much as possible. For these reasons we rejected the use of questionnaires. In order to explore the use of de Bono's tool, an open, but guided, interview with the expert needs be conducted, hence the development of the PMI program.

4.3 Ontology

The experiment with the questionnaires, and the considerations described in the previous section, led us to develop an ontology of the domain (Regoczei & Plantinga 1988) which would be accessible to the engineer only. The two main actors in the scenario of eating out are obviously the restaurant and the eater. What relates these two entities is the world they are both in and the food to be eaten. Studying the answers received from the test subjects helped us to arrive at the provisional ontology shown in figure 1.

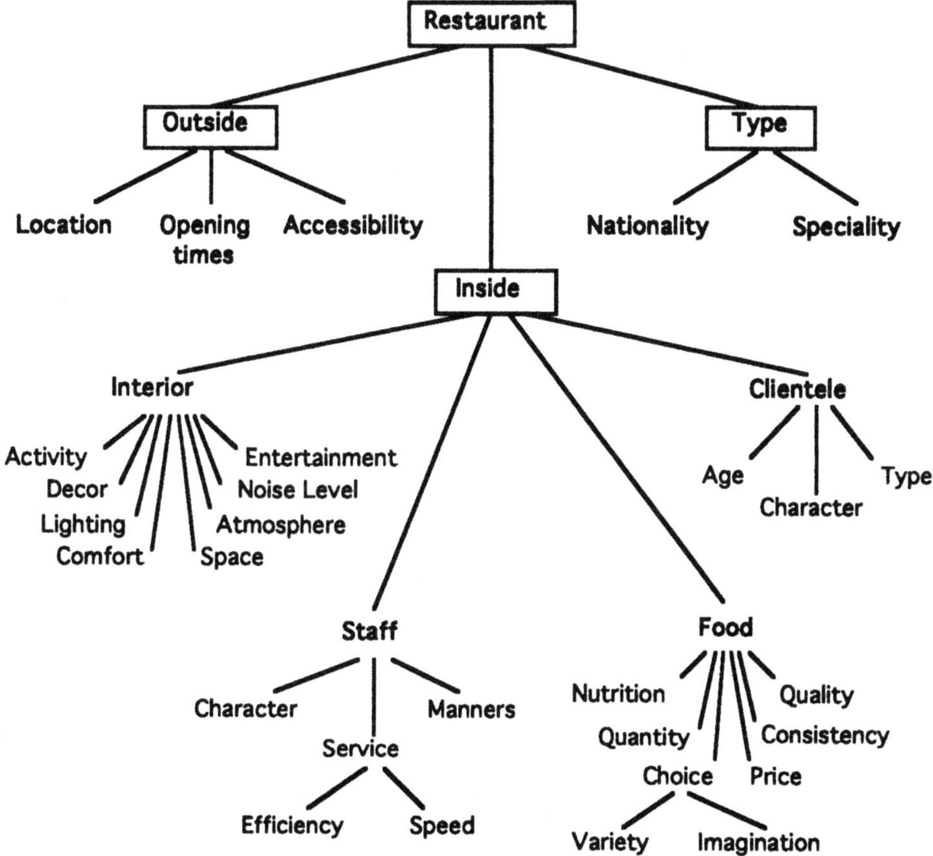

Fig. 1. A possible (hidden) ontology for the restaurant domain

At no time should the knowledge engineer force the expert's answers to fit the ontology. On the contrary, the ontology is flexible and will continue to evolve during the process of doing the PMI. Aspects commented on which are not in the ontology should be added to it. Certain groupings of aspects might have to be changed. Originally, the ontology included the aspect 'Menu'. After use of PMI with a number of experts, this was changed to 'Choice' and made a dependent of 'Food': people did not refer to the menu of a restaurant, but to the variety of dishes and the interestingness of choice.

The ontology should at most be used to provide consistency in the naming of aspects. When an expert refers to 'Price' he actually means a feature of the aspect 'Food', as this is what the restaurant sells. Hence 'price' would be entered as 'Food_price'. Again, this is not a matter of course, as the restaurant could be within a club which charges an entrance fee, in which case 'Price' could refer to this fee, or to the food. If it refers to the fee, then a new aspect 'Entrance_price' would have to be added to the ontology.

The ontology exists only on paper so far. It could be implemented as a look-up table, or as a hypertext. For the restaurant domain, the engineer can just about cope with it being on paper. In a domain with a large number of aspects to be discussed and where relationships between entities are more intricate, implementation would be a must. The structure would have to be flexible and updatable.

5 Implementation

The PMI knowledge elicitation tool consists of two modules, the first to gather the information, the second to analyse it. The first module can be said to be a prototype elicitation tool, the second module is still in its very early stages. The advantage of the use of PMI the thinking tool can be seen in the organisation of the elicited knowledge in the first module.

5.1 Module I - Elicitation

Doing the PMI. The data is collected via a straightforward interview between the knowledge engineer and the expert, with the engineer recording responses by interacting with the program, so that the expert is not distracted. The engineer explains the use of the PMI briefly to the expert, and - as far as is possible - unobtrusively monitors the amount of time spent on each of P, M and I. He should give the expert roughly the same amount of time for each of the three, even if the expert thinks he has no more comments to make.

At the start of the interview, the name of both the expert and the restaurant are recorded. The data collected will consist of lists of Plus, Minus and Interesting points. The expert is then asked whether he liked the restaurant or not. We could not avoid asking this yes/no question, as the answer to it will affect the way the information gathered will be used in the later analysis. However, it was important that the question should be asked as late as possible during the interview so as not to distract from the PMI.

In seeking alternatives to a closed question of liking or disliking a restaurant, we considered the possibility of asking whether the expert would *object* to eating in the restaurant under discussion, as this might disguise the like/dislike question. It turned out that the two questions elicit different answers: an expert might dislike a restaurant but not object to eating there. Although this fact could have been exploited in the analysis, for the purpose of this project we just used the like/dislike question. In fact, the pervasiveness of this question establishes the need for the PMI: as de Bono points out, the PMI is most useful when a person is in no doubt about something.

Building the Entities. The elicited knowledge sheds light both on the restaurant and on the expert or 'eater'. The information gathered in the PMI constitutes the eater's opinion on a restaurant (see figure 2). This is then used to characterise both the eater and the restaurant. Eventually, we want a fine-grained description of the restaurant which takes into account both people who like it and who dislike it. We also want a fine-grained description of a stereotypical eater who likes the restaurant, and a stereotypical eater who dislikes it. Stereotypes could of course be built up according to different criteria; for instance the stereotype "Student eater", or the stereotype "Businessman eater". Both the

Eater stereotypes and the Restaurant entities are made up of more than one person's information.

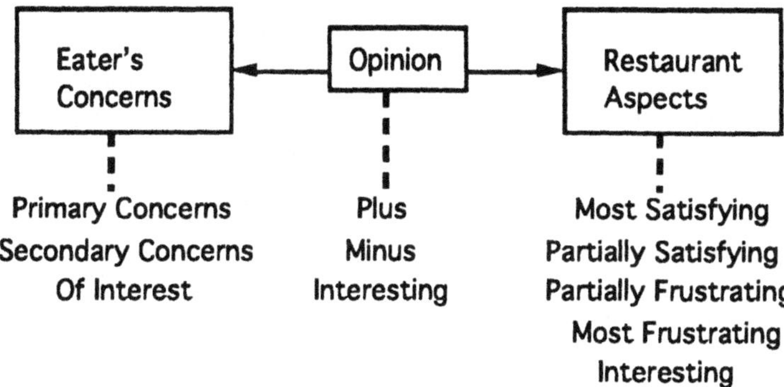

Fig. 2. The PMI gathers information about an eater's opinion on a restaurant, which is then used to build eater stereotypes and restaurant descriptions.

Figure 3 shows the headings used for the eater stereotypes (Expert) and for the restaurant descriptions (Restaurant). Plus, Minus and Interesting are the lists of aspects (represented in the ontology), with the values the expert attaches to them. The three categories that make up the eater's concerns are lists of aspects without corresponding values, as they abstract away from the particular restaurant. The categories provide information about which of the eater's concerns are more likely to influence a decision about whether a restaurant is liked or disliked. The categories of the restaurant description are made up of aspects and the values attached to them, and provide information about which how different aspects affected eater's opinions of the restaurant.

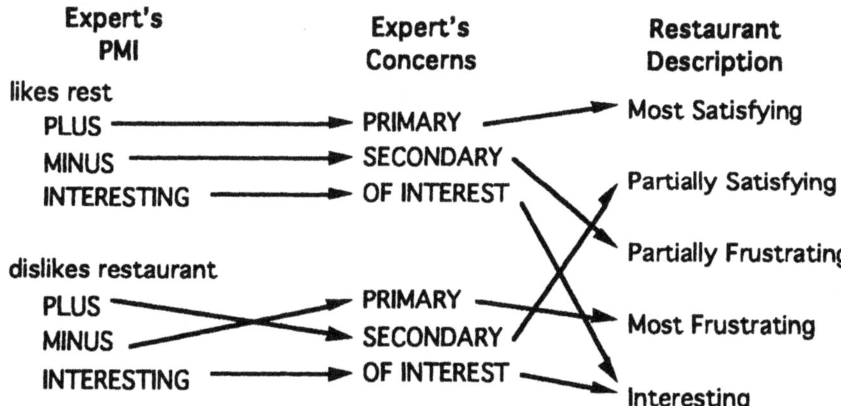

Fig. 3. Relationships between the P, M and I, and the Eater's concerns and the restaurant description.

The headings specify the relationship between expert and restaurant, but they might equally generalise as the relationship between restaurant and client. In generating these headings, we have made some assumptions about the expert's responses. In particular, we assume that there is a causal relationship between the plus and minus points elicited and whether the expert likes or dislikes the restaurant. For example, plus points for a restaurant that is liked overall are likely to be of greater importance to the expert than the minus points for that restaurant, while the reverse applies to minus points.

The following will clarify the considerations that led us to this choice of headings:

Expert

Primary Concerns are those points which need to be to the expert's satisfaction for him to like the restaurant. We assume that the plus points for a liked restaurant and the minus point for a disliked restaurant are significant enough to affect the expert's choice: they are primary concerns.

Secondary Concerns means the expert is not too bothered with these, whether they are to his general satisfaction or not. He will either like this restaurant, even if he is not satisfied by these points, or he will refuse to go to the restaurant, even if these points are to his satisfaction.

Of Interest are those points the expert finds interesting, whether he likes the restaurant or not.

Restaurant

Most Satisfying needs to be understood thus: If all these points are to the expert's or client's satisfaction, he will be satisfied by the restaurant and will like it. These are the plus points that caused people to like a restaurant.

Partially Satisfying reads: even if all these points are to the expert's or client's satisfaction, he may not be satisfied by this restaurant and may dislike it. While these may affect a person's opinion about a restaurant, they are not decisive enough to guarantee liking a restaurant.

Partially Frustrating reads: Even if all these points are frustrating the expert or client, he will still like the restaurant and be satisfied by it. These are the minus points that were not decisive enough for a person to dislike a restaurant.

Most Frustrating reads: if all these points are considered as minus points by the expert or client, he will find the restaurant frustrating and will dislike it. These are the minus points that caused a person to dislike a restaurant.

Amendments Options and General Concerns. PMI provides the expert with two amendment options: the Restaurant entity is built up after the first stage of the amendments option, the Expert entity gets built up after the second stage of the amendments option.

First Stage: Points can be added or deleted under any of the three P, M or I headings. Points can be moved from one heading to another. The wording used for listing the points can be altered. After each alteration, the new arrangement of the information is displayed.

The decision to give the expert this chance at all was considered carefully. One the one hand, this gives an expert who is not used to being interviewed the chance to avoid omitting the obvious. On the other hand, it could turn the whole of the PMI into what it tries not to be. Hence the expert should not be encouraged to add many aspects, nor should he be encouraged to re-classify them. The option to make changes should mainly be used to rectify mistakes the expert was aware of making during the PMI.

Up to this stage, the relationship between the entries under the 'Expert' headings and the entries under the 'Restaurant' headings correspond to the one described in Figure 3.

Second Stage: Any alterations made in this stage will change the entries for the expert's concerns, but NOT the entries under the 'Restaurant' headings. The reason for this way of doing things is that eventually we want to build up a stereotype of a *person* liking or disliking a restaurant, not a stereotype of a *relationship* between that person and the restaurant. Although the concerns have been extracted from the expert's discussion of the restaurant, they now no longer relate to that particular restaurant, but to eating out in restaurants generally.

The expert is given the chance to state what he is most concerned with when going to eat out. He is presented his primary concerns and his secondary concerns in relation to the restaurant discussed, and asked for changes to be made. The wording of the questions had to be carefully thought out and tested with several interview subjects in order to make them not too direct, yet to get a clear answer.

When an expert likes a restaurant, we know that he is obviously not too bothered by the Minus points he lists for it. But this does not mean that he is *generally* not bothered about these points. He may be bothered about them in principle but willing to ignore them in relation to a specific restaurant. We want to know which aspects might nevertheless be crucial for him generally. In other words, he is allowed to be human, which is to be inconsistent and ambiguous.

Similarly, if an expert dislikes a restaurant, we can be sure that he is not too bothered about the Plus points listed in relation to that restaurant. But we cannot know whether he is *generally* not bothered by these concerns. Some of them might be crucial for him in principle. We want to know which ones.

On the other hand, we know that all Plus points listed are to the satisfaction of the expert who likes the restaurant. But we cannot be sure that all of these points are equally important for the expert generally. Some of them might not need to be to his satisfaction for him to like the restaurant. We want to know which ones.

Similarly, if an expert dislikes a restaurant, we can be sure that in relation to that restaurant, he would be most concerned about the Minus points listed. (After all, he has rejected the restaurant despite its Plus points). But again, this does not mean that he is necessarily bothered about them *in principle*. Some of them might not generally bother him: we want to find out which ones.

This approach offers a useful compromise between open questions and closed questions: the expert could not possibly be presented with an selection menu of all the points he might be concerned with when eating out. At the same time, we don't want the expert to have to think of points he might be concerned with *generally* in the middle of an interview about a *specific* restaurant. Thus *some* general concerns are extracted from the concerns emerging during the discussion of points relating to a specific restaurant.

Additional Information and Storage. The last section of Module I extracts some additional information about the expert such as age, gender, occupation, and the occasion of eating in the restaurant under discussion. This information may be used later in the analysis model for clarifying the stereotypes. For example, commonalities in the experts that contribute to a particular stereotype might be used to give a meaningful label to that stereotype. The tool then gives the engineer a chance to store the information extracted in the current interview cycle. The storing facility provides for data to be retrieved for use in a later interview session, and enables the engineer to gather and store a mass of information before analysing it in a separate session.

5.2 Module II - Analysis of Information

This module is under development. It is to provide retrieval facilities and information about data stored. It is also to prepare data for analysis and conflict resolution. Only some rudimentary facilities have so far been implemented, such as options to count and display items referred to several times, be they aspects of a restaurant, concerns of an expert, or values attached to aspects and concerns.

The main feature of this phase of the analysis is the combination of several entities into one. This is a must, as the analysis will be concerned with *stereotypes* of experts and *collective descriptions* of restaurants.

Stereotypes of experts. These are built up from many experts according to varying criteria: the stereotype liking or disliking a restaurant, the stereotype of a student, the stereotype of a twenty year old eating out, the stereotype female liking a particular restaurant, and so on. Many attributes of the eaters might be taken into account here: one might want the collective description of a restaurant given by all males between twenty and thirty, by all single people, by all couples with children. The choices will clearly depend on which characteristics were recorded for the experts in the interview: for the present study we selected a few of the more obvious ones. This provision is especially important in domains where there are reasons to believe that significant differences in description should emerge between groupings of experts according to different criteria.

Figure 4 shows an example of an stereotype eater from the restaurant domain. This stereotype is based on the criterion of liking a particular restaurant, and was built from five different experts' knowledge. The experts used for this example were all students, of roughly similar age. It is interesting to note that other commonalities occur across these experts, for instance, that in all cases the occasion was an evening meal. This tells us something about the relationship between this stereotype and the restaurant, ie. this particular restaurant is not frequented by this stereotype for lunch or tea.

General Information	
restaurant:	bystander
restaurant_type:	vegetarian (4); caribbean (1);
experts:	5
likes:	bystander (5);
gender:	female (4); male (1);
age:	25 (1); 23 (1); 27 (1); 28 (1); 26 (1);
occupation:	student (5);
occasion:	evening_meal (5);
Concerns of the Stereotype	
primary_concerns:	staff_manners (1); location (1); setting (1); lighting (1); atmosphere (3); food_choice (2); food_quality (4); food_price (5); service (2); food_choice_diet (1);
secondary_concerns:	space (2); accessibility (2); lighting (1); privacy (1); service_speed (4); food_choice_diet (1); windows (1);
of_interest:	music (3); flavouring (1); food_variety (2); food_choice (1);

Fig. 4. Stereotype of an Eater liking a particular Restaurant. The figures in brackets indicate how many experts have referred to a particular aspect.

Restaurant Descriptions. The collective restaurant descriptions are built up from the PMI points of many experts liking *and* disliking a restaurant (see figure 5). Storing expert and restaurant entities individually facilitates combination of entities in many different ways for many different purposes.

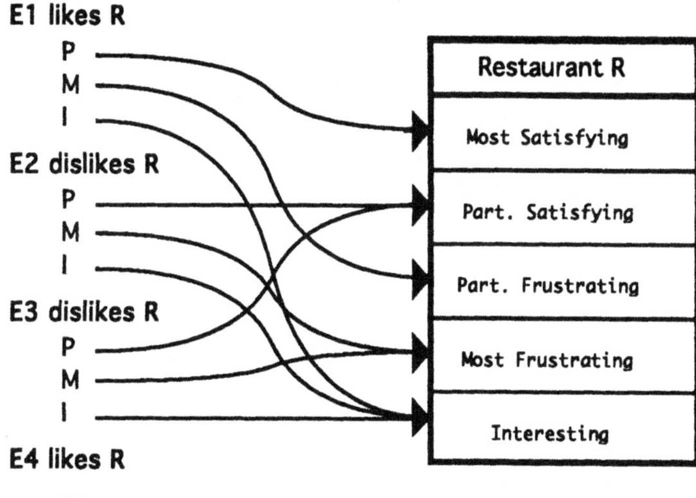

Fig. 5. A collective Description of a restaurant is build up from experts both liking and disliking the restaurant

Figures 6 gives an example of a restaurant description using the knowledge of ten experts. The aspects (in capitals) in this example will be part of the ontology, as described in section 4.3. The values attached to these aspects are not part of the ontology, and it can be seen from the example that different experts might use different terms for roughly the same value. The assumption that these various terms might refer to the same value cannot be made before close scrutiny of the terms and their meaning. Hence, the terms have not forced to conform to a common vocabulary.

6 Conclusions

We have described a tool for elicitation of knowledge suitable for an advice giving system. The tool is based on de Bono's thinking tool PMI, and serves to elicit finer grain detail about an expert's opinion, especially where an expert would not normally have cause to question that opinion. The tool also provides a way of gathering information about the expert, so that generalisations about the experts can be used when applying their knowledge, for example, by comparing the experts' concerns with a client's. The elicitation tool has been used on a sample domain, that of choosing a restaurant, and we have shown how the tool can be used to analyse the domain, building up descriptions of both the experts and the restaurants they are discussing.

Simplicity of conception has been achieved: basically, the interview cycle is simply *one* expert giving information about *one* restaurant, whether or not that expert has been interviewed before, and whether or not that restaurant has been discussed by someone else before.

The tool has not been tested extensively yet, but from our initial observations with one study group, we have been able to deduce some characteristics of the expert from the information he has given. The information received has been found to be more balanced than it would have been with more directed questioning methods. Of course, for a realistic

Information relating to the Experts

name	- bystander
type	- vegetarian (8); caribbean (1); mexican (1);
interviewees	- 10
gender	- female (6); male (4);
age	- 28 (2); 25 (2); 27 (1); 26 (3); 23 (1); 22 (1);
occupation	- student (10);
bias	- likes (5); dislikes (5);
occasion	- evening_meal (10);

Categories of Satisfaction/Frustration

most_satisfying
PRIVACY has (1);
ATMOSPHERE relaxed (1); friendly (1); informal (1);
FOOD_CHOICE good (1); varied (1);
LIGHTING nice (1);
SERVICE friendly (2);
FOOD_CHOICE_DIET serve_vegan (1); vegetarian (1);
SETTING small (1);
FOOD_QUALITY good (3);
FOOD_PRICE good (1); reasonable (2); cheap (2);
STAFF_MANNERS friendly (1);
LOCATION easy_to_get_to (1);

partially_satisfying
FOOD_PRICE cheap (2); reasonable (1);
ATMOSPHERE good (1); friendly (1); cosy (1);
MUSIC play_your_own (1);
SETTING good_for_party (1);
STAFF_MANNERS friendly (3);
ATTITUDE tolerant (1); congenial (1);
LOCATION near_station (1); easy_to_reach (1);
WINE reasonable (1);

most_frustrating
FOOD_QUALITY bad (1); poor (1);
FOOD_CHOICE small (1); unimaginative (1);
LOCATION unpleasant (1);
SPACE cramped (3);
FOOD_QUANTITY small (1);
WINE expensive (1);
SERVICE_QUALITY abysmal (1);
SERVICE disorganised (1);
SERVICE_SPEED bad (1); slow (2);

partially_frustrating
ACCESSIBILITY no_disabled (2);
LIGHTING dark (1);
WINDOWS absent (1);
SERVICE_SPEED slow (4);
FOOD_QUALITY average (1);
SPACE cramped (2);

interesting
FOOD_TYPE interesting (1);
ATTITUDE casual (1);
FLAVOURING coconut (1);
FOOD_CHOICE interesting (1);
FOOD_VARIETY unusual (1); west_indian (1); interesting (1);
MUSIC play_your_own (3); varied (1);
DECOR unusual (1);
INTERIOR curious (1);

Fig. 6. Example of the contents of a restaurant description. The figures in brackets indicate how many experts have referred to a particular aspect.

advice giving system, larger study groups, and many grouping criteria, would have to be used. This would require more time, and it is not clear whether the use of the PMI would, in the long run, save time and/or money.

Getting the experts to do the PMI was fairly easy and proved to be a relaxed way of getting the experts to talk. Once the subjects had understood the difference between "finding points through looking in the direction of Plus, Minus and Interesting" and "listing positive, negative and interesting points", and once they were told that what mattered was not the number of points found, but the concentration on *one* direction at a time, they relaxed and seemed to enjoy the session.

The tool provides a novel approach to Knowledge Acquisition. At the same time as building up information about the domain, we collect information about the expert and the expert's perspective on that domain. The more experts that contribute to the system, the richer a picture we achieve. The success of the system, i. e. the number of clients satisfied, increases proportionally with the number of experts consulted. This contrasts with other expert systems for which the difficulties in integrating knowledge increase if more experts are consulted.

The project stops just when things would start to become interesting: the evaluation and analysis of data collected. Further work is needed to develop the analysis phase, and to apply the knowledge elicited in a real advice-giving system. When we reach that stage, we will be ready to test whether our hypotheses are correct, by observing how the advice giving system performs. In particular, we would need to test whether the analysis we described above provides sufficient detail for advice to be matched to the client's needs, and also whether such a system can successfully deal with conflicts between the needs of a group of clients.

References

Boose, J. H. (1989) A survey of Knowledge Acquisition Techniques and Tools, *Knowledge Acquisition: An International Journal*, Vol 1, No 1, pp3-38.

De Bono, E. (1985) *De Bono's Thinking Course*, London: Ariel Books.

De Bono, E. (1988) *Letters to Thinkers: Further Thoughts on Lateral Thinking*, London: Penguin Books.

Du Boulay, B., and Ross, P. (1991) booknotes for MSc Intelligent Tutoring Systems, School of Cognitive and Computing Sciences, University of Sussex.

Brenner, M. (1982) "Response Effects of 'Role-restricted' Characteristics of the Interviewer", in W. Dijkstra and J. Van der Zouwen, eds., *Response Behaviour in the Survey Interview*, London: Academic Press.

DeLamater, J. (1982) "Response-effects of Question Content", in W. Dijkstra and J. van der Zouwen, eds., *Response Behaviour in the Survey Interview*, London: Academic Press.

Easterbrook, S. M., (1991) "Handling Conflict Between Domain Descriptions with Computer-Supported Negotiation", *Knowledge Acquisition: An International Journal*, Vol 3, pp 255-289.

Gammack, J. G. & Young, R. M. (1985) "Psychological Techniques for Eliciting Expert Knowledge", in M. A. Bramer, ed., *Research and Development in Expert Systems*, British Computer Society Workshop Series, Cambridge: Cambridge University Press.

Greenwell, M. (1990) "Knowledge Elicitation: principles and practice" in M. F. McTear and T. J. Anderson, eds., *Understanding Knowledge Engineering*, Chichester: Ellis Horwood.

Kelly, G.A. (1955) *The Psychology of Personal Constructs*, New York: Norton.

LaFrance, M. (1988) "The Knowledge Acquisition Grid: a method for training knowledge engineers", in B. Gaines and J. Boose, eds, *Knowledge Acquisition for Knowledge Based Systems, Vol. 1*, London: Academic Press.

Molenaar, N. J., (1982) "Response-effects of 'Formal' Characteristics of Questions", in W. Dijkstra and J. Van der Zouwen, *Response Behaviour in the Survey Interview*, London: Academic Press.

Regoczei, S. and Plantinga, E.P.O. (1988) "Ontology and Inventory", in B. Gaines and J. Boose, eds, *Knowledge Acquisition for Knowledge Based Systems, Vol. 2*, London: Academic Press.

Shaw, M. L. G. (1980) *On Becoming A Personal Scientist*, London: Academic Press.

Shaw, M. L. G. (1981) "Conversational Heuristics for Eliciting Shared Understanding", in M. L. G. Shaw, ed., *Recent Advances in Personal Construct Technology*, London: Academic Press.

Shaw, M. L. G., and Gaines, B. R. (1988) "A Methodology for Recognising Consensus, Correspondence, Conflict and Contrast in a Knowledge Acquisition System", Proceedings of the Workshop on Knowledge Acquisition for Knowledge-Based Systems, Banff, Nov. 7-11.

Wittgenstein, L., (1984) Ueber Gewissheit, Eds. G.E.M. Anscombe & G.H. von Wright, Suhrkamp Verlag.

Winograd, T., and Flores, F., (1986) *Understanding Computers and Cognition*, Reading MA: Addison Wesley.

A New Approach to the Solution of Expert Classification Problems

Oleg I. Larichev

25 Tchaikovsky str.
bl.10 fl.46
123242 Moscow, Russia

Criteria for knowledge base construction

Knowledge base (KB) is a principal component of expert systems and many decision support systems. For these systems to be at a high level of sophistication, KB must meet the following set of requirements:

1. KB must be valid: it should be built on the basis of knowledge of a highly skilled expert;
2. KB must be full: it must contain answers to all possible questions within a preliminary outlined and structured problem area;
3. KB must be consistent: it must contain consistent answers to any questions put to it;
4. KB must be reliable. First, in the course of its construction, use is made of only those questions to the expert which are permissible from the standpoint of human information processing system. Second, any expert responses should be tested for consistency. Third, the answers to the experts should imitate a routine activity performed by experts within the frameworks of their professional activities.

Expert classification problem

Diagnostic problems constitute a sizable share of problems the expert systems are designed for. Thus, for example, in medicine it is necessary to diagnose on the basis of examination results, i.e. identify a concrete type of disease (Shortliffe et al., 1979), in chemistry the data on chemical compound structures lead to a conclusion on certain properties (Rosenblitt & Holender, 1983), in technical diagnostics a number of indirect characteristics make it possible to determine the cause of system breakdown or failure, or to conclude on the correspondence of the article to certain requirements, socio-economic studies aim at identifying homogeneous groups of population, economic regions etc.

The diagnostic expert systems are in effect intended for solution of classification problems: they put each object (situation) out of some problem area in correspondence with its diagnosis (property, course of actions).

Classification problems were traditionally considered within the pattern recognition theory. Characteristic of the models employed is a common approach to classification problems. It assumes a preliminary structuring of the problem by way of assigning a variety of potential membership classes of objects under study, a set of attributes describing these objects, and their scales. In some classification problems recognition is exercised automatically. In others, membership classes for a number of objects are assigned (learning sample) and used as a foundation for the recognition algorithm, capable of identifying the membership class of an arbitrary object on the basis of its description.

The pattern recognition approach proved rather productive. The development of algebraic approach (Juravlev, 1978) and of structural minimization method (Vapnik, 1979) permitted construction of efficient classification algorithms for a wide range of problems. At the same time, the experience gained in application of the pattern recognition techniques exposed some of their weaknesses.

This is primarily the case when the available empirical material (learning sample) is clearly insufficient for the construction of reliable classification algorithms. As applied to many problems, the generation of large homogeneous samples runs into considerable difficulties.

On the other hand in many areas dealing with classification problems, there are highly skilled specialists successfully performing their professional duties. A more efficient utilization of their knowledge could considerably improve solution of diagnostic problems. It is not always possible to use effectively the pattern recognition methods in the computational classification algorithms.

Finally, note a rather significant psychological constraint. The use of mathematical methods in applied research indicates that the rate of application of the decision methods and procedures largely depends on their clarity and explicability (Larichev, 1979). To be confident in the produced results, the user ought to understand the procedure of their generation and be able to verify them.

As is known, pattern recognition models are not, ordinarily, used by professionals in solving classification problems: the expert judgements in analyzing complex, ill-structured situations mostly result from logical reasoning rather than numerical procedures (Hayes-Rott, Waterman and Lenat, 1983). Therefore, the complex numerical methods of information processing related with pattern recognition models do not represent the real inferences of the experts, hence the logics of results derived by these methods sometimes engender their distrust and find no adequate application.

The recent development of interactive systems based on expert knowledge gave rise to a quite different approach to solution of classification problems (Alty & Coombs, 1981; Feigenbaum & McCorduck, 1983). This approach assumes the availability of skilled professionals in each problem area whose knowledge and experience are helpful for the less skilled specialists in solving similar problems.

The knowledge-based systems (KBS) apply their heuristic rules and simulate the substantive process of problem solution by experts. Thus, in contrast to formal algorithm approach based on quantitative information processing, the problem is solved directly by descriptive methods: it is assumed herewith that this would improve the quality and validity of the respective problem solution.

In spite of the before mentioned KBS advantages underlying their wide-ranging popularity and intensive development, a significant shortcoming of such systems is that the existing methods of their construction do not guarantee classification of each object studied by the system. The KBS are usually not designed to deal with the problem of full classification of the object under study. As was mentioned earlier, the major purpose thereof is to fix the expert knowledge in some subject area. The knowledge makes it possible to classify some object states leaving all other potential states beyond the developed system. Obviously,the very formulation of complete classification problem is feasible only when the subject area was structured in advance (definition of a set of attributes of their values) as is done, for example, in pattern recognition.

Thus, the strong point of pattern recognition approach is an explicit structuring of classification problem permitting full classification, whereas the major weakness is the construction of classification rules based on formal models. In recent years this shortcoming has been increasingly recognized by the pattern recognition specialists themselves. This is manifested in the fact that the methods oriented at expert information, logical decision rules are gaining an ever wider acceptance.

On the other hand, the principal advantage of KBS is an opportunity for a flexible and convenient presentation of expert information, utilization of logical inference rules permitting descriptive explanations of the decisions made. At the same time, the fragmentary nature of expert knowledge elicitation is a KBS shortcoming practically ruling out construction of full KB. In this connection, the KBS studies generated approaches where the process of knowledge elicitation from the expert is organized in a structured form, i.e. concrete answers to clear questions.

Thus, the considered statements of classification problem tend to draw nearer. We believe that the problem statement representing the basic requirements of the both approaches should have the following form.

There is a set of attributes describing various states of the object under study. Each attribute is assigned a range of potential values. The Cartesian product of attribute scales determines a combination of potential object's states. It is necessary, on the basis of expert knowledge, to determine the properties of the object in each of its states, and so, classify all states of the object under study.

This statement of the problem will hereafter be referred to as expert classification problem. Note that in (Clancey, 1984) it is suggested a term "heuristic classification". It was shown in (Yagmai & Maxin, 1984) that irrespective of the form of knowledge presentation (frames, networks, products) a KB can be viewed as a totality of states of an object under study classified by the expert. We maintain that the term "expert classification" more intimately corresponds to the specifics oft he considered problem.

The formulated expert classification problem requires definition of various properties of the studied object which is the part of a traditional diagnostic problem. We shall treat it as the key classification problem. Besides, in handling practical problems a necessity may arise to specify the degree of manifestation of the examined properties which can be ordered in a natural manner. Note that the definition of groups of object's states in which the examined property manifests itself to one and the same extent, implies classification of the object states into a set of ordered groups. We shall refer to this expert classification problem as ordinal classification problem.

Approach to problem structure elicitation

The first stage in expert classification task solution is the determination of the problem structure set of diagnostic attributes, analyzed by the expert and describing different object's states.

Usually while constructing the knowledge base for expert systems, this set is defined in an informal way - the knowledge engineer asks the expert to give attributes necessary to take into account in the task of expert classification. It is clear that part of attributes may be omitted, and some auxiliary ones may be included into this set. In the other way of fulfilling this task the expert is asked to give the description of one of the situations to be classified and take attributes from this description. Let us note that usually such description reflects the typical, ordinary cases and, as so, some important attributes may be absent in this description.

The full set of necessary attributes may be formed to our mind as a result of logical combination of process of problem structuring with the routine for the expert diagnostic task. In accordance with such approach is the idea of diagnostic games, described above (see Gelfand, Rosenfeldt and Shifrin, 1985).

The main peculiarity of the diagnostic games is the simulation of a dialogue (in a distance) of an experienced expert with unexperienced specialist, who is to examine the object. The solution of a diagnostic task at a distance (upon telephone, radio, etc.) is rather popular, i.e. in medical diagnostics. It is possible to use this idea but for classification of a specially formed sample of such objects, so as to receive the mostly informative data on necessary attributes.

The proposed approach is the following. With the help of a computer the situation of a "remote consultation" is simulated. The computer informs about the probable class of decision and asks the expert to put necessary questions (parameters). After receiving the current parameter, the computer displays the question about its possible values (estimates), especially characteristic of the class under consideration. The sequential combination of characteristic parameters' values forms an image of the object under study from the analyzed class. After the set of attribute is full enough to make the decision (to put the diagnosis), the experts informs the system. Then the computer selects less characteristic values for parameters and the expert is able to add new attributes, necessary to make the decision in such, more complicated situation. The process is over when the expert does not add new attributes, but simply identifies another class for some untypical (for the class under consideration) situation.

Approach to expert knowledge elicitation

Two principal actors take part in knowledge base construction. These are, first, an expert or a group of experts whose knowledge is used in designing KBS and, second, a system designer or knowledge engineer determining the method of knowledge representation, system structure, requirements to the contents and format of expert information. The KBS development requires a large volume of expert information, therefore the organization and execution of expert interviews require considerable efforts on the part of both designers and experts.

Only a structured procedure of the expert's polling can provide a basis for a full and consistent diagnostic system KB, for it allows elicitation of all necessary information from the expert to fill in the KB. Naturally, the logics of such procedure must be related to that of KBS organization.

The expert knowledge elicitation system must be capable of analyzing the available information, determining its missing fragments, and enquiring the expert in a form so that the obtained expert information could be used for the construction of a full KB of the system. Thus, in contrast to the first method of knowledge elicitation whose pattern is determined by the expert himself the requirements to the format of expert information must in this case be determined by the interactive knowledge elicitation system which would have allowed systematization of the process of expert information elicitation.

In arranging an interview with the expert a considerable attention should be given to reliability of information elicited from the expert which, as is seen from descriptive research, is largely determined by the methods of its elicitation. As is known, building up of professional experience boils down to mastering skills in solving a certain range of problems. In the process of communication they use concrete forms of questions and messages which are customary in the given professional area. As is indicative by the experience of interaction with experts, the use of traditional methods of information acquisition, they are familiar with, essentially improves its reliability and validity (Larichev, 1979).

In their practical activities, experts dealing with diagnostic problems have to determine classes of diagnosed objects membership on the basis of their description. In medicine, for example, the physician makes a diagnosis only following the patient examination. Hence, classification on the basis of some object description is common practice for experts in solving diagnostic problems. It seems more reasonable, in this connection, to organize the process of expert knowledge elicitation by rating (classifying) the concrete object states, i.e. to obtain information from the expert in the form of a list of membership classes of object states.

Note that in order to ensure the maximum approximation of the problem, suggested to the expert in the process of interview, to the form he (she) is accustomed to, it makes sense to use discrete scales of potential attribute value estimates expressed verbally. For example, in diagnosing heart diseases, the "Localization of pain" sign may have a scale of the following three values: (1) retrosternal pain; (2) heart pain; (3) pain elsewhere in the chest. In cases where there is a continuous scale of attribute values, it can frequently be transformed into discrete, for the expert usually takes account of only definite value gradations on the continuous scale. Thus, for the sign "Patient temperature" the following value scale often suffices: (1) higher temperature (over 37.0), (2) normal temperature, (3) lowered temperature (below 36.0).

Given this statement of the problem, an expert can easily apply his intuition, experience, etc. Note that the physician has to communicate information in a language close to the one he is accustomed to - assume a disease and the degree of the assumption which highly resembles his routine activities. This makes it possible to consider the thus elicited information reliable.

Hence, given the traditional approaches to the construction of a diagnostic system KB, the expert has to solve a problem of his (her) knowledge synthesis, which is rather complex for him (her), while the suggested method corresponds to his routine case studies. Here he (she) unconsciously uses many of his skills and devices which can hardly be explicitly formulated. Therefore, we treat construction of a diagnostic system KB as an expert classification problem to be solved on the basis of a direct expert evaluation of the states of the object under study.

The implementation of the advanced approach to KB construction, however, faces a number of problems. The first one is conditioned by the dimension of the problem solved. The point is that the real expert classification problems are of large size determined by the number of properties, attributes and possible values on their scales. Accordingly, a direct classification of all states of the object is infeasible.

The second problem is associated with possible expert errors made when assessing complex, multiattribute situations. The psychometric experiments conducted thus far produced an extensive material relative to elicitation of reliable information from experts and decision makers. The principal output of the studies was a conclusion on the presence of a series of constraints on human capabilities to process huge volumes of information (Larichev, 1982b).

According to a hypothesis advanced in (Simon, 1981) the constraints are largely conditioned by a limited capacity of short-term memory of people, their inability to handle a huge amount of unstructured information at a time. As experiments indicate, in facing complicated situations people use diverse simplifying heuristic rules aimed either at information aggregation or its sequential consideration (Kahnemann, Slovic & Tversky, 1982). The application of such rules can distort the obtained expert estimates, reduce their accuracy, lead to errors.

Thus, the developed procedures of the expert's polling must, on the one hand, minimize the scope of expert efforts and, on the other, facilitate the analysis of information elicited from the expert with respect to its consistency.

Approach to organization of the expert's polling

In structuring an expert classification problem we use a hypothesis that estimates upon different attributes' scales may be differently inherent in one and the same property (or, which is the same, class) (Larichev et al. 1987). The expert is assumed to be able to order estimates upon each attribute scale with respect to their inherence for the corresponding class, and this ordering is independent of the estimates upon other attributes.

Let us explain the suggested approach for medical diagnostics as an example. As may be seen from Table 1, the estimates upon attribute "Pain localization" are differently inherent to the three different diseases: "myocardial infarction, stenocardia, and cardialgia.

Most inherent to myocardial infarction is, according to the expert judgement, retrosternal pain (1). Less inherent is pain to the left of sternum (2), and much less - pain elsewhere in the chest (3). As for stenocardia and cardialgia, various localizations of pain manifest themselves in a somewhat different manner (see Table 1). Similar information about various attribute estimates for different diseases can be obtained for all other attributes.

	Retrosternal Pain	**Pain to the left of sternum**	**Pain elsewhere in the chest**
Myocardial infarction	*1*	*2*	*3*
Stenocardia	*2*	*1*	*3*
Cardialgia	*3*	*2*	*1*

Table 1: Different inherence of estimates in different diseases

The experience gained in solving expert classification problems (classification of R&D projects (Larichev, 1982a), architectural designs (Larichev, Naginskaya and Mechitov, 1987), scientific publications (Larichev, Grechko and Furems, 1981) expert classification in medical diagnostic problems (Kim et al., 1987), etc.) indicates that the assumption about ordering of estimates upon attribute scales for different properties holds for many practical problems and, naturally, the considered statement encompasses a wide range of expert classification problems.

Such information may be used for an indirect classification of a number of objects without presenting them to the expert. Let the expert, following examination of a patient condition (an earlier presented example) arrive at a conclusion that this condition is indicative of myocardial infarction. Then all conditions with more inherent in infarct estimates indicate this disease. Should the expert conclude that the presented condition is not characteristic of cardialgia, then all conditions with less inherent to cardialgia estimates than the present one, do not relate to cardialgia either.

The possibility of obtaining indirect information about the classes of objects membership makes it possible to design a rational procedure of expert interview with a view to minimizing the number of questions to him (her). Besides, as will be seen further, this information is also conducive to identification of potential errors in expert responses.

Informativeness of expert responses

The problem of choice of the object to be presented to the expert is analogous to the problems of search for the most informative points traditionally handled by the information theory for the purpose of code construction (Yaglom & Yaglom, 1973), problems of decoding monotonic functions of the algebra of logic (Sokolov, 1980), problems of questionnaire compilation (Parhomenko, 1970), etc.

The general concept of the problem solution implies identification of information obtained from the test in some point (i.e. putting the given question, computation of function in the given point, etc.) and choice of the search principle for the most informative point. As a matter of fact, the obtained information is dependent not only on the point chosen for the test, but also on the outcome of the test (i.e. what answer will be given to the question, or the obtained function value, etc.). Thus, each test is associated with a kind of uncertainty leading to the necessity of estimating the information obtained under each potential outcome of the test.

There are quite various approaches to determining the general informativeness of the conducted tests. The choice of the most informative point often employs the maximum principle implying the following. Each point is assigned a guaranteed minimum of the obtained information in conformity with potential outcomes of the test. At each step a point with a maximum estimates is chosen. Thereby, the maximum criterion secures elicitation of a guaranteed minimum of information.

Yet another widespread approach is maximization of the expected amount of information generated by an individual test. Herewith use is made of the probability estimates of occurrence of each outcome. The sum total of products of probability estimates of each outcome by the amount of information generated from it serves as a measure of test informativeness.

As was noted above, information elicited from the expert in classifying one object's state may be extended to other states. The expert classifies these states in an indirect manner. The number thereof is dependent on the state presented to the expert and the answer of the latter, i.e. to what class and with what degree of confidence he (she) placed the analyzed state.

Thus, in the considered problem the test is presentation to the expert of an individual state of the object, the test outcome consists in the state classification, and the potential measure of the test informativeness is the number of indirectly classified states on the basis of inherence relation. It is possible to find this number for each state given any potential answer of the expert, and calculate the mean or minimal value. By making use of these variables, one may compare all unknown states of the object with respect to their informativeness and select the most informative state. The presentation of the most informative states to the expert produces on the average the maximum amount of information given any answers of the expert.

Search for and elimination of errors in expert answers

Any procedure of expert questioning should account for possible errors in his answers. The errors arise due to his (her) carelessness, fatigue, as well as complexity of the handled problem (see below). Since the KB must be consistent, there is a need for the analysis of information elicited from the expert, identification of inconsistencies. The possibility of a direct determination of classes of state membership makes it possible to verify the consistency of expert estimates. Should there be discrepancies between indirect and direct state estimates, this is indicative of an error (errors) in his answers.

The conflicting answers should be presented to the expert with a view to understanding and finding a correct means for the assessment of a series of states. Here we proceed from the fact that though experts use different decision rules, they do their best to make them consistent and logical.

There are two strategies for eliminating inconsistencies in KB. One assumes a continuous comparison of information elicited from the expert with that obtained earlier, and checking for consistency. Should there be an inconsistency between the last answer of the expert and the preceding information, this inconsistency is presented to the expert for analysis and selection of a consistent policy. Another strategy envisages elicitation of either a portion or all necessary information from the expert followed by the location of inconsistencies in it and a stepwise elimination thereof. The first strategy is good in that in the course of the interview the expert as if learns, he is assisted in elaboration of a consistent policy. In some cases, however, the second strategy is more suitable (see chapters that follow).

Note that the problem of search for and elimination of inconsistencies in identifying decision rules was first stated in (Larichev et al., 1978; see also Larichev,

1982b). As applied to classification problem, these concepts were further developed in (Larichev & Moshkovich, 1986).

Specifics of human behaviour in solving classification problems

Though there is a voluminous literature on human behavior in solving multiattribute, multidimensional problems (see review Larichev, 1982b) only a few dealt with problems of expert classification of multidimensional objects. Note that a systematic study into human behaviour in solving multidimensional classification problems was first undertaken in (Larichev et al., 1980, Larichev, 1982b).

In (Hoffman et al., 1968) it was showed that people fail to cope with classification problem given more than 5 criteria and 7 decision classes. As is seen from (Larichev et al., 1980) however, given 7 criteria and 2 decision classes the subjects succeed in solving classification problems.

One of the purposes of the present research effort was to study human behaviour in handling ordinal expert classification problems. A hypothesis was advanced that there is a certain limit to human information processing capacities in these problems, and that this limit is a function of problem size. With a view to verifying this hypothesis we conducted a large number of experiments (see below). The procedure of the latter was as follows. A complete set of potential states was generated for various problems differing in the number of attributes, number of estimates on the attribute scales, and the number of classes. The topic of experiments was chosen so that the estimated object was quite familiar to the subjects. Special measures were taken to motivate subjects for a successful solution of the problem: the problems constituted a part of instruction assignments to students or pupils, or were secretly introduced in the real-life problems handled by decision makers.

The results of experiments really showed that depending on the size of problem the subjects' behaviour changes sharply, though differently for ordinary people and experienced decision makers. Should a certain dimension be exceeded, the problem came to be too complex for the subjects. The students and pupils experienced a sharp increase in the number of inconsistencies such that the conflicting estimates simply did not allow to discern a line between the classes. The experienced managers generally retained the policy consistency but it became primitive attributes were substituted by one estimate on the scales. The experiments made it possible to define variable limits to human capabilities in ordinal classification problems.

Approach to construction of explanation system

The new opportunities provided by expert systems consist in explanation of the system operations. The system must not simply answer the user question but render this answer understandable for him (her). Two goals are pursued herewith:

- to win the user confidence, explain the rationality of the system operation to him;
- to train the user, i.e. help him get an insight into the expert logics built in the system.

Let us focus on the approach to explanations typical for the majority of existing expert systems. Explanation in these systems is generally defined as demonstration of the system behavior logic to the user. And since the system has a collection of rules, the user is given information on the rule that was behind the concrete answer to the user question. This rule is presented as the system "track of actions" ((Hayes-Rott, Waterman and Lenat, 1983), i.e. a totality of states (usually arranged in an order from the more general to the more particular) that resulted in the outcome. In other words, the user is offered a portion of the relevance tree where in the general goals precede particular ones.

It is precisely this explanation pattern - demonstration of the sequence of system logical steps leading to a conclusion that is considered a characteristic feature of the expert system.

Now consider generation of explanations as a standard problem of human behaviour. Recall the way people usually explain the logics, the causes of their actions. Usually a human being exemplifies solution of an expert classification problem and explains the characteristic attributes behind the object classification. Thus, in teaching medical students an experienced physician suggests a diagnosis and points out to the characteristic signs in the patient's states that led him to that conclusion. He also answers to the question "Why this rather than the other disease?" in the language of attributes.

This approach to explanations has gained wide practical acceptance, therefore it is customary for users of expert system. In comparing this approach and explanations generally employed in expert systems, it can be easily seen that the explanations of expert systems /a fragment of relevant tree) are far from most effective. In response to a question "Why", the expert system presents the entire "track of actions to the user, involving a large amount of general information, without identifying attributes particularly characteristic of the considered situation. Given this method of explanation, an attempt is made to teach the user "to think like machine", i.e. marshal one's knowledge in conformity with the relevance tree. It is clear that this method of knowledge storage is not characteristic of human beings.

The suggested approach to KBS construction, containing a full and consistent expert knowledge base, is also conducive to the most natural approach to explanation generation. At a stage of knowledge elicitation, we constructed a matrix of individual signs typicality with respect to individual diseases. It is precisely this matrix, repeatedly verified in the course of knowledge base construction, that is capable of generating effective explanations to the user. These explanations take form of indications to the most characteristic attributes for the given class of decisions. Thus, for example, for a situation:

- pain localization - not retrosternal and not in the area of heart
- but elsewhere in the chest;
- cause of the pain - pain occurs in the course of palpation;
- pain lasts for over 15 minutes following nitroglycerin treatment;
- normal pressure;
- normal temperature;
- moist skin;
- ECG data - normal,

the knowledge-based system states that there are strong indications to cardialgia, and in response to a question "Why" issues the following answer: "Because the given situation is dominated by a set of attribute values: pain localization - notretrosternal and not in the area of heart but elsewhere in the chest; the cause of pain - pain occurs in the process of palpation; pain duration - more than 15 minutes following nitroglycerin treatment; ECG is normal" which are most characteristic of cardialgia. Such explanation corresponds to a natural situation of teaching a man the decision rules.

Conclusions

Above we stated a set of concepts conducive to:

- formation of the set of diagnostic attributes;
- correct elicitation of information from the expert;
- valid dissipation of this information;
- search for the most informative states to be presented to the expert;
- detection and elimination of errors in the expert's response;
- due regard to capacities of human information processing system.

The above set of concepts provides a real opportunity for designing a man-machine system of KB construction meeting a set of requirements (see details in Larichev et al., 1991).

First, it is necessary to structure the problem, identify a set of attributes and scales, determine decision classes. The attributes and scales of their estimates determine a complete list of potential states of the object under study. In line with the available algorithm, computer assesses the potential informativeness of all feasible states and selects the most informative one. This state is presented to the expert. The latter classifies the presented state. Then the expert's answer is verified for consistency (note that verification may be carried out following a series of answers of the expert). Once the inconsistencies are eliminated, the following informative point is determined, etc. until all states are classified.

Note that the suggested approach makes it possible to rather adequately imitate the activities the expert is accustomed to in solving classification problems. It takes into consideration the specifics of human information processing system. It is helpful in constructing full and consistent knowledge bases.

REFERENCES

Alty J., Coombs M. (1981) *Computing skills and the user interface* London: Academic press.

Clancey W.J. (1984) Classification problem solving. In proceedings of the *National Conference on Artificial Intelligence*, IAAAAI, University of Texas at Austin.

Feigenbaum I.A., McCordack P. (1983) *The 5th generation.* Mass.: Addison Wesley.

Gelfand I.M., Posenfeldt B.I., Shifrin M.A. (1985) Structural organization of data in medical diagnostic and forcasting tasks. In: Gelfand I.M. (ed.) *Questions of cybernetics and medical diagnostic tasks from the point of view of a mathematician.* Moscow: Kibernetika, p.5-64 (in Russian).

Hayes-Roth F., Waterman D.A., Lenat D.B. (1983) *Building expert systems.* Mass: Addison-Wesley.

Hoffman P.J., Slovic P., Rorer L.G. (1968) Analysis -of-variance model for assessment of of conficural cue utilization in clinical judgement. *Psychological Bulletin*, No.69, p.338-349.

Juravlev Yu.I. (1978) About an algebraic approach to tasks of recognition and classification. In: *Problems of cybernatics.* Moscow: Nauka press (in Russian).

Kahneman D., Slovic P., Tversky A. (eds) (1982) *Judgement under uncertainty: heuristics and biases.* Cambridge: Univ. Press.

Kim V.N., Malygin V.P., Larichev O.I. et al., (1987) Implementation of a computarized system in diagnostic of cardial ishemia on the prior to hospital stage. *Naval medical journal*, 1, p.23-26 (in Russian).

Larichev O.I. (1979) *Science and art of decision making.* Moscow: Nauka press (in Russian).

Larichev O.I. (1982a) *A method for evaluating R&D proposals in large research organizations.* Collaborative paper CP-82-75. Laxenburg, Austria: IIASA.

Larichev O.I. (1982b) About the human capacities in multicriteria decision making. In: *Problems and methods of decision making*. Moscow: VNIISI press (in Russian).

Larichev O.I. (1987) *Objective models and subjective decisions*. Moscow: Nauka press (in Russian).

Larichev O.I., Boichenko V.S., Moshkovich H.M., Sheptalova L.P. (1978) *Method of hierarchical schemes in goal programming planning*. Moscow: VNIISI press (in Russian).

Larichev O.I., Boichenko V.S., Moshkovich H.M., Sheptalova L.P. (1980) Modelling multiattribute information processing strategies in binary decision task. *Organizational behavior and Human Performance*, 26.

Larichev O.I., Grechko V.M., Furems E.M. (1981) *Problems of publishing activity planning*. Moscow: VNIISI press (in Russian).

Larichev O.I., Mechitov A.I., Moshkovich H.M., Furems E.M. (1987) Systems of expert knowledge elicitation in classification problems. *Tehknicheskaya kibernetika*, 2, p.44-52 (in Russian).

Larichev O.I., Moshkovich H.M. (1986) Task of direct classification in decision making. *Dokladi Academii nauk SSSR*, 287, No.6, p.567-570 (in Russian).

Larichev O.I., Moshkovich H.M., Furems E.M., Mechitov A.I., Morgoev V.K. (1991) Knowledge aquisition for the construction of full and conradiction free knowledge bases. Groningen (the Netherlands): iecProGamma.

Larichev O.I., Naginskaya V.S., Mechitov A.I. (1987) An interactive procedure for industrial building design choice. *Journal of Applied Systems Analysis*, 14,,p.33-40.

Parhomenko P.P. (1970) Theory of questionnaires: a survey. *Automatika i telemekhanika*, 4, p.140-159 (in Russian).

Rosenblitt A.B., Holender V.E. (1972) *Logico-combinatorial methods in medicines' construction*. Riga: Zinatne press (in Russian).

Simon H.A. (1981) *The sciences of the artificial*. (2nd ed.). London: MIT.

Shortliffe E.H., Buchaman B.G., Feigenbaum E.A. (1979) Knowledge engineering for medical decision making: A review of computer-based clinical decision aids. 67, No.9, p.1207-1223.

Sokolov N.A. (1980) *About the solution of some optimizational tasks.* Moscow: VNIISI press (in Russian).

Vapnik V.N. (1979) *Finding the dependencies upon empirical data.* Moscow: Nauka press (in Russian).

Yaghmai N.S., Maxin J.A. (1984) Expert systems: a tutorial. *Journal of Amer.Soc.Inform.Sci.*, 35, No.5, p.297-305.

Yaglom A.M., Yaglom I.M. (1987) *Probability and information.* Moscow: Nauka press (in Russian).

Zagoruiko N.G. (1972) *Methods of recognition and their implementation.* Moscow: Sovetskoe radio (in Russian).

Knowledge Acquisition for Explainable, Multi-Expert, Knowledge-Based Design Systems

Rose Dieng, Alain Giboin, Paul-André Tourtier, Olivier Corby
SECOIA Project, INRIA - CERMICS
2004 Route des Lucioles, 06561 VALBONNE CEDEX, FRANCE
E-mail: {dieng, giboin, tourtier, corby}@sophia.inria.fr
Fax: (33) 93 65 77 83

Abstract

In order to help the knowledge engineer and the expert during knowledge acquisition phase, the ACACIA Group is working on a knowledge acquisition methodology and tool (*KATEMES*) allowing knowledge acquisition from multiple experts, exploiting the specificities of design problems and preparing the assistance to the end-user and the quality of explanations he will be provided with. This paper describes our research program. After a brief description of our previous knowledge acquisition tool *3DKAT*, we will present the primitives of *KATEMES* and the problems we intend to study and the ideas we intend to deepen about the link between knowledge acquisition and explanations, knowledge acquisition from multiple experts and methodological aspects.

Keywords: knowledge acquisition and explanations, knowledge acquisition from multiple experts, knowledge graphs, cognitive agents, design applications

1 Introduction

During the phase of knowledge acquisition and specification of a multi-expert knowledge-based design system, how to prepare the quality of the final system (concerning as well its reasoning capabilities or the explanations it will be able to generate)? This question guides the research of ACACIA group, research summed up as follows:

> In order to help the knowledge engineer and the expert during knowledge acquisition phase, we are working on a knowledge acquisition methodology and tool (*KATEMES*) allowing knowledge acquisition from multiple experts, exploiting the specificities of design problems and preparing the assistance to the end-user and the quality of explanations he will be provided with.

Some knowledge acquisition tools don't rely on the problem class while other researchers focus on a given problem class by proposing tools dedicated to this problem class: for example, *SALT* [50,51] is aimed at design applications. We will adopt this last approach and try to deepen design applications, for which our team had a number of experiments in the past [59,58,60]. Notice that very few knowledge acquisition tools concern design task, that is considered as very difficult to tackle: *DSPL ACQUIRER* [13], *SALT* [51], *CANARD* [69].

Here are the main questions we will study: 1) How to elicit and model knowledge from several experts? 2) How to take into account the users of the final knowledge-based system (KBS) and, in particular, to prepare the quality of the future explanations in the earlier knowledge acquisition phase? 3) How to validate the acquired knowledge? 4) How to design the final multi-experts system? 5) Can we propose a methodology taking into account explanations and multi-expertise?

KATEMES (Knowledge Acquisition Tool for Explainable, Multi-Expert Systems) will be the result of this research.

This paper will describe our research program. After a brief description of our previous knowledge acquisition tool *3DKAT*, we will present the primitives of *KATEMES* and the problems we intend to study and the ideas we intend to deepen about the link between knowledge acquisition and explanations, knowledge acquisition from multiple experts and methodological aspects. Very-long-term research topics such as validation of the acquired knowledge and design of the final system will also be mentioned in order to give a complete idea of the ACACIA program. At the end of each section, we indicate related work, in order to recapitulate the points for which similar ideas were already evoked by other researchers and to highlight those for which we propose an original approach.

2 From 3DKAT to KATEMES

2.1 3DKAT

In our past work, we developed a knowledge acquisition tool aimed at design applications, *3DKAT* [1] [24,1]. It allows to describe the structure of the designed system and of its components, and to represent explicitly the dynamic model used by the expert during the design process. It relies on the observation that, for a design application, the knowledge engineer seems to reconstruct a model of the system to be designed, using what he understood from the information provided by the expert. *3DKAT* allows the knowledge engineer to make this model explicit and to let the expert validate it.

This model is based on the dependencies among the main parameters occurring during the problem solving and can be represented through a *dependency graph* called PDOG (Parameter Dependency Oriented Graph). A node of the graph corresponds either to an attribute of the object to be designed or to one of its components, or to a parameter issued from the external environment. *3DKAT* proposes a typology of relations possible among the nodes. This hierarchy of links can be extended by application-specific relations. A particular relation, called *topos*, allows to express how a parameter influences another. The influence of a given parameter modification can then be visualized dynamically.

During knowledge acquisition phase, through a PDOG, the knowledge engineer

[1] 3DKAT was designed by Rose Dieng and Brigitte Trousse and implemented by Marie-Paule Epp, Nathalie Riera and Eric Faisandier.

makes the model he built from the interviews with the expert, explicit. Then he presents this dependency graph to the expert in order to complete it or correct it with him. Several types of qualitative reasoning are possible on the graph. The knowledge engineer can simulate the effect of increasing or decreasing a parameter (*what-if* reasoning), or simulate how to increase or decrease a parameter (*how-to* reasoning). Both kinds of reasoning are useful as well in design as in re-design from an existing solution. Thanks to a graphic, qualitative, parameterized simulation of the expert's reasoning, the macroscopic behaviour of the future expert system can thus be simulated and validated before effective implementation.

3DKAT also allows to model the ***subpart graph*** of an object as it is important in design applications. It offers a language of description of the expert's tasks and a notion of task graph, called TDOG (Task Dependency Oriented Graph).

The modelling of dynamic knowledge through PDOGs and the macroscopic validation thus allowed are one of the main interests of *3DKAT*. Another strength is the ability to tackle some kinds of design tasks such as configuration of a composite system made of several components.

2.2 Extensions of 3DKAT to KATEMES

The part 2 of the SISYPHUS'91 project aimed at deepening various models of problem solving in knowledge-based systems, so as to analyse their influence on knowledge acquisition activities. A comparison of such models was performed through an example of office assignment. Our participation to this project [1] allowed us to analyse the differences between *3DKAT* approach and generic approaches such as Chandrasekaran's generic tasks [11,12] or *KADS* interpretation models [64]. We could also distinguish the aspects rather design-oriented in *3DKAT* (the PDOGs, the subpart graphs) and the more general aspects (the task language, the use of semantic networks): PDOGs or subpart graphs are mainly useful in design problems consisting of building a composite system made of several components.

3DKAT allows to model one expert's vision only and the possibility of knowledge acquisition from several designers cooperating for a design task is not offered explicitly. Last, *3DKAT* does not take into account the future KBS user and it does not help the knowledge engineer to prepare the explanations this user would need.

Therefore, we will propose several extensions of *3DKAT* so as to constitute a new tool *KATEMES* (*Knowledge Acquisition Tool for Explainable, Multi-Expert Systems*). This new tool will be more ambitious than *3DKAT*. It will also focus on design applications but in addition, it will tackle the problems of explanations and multi-expertise.

The following sections will describe the main planned research topics: a) choice of the primitives of the knowledge acquisition tool, b) preparation of the assistance to the end-user, c) study of multi-expertise, d) methodological aspects.

3 The Primitives of KATEMES

3.1 Knowledge Graphs and Links

KATEMES will offer the knowledge engineer a knowledge representation formalism and various libraries. Knowledge will be described through semantic networks, called ***knowledge graphs***. Several types of knowledge graphs will be possible, according to the nature of nodes and links. The nodes of a knowledge graph can be: a) ***parameters*** of the system to be designed, b) ***tasks*** of the experts or of the users, c) ***agents*** (allowing to represent the experts).

As in *MACAO* [2], we will admit ***generic graphs*** (where nodes correspond to classes) and ***instantiated graphs*** (where nodes are associated to instances).

We will extend the taxonomy of links previously offered by 3DKAT: the knowledge engineer will then use this link library and will be able to complete it by application-specific links.

We will distinguish: a) ***static links*** (such as the ***subpart*** link): no behaviour will be associated to them and they will help to constitute static knowledge graphs. b) ***dynamic links*** (such as ***topoï***): a behaviour will be associated to such links, so that a simulation can be performed on the dynamic graphs where such links will appear.

Some links will be general (interesting for various classes of problems) while others will be specially offered for design applications. Some links will be generic while others will be application-specific and added by the knowledge engineer.

Some kinds of important links will be stressed and considered as viewpoints: for example, *electrical-link*, *mechanical-link*, *family-link* are examples of such viewpoints that may be considered as interesting in an application. It will then be possible to associate knowledge graphs to these types of links. For example, in *3DKAT*, there were three kinds of knowledge graphs: the subpart graph, the PDOG and the TDOG. The only kind of static link emphasized was the *subpart* link. The PDOG was gathering all kinds of links among parameters (*allows-to-calculate*, *influence relation*...). The TDOG was stressing links among tasks such as *followed-by*, *is-palliated-by*... In *KATEMES*, it will be possible to emphasize other kinds of links: instead of gathering all kinds of links in the PDOG, we will distinguish as many types of knowledge graphs as important links. For example, the knowledge engineer can decide to stress the links expressing "electrical relationships" and thus to handle an "electrical viewpoint knowledge graph".

Links can concern parameters or tasks or other entities. Links concerning entities of the same nature will lead to ***homogeneous*** knowledge graphs, while ***heterogeneous*** knowledge graphs will admit nodes of different natures.

As ***case-based reasoning*** is important in design applications [74,48], *KATEMES* will allow the knowledge engineer to elicit and store descriptions of ***typical solutions*** that may be used later for explanations. A typical solution will be a kind of knowledge graph, with a context describing its application conditions.

Remark:

We consider that this research, aiming at finding the adequate kinds of links and of knowledge graphs to emphasize, holds at a "knowledge level" [61]. We are aware of the complexity of this problem and we don't claim to find a general solution. But focusing on design applications should help us to determine links or knowledge graphs useful for this class of problems at least.

3.2 Tasks and Agents

KATEMES will offer a language for describing the experts' tasks (as in *3DKAT*) and the users' tasks, and it will handle homogeneous knowledge graphs of tasks, as *3DKAT*'s TDOGS.

To take into account multi-expertise, we will introduce the notion of *agent*, having knowledge graphs, representing its vision of the domain and of its reasoning in the domain. We will give a more detailed description of this notion of agent later, in the section concerning multi-expertise.

Some homogeneous knowledge graphs may have agents as nodes and represent networks of cooperating agents. Some heterogeneous graphs may emphasize the links among agents and tasks.

3.3 Models of Reasoning

KATEMES will offer a qualitative reasoning on dynamic knowledge graphs. The relationships between the qualitative simulation offered by *KATEMES* and *qualitative physics* [18,42] will be studied. In particular, we will compare our notion of knowledge graphs and the qualitative representation of a physical system.

A theoretical study of knowledge graphs, perhaps inspired of graph theory, will also be performed, as in [32].

We will study the *consistency* of *KATEMES* graphs through *Petri nets*: if we establish a correspondence between some classes of knowledge graphs and some known classes of Petri nets, we hope to take benefit of theoretical work already existing on Petri nets in order to deduce various properties of our knowledge graphs.

3.4 Related Work

The use of semantic networks or knowledge graphs for knowledge acquisition is quite frequent [2,32] but proposing qualitative graphs on which a qualitative simulation is carried out seems an original idea, as well as the highlighting of particular links in a given knowledge graph. In [32], graph theory is used in order to analyse the properties of knowledge graphs.

Several typologies of links were already studied, in the framework of knowledge acquisition [2] or in a more general context [27,28].

3.5 Conclusions

We unify several notions in this basic notion of knowledge graph: the choice of the kinds of nodes, relations and knowledge graphs to emphasize for a given relation will result from a work at a knowledge level [61].

At the "symbol" level, we will use an object-oriented representation and implement agents, tasks, links, knowledge graphs as objects.

4 Knowledge Acquisition and Explanations

There may be different types of end-users of the final KBS. Such users may have various purposes and need different forms of help. We rely on the principle that the quality of the final KBS future explanations must be prepared in the early knowledge acquisition phase: some information not necessarily useful for problem solving but important for the future explanations must be elicited from the experts. We will determine what this explanatory knowledge consists of and study how to elicit it, what influence it will have on the methodology and what formalisms will allow to represent it. This necessity to take into account the explanations as soon as the knowledge acquisition phase is recognized by researchers on explanations and the EES project [57,56] relies on this idea.

4.1 Explanatory Knowledge

The analysis of the different steps leading to the production of an explanation (analysis of the user's request, generation of the explanation contents and presentation of the answer, using an adequate medium) can give indications on the explanatory information needed in each of such phases.

We will study the following points :

- *Which explanatory knowledge elicit, when and how?* In [14], the necessity to represent deep knowledge, domain principles, causal or mathematical models, and world knowledge for explanations was emphasized and is one of the interests of research on second generation expert systems [72]. So, deep models can be considered as explanatory information [14,15]. In [54], the author distinguishes missing knowledge (such as deep knowledge) and implicit knowledge embedded in the implementation (such as the rule choice criterion,...). In [57], different kinds of knowledge useful for explanations are stressed: domain model, domain principles, tradeoffs, preferences, terminological definitions, integration knowledge and optimization knowledge. In [20], the knowledge engineer must indicate application-specific relations, in prevision of future explanations. In [45], different types of explanatory knowledge useful for producing explanations are distinguished: explanatory principles, discourse structures, explanation strategies and factual knowledge.

  Notice that explanatory knowledge may be dependent or not on the application or on the problem class: generic explanatory knowledge can thus be offered by a knowledge acquisition tool while application-dependent explanatory knowledge needs be elicited from domain experts and from future users. We must study if this elicitation depends or not on the problem solving knowledge elicitation and if it must take place simultaneously or later. We must also study how to link explanatory knowledge to problem solving knowledge. If some explanatory information is stored in electronic documents, it is possible to link portions of text to the entities handled by the knowledge acquisition tool and to exploit hypertext links for later explanations.

- *How to take into account the needs of the future user?* Using elicitation techniques (interviews, activity analysis...) can allow to extract various information from the intended end-users of the final KBS: their expertise level in comparison with the system, the assistance they need from the system, their needs in explanations... We will study how the analysis of the end-users' activity can be integrated in the knowledge acquisition methodology. Determining the end-users' possible requests and the possible forms of answers they need will help the knowledge engineer specify the future user - KBS interaction and the system interfaces. He must also specify the way the system task will be integrated in the expert's one. The information elicited from the users may also be analysed to compare the users' knowledge and the experts' one about the domain and the problem solving, so as to exploit it in the explanatory module of the final KBS: for example, it could be a basis for correcting the misunderstandings of the non expert end-users of the final KBS or for filling in the deficiencies of such users. On the contrary, if the expertise level of the intended user is higher than the system's one, the system will be rather a kind of assistant for this user and offer him other kinds of explanations.

- *How to elicit and combine the explanatory knowledge coming from several experts or users* (consistency checking, choice between several explanations...)?

Remarks:

The cognitive study of explanatory dialogues among humans [40,34] can give ideas on the adaptation of explanations to the interlocutor. The explanations given by the expert to another expert, to a non expert or to the knowledge engineer are examples of explanations offered to different types of users performing different tasks and having different goals when they ask explanations. The analysis of the differences of vocabulary and of explanatory strategies can indicate how the adaptation to the user is carried out. Some researchers consider the explanatory process as a cooperation among the explainer and the explainee: therefore, the nature and the role of both interlocutors affect the cooperation mode.

The interest of a multidisciplinary approach (in particular, the usefulness of cognitive psychology for knowledge acquisition) is more and more recognized [2,76].

Conclusions

Our study on explanatory knowledge should help us to propose:
- a typology of explanatory knowledge,
- a methodology taking into account the end-users,
- techniques of elicitation of explanatory knowledge from several experts,
- techniques for checking the consistency of explanatory knowledge elicited from several experts.

4.2 Adaptation of Explanations

We consider that explanations can depend on both the KBS task and the user's task. We will try to offer tools for improving the adaptation of the future explanations to the problem class or to the users.

4.2.1 Adaptation to Problem Classes

Deepening classes of problems will allow us to constitute a library of *"generic explanations"*. As a reflection on classes of problems and generic tasks was already carried out in the knowledge acquisition method *KADS* [9], we will rely on *KADS* generic tasks: our library will contain information on types of questions, users' goals, explanatory schemata and explanation presentation media advised for each *KADS* generic task.

For example, here is a list of various explanatory questions adapted to the design task [20]: a) the genesis and the evolution of designed objects [16], b) the relations between objects (cf their role, their evolution...), c) the different viewpoints on a given object, d) the comparison with typical solutions or typical cases, e) the justification of the choice between several alternatives, f) the failures, and in particular, those requiring a relaxation of constraints or a redesign, g) the transformation of a preliminary design into a detailed one, h) the influence of a modification of specifications or of constraints...

Discussions with some experts in civil engineering design convinced us that such experts often use analogies with typical solutions, when they give explanations to other experts of the same domain [16]. So, an explanatory mechanism for explaining some design choices may be based on such analogies, when the end-user is also an expert of the same domain.

As graphical explanations seem very useful for designers in civil engineering, graphics can be used as a medium of presentation, in addition to text.

Such examples of questions, explanatory mechanism and presentation medium for specific kinds of design task can be exploited for building the "generic explanations" associated to the design generic task.

Our library of "generic explanations" will contain such information, expressed using *KADS* vocabulary and it will guide the knowledge engineer for acquisition of explanatory knowledge, and for specification of an application-specific explanatory module.

Remarks:

This research of generic explanations associated to different classes of problems seems to be a new idea: generally, researchers study explanations regardless of the problem class. In [5], types of questions (such as "*why metaclass*" or "*justify knowledge source*" are associated to entities handled by *KADS*, but without linking explanations to generic tasks of *KADS*. The authors study model-based explanations, described at a knowledge level instead of a symbol level and we do approve this reflection at a knowledge level.

Most researchers don't take into account the problem class for explanations or study diagnostic tasks. Very few research on explanations tackle specificities of design task: let us cite [38,21] and [46] that is interested in the users of a CAD environment.

4.2.2 Adaptation to the Users

Many researchers study user models [53,35,36,37,49]. For a given application, some user's characteristics are interesting to be extracted and analysed during knowledge acquisition phase and stored. To deal with such users' characteristics, we will deepen the notion of ***user model*** [36] and try to offer a library of user models. We will distinguish generic user models and application-specific models and study techniques for acquiring and exploiting such user models.

In *KATEMES*, the viewpoint of a category of user will be constituted by its associated knowledge graphs. Techniques of comparison of knowledge graphs will allow us to compare the user's viewpoints and the expert's ones. We will then be able to determine a model common to the expert and to the user, as well as a model of the knowledge specific to each of them.

The correspondence between the users' viewpoints and the experts' ones may allow a better adaptation of the future explanations: for example, the KBS will be able to play on the vocabulary, the concepts understandable by a category of users, the simplified viewpoint that the user has on the expert's reasoning...

This study will end up in:
- a library of generic user models, that will be linked to the library of "generic explanations",
- techniques of comparison of users' knowledge graphs and experts' ones.

4.3 Interest of KATEMES for Explanations

The primitives of *KATEMES* are partly inspired from explanatory needs: for example, the description of ***typical solutions*** with their contexts of application is provided mainly for explanatory reasons, since references to typical cases seem to be often used by experts giving explanations to other experts in design applications [16].

The description of the tasks of the experts and of the end users can also facilitate the explanations, as well as the exploitation of different knowledge graphs extracted using *KATEMES*: simulations on knowledge graphs may sometimes be used as a kind of explanation.

During knowledge acquisition phase, we will allow the construction of a ***structured documentation***, based on ***hypertext techniques*** and useful later for the future explanations.

Among other modules, *KATEMES* will contain:
- a module allowing the exploitation of typical solutions for explanations,
- a module of exploitation of the knowledge graphs for explanations, with a specification of its use in the final KBS,
- a module exploiting such a hypertext-structured documentation, for explanations, with a specification of its use in the final KBS.

4.4 Related Work

The distinction between explanatory knowledge and problem solving knowledge was one of the basic ideas of the EES project [57,56,73] and allows, in [62], to differentiate the explanation line from the reasoning line.

For a second generation expert system, once acquired, the deep knowledge (i.e causal model or qualitative model of a system) will be available for later explanations. Model-based explanations are offered in [4].

In [52], explanations and knowledge acquisition are considered as two aspects of the same problem. Taking into account explanations in the earlier knowledge acquisition phase [57,56,39] eases the later maintenance of the KBS. The notion of explanation structure extracted from the expert is proposed in [41]. In [30], the author proposes a knowledge acquisition technique based on elicitation of justifications from people. In [5], a model-based approach allows to anticipate the user's questions and to design mechanisms of answers as soon as the knowledge acquisition phase. Types of questions are identified and their semantics linked to the components of *KADS* method. Another way of linking knowledge acquisition and explanations is to exploit explanations in order to guide knowledge acquisition: *ADELE* [15] is a tool for helping to knowledge acquisition, relying on the exploitation of justifications or explanations in order to ratify knowledge. On the contrary, our approach consists of exploiting knowledge acquisition in order to prepare and improve future explanations.

The use of hypertext techniques for explanations was already proposed [33]. Such techniques are also more and more used for knowledge acquisition [43,44]: *K-STATION* (tool supporting the method *KOD*) and *SHELLEY* (tool supporting the method *KADS*) use such techniques. But the idea of exploiting the documents obtained during knowledge acquisition phase for later explanations don't seem to have yet been proposed.

5 Knowledge Acquisition from Several Experts

5.1 The Problem

The elicitation of knowledge from multiple experts was recently studied [31,8,65, 68,66,67,55,70,77]. Sometimes, it is interesting to extract knowledge from several experts. They can be: a) either several experts working on the same domain and able to solve the same kinds of problems (but perhaps using different problem solving methods), b) or on the contrary specialists having different competence domains, each of them taking part in the solving of a more global problem.

The experts may disagree on the vocabulary or on some concepts or on limit cases. The knowledge engineer can try to model the common part of their knowledge as well as more specific aspects of this knowledge. He can detect possible conflicts and, according to the case, try to obtain a consensus or to keep the different viewpoints of the experts. So we must study how to represent the viewpoints of the different experts, the different possibilities of cooperation or of conflicts among the experts as well as the combination of their respective tasks.

We will study problems due to elicitation and analysis of knowledge of several experts: for example, can the analysis of the data elicited from an expert occur before and guide the elicitation of another expert knowledge or must the knowledge engineer avoid the biases that may be introduced by this way? We could benefit from previous experiments of knowledge elicitation from multiple experts [65] and from studies of cognitive psychologists for avoiding bias in knowledge elicitation. The analysis of the elicited data must allow to build: a) a *common model* corresponding to the kernel of knowledge common to all experts and perhaps models common only to sub-groups of experts, b) *specific models* corresponding to knowledge specific to an expert and not shared by other experts.

5.2 Multi-Expertise in *KATEMES*

The viewpoint of an expert will be constituted by his vision of the structural knowledge of the system to be designed (in the case of a design application), by his dynamic knowledge represented by dynamic knowledge graphs, by the description of his tasks and by his interactions with other experts.
We will compare the viewpoints of different experts, in order to detect and solve potential conflicts among them. Therefore, a correspondence may be established among the entities handled in the different knowledge graphs. We will propose *techniques for managing consistency of several knowledge graphs.*

We will extend the *language of description of the expert's tasks*, in order to take into account possible cooperation among several experts (for example, call to other experts, distribution of a task among several specialists...).

In order to tackle this multi-expertise problem, *KATEMES* handles the notion of *agent* to which a set of knowledge graphs will be associated. An agent may represent an expert totally or partially. More precisely, an expert may be represented by a compound agent, made of: a)an agent common to all experts, b) agents common to this expert and to other experts, c) and an agent representing the specificities of this expert.

The model of agent that we will propose will be described, among other features, by (a) its competences, (b) its vision of the domain and of its reasoning (cf its knowledge graphs), (c) its vision of other agents, (d) its interactions with the other agents [23].

In addition, we will propose a *hierarchy of agents* as well as a *typology of relations* that can link several agents. We will use this typology to describe *semantic networks of agents* [21,22], allowing to describe the way several experts work together, share their tasks, cooperate or communicate in real life.

Some knowledge graphs will have agents as nodes and represent networks of cooperating agents. We will study the possibility of qualitative simulation on agent knowledge graphs. The architecture of the final expert system will take inspiration of such networks if it intends to reflect the real behaviour of the experts in their activity.

5.3 Notion of Composite System

The cooperation of the users with the system can be described through a knowledge graph: the nodes will be agents representing the users or the system, and the arcs will be the relations between the users and the system.

In [23], we described our view of the process of knowledge acquisition as the behaviour of a composite system made of several human agents (experts, knowledge engineers and users) and software agents (the knowledge acquisition tool, the final system and the software where the final system will be integrated). This notion of composite system made of heterogeneous, interacting agents helps us to model the main relations between such agents (knowledge transfer, explanation, validation, assistance to problem solving...) and to analyse the cooperation underlying the process of knowledge acquisition. Our notion of agent should allow us to model the user as an agent and ease the description of a knowledge acquisition methodology involving several human agents.

5.4 Related Work

In the framework of distributed artificial intelligence [7,29,19], we are related to research on distributed knowledge acquisition [26], that emphasizes the link between knowledge acquisition and multi-agent systems. The modelling of knowledge acquisition process using a composite system comprising interacting human or software agents is a new idea, as well as the notion of agent to which knowledge graphs are associated. The vision of the user as an agent of a composite system seems original.

A methodology for acquiring knowledge from a group of experts working together towards common goals is presented in [47]. The integration of knowledge from multiple knowledge sources is studied in [55]. A method allowing to detect consensus, conflicts, correspondences et contrasts is proposed in [67]. Experiments based on grid repertories used by several experts are described in [68,66]. Techniques for comparing several viewpoints and solve conflicts among them are depicted in [25]. But techniques of comparison between several knowledge graphs representing the viewpoints of several experts don't seem to have been studied. The *EMA* knowledge acquisition method handles a notion of agent [71].

5.5 Expected Results

This research should lead us to propose:
- a formalism of multiple expert knowledge representation,
- a language of description of the tasks of several experts,
- a model of agent comprising, among others, a hierarchy of agents and a typology of relations among agents (cooperation, conflicts ...),
- techniques of comparison of several knowledge graphs,
- techniques for managing the consistency among the knowledge graphs.

6 Methodological Aspects

Several knowledge acquisition methods were proposed recently (*EMA* [71], *KADS* [9], *KOD* [76], *MACAO* [2]...) but none focus on design applications and takes into account the explanations and multi-expertise aspects. A top-down approach for knowledge acquisition for a design application was proposed in [10]. A few methodologies handle multiple experts explicitly [68,47,77]. *EMA* handles a notion of agent.

We will study methodological aspects, by taking into account the characteristics of design applications, explanations and multi-expertise.

We already noticed several questions linked to the methodology: a) How to elicit and model knowledge stemming from several experts? b) When and how must the acquisition of explanatory knowledge be carried out? c) When and how must deep knowledge be elicited?

This seems rather ambitious. So, our work will be perhaps a study of the influence of such aspects on a methodology, and what extensions or deepenings the existing methodologies need to tackle such problems.

How would an original methodology be related to other existing methods? *KADS* proposes a general methodology, and adapts the knowledge acquisition mode to each identified generic task. So we will compare our approach with the propositions of *KADS* concerning design applications. *KOD* is a general method for knowledge modelling and is independent of the kind of application. At present, we don't see any connection between our approach and *KOD* approach. As *MACAO* is based on a cognitive model and aims at generality, we can study if this cognitive model needs to be adapted in order to take into account the specificities of design process.

7 Very-Long-Term Research Topics

7.1 Validation of Acquired Knowledge

The necessity to link knowledge acquisition and validation is recognized. During expertise transfer, the knowledge engineer will present the knowledge graphs obtained during the interviews, to the expert. In addition to this incremental validation of problem solving knowledge by the experts, explanations will have to be validated both by the experts and by the users.

Once the final KBS effectively built, the knowledge base will be validated relatively to the specifications constituted by the results of *KATEMES*. This link between knowledge acquisition, specification of the KBS and validation of the acquired and implemented knowledge is the basis of a "software engineering" approach during the development of the KBS.

We can also think about the *a posteriori construction of the macroscopic description of an already existing expert system*, developed without the help of *KATEMES*, in order to have it validated by the expert: it may be seen as a kind of "reverse engineering", allowing to verify if the KBS satisfies the macroscopic behaviour the expert had in mind, when describing his activity.

So we will propose rules of *macroscopic validation* of the KBS. In a very long term, we intend to exploit the research already performed in order to clarify the notion of validation and try to have a more formal vision of this notion [3,63,6,75,17].

7.2 Design of the Final Multi-Expert System

Figure 1 describes our vision of the whole development of the final KBS.

The multi-expert aspect appearing in the knowledge acquisition phase can be translated in different architectures of the final KBS: several cooperating knowledge bases, a blackboard architecture, a multi-agent architecture... We don't intend to study these aspects. But in a very long term, we could study the possibility of automatic translation at least into the target shell *SMECI* that had been developed in our team [60]. Probably, this automatic translation will be able to tackle only a part of the final KBS.

Figure 2 sums up the main tools to be realized.

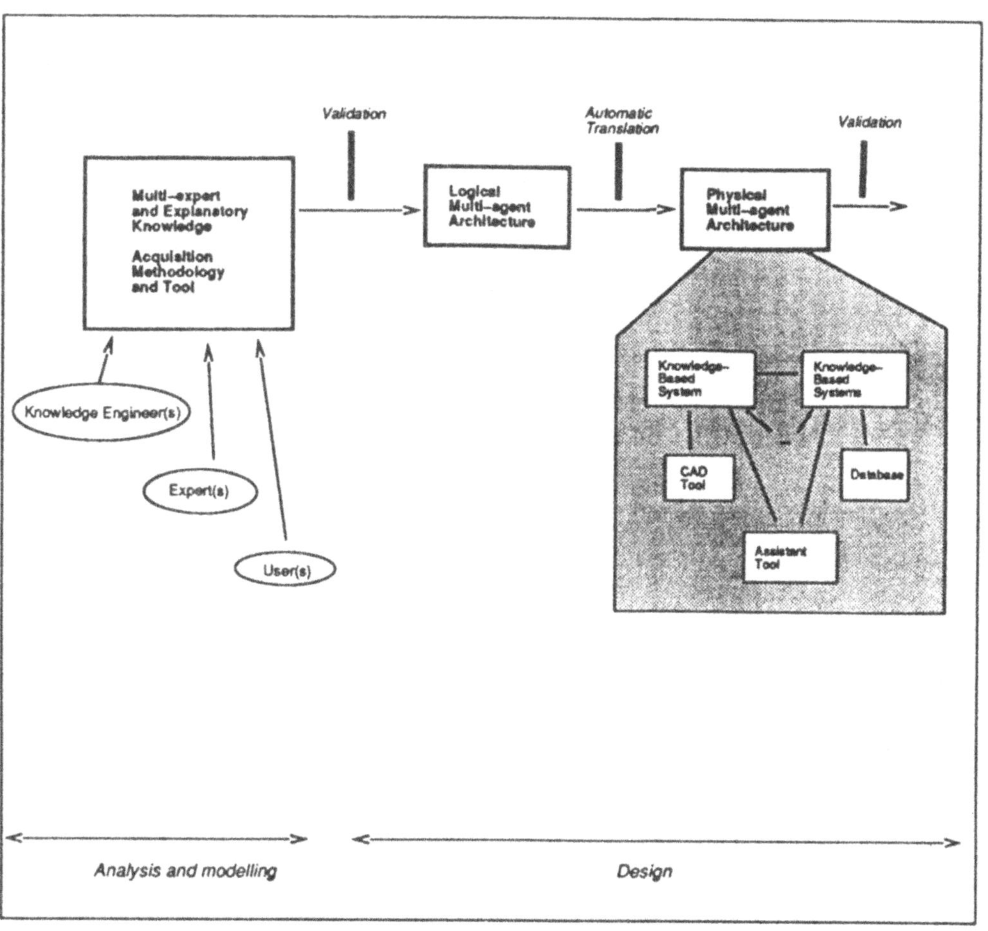

Figure 1: Phases of development of the multi-expert system

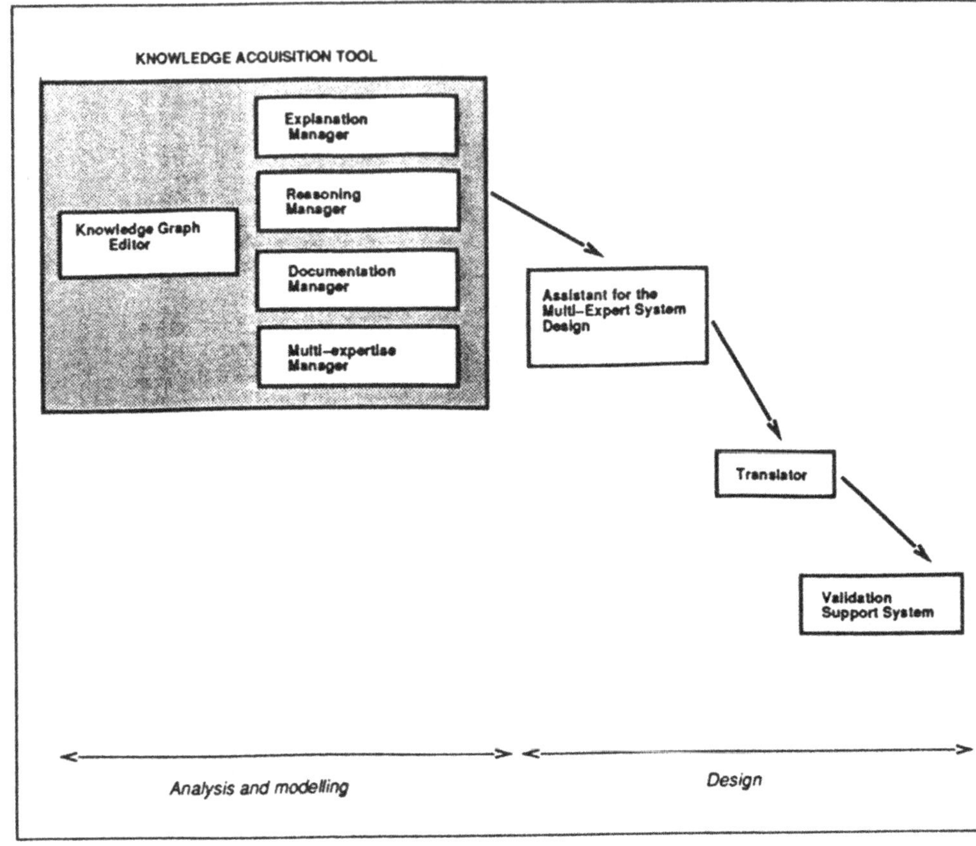

Figure 2: Tools to be realized

8 Conclusions

This paper presented our ideas on the various problems we intend to study in order to build *KATEMES*, a tool able to tackle specificities of design applications, explanations and multi-expertise. We are aware that this project is very ambitious and attacks several difficult problems. But it is important for us to think of such problems as soon as knowledge acquisition phase, so as to offer adequate primitives in our tool. Our previous experience in design applications, knowledge acquisition, explanations, and cooperation among cognitive agents will guide us. We will exploit, generalize and try to unify this previous work that inspired the key notions of *KATEMES*: ***agents***, ***relations*** and ***knowledge graphs***. The dependency on the problem class will help us to simplify some problems: each time we will try to build a library of generic, predefined entities (such as links, knowledge graphs, explanations...), we will deepen design applications, so as to offer the part of the library specially adapted to such applications, at least.

Acknowledgements

We thank very much all our colleagues that helped us for the definition of this project:

- François Rechenmann for his careful rereading of the ACACIA program and his remarkable comments,
- Pierre Bernhard, André Bisseret, Gilles Kahn, Bernard Larrouturou and Alain Michard for their extremely judicious advices on the building of the ACACIA Group,
- the laboratories ARAMIIHS (in particular Nathalie Aussenac), LAFORIA (specially Patrick Brézillon) and LIRMM (in particular Danièle Hérin-Aimé, Joel Quinteton and Jean Sallantin) for fruitful contacts and discussions,
- Leila Alem, Franck Lebastard, Mireille and Claude Fornarino, Anne-Marie Pinna, Odile Pourtallier and the PhD students of the SECOIA team for their constant, friendly support,
- Christelle Amergé, Fatiha Belaid and Sofiane Labidi thanks to whom the ACACIA Group exists.
- Philippe Martin, Philippe Navarro and Jean-Christophe Pazzaglia who are implementing *KATEMES*.

References

[1] N. Aussenac and R. Dieng. Models of problem solving for knowledge acquisition: comparison of MACAO and 3DKAT. In *SISYPHUS PROJECT, Part II, EKAW-91*, Crieff, Scotland, UK, May 1991.

[2] N. Aussenac, J.L. Soubie, and J. Frontin. A mediating representation to assist knowledge with MACAO. In *Proc. of KAW-89*, pages 2.1–2.17, Banff, Canada, October 1989.

[3] M. Ayel. Protocols for Consistency Checking in Expert System Knowledge Bases. In *Proc. of the 8th ECAI Conf.*, pages 220–225, Munich, August 1988.

[4] D.Y. Bau and P. Brézillon. Explanation-based diagnosis with the use of a model in control systems. In *Proc. of the 11th Int. Workshop on Expert Systems and their Applications, Spec. Conf.: Artificial Intelligence & Electrical Engineering*, pages 33–42, May 1991.

[5] A. Baumewerd-Ahlmann, P. Jaschek, J. Kalinski, and H. Lehmkuhl. Embedding Explanations into Model-Based Knowledge Engineering - Improved Decision Support in Environmental Impact Assessment. In D. Hérin-Aimé, R. Dieng, J.-P. Regourd, J.-P. Angoujard eds, *Knowledge Modeling and Expertise Transfer*, ISO Press, pages 269–284, Sophia-Antipolis, France, April 1991.

[6] I. Benbasat and J. S. Dhaliwal. The Validation of Knowledge Acquisition : Methodology and Techniques. In *Proc. of EKAW-89*, pages 60–74, Paris, July 1989.

[7] A. H. Bond and L. Gasser, editors. *Readings in Distributed Artificial Intelligence.* Morgan Kaufmann Publ., San Mateo, CA, 1988.

[8] J. H. Boose. A Survey of Knowledge Acquisition Techniques. *Knowledge Acquisition*, 1(1):3–37, March 1989.

[9] J. Breuker and B. Wielinga. Models of Expertise in Knowledge Acquisition. In Guida and Tasso, editors, *Topics in Expert System Design.* North-Holland, Elsevier Science Publishers B.V., 1989.

[10] P. Buck, B. Clarke, and G. Lloyd. A Top-down Approach for Capturing Design Knowledge. In *Proc. of EKAW-91*, Crieff, Scotland, UK, May 1991.

[11] T. Bylander and B. Chandrasekaran. Generic Tasks in Knowledge-Based Reasoning : the 'Right' Level of Abstraction for Knowledge Acquisition. *International Journal of Man-Machine Studies*, 26:231–244, 1987.

[12] B. Chandrasekaran. Towards a Functional Architecture for Intelligence Based on Generic Information Processing Tasks. In *Proc. of the 10th IJCAI*, volume 2, pages 1183–1192, Milan, Italy, August 1987.

[13] T. Y. L. Chiang and D. C. Brown. DSPL ACQUIRER - A System of the Acquisition of Routine Design Knowledge. In Sriram and Adey, editors, *Proc. of the 2nd Conference on Applications of Artificial Intelligence in Engineering*, pages 95–110, Cambridge, MA, USA, August 1987. Mech. Comp. Publ.

[14] W. J. Clancey. The epistemology of a rule-based expert system - a framework for explanation. *Artificial Intelligence*, 20:215–251, 1983.

[15] M. O. Cordier and C. Reynaud. Knowledge Acquisition Techniques and Second-Generation Expert Systems. In *Proc. of EKAW-91*, Crieff, Scotland, UK, May 1991.

[16] R. D. Coyne. Design Reasoning Without Explanations. *AI Magazine*, pages 72–80, Winter 1990.

[17] H. Davis. Using models of dynamic behavior in expert systems. In *9th Int. Workshop Expert Systems & their Applications*, pages 393–404, Avignon, France, May-June 1989.

[18] J. de Kleer and J. S. Brown. A qualitative physics based on confluences. *Artificial Intelligence*, 24:7–83, 1984.

[19] Y. Demazeau and J.-P. Muller, editors. *Decentralized AI, 2*. North-Holland, Elsevier Science Publ., 1991.

[20] R. Dieng. Knowledge-based, relation-based and learning-based explanations. In *Proc. of the 5th Workshop on Explanations*, Manchester, UK, April 1990.

[21] R. Dieng. Relations linking Cooperating Agents. In Y. Demazeau and J.P. Muller, editors, *Decentralized Artificial Intelligence, 2*, Elsevier Science Publ. B.V., North-Holland, 1991

[22] R. Dieng. Semantic network of expert systems. In Kohonen and Fogelman-Soulié, editors, *COGNITIVA 90*, North-Holland, Elsevier Science Publ. B.V., 1991

[23] R. Dieng and P.A. Tourtier. A Composite System for Knowledge Acquisition and User Assistance. In *Proc. of AAAI Spring Symposium on Design of Composite Systems*, pages 1–5, Stanford, CA, March 1991.

[24] R. Dieng and B. Trousse. 3DKAT, a Dependency-Driven Dynamic-Knowledge Acquisition Tool. In *Proc. of the AAAI-88 Workshop on Integration of Knowledge Acquisition and Performance Systems, St-Paul, Minnesota*, August 1988.

[25] S. Easterbrook. Handling conflict between domain descriptions with computer-supported negotiation. *Knowledge Acquisition*, 3(3):255–289, September 1991.

[26] S. M. Easterbrook. Distributed Knowledge Acquisition as a Model for Requirements Elicitation. In *Proc. of EKAW-89*, pages 530–543, Paris, July 1989.

[27] M. Fornarino and A.M. Pinna. An original object-oriented approach for relation management. In *Proc. of EPIA-89*, Springer Verlag, Lecture Notes on Artificial Intelligence, n. 390, Lisbonne, Portugal, September 1989.

[28] M. Fornarino and A.M. Pinna. *Un modèle objet logique et relationnel : le langage OTHELO*. PhD thesis, Université de Nice, Avril 1990.

[29] L. Gasser and M. N. Huhns, editors. *Distributed Artificial Intelligence, vol. II.* Pitman / Morgan Kaufmann Publishers Inc., London, 1989.

[30] T. Gruber. Justification-based Knowledge Acquisition. In H. Motoda, R. Mizoguchi, J. Boose, and B. Gaines, editors, *Knowledge Acquisition for Knowledge-Based Systems (Proc. of JKAW-90)*, pages 148–158. IOS Press, 1991.

[31] V. Jagannathan and A. S. Elmaghraby. MEDKAT: multiple expert DELPHI-based Knowledge Acquisition Tool. In *Proc. of the ACM NE Regional Conference*, pages 103–110, Boston, MA, October 1985.

[32] P. James. Structuring Knowledge using Knowledge Graphs. In *Proc. of EKAW-91*, Crieff, Scotland, UK, May 1991.

[33] P. W. Jamieson. HyperExplain: A New Method for Natural Language Generation. In *Proc. of the AAAI'88 Workshop on Explanation*, pages 59–62, Saint-Paul, Minnesota, August 1988.

[34] H. Johnson and P. Johnson. Explanation Dialogues for Explanation and Learning (IDEAL): The Effects of Different Explanatory Dialogue Styles on Learning by Non-Experts. In *Proc. of the 5th Workshop on Explanations*, Manchester, UK, April 1990.

[35] R. Kass and T. Finin. Rules for the Implicit Acquisition of Knowledge about the User. In *Proc. of AAAI-87*, volume 1, pages 295–391, Washington, DC, July 1987.

[36] R. Kass and T. Finin. Acquiring User Models for Tailoring Explanations. In *Proc. of the AAAI'88 Workshop on Explanation*, pages 48–54, Saint-Paul, Minnesota, August 1988.

[37] R. Kass and T. Finin. A general user modelling facility. In *Proc. of the CHI'88*, 1988.

[38] A. Kassatly and D.C. Brown. Explanation for Routine Design Problem Solving. In D. Sriram and R.A.Adey, editors, *Knowledge Based Expert Systems in Engineering: Planning and Design*, pages 225–239, Cambridge, MA, August 1987. Mech. Comp. Publ.

[39] C. Kellog, R. A. Gargan Jr, W. Mark, J. G. McGuire, M. Pontecorvo, J. L. Schlossbeg, and J. W. Sullivan. The Acquisition, Verification And Explanation Of Design Knowledge. *SIGART Newsletter, Knowledge Acquisition Special Issue*, (108):163–165, April 1989.

[40] A. Kidd. The Consultative Role of an Expert System. In P. Johnson and S. Cook, editors, *People and Computers: Designing the Interface, Proc. of the Conference of the British Comupter Society, Human Computer Interaction Specialist Group*, pages 249–254, University of East Anglia, September 1985. Cambridge University Press.

[41] O. Kuhn, M. Linster, and G. Schmidt. Clamping, COKAM, KADS and OMOS: The Construction and Operationalisation of a KADS Conceptual Model. In *Proc. of EKAW-91*, Crieff, Scotland, UK, May 1991.

[42] B. J. Kuipers. Qualitative simulation. *Artificial Intelligence*, 29:289–338, 1986.

[43] L. Lafferty, Jr Koller, A. M., G. Taylor, R. Schumann, and R. Evans. Techniques for capturing expert knowledge: an expert systems / hypertext approach. *SPIE, Applications of Artificial Intelligence VIII*, 1293:181–191, 1990.

[44] H. Langendørfer, U. Schreiweis, and M. Hofmann. Knowledge Acquisition with a special Hypertext System. In H. Motoda, R. Mizoguchi, J. Boose, and B. Gaines, editors, *Knowledge Acquisition for Knowledge-Based Systems (Proc. of JKAW-90)*, pages 249–258. IOS Press, 1991.

[45] B. Lemaire and B. Safar. An architecture for representing explanatory reasoning. In D. Hérin-Aimé, R. Dieng, J.-P. Regourd, J.-P. Angoujard eds, *Knowledge Modeling and Expertise Transfer*, IOS Press, pages 327–332, Sophia-Antipolis, France, April 1991.

[46] S. Line and J. Ferrans. Explanation In a CAD Environment: Surveying User Requirements. In *Proc. of the 5th Workshop on Explanations*, Manchester, UK, April 1990.

[47] Y. I. Liou, E. S. Weber, and Jr J. F. Nunamaker. A methodology for knowledge acquisition in a group decision support system environment. *Knowledge Acquisition*, 2(2):129–144, June 1990.

[48] M.L. Maher. Process Models for Design Synthesis. *AI Magazine*, pages 49–58, Winter 1990.

[49] C. Maïs and A. Giboin. Helping users achieve satisficing goals. In M.J. Smith and G. Salvendy, editors, *Work with Computers: Organizational, Management, Stress and Health Aspects, Advances in Human Factors/Ergonomics Series 12A (Proc. of the Third Int. Conf. on Human-Computer Interaction)*, pages 98–105, Boston, MA, September 1989. North-Holland, Elsevier Science Publishers B.V.

[50] S. Marcus. Taking backtracking with acquisition grain of SALT. *International Journal of Man-machine Studies*, 26(4):383–398, 1987.

[51] S. Marcus and J. McDermott. SALT: A knowledge acquisition language for propose-and-revise systems. *Artificial Intelligence*, 1988.

[52] B. Mark. Explanation and Interactive Knowledge Acquisition. In *Proc. of the AAAI'88 Workshop on Explanation*, Saint-Paul, Minnesota, August 1988.

[53] K. R. McKeown and R. A. Weida. Highlighting User Related Advice. In *Proc. of the AAAI'88 Workshop on Explanation*, pages 38–43, Saint-Paul, Minnesota, August 1988.

[54] C. Millet. A study of the knowledge required for explanations in expert systems. In *Proc. of the 5th Conf. on Artificial Intelligence Applications*, pages 83–90, Miami, Florida, March 1989.

[55] K. Morik. Integration Issues in Knowledge Acquisition Systems. *SIGART Newsletter, Knowledge Acquisition Special Issue*, (108):124–131, April 1989.

[56] R. Neches, W. R. Swartout, and J. Moore. Enhanced Maintenance and Explanation of Expert Systems through Explicit Models of their Development. *IEEE Transactions on Software Engineering*, SE-11(11):1337–1351, November 1985.

[57] R. Neches, W. R. Swartout, and J. Moore. Explainable (and maintainable) expert systems. In *Proc. of the 9th IJCAI*, pages 382–389, Los Angeles, CA, 1985.

[58] B. Neveu. EXPORT: an expert system in breakwater design. In *ORIA 87, Artificial Intelligence and Sea*, pages 11–I7, 1987.

[59] B. Neveu and P. Haren. SMECI : an Expert System for Civil Engineering Design. In *Proc. of the 1st Int. Conf. on Applications of Artificial Intelligence to Engineering Problems*, Southampton, UK, April 1986.

[60] B. Neveu, B. Trousse, and O. Corby. SMECI : an Expert System Shell that fits Engineering Design. In *3er Simposium Internacional de Inteligencia Artificial*, Monterrey, N.L., Mexique, October 1990.

[61] A. Newell. The knowledge level. *Artificial Intelligence*, pages 87–127, 1982.

[62] C. L. Paris, M. R. Wick, and W. B. Thompson. The Line of Reasoning Versus the Line of Explanation. In *Proc. of the AAAI'88 Workshop on Explanation*, pages 4–7, Saint-Paul, Minnesota, August 1988.

[63] M. C. Rousset. On the Consistency of Knowledge Bases: the COVADIS System. In *Proc. of the 8th ECAI Conf.*, Munich, 1988.

[64] G. Schreiber, B. Wielinga, and J. Breuker. The KADS Framework for Modelling Expertise. In *Proc. of EKAW-91*, Crieff, Scotland, UK, May 1991.

[65] M. L. G. Shaw. Problems of Validation in a Knowledge Acquisition System using Multiple Experts. In *Proc. of EKAW-88*, pages 5.1–5.15, Bonn, RFA, June 1988.

[66] M. L. G. Shaw. A Grid-Based Tool For Knowledge Acquisition : Validation with Multiple Experts. *SIGART Newsletter, Knowledge Acquisition Special Issue*, (108):168–169, April 1989.

[67] M. L. G. Shaw and B. R. Gaines. A methodology for recognizing conflict, correspondence, consensus and contrast in a knowledge acquisition system. *Knowledge Acquisition*, 1(4):341–363, December 1989.

[68] M. L. G. Shaw and J. B. Woodward. Validation in a knowledge support system: construing consistency with multiple experts. *International Journal of Man-Machine Studies*, 29:329–350, 1988.

[69] D. B. Shema, J. M. Bradshaw, S. P. Covington, and J. H. Boose. Design knowledge capture and alternatives generation using possibility tables in Canard. *Knowledge Acquisition*, 2(4):279–390, December 1990.

[70] B. G. Silverman, R. G. Wenig, and T. Wu. COPEing With Ongoing Knowledge Acquisition From Collaborating Hierarchies of Experts. *SIGART Newsletter, Knowledge Acquisition Special Issue*, (108):170–171, April 1989.

[71] S. Spirgi and D. Wenger. Generic techniques in EMA: A model-based approach for Knowledge Acquisition. In *Proc. of EKAW-91*, Crieff, Scotland, UK, May 1991.

[72] L. Steels. Second Generation Expert Systems. In *Future Generation Computer Systems*, volume 1, pages 1213–1221, 1985.

[73] W. R. Swartout. Knowledge needed for expert system explanations. In *AFIPS Conf. Proc., Nat. Computer Conf.*, pages 93–98, Chicago, IL, July 1985.

[74] K. Sycara and D. Navichandra. Integrating Case-Based Reasoning and Qualitative Reasoning in Design. In Computational Mechanics, editor, *AI in Design*, pages 231–250, Southampton, UK, 1989.

[75] S. Twine. A Model for the Knowledge Analysis Process. In *Proc. of EKAW-89*, pages 253–268, Paris, July 1989.

[76] C. Vogel. How to Qualify Knowledge-Based Systems. In *Proc. of the 4th COMPASS Conference (COMPASS-89)*, 1989.

[77] W. A. Wolf. Knowledge Acquisition From Multiple Experts. *SIGART Newsletter, Knowledge Acquisition Special Issue*, (108):138–140, April 1989.

Causal Model-Based Knowledge Acquisition Tools: Discussion of Experiments

Jean Charlet*, Jean-Paul Krivine†, and Chantal Reynaud‡

* DIAM, INSERM U194 & Service d'Informatique Médicale de l'AP-HP
91, Bd de l'Hôpital - 75634 Paris Cedex 13 - France
charlet@frsim51.bitnet
† E.D.F. Direction des Etudes et Recherches
1, Av. du Général de Gaulle - 92141 Clamart Cedex - France
krivine@clr34el.edf.fr
‡ Laboratoire de Recherche en Informatique, Bât. 490, Université Paris-Sud
91405 Orsay Cedex - France
reynaud@frlri61.bitnet

Abstract. The aim of this paper is to study causal knowledge and demonstrate how it can be used to support the knowledge acquisition process. The discussion is based on three experiments we have been involved in. First, two classes of Causal Model-Based Knowledge Acquisition Tools are identified: bottom-up designed causal models and top-down designed causal models. The properties of each type of tool and how they contribute to the whole knowledge acquisition process is then discuted.

1 Introduction

The aim of this paper is to study causal knowledge and demonstrate how it can be used to support the *knowledge acquisition* (KA) process. The discussion is based on three experiments we have been involved in: the ADÈLE tool [11] and the ACTE tool [4, 5] in the field of medical diagnosis, and the DIVA experiment for turbine-generator diagnosis [12]. These experiments were carried out separately and independently. Discussion takes place in the framework of the new paradigm of "task and method specific tools" for KA [27].

We present KA through a conceptual model of possible processes for the building of an expert system (Sect. 2), then we use this framework to localize the role and the place of *Causal Model-Based Knowledge Acquisition Tools* (CMBKATs) (Sect. 3). Such KA tools have two major roles depending on the way they are built. They can be useful in validating the heuristic knowledge being acquired, although this supposes firstly that the causal KA process has been developed quite independently of the heuristic KA process, and secondly that connection between the two knowledge bases is nevertheless possible. In this paper, such models are termed "bottom-up designed causal models". Causal models can also be used to ensure consistency in the expert discourse, but this supposes that they are connected with the heuristic level by construction. Such causal models, termed "top-down designed causal models", are often built using expert justifications during the interviews.

The two roles described above are important and useful in the KA process, and particularly in what we call the "instantiation of the conceptual model". The two kinds of tools which can be built according to these different approaches can contribute significantly to the enhancement of capabilities during the KA process. ACTE and ADÈLE, described in Sect. 4, are appropriate illustrations of both kinds of tools. However, a single CMBKAT can not assure the two above roles. We therefore consider that it would be useful to study how both tools can be integrated or can work together in the same KA workbench. Similarly, a promising research path would be to investigate how CMBKATs can be made to work with more conventional KA tools, with explicit reference to the underlying conceptual model.

In the last section of the paper, we discuss causal models (still in the KA context) and a few specific points based on the three experiments, the content and the use of CMBKAT causal models, how CMBKATs manage a conceptual model of expertise, how they deal with uncertainty, and the determination of an accurate causal model for KA. This leads to the identification of three important properties: connection, consistency and completeness. Finally, we note the advantages of causal models.

2 Knowledge Acquisition as Conceptual Model Design

A new and fruitful paradigm for KA has emerged in recent years. This paradigm, sometimes called "task and method specific tools", aims at filling the conceptual gap between the form in which knowledge is described in the natural discourse of domain specialists, and the form in which it is represented in Knowledge Based programs. This approach is based on the design of a *Conceptual Model* which tries to describe the problem solving process at a better level of abstraction. This conceptual model can either be designed by selection and refinement from a predefined library of generic tasks, or can be built from scratch when no appropriate generic tasks are available. Of course, the former case is preferable, and most attention is paid to the development of such a library (see the Esprit Project CONSTRUCT, project P5477). Thus, KA becomes a modelling task, and once the conceptual model has been designed the process is largely dependent on the role and type of knowledge required. This issue has been widely examined. Clancey (Heuristic Classification), Chandrasekaran (Generic Tasks), Breuker and Wielinga (Models of Expertise and the KADS Methodology) and McDermott (Role Limiting Methods and KA Tools) were among the forerunners in this field [7, 33, 3, 25].

KA, as a cognitive task, can also be modelled in the same framework. Figure 1 from Aussenac et al. [1] proposes a "conceptual model" for an expert system building process. This decomposition is not wholly original, and is neither a generalization of previous descriptions nor an alternative description. It no longer attempts to come up with a new KA theory, but is simply a re-formulation of a shared framework that enables discussion and comparison of KA tools and methods. For this reason, it is relevant to our discussion on causal models in KA. Before commenting further on this decomposition, let us explain why such decomposition and analysis of the KA process can be useful and interesting.

Firstly, *such an analysis provides a better delimitation of the role and contribution that each tool and method can play.* The increasing number of tools and methods for KA make it essential for us to be able to delimit the respective role of each one, and to better define the domain of applicability. This is the basis for the comparison of tools and methods if we are to avoid comparing too distinct types of element.

Secondly, *such a framework is useful for specifying how several tools or methods can be used together.* It attempts to specify the inputs and outputs of each step, and then to specify how complementary or redundant the various tools are. More generally, a modelling of the KA process itself is necessary when designing a general KA workbench, where the various tools supplied should be recognizable by the role they can play during *knowledge base system* (KBS) design.

Lastly, and this is the purpose of our paper, *such a framework is useful for the specification of the benefit and the role of a specific approach*, and its comparison with existing ones.

We will now describe the four steps of the Fig. 1, as given by Aussenac et al. [1]. These steps are naturally not sequential, and should instead be seen as a breakdown of the KA task, rather than a linear procedure for KA.

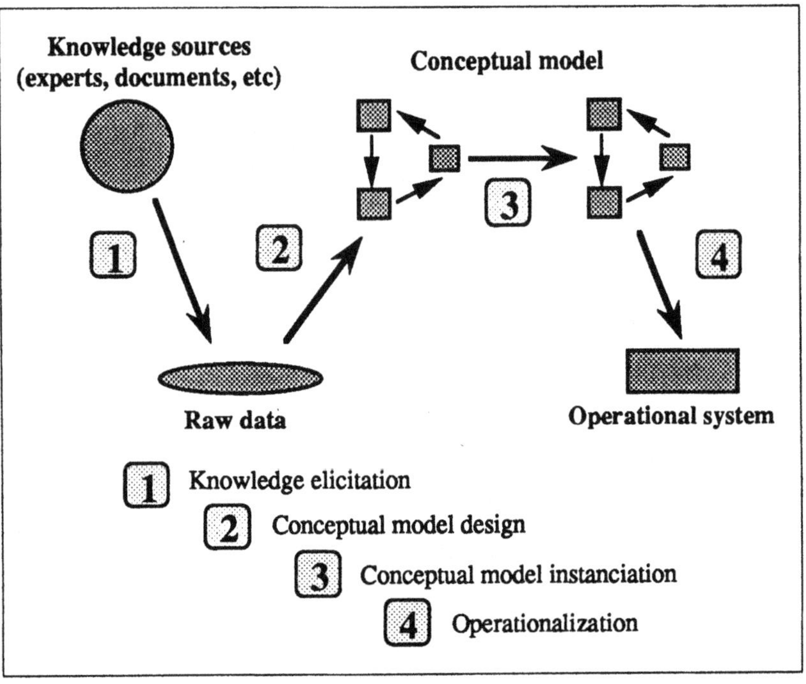

Fig. 1. Knowledge Acquisition (from Aussenac et al.)

1. **Knowledge Elicitation.** Some authors like Motta et al. call this phase "bottom-up elicitation" [26]. The output consists of "raw data" that can be more or less self-organized, depending on the tools or the method used. This data serves as a basis for the construction of the conceptual model. Further elicitation will then become "model-driven" (conceptual model-driven) and is included in step 3 (termed "top-down elicitation" by Motta et al.). The main characteristic of this phase is that no a priori model is assumed. Methods such as interviews or think

aloud protocols are the most frequently used at this stage. Motta et al. consider these techniques to be "weak" because they are domain-independent. This step also includes "data analysis", aiming to remove the background noise in raw data, and outputting the first set of organized elicited knowledge.

2. **Design of the Conceptual Model.**[1] Based on the first set of data and knowledge gathered from step 1, the aim of step 2 is to provide a framework for the representation of these pieces of knowledge and for the description of the way in which this knowledge will be used (the problem solving process). This is certainly one of the most difficult tasks in this paradigm (how to select the appropriate methods when faced with a concrete problem). Many approaches try to convert this task into a selection and refinement process in a library of generic methods. The KADS methodology also takes this approach, and several projects aim at increasing the number of available libraries [2], Esprit Project Construct or the various "KADS user groups". The underlying approach of Chandrasekaran's Generic Task is very similar (selection and refinement of generic methods[2]).
3. **Instantiation of the Conceptual Model.** The conceptual model defined in step 2 provides a very solid foundation for KA. The role and place of knowledge still to be acquired is clearly defined. For this reason, many tools and methods exploit this fact, and most KA tools can be classified in this category. The most typical are certainly those from CMU (MOLE [15], MORE [19] and SALT [24]). Motta et al term this step "top-down elicitation".
4. **Operationalization.** This phase consists of translating the conceptual model and the associated knowledge into a running system. It is no longer directly a matter of "knowledge acquisition". However, since it is very frequently the case that KBS design needs feedback and looping, it would appear useful to design an operational system that is the best possible reflection of the conceptual model. Some authors refer to a "semi isomorphism" [17]. This is mostly a matter of architecture or language, and an important line of research is taken up by this subject [21, 29].

These four steps are not, of course, sequential, and iterations are frequent. They can be seen as a kind of conceptual model of the KA process itself. Of course, the human expert has to intervene during all the four steps (at least during the first three ones).

3 Causal Models and their relations with KA

3.1 Two classes of Causal Models for KA

In our discussion, causal models are examined for their role in the KA process. Thus, "heuristic level" or "heuristic knowledge base" is used to refer to the knowledge that needs to be acquired (the knowledge that causal models are supposed to improve), while a "causal knowledge base" is used to refer to the causal level.

[1] Conceptual model is now a term largely used. However, it may still give rise to some confusion. For a deeper discussion on how various approaches refer to it, see Karbach et al. [20].

[2] Chandrasekaran refers to Generic Task, but like Karbach et al. [20] we prefer to use method.

Before discussing the place of causal models for KA in the framework laid out above, and before commenting on our experiences, let us first briefly define what we mean by causal models. Firstly, following Davis [14], we reject the terms "deep models" and "shallow models". These notions are relative. As Sticklen et al state [30], one model is deep only in relation to another, and may well be shallow compared to a third one. Another point of view concerns the function of the expressed knowledge (the "teleology"). What we term in our discussion *"causal models" are models that express causality at a certain level of abstraction, without referring to the goal of the final system in which they will be used (e.g. diagnosis or classification in a medical* KBS*)*. Intuitively, causal models express knowledge that can be relevant over a wide range of applications and so appear to be more "generic". They often try to represent "domain theory". For this reason, the term "deep knowledge" is sometimes applied. This kind of knowledge seems to be very naturally available, often appearing as a background to a number of interviews for KA ("why are you telling me that?"). They also serve to justify acquired knowledge and to provide new clues and new directions for broadening the KA process itself.

From our experience, we can distinguish two classes of causal models in KA. Each of them is of interest and raises different kinds of difficulties.

Top-down designed causal models: these models come directly from the main KA process. They frequently appear as justifications of elicited knowledge ("why are you telling me that?"). Thus, using top-down designed causal models often leads to the simultaneous running of two distinct KA processes: the main KA process (to acquire what we have called "heuristic knowledge"), and the process of the design of the causal model itself.

Bottom-up designed causal models: these models are designed independently of the KA process. They generally develop out of existing models (design models, handbooks or tutorial manuals). These models often describe "how things work" or "how things fail".

Bottom-up designed causal models provide a different viewpoint (different according to the heuristic knowledge base and because the source is different from the (generally expert) source which provides heuristic knowledge). The combination of two views of the same subject area may prove to be very fruitful, especially in terms of validation of the heuristic level, but may also be difficult to achieve. Conversely, although top-down designed causal models and heuristic levels represent two different points of view, the former is derived from the later, and thus its role is a role of "internal consistency in the expert discourse" rather than a validation of what is acquired.

3.2 Place and interest of Causal Models for KA

In this paper, we aim to present and then comment on the argument for the three following assertions:

- *Causal models can be very useful for* KA *because they provide another and complementary viewpoint on the knowledge being acquired.* Several issues have been quoted: (i) the use of justifications of expert knowledge for the validation of acquired knowledge or for the extension of an existing knowledge base [28], (ii) the acquisition of heuristic knowledge [14], and (iii) the acquisition of strategic knowledge [16].

- *Most causal model-based knowledge acquisition tools or methods (*CMBKAT*s) play a major role during the "instantiation" of a conceptual model* and are therefore relevant for step 3 in the framework described in Fig. 1 (conceptual model instantiation). We will see that the various experiments use pre-existing conceptual model. Gruber assumes that an initial amount of knowledge has been collected before the system (the ASK system) can be used [16]. In the ACTE tool, a conceptual model is assumed (a kind of classification) and an initial set of knowledge (hypothesis and symptoms) is still specified when building and using the causal model. Similarly, ADÈLE can run only when a first set of rules is present in the HKB.
- However, CMBKAT*s do not perform this instantiation automatically, but help to achieve it.* They therefore have to be used in collaboration or interaction with other tools or methods, and benefits come from an explicit reference of these tools or methods, to the underlying conceptual model.

4 Three experiments

We will now present the three experiments our discussion is based on. Two of them are complete KA systems. They have been fully described elsewhere in [11] for the ADÈLE system and in [5] for the ACTE system. ADÈLE and ACTE were designed to support the KA activity in an interactive way in architectures combining heuristic and causal knowledge (often termed "Second Generation Expert Systems"). Both of these systems are used in medical diagnosis applications. In this section we simply want to list the main features of these systems. The third experiment is described in [12, 13] and is an experiment in combining causal models and heuristic levels for KA purposes rather than a pure KA tool.

4.1 The ADÈLE system

4.1.1 Description. ADÈLE is a causal model-based knowledge acquisition tool (CMBKAT) with two main features. Firstly, it is designed inside the framework of Second Generation Expert Systems, particularly in the framework of systems in which heuristic and causal models cooperate. Secondly, it contributes to the design of a heuristic knowledge base, an equivalent to an instantiated conceptual model.

The basic idea in ADÈLE is to use causal models to make the main (heuristic) KA process easier. This does not mean that problems of the (main) KA process will entirely disappear. ADÈLE does not generate the heuristic level from a causal one. On the contrary, heuristic and causal models are represented by two quite independent knowledge bases with their own KA process: the *heuristic knowledge base* (HKB) is represented by production rules (and will form the operational knowledge base), the *causal knowledge base* (CKB) is composed of causal models and is represented in a formalism closely related to that of the semantic network. Being issued from different sources, there is every chance that these knowledge bases model various viewpoints and then, the objective of ADÈLE is to profit from these different but maybe complementary viewpoints to help the main (heuristic) KA process while it is in progress.

So, ADÈLE supplies the knowledge engineer (who is assumed to be the system user) by providing control and understanding of the (heuristic) knowledge being acquired. Furthermore, it can provide suggestions to complete the HKB. It is a tool for the refining and extending of an already existing HKB, using causal models. Moreover, this tool makes communication with the domain expert easier, because it is based on a causal level assumed to be more tractable. In addition, it contributes to easier expression and validation of the (heuristic) knowledge base.

The KA process in ADÈLE is as follows: the expert expresses a production rule encoding some piece of heuristic knowledge. Each rule is then considered separately. When a new production rule is acquired (let us remain that the heuristic KA process is in progress when ADÈLE operates), abductive reasoning based on the causal knowledge base provides justifications that can be regarded as proofs of the association between the conditions and the conclusion of the rule. A precise analysis of the justifications provides the expert with interesting results concerning the nature of the link between conditions and conclusion, the strength of this link, the roles played by the conditions and the discriminating power of the conditions over the conclusion. ADÈLE takes advantage of this analysis to explain the rule, comment on it, check it, and to suggest modifications or new rules. ADÈLE can also be used in the design of the knowledge base and for maintenance purposes of an existing knowledge base. Such an approach can not be used without any heuristic knowledge. Reasoning on causal models which have been acquired separately from the heuristic level, has to be controlled. In the ADÈLE approach, heuristic level is used to support reasoning on causal models.

This approach has been experimented on a medical diagnosis application in electromyography, diagnosing muscle and peripheral nerve disorders by electrical measurements. An example of session in this field is described below (see Fig. 2).

4.1.2 Causal Knowledge Base in ADÈLE. The CKB models the domain knowledge. In the CKB, causal relations co-exist with descriptive or definition relations. In addition, the CKB is not composed of a unique causal net, but may contain several competitive models. It corresponds to the fact that a model is always designed from a particular viewpoint and a variety of viewpoints may be possible. In ADÈLE, we would like to take advantage of the multiplicity of available domain models.

Nonetheless, any causal model will not always be useful for the heuristic KA process. The knowledge engineer has to choose the most appropriate models, those most closely related to the heuristic knowledge being acquired.

With reference to the classification of causal models given in Sect. 3, causal models used in ADÈLE can be qualified as bottom-up designed causal models. CKB has its own KA process and it is quite independent of the main KA process. CKB is born out of pre-existing models directly extracted from medical textbooks. Obviously, such existing models are not directly connected with the heuristic level. Therefore, the approach is extended by a connection phase where the knowledge engineer tries to reformulate the initial and "raw" causal models to enable connection with the HKB.

The CKB is a two-level modelization and is represented by two kinds of models. "Instantiated Causal Models" model objects and relations between objects of the subject domain. These objects refer directly to the conditions and the conclusions of the production rules of the HKB. "Generic Causal Models" which model classes of objects and relations between them, are obtained from "Instantiated Causal Models". Classes of objects stem from grouping together objects, and relations between classes of objects stem from generalizing relations between objects. Relations of the models (whatever kind of model it is) are described by a name in a literal form, a type which denotes the type of domain knowledge that the relation refers to (neuroanatomical, pathophysiological, etc.) and its nature (hierarchic, descriptive, functional, causal, evocative). The value of these attributes are exploited when analyzing explanations provided by CKB. Relations between Generic Model and Instantiated Model are exclusively "is-a" relations between classes of objects and objects which belong to them.

Using such causal models was helpful in our medical application – medical diagnosis is a suitable domain, and one for which causal models are available. We worked on a medical diagnostic reasoning system for electromyography. The CKB is composed of:

- anatomical model which models which muscle is innervated by which nerve,
- model which describes an electrical schema of diseases, and which in particular describes electrical measurements which are abnormal when a disease appears,
- model of localization which shows in which muscular region a symptom appears,
- pathophysiological model which indicates the effects of the diseases on nerves, on electrical measurements and on the clinical schema of a patient.

4.1.3 Using ADÈLE. ADÈLE improves communication with the domain expert. It provides the knowledge engineer with a deeper background to understand the acquired expert knowledge. By giving explanations and making comments, it helps to avoid potential misinterpretations and modelling errors[3]. Moreover, the knowledge engineer will be able to detect strange combinations of knowledge elements, which are expressed at different levels of abstraction. Expressing knowledge with the production rule formalism is sometimes difficult for an expert and can lead to imperfections [8]. The results provided by ADÈLE can serve as the basis of a discussion between the expert and the knowledge engineer, that can lead the expert to reformulate the system's knowledge. In addition, ADÈLE provides the knowledge engineer with the possibility of checking the acquired expert knowledge by using the causal knowledge base; this is a way of validating the acquired heuristic knowledge.

ADÈLE has a very interesting structure both from a methodological and a computational viewpoint. At first, explanations are looked for on the generic level and then, when (at least) one has been found (termed generic explanation), further explanations are sought on the instantiated level. This approach does not explore all instantiated models, but rather looks for instantiations of generic explanations.

[3] As far as the design of a knowledge base is considered as a modelling process.

The knowledge engineer gives the rule described below. ADELE immediately operates on it.

If not Paresthesie in the median distal region
and if Woman
then Carpal channel syndrome

This rule expresses the relation between paresthesie (prickling) confined to a part of the arm, the fact that the patient is a woman and carpal channel syndrome being an obstruction of the channel of the median nerve at the wrist.
The results of ADELE are:

This rule is not valid, it can not be explained.
(Not any explanation has been found for the association between the conditions and the conclusion of the rule in instantiated causal models)
Nevertheless,one (partial) generic explanation exists: "A clinical symptom is localized in a muscle ; a muscle is innervated by nerves ; a nerve can be damaged by diseases".
(This generic explanation has been provided by generic causal models)
...
Not any explanation has been found for "woman". Is "woman" a condition which reflects heuristic context?
...

ADELE has identified generic concepts which can be associated with the terms of the rule: clinical symptom for Paresthesie in the median distal region and disease for Carpal channel syndrome. Its justifies the association between these concepts. This helps the knowledge engineer by providing understanding of the rule being acquired. Let us note that the explanation is partial. No concept has been found for the condition "woman" and then, no explanation which refers to this condition, has been delivered. adele deduces that the condition "woman" could reflect a heuristic context.
Results of ADELE are analyzed. The knowledge engineer decides to modify the rule (to remove the "not" in the conditions of the previous rule) and proposes ADELE to validate the modified rule.

If Paresthesie in the median distal region
and if Woman
then Carpal channel syndrome

The results of Adèle *are:*

This rule is partially valid.
(One partial explanation has been found in instantiated causal models)
"Paresthesies in the median distal region are localized in the muscle in the median nerve ; the muscle in the median nerve is innervated by the median nerve; the median nerve can be damaged by carpal channel syndrome"
...
According to this explanation, no additive condition is required to explain the conclusion of the rule.
...
The explanation below suggests the rule is an evocative one.
...
Here is an analogous rule:
If Hypoesthesie in the median distal region
then Carpal channel syndrome
...
etc.

Fig. 2. An example of session with the ADÈLE system, in the field of electromyography

4.2 The ACTE system

4.2.1 Description. ACTE is a KA tool in a medical diagnostic domain. The resulting knowledge-base system is aimed at doing a heuristic classification. The approach is based on the interpretation of a causal model. The aim of this interpretation is twofold: on one hand, it facilitates the checking of the causal model, on the other hand, it generates heuristic knowledge which is usable for a specific task.

ACTE deals with two knowledge bases: the *causal knowledge base* (CKB) – i.e. the causal model – which is the input to the KA process, and the ***heuristic knowledge base*** (HKB) which is the output of this process and will constitute the operational knowledge base. The CKB is represented in a semantic network formalism while the HKB is represented by production rules. The following steps describe ACTE's KA process:

1. The conceptual model is first defined so as to describe the problem-solving methods that accomplish the diagnostic task. These methods deal, for example, with "data-abstraction" or the "unicity of the fault process".
2. The expert provides domain knowledge in a causal model framework. This causal model is the CKB.
3. The CKB is taken as a whole and globally analyzed in interaction with the expert in order to check its consistency.
4. Each relation is analyzed separately and interpreted by the problem-solving methods of the conceptual model. This generates both immediate (obvious) and heuristic knowledge. Depending on the nature of the heuristic knowledge – i.e. the nature of the causal relationships and problem-solving methods which have generated this heuristic knowledge – it may be checked and refined by the expert.

The conceptual model is therefore instantiated on the CKB and the final HKB is built. ACTE has been applied to LÉZARD, a medical diagnostic reasoning system for discriminating between diseases in the domain of acute abdominal pain. We will illustrate various features of ACTE with examples from the knowledge-base of the LÉZARD system [5].

4.2.2 Causal Knowledge Base in ACTE We have seen that CKB modelizes the domain knowledge. This knowledge is pathophysiological and semiological knowledge. Both knowledge are represented in a causal network.

The pathophysiological part of the network is made up of causal and hierarchical relationships between diagnoses. Causal relationships describe the etiology of diagnoses. Hierarchical relationships are tangled taxonomies based on anatomical or pathological considerations. These tangled taxonomies express multiple viewpoints on the same set of diseases. In ACTE we chose both an anatomical description of the diseases – e.g. DIGESTIVE-DISEASE or URINARY-DISEASE – and a description by the process – e.g. ORGANIC-OBSTRUCTION or FUNCTIONAL-OBSTRUCTION.

Semiological knowledge is described by relationships between signs and diagnoses. These signs are symptoms (input-data) or syndromes (abstracted data). Furthermore, the nature of these relationships is twofold: some qualifying conditions which express that a sign must be observed before evoking a disease [15] or some triggering conditions which evoke some hypotheses [32]. Figure 3 gives an illustration of such a knowledge.

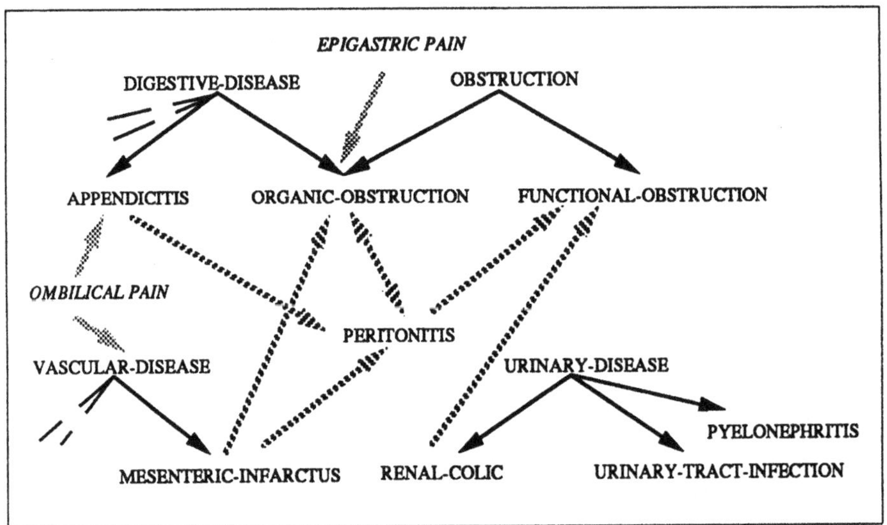

Fig. 3. Causal network representation. Dotted lines represent causal links, Black lines taxonomic links and gray lines evocation links

4.2.3 Using ACTE. ACTE is closely related to a type of conceptual model (a type of heuristic classification applied to medical diagnosis). This domain is characterized by its uncompleteness and uncertainty[4]. Problem solving methods, which are now described, have been influenced by previous works [22, 7, 3, 32]:

- generalizing from specific observations with the "data-abstraction" method;
- focusing on the highest abstraction levels – i.e. trying to decide if the classes of the most widespread diseases are present before deciding on more specific classes;
- using Trigger or necessity signs to evoke hypotheses;
- applying the unique fault process hypothesis – i.e. attempting to create a unique causal chain to explain the observed symptoms.

The last method intervenes, among others, in the validation of CKB. This method is used in several diagnostic systems, and particularly in the medical field [22, 32]. According to this hypothesis, multiple disorders (in medicine, multiple diseases) may occur simultaneously if, and only if, they are connected by causal relations. ACTE's interpretation of the causal network is based on this last hypothesis.

[4] Not all medical domains are characterized by uncompletness and uncertainty – e.g. cardiac pathophysiology which may address "qualitative physic" problematic.

The interpretation algorithm is the *exclusions calculus*. The basic idea is to use the unique fault process in two ways: either to seek diagnoses which may appear in the same causal process or to seek diagnoses which may not appear in the same causal process; a simplified formulation is: "two concepts without causal relationships are exclusive". Practically, the results of this interpretation consist of *mutual-exclusions* – i.e. two concepts of the domain cannot belong to the same solution – as opposed to *mutual-compatibilities*. The reality is Obviously more complex insofar as the causal relationships may be transitive or not: "A may cause B" and "B may cause C" do not imply "A may cause C". These problems of "weak transitivity" have been treated in cognitive science by Johnson-Laird [18] as well as in the AI framework [32, 12]. Our choice is to ask the expert about the plausibility of chains of causally-related events such as A and C. Also, mutual-exclusion or mutual-compatibilities are retained conditional to the transitivity (or non transitivity) attributed by the expert to the successive causal relationships. The benefit of this interpretation is twofold:

- The causal network is validated. For example, the expert may not agree with the result of the system – e.g. a mutual-exclusion relation between two diagnoses – and be led to add new causal relationships to justify its position – e.g. that the two concepts above are compatible.
- The unique fault process hypothesis is operationalized in heuristic knowledge through mutual-exclusions.

The exclusion calculus algorithm is optimized for computing this knowledge at the highest level in the hierarchical representation of the domain concepts [6]. For example, based on the causal network represented in Fig. 3, we have the interaction between the expert and the system described in Fig. 4. Similarly, the other methods of the conceptual model lead to a particular interpretation of each of the relations of the CKB. For example, the CKB may be analyzed in search of new data-abstraction (e.g. gathering of observations) with regard to the diseases they trigger. In an other way, based on the causal network represented in Fig. 3, the hierarchical links are analyzed with regard to their structure to generate immediate (obvious) knowledge – e.g. "FUNCTIONAL-OBSTRUCTION $\Rightarrow$ OBSTRUCTION" – and to propose new heuristic knowledge – e.g. "URINARY-DISEASE $\wedge$ $\neg$RENAL-COLIC $\wedge$ $\neg$URINARY-TRACT-INFECTION $\Rightarrow$ PYELONEPHRITIS".

With reference to the classification of causal models in Sect. 3, the causal model used in ACTE can be qualified as a bottom-up designed causal model, because CKB may well come from existing models directly extracted from medical textbooks. Nevertheless, such a model has been designed for a particular discrimination diagnostic task, with well known signs and diagnoses. Moreover, the CKB is checked during the knowledge KA process. In this way, we can say that the term causal model, in ACTE, mainly refers to a top-down designed causal model.

This illustrates how a causal model, not oriented by the task to be performed, can help to instantiate a conceptual model in order to create an operational and heuristic knowledge base. Further work will be carried out to make the conceptual model in the program more explicit, as for heuristic knowledge. This may prove to be difficult, but the result should enhance the performance and the understanding of the interpretation process – i.e. in making the nature of the knowledge provided

Do you agree with the following mutual-compatibilities:
APPENDICITIS and OBSTRUCTION are compatible (y/n)? y
VASCULAR-DISEASE and FUNCTIONAL-OBSTRUCTION are compatible (y/n)? y
ORGANIC-OBSTRUCTION and FUNCTIONAL-OBSTRUCTION are compatible (y/n)? n
Caution. Refusing this compatibility may question the model or generate an exclusion relationship between the two above diagnoses. (1) You refuse the model, (2) you refuse only the compatibility, (3) you agree with the compatibility (1/2/3)? **2**

Do you agree with the following mutual-exclusions:
DIGESTIVE-DISEASE and URINARY-DISEASE are exclusive (y/n) ? y
VASCULAR-DISEASE and URINARY-DISEASE are exclusive (y/n) ? y
OBSTRUCTION and URINARY-TRACT-INFECTION are exclusive (y/n) ? y
OBSTRUCTION and PYELONEPHRITIS are exclusive (y/n) ? y
RENAL-COLIC and URINARY-TRACT-INFECTION are exclusive (y/n) ? y
URINARY-TRACT-INFECTION and PYELONEPHRITIS are exclusive (y/n) ? n
RENAL-COLIC and PYELONEPHRITIS are exclusive (y/n) ? y
VASCULAR-DISEASE and APPENDICITIS are exclusive (y/n) ? y
ORGANIC-OBSTRUCTION and URINARY-DISEASE are exclusive (y/n) ? y
PERITONITIS and URINARY-DISEASE are exclusive (y/n) ? n

Generated mutual-exclusions :

ORGANIC-OBSTRUCTION and FUNCTIONAL-OBSTRUCTION are exclusive
DIGESTIVE-DISEASE and URINARY-DISEASE are exclusive
VASCULAR-DISEASE and URINARY-DISEASE are exclusive
OBSTRUCTION and URINARY-TRACT-INFECTION are exclusive
OBSTRUCTION and PYELONEPHRITIS are exclusive
RENAL-COLIC and URINARY-TRACT-INFECTION are exclusive
RENAL-COLIC and PYELONEPHRITIS are exclusive
VASCULAR-DISEASE and APPENDICITIS are exclusive
ORGANIC-OBSTRUCTION and URINARY-DISEASE are exclusive

Fig. 4. Interaction between ACTE and the expert about the causal network described in the preceding figure

explicit in terms of the conceptual model – of semiological and pathophysiological relations.

4.3 Comparison between ACTE and ADÈLE

ADÈLE and ACTE are two very similar CMBKATs; in particular their CKB and HKB are the same as regards the nature of the modelized links. Nevertheless some specific differences must be noted.

Firstly, ADÈLE and ACTE do not refer in the same way to the conceptual model of the task being modelized. Neither takes advantage of an explicit representation of the conceptual model (it is one of the forecasted development). ACTE, however, assumes a fixed conceptual model and interprets the causal model in this framework in order to create some, often heuristic, rules, even if the conceptual model is not explicit. Conversely, ADÈLE takes heuristic rules – i.e. a partially instantiated conceptual model – and verifies that these rules are plausible interpretations of a causal model. In this sense, ADÈLE has the potential to be used for a number of different tasks.

Moreover, ACTE works from a causal model towards heuristic rules, while ADÈLE attempts to work in the opposite direction (from heuristic rules towards a causal model). In the former case, an examination of the CKB can help to generate new pieces of heuristic knowledge. In the latter case, the starting point is the heuristic knowledge and CKB is used for various checking procedures. These approaches are complementary: ACTE allows the instantiation of a conceptual model on a domain in order to build a heuristic and operational knowledge base, while ADÈLE enables the validation of chunks of an implicit conceptual model included in new heuristic rules, [4, 11].

Finally, the causal model in ACTE is mainly what we have termed a "top-down designed causal model", while the one in ADÈLE refers to a "bottom-up designed causal model". As we will see in the next section, the latter is more appropriate for validation, while the former is more useful for internal consistency checking or for the extension of the knowledge base over a broader domain area.

4.4 Causal Models in the DIVA experiment

DIVA is an expert system for vibration-based monitoring of turbine-generator. It is currently in an industrialization phase. DIVA is built around an explicit conceptual model. The main task is a classification task of typical situations which represent possible states of the machine. The system tries to identified the situations which account the best for concrete symptoms present on the machine. Te description of the task characterizes the type of knowledge that must be acquired (according to this, a strong protocol has been defined to guide the KA process [12]).

However, during this process that led to the construction of an important knowledge base, it appeared that the experts often provided justifications for the elicited knowledge. Thus, in order to support the KA process, an attempt to gather all justifications in a causal network was made [13].

According to our classification of causal models for KA, the DIVA causal model is clearly a top-down designed causal model. The start point is the heuristic level, and the causal models are derivated from this heuristic level. The Sect. 5 will discuss the problem we were faced on during this experiment.

5 Discussion

Before discussing CMBKAT, let us remember that our discussion on causal models is in the framework of KA. We are not commenting on causal knowledge alone. This is a very broad area, ranging from qualitative physics to causal nets, and a large amount of literature is available.

5.1 Relation to the Conceptual Model

We have seen that neither ADÈLE nor ACTE benefits from an explicit conceptual model (even if ACTE assumes that the task is a kind of heuristic classification).

However, making the underlying conceptual model explicit appears to be a promising path for research. The "knowledge level approach", briefly described in Sect. 3, allows a precise role to be assigned to problem solving for each chunk of acquired knowledge. It can also provide a way of "labelling" the outputs of the various CMBKATs. Viewing KA in terms of "acquiring knowledge for a specific task in a specific conceptual model" has meant that another step forward was necessary, by comparison with "acquire rules" as in the first generation of expert systems. Similarly, ADÈLE and ACTE "acquire rules" and the same step forward can be imagined. In the same way, it may appear interesting to look at how CMBKATs can work together with other, more conventional KA tools performing instantiation of conceptual models (with explicit use).

However, it may become difficult to identify and characterize the nature of the knowledge or comments provided by the CMBKATs in terms of the conceptual model. This is currently being looked into the ADÈLE and ACTE experiments.

Let us now provide a more concrete example of how CMBKATs can deal with an explicit conceptual model. Part of the conceptual model of the DIVA system is a classification task. This classification task requires a set of well identified types of knowledge: knowledge to decide if a specific typical situation accounts for the concrete symptoms gathered on the machine, knowledge to refine a situation that has been recognized, knowledge to "abstract data" to be interpreted, etc. The causal model provide the basis for a global explanation of symptoms. Thus, it is strongly related to the first type of knowledge quoted above (knowledge to decide if a specific typical situation account for the concrete symptoms gathered on the machine). In other words, if the classification is mainly based on a heuristic matching, a causal explanation may help to acquire this heuristic knowledge. In this example, the causal model is of no help for other types of knowledge identified in the conceptual model.

5.2 Dealing with uncertainty

It is widely recognized that reasoning on causal nets is a difficult process. However, in addition to the classical difficulties (often in terms of complexity), causal models for KA are frequently required to deal with uncertainty (especially for top-down designed causal models, more closely related to the heuristic level). Weak causality appears in the form of relations such as "A may cause B under conditions C or D". These conditions can be either explicit (the conditions are explicitly represented) or implicit (e.g. a certainty factor). In the former case, the complexity of the network may increase and render design difficult. In the latter case, classical problems of weak transitivity have to be dealt with (see ACTE, Sect. 4.2). Nevertheless, the need to represent this uncertainty is widely recognized [32]. Using uncertain relations in causal nets has been attempted in several experiments (for example in CHECK [10], in DIVA [13], and in ACTE [5]). With its probabilistic causal networks Long has been tried to determine a global and incrementally solution to the uncertainty management [23].

5.3 What is an accurate Causal Model for KA?

Designing a causal model is a process of KA that comes in addition to the main process that aims at eliciting the HKB. These two processes may be completely separate or inter-related, depending on the type of model (top-down and bottom-up). But for both of them, three properties are expected:

Connection. This property refers to the degree of connection between the CKB and the HKB. Obviously, connection is expected to be strong in order to further improve the KA process.

Consistency. This property refers to the whole causal model itself and its internal consistency. This property is not essential. A CMBKAT can operate on several partial justifications or several competitive networks.

Completeness. This property refers to the knowledge present in the causal model or part of a causal model. A certain kind of completeness is expected (completeness is relative, just like the "deep model" – at least completeness regarding the role the causal model has to play for KA).

These three properties are discussed with the two classes of causal model defined in Sect. 3.

5.3.1 Obtaining Causal Models by a "top-down approach". The first class of causal model for KA identified above is obtained from the "heuristic level" (the knowledge used in the KBS under construction). These causal models are termed "top-down designed causal models". They are mostly the direct justification of the chunks of knowledge already acquired ("why are you telling me that?"). This process of construction has some important consequences in terms of connection, consistency and completeness:

- the connection between the causal model and the heuristic level is easy to produce (one is derived from the other). Connection is "by construction".
- however, it may be difficult to design a coherent and only causal network. Each justification is strongly related to the heuristic level, but there is no reason for the set of justifications to become coherent. This problem has been encountered in the DIVA experiment where it was not easy to connect concepts belonging to a local justification with similar (but slightly distinct) concepts in another local justification. Experimentation has led to the design of several local causal networks, attached to the various diagnosis hypothesis. Therefore, consistency is hard to achieve, but is not essential, and partial models can be used [9].
- the completeness of the network may sometimes appear as a challenge as difficult to meet as the design of the "main knowledge base " (i.e. what we have called the "heuristic level" and which the causal model is supposed to help). This the case in the DIVA experiment, and so the advantages of using causal models need to be reconsidered in the light of the costs involved in designing such models.

5.3.2 Obtaining Causal Models by a "bottom-up approach". Bottom-up causal models are designed (or are pre-existing) independently of the heuristic level. This is typically the case for causal models obtained from tutorial manuals (for instance medical treatises) or resulting from material design. In this case, connection becomes a major problem. This is illustrated by ADÈLE. A connection step, following the selection of pre-existing causal models, aims to connect the HKB with the CKB.

The process of designing the two levels is quite separate from the initial stages. It is not surprising that connection does not always come naturally.

As opposed to top-down designed causal models, consistency and completeness are often a major pre-requisite of such pre-existing causal models, especially when they are also correct behavior models. This remark must be relativized with fault models which are partial by nature. Therefore, in ADÈLE for example, the approach suffers from the incompleteness of the CKB. Incompleteness of CKB is shown when some piece of heuristic knowledge cannot be or is only partially justified. In this case, CKB must be increased with new, more appropriate causal models. ADÈLE does not help to add this knowledge, but it does allow the user to localize the missing knowledge. The notion of consistency can be illustrated by the "top-down" designed causal models of ACTE. At the beginning of the KA process they may not be consistent, but the approach helps the expert to create consistency.

5.4 Advantages of Causal Models

Firstly, CKB and HKB are two modelizations of the same domain, at different levels of abstraction (CKB is "deep" with regard to heuristic knowledge). Thus, CMBKATs provide the opportunity to build KBS in a more consistent and complete way by having a separate specification of the problem. In particular, causal models can be useful for the validation and consistency of the HKB. As we have seen, for validation purposes, a "bottom-up designed causal model" is certainly better suited, while consistency is more easily attainable using a "top-down designed causal model". This is what we have observed on the ADÈLE and ACTE experiments. This is not really surprising, since validation requires an independent reference, and "bottom-up designed causal models" have this property; consistency, on the other hand, requires a strong connection between the HKB and the CKB, and "top-down designed causal models" have this property from their construction.

Secondly, CKB contains knowledge which is supposed to be more readily available. In this way, acquisition of CKB is assumed to be easier than acquisition of HKB (even if the DIVA experiment proves the contrary), and this is one of the expected advantages of using a causal model for KA.

Finally, CKB is a KA support, but it can also be very useful for other tasks. Justifications can be used for explanation [31], and also for the operational system itself, covering atypical problems the HKB is unable to solve.

6 Conclusion

This paper is the result of a recent comparison of several experiments on the use of causal models for KA. We have tried to place the various CMBKATs in the paradigm of "task and method specific tools". We have outlined the fact that they do not generally use explicit reference to any underlying conceptual model. We have noted how such a relation might be a promising path of research. In particular, we think that it will be of great help to study how a set of tools can be integrated or can collaborate in the same KA workbench. Further work should be done in this direction.

We have also identified two different types of CMBKAT. Of course, such a classification is not strict, and very often tools can be either "top-down designed" or "bottom-up designed". However, we have also noted how the former are more appropriate for checking "internal consistency", and how the latter are better suited for validation. We have also seen some of the properties that such tools may have. Connection, consistency and completeness have been identified with the two classes of tools.

References

1. Nathalie Aussenac, Jean-Paul Krivine, and Jean Sallantin. Introduction to the special issue on knowledge acquisition. *Revue d'Intelligence Artificielle*, 1992. *(To appear)*.
2. Joost A. Breuker and Bob J. Wielinga. Models of expertise in knowledge acquisition. In G. Guida and C. Tasso, editors, *Topics in Expert System Design: Methodologies and Tools*. North Holland Publishing Company, The Netherlands, 1989.
3. B. Chandrasekaran. Towards a functional architecture for intelligence based on generic information processing tasks. In *Proceedings of the 10 th International Joint Conference on Artificial Intelligence*, pages 1183–1192, Milan, Italy, 1987.
4. Jean Charlet. ACTE: a strategic knowledge acquisition method. In *Proceedings of the 5 th European Workshop on Knowledge Acquisition for Knowledge-Based Systems*, Glasgow, UK, 1991. Springer Verlag. *(To appear)*.
5. Jean Charlet. ACTE: une méthode d'acquisition des connaissances pour un système de diagnostic. *Revue d'Intelligence Artificielle*, 1992. *(To appear)*.
6. Jean Charlet and Olivier Gascuel. Knowledge acquisition by causal model and meta-knowledge. In John H. Boose, Brian R. Gaines, and Jean G. ganascia, editors, *Proceedings of the 3 th European Workshop on Knowledge Acquisition for Knowledge-Based Systems*, pages 212–225, Paris, France, July 1989.
7. W. J. Clancey. Heuristic Classification. *Artificial Intelligence*, 27(3):289–350, 1985.
8. Luca Console, Mauro Fossa, and Pietro Torasso. Acquisition of causal knowledge in the CHECK system. *Computers and Artificial Intelligence*, 8(4):323–345, 1989.
9. Luca Console and Pietro Torasso. A logical approach to deal with incomplete causal models in diagnostic problem solving. In *Lecture Notes in Computer Science, 313*. Springer-Verlag, 1988.
10. Luca Console and Pietro Torasso. Hypothetical reasoning in causal models. *International Journal of Intelligent Systems*, 5, 1990.
11. Marie-Odile Cordier and Chantal Reynaud. Knowledge acquisition techniques and second generation expert systems. *Applied Artificial Intelligence*, 5(3):209–226, 1991.
12. Jean-Marc David and Jean-Paul Krivine. Augmenting experience-based diagnosis with causal reasoning. *Applied Artificial Intelligence*, 3(2-3):239–248, 1989.
13. Jean-Marc David and Jean-Paul Krivine. Designing knowledge-based systems within functional architecture: the DIVA experiment. In *Proceedings of the 5 th IEEE Conference on Artificial Intelligence Applications*, Miami, Florida, USA, March 1989.
14. Randall Davis. Form and content in model based reasoning. In *Proceedings of the IJCAI workshop on Model-Based reasoning*, 1989.
15. Larry Eshelman. MOLE: a knowledge acquisition tool for cover-and-differentiate systems. In Sandra Marcus, editor, *Automating Knowledge Acquisition for Expert Systems*. Kluwer Academic Publishers, 1988.
16. Thomas Gruber. Learning why by being told what. *IEEE-Expert*, pages 65–75, 1991.

17. Franck R. Hickman, Jonathan L. Killin, Lise Land, Tim Mulhall, David Porter, and Robert M. Taylor. *Analysis for Knowledge-Based Systems, a Practical Guide to the KADS Methodology*. Ellis Horwood, 1989.
18. P. N. Johnson-Laird. Mental models in cognitive science. *Cognitive Science*, 4:71–115, 1980.
19. Garry Kahn, S. Nowlan, and John McDermott. MORE: an intelligent knowledge acquisition tool. In A. Joshi, editor, *Proceedings of the 9 th International Joint Conference on Artificial Intelligence*, pages 581–585, Los Angeles, CA, August 18–23 1985. M. Kaufmann, Inc.
20. Werner Karbach, Marc Linster, and Angi Voss. Models, methods, roles and tasks: many labels – one idea? *Knowledge Acquisition*, 2:279–299, 1990.
21. Werner Karbach, Angi Voss, Ralf Schuckey, and Uwe Drouven. Model-K: Prototyping at the knowledge level. In D. Herin-Aimé, R. Dieng, J.-P. Regouard, and J.P. Angoujard, editors, *Proceedings of the 1 st conference on Knowledge Modeling & Expertise Transfer*, pages 195–208. IOS Press, 1991.
22. W. Long, S. Naimi, M. G. Criscitiello, S. G. Pauker, and P. Szolovits. An aid to physiological reasoning in the management of cardiovascular disease. In *Proceedings of the Computers in Cardiology Conference*, 1984.
23. William Long. Medical diagnosis using a probabilistic causal network. *Applied Artificial Intelligence*, 3(2-3):367–383, 1989.
24. Sandra Marcus and John McDermott. SALT: a knowledge acquisition language for propose-and-revise systems. *Artificial Intelligence*, 39(1):1–37, 1989.
25. John McDermott. Preliminary steps towards a taxonomy of problem-solving methods. In Sandra Marcus, editor, *Automating Knowledge Acquisition for Expert Systems*. Kluwer Academic Publishers, 1988.
26. Enrico Motta, Tim Rajan, and Marc Eisenstadt. Knowledge acquisition as a process of model refinement. *Knowledge Acquisition*, 2:21–49, 1990.
27. Mark A. Musen. Conceptual models of interactive knowledge acquisition tools. *Knowledge Acquisition*, 1:73–88, 1989.
28. R. Neches, W.R. Swartout, and J. Moore. Explainable (and maintainable) expert systems. In A. Joshi, editor, *Proceedings of the 9 th International Joint Conference on Artificial Intelligence*, pages 382–389, Los Angeles, CA, August 18–23 1985. M. Kaufmann, Inc.
29. M. Reinders, E. Vinkhuyzen, A. Voss, H. Akkermans, J. Balder, B. Bartsch-Spörl, B. Bredeweg, U. Drouven, F. van Harmelen, W. Karbach, Z. Karssen, G. Schreiber, and B. Wielinga. A conceptual modelling framework for knowledge-level reflection. *AI Communications*, 4(2/3), 1991.
30. Jon Sticklen, B. Chandrasekaran, and W. E. Bond. Distributed causal reasoning for knowledge acquisition: A functional approach to device understanding. In *Proceedings of the 3 rd Banff Workshop for Knowledge Acquisition*, Banff, Canada, 1988. (revised version: *Applied AI* 3(2-3):275–304,1989).
31. W.R. Swartout. Xplain: A system for creating and explaining expert consulting programs. *Artificial Intelligence*, 21(3):285–325, 1983.
32. P. Szolovits, Ramesh S. Patil, and W. B. Schwartz. Artificial intelligence in medical diagnostic. *Annals of Internal Medicine*, 108:80–87, 1988.
33. B. J. Wielinga and J. A. Breuker. KADS: Structured knowledge acquisition for expert systems. In *Proceedings of the 5 th International Workshop Expert Systems & their Applications*, Avignon, France, 1985. Gerfau.

This article was processed using the LaTeX macro package with LLNCS style

Knowledge Base Maintenance and Consistency Checking in MOLTKE/HyDi

Frank Maurer

Dept. of Computer Science, University of Kaiserslautern
P.O. Box 3049, D-6750 Kaiserslautern, Germany
e-Mail: maurer@informatik.uni-kl.de

Abstract. This paper deals with special problems of knowledge base maintenance which have to be solved within the knowledge acquisition process. We illustrate that aspects of maintenance must be taken into account by the design model construction because dependencies between pieces of knowledge can result in inconsistent states of a knowledge base. We describe a *Knowledge Dependency Network* which extends ideas from truth maintenance systems to detect and manage these inconsistencies. The network allows formal definitions of inconsistency conditions and checks them automatically preserving the integrity of the knowledge base. As a fundamental part of the acquisition and maintenance environment the knowledge dependency network supports the conventional development and editing of a knowledge base.

1 Overview

This paper deals with aspects of knowledge acquisition, knowledge base maintenance and consistency checking. Our experience in expert system projects showed that aspects of knowledge maintenance must be considered while constructing the design model of the domain. After defining appropriate knowledge structures, there are often troubles with inconsistencies in the knowledge base because of dependencies between knowledge objects. Often only the co-existence of a few objects results in an inconsistent state.

Our general approach to knowledge acquisition and maintenance is described in chapter 2. We illustrate the approach by following the development of the MOLTKE shell for technical expert systems. In paragraph 2.1 we introduce the basic representation language for which an interpreter is presented in 2.2. Then we present our general approach to knowledge maintenance (2.3). We define the knowledge dependency network (2.4) and the concept of graph consistency (2.5). The network enables the knowledge engineer to specify conditions of consistency for knowledge bases. It manages the dependencies of knowledge objects and automatically maintains the consistency of a knowledge base. The network is an extension and a new application of the ideas of truth maintenance systems [8, 9]. The resulting maintenance component supports the user while inserting and deleting objects preserving the consistency of the knowledge base. Paragraph 2.6 gives some complexity estimations. Chapter 3 of this paper presents an overview on the other parts of the MOLTKE workbench for technical diagnosis. The workbench is a complex, fully implemented expert system toolbox which integrates several second generation expert system techniques. In chapter 4 we discuss results and compare our approach with related work. Chapter 5 gives an overview on our ongoing work and the state of realization. An example is given in the appendix.

2 Requirements of Knowledge Acquisition and Maintenance

In general the building of experts systems consists of two main parts. First, a model of the domain has to be constructed. The expert(s) and the knowledge engineer usually work together in this phase. This model is implemented on a computer by the knowledge engineer who usually has a background in computer science and artificial intelligence. The second part includes the filling of the model with the expert´s knowledge. Ideally, the domain expert himself fills the knowledge base because:

- only he can guarantee for the correctness of the system,
- he is able to test whether the system acts appropriately,
- he often has to maintain the knowledge base (in fact: he is the only person who can decide whether the represented knowledge has to be changed).

A problem is that experts usually do *not* have any background knowledge concerning expert systems. Therefore, the representation formalism must reflect the experts own terminology. This observation was our reason to develop the design model for technical diagnosis described in 2.1 and 2.2.

To summarize the above mentioned one can say that if the representation formalism uses the terminology of the domain, the understanding of the knowledge base and the process of inference is simplified for the expert. Therefore, maintenance is made easier. At least, the testing and debugging of the knowledge base may be better supported by the expert then.

Furthermore, a development tool has to support the editing and maintenance of the knowledge base, especially if used by a domain expert who is normally not used to work with computer systems. A knowledge maintenance component has to include facilities which easily allow to create and test knowledge bases. It has to satisfy the following requirements:

- incremental input of the knowledge in an *user-determined* order (this is the natural way of editing a knowledge base for an expert),
- managing the changes which follow an insertion or deletion of an object,
- showing dependencies of the represented pieces of knowledge,
- showing the effects of changes in the knowledge base (often the overview is lost if much knowledge is represented),
- checking the syntactic correctness and the semantic consistency (see 2.4) of the knowledge base.

Watching the knowledge acquisition process we find several steps which possibly must be repeated. At first we construct a conceptual and a design model of the domain (cf. also KADS [6, 21]) which collect all relevant concepts of the domain (within the MOLTKE project for diagnosis we developed the representation language described below)[1]. The model does not include all facts of the domain. It is only a frame which will be filled in a later step. But it is immediately refined to the implementation level.

Extending the KADS framework we now ask for dependencies between the relevant aspects of the domain and for inconsistency conditions (chapter 4 includes a discussion of

---

[1] These steps will be supported by our hypermedia-based knowledge engineering environment HyperCAKE which is briefly described in chapter 5.

the use of a truth maintenance system for managing the dependencies). The next step is to implement a domain-dependent acquisition interface which is used to fill the knowledge base. Thereby the consistency of the entered knowledge is automatically preserved by the knowledge dependency network described below.

We now illustrate the knowledge acquisition process described above by tracing the development of the MOLTKE shell for technical diagnosis, with a special focus on the knowledge base maintenance component.

2.1 Basic Definitions

In the MOLTKE project we developed a design model for technical diagnosis. We believe that diagnosis can be described as follows:

Diagnosis = Classification + Test Selection.

A knowledge base represents the knowledge about the technical system divided into these two parts. Now we describe the basic vocabulary:

A *symptom class* relates a name to a list of possible values, its *type*, (e.g.Valve --> {open, closed}) whereas *symptom instances* reflect the actual state of a part of the technical device (e.g. Valve 21Y5 --> open). The actual value may be either *unknown* or an element of the list of possible values in the corresponding class.

The set of all symptom instances is called a *situation*. Within the context of predicate calculus the actual situation is the base for the interpretation of a *language of formulas*. It stores the variable bindings (every symptom instance is a variable in the calculus). For the evaluation of formulas we use a three-valued logic with *true*, *false* and *unknown*.

A *test* ascertains the value of one or more symptom instances. Usually, a test asks the user for the value of the symptom instance. The sequence of testing is determined by a set of ordering rules where the left hand side is a formula and the right part contains the symptom instance to test (e.g. (if (= Valve 21Y5 open) then relais test)).

To express relations between symptom values *shortcut rules* are used (e.g. (if (= light room-1 on) then wires := working)).

Contexts are one of the means for modularization in MOLTKE. A context represents a rough, intermediate, or final diagnosis. If its precondition is true, the associated failure is said to be proven and the related *correction* is executed. Any context contains a set of ordering rules which locally prescribe the strategy of testing. Additionally, a context includes a set of shortcut rules. A correction describes what has to be done when a special fault occurs. For example, a context (without rules) is defined by the following statement:

```
Context  name: LIGHT-BULB
         precondition: (SWITCH = CLOSED) & (LIGHT = OUT)
         correction: "Change the light-bulb"
```

The contexts are organized in a *context graph*. Its arcs have the semantics "is-refinement-of" (e.g. the context *failure-in-electric* is a refinement of *failure-in-car*.).

2.2 The Interpreter

A global interpreter, which is easy to adapt and to maintain because it is organized in small modules, processes the knowledge base. The interpreter uses an establish-and-refine strategy.

The diagnostic process goes through the context graph by testing symptoms according to the ordering rules of the actual context and switching to a refinement when its precondition becomes (the logical value) true. If a leaf of the context graph is reached the system prints the diagnosis and terminates.

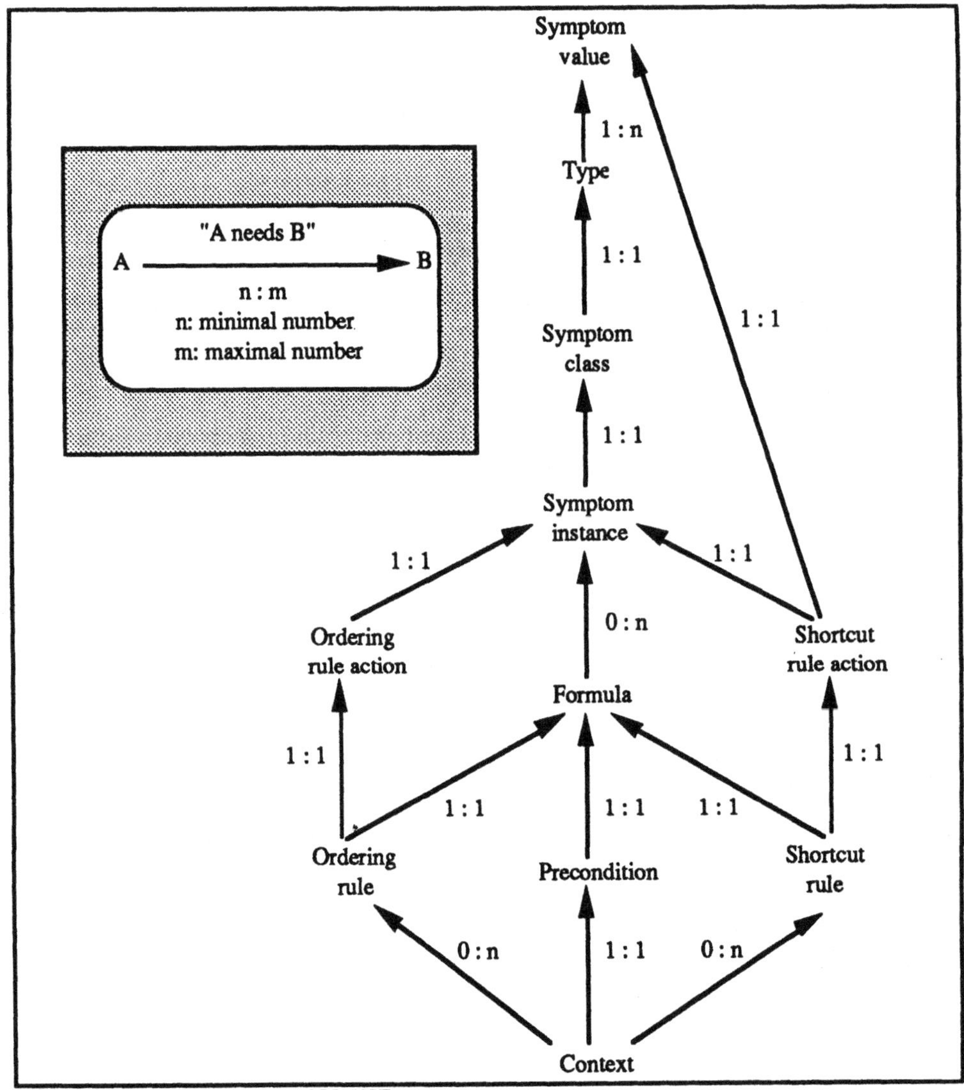

Fig. 2.1. Dependencies of MOLTKE objects

2.3 Knowledge Maintenance in MOLTKE

After developing the basic representation language and implementing the appropriate parsers for the domain-dependent acquisition interface we asked our engineers for the dependencies of the defined structures. The answers are shown in figure 2.1.

Extending the acquisition interface which uses the parsers for checking the syntactic correctness of a knowledge base we built the MOLTKE maintenance component[2] which checks two further aspects of consistency:

- node consistency: a piece of knowledge is used in the inference process only if all referred objects are correctly defined
- graph consistency: the knowledge base must not contain redundancies and contradictions

In the following paragraphs we illustrate these concepts of consistency.

2.4 Knowledge Dependency Network

To ensure the integrity of a knowledge base we build up a knowledge dependency network, which supervises dependencies between knowledge chunks.

For each kind of knowledge objects (e.g. in MOLTKE types, rules, contexts, etc.) a node class is defined which is used as a pattern for the definition of instances for the knowledge base. Figure 2.2 shows two examples for node class definitions.

```
(1)   Symptom-Instance-Node
          needs: (Symptom-Class-Node(1:1))
          needed-by: ()
          is-a-source: ()
(2)   Context-Node
          needs:        (Precondition-Node(1:1)
                 Shortcut-Rule-Nodes(0:n)
                 Ordering-Rule-Nodes(0:n)....)
          needed-by: ()
          is-a-source: ()
```

Fig. 2.2. Node class definitions of the knowledge dependency network for MOLTKE objects

Instances of these classes are used to represent all knowledge objects defined by the user. But only "correct" objects (e. g. objects which are consistent with the rest) will be inserted into the knowledge base. E. g., example (1) in figure 2.2 states that a symptom instance node is only correctly defined if the needed symptom class was inserted into the knowledge base before.

The instances are the nodes of the knowledge dependency network. For each node exists an unambigous identifier, usually the name of the corresponding knowledge object. Arcs represent three different relations: needs, needed-by, and is-a-source. The needs-relation expresses the necessary preconditions for a correct object. The creator of a node is referred to by the is-a-source-relation. The needed-by-relation shows where a node is used.

Each node instance stores three lists (needs-, needed-by- and is-a-source-list) which contain

---

2 Actually, the maintenance component is only implemented for HyDi, the successor of the MOLTKE system.

the anchors of the above described relations[3]. These lists are filled by the insertion of new nodes into the network (see below).

The knowledge dependency network separates the knowledge base from the developer of the expert system (see figure 2.3). It stores all syntactically correct object definitions. But objects are only inserted into the knowledge base if their definition is consistent with the rest of the knowledge base. Only objects in the knowledge base are used in the inference process. In fact the network supervises the non-monotonic process of filling a knowledge base[4]. Additionally, an agenda stores objects which are needed but not defined. Entries in the agenda contain the name of the needed object, its type and the node where it is referred.

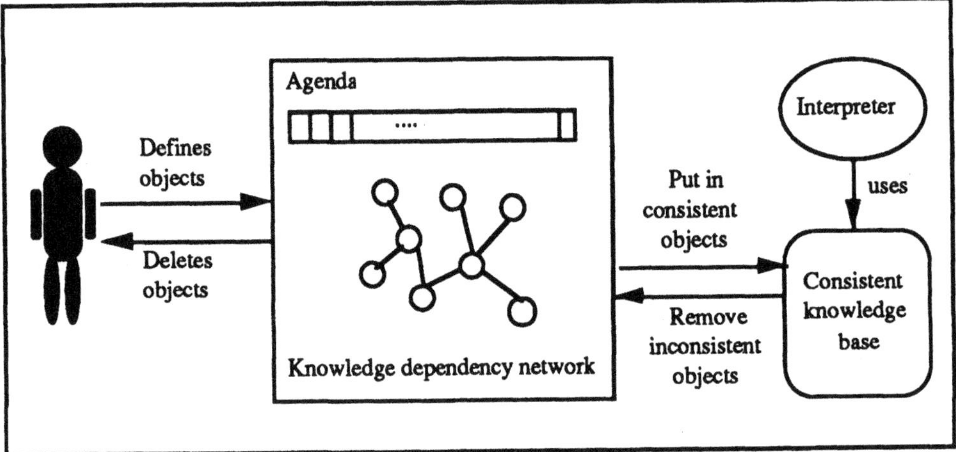

Fig. 2.3. Separating the expert from the knowledge base

The approach of knowledge dependency networks may always be used in domain-dependent models because we also found the defined relations when we talked with our experts in construction and planning domains. Also, the algorithms for the creation and deletion of new knowledge objects are general and not domain specific. They do not use references to the special kind of objects used in diagnosis.

Defining new Knowledge Objects. If the user wants to create a new object for the knowledge base the system first checks the syntax of the definition. Then all entries of the needs-list must be filled with an object corresponding to the type used in the node class (e.g. a symptom-instance-node needs a symptom-class-node as the corresponding anchor).

If all referred objects are already included in the knowledge base, the new object will also be put in. Otherwise the user is informed and the needed anchors are put on the agenda of objects which must be defined in the future. In this case the new object is not put into the knowledge base (preserving its consistency). This feature allows the user to define new pieces of knowledge in whatever order he wants and, nevertheless, only consistent

---

3 For the relation *rel(A,B)* we define object *B* as the anchor of object *A* and the other way round.

4 Inserting or deleting an object may result in an inconsistent state of the knowledge base. Conclusions drawn from a prior state may then be faulty. In fact, dependencies of objects may be viewed also as inferences (e.g. from the existence of one object the system may infere that another object has to exist, too).

knowledge bases are used for inference. If all nodes are completely anchored we call the network *node consistent* .

A node consistent state may also be reached by a given order of definitions, which means that an object may only be defined if all needed objects are already existing. The knowledge dependency network supports the construction of a knowledge base because the developer is not unnecessarily restricted.

Then the is-a-source-list is filled with the origin of the object. Usually, the source is the expert who edits the knowledge base. The is-a-source-list is used if an object shall be deleted. Only the creator of an object may remove it.

At the end of an object's insertion into the knowledge dependency network the system checks if it is already needed in another node (which means that a reference is included in the agenda). If so, the needs- and needed-by-lists of the two objects are updated. Possibly, the other object is now node consistent. Then it will be put into the knowledge base and its needed-by-list is checked for other nodes which may change into a consistent state. Figure 2.4 shows the algorithm for inserting a new node into the network[5].

1.	Parse the definition of the new object generating a list of all referenced node instances
1.1.	Parsing ok: Mark the new node as consistent
1.2.	else: reject the new definition
2.	**For all** needs-relations of the class corresponding to the new node instance **do**
2.1.	Check if the referenced object is still in the network
2.1.1.	**If true:** Create the needs- and needed-by-relations between the two nodes;
2.1.2.	**If false:** Enter the referenced node into the agenda and mark the new node as inconsistent;
3.	**If** the new node is consistent **then** it is put into the knowledge base;
4.	Store the source(s);
5	**For all** references to the new node in the agenda **do**
5.1.	Create the needs- and needed-by-relations between the two nodes;
5.2.	**If** the object from the agenda is consistent **then** put it into the knowledge base (then all dependent objects must also be checked for consistency and possibly are entered into knowledge base);

Fig. 2.4. The algorithm for inserting of a new node into the knowledge dependency network

Deleting Knowledge Objects. While the need-list stores the essential preconditions of an object and is filled by insertion, checking the pattern of the node class, the dependent objects are included in the needed-by-list which helps the developer to delete objects.

If an object is removed by the user the system checks if it is referred to anywhere. If so, the user is informed about this fact and may decide if he really wants to delete the object. As a result of a following deletion the dependent objects are marked as inconsistent and removed from the knowledge base. Figure 2.5 shows the algorithm for deleting a node.

5 See appendix for a detailed example.

1.	**For all** objects stored in the needs-list **do**
1.2.	Remove the needs- and needed-by-relation between the two objects;
2..	**If** the node was consistent **then** remove it from the knowledge base;
3	**For all** objects *o* stored in the needed-by-list **do**
3.1.	Remove the needs- and needed-by-relation between the two objects;
3.2.	Generate an entry in the agenda that the deleted node is referenced;
3.3.	"object *o* is inconsistent" remove o from the knowledge base (then all dependent objects also must be marked and removed)

Fig. 2.5. The algorithm for deleting a node from the knowledge dependency network

2.5 Graph Consistency of a Knowledge Base

A node consistent network includes locally correct nodes, which means that all their preconditions are fulfilled. Additionally, the integrity of a knowledge base must also be guaranteed for relations between more than two objects. The system must prevent that the combination of several objects results in an inconsistent state where the concept "Inconsistency" may only be defined according to the domain. A MOLTKE knowledge base for diagnosis must not contain for example

1. types with different names and same values,
2. symptom classes with the same type,
3. shortcut rules with the same precondition and different values for the same symptom instance on the right hand sides,
4. more than one context with the same precondition.

Based on the knowledge dependency network these conditions may be checked by a matching of subgraphs. This fits into our perspective of knowledge engineering which is strongly influenced by object-oriented analysis and object-oriented design. Therefore, our approach is a little bit different from more logic-based validation techniques.

Figure 2.6 shows the structure of inconsistent subgraphs corresponding to the above conditions. Our default assumption is that all graphs which do not contain inconsistency subgraphs represent consistent states of a knowledge base. A knowledge dependency network which does not contain *inconsistency graphs* is called *graph consistent.*

While developing a design model of the domain we also acquire knowledge about inconsistencies and define the appropriate inconsistency subgraphs for the network. When a new node enters the network, the system, after having checked for node consistency, tests via graph matching if the network stays graph consistent. Otherwise, the user is informed and has to resolve the inconsistency.

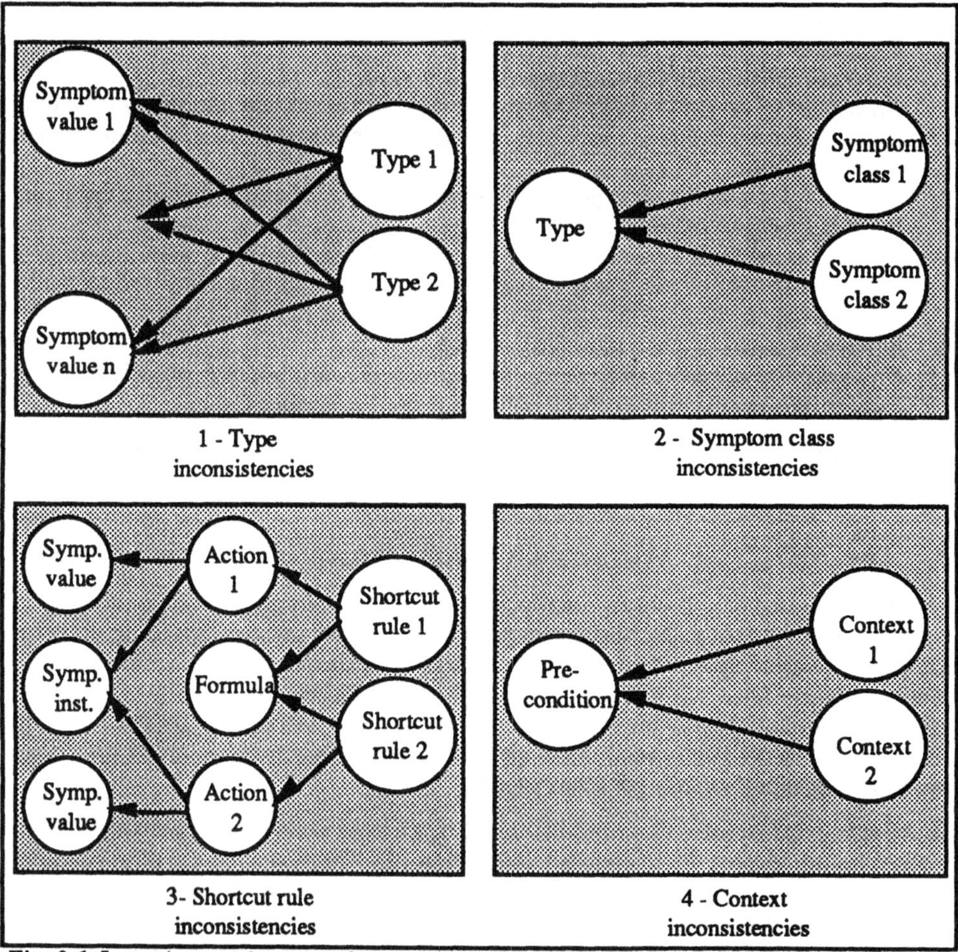

Fig. 2.6. Inconsistent subgraphs of a knowledge dependency network for MOLTKE KBs

2.6 Complexity Estimations

The time needed for node insertion depends on the number n of entries into the needs-list, the size of the agenda a and the number of objects o which are dependent from the new object. Thus, inserting a new node needs at most $O(n*a+o*a) = O(a*(n+o))$ steps. The algorithm for deleting a node needs $O(n+o)$ steps.

In our applications these estimations result in small numbers. E. g. in our CNC machining center domain (cf. [19]) both, n and o, are smaller than 10. Checking graph consistency appears to be more problematic because it is reduced to graph matching. It is known that graph matching in general takes an exponential number of steps. In MOLTKE knowledge bases this effort is in fact drastically reduced because we first take advantage of having typed nodes. Therefore, not all nodes need to be used as a starting point for a check. Second, the subgraphs are not very complex.

For the inconsistency graphs described above we have the following upper limits:

1. types with different names and same values:
   *O(|number of types| * |maximal size of types|)*
2. symptom classes with the same type:
   O(|number of needed-by-relations of the type|), because when inserting a symptom class the system needs to check only for the referenced type if it is used in another symptom class
3. shortcut rules with the same precondition and different values for the same symptom instance on right hand sides
   O(|number of needed-by-relations of the precondition|), because when inserting a shortcut rule the system needs to check only if it is used in another shortcut rule with a different value for the same symptom instance on right hand side
4. different contexts with the same precondition
   O(|number of needed-by-relations of the precondition|), because when inserting a context the system needs to check only if it is used in another context.

All in all we have a tolerable[6] time complexity for consistency checking of MOLTKE knowledge bases.

3 The MOLTKE Workbench for Technical Diagnosis

The work reported here is only a small part of the MOLTKE project. Within this project we developed the above described conceptual model (in the sense of KADS [6, 21]) for diagnostic expert systems in technical domains. This model was refined to the implementation level via a design model. Then we added qualitative reasoning and machine learning techniques to the model. A detailed description of the resulting MOLTKE workbench is beyond the scope of this paper. Therefore, we only give a brief overview and refer to already published papers.

In addition to the facilities described in this paper, we use second generation expert system technology to support the knowledge acquisition [2]. These include a model compiler which generates the core of a knowledge base out of a deep model of the technical system [16, 17]. This basic expert system is improved and extended by machine learning methods. We implemented a case-based reasoning system which supports the diagnostic process [4, 22]. [3] and [1] describe a system which learns relations between symptom patterns and the work of [12] covers a system which learns diagnostic strategies based on neural network methods. The representation of temporal knowledge in the MOLTKE system is subject of [15].

4 Discussion and Related Work

The MOLTKE workbench was developed in cooperation with the WZL, a mechanical engineering institute at the technical university of Aachen, following a pragmatic approach. Because of the integration of several advanced expert system techniques, the workbench contributes to the state of art in knowledge acquisition (following, e. g., the requirements of [20]).

In this paper we described the maintenance component which supports the elicitation and coding of the knowledge by a knowledge dependency network. The network is especially

---

6 Tolerable means that an interactive development of the knowledge base is possible.

helpful if

- several persons work together to build the knowledge base,
- the knowledge base is filled directly by the domain expert.

The network meets the above stated requirements on a maintenance component. Based on the network, we are developing an interface which shows the effects of changes in the knowledge base. The network shows and supervises the dependencies of the pieces of knowledge and allows the user to define objects in an arbitrary order. Additionally, it checks the represented knowledge for inconsistencies. Therefore, it supports the construction of a knowledge base, especially if the builder of the domain model is different from the one who has to fill it.

Seeking in knowledge acquisition literature we find many contributions which are concerned with the more or less automatic acquisition of the domain models itself (e.g. [13, 21]. We agree with the KADS group that a methodology for knowledge acquisition exists. We extend their approach by emphasizing aspects of maintenance which are very important if the expert system is supposed to live for a longer period of time.

The MOLTKE workbench can be used at least for every technical system of a similar complexity as a CNC machining center, which was our first application[7]. So we followed a more generic approach than [14].

Our approach based on the knowledge dependency network is to fill and maintain a given domain model preserving formally defined consistency conditions. Scanning knowledge acquisition literature we did not find many papers on knowledge dependency supervising and consistency checking. Comparing our maintenance component with the approach of [10] we find two main differences. First, we use dependencies between pieces of knowledge for consistency checking, they mainly build cross references (which is only the first step of our approach). Second, they want to integrate different general representation formalisms (e.g. production rules, semantic nets, frames, etc.) whereas we want to ease the development of a knowledge base within a domain-dependent representation.

Supervising dependencies and backtracking to consistent states is the subject of truth maintenance systems (ATMS [8], TMS [9]). Usually, truth maintenance systems are used within one (dynamic) inference process. We need it for preserving a consistent state of a (static) knowledge base. Thus, our system would be at least a new application of TMS.

Although we took a lot of inspirations from TMS approaches, we had to extend them. We have to deal with consistent and inconsistent states of the knowledge base. A currently inconsistent state may be consistent in the next step and then again become inconsistent (e.g the user defines an object, removes it and then redefines it). This swapping between consistency and inconsistency is not well handled by truth maintenance systems. Furthermore, a TMS does not find the inconsistencies. It is externally told that the actual state is inconsistent and then backs up to a consistent state. We need a system where we can define what is inconsistent and which then checks this by itself. Therefore, we developed the knowledge dependency network.

A problem in the discussion of the MOLTKE workbench is that it consists of several complex components which deal with different topics from the field of expert systems

---

7 Additionally, we implemented an expert system for fault diagnosis in heterogenous computer networks.

(e.g. deep modelling, qualitative reasoning, representation, acquisition, machine learning, knowledge maintenance and compilation). The integration of the components is an advantage over any stand-alone solution (in the sense of: "The whole is more than the sum of its parts"). But this advantage cannot be presented successfully within one paper dealing with special aspects of the whole system.

5 State of Realization and Ongoing Work

The MOLTKE base system for diagnosis (i.e. the above described representation formalism) is fully implemented in Smalltalk-80. Its graphic-oriented acquisition interface uses different parsers for checking the syntactic correctness of an object definition. The deep modelling and machine learning facilities are implemented, too.

Based on our experience we are developing a hypermedia-based knowledge engineering environment (called CAKE or HyperCAKE) which supports the knowledge acquisition process [11]. The maintenance network will be integrated in this environment to support multiple experts and multiple knowledge engineers working together to build an expert system. It will support the process of model construction by allowing a smooth transition from informal (data level) descriptions via a semi-formal conceptual model to formal design models.

The HyperCAKE system uses the hypertext abstract machine (HAM) for storing and retrieving information (following the ideas of [7]). We extend the HAM by facilities for typing nodes, links and contexts. Additionally, we integrate a rule interpreter into the hypertext machine.

We finished the implementation of the HAM and the integrated rule interpreter. The implementation of the maintenance component (which includes the described knowledge dependency network and consistency checkers) will be finished this summer.

We are re-implementing the MOLTKE shell based on the HyperCAKE system until the october 1992. The resulting system is called HyDi (Hypermedia-based Diagnostic Expert System).

6 Acknowledgements

I would like to thank the research group of Prof. Richter for the excellent working climate. Especially, I want to thank Prof. Richter for a lot of advices on this paper and Klaus Althoff, Alvaro de la Ossa, Hans Lamberti, Erica Melis, Scarlet Nökel, Jürgen Paulokat, Reinhard Praeger, Robert Rehbold, Mike Stadler and Holger Wache for discussing preliminary versions of this paper written in a really ugly English. Last but not least I would like to say a big "thank you" to Claudia Dell for the time she spent in maintaining me when I was writing this paper on knowledge base maintenance.

Appendix

In the following we give an example how the editing of a knowledge base is supported by a knowledge dependency network. First, we define the node classes. For checking graph consistency the inconsistent subgraphs of figure 2.6 are used. Last, we define a few objects and show how the knowledge dependency network developes. The description of the needed parsers is left out.

Node class definitions:

Type-Node needs: ()
Symptom-Class-Node needs: (Type-Node (1:1))
Symptom-Instance-Node needs: (Symptom-Class-Node (1:1))

Defining objects for the knowledge base:
Step 1: Symptom-Instance new_with_name: SWITCH-1 for_class: SWITCH
What happens? A symptom instance node is put in the empty knowledge dependency network and marked as inconsistent. An entry for the needed symptom class is put into the agenda.

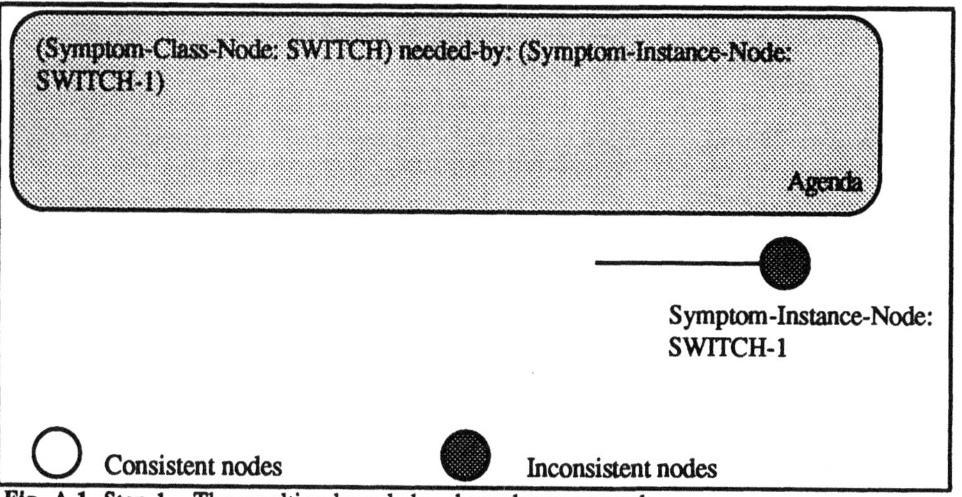

Fig. A.1. Step 1 - The resulting knowledge dependency network

Step 2: Symptom-Class new_with_name: SWITCH with_Type: SWITCH-TYPE
What happens? A symptom class node is put in the knowledge dependency network and marked as inconsistent. An entry for the needed type is put into the agenda. Then the system finds out that the new node is already referenced in the agenda and the appropriate connections are established.

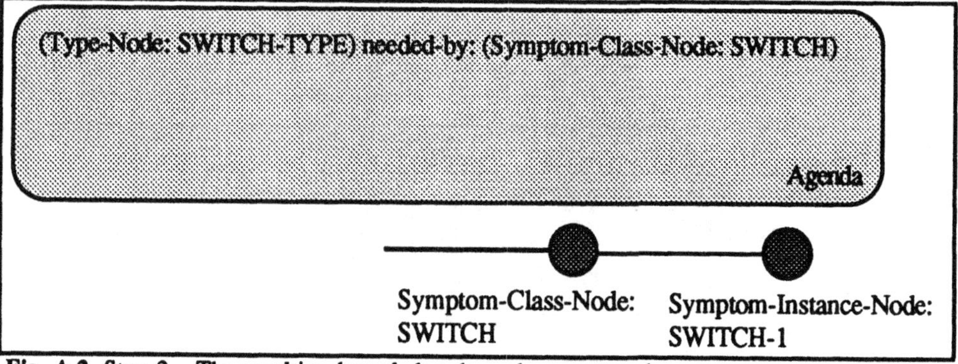

Fig. A.2. Step 2 - The resulting knowledge dependency network

Step 3: Type new_with_name: SWITCH-TYPE values: (open closed)

What happens? A type node is put in the knowledge dependency network and marked as consistent. Then the system checks the agenda for an entry which matches the new type. This entry is removed from the agenda and the (referenced) symptom class node is marked as consistent. From this results that also the symptom instance node is consistent. All nodes enter the knowledge base.

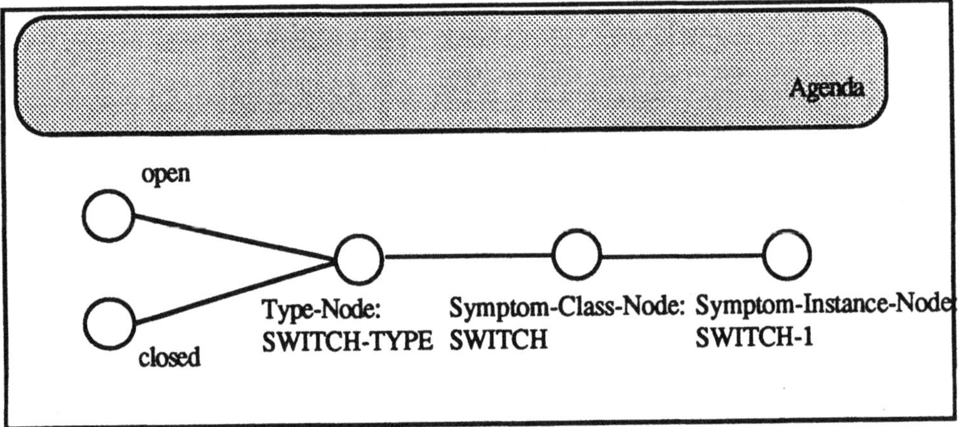

Fig. A.3. Step 3 - The resulting knowledge dependency network

Step 4: Symptom-Class new_with_name: POWERSWITCH with_type: SWITCH-TYPE

What happens? The user tries to define a symptom class node. The system checks the inconsistency graphs and detects a contradiction to graph 2 of figure 2.6. Thus, the new node is rejected.

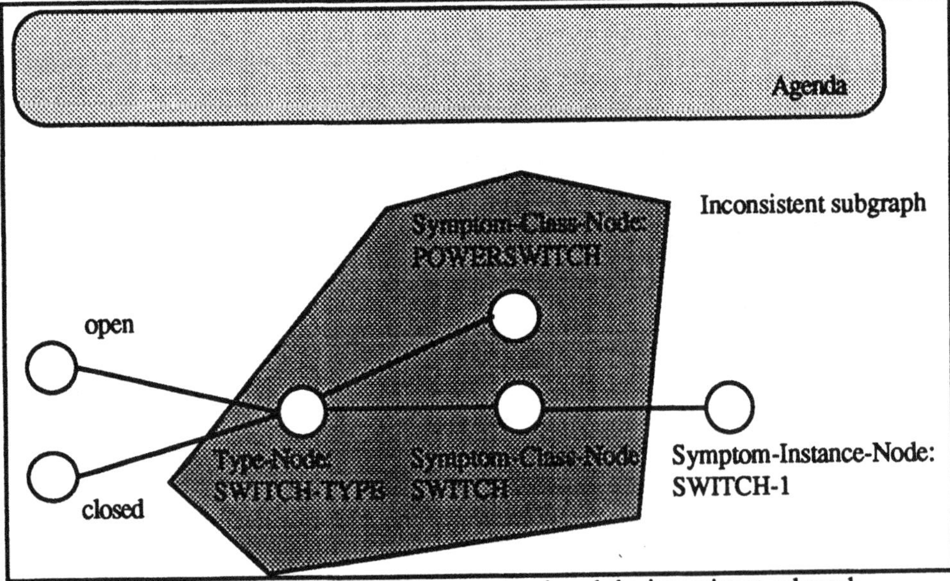

Fig. A.4. Step 4- The knowledge dependency network and the inconsistent subgraph

Step 5: Type new_with_name: POWERSWITCH-TYPE values: (open closed)
What happens? The user tries to define a type node. The system checks the inconsistency graphs and detects a contradiction to graph 1 of figure 2.6. So, the new node is rejected.

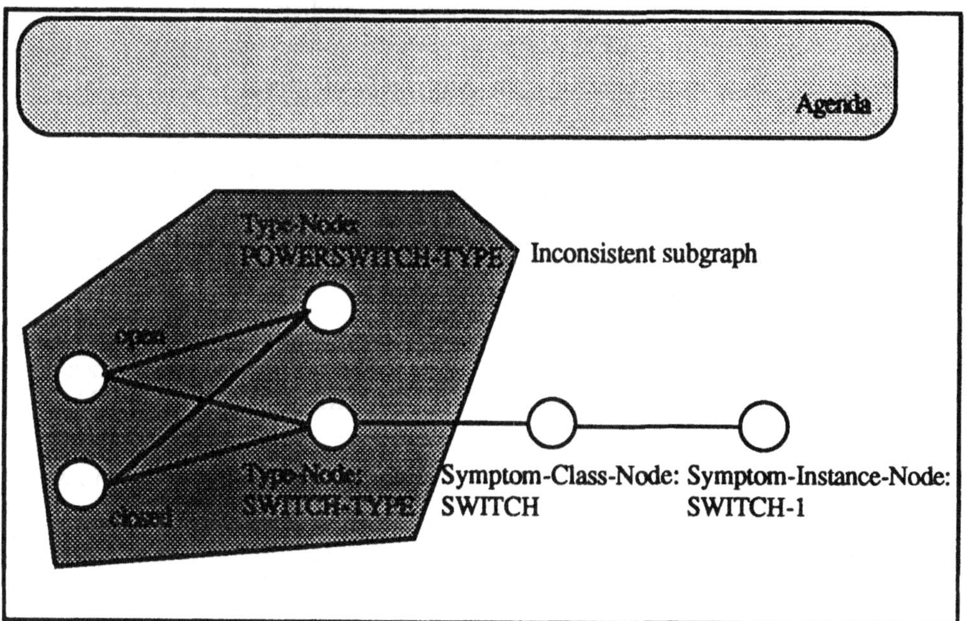

Fig. A.5. Step 5- The knowledge dependency network and the inconsistent subgraph

References

1. Althoff, K.-D.: Eine fallbasierte Lernkomponente als ein integrierter Bestandteil der MOLTKE-Werkbank für die Diagnose technischer Systeme, Doctoral Dissertation University of Kaiserslautern, 1992 (to appear)

2. Althoff, K.-D., Maurer, F., Rehbold, R.: Multiple Knowledge Acquisition Strategies in MOLTKE, in: Proc. EKAW 90, 1990

3. Althoff, K. D., Maurer, F., Traphöner, R., Weß, S.: The learning component of the $MOLTKE_3$ workbench for the diagnosis of technical systems (in German: Die Lernkomponente der $MOLTKE_3$ Werkbank für die Diagnose technischer Systeme), KI, special edition on Machine Learning, Baden-Baden: FBO-Verlag, No. 1, 1991; also: SEKI-Report SWP-90-08, University of Kaiserslautern

4. Althoff, K.-D., Maurer, F., Weß, S.: Case-Based Reasoning and Adaptive Learning in the $MOLTKE_3$ Workbench for Technical Diagnosis, SEKI Report SR-91-05, University of Kaiserslautern, 1991

5. Althoff, K.-D., Traphöner, R.: GenRule: Learning of Shortcut-Oriented Diagnostic Problem Solving in the $MOLTKE_3$-Workbench, SEKI Report SR-91-04, University of Kaiserslautern, 1991

6. Breuker, J., Wielinga, B.: Model-Driven Knowledge Acquisition: Interpretation

Models, Memo 87, Deliverable task A1, Esprit Project 1098; 1987

7. Campbell, B. , Goodman, J. M.: HAM: A General Purpose Hypertext Abstract Machine, Communications of the ACM, July 1988, Vol. 31, No. 7, 1988

8. de Kleer, J.: An assumption-based TMS, Artificial intelligence, Vol. 28, P. 163-196, 1986

9. Doyle, J.: A truth maintenance system, Artificial intelligence, Vol. 12, P. 231-272, 1979

10. Jansen, B., Compton, P.: The Knowledge Dictionary: Storing Different Knowledge Representations, in: Proc EKAW 89, 1989

11. Maurer, F.: CAKE: Computer-aided Knowledge Engineering, Proc. of IJCAI-91 Workshop on "Software Engineering for Knowledge Base Systems", 1991; also: SEKI Report SR-91-09, University of Kaiserslautern

12. Maurer, F. , Ruppel, A., Weß, S.: Learning of diagnostic strategies with neural networks in the MOLTKE 3.0 expert system toolbox (in German: Lernen von Diagnosestrategien mit neuronalen Netzen in MOLTKE), SEKI Report SWP-91-02, University of Kaiserslautern, 1991

13. Morik, K.: Acquiring domain models, in: Knowledge Acquisition Tools for Expert Systems, Academic Press, 1988

14. Musen, M. A., Fagan, L. M., Combs, D. M., Shortcliff, E. H.: Use of a domain model to drive an interactive knowledge-editing tool, in: Knowledge Acquisition Tools for Expert Systems, Academic Press, 1988

15. Nökel, K.: Temporal Matching: Recognizing Dynamic Situations from Discrete Measurements, in: Proc. IJCAI 1989, 1989

16. Rehbold, R.: Model-Based Knowledge Acquisition from Structure Descriptions in a Technical Diagnosis Domain, Proc. Avignon 1989, 1989

17. Rehbold, R.: Integration of model-based knowledge into technical diagnostic expert systems (in German: Integration von modellbasiertem Wissen in technische Diagnostik-Expertensystem), Doctoral Dissertation, University of Kaiserslautern, 1991

18. Richter, M.M.: Principles of artificial intelligence (in German: Prinzipien der künstlichen Intelligenz), Teubner Verlag, 1989

19. Richter, M. M. (ed.): MOLTKE - Methoden zur Fehlerdiagnose technischer Systeme, Springer Verlag, (to appear), 1992

20. van Someren, M. W., Zheng, L. L., Post, W.: Cases, Models or Compiled Knowledge; a Comparative Analysis and Proposed Integration, in: Proc. EKAW 1990

21. Wielinga, B., Schreiber, A Th., Breuker, J.: KADS: A Modelling Approach to Knowledge Engineering, KADS-II/T1.1/PP/UvA/008/1.0, Esprit Project P 5248 KADS-II, 1991

22. Althoff, K.-D., Weß, S.: Case-Based Knowledge Acquisition, Learning, and Problem Solving for Diagnostic Real World Tasks, in: Proc. EKAW 91, 1991; also: SEKI Report SR-91-07, University of Kaiserslautern

Acquiring Knowledge of Knowledge Acquisition: A Self-Study of Generic Tasks

Dean Allemang[1] *and Thomas E. Rothenfluh*[2*]

[1] Istituto Dalle Molle di Studi sull'Intelligenza Artificiale
Corso Elvezia 36, CH-6900 Lugano, Switzerland
dean@idsia.ch

[2] Laboratory for Artificial Intelligence Research, Department of Computer Science
The Ohio State University, 2036 Neil Ave. Mall
Columbus, Ohio 43210-1277, United States
rothen@cis.ohio-state.edu

Abstract In this paper we describe an experiment to study the problem solving behavior of a group of knowledge engineers. The subjects are knowledge engineers trained in the Generic Task framework [4]. The study has two aims: (1) to evaluate the degree of consistency among a set of engineers trained in the same high-level framework in order to assure the presence of a consistent methodology within such a group, and (2) to develop methods for studying knowledge engineering activity, which can also be applied to practitioners trained in other paradigms of knowledge engineering. Since such an analysis is exactly the domain of knowledge engineering, we use a knowledge level framework to model the knowledge engineering task. The use of the Design Model of the Generic Task theory [5] as an analysis framework for the knowledge engineers' problem solving process is motivated and its application demonstrated by in-depth analyses of solutions produced by our subjects. The results of our empirical study and its interpretations as well as methodological questions are discussed. It is concluded that the analysis of the knowledge engineers' task with the Generic Task Design Model provides interesting insights, but it also needs to be refined and complemented with more empirical evidence.
Keywords: Generic Tasks, knowledge engineering methodology, models of problem solving.

1 Introduction

A recent movement in knowledge acquisition has been toward "models of problem solving". In general, such models are intended to provide some sort of framework into which knowledge from an expert can be incorporated. We focus on the claim that these models are also aimed at structuring the task of knowledge acquisition so that it is more directed than the simplistic, albeit commonly used "ask for some knowledge, implement, repeat" prototyping approach. Several models have been proposed and attempts have been made to evaluate and compare these models. Along with each model comes a methodology for its use and—of particular interest here—guidelines to direct knowledge acquisition. Unfortunately, the models are usually very general theories and the associated methodologies are rarely well-defined

* Supported by the Swiss National Science Foundation, grant #8210-028342.

procedural descriptions. Therefore, any fruitful evaluation seems to need empirical evidence of the "usefulness" and "adequacy" of a particular model. However, such empirical evidence is hard to get and only occasionally reported in the literature, a recent exception being the Sisyphus'91 project which tried to compare such models by applying them to a common problem.[3]

Even if the evidence were available, the desire to assess commonalities and differences of problem solving at a conceptual level reaches beyond the currently available methods of comparison which operate on a lower level (e.g., statistical techniques used on quantifiable data). Thus, in addition to the question about the models, a more fundamental question arises:[4] *How can one evaluate the performance of a methodology in an experimental setting*? For example, how can the different "solutions" to the very same problem be compared? Surely, a contest among researchers is not of scientific interest; the real question is whether a methodology has the power to assist in a solution. The customers in the methodology market want tools that will help them do the analyses they want to do. How can we tell if we are evaluating a methodology and not individual researchers, research traditions, implementations etc.?

In order to count as a methodology, a commonly suggested criterion would require that it should be the case that any practitioner who is appropriately trained in that methodology, when given a particular problem, will produce the same result. Only if such a statement is true of a proposed methodology, can a prospective customer feel any inclination to buy, i.e., to invest the (usually huge) effort in becoming "appropriately trained".

This characterization of methodology (which we will designate as the "result criterion") seems a bit too rough for most uses of the word (consider the case of "top-down programming methodology": Two practitioners trained in this methodology can produce quite different, but still correct solutions, though both are following the methodology correctly), however the question is still well-taken; is there a commonality of process among the "appropriately trained" practitioners of some proposed methodology?

In this paper we provide an outline of a framework for doing such an analysis and report an experiment which was conducted to determine the commonality among a group of "appropriately trained" practitioners of one proposed methodology, namely the Generic Task methodology [4].

Due to the reasons mentioned above, we cannot expect the results themselves to match, although there should be something methodical about how the practitioners proceeded that can be compared. The framework proposed in section 2 puts knowledge acquisition into the perspective of the modeling view in knowledge engineering and identifies the Generic Task model of design as a useful tool for analyzing and comparing different outcomes from a common knowledge acquisition problem.

---

[3] The focus of Sisyphus'91 as stated in the description of the project: "...we want to compare different approaches to the modeling of problem solving in knowledge based systems and the influence of the models on the knowledge acquisition activities" [8].

[4] The question—in a slightly different form than presented here—was first posed by Max Bramer during a discussion at EKAW'91.

In section 3 an empirical study is reported where a number of researchers, all experienced in the use of the Generic Task methodology, were asked to analyze a common problem (For various reasons outlined later, the Sisyphus'91 problem was selected), and subsequently report on several questions concerning their knowledge acquisition process. A first analysis of the results is presented in section 4 and discussed in section 5 with respect to the evaluation of problem solving methods and their associated knowledge acquisition methodologies.

2 Framework

2.1 Knowledge acquisition in perspective

Knowledge acquisition research has been focussed on the improvement of manual and automated knowledge elicitation methods and the development of tools which support the knowledge acquisition and knowledge representation process. By exploiting computational and psychological approaches to knowledge elicitation and knowledge modeling, a refinement of earlier, rather crude knowledge acquisition methods has been achieved. Today's knowledge engineers have quite a repertoire of various different ways at hand to "attack" the knowledge acquisition phase (to quote but one source, see e.g. [6]).

Ideally, knowledge acquisition and knowledge engineering methodology should co-develop in research and practice. Innovations and evolutions in one field should have—hopefully beneficial—impacts on the other and spur further research. In the current renaissance of awareness for the subtleties of human problem solving, the constructive and social nature of knowledge and the emergence of expert-friendly and user-centered knowledge-based systems, it seems odd to view knowledge acquisition purely as a subordinate technology to aid knowledge engineering.

The development of knowledge engineering methodologies has changed its main focus from the basic problems of *knowledge representation* and *inference methods* to a more *knowledge-oriented view*. Current approaches try to capture the difficult "middle-ground", that is, they try to conceptualize the "right level of abstraction" of intelligent problem solving, which lies somewhere between specialized, domain-dependent knowledge and general-purpose problem solving methods. Various models for problem solving have been incorporated in quite a few different theoretical frameworks, methodologies, and tools (such as KADS, Components of Expertise, Generic Tasks, Role-Limiting Methods, Method to Task; for a short evaluation and a comparison of the key concepts see e.g. [7]).

An important consequence of all these proposals is the refutation of a "mining" or "transfer" view of the knowledge acquisition process in favor of a "modeling" view.[5] Conceptual modeling becomes the main issue for knowledge acquisition and the respective frameworks should thus provide useful and applicable guidelines for the elicitation, analysis and structuring of problem solving knowledge.

[5] In fact, one of the unifying features of all these frameworks—despite all other differences—is the claim that knowledge modeling is separable from the domain and implementational levels and thus their conceptual models can be used for *guiding* and *focusing* knowledge acquisition.

However, as these approaches are still evolving, they lack a stable and fully specified methodology for doing knowledge acquisition and there are only anecdotal reports on pertinent experiences available. This makes it difficult to *compare* the proposed frameworks in terms of their usefulness and their impacts for knowledge acquisition. More specifically, is seems crucial for the long-term survival of the modeling approach that not only are successful systems being built, but that a reliable methodology is available which ensures a reasonable training effort for learning these frameworks.[6] The integration of specifically designed knowledge acquisition tools, such as SHELLEY [2], may support knowledge engineers in applying the conceptual modeling. However, the core problem of when to select what particular (sub-)tool and how to map the real-world problem solving behavior onto conceptual structures remains in the duty of the (human) knowledge engineer.

It is still under discussion what exactly constitutes an adequate knowledge acquisition methodology for this modeling view—even worse, there is little agreement on what the criteria to evaluate and compare different approaches would be. One of the most critical problems for knowledge-level models is the difficulty in applying their generic, conceptual structures to a particular domain. The mapping of real-world expert problem solving behavior onto a particular framework and the identification of the "right" conceptual entities is not a straightforward task and needs special consideration[9]. Usually, the lack of a full-fledged specification for the knowledge acquisition process is counterbalanced by the excessive training and hands-on experience of knowledge engineers. Eventually, these knowledge engineers will become experts of that task (i.e., applying a knowledge-level framework to a given problem) and produce the desired results. A slightly exaggerated characterization of the presently available "solution" is thus that *good knowledge acquisition can be done with a clever knowledge engineer, who has in-depth knowledge about all the conceptual models available and has enough experience to pick reasonably adequate abstract task-structures and then uses the particular framework or methodology to appropriately refine them*[7].

To overcome the problems that necessarily appear with any violation of these ideal conditions, it seems to be fruitful to push the development of knowledge acquisition methodologies from a prescriptive, normative and top-down process to a descriptive, modeling and more bottom-up process. Nevertheless, the performance of experienced knowledge engineers is a useful starting point to explicitly develop and improve such a methodology. During their training, they must have developed means

[6] Interestingly enough, the lack of systematic validation gave rise to special workpackages and projects in several ESPRIT-II projects, which hopefully provide more systematically collected empirical data and pertinent results.

[7] It is astounding how many papers proposing a modeling view for knowledge acquisition only glimpse at the actual support for doing knowledge acquisition in one or two paragraphs in order to quickly shift gears to discuss their conceptual frameworks and representations at considerable length. We suspect that this might be due to the fact that many knowledge-based systems are not built around expert problem solving behavior but around well-defined problems and well-defined, formal domain knowledge. Therefore, knowledge acquisition is mainly reducible to *domain* modeling, not to *problem solving* modeling and can dispense with most of the tedious analysis work.

to overcome the aforementioned problems. We propose to study the problem solving behavior of knowledge engineers as (implicit) instantiations of the sought-after methodological guidelines. A "unified", generic description of *their* tasks, problem solving methods and relevant domain knowledge would be very helpful in assessing the particular means and methods used by a knowledge engineer.

It is also worthwhile to contrast this *"empirically grown"* methodology of knowledge acquisition with the idea of *automated* knowledge acquisition. The purpose of the latter—taken to its extreme—is to eliminate the need for (human) knowledge engineers to do knowledge acquisition by replacing them with an information-gathering expert knowledge acquisition system. This system is to ask all the relevant knowledge required for the construction of a knowledge-based system from the appropriate sources (experts, users, databases, etc.) and to come up with an adequate (conceptual) model of the problem solving process, specifying all the information that is required by the respective framework (e.g., external requirements, domain facts, knowledge sources, task features). Thus, the answers to the crucial question "Do these frameworks provide enough (informal or formal) guidelines to make the outcomes of the knowledge acquisition process *consistent* and *reliable*?" could also be used to refine the development of knowledge acquisition support tools as well as to improve the frameworks themselves.

2.2 Generic Tasks as an analysis tool

In order to describe uniformly and consistently the problem solving behavior of knowledge engineers doing knowledge acquisition, a language has to be used which is powerful enough to characterize human problem solving behavior in generic terms but also constrained enough to allow us to focus on the aspects we expect to be similar or different across individual knowledge engineers (or groups of knowledge engineers). In this section, we will motivate our use of the Generic Task (GT) framework as an analysis tool to study knowledge engineers. GT provides a language in which to describe the problem solving activity, so that a modeling of their activity can be done. Since that description is made on a generic level, a GT model can also be used for comparisons of different experts. Furthermore, in the case that there is considerable similarity in the experts' problem solving activity, then it provides a context in which the knowledge is used, and allows the *integration* of such knowledge. That is, if one expert has considerable knowledge in one part of the (revealed) common structure, while another has knowledge in another part, this structure shows whether the knowledge of one expert makes the knowledge of the other obsolete, or if the knowledge can be combined, or if it is in conflict.

The basic task model for the knowledge acquisition process can be described in terms of a general problem solving model. First, a knowledge engineer has to *understand* the problem at hand. Once the domain and the problem solving processes have been captured appropriately, a set of possible solutions is *generated* and maybe *refined* into a final solution. However, in order to compare different knowledge engineers performing this task, a more precise description of that almost universal *generate-and-test* process is needed. It is a basic claim of the GT framework that (generic) problem solving models cannot be separated from their use (the interaction hypothesis). Consequently, we have to identify the appropriate task-model for the knowledge acquisition process. In the sequel, we will show that the GT model for design [5] is a useful tool for such an analysis.

A design task is defined as and specified with (1) a set of functions to be delivered by an artifact and (2) a set of constraints to be satisfied and (3) a technology. By translating this generic definition of design problem solving to our study of the knowledge acquisition process, knowledge engineers are conceived of as experts in the domain of knowledge acquisition solving the problem of constructing a conceptual model of a domain expert. The artifact to be constructed is a conceptual model of the domain expert's problem solving process. The constraints are given by the task features of the knowledge acquisition process itself and will be discussed in more detail in the following section. However, most important to our current study is the fact that the technology should be specified as "a repertoire of components assumed to be available and a vocabulary of relations between components" [5]. That is exactly what these various modeling frameworks are supposed to provide. Both the general design problem and the knowledge acquisition problem also share the crucial property that they require a generative component to provide solutions and that a prespecified set of (partial) solutions or operators are already given. The main design problem—that is, to reduce the complexity and size of a usually huge solution space—is present (and to be solved) in both instances. We thus employ the GT model of design problem solving to find the similarities and differences between different knowledge engineers who have been trained in the same modeling framework.[8] In the following section, we will present an experiment which has been conducted to provide empirical material about the knowledge acquisition process as proposed by the GT model (and as used by experienced GT knowledge engineers). The framework as outlined above is then used to analyze the resulting material.

3 Experiment

3.1 Goal, selection of subjects and task

The goal of the experiment was to get empirical evidence on how experienced knowledge engineers apply the methodology suggested by their general framework. GT researchers were considered being suitable subjects for this study for practical reasons of accessibility, and that the GT community is homogeneous; there are no radically different "schools of thought" within that approach.

Since one of the authors already participated in a similar experiment [1] and we tried to maintain some comparability with other conceptual frameworks, the same task as posed to the participants of Sisyphus'91—an office assignment problem, see [8] for more details—was used.

[8] Which, to complicate things slightly, happens to be very same framework as the one employed by our subjects, namely, the Generic Task framework, see the section describing the method.

3.2 Method

The use of the GT framework as a tool for the analysis of expert knowledge acquisition behavior suggests the following methodological procedure for the experiment:

1. Find a number of appropriately trained GT practitioners who provide solutions to one single application problem. Then perform an analysis of each submission by using the GT Design Model (as outlined in [5], [1] and in section 2.2).
2. Examine these analyses for noticeable differences; are they basically similar, or widly different? Does one (or just a few) of them stand out as very different? If they are the same, then we can make a statement about "what GT researchers are doing". If they are very different, either there is no consensus among GT researchers, or the consensus is not made apparent by the GT tool we are using to analyze the results. A small number of standouts would be expected; not everyone who has undergone training manages to be appropriately trained.
3. If there were considerable similarities in the analyses, examine the differences more closely. Were they simply differences in knowledge used, or differences in task structure? E.g., one practitioner chose the GT tool for Abduction while others chose Routine Design. Is this a difference in knowledge (e.g., when time came to choose a tool, this practitioner used different knowledge to identify which one to use), or a difference in task structure (e.g., this practitioner is not choosing a tool at all, rather simply always views the world as abduction)?
4. Whenever the difference is simply that of knowledge applied, then it is possible to construct a conglomerate task structure for the expertise of the experts. For example, if respondent 2 says that Abduction is good for any synthetic task, but respondent 1 says that for problems with a topological model, Routine Design is more appropriate than Abduction, it could be that respondent 2 would say, "I didn't know that", and the two pieces of knowledge could be combined in a single matching agent. If on the other hand, respondent 2 says that even for problems with a topological model, Abduction is better, this is clearly a collision, a disagreement. Some knowledge will be prevented from clashing just from the task structure, e.g., respondent 3 might state that the existence (or lack thereof) of failure modes indexed on a particular design decomposition level (in Routine Design) is a good way of verifying that the level is necessary (or not, respectively.). There is no way that respondent 2 could have reported this knowledge, given her/his earlier decision to use abduction.

The format of the solution was (unlike in the Sisyphus experiment) not predefined. This was done deliberately to allow the respondents to structure their argumentation as they saw fit. After having received the initial solutions, a set of follow-up questions was sent to all contributors in order to ask some general questions and to clarify individual statements. Our analysis was based on both the responses as structured by the subjects and on their answers to the follow-up questions.

Since the analysis of the GT-experts was also done by a former student of Chandrasekaran, who is personally acquainted with the researchers in the study, we installed a "single-blind" condition in the experiment[9] to protect from biases based on earlier familiarity with the work and individual style of particular respondents.

3.3 An overview of the use of the GT Design Model as an analysis tool

The graphical presentation of generic tasks analyses used in this paper is described in [1] and based on [5]. In this section we briefly review the conventions of these diagrams.

Each diagram is a tree, whose nodes contain *tasks* and *methods*[10]. The only tasks we use in these diagrams are related to the DESIGN task, that is, Design, Propose, Critique, Verify, Modify, Generate Specifications, Select Plan, and Compose. These are always printed in *italics* in the figures. The methods used in these diagrams are PVCM, Decomposition (and a special case of Decomposition, Design Plan) and Sponsor/Select. These are printed in **boldface** in the figures. Each of these methods specifies a set of subtasks which must be performed in order to accomplish it; for example, PVCM specifies subtasks Propose, Verify, Critique, and Modify. The task decomposition is constant for any method. The decompositions for these and other tasks are given in [5].

Thus our method for analyzing each submission is as follows:

1. Decide which Generic Task best describes the problem solving behavior of the respondant (in this experiment, the answer is always DESIGN). Start an analysis tree with a single node labeled DESIGN.
2. For each outstanding node in the tree, select a method appropriate for it. In the case of *Design* nodes, only PVCM is applicable. For a *Propose* node, a choice of method must be made among **Decomposition Methods, Design Plans, Case-based Methods**, etc. (see [5]). This choice is made by examining the knowledge used by the respondant to solve this task.
3. Look up the method in table 1. Complete the node as directed; if the method spawns new tasks, then make new nodes in the analysis tree corresponding to each task mentioned.
4. If any outstanding nodes remain in the tree, go to step 2.

The goal of analyzing the responses in this way is to have a deeper structure for comparison than simply the results themselves. Expressing all the responses in a common language will help us do comparisions, and eventually, combine the knowledge from the various sources.

4 Results

4.1 Subjects

The first step was done by sending a call to (former) students of Chandrasekaran, who were asked to forward the call to other parties who they felt qualify. To qualify

[9] By channeling all communications through a "neutral" messenger who anonymized them accordingly.

[10] In this discussion, I do not distinguish between methods and 'families of methods'

PVCM	Spawn tasks Propose, Critique, Verify and Modify
Decomposition	Spawn tasks Generate Specifications, Design*, and Compose
Design Plan	Spawn tasks Select Plan, Design*, and Compose
Sponsor/Select	Specify criteria for plan selection (plan steps are summarized under corresponding *Design** task).

Table 1. Methods and actions to be taken. 'Spawn tasks' indicates that new task nodes will be added to the analysis tree.

as "appropriately trained GT expert", at least two years of work at a GT-developing site (e.g., the Laboratory of Artificial Intelligence Research at The Ohio State University) were required. 14 practitioners expressed interest and received detailed instructions on their task. 5 solutions were submitted within the given time-frame (2 months); two of these came late (in response to a second call). Of all five submissions received, only 3 were in sufficient detail to support the sort of GT analysis that we outlined in section 2 and wanted to apply in its first step.

In further studies, it would be desirable to perform a follow-up study also on the non-responding subjects. Besides time and other resource limitations and beyond the limitations imposed by the study's design (i.e., the type and amount of information the subjects were given as problem statement), more insight into reasons for not submitting a solution could illuminate possible fundamental problems of the framework to be used. For example, reasons for not participating might include a (presumed or real) lack of individual knowledge of the GT framework, a feeling that the GT model is inappropriate to solve that particular application problem (e.g., that it lies outside the scope of currently defined tasks), a lack of an adequate framework to describe a solution or an inability to find a reasonable solution to the problem. These (and other) shortcomings may cause changes which are specific for problems with the GT framework, for example, the development of a more straightforward notational language or the extension of the theory to other generic (sub-) tasks.

4.2 Synopsis of the responses

With respect to our main goal, that is, to evaluate whether the subjects use a methodologically similar approach to make their GT analysis, we will focus on the process of how the GT analysis was done. Due to the nature of our experiment (only written statements, no data on the dynamic construction process available), this analysis is based on the respondents written solution statements, the answers to the follow-up questions and the structure of their argumentation. First, we will give synopses of the responses and provide illustrative examples. Then, we will present our GT analyses of the respondents' problem solving process, that is, a description of their argumentation in terms of a design task.

Since the subjects had no prior knowledge of the task and of the solution provided earlier by [1], we also included his results to enrich our study of GT researchers. Thus, six descriptions of generic task experts describing their way of tackling the office assignment problem were available for our analysis. The small number of responses and the fact, that we did not require a specific format for the solutions does not allow for a meaningful quantitative evaluation.

Because of the "single blind condition" and in order to clearly separate the experts' contributions from our interpretations, code numbers are used to identify the individual contributions.

- *Respondent 1* identified the Sisyphus problem as a DESIGN TASK[11], where the offices form the 'primitive components' of the design, and the floor plan constitutes a 'topographic model' of the artifact to be designed. People and their organizational relations were conceived of as a 'set of inter-related functional constraints' and the expert's office-assignment policies as 'design guidelines'. The Sisyphus problem/task was then re-stated as 'map the functional constraints on to the topographical model in accordance with the guidelines'. The method of solution was identified as 'Plan Selection Instantiation and Expansion (PSIA) (sic)'. A hierarchical plan structure (i.e. a tree of DESIGN PLANS) based on the topographic model was constructed, and filled in according to the dictates of PSIA.
- *Respondent 2* identified the task as an ASSEMBLY PROBLEM, and used the GT tool PEIRCE as the method of solution. Respondent 2 then mapped the parts of the PEIRCE problem to the parts of the Sisyphus problem. Remaining aspects of the Sisyphus problem were added into the architecture defined by PEIRCE. Possible uses of the aspects of the PEIRCE architecture that did not have obvious correspondences in the Sisyphus problem were discussed.
- *Respondent 3* identified the task as a ROUTINE DESIGN TASK, and chose DSPL as the method. The rest of the activity was involved in identifying DESIGN PLANS and the hierarchy of DESIGN PLANS.

Respondents 4 and 5 gave very brief answers; synopses are difficult.

[11] To ease the readability of the following discussion, we will designate the problem which the GT-experts had to solve the 'Sisyphus problem' (instead of the more precise description "the office-assignment problem solved by a particular domain expert as documented in the Sisyphus'91 assignment") and their task as the 'Sisyphus task' (instead of the more precise description "the task to find a GT model for the office-assignment problem solved by a particular domain expert as documented in the Sisyphus'91 assignment"); 'Siggi' is the reference to the (office assignment domain) expert for the Sisyphus. Furthermore, special typesetting (e.g., PROPOSE or DSPL) is used to indicate concepts with a specific meaning in the GT methodology as used by the subjects.

- *Respondent 4* seems to view the problem as bin-packing, and selects a 'canned-plan' approach to the solution. Then a plan structure is determined, with plans being run by a constraint handler.
- *Respondent 5* identified DSPL as the tool to use for the problem. Aspects of the problem were mapped to DSPL entities (parameters). One plan is identified, the solution is not pursued further.
- *Respondent 6* provided the most elaborate description of a GT analysis of the Sisyphus problem. First, he identified the knowledge available (and missing) in the problem statement and made some of his own additional assumptions explicit. He matched the reported "large number of attempted solution" and the fact that "there is apparently a vanishingly small number of satisficing solutions" to the formal description given for a DESIGN TASK. The further decomposition of that task followed strictly the guidelines given for the PROPOSE, VERIFY, CRITIQUE, MODIFY family of methods with the important quality that the use of GT concepts (such as DESIGN PLANS) were explicitly justified by referring to Siggi's protocol statements. Respondent 6 also provided an evolving set of graphical, tree-like structures to describe the construction of his solution.

4.3 Analyses

As described in step 1 of the method (section 3.2, above), the first analysis of the data is to produce a Generic Tasks analysis of each respondent. Only the results for respondents 1, 2, 3 and 6 were presented in enough detail for such an analysis.

Respondent 1 Respondent 1 seemed willing to respond in great depth, usually about how the solution was constructed, but not how it was tested or corrected. This may well be due to the fact that respondent 1 did not complete the knowledge engineering task by actually checking its performance. Nevertheless, an analysis of the problem solving activity of respondent 1 was possible.

Respondent 1 chose PSIA to solve the Sisyphus problem. This choice is justified on the grounds that a 'topographic model' of the domain was available. The choice of PSIA cuts the problem into one of designing a number of abstract PLANS, and putting them into a design hierarchy (also referred to as 'tree'). These three steps, that is, choose a decomposition of the problem (the decomposition is called 'PSIA'), solve the subproblems, which are in themselves DESIGN TASKS (an indefinite number of abstract PLAN designs), and combine the solutions (put the abstract PLANS into a hierarchy), are the subtasks of the 'Decomposition' family of methods for the PROPOSE task from the table in [5, 1].

The construction of a PLAN NODE itself is a DESIGN TASK (as specified in [5, 1], and shown in figure 1). This design plan again is done by a PVCM family of methods, the Propose being done as a decomposition method. In particular, the decomposition is done as a single design plan; every abstract node is designed in the same way, by determining the PLAN SELECTOR, INSTANTIATION and EXPANSION for the node. The last two of these are declared trivial in this case. The actual content of the PLAN was left to the *Compose* step higher in the diagram; the contents of a particular PLAN are exactly its children in the tree. The expert could not report on how this tree was constructed, i.e., whether it was constructed first, and then the PLANS were put in, or whether the PLANS were constructed, then a tree was built to accommodate them. This information could have been made available from a finer-grained experimental setup; that is, by asking the expert to write down intermediate stages of the modeling process, or with a more challenging domain problem that would involve having to revise the constructed system.

The complete task structure for respondent 1 appears in figure 1.

Respondent 2 Respondent 2 chose to model the Sisyphus problem as an ABDUCTIVE (ASSEMBLY) problem, and used the GT tool PEIRCE for the basis of the model. The reason s/he gave for this was that any problem that can be seen as a problem of coverage can be viewed as abductive assembly. Then s/he solved a number of small subproblems of mapping the features of the problem to the known features of assembly, that is, s/he identified the observations, hypotheses, causal connections, etc. of the Sisyhpus domain. Forming a solution from these decisions involved simply tabulating them together. Logically, it would have been useful had the respondent shown how, under this mapping, the result provided by the assembly mechanism of PEIRCE corresponds to a solution of the Sisyphus problem. Such an exposition was not provided, even in response to a directed question. Thus this solution is at best radically incomplete. Our own attempts to complete the solution by reference to published formal descriptions of abduction [3] were unsuccessful.

Nevertheless, the solution was complete enough to provide some insight into the verification, critique and modification phases of the respondent's reasoning. The support that was provided by the model (e.g., parsimony and essentialness critics) were interpreted in light of the mapping determined in the *Propose* phase. The modifications that the respondent made were of three sorts; the essentialness critic was discarded (pending data that might reinstate it), the parsimony critic was used to search for possible problems that were not brought out by this example, and two new critics, for compatibility and synergy were introduced into the architecture. The task analysis for respondent 2 appears in figure 2.

Respondent 3 In contrast to the report given by respondent 1, respondent 3 gave a thorough report of each step taken, but did not go as deeply into detail of any of them.

Respondent 3 also chose among a number of possible tools, and chose the tool DSPL to solve the problem. Respondent 1 identifies DSPL as the tool for the problem solving method model, PSIA. However, respondent 3 gives completely different reasons for choosing DSPL than 1 does, and explicitly compares its value in this circumstance to another possible choice, the GT tool PEIRCE. It is the synthetic rather than interpretative nature of the task that respondent 3 claims makes DSPL a good choice. As in PSIA, the 'subcomponents' are the PLANS that will be put into a design tree.

At the top level, respondent 3 mentions how the structures that are to be proposed can be verified. The verification is done by implementing the system. The critique is done by asking the expert to supply particularly difficult cases (presumably the strictly unsolvable problem proposed in Sisyphus 92 would be such a case). Finally, the system would be modified by re-arranging the system to accommodate the new data.

At the next level down, the proposal for each plan is done by concentrating on the plan content, i.e., determining the subplan structure. No comment is made about plan selection here, in contrast to respondent 1 who concentrated entirely on plan selection at this point (though it decomposed into trivial tasks one level down).

The plan construction of respondent 3 makes ample use of all phases of PVCM. The expert seems to have very little knowledge of proposing such a plan, and mentions 3 provisional plan structures that were considered, and the knowledge used to rule two of them out. One plan was ruled out because an implementation seemed too difficult. Another provisional plan was critiqued on the basis of having levels of distinction that were deemed unnecessary; DSPL organizes error handling through these levels, as well as using them to order subgoals. Siggi's protocol shows no error handling, and no useful ordering changes (no 'leverage', to use the respondent's term), so the extra level was removed.

At another point, the respondent conjectured that the most constrained decisions were to be made at the lowest levels (that of assigning researchers), and that propagating these constraints might well be costly, and introduced an extra level to control such propagation. In fact, Siggi comments in the original assignment that projects are better separated than kept together, and hence during the implementation/verification phase in the first level, a discrepancy was noticed between the system's answer and Siggi's. The expert, having overlooked Siggi's comment, wondered aloud whether this difference was important. In a follow-up question, we pointed out Siggi's comment, which allowed us a glimpse of the expert's own failure modes. The patch was done with the minimal amount of effort, in this case, rebuilding plan specialists to work from the new constraint rather than the old.

The complete task structure for respondent 3 appears in figure 3.

Respondent 6 As was mentioned in the synopsis, respondent 6 used (again) a hypothesis match (based on the knowledge-level properties of the task, i.e., characteristics of the solution space) to select DESIGN as a candidate task structure. This DESIGN TASK is identified as being a general, hierarchically structured DESIGN PLAN which is then decomposed with a weaker decomposition method according to design steps identified from Siggi's protocol. Similar to respondents 1 and 3, respondent 6 developed a hierarchical structure of such specialized DESIGN PLANS. The construction of these nodes is done by examining the domain expert behavior for each plan, one by one.

This was followed by the discussion of PLAN NODES. However, in contrast to respondent 3 who focused on the same part, these PLAN NODES were developed by abstracting PLANS and CONSTRAINTS from Siggi's protocol statements and matching them to the knowledge roles prescribed by the PVCM subtasks. For a special case (completion of the DESIGN RESEARCHERS task in the Sisyphus problem), an elaboration on the Verify, Critique and Modify steps for the construction of the DESIGN PLAN was discussed. The Propose step generated two alternative DESIGN PLANS, because Siggi's protocol did not specify all necessary details (e.g., an ordering of constraints) to fully define DESIGN PLAN NODE. Respondent 6 suggested further questions to Siggi to resolve (i.e., Verify, Critique, Modify) that problem.

At the more global level of the whole Sisyphus task, respondent 6 mentioned (briefly) that DSPL would be suitable to assist in the development of the top-level plans and could also be used to support the backtracking knowledge.

Respondent 6 also comments on the fact that Siggi's protocol does not show any verification, critiquing, or modification at any stage, which would be expected if Siggi really did DESIGN. Together with the fact that some important aspects of the knowledge (required to solve a more general version of the Sisyphus problem) were not deducible from statements in Siggi's protocol, respondent 6 suggested a Verify/Critique step for the design of the system. The "numerous loose ends" which were identified during the analysis of the Sisyphus problem would require more flexible tools, which are not (yet) available in the GT framework. That prevents the task from being implemented and thus prevents the structure from being critiqued on the grounds used by repondents 1 and 3, namely, implementation. Similar to the strategy used by repondent 2, respondent 6 compares the support provided by the selected model, so instantiated, with the requirements of the Sisyphus problem. Respondant 6 gives similar options for modification as are given by respondant 2, that is, s/he generates possible scenarios in the problem domain that correspond to the predictions made by the model, and considers changing the model (though not as drastically as respondent 2 does) in the face of contradictory data.

4.4 Combining analyses

A number of comparisons between respondents 1 and 3 have already been made, based on the task decomposition diagrams. Some of these differences may be simply artifacts of the small experimental setup (most notably, the omissions in breadth from respondent 1), while others are clearly somewhat deeper (e.g., the lack of discussion from respondent 1 about how the plan node children were formed, while for respondent 3, this was the central concern).

But in fact, the two solutions are strikingly similar, despite some large differences. Many of the differences (e.g., the difference in breadth-first versus. depth-first presentation) can be easily assimilated into a single knowledge base; that is, since both experts are performing a PVCM method to solve the task, the verification, critique and modification methods used by respondent 3 are applicable to solutions proposed by respondent 1 as well. For these two, the criteria for selection a GT tool seem compatible as well, though they did not cite any of the same criteria for making the decision. In particular, we learn that in favor of DSPL as a model are the existence of a topographical model of the solution, design guidelines, (these from respondent 1), and synthetic tasks in general (respondent 3).

Respondent 1 was unable to respond to questions about how the plan tree was constructed, even when asked a pointed question on the subject. This is a strike against our use of Generic Tasks as an analysis took (in fact, against Generic Tasks as a knowledge acquisition tool in general), since we use such tools to help us to ask questions that are focused, and answerable by the expert. But we find that respondent 3 was quite willing to write at great length on this topic (even before the follow-up question). This suggests that possibly one of the design subtasks for proposing a plan in figure 1 should be examined more closely; in fact 'expanding' a plan is only a trivial operation if one already knows the contents of the plan. We see that respondent 3 spent a great deal of time filling in that content, or in fact, designing the plan expansion. This mitigates the strike against GT theory, since it makes it possible for one expert to provide answers to questions left unanswered by another expert.

Furthermore, although respondent 2 constructed a solution that was considerably different from that of 1 and 3, it is still possible to combine some of respondent 2's knowledge with the others. In particular, his/her treatment of the solution, not necessarily to be verified by implementation, but also verifiable by means of its predictive power with respect to interpreting the problem domain, is similar to the treatment made by respondent 6, and is applicable to the models built by any of the respondents.

This allows us to draw an amalgamated task diagram, containing the knowledge of all four experts, shown in figure 4. Respondents 1, 3 and 6 were in considerable agreement, making this synthesis quite straightforward, once the task components had been identified.

5 Conclusions

This experiment actually evaluates the Generic Tasks framework twice; once as the subject of the experiment (in response to the original motivation, to determine to what extent something like Generic Tasks can be considered to be a methodology), and again as the tool of analysis of the results of the experiment. Had Generic Task theory been seriously deficient in its claims to assist in the organization of knowledge, an analysis of the sort we have made would have been impossible. We will discuss the aspects of Generic Tasks learned by each of these examinations separately.

For the unity of application of Generic Tasks theories by Generic Tasks researchers, we have found that there is considerable agreement about how to proceed in a knowledge acquisition task, as described by the subjects. There is considerable disagreement about the details of how to proceed, but for the most part these can be reconciled. Some disagreements arose right away, before the analysis phase; for example, one subject stated that Generic Tasks were not intended to support, and were in principle incapable of supporting, knowledge acquisition.

Whether our analysis method is transferable to other knowledge level frameworks has to remain an empirical question. However, the GT Design Model and the methods described in this paper seem to provide sufficient guidelines to analyze the problem solving of knowledge engineers doing initial knowledge acquisition with the GT framework. The role of the GT Design Model in this study was to move away from the simple 'result criterion' for consensus of expert activity. It is important to emphasize that the use of the GT Design Model as an analysis tool does not restrict the frameworks which the knowledge engineers themselves use to analyze the original application problem. For example, there should be no fundamental problem with analyzing KADS-trained knowledge engineers, using the GT Design Model as a "meta-model" of the knowledge engineering process.

As it quickly became apparent that the 'result criterion' for judging a methodology was too strict, a more abstract method of comparison was needed. As can be seen by the commonality, and to some extent composability of the solutions, the intermediate abstractions that appear in a Generic Tasks analysis are in fact useful for clarifying the relationships between different knowledge engineers.

However, we are also aware of some shortcomings in our analysis. The responses analyzed in this paper are entirely based on the knowledge engineer's introspection and constitute at best a "post-hoc rationalization" of their own problem solving activity. The different *formats* used by the respondents (i.e., plain English description, DESIGN HIERARCHIES, tables, (pseudo-) traces, problem solving decomposition trees) indicate that the GT framework could profit from a unified way of describing the conceptual model (a design description language), whereas the more rigid, formal description languages (e.g., the proposed ML^2 language for KADS models) do not fit into GT's modeling phase (since GT's are more like *prescriptions* for a conceptual model and are not composed in a bottom-up manner; the different decompositions are selected in the design phase according to the knowledge available in the domain). A uniform description of the respondent's analysis would have eased our own analysis considerably. For future studies, one might also consider the inclusion of some of the more traditional reviewing techniques (e.g., the walkthrough techniques for software development as described in [10] or other consensus-finding techniques) to arrive at a more "objective" analysis. However, the use of the GT Design Model provided a useful "normative" (but still general and not too restrictive) guideline to accomplish our analysis.

Though the abstractions were of use in the comparative analysis, the Generic Task analysis tool was not uniformly successful in all phases of the analysis. One of the advantages of having a task structure is that it suggests pointed questions about the problem solving process, that should be answerable by the expert. As we saw in the analysis of response 1, at least one such question was not easily answered.

In spite of these methodological problems, we are most encouraged by the possibilities for combining the knowledge of several experts offered by this approach. This suggests that such an analysis might be useful for comparing, and eventually combining the expertise of knowledge engineers who come from differing knowledge acquisition backgrounds.

This is not only true for models which embody similar results or have only minor diversions but also for "failures", that is, for solutions which are not conforming (and cannot be forced to conform) the overall consensus. Our use of the DESIGN MODEL as an interpretation model for the knowledge engineers' activities allows to identify points of departure from a common path and may even help to identify wrong assumptions or potential misconceptions. It may even turn out that some apparent differences are not truly relevant to solve the application problem (e.g., they constitute viable alternatives due to the availability of redundant knowledge).

In certain circumstances, such "failures" could also be used to detect (i.e., acquire knowledge about) important default assumptions being made by the knowledge engineers or by the frameworks used for analysis. To be able to make these things more explicit and to point at shortcomings of the current usage is of course in service of refining the knowledge level frameworks under study and not to blame the individual knowledge engineers—theoretical models of problem solving are only as good as their accompanying methodologies.

6 Acknowledgments

We gratefully acknowledge the assistance of the researchers who participated in the experiment. In particular, we would like to thank Tom Bylander, B. Chandrasekaran, Ashok Goel, Michael Tanner, Michael Weintraub and other members of the GT community for their contributions and discussions. Of course, any errors in interpreting their results are the fault of the authors. We also wish to acknowledge Max Bramer, for his insightful comments that inspired this work.

References

1. Dean Allemang. Sisyphus'91, generic tasks. In *Sisyphus Working Papers Part 2: Models of problem solving*, 1991.
2. Anjo Anjewierden and Jan Wielemaker. SHELLEY—Computer Aided Knowledge Engineering. In Bob Wielinga, John Boose, and Brain Gaines, editors, *EKAW'90. Proceedings of the Fourth European Workshop on Knowledge Acquisition*, pages 41–59, 1990.
3. Tom Bylander, D. Allemang, M. C. Tanner, and J. R. Josephson. The computational complexity of abduction. *Artificial Intelligence*, 49:25–60, 1991.
4. B. Chandrasekaran. Generic tasks as building blocks for knowledge-based systems: The diagnosis and routine design examples. *Knowledge Engineering Review*, pages 183–219, 1989.
5. B. Chandrasekaran. Design problem solving: A task analysis. *AI Magazine*, 11(4):59–71, 1990.
6. Dan Diaper, editor. *Knowledge elicitation. Principles, techniques and applications.* Chichester: Ellis Horwood, 1989.
7. Werner Karbach, Marc Linster, and Angi Voss. Models of problem solving: One label - one idea? In Bob Wielinga, John Boose, and Brain Gaines, editors, *EKAW'90. Proceedings of the Fourth European Workshop on Knowledge Acquisition*, pages 3–18, 1990.
8. Marc Linster. Statement of the sample problem. In *Sisyphus Working Papers Part 2: Models of problem solving*, 1991.
9. Rolf Pfeifer, Thomas Rothenfluh, Markus Stolze, and Felix Steiner. Mapping expert behavior onto task-level frameworks: The need for 'eco-pragmatic' approaches to knowledge engineering. In Franz Schmalhofer, Gerhard Strube, and Thomas Wetter, editors, *Contemporary knowledge engineering and cognition*. Springer, 1991.
10. Edward Yourdon. *Structured walktroughs*. Yourdon Press, New York, 3rd edition, 1985.

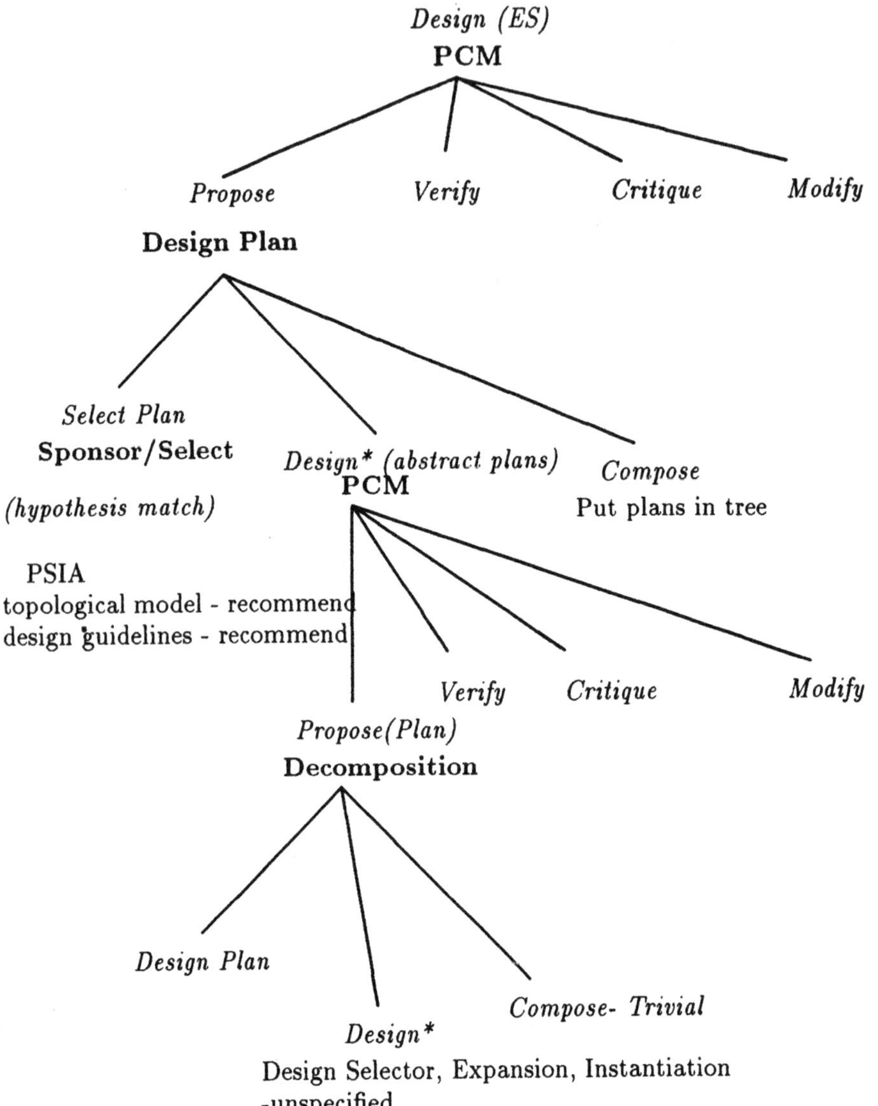

Fig. 1. GT analysis of Respondent 1's knowledge engineering activity. 'Design*' denotes that this design could be done by several design subtasks. Except for hypothesis match (which is shown as a table), all expansions come from the table in [5].

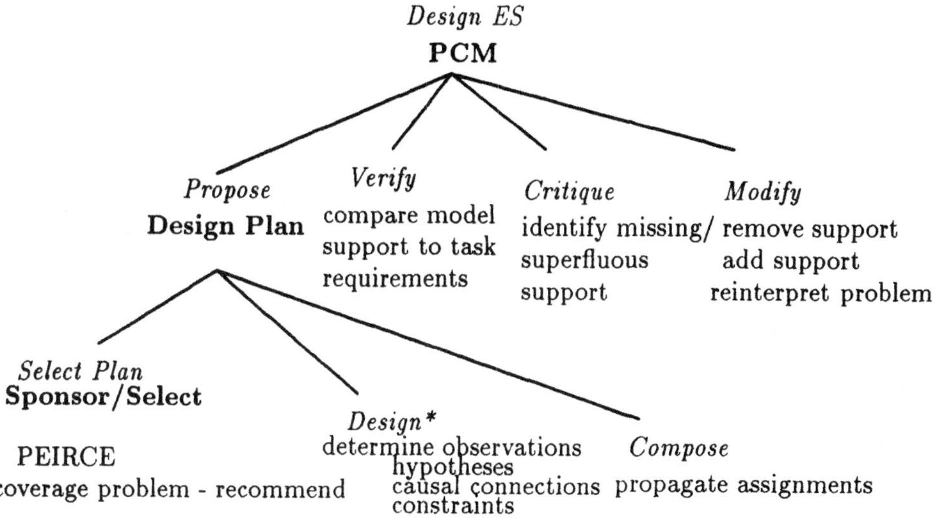

Fig. 2. GT analysis of Respondent 2's knowledge engineering activity.

Design (ES)
PCM

Propose
Design Plan

Verify
implement

Critique
special cases
from expert

Modify
Hack structures

Select Plan
Sponsor/Select

(hypothesis match)

DSPL
interpretive - discoruage
synthetic - recommend

Peirce
synthetic - recommend

Design (abstract plans)*
PCM

Propose(Plan)
Case-based?

Verify

Critique
- Useless levels:
  no decisions made
  no failure modes
- nonlocal constraint
  propagation

Modify
- Remove level
localize (new level)

Compose
Put plans in tree

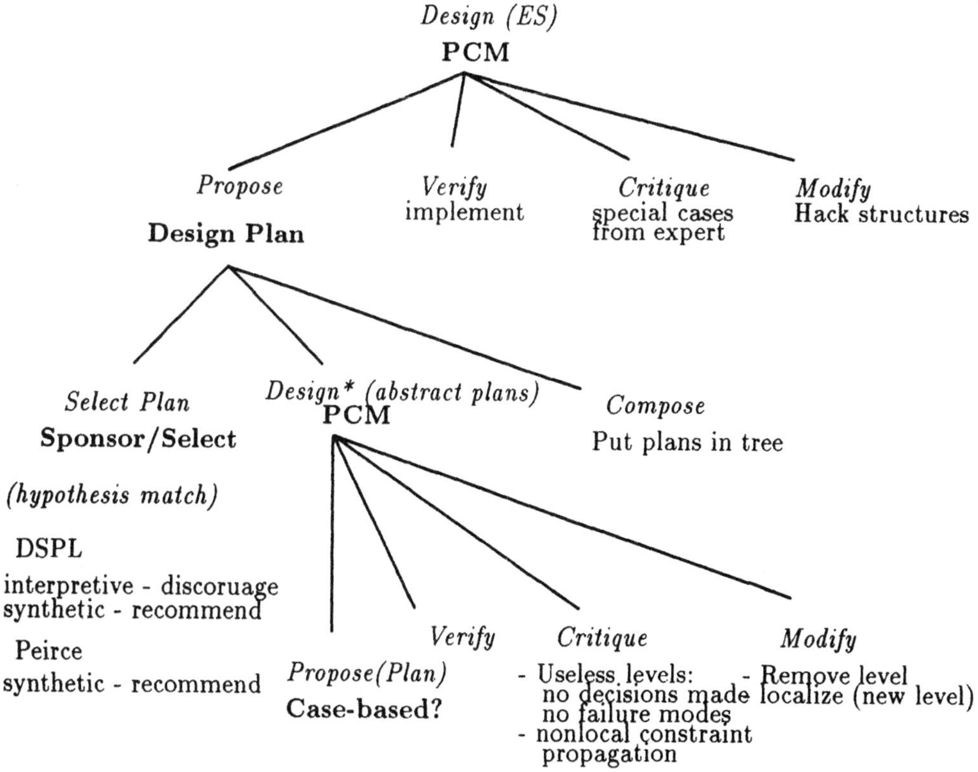

Fig. 3. GT analysis of Respondent 3's knowledge engineering activity.

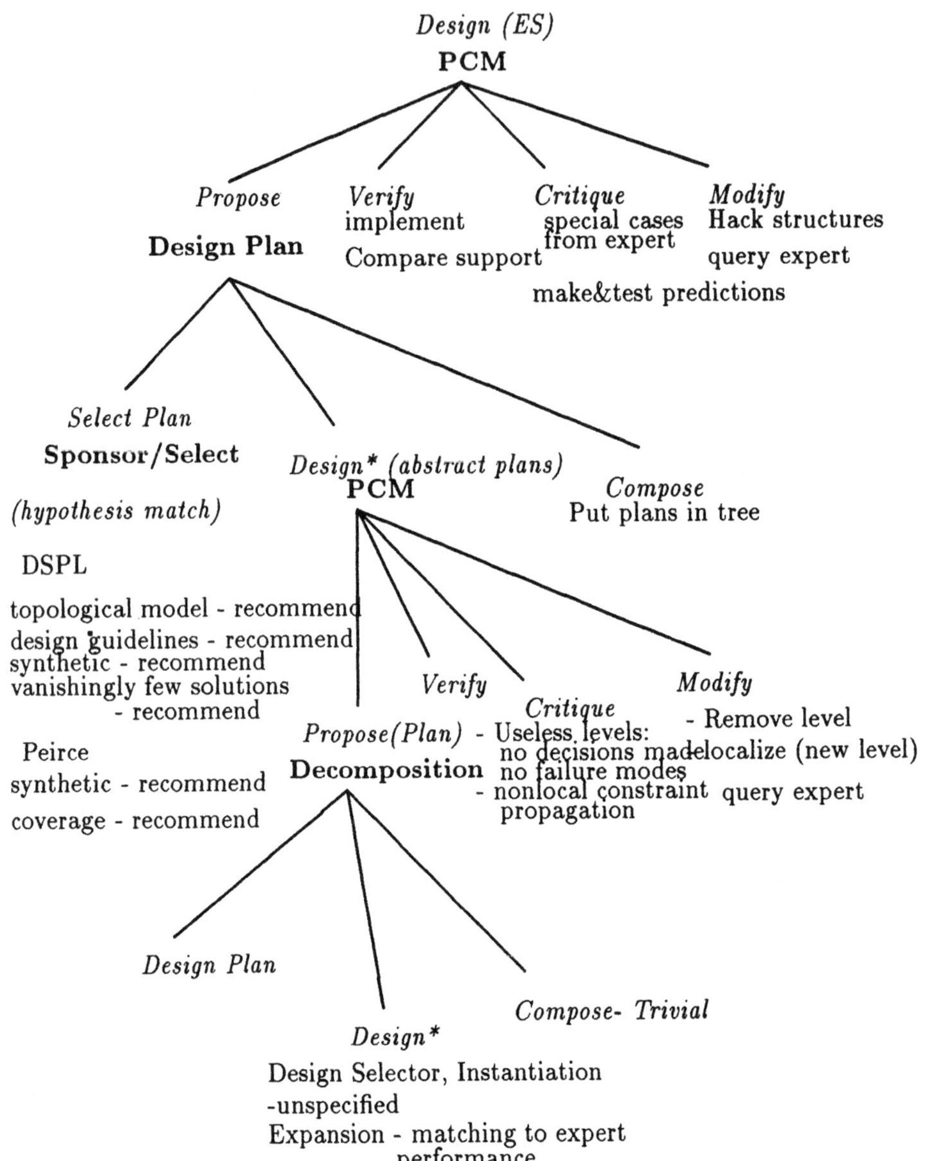

Fig. 4. Amalgamated task diagram from respondents 1, 2, 3 and 6, containing knowledge from all protocols.

Reusable analysis and design components for knowledge-based system development

David Porter

The Knowledge-Based Systems Centre, Touche Ross Management Consultants
London, U.K.

Abstract. A key feature of the KADS method for knowledge-based system development is the concept of a library of reusable generic models of expertise which are used to bootstrap and guide the analysis process. These are accompanied by a set of generic design frameworks which can be used as a starting point for the design process. This paper describes how the analysis and design components relating to the KADS *assessment* model, originally used in the domain of credit card fraud detection (the Fraudwatch system), have been successfully reused in the domain of share application fraud detection (the TRAP system).

1 Introduction

1.1 Reusability and the KADS Method

The concept of reusability is becoming increasingly important in software engineering, witnessed by the growing use of object-oriented analysis, design and programming techniques. Reusability applies equally well to knowledge-based system (KBS) development, and is a central aspect of the KADS[1] method for developing knowledge-based systems which provides support for the reuse of both analysis and design material across different KBS development projects. This paper describes how reusability in a KADS development project can take the following forms:

- reusable models of expertise;
- reusable methods of instantiating a particular type of model of expertise;
- reusable design frameworks, both generic and expertise model-specific variants.

In this paper the reuse of generic analysis and design components is illustrated with reference to a recent commercial knowledge-based system development called TRAP. For reasons of commercial confidentiality, only a certain level of information can be disclosed. However, it is hoped that the information that is presented will be of practical use to other members of the knowledge engineering community. Having the components and techniques to support reusability (whether in KADS or in general object-oriented programming) is one thing, knowing how to select and apply them is quite a different matter.

---

[1] A brief overview of KADS is presented in section 1.4 for readers not familiar with this method.

1.2 Overview of TRAP

TRAP (Touche Ross Applications Processor) is a knowledge-based system recently developed by chartered accountants Touche Ross for use in detecting fraudulent multiple share applications. TRAP has been recently used to support a team of Touche Ross forensic accountancy experts in their search for fraudulent share applications relating to the 1991 privatisation of the UK Regional Electricity Companies and Generating Companies. This flotation, valued at £8 billion, was Britain's largest-ever privatisation involving some twelve million share applications across twelve different companies. It follows that there was considerable scope for potential fraud among the applications for this share issue.

TRAP has been implemented on a high-performance PC, using a hybrid combination of knowledge-based and conventional database techniques to detect individual fraudsters and larger coordinated fraud "rings". It operates in batch mode on a large database (of the order of 500 Mbytes) of application data downloaded from a mainframe computer. The TRAP knowledge base encapsulates the Touche Ross forensic team's compiled knowledge and expertise from previous fraud audits (e.g. British Gas, British Steel and Rolls Royce) and also makes use of techniques which were pioneered during the Touche Ross/Barclaycard Fraudwatch KBS project (described later).

The TRAP knowledge base contains descriptions of patterns of fraudulent behaviour which are applied to a set of applications in order to assess the likelihood of fraud. TRAP provides the forensic team with a hardcopy report listing all suspicious cases, ranked according to severity of fraud, and accompanied by reasons for the suspicion. TRAP also provides the facility to "cleanse" the application data during data take-on and after the production of the final reports. An on-line search facility is also provided which enables the experts to interrogate the database when following up particular lines of investigation. Finally, reports produced by TRAP can be transferred into a word processing package to enable the preparation of final reports destined for the appointed prosecuting authority. An overview of the TRAP system is given in figure 1.

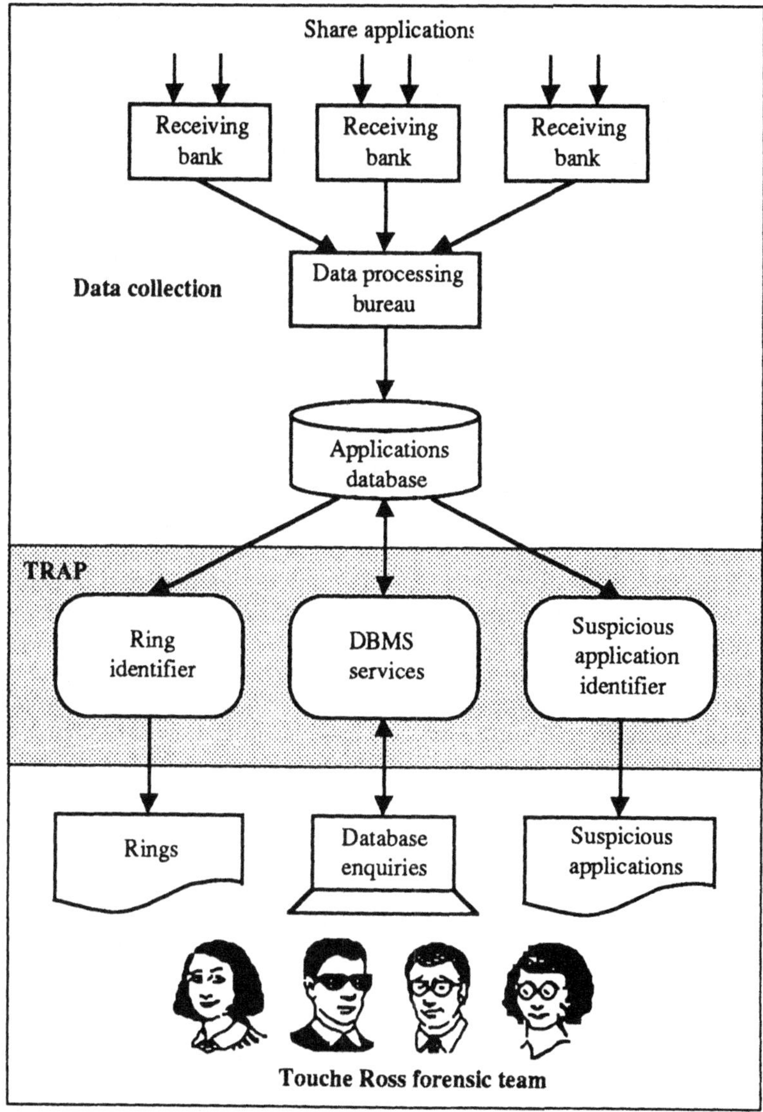

Fig. 1. Overview of the TRAP system

1.3 TRAP, Fraudwatch and Reusability

TRAP shares many similarities with the Fraudwatch credit card fraud identification system previously built by Touche Ross and Barclaycard. Fraudwatch is a KBS which detects the fraudulent use of a credit card before the card has been reported by the cardholder as lost or stolen. Fraudwatch has achieved dramatic success in detecting fraud at an early stage (current payback is in excess of £1 million per annum) and a detailed account of this system can be found in [5]. The similarities shared between the Fraudwatch and TRAP systems are as follows:

The problem. In both cases a small number of experts have the task of sifting through a large quantity of computer printout, with the aim of identifying suspicious cases which should be investigated further. The volumes of data involved are considerable (one million accounts trading daily in Fraudwatch, twelve million total applications in TRAP), the sophistication of the fraudster has increased, and the time available in which to solve the problem is very limited. Any improvement in performance will therefore be beneficial.

The expert task. The task used in the solution of this problem is the expert task of *assessment*, in which a set of case data is examined for evidence of fraud on the basis of pre-defined models (or patterns) of fraud.

The KBS solution. Both systems support the expert during the early stages of the fraud detection process, in which a large set of cases have to be reduced to a more manageable set of suspicious cases within a short period of time. Both systems are hybrid systems making use of knowledge-based techniques in conjunction with conventional algorithmic techniques to batch process a very large database.

Given the similarity of the two applications, and the previous experience and success of the Fraudwatch project, it was possible for the development team to reuse a number of generic components of the Fraudwatch analysis and design material, in particular the underlying model of assessment expertise and the method used to instantiate this model. It should be stressed that the reused material consists of an empty *generic framework* for the analysis and design specification of an assessment-type knowledge base, not the actual domain-specific *contents* of the knowledge base, which is of course proprietary to Fraudwatch and applicable only to credit card fraud identification. Such reuse was made possible by the fact that both systems were built using the KADS KBS development methodology.

1.4 The KADS Methodology

This section provides a brief overview of the KADS methodology. For further details the reader is referred to [2]. KADS is a methodology for the development of knowledge-based systems, originally developed under ESPRIT project 1098[2] and currently under further development, in the form of KADS-II, under ESPRIT project 5248[3]. It is based on best conventional software engineering practices but includes additional methods and techniques for meeting the special needs of knowledge engineering projects. In particular KADS insists on a thorough analysis of the problem before design and coding, rather than the more commonly adopted "rapid prototyping" approach. Central to KADS is the view of KBS development as a *modelling process*. System development is viewed as a steady

[2]KADS was a research project partially funded by the ESPRIT programme of the Commission of the European Communities as project number 1098. The partners in this project were: University of Amsterdam (NL), STC Technology Ltd (UK), SD-Scicon Ltd (UK), Cap Sesa Innovation (F), NTE NeuTech Gmbh (D) and Touche Ross Management Consultants (UK).

[3]KADS-II is a research project partially funded by the ESPRIT programme of the Commission of the European Communities as project number 5248. The partners in this project are: Cap Gemini Innovation (F), Cap Gemini Logic (S), Netherlands Energy Research Foundation ECN (NL), ENTEL SA (ESP), Lloyd's Register (UK), IBM France (F), Swedish Institute of Computer Science (S), Siemens AG (D), Touche Ross Management Consultants (UK), University of Amsterdam (NL) and Free University of Brussels (B). This paper reflects the opinions of the author and not necessarily those of the consortium.

progression of models from initial analysis through to detailed design. There are two main types of model produced during development [8]:

The conceptual model. This is produced during analysis, consisting of a description of the expert problem-solving behaviour and the user-system interaction (modality). It is expressed in real world-oriented terms, independent of any computational considerations.

The computational model. This is produced during design, consisting of functional, behavioural and physical design specifications. The model is expressed in computer system-oriented terms, in which computational techniques (both AI and conventional) are used to realise the requirements of the conceptual model.

The component of the conceptual model which describes the expert's problem-solving behaviour is central to KADS KBS construction. As an abstract description of the expert's problem-solving behaviour it corresponds with Newell's *knowledge level* [3]. An alternative approach, as exemplified by rapid prototyping, is to concentrate from the outset of system development on the computational AI processes and data structures required to directly implement an executable system. This approach, in direct contrast to KADS, is oriented towards Newell's *symbol level* [3]. The KADS conceptual model of expertise is based on the following two principles [8]:

- The distinction between different *types* of knowledge according to the *roles* they play in a problem-solving process;

- The organisation of knowledge types into a number of *layers* with *limited interaction.*

The typing of knowledge is based on epistemological distinctions, and at the highest level divides into *domain* and *control* types, with *control* being further divided into three sub-types. The four types of knowledge are arranged into a four-layer model as follows [8]:

Domain layer. Static knowledge describing a declarative theory of the domain.

Inference layer. Knowledge of different types of inference that can be made on the domain theory (first type of control knowledge).

Task layer. Knowledge representing tasks and problem-solving methods which are applied to the inference layer (second type of control knowledge).

Strategy layer. Strategic knowledge which controls the task layer (third type of control knowledge).

The organisation of the KADS four layer model of expertise is shown in figure 2.

Knowledge Category	Organisation	Knowledge Types
strategy ↓ *controls*	strategies	plans meta rules assumptions
task ↓ *applies*	task decomposition	tasks problem solving methods control structures control roles
inference ↓ *uses*	inference structure	primitive inference actions dynamic knowledge roles
domain	domain theory domain model user theory case model user model	concepts properties relations situation-specific information

Fig. 2. Organisation of the KADS four layer model of expertise (taken from [8])

KADS defines a taxonomy of generic expert problem-solving tasks whose leaf nodes consist of tasks such as *diagnosis, prediction, monitoring, classification, assessment, design,* etc. Each task has an associated four-layer model, which is "empty" except for the inference layer which contains an *inference structure diagram* describing the inferences involved in the execution of that particular task[4]. These are known as "interpretation models" because they help the knowledge engineer to *interpret* the expert's verbal data.

KADS analysis begins with the selection of an appropriate interpretation model from the library which is then used as a "template" for driving the knowledge acquisition process (i.e. eliciting and analysing verbal data from an expert). The knowledge engineer's task is to instantiate the layers of the model and so build a complete model of the expert's problem-solving behaviour. During this process the original "high grain" model undergoes a process of "lower grain" refinement and differentiation. The interpretation model is used to support knowledge elicitation in much the same way as an expert system shell, with the vital difference that the KADS four layer model is not tied to any particular computational formalism and is able to act as a single unifying framework for *all* elicited knowledge, ready for subsequent transformation into a design model.

As already mentioned, the original KADS methodology is now undergoing further development in the KADS-II project. Major enhancements include the revision, extension and formalisation of the modelling language, development of the life-cycle model with particular emphasis on project management and quality issues, synthesis of the methodology with other approaches to KBS and conventional systems development, and

[4]The KADS-II project is currently extending the library to include generic domain and task layer elements of variable grain size.

provision of comprehensive CASE tool support. Readers already familiar with KADS should note that some of the original KADS terminology is in the process of being renamed under KADS-II, and this is indicated where appropriate by a footnote. For further information on the KADS-II project and the latest state of the developing *CommonKADS* method, the reader is referred to [4].

2 Reusability in Analysis

2.1 The Reused Interpretation Model

The selection of an appropriate interpretation model as a candidate for reuse is an important first step in KADS analysis since it acts as the foundation for subsequent development work. In the Fraudwatch project the generic KADS *assessment* interpretation model was selected an appropriate starting point for further refinement. This model was selected as a result of an initial technical scoping study in which the nature of the expert task and the application domain were investigated in sufficient detail. It is very important that the correct model is selected for reuse, since the selection of an incorrect model will ultimately lead down a "blind alley" and waste project resources. This selection activity is still very much an expert task in itself. The inference structure diagram for the assessment task is shown in figure 3.

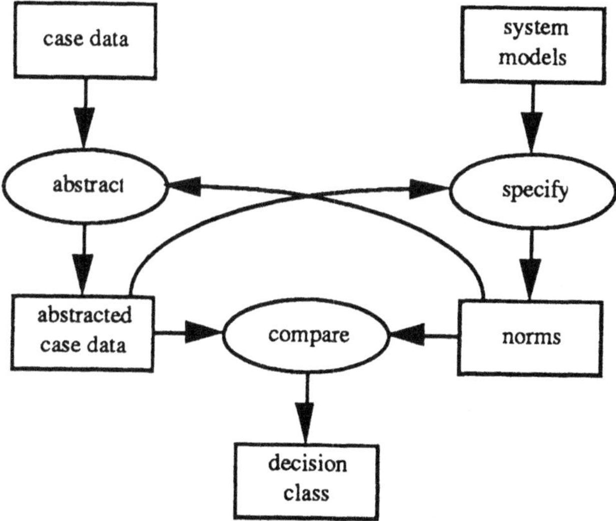

Fig. 3. KADS assessment inference structure (taken from [2])

The inference structure consists of *dynamic knowledge roles*[5] (rectangles), which are the roles that domain elements can take in the inference process, and *primitive inference actions*[6] (ellipses), which are primitive inferences that are applied to domain layer elements. Each inference action is supported by one or more *methods* (usually AI-based) together with *support knowledge* for that method. A brief explanation of the assessment

[5] Original KADS term: *metaclasses.*

[6] Original KADS term: *knowledge sources.*

inference structure is as follows. The *case data* contain details of the current case under assessment. The comparison of the *case data* with one of the *system models* is done at a level of abstraction away from the data *(abstract)*, and only those aspects of one of the *system models* that apply to the particular case *(norms)* are used in the comparison *(specify)*. The arrows in the inference structure diagram show the input and output to each inference action rather than execution order. The actual invocation of each inference action is specified by an overlying *task structure*. The inference structure can be driven by a task structure in a number of ways:

Data-driven (or forward chaining. Evidence from *case data* leads to a conclusion in the form of a proven *system model*.

Goal-driven (or backward chaining. A *system model* hypothesis is initially selected and then proved true or false according to the *case data* evidence.

Combined data- and goal-driven. Initial evidence from key items of *case data* is used to select a candidate *system model* hypothesis, which is then proved true or false according to further *case data* evidence. This was the task structure which was used in both the Fraudwatch and TRAP projects and is specified as follows:

```
assess(case_data → decision_class) =
   abstract(case_data → abstracted_case_data)
   specify(fraud_model + abstracted_case_data → fraud_norms)
   do for each norm ∈ fraud_norms
      abstract(case_data + fraud_norm → abstracted_case_data)
   compare(abstracted_case_data + fraud_norms → decision_class)

compare(abstracted_case_data + fraud_norms → decision_class) =
   do for each norm ∈ fraud_norms
      match(abstracted_case_data + fraud_norm → degree_of_fit)
   rank(degree_of_fit → decision_class)
```

The KADS assessment model selected as a candidate for reuse was subsequently modified, according to the nature of the Fraudwatch domain, to support *the assessment of fraudulent cases contained within a large volume of data*. The two main refinements to the original assessment model are as follows:

- The addition of an initial *select* inference process which acts as an initial "filter" in order to prevent processing overload;

- The decomposition of the *compare* inference into *match* and *rank* inferences in order to rank cases according to the suspected degree of fraud. *Match* matches the *abstracted case data* against the selected *norms* to determine the *degree of fit* and from this *rank* produces a *decision class* representing the overall level of suspicion assigned to the assessed case.

Other refinements are more "cosmetic", for example the use of the term *fraud models* rather than *system models* to describe one of the knowledge roles, which reflects the characteristics of the fraud identification domain. The resulting *selective assessment* inference structure is shown in figure 4.

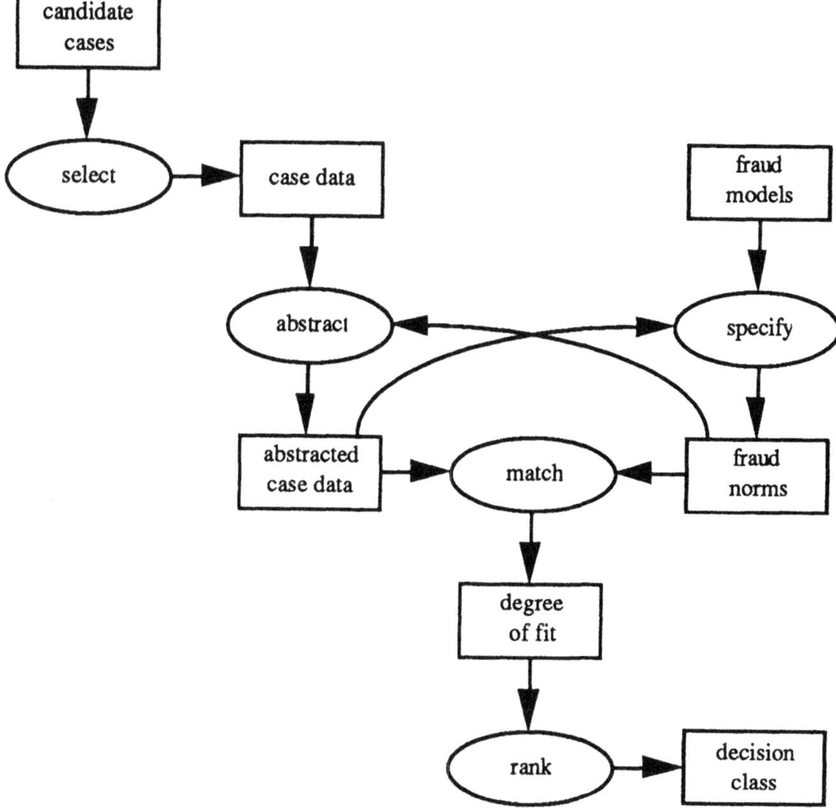

Fig. 4. Selective assessment inference structure (adapted from [5])

In the TRAP project the selective assessment model, originally defined in the Fraudwatch project, was selected as an appropriate model for reuse because of the similarities between the two applications already discussed in section 1.3. In summary, these similarities related to the nature of the *expert task* (selective assessment) and that of the *domain* (fraud identification).

To summarise this section, the Fraudwatch project reused the KADS generic assessment model and subsequently refined it to form the selective assessment model for use in the domain of credit card fraud identification. The TRAP project reused the Fraudwatch selective assessment model for use in the alternative domain of share application fraud identification. In "classical" object-oriented programming terms, we could think of the assessment and selective assessment interpretation models as being equivalent to "classes", and the Fraudwatch and TRAP realisations of these models (i.e. instantiated with the appropriate knowledge) as different "instances" of the selective assessment "class". This is illustrated in figure 5.

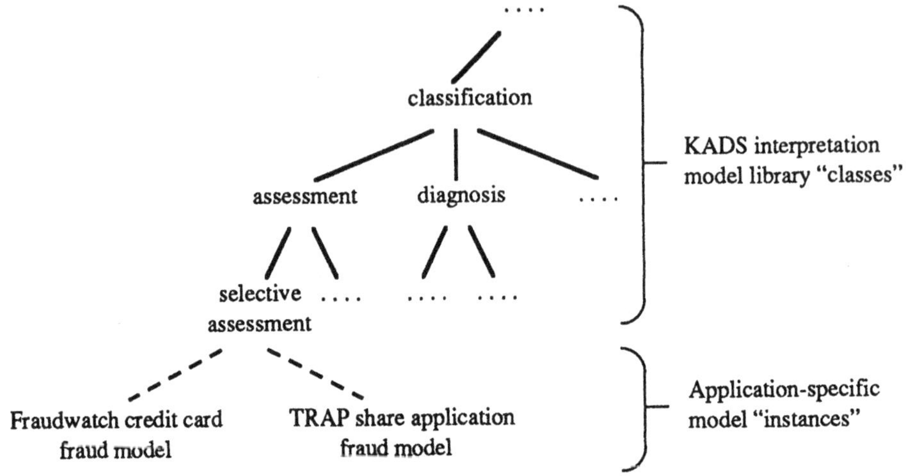

Fig. 5. An object-oriented interpretation of the Fraudwatch and TRAP systems

2.2 Instantiating the Reused Model

In addition to reusing the selective assessment model from the Fraudwatch project, the method of instantiating the main assessment component of that model was also reused in the TRAP project and this will now be described. The most practical entry point into an interpretation model, for instantiation purposes, is often at the inference layer, from where the knowledge engineer can progress "down" to the domain layer and then "up" to the task and strategy layers. This is illustrated in figure 6.

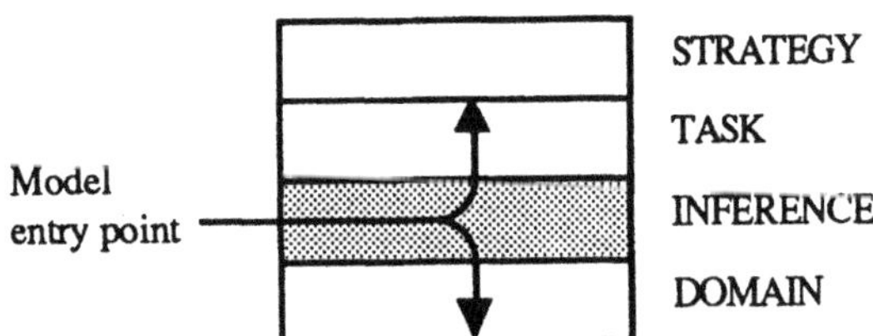

Fig. 6. Entry point into the interpretation model

The process of instantiating or "fleshing out" the model in both Fraudwatch and TRAP projects began with the instantiation of the domain and inference layers of the model, followed by the instantiation of the task and strategy layers. Instantiation of the elements of the inference layer and domain layer took place mainly in parallel, with most emphasis on the domain layer. The inference structure acts as a useful "roadmap", providing the knowledge engineer with vital clues concerning *what* sort of domain knowledge is used in the problem solving process and *how* that knowledge is used. For example, each inference action provides clues as to what sort of methods and support knowledge are required in the domain layer to support the inference. Similarly, each knowledge role provides clues as to which domain layer elements can fulfil that particular role. This facilitates the planning of knowledge elicitation and the structure and contents of each expert interview according to which part of the inference structure we wish to instantiate, such as case studies (which are always required when a *system models* knowledge role is present), self report, teachback and structured interviews. The extent to which the layers of the model and their component parts are instantiated enables the analyst to quantify the "completeness" of the model and enables the project manager to judge the state of progress of the analysis work[7].

At the highest level, it is possible to identify two main steps involved in the instantiation of the assessment inference structure:

- First tackle the *abstract* and *specify* components at the "top" of the structure;

- Then tackle the *compare* component at the "bottom" of the structure.

This is illustrated in figure 7.

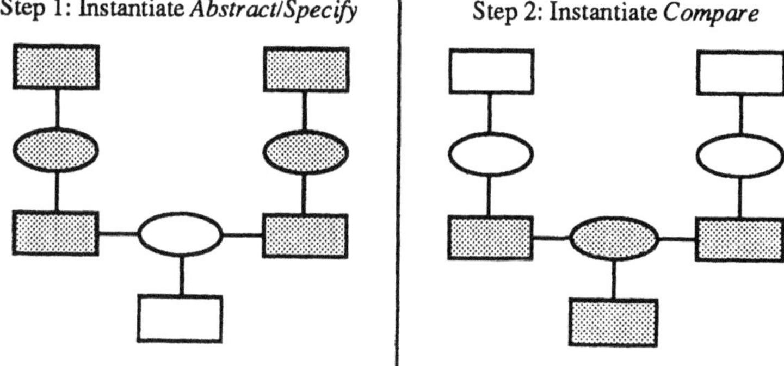

Fig. 7. Top-level instantiation of the assessment inference structure

At a more detailed level, it is possible to specify a number of lower-level steps involved in the instantiation process. Before these steps are described, the reader should note that the following should not be taken as a definitive prescriptive statement of how the assessment model should be constructed. Depending on the characteristics of the development, steps may often be repeated, executed in a different order or in parallel with other steps, or combined together. However, it does illustrate the general approach used in both the Fraudwatch and TRAP projects which could potentially be reused in future developments.

The first point to make is that the contents of the *system models* knowledge role constitutes the foundation of the entire inference structure. Every other element of the inference structure is dependent in some way on the system model definition and in this respect it is a key component. Instantiating the *system models* knowledge role is one of the most difficult and important tasks to be performed. An illustration of this dependency is illustrated in figure 8.

---

[7]The concept of successive model states and their quantification as a basis for project management and quality assurance is currently a major topic in the KADS-II life-cycle model work.

1: Specification of norms for a particular system model

2: Specification of abstractions required to match with norms

3: Specification of case data upon which abstractions are made

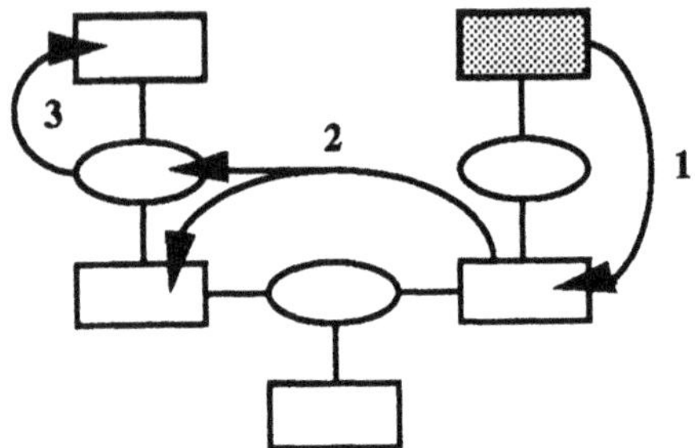

Fig. 8. *System models* as the primary inference structure component

The four detailed steps in the instantiation of the components of the assessment inference structure are illustrated in figure 9. For each step the element of the inference structure currently being instantiated is shaded and arrows are used to indicate how the instantiation of that element feeds into the instantation of other elements.

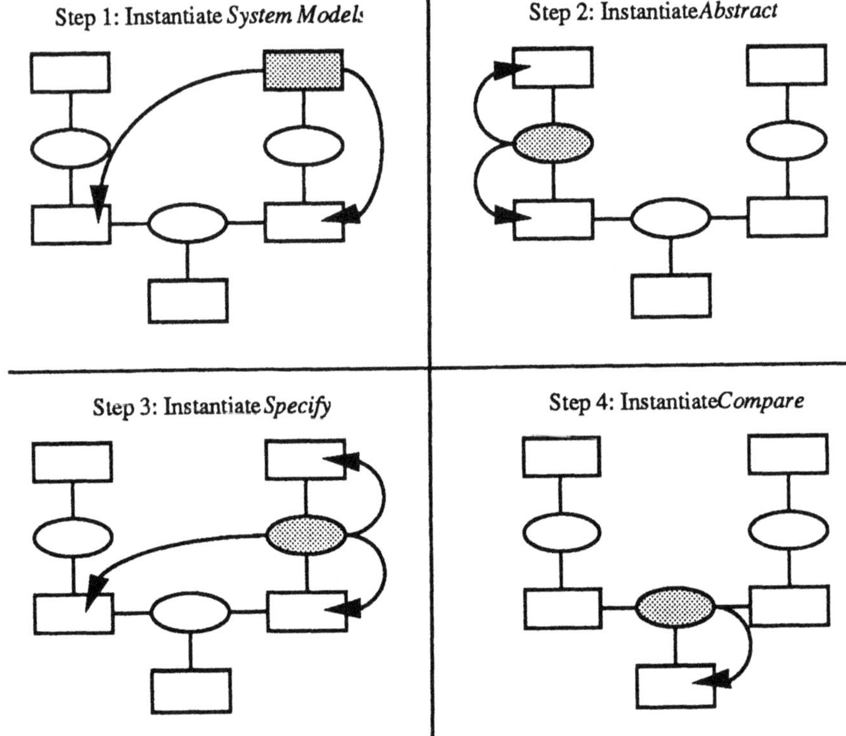

Fig. 9. Detailed instantiation of the assessment inference structure

A brief description of each of these steps as they were applied during the TRAP analysis is as follows:

Instantiate system models. *System models* defines models (or patterns) of fraudulent behaviour in the form of conceptual structures located in the domain layer. It guides us towards the *norms* which relate to the currently hypothesised fraud model (defined using a subset of the *system models* domain layer notation) and the *abstracted case data* which represent qualitative descriptions of *case data* observables. The aim is to elicit statements from the expert such as: *"There are basically three types of fraud in this area, X, Y, and Z..."*.

Instantiate abstract. *Abstract* defines, in the form of heuristic rules, the abstractions needed to produce *abstracted case data*. This inference action is often the largest with regard to the body of support knowledge upon which it is based. It guides us towards the relevant *case data* upon which abstractions are based, which in the cases of Fraudwatch and TRAP are ultimately represented by database file and record definitions. The aim is to elicit statements from the expert such as: *"A is a particularly important aspect of fraud type X, and a very good sign of A is if case datum D is..."*.

Instantiate specify. *Specify* defines, in the form of discrimination rules, how a candidate system model is selected on the basis of current abstractions. The instantiation of this inference action has a useful refinement effect on *abstracted case data, system models* and *norms*. The aim is to elicit statements from the expert such as: *"If A, B and C abstractions can be made then I would suspect that this is fraud type Z..."*.

Instantiate compare. *Compare* defines the way in which *abstracted case data* are matched with *norms* relating to the currently hypothesised *system model* and the assignment of a final *decision class* value representing the degree to which a case is fraudulent. This takes the form of pattern matching and the algorithmic combination of weightings assigned to *norms*. The aim is to elicit statements from the expert such as: *"Depending on how the abstractions match the characteristics of the fraud type, I would rank the case as follows..."*.

The method of instantiating the assessment inference structure described in this section can potentially be modified and reused for other generic tasks such as *diagnosis* and *planning*, since inference actions such as *abstract, match* and *specify* are common across a number of these tasks.

3 Reusability in Design

3.1 The KADS Design Process

For the benefit of readers not familiar with the KADS design process, a brief overview now follows. KADS design, like analysis, is a modelling activity although the design model is system-oriented rather than real world-oriented. In the design phase the output of analysis — the conceptual model — is transformed into a design model. The design model is at a higher level of abstraction than an implementation formalism but remains specific enough to constrain the implementation process [6]. The KADS design model consists of three different specifications:

Functional specification. This is the functional (logical) description of the prospective system in the form of a decomposition hierarchy of functional blocks (or "what" is required of the system). This is augmented with descriptions of control and data flow relations between functional blocks. Each leafnode functional block is specified in detail.

Behavioural specification. This involves the selection of a set of both AI and conventional *methods* and *design elements* (building blocks) which are capable of realising the behaviour of the leaf node functional blocks in the functional decomposition hierarchy.

Physical specification. This is a physical specification of "how" to implement the design elements of the behavioural specification using appropriate KBS and conventional programming tools. Design elements in the behavioural layer are aggregated into a number of discrete *physical modules* which represent the final system architecture. Each physical module is then specified in detail.

3.2 Generic Functional Design Frameworks

Reusability in KADS has mainly been focussed on the analysis phase of development, in the form of generic interpretation models as described in section 1.4[8]. However, the experience of the TRAP and Fraudwatch projects is that reusability in KADS is also possible during the design phase of development. The key to reusability here lies in the *KADS design paradigm,* which is founded on the preservation of the structure of the four layer model during design. There is usually a near-isomorphic mapping between the elements of the conceptual model and the elements of the design model, which is very beneficial for explanation, testing, debugging, maintenance and knowledge refinement purposes.

To help guide the designer during the early stages of functional design, KADS provides three generic frameworks, each of which concentrates on a particular aspect of functional design. These can be used as starting points for the design process, being further refined as appropriate. In addition to reusing these frameworks during the TRAP project, the problem solving components of the Fraudwatch functional design models were also reused as starting points for the TRAP design. In this section the three reused design frameworks, all oriented towards the assessment problem solving task, will be presented.

The first reusable KADS design framework is the top-level functional decomposition framework which recommends that the system is partitioned into the following functional groupings:

Cooperation. Modality or KBS–user cooperation management functions.

Communication. Interface functions (e.g. with the user, sensors, databases, other systems, etc).

Problem solving. Core problem solving functions (derived from the strategy, task and inference layers of the four layer model of expertise).

[8]The KADS-II project is addressing the issue of generic computational (design) elements with the aim of providing a library of such elements to accompany the existing library of generic analysis elements.

The adoption of the KADS design paradigm results in a very close mapping between the inference layer of the four layer model and the functional decomposition of the problem solving functional block listed above. Figure 10 shows a simplified version of the functional decomposition design framework which was used as a starting point for the TRAP design. The assessment problem solving component of the framework is shaded.

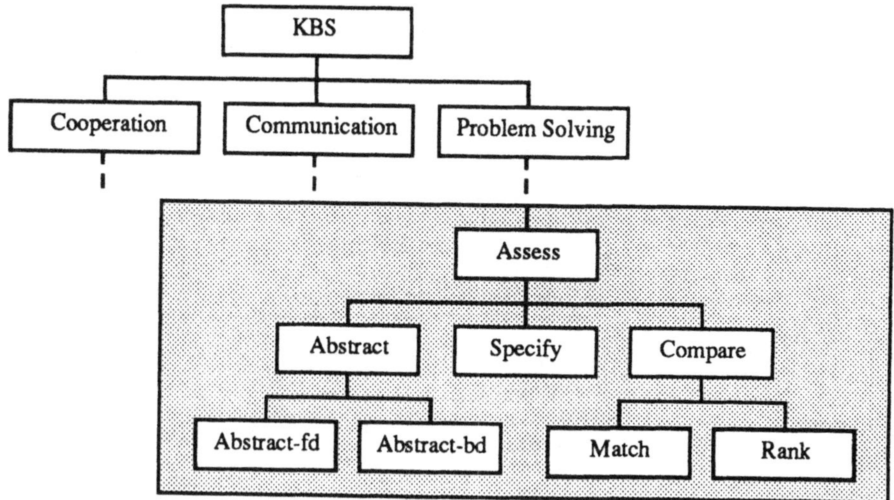

Fig. 10. Generic functional decomposition framework for assessment

The second reusable KADS design framework is the top level dataflow framework which recommends the overall data flow between different parts of the system. The recommended data flow chain is as follows: *User, Communication, Cooperation, Problem Solving,* and *Domain Model.* Again, if we focus in on the problem solving functional block we can see that the adoption of the KADS design paradigm results in a strong mapping between the I/O relations in the assessment inference structure and the dataflow relations in the functional design model. Figure 11 shows the dataflow design framework which was used as a starting point for the TRAP design. The arrows linking functional blocks represent data flows, and the assessment problem solving component of the framework is shaded.

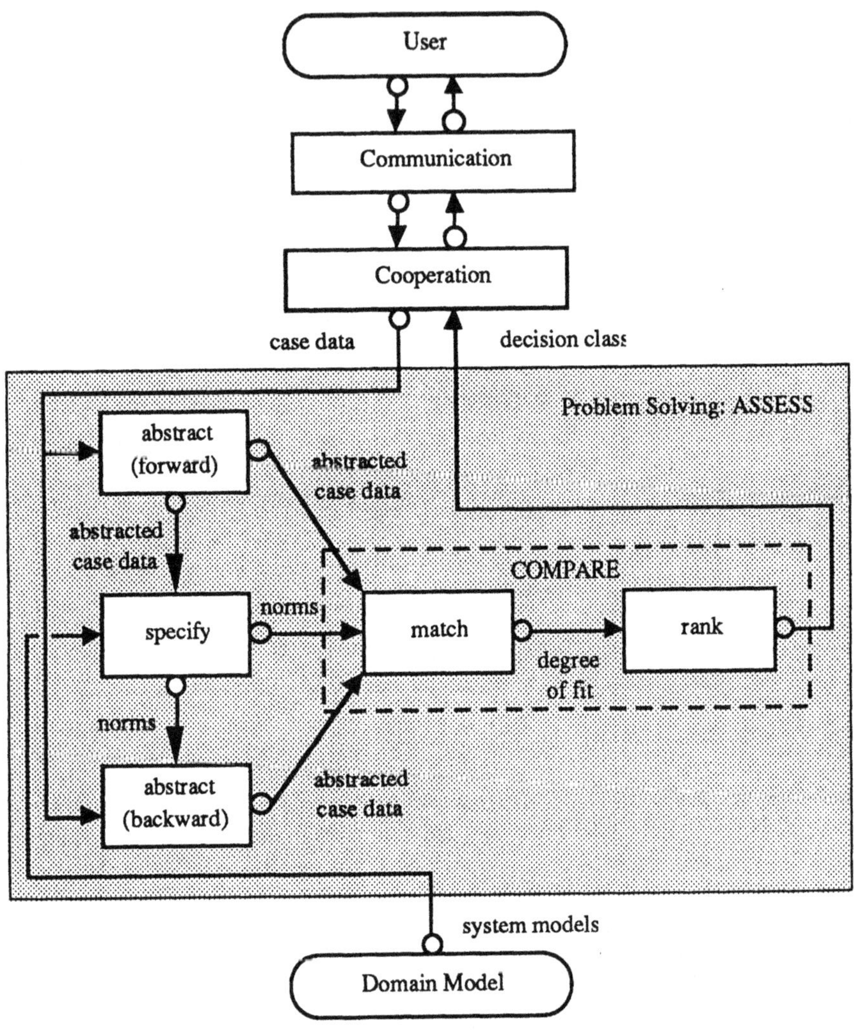

Fig. 11. Generic dataflow design framework for assessment (adapted from [1])

The third and final reusable KADS design framework is the top level control framework which recommends the overall control flow between different parts of the system. There is a strong mapping between the four level control structure of the conceptual model and that of the design model. Again, if we focus in on the problem solving functional block we can see that the adoption of the KADS design paradigm results in a strong mapping between the design model control structure and the task structure of the conceptual model previously shown in section 2.1. Figure 12 shows the control design framework which was used as a starting point for the TRAP design. The arrows show the flow of control down the hierarchy, from the overall strategic planner down to lower-level inference and communication functions. The assessment problem solving component of the framework is shaded.

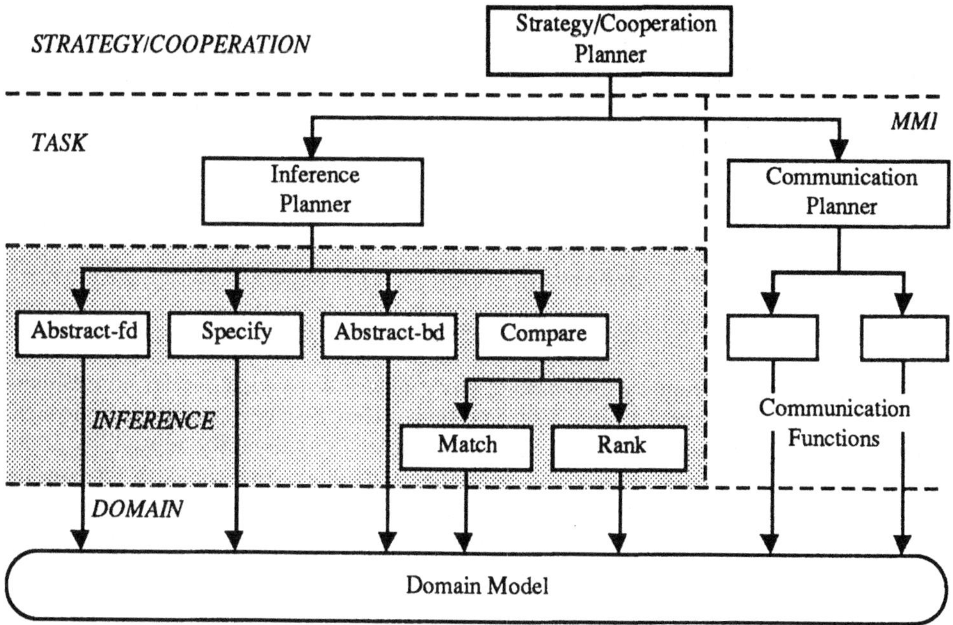

Fig. 12. Generic control design framework for assessment (adapted from [7])

3.3 Reusability in Behavioural Design

A degree of reusability is also possible during behavioural design. The behavioural design model of the Fraudwatch system provided useful indications of the kinds of AI methods and design elements which could be used to realise the problem solving functional blocks for an assessment problem solving model. Examples are *forward and backward chaining rule-based system* and *combinational weighting algorithm*. These methods and design elements will of course vary across different designs, depending on the conceptual model and various non-functional requirements. Nevertheless, they were a useful starting point for the TRAP designers.

3.4 Reusability in Physical Design

Reusability is really only possible during physical design if the same programming environments are used across two projects. This was not the case in the Fraudwatch and TRAP projects, as shown in table 1.

System	KBS routines	Conventional routines	Hardware/OS
Fraudwatch	KnowledgeTool™ PL/1	PL/1 COBOL IMS	IBM 3090 MVS/XA
TRAP	Leonardo™	Clipper™	IBM 80386 PC MS-DOS

Table 1. Summary of Fraudwatch/TRAP programming environments

Each project used a different programming environment to provide the design elements specified in the behavioural design, therefore they differed with regard to their physical module specifications and reusability was not possible. With regard to reusability at the coding level, this would depend on both projects using the same programming environment, as already discussed, as well as the degree of modularity of the coded routines (i.e. a structured or object-oriented programming approach would be essential). This last point obviously applies to all software development, conventional as well as KBS.

4 Conclusions

The TRAP project has shown that there is considerable potential for reusability during both the analysis and design stages of a KADS system development, in the form of generic interpretation models and design frameworks. These act as powerful support tools for the knowledge engineer, providing useful starting points for further development and refinement. The knowledge and experience relating to the selection of the correct components for reuse and subsequent refinement and instantiation of these components is continuing to grow as more and more KADS-based systems are developed.

TRAP has been used with great success on the UK Electricity privatisation project. Latest results have shown that TRAP can reduce the amount of initial paperwork that the expert has to go through by up to 75%. TRAP has already identified a number of highly suspicious multiple applications which are being further investigated, and its performance continues to improve with knowledge refinement. There is no doubt that the development of TRAP benefited from shorter development times as a result of reusing existing KADS-based components. A particularly attractive feature of KADS is that as well as providing a library of such components, these components are expressed at an *implementation-independent* level and can therefore be reused across a variety of hardware and software platforms (as shown in table 1, section 3.4).

A major benefit of TRAP is the potential reusability of the system. The TRAP knowledge base can be refined, scaled and adapted for use on subsequent privatisation projects. It has already been reused for analysing applications for the UK Generating Company share issue and is currently being reused in the British Telecom share offer. At a more generic level, the foundation *selective assessment* or *assessment* models upon which TRAP is based can be applied to other areas of fraud detection (e.g. computer fraud, retail product shrinkage, etc) as well as non-fraud domains (e.g. bad debt, loan risk, product performance, market trends, etc).

The theme of reusability is continuing to play a central part within the KADS-II project, with the addition of generic, variable grain size, domain and task layer elements to the library of reusable components, as well as the creation of a complementary library of generic design elements [4]. This will make possible "middle-out" reusability in addition to the more traditional "top-down" KADS approach, offering a new challenge to the knowledge engineers of the 1990s.

Acknowledgements

The TRAP system described in this paper was the result of a team effort and the author would like to acknowledge the other members of the Touche Ross TRAP/KBS development team. The author would also like to thank Lise Land and Tim Mulhall of Touche Ross for their comments on this paper.

References

1. Y. Chon, K. Streng, R. Nobis: *Process monitoring and preventative maintenance: System document.* ESPRIT Project 1098, Deliverable E10.1, NTE NeuTech, 1989.

2. F. Hickman, J. Killin, L. Land, T. Mulhall, D. Porter, R. Taylor: *Analysis for knowledge-based systems: A practical introduction to the KADS methodology.* Ellis Horwood, 1989.

3. A. Newell: 'The knowledge level'. *Artificial Intelligence,* **18**, pp. 87–127, 1982.

4. D. Porter: *KADS-II: Towards the CommonKADS method.* ESPRIT Project 5248 KADS-II, Public Paper KADS-II/T5.1.2/PP/TRMC/001/1.0, Touche Ross Management Consultants, 1992.

5. D. Porter, R. Taylor: 'A knowledge-based system for identifying credit card fraud'. *Business benefits of expert systems (BCS Expert Systems 90): Papers from the applications stream,* Clearway International, 1990.

6. G. Schreiber, B. Bredeweg (Eds.), M. Davoodi, B. Wielinga: *Towards a design methodology for knowledge-based systems.* ESPRIT Project 1098, Deliverable D8, University of Amsterdam and STC plc, 1987.

7. G. Schreiber, G. (Ed.), B. Bredeweg, P. de Greef, P. Terpstra, B. Wielinga, E. Brunet, A. Wallyn: *A KADS approach to KBS design.* ESPRIT Project 1098, Deliverable B6, University of Amsterdam, 1989.

8. B. Wielinga, W. Van de Velde, G. Schreiber, H. Akkermans (Eds.): *Towards a unification of knowledge modelling approaches.* ESPRIT Project 5248 KADS-II, Deliverable D1.1, University of Amsterdam, Free University of Brussels and Netherlands Energy Research Foundation, 1991.

Acquiring descriptive knowledge for classification and identification

Michel MANAGO, Noël CONRUYT

ACKNOWLEDGE, 16 Passage Foubert, 75013 Paris France.

Jacques LE RENARD

Muséum d'Histoire Naturelle, Laboratoire de Biologie des Invertébrés Marins et Malacologie, 55 rue de Buffon, 75005 Paris France.

Abstract: During the past decade, numerous real world knowledge-based systems have been built for the purpose of identification. Although most identification systems are based on the ability to observe and describe, few systems adress one of the first steps in knowledge acquisition which is how to acquire descriptions. Collecting this *descriptive knowledge* (observed facts) requires that a *descriptive model* (observable facts) has been previously defined. In addition, experience shows that the model depends on the goal which is pursued. In this paper, we present a tool and a methodology for the acquisition of the descriptive knowledge and the corresponding model which was designed primarily for identification. To achieve this goal, we have first used induction and have ran into redhibitory problems due to some limitations of this technology for processing incomplete descriptions. We present how we have stretched the technology in a case-based reasoning fashion to overcome these limitations. The tools and methodology have been developped and validated in the context of several real world applications.

1 Acquiring descriptions

The activity of describing is taking place each time it is necessary to characterize, to recognize or to identify something. The mental description process could appear to be quite random, but in fact it implies the reference to a structured model. Acquiring this model, for a given kind of object, is a fundamental step in the cognitive development of observation. For example, in biology, a description is generally used for classifying and/or identifying. While the latter activity may be done by practically everybody, classification is reserved to a small number of specialists. Each of these specialists has developped his own method for characterizing the different classes of biological objects or individuals he is dealing with. There exist few tools to help him, apart from classical data analysis software which only allow a limited and restrictive data representation.

The aim of our project is to provide the expert with a set of tools which let him collect and handle all the descriptions he wants, without artificial limitations. Once the particular domain has been delimited (according to the expert's area of interest), the global goal to be achieved is to accumulate a number of observations, which constitutes the *descriptive knowledge*, in what is called a case base. This knowledge must be expressed in such a way that it allows various usages. For instance, comparisons between cases, automated edition of descriptions and diagnoses, classification (i.e. characterization of the distinguished classes), inductive generation of trees, and identification (by a specialist as well as a

Section 5.3 has been further developed in ***Michel Manago and Noël Conruyt; Using Information Technology to Solve Real World Problems; in Schmalhofer, F., Strube, G., and Wetter, Th. (eds.); Contemporary Knowledge Engineering and Cognition; Berlin: Springer 1992*** newcomer). Thus the descriptive knowledge has to be exhaustive, precise and flexible, and it cannot be stored randomly but structured according to a logical frame. The activity of describing implies such a reference to a more or less explicit model of description, what we call the *descriptive model* of the domain. While this model is often reduced to a mere table of characters (attributes) in most tools for data acquisition or analysis, we have deliberately used a richer knowledge representation which can take into account the great diversity of biological or natural characters (in terms of values, ranges, precision, relations etc.). A particular care is payed to *incomplete observations*.

In the first part of this paper, we present a methodology for gathering the descriptive model (phase 1) and a tool to collect the case database (phase 2). Both are expressed in an object-based representation language. There are interdependancies between phases: phase 2 depends on the completion of phase 1. However, phase 1 also depends on phase 3 because the descriptive model varies according to the final goal that is to be achieved (identification). Therefore, although we have made a sequential presentation the different phases, in reality this process is incremental: one builds an initial descriptive model, collect cases, build an identication system and often modify the model or the case library depending on the results.

Phase	Task	Outcome
❶	Building the descriptive model	Questionnaire
❷	Collecting case descriptions (descriptive knowledge>)	Case database
❸	Generating the identification or classification system	expert system, *identification* system, or classification of the data

Case descriptions are made out of objects and relations between objects. The terms (vocabulary) used to describe the training cases are the names of the objects, the names of slots and slot values. Additional knowledge can be expressed in this language. For instance, constraints on descriptors which are relevant for describing a particular object, constraints on the values which are possible for a descriptor in a certain context, rules to deduce the value of a descriptor from other descriptor values, hierarchies of objects and so on.

2 What is a description?

We have first to analyze the elementary phases that are involved during the activity of describing, in order to specify what is involved in a description.

The most obvious phase consists in splitting the description into a set of more or less independant sub-descriptions, that we call local descriptions. This is obtained by decomposing the whole physical object that is being studied into parts and subparts, each of them giving rise to its own local description and which may in turn be divided into subparts. These subparts are rarely independant from each others, and their relations have to be established (e.g. conditions of mutual significance, conditionnal values, inheritance etc). A subpart either exists in one or more instances (in which case it/they can be described), be absent (object = none; this is an information), or we may ignore wether or not it exists (object = unknown; in that case, all its own subparts are also unknown). Each local description is formed by a list of local characters, represented by slots.

Another elementary descriptive phase is the distinction between several kinds of the same generic subpart. Each of these only differs from the others by some details, which implies that we should not introduce different high level concepts for these. This is merely an instantiation process.

The last descriptive mechanism is the progressive characterisation of an object, following a particular graph of generality. Objects lower down in the graph inherit the more general characters from their parents, and have some additional characteristics of their own. This is classically implemented in frame-based languages [Minsky, 1975].

In order to illustrate these three elementary descriptive phases with something that everyone can understand, let us imagine that we have to describe some mammal. If we begin in distinguishing a head, a trunk, members and a tail, and then if we consider that the head consists of eyes, ears, a nose and so on, we are engaged in the first process. Now, we have to open the mouth and describe what we see. Several kinds of teeth are present , and it is usefull to describe separately each of these kinds (even if we have forgotten their name) by following the same schema. Doing so, we have followed an instantiation process. Finally, if we discover that the anterior members are in fact a pair of fins (if our mammal is a whale!), we would like not to be asked about subparts like arms or hands: the fact that a fin is "a kind of" member, with particular characters, can be taken in account by the specialisation process.

Following these three phases, we can deduce the corresponding structure of a generalized descriptive model, the way such a model can be designed for a particular domain, and the specifications of a tool allowing the instanciation of this model for a particular description.

3 Designing the descriptive model

One must pay particular attention when creating the descriptive model for a new domain. It is essential at this point to work with at least one domain expert. In the case of the application described in this paper, the descriptive model has been designed by us, acting as "knowledge engineers", following a similar iterative method as for creating a regular expert system. The application used to illustrate our presentation has been developped with Pr. Claude Lévi, a renowned specialist of the Spongia (a group of marine animals). We present it in more details in section 6.5.

The first step is to identify the basic objects presently used (as concepts) by the expert or appearing in the various descriptions already published in the specialized literature. The structure and relations that can exist between these objects are critically defined by the expert, and a preliminar descriptive model is proposed for progressive improvement. In our example, it appeared that the decomposition of the object "body of the sponge" into subparts was to be completed by a decomposition into macro- and micro-elements (correspondind to different and independant scales of observation). The main difficulty at this point is to correctly distinguish objects and slots (i.e. features of objects): this is helped by drawing the pattern of the different relations between objects, which locate the slots as terminal leaves of the description tree (see figure 3).

The second step is to define the different features of the objects (represented as slots). This implies defining the type of the slot (i.e. wether it expects an integer or a real value, an interval, a nominal/symbolic slot, a structured value), the range of the slot, the number of values it can have (zero, a single value, or several). When a feature is shared by several objects, these definitions can be further refined for each object. For example, the allowed values for the "longueur" (length) slot depend on the object ("marginalia" or "tignules") that is being described:

```
(defslot longueur real Interval
    (range
       (object   (marginalia 0.1 2.5)
                 (tignules 1.0 10.0)))
    (unit mm))
```

The second step also corresponds to listing the different values that each nominal feature can take. The symbolic nature of such an information is better illustrated by schema or figures, which can be grouped into an album for further integration in the description guide (see below). Finally, we also identify logical relations to deduce slot values from other slot values, and constraints between slot values (i.e. when two values cannot occur simultaneously). Note that there can be several iterations between the first and second steps. For example, we use different "cooking receipes" such as "if an object does not have slots and subparts, it probably should not be defined as an object but should be turned into an attribute value". Thus, a relation can become a slot and an object a slot value during this process.

The third step is to identify generalization structures among the objects or among the slot values. Hierarchies of objects are classically modelled by subsumption links between concepts in frames ("A kind of" link); frames lower down in the subsumption hierarchy inherit slots from frames higher up. In addition, we can express hierarchies of values. The following representation illustrates how "renflee" (= inflated), which is one of the values of the feature "shape" of the object "body of the sponge"), can be decomposed in several subvalues (we show the drawings of the subvalues of "inflated" in figure 2). These subvalues are not mutually exclusive and up to 3 subvalues can be selected simultaneously (note that it means that the slot value is a conjunction of subvalues and not a disjunction due to some uncertainty/noise) :

```
(defvalue renflee
        (subValue en-flute en-corolle piriforme ovoide bulbiforme)
        (cardinal 1 3))
```

The fourth step is to generate an interactive questionnaire, which will direct the description of any individual (physical object), according to the descriptive model. Using this methodology with actual cases allows a rapid verification that the descriptive model is sufficiently exhaustive and consistent.

4 Collecting case descriptions

Once the descriptive model has been designed, it can be used in a tool which automatically builds an interactive questionnaire for collecting the database of cases. This hypermedia tool called HyperQuest, generates automatically such a questionnaire (HyperQuest is implemented in C and Hypertalk).

Entities of the descriptive model (knowledge base, objects, slots, slot values) map onto Hypertext entities (stack, cards, buttons etc.). Additional domain knowledge (rules to deduce slot values from other slot values, constraints on relevant descriptors) are compiled into hypertalk scripts. What follows is the mapping between these entities:

knowledge base ----> stack (questionnaire)
slots of an object -----> card with scroll field for the slot names
components of an object ------> card with buttons for the components
subobjects --------------> card with buttons for the subobjects
slot --------> item in the scroll field of the object card
slot values (qualitative) ------> card with buttons corresponding the values
slot values (string/comment) -------> card with an edit box
slot values (numeric) --------> card with ruler for entering the value
rules and constraints ----------> compiled scripts

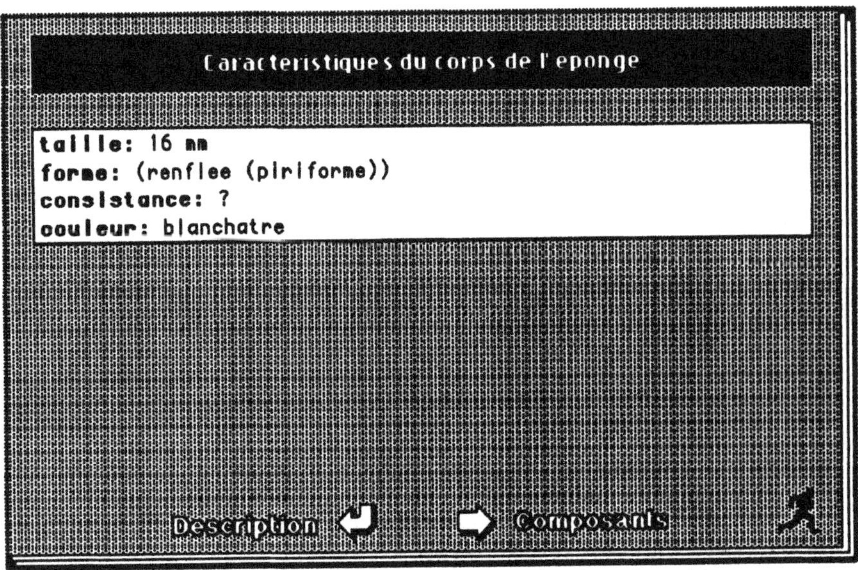

Figure 1: A card which corresponds to the slots of an object

The following object definition maps onto the hypertext entities shown in figure 1. Note that the slots are defined elsewhere (whether the slot is numerical, structured or qualitative, the range for the slot, whether it expect a single or several values and so on).

```
(defobject corps
        (part-of    eponge)
        (gender     ms)
        (subparts   macro-constituants
                    micro-elements)
        (slots      taille
                    forme
                    consistance
                    couleur))
```

Using the usual hypercard tools, the user can customize the questionnaire by adding text, graphics or multi-media facilities. He can associate images (pictures or drawing), define sensitive parts of the images with arbitrary shapes, move buttons etc.

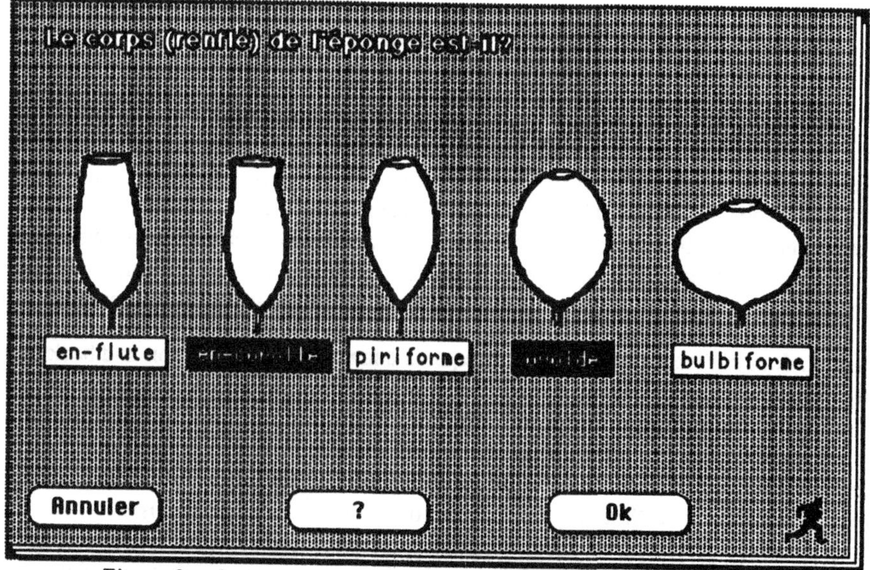

Figure 2: pictures can be associated to objects and slot value cards

These changes are saved automatically in another stack. The reason for recording the changes is that if the descriptive model is modified (for instance, if a new descriptor is added) and the questionnaire is generated again, the new questionnaire will be updated with the changes that were made by the user. This is important since there are many iterations before completing the design of the descriptive model and as a consequence many intermediary questionnaires are built. The process is as follow: build an initial descriptive model, generate a questionnaire, record cases, notice gaps in the model, change the model and iterate. We are currently implementing an additional module which interactively updates the cases which have been already entered when such a change occur.

5 Why do we need descriptive knowledge?

5.1 Descriptive knowledge is useful on its own

As stated previously, developing tools and methods for acquiring the descriptive model and building a case database has an interest on its own. For example, biology is a science where observing and describing nature is a goal on itself. Generating and refining a descriptive model is interesting for recording observations, comparing them and so on. There are other domains where the acquisition of a descriptive model has an interest on its own. For example, this might be valuable for an intelligent system which manages technical documentation and is used, among other things, for justifying design rationale (see the section written by Mrs C. Baudin in [Gruber et al 1990]). This would require integrating the method with a documentation system as done in [Schmalhoffer et al 1991].

5.2 Descriptive knowledge for induction

Another practical interest of the methodology and tools presented above is for learning by induction. Induction can be used to build a knowledge-based system from a case database (called *training examples*). From a set of examples, an induction system automatically generates a knowledge base in the form of a decision tree or a set of production rules. For instance, from a database of case records of patients whose diseases are known, the induction engine learns a procedure to diagnose the unknown diseases of new incoming patients. In our application, induction has been used to learn how to efficiently identify marine sponges.

Induction does not learn from scratch. It requires a language of description and background knowledge (what we call a descriptive model) and a database of examples. In many applications where induction has been used, the database of examples already existed in a form or another. Most of the work for acquiring the initial information needed for using an induction tool was devoted to interfacing the induction tool with an existing database. However, induction is still a very useful technology for knowledge acquisition even when such a database of examples does not pre-exists. As shown in [Rouveirol & Manago, 1988], induction provides methodologies for knowledge acquisition, validation and maintenance. The tools and methodology presented here are thus useful for building the initial information (language of description & database of training examples) required for using an induction tool such as KATE. In this paper, we do not describe how KATE builds decision trees from examples with complex objects (see [Manago & Conruyt, 1992]).

5.3 Descriptive knowledge for case-based reasoning

KATE presents some limitations for building an identification system ; this is inherent to the inductive approach we have implemented. Consider the following database of examples:

CASE	CLASS	FORME(CORPS)	TEETH-TIP(MACRAMPHIDISQUES)	...
Ex1	PARADISCONEMA	ELLIPSOID	LARGE	...
Ex2	COSCINONEMA	CONICAL	LANCET-SHAPE	...
Ex3	CORYNONEMA	ELLIPSOID	LANCET-SHAPE	...
...	...	...	...	...

KATE works in two stages: it first learns the decision tree, such as the one shown below, from the examples and then uses the tree (and not the examples) to identify the class of a new incoming sponge. Consider what happens if the user does not know how to answer the first question.

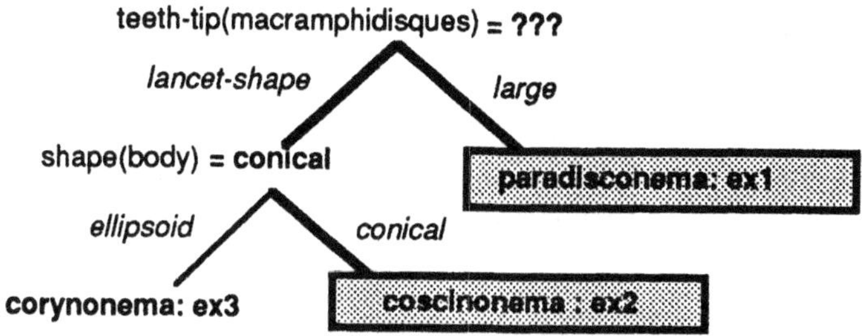

Figure 3: A consultation of the tree

When the user answers "unknown" to the first question about "teeth-tip" of object "macramphidisques", KATE proceeds by following both the "lancet-shape" and "large" branches and combines the answers at the leaf nodes. In the "large" branch, it reaches the "Paradisconema" leaf node. In the "lancet-shape" branch, we reach a test node and the user is queried for the value of the "shape" of the object "body". He answers "conical". The system follows that branch and reaches the "Coscinonema" leaf node. It then combines the two leaf nodes and concludes that it is "Paradisconema" with a probability of 0.5 and "Coscinonema" with a probability of 0.5. However, if we consider the case at the "Paradisconema" leaf node (ex1), we note that its characteristic "shape(body)" has the value "ellipsoid", unlike the current case where it is "conical". Therefore, the correct conclusion should have been "Coscinonema" with a probability of 1 since the current case is similar to ex2 but not to ex1. Unfortunately, the information about the body shape of ex1 was generalized away during the induction phase and is no longer available during consultation.

The problem described above is not due to a flaw in the induction algorithm nor is it a flaw of the decision tree formalism (we could have obtained the same conclusion if we had used production rules instead). It is due to the fact that we are reasoning using some abstract knowledge (an abstraction of the information contained in the examples) instead of reasoning directly using the information contained in the training cases. The reasoning system uses general knowledge and not the actual examples. This tree, or rules, could have been entered by hand instead of being derived from the examples by induction. It is therefore a flaw of the knowledge-based system approach to problem solving (reasoning about a problem using general knowledge). We argue that in order to provide a general solution to this problem, we must adopt a case-based reasoning approach instead of a knowledge based system approach.

One might object that if we had the same configuration of unknown values in the training cases (for instance, a fourth case with unknown "teeth-tip(amphidisques)"), the conclusion would have been correct. Unfortunately, this is not realistic for many practical applications. Consider an application where we try to assist a user in identifying a sponge on a photo. We are dealing with a three-dimensional objects from which we can only see one part (ex: the right side). Furthermore, parts of the object may be hidden by other objects which are on the first plan. What would be the size of the database of training cases if we wanted to enter all the configurations of unknown values which could possibly occur on such a picture? We were faced to this problem in practice. In an application we had to deal with, an object is described by 58 characters. Since the characters of the object can be hidden in any combinations, there are 2^{58} ($\approx 2{,}8 * 10^{17}$) combinations of unknown values (i.e. a character is known versus it is unknown) per class which is a very large number. In order to provide an exhaustive database we must collect at least that many examples for *each example* to identify. This is clearly not possible. Instead, we prefer to enter 91 prototypical cases (reconstructed from several photos) and index them dynamically in order to retrieve past cases which best match the current picture.

As pointed out in [Bareiss, 1989] "case-based reasoning is the usual name given to problem solving methods which make use of specific past experiences rather than a corpus of general knowledge. The key distinction between case-based methods and other forms of automated reasoning is that in the former, a new problem is solved by recognizing its similarities to a specific known problem then transferring the solution of the known problem to the new one (...) In contrast, other methods of problem solving derive a solution either from a general characterization of a group of problems or by search through a still more general body of knowledge". We believe that this key distinction is essential to understand the fundamental differences between induction and case-based reasoning. Note that the two technologies are often confused and some induction products appearing on the market are presented with the label "case-based reasoning tool".

We have developped the CASSYS module which does some form of case-based reasoning. CASSYS was specifically developped for identification problems. The distinction between KATE and CASSYS is not the underlying technology (both use similar information metrics to find the most discriminant characteristics) but how the technology is used. KATE builds a static decision tree and uses the tree for consultation. CASSYS reasons directly from the case library and dynamically builds a path in the implicit tree which corresponds to the current case. At the root node, it computes information gain for all the features. It then ask the user for the value of the most discriminant one. If the user answers, it develops the corresponding branch. However, if the answer is unknown, then the next best test is tried and we iterate the process until the user is able to give an answer.

For identification problems, such as the application at the "Muséum d'Histoire Naturelle", CASSYS performs better than KATE whenever there are unknown values during consultation. It is incremental and new cases can be added without having to reconstruct the whole decision tree like in KATE. On the other hand, KATE can extract explicit knowledge from the case database. It can detect inconsistencies in the case library: a leaf node in the decision tree covers two different classes with some probabilities attached to the classes. There can be several causes for such an inconsistency such as errors in the case description, uncertainty in the domain or the expert forgot an important descriptor which would allow to discriminate between the inconsistent examples. In the latter, the case representation will be modified by adding new slots to objects. Thus, HyperQuest and KATE can be used as knowledge acquisition front-ends for a case based reasoning tool such as CASSYS. In addition, the questionnaire generated by HyperQuest can be used to consult the case-based reasoning system and enrich the case database incrementally.

6 Applications

The methodology presented in this paper was used for building several applications in various domains. The hypermedia questionnaire generator became available recently and the interactive questionnaire was built by hand for some of the applications below (e.g. plant diseases). The HyperQuest tool was tested on these applications afterward.

6.1 Diagnosis in Plant Pathology

In the tomato application developped for the "Institut National de Recherche Agronomique" (INRA), there is a small number of examples per concept (there are less than 400 case for 60 diseases). However, each case is extremely complex as stated in details in [Manago & Kodratoff, 1991]. There are 147 different kinds of symptoms (types of objects) and each plant (example) can be affected by up to six symptoms. On the average, each symptom is described by 9 features (slots). There is a total of 80 different features (i.e. many symptom objects have some features in common). Thus, the questionnaire is a very useful tool in this application.The user answers only 6*9= 54 questions for each example instead of the 6*80 = 480 that he would have had to answer if we had not used the object structure. The descriptive model, implemented on the computer as an interactive questionnaire, is thus used to quickly restrain the description of the current object.

In this domain, it is not unusual that a new disease appears or that an existing disease mutate and presents some unseen features. Thus, maintaining rapidly the knowledge base from one crop season to the other is of vital importance. As a consequence, the on-line interactive questionnaire, that is normally used to collect the description of a training example, is used for entering the full description of the case to identify. The user then chooses to record the description as a training example (the expert provides his diagnosis in a second stage) or to consult the case-based reasoning engine.

6.2 Credit assesments

The french "Société d'Informatique et de Système (SIS)" has tested KATE on an application delivered to one of France's major bank. The expert system's task is to evaluate financial risks when the bank covers credit assessed by a supplier to one of its customer. The training set contains 700 examples described by one object with 31 slots: 12 slots with integer values, 2 slots with real value, 17 slots with nominal values (with an average of 5 values per slot). There are 7 concepts to identify. KATE was ran three times and the descriptive knowledge was modified in between each run. Note that, although, a case database already existed, the questionnaire was used to interface with the external database and for inspecting the cases during iterations of the learning cycle (generation of a knowledge base, modication of the background knowledge etc.). This allowed to notice useful additional knowledge: the expert had provided the descriptor "revenue of the company" and "number of employees" but the interesting descriptor was actually the ratio of the two quantities. By inspecting the cases at the leaves of the decision tree, the expert was able to notice this and to fill this gap in the descriptors (KATE does not generate new descriptors automatically, but the partitions of examples at the leaf nodes interactively help him choose a new descriptor).

6.3 Military Applications

KATE has been used for building two military applications. The training data is represented by complex objects and a flat attribute-based representation would not have adequately captured the information contained in the data. The description of an example varies drastically depending on the type of objects involved.

6.4 Failure analysis in a telecommunication network

We have also used the method for an application which analyzes failures in a telecommunication network. The objective is to identify in the history database, faults (cases) which are similar to the current fault and browse through these cases using the questionnaire. Thus, in this application, the two tools (questionnaire and the case-based reasoning engine) are integrated. The database of examples contains 160 examples with 7 different faults and most of the features are numerical.

6.5 Classification and identification of marine sponges

This application has been chosen as the support for developping and testing the most recent aspects of our project, because the well delimited and well covered domain of marine sponges brings a good illustration the great variability and complexity of a natural biological group. The structure of the descriptive model (subpart relations) is shown in figure 3. The model has been elaborated in order to match as precisely and freely as possible the phenetic (morphological, descriptive) concepts and relations actually used by a great specialist of marine sponges: Prof. Claude Lévi at the Museum of Natural History in Paris.

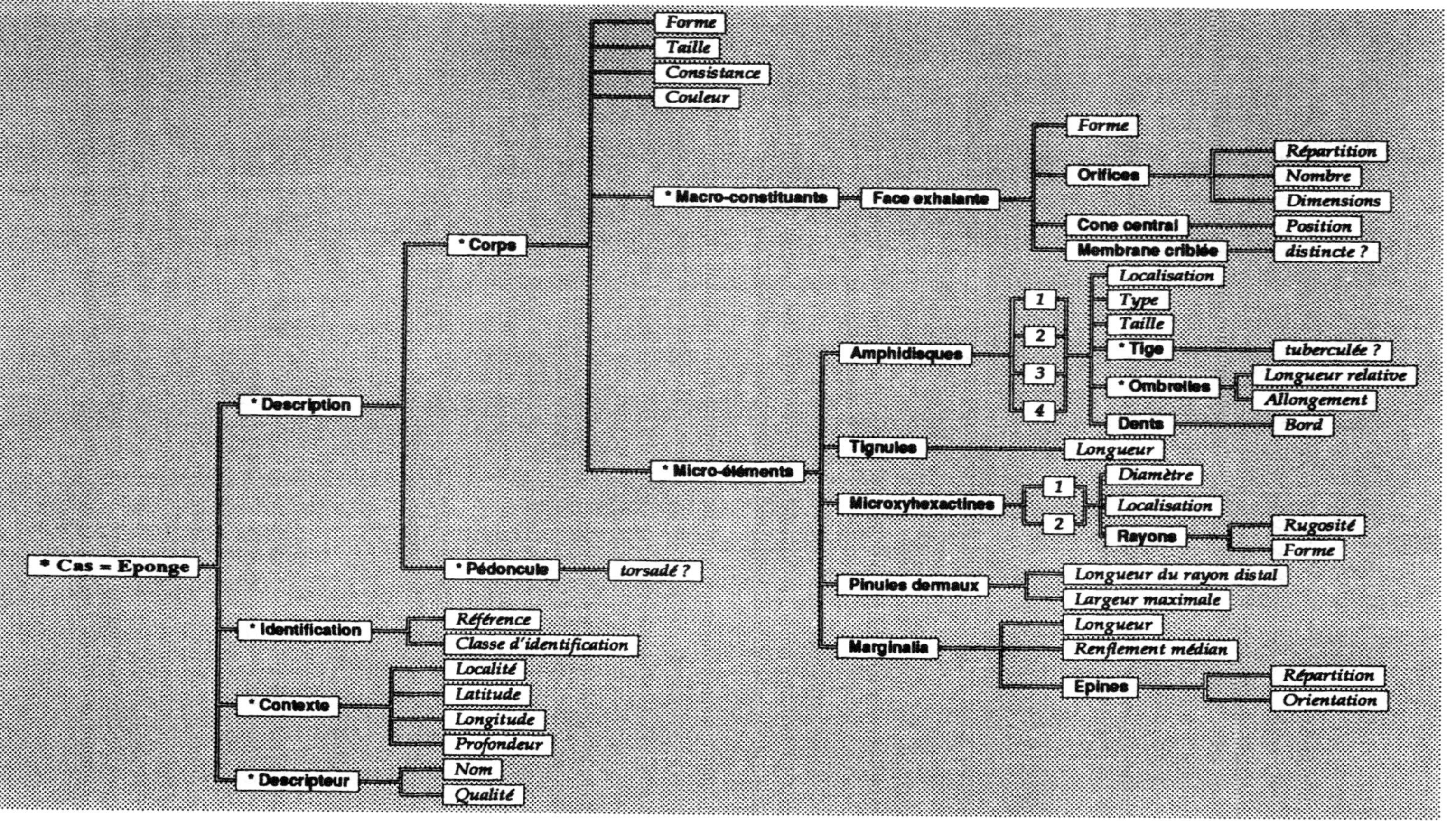

Figure 3 : The descriptive model of the marine sponges application
(objects in bold, slots in italics, values not shown, cardinals as numbers in boxes ; presence/absence of an object with a star is not a descriptor)

This expert who has experienced numerous ways of describing these sponges for several decades has realised that the effort payed to formalizing the descriptive model now allows him to work more efficiently and produce more comprehensive and homogeneous descriptions while pointing out some defaults of previous works (by other authors or by himself). The questionnaire which has been derived from the descriptive model and which includes many drawings, has allowed to collect a large number of descriptions of individual sponges. This work was done directly by the expert without particular external assistance. The data has been processed by our inductive tool KATE giving rise to decision trees. While these trees were primarily intended to be translated into identification systems, they have been found to be helpful for classication purposes. An interactive tree editor with on-line assistance from the induction tool allows to evaluate different characters in terms of predictivity, sensitivity, discriminatory weight etc.

7 Conclusions

We have presented a method for building a descriptive model of a domain. This descriptive model can be used to build an interactive questionnaire to collect case descriptions. The HyperQuest tool automatically builds such an interactive questionnaire from the descriptive model. Hypertext entities are associated to entities of the descriptive model. The hypertext environnement allows rapid customization of the questionnaire by the user. Generating a descriptive model and a case database is interesting on its own in several domains, for building expert systems using knowledge acquisition techniques such as inductive learning, and for building identification systems using case-based reasoning.

Currently, the three phases of building a descriptive model, a case library and an identification system are more or less sequential (although new cases can be added incrementally). A modification in the descriptive model after a case database has been built is still viewed as a "patch" and the cases are not updated accordingly. However, as we have stated previously, the descriptive model heavily depends on the final goal which is pursued (identification). Thus, after the identification system has been ran, one often notices gaps in the descriptive model (lack of a useful descriptor, need to intoduce a new object etc.) and make changes in it. As a consequence, our next objective is to upgrade the system so that it is fully interactive and incremental and is able to update the description of the cases which have been already entered when the expert changes the descriptive model. This could be performed semi-automatically and/or interactively.

Acknowledgements

We would like to thank Prof. Claude Lévi who developped the application on marine sponges presented here. This research has been supported by an ARITT from CRITT-CCS and by ANVAR. We would like to thank Prof. Edwin Diday and Dr Jacques Lebbe at INRIA for their numerous scientific advices. Michel Manago would also like to thank the European Economic Community which supported its PhD research between 1985 and 1988 (ESPRIT contract P1063, the INSTIL project with the General Electric Company, CNRS and Cognitech [INSTIL, 1989]) and Dr Y. Kodratoff who was his mentor during this period. KATE is a trademark of Michel Manago, HyperQuest is a trademark of Acknowledge.

References

Bareis R. (1989). Exemplar-Based Knowledge Acquisition: A Unified Approach to_Concept Representation, Classification, and Learning. Academic Press.

INSTIL (1989). Project Summary. ESPRIT Deliverable. Brussel, Belgium: Commission of Economic Communities.

Manago, M. (1986). Object-oriented Generalization: A Tool for Improving Knowledge Based Systems. *Proceedings of the International Meeting on Advances in Learning*, Les Arcs, France.

Manago, M. (1988). Intégration de Techniques Numériques et Symboliques en Apprentissage Automatique. PhD dissertation, University of Orsay, France.

Manago M., Kodratoff Y. (1990). "KATE: A Piece of Computer Aided Knowledge Engineering", Proceedings of the fifth AAAI workshop on knowledge acquisition for knowledge based systems, Gaines B. & Boose J. eds, Banff (Canada).

Manago, M. & Conruyt, N. (to be published). "Using information technology to solve real world problems", KEKOG, Schmalhoffer F. (ed), Springer Verlag.

Gruber T., Baudin C., Boose J., Weber J. (1991). "Design Rationale Capture as Knowledge Acquisition: Tradeoffs in the Design of Interactive Tool," *proc. of the eigth international workshop on Machine Learning*, Morgan Kaufmann.

Minsky, M. (1975). "A framework for representing knowledge," in The Psychology of Computer Vision, Winston P. H. ed, Mc Graw-Hill, New York 1975.

Nilsson, N. (1980). Principles of Artificial Intelligence. San Matteo, CA: Morgan Kaufmann.

Perray, M. (1990). "Etude Comparative Entre Trois Techniques d'Acquisition des Connaissances: Interview, Induction et Analyse Statistique pour Construire une Même Base de Connaissances". *Proceedings. of the Journées Informatique et Intelligence Artificielle*. Paris, France.

Quinlan, J. R. (1983)." Learning efficient classification procedures and their application to chess end games". In R. Michalski, J. Carbonell & T. Mitchell (eds), *Machine Learning: An Artificial Intelligence Approach* (Vol. 1). San Matteo, CA: Morgan Kaufmann.

Rouveirol C., Manago M. (1988). "Widening The Knowledge Acquisition Bottleneck", proceedings of the third AAAI workshop on knowledge acquisition for knowledge-base systems, Banff (Canada), .

Schmalhofer F., Kühn O., Schmidt G. (1991). "Integrated knowledge acquisition from text, previously solved cases and expert memories". *Applied artificial intelligence* 5, pp 331-337.

Intelligent Documentation as a Catalyst for Developing Cooperative Knowledge-Based Systems

Franz Schmalhofer, Thomas Reinartz, and Bidjan Tschaitschian

German Research Center for Artificial Intelligence
University Building 57
Erwin-Schrödinger Str.
W-6750 Kaiserslautern
Germany

e-mail: schmalho@informatik.uni-kl.de

Abstract. In the long run, the development of cooperative knowledge-based systems for complex real world domains such as production planning in mechanical engineering should yield significant economic returns. However, large investments have already been made into the conventional technology. Intelligent documentation, which abstracts the current practice of the industry, is suggested as a stepping stone for developing such knowledge-based systems. A set of coordinated knowledge acquisition tools has been developed by which intelligent documents are constructed as an intermediate product, which by itself is already useful. Within the frame of the conventional technology, the task- and domain specific hypertext structures allow the reuse of production plans while simultaneously starting the development process for knowledge based systems.

1 Introduction

While the specific needs of human problem solvers have often been ignored in expert systems, the pivotal importance of system-user interactions is now well recognized. The more recently developed cooperative knowledge-based systems indeed support the users in their problem solving and learning activities (Fischer, Lemke, Mastaglio & Morch, 1990; Reiser et al. 1988).

The application of such concepts to complex real world problems would yield significant economic benefits in the long run. With these knowledge-based systems a user could solve complex problems faster and more reliably. In addition, the expertise of the domain would be better documented, which would facilitate its communication and also allows the reuse of old problem solutions in related contexts.

Nevertheless, the potential sponsors and customers of cooperative knowledge-based systems hesitate to introduce this innovation on a large scale to their companies. Since the conventional procedures, which are currently in practice are perceived as quite adequate, hardly anybody feels a need for change. Practitioners may even fear the uncertainties, which could arise when knowledge-based systems are introduced into their field. When innovation is introduced the established competence of a company could even be lost. Maturing innovative approaches so that they work well in practice requires long development periods which are very expensive and disruptive to the current technology. Potential customers may therefore doubt that an innovation can be successfully applied to their domain. There is obviously a high barrier for introducing knowledge-based systems into the industry.

This barrier is particularly severe for complex real world domains, where sophisticated competence has been accumulated over long time periods. For example the competence in the field of mechanical engineering is extremely elaborate and detailed and has matured over at least hundred years (Spur, 1979).

Over the last few years our knowledge acquisition group has developed an integrated knowledge acquisition method. The current paper describes how an intelligent documentation in form of a domain-specific hypertext structure is formed with this method as an intermediate knowledge representation. Since such an intelligent documentation will yield direct benefits in its own right, it will lower the barrier for introducing knowledge-based systems. First we describe the complex real world domain of mechanical engineering, in order to show the necessity of an intelligent documentation. Thereafter the integrated knowledge acquisition method with its three coordinated tools is explained, and the resulting domain- and task-specific hypertext as the intelligent documentation is presented.

2 The Real-World Domain of Mechanical Engineering

In the field of mechanical engineering numerous descriptions exist as written documents and through the explanations of various domain experts. Such descriptions are usually uncommittal: imprecisely stated, at different levels of generality, overall incomplete and at times even contradictory. In other words, the knowledge of the field is quite badly documented. This knowledge is nevertheless needed for solving specific problems such as for example the manufacturing of rotational parts. Because of the quantity and variety of knowledge which enters into solving such problems, the planning of the manufacturing process is itself complex.

2.1 The Manufacturing of Rotational Parts

The technique for manufacturing a rotational part is best understood by a comparison to pottery. The manufacturing processes are similar to making a pot in the following way: One puts or attaches a piece of clay to a potter's wheel and shapes the clay to a specific form, *only by removing* some parts of the clay while the potter's wheel is turned. Contrary to the soft clay, which also allows a potter to push some material to a neighboring position, a rotational part or workpiece (metals) is shaped, *solely by removing materials with a hard cutting tool.*

Figure 1 shows a graphical representation of a (partial) workplan for a rotational part. The geometric form of the mold and the target workpiece are overlayed and shown at the top part of the figure (in the middle). The chucking fixture (seen as the black area on the left and the black triangle on the right side) is rotated with the attached mold (a 500 mm long cylinder indicated by the shaded area) with the longitudinal axis of the cylinder as the rotation center. The sequence of cuts are indicated by the numbers 1 to 7. For each cut the cutting tool, the cutting parameters, and the cutting path are also shown in the figure. For example, the cutting tool number 1 has the specification "CSSNL 3232 C15 SNGN151016 TO 3030". It is applied to remove a part of the upper layer of the cylinder with a rotation speed of $v_c = 450$ m / min, a feed of f = 0,45 mm/U and a cutting depth of $a_p = 5$ mm. A complete description of the real world operations would also include further technological data of the workpiece (surface roughness, material, etc.) and precise workshop data (CNC machines with their rotation power and number of tools and revolvers, etc.).

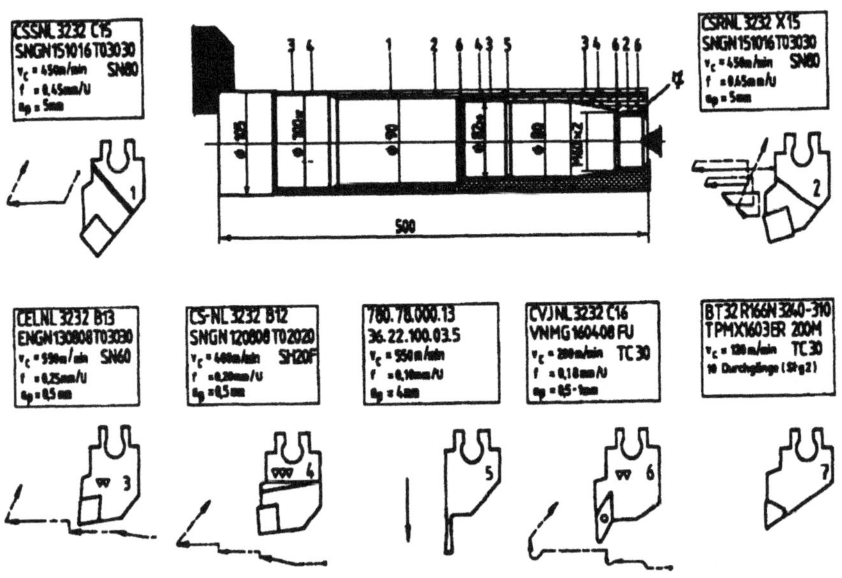

Figure 1: Graphical representation of a typical workplan for a rotational part (From "Examples for Application" (pp. 25-27), Plochingen Neckar, Germany: Feldmühle AG. Copyright 1984 by Feldmühle AG. Reprinted by permission.)

This plan is relatively simple in comparison to the planning processes by which it was generated. Human experts require several hours to produce the first complete version of the plan. A total of two days is spent before it is successfully tested and a qualitatively good plan is obtained. The following facts of the application domain may explain why these planning processes are so time consuming.

About $1.8 * 10^7$ toolholders and $1.5 * 10^8$ tool inserts can be specified within the ISO norm 5608 and the ISO norm 1832. However, only $3.5 * 10^{12}$ cutting tools are potentially usable. The very large number ($2.6965*10^{15}$) of meaningless specifications (i.e. specifications for which no cutting tool can be physically assembled) shows the inadequacy of the ISO notations. From the potentially useful cutting tools 40 000 tools are commercially available and a medium sized company will typically apply 5000 tools in their production. Some highly specialized cutting tools may in addition specifically be constructed for the manufacturing of some workpiece. A workplan typically uses between 6 and 16 tools. Since a number of parameters have to be determined from a continuum (chucking force, cutting speed, feed and path, etc.) the number of possible alternatives can be considered arbitrarily large. Depending on the various cutting parameters (see Figure 1) each of the tools can be used in different ways to produce different effects. Although they provide a structure into which the tools can be sorted, the existing ISO norms are not sufficiently tailored to the needs of the planning process.

The production plan must also fit the specific CNC machine which is used for manufacturing the workpiece. For each company the CNC machines are individually configured from a set of different components. The configuration of a machine depends on the spectrum of workpieces and the lot size which the company expects to produce. Therefore rarely two lathe machines of a company are completely identical.

A company has a typical history and profile with respect to the workpieces it usually produces. The typical manufacturing cases of a company can therefore be found in firm records so that they can be reused when a similar workpiece needs to be produced.

There are a number of interdependencies between the tools, the CNC machines and the workpieces to be produced. CNC machines must have a large enough revolver to keep all the necessary tools. In addition, the CNC machine must have enough power to achieve the required cutting speed and force for the operations specified in the plan.

Since the quality of the resulting plan is very high whereas the planning processes themselves are not completely knowledge-based in the sense that the plans have to be developed to some degree by trial and error in the real world, human experts often obtain a new plan by modifying previous planning products to the new problems. The information and the knowledge which is needed for production planning is distributed among at least three different sources.

2.2 Characterization of the Relevant Information Sources

Human Experts. Human experts are known to form and utilize concept hierarchies (Chase & Ericcson, 1982; Chi, Feltovich & Glaser, 1981) in such a way that the most useful distinctions are made for their domain of expertise (de Groot, 1966). Within this concept hierarchy there exist so called basic level categories (Rosch, 1978; Hoffmann & Zießler, 1983). These categories tend to be formed so that the associated task related operations can be successfully applied to the members of each category (Chi, Feltovich & Glaser, 1981). An expert's concept hierarchy should thus have uniform solution methods stored with each concept (Anderson 1990, Chapter 3). Usually, these solution methods consist of compiled knowledge and cannot be directly expressed verbally. An expert's judgements about problem similarities may, however, be used to infer the underlying hierarchical organization.

Written Documents. In mechanical engineering written documents exist in the form of text books for engineering students, practical guidelines for the various applications in the domain and catalogues from tool manufacturers. The text books present the relevant knowledge from geometry and physics in a task independent way such as the calculation of angles, the decomposition of forces and classifications of materials on the basis of physical and chemical properties. There are also descriptions of application specific models and summaries of experiments about the applicability of different types of tools. In the catalogues of the tool manufacturers, the more specific experimental results about the offered tools are published. The practical guidelines describe particular problems and present relevant criteria which should be considered when tackling these problems.

Solutions of Previous Manufacturing Problems. The solutions of previous manufacturing problems (i.e. manufacturing plans) which have been proven successful by numerous applications in the real world can be found in databases (or filing cabinets) of the different manufacturers. A set of qualitatively good cases which is representative of the desired competence of the future knowledge based system can provide important information.

The large amount of different types of information, which are used according to some conventional procedures, emerged over a long development period. The large number of interdependencies among the components of the planning procedure and the different types of information also make it difficult to introduce a differently structured innovative procedure, without a long period of preparation. Because of the forbidding high investment cost, it is almost impossible to successfully introduce knowledge-based systems into such complex real world domains by a single software project.

In order to overcome this barrier, one would therefore need to make some preparatory steps, which are beneficial in their own right. We thus suggest to define a milestone for introducing knowledge-based systems, which, however, can be seen as a goal of its own. An intelligent documentation of the actual procedures, which is organized according to the structure of a possibly future knowledge-based system is such an intermediate step. The following section describes how an integrated knowledge acquisition method can be used to develop an intelligent documentation of production planning, from which a knowledge-based system can be subsequently constructed.

3 Integrated Knowledge Acquisition Method

When knowledge is independently acquired from different, but equally respectable sources (e.g. different experts, different information sources) or with different and equally profitable tools, knowledge may be integratively analyzed. Since several relevant information sources have been identified, an integrated knowledge acquisition method has been developed, that uses several tools to accomplish intelligent documentation and an efficient utilization of these sources, as well as an early verification of the elicited knowledge.

The purpose of intelligent documentation as well as documentation in general is to support users in their problem solving activities. In order to support the human problem solving strategies for production planning, an intelligent documentation of the relevant information sources should be oriented towards the human problem solving activities.

In the following, some important issues from investigations of expert's problem solving behavior are presented, resulting in a model of expertise for production planning. Then the requirements for an integrative approach are addressed, followed by the introduction of the integrated knowledge acquisition method. Finally, a brief description of their tools is given.

3.1 Basic Requirements

Supposedly an expert's memories include a hierarchy of workpiece classes. Results from cognition (Chi, Feltovich & Glaser, 1981; Egan & Schwartz, 1979; de Groot, 1966; Chase & Ericcson, 1982) provide substantial evidence that these classes have been formed according to skeletal production plans.
In an empirical investigation (Thoben, Schmalhofer & Reinartz 1991), and a related think-aloud study (Schmidt, Legleitner & Schmalhofer, 1990), the expert's problem solving behavior for finding a production plan was investigated in detail. The results showed that nearly all production planning can be seen as modification planning, i.e. a more or less abstract skeletal plan (Friedland & Iwasaki, 1985; Chien, 1989) is retrieved and subsequently refined to a specific workplan. When the skeletal plan is quite general, skeletal plan refinement, which relies on generative planning processes, plays the major role. When the skeletal plan is so specific that it is very close to a detailed production plan, the memory retrieval accomplishes the planning goal (replication planning). Replication planning is thus a special case of modification planning (Hammond, 1989), where a complete plan is already available. Between these two extremes the various forms of modification planning occur, where the planning effort is differently distributed between the retrieval of the skeletal plan and its refinement.

Model of Expertise. From these investigations a model of expertise (Breuker & Wielinga, 1989) has been developed (see Figure 4, left side): The problem of production planning consists of finding an adequate production plan for a given workpiece which is to be manufactured in some given factory. The description of the workpiece is presented by the workpiece model and the description of the factory (i.e. the available machines and tools) by the factory model. From these concrete data an abstract feature description of the workpiece and an abstract context specification are obtained through the application of abstraction or classification rules. To these abstract workpiece and context descriptions a skeletal plan can be associated which may be seen as an abstraction of a concrete production plan. The skeletal plan is then refined with the help of the workpiece and the factory models so that an executable production plan is obtained.
In order to develop a documentation which fits the described human problem solving strategies, the different information sources should be documented with respect to this model, i.e. elicited knowledge units have to be categorized according to the knowledge sources and meta-classes in the model of expertise.

With the previously developed integrated knowledge acquisition method (Schmalhofer, Kühn & Schmidt, 1991) the relevance and sufficiency of the elicited knowledge, and problems with redundancies and contradictions can be assessed. Consequently, a respective intelligent documentation will also provide an assessment of the relevance and sufficiency of the information and the elimination of redundancies and contradictions.

Relevance and Sufficiency Assessment. The relevance and the sufficiency of general knowledge units can be determined by having an expert explain prototypical target tasks (cases) with the general knowledge units. These units (e.g. general statements from a text or general experiences from human experts) are elicited, because of their great generality and high reliability. High quality task solutions are selected, so that the specific set of examples forms a base for all problems which the expert system is supposed to solve. Because the set of examples defines the particular area of competence of the knowledge-based system, they can be used as a guide for selecting those general knowledge units which constitute the relevant knowledge. By having the expert instantiate the general knowledge with respect to the specific cases and by performing constructive explanations, a bridge is built between the general knowledge units and the specific cases. Thereby a knowledge integration can be performed between a case base and a text, or a case base and general expert experiences. Relevance and sufficiency are consequently assessed with respect to the selected cases.

Elimination of Redundancies and Contradictions. In order to eliminate major redundancies and overt contradictions the various knowledge units must be compared in a systematic way. The model of expertise together with the domain oriented decomposition into subtasks provides a useful categorization for the elicited knowledge units. By comparing the knowledge units of a category with all other knowledge units of the category the most critical redundancies and contradictions are eliminated.

Early Knowledge Verification. Through the application of these principles an early knowledge verification is performed. With informally presented knowledge (e.g. natural language sentences and rules), which is often more comprehensible to a human expert (Schmidt & Wetter, 1989) relevance, sufficiency, redundancies and contradictions can be identified relatively soon. Formal considerations (i.e. completeness and consistency of the knowledge base) are thereby already treated with informally denoted knowledge. Performing such formal considerations at an informal level is termed early knowledge verification.

3.2 Acquisition Method

These requirements are met by the integrated knowledge acquisition method (Schmalhofer, Kühn & Schmidt, 1991), which has been developed for constructing cooperative knowledge-based systems. This general method can be applied for constructing an intelligent documentation. We propose to combine knowledge units, elicited from several information sources, with different acquisition tools and on various levels of abstraction, with respect to the model of expertise and the elicitation history. Thus we get means to provide high-level explanation facilities (Yetim, 1991) and to store suitable information about interdependencies of the knowledge units.

In the following we describe two coordinated knowledge acquisition tools, which were designed to construct an intelligent documentation on route to a formal knowledge base: The case experience combination system or CECoS (Bergmann & Schmalhofer, 1991) and the case oriented knowledge acquisition method from texts or COKAM+ (Schmidt & Schmalhofer, 1990). After the documented information has been formalized a skeletal plan generation procedure SP-GEN (Schmalhofer, Bergmann, Kühn & Schmidt, 1991) can be applied to construct skeletal plans for the different problem classes.

Figure 2 shows how CECoS and COKAM+ are used to construct an intelligent documentation of human problem solving strategies and related information for production planning on route to the development of a knowledge-based system. A hierarchy of problem classes from the set of selected cases and a hierarchy of operator classes from the set of operations, which occur in the plan of the selected cases, are delineated by CECoS.

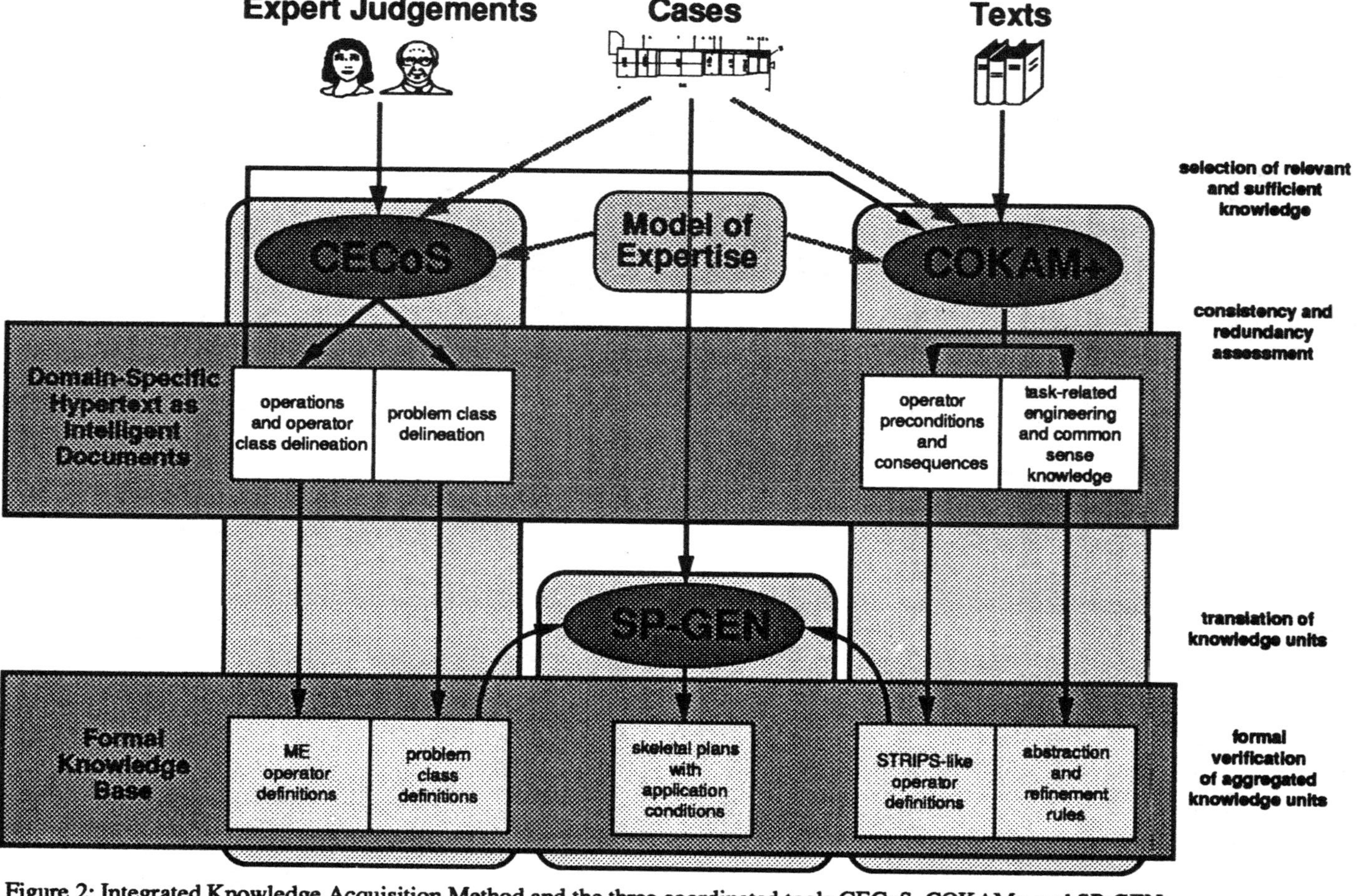

Figure 2: Integrated Knowledge Acquisition Method and the three coordinated tools CECoS, COKAM+ and SP-GEN

With COKAM+ the set of operations and the operator classes which have so far only been delineated by their extensions are now specified in terms of preconditions and consequences, which have to be formalized to STRIPS-like operator definitions. The preconditions and consequences at the various levels of generality are related by common sense and engineering knowledge. Both types of knowledge are interactively extracted from written documents.

The knowledge acquisition tools COKAM+ and CECoS are applied to the same set of cases so that the knowledge acquired with these tools will complement one another. The domain and common sense knowledge is supplied by COKAM+. The definition of operator classes and the definition of production classes are obtained through CECoS. The white boxes of Figure 2 show the global structure of the intelligent documentation and the grey boxes below show the corresponding entities in the knowledge-based system.

3.3 The Acquisition of Problem Classes and Operator Classes with CECoS

With the interactive tool CECoS hierarchically structured problem and operator classes are obtained which closely correspond to the hierarchical organization in the expert's memory.

Similarity Judgements. In the first step of the CECoS procedure a human expert judges the similarity of pairwise presented problems or operators on a discrete scale between 1 (very different) and 7 (very similar). Since a complete comparison yields n*(n-1)/2 judgements for n items, it may be useful to group items in classes with respect to global and obvious similarities as a primary step, and to take these classes as the items of the initial paired comparison. Later on CECoS may be applied to each class separately and the resulting tree structures can be joined (see Schmalhofer & Thoben, in press). Thus the complexity is now basically linear instead of a polynomial increase with the number of items (cases or operators) being considered.

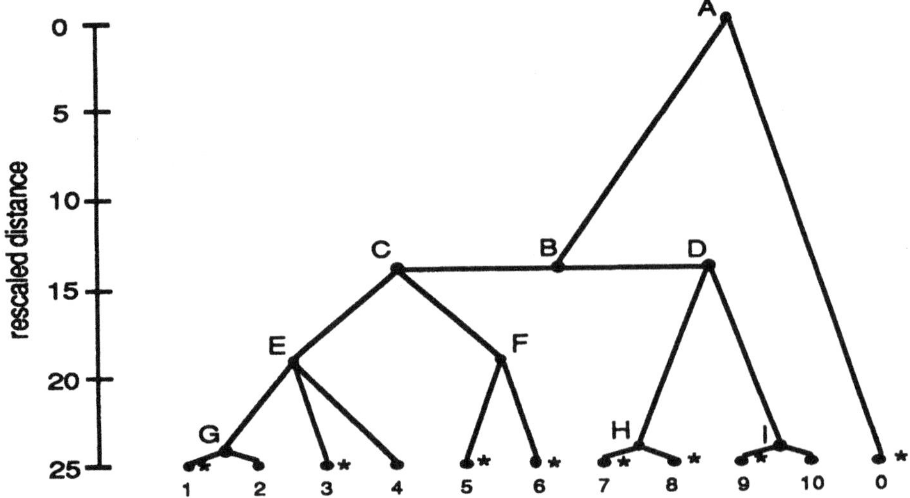

Figure 3: Resulting hierarchy of problem classes for rotational parts in mechanical engineering from an example application of CECoS

Hierarchical Cluster Analysis. A hierarchical cluster analysis is separately applied to each of the resulting similarity matrix. The outcome is a hierarchy of problem or operator classes which are extensionally defined by their reference to the items, for which similarity judgements were given in the first step. Each class subsumes its subordinate classes and instances, i.e. every item, which belongs to a certain class within the hierarchy, is also a member of all classes from the root to the specific class. Figure 3 shows such a hierarchy of problem classes for rotational parts, which was received by an example application to CECoS on 60 different cases, which varied in five geometries, four workpiece materials, and three turning machines. Each terminal problem class 0 to 10 consists of several single cases, which have been grouped in a primary step. The CECoS procedure has also been applied to the classes 5 and 6 (see Reinartz, 1991). The vertical distance between two classes within the hierarchy shows the grade of similarity. Thus the classes 1 and 2 are more similar than the classes 3 and 4. Classes marked by an asterisk include some cases with corresponding skeletal plans acquired in a related study (Thoben, Schmalhofer & Reinartz, 1991; Schmalhofer & Thoben, in press).

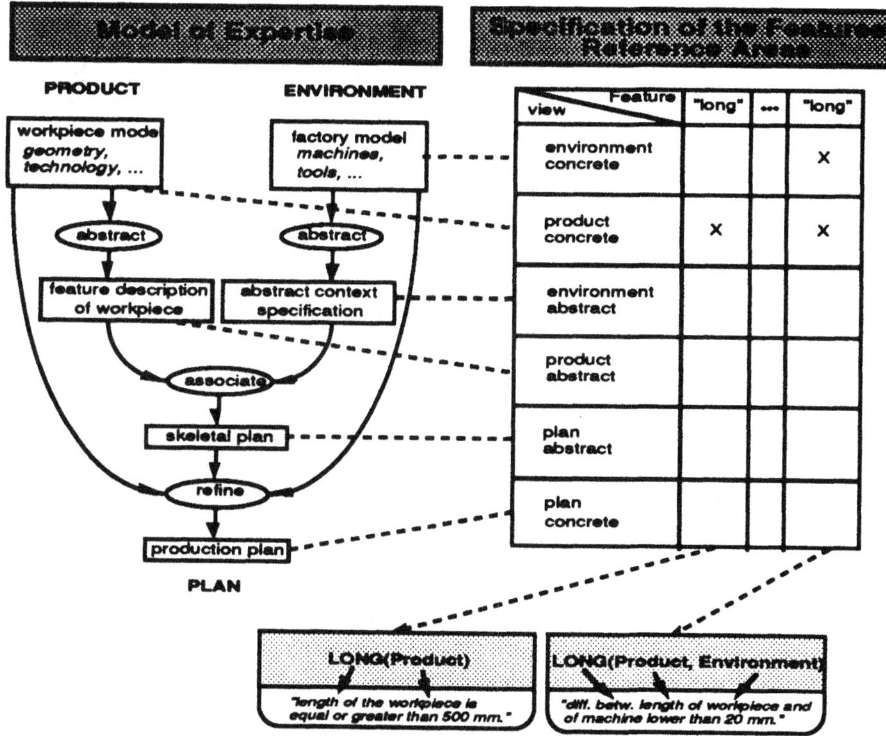

Figure 4: How the model of expertise yields different views and guides the intensional definitions of problem classes in CECoS

Acquisition of Features. After the extensional definition of the problem classes the expert is asked to define each class intensionally by naming several features. CECoS presents a certain class and the expert can type some features, but has to take into account that every named feature has to fit all subordinate problem classes, since the subsumption principle holds. For example "long workpiece" is a quite general feature, which belongs to class B (and hence to all classes in the subtree of class B), whereas "threat M60x2" is more precise and describes a terminal class in the (not shown) subtree of class 6. The operator classes, on the other hand, are intensionally defined within the tool COKAM+ (see section 3.4).

Views. Each feature can be seen as a single knowledge unit, which is used to explain a certain problem class. The next step on route to develop a formal knowledge-base is to structure these units according to the model of expertise. For large and complex real world domains such as mechanical engineering it is necessary to divide the knowledge base into several specific reference areas. This strategy can be compared with modularization for large programming tasks in Software Engineering (Wachsmuth & Meyer-Fujara, 1990). The main reason for modularization is to reduce the complexity of the resulting system. A structured knowledge base may also easily be developed and changed, since each 'module' can be treated more or less independently. Thus the following steps in CECoS are less complex, if the knowledge base has been appropriately partitioned before.

A model of expertise (Kühn & Schmalhofer, 1992) whose general structure is shown in Figure 4 guides our modularization of the knowledge base. Since each reference area can be interpreted as one special view of the knowledge base, we call our 'knowledge modules' *views*. Each rectangle of the model of expertise defines one *single view*. Thus we distinguish *product*, *environment* and *plan view*, and *concrete* and *abstract views*, so that all in all six single views exist. The expert has to assign every feature to one of these views by marking the corresponding field in a table (see Figure 4). For example the feature "long" with its absolute meaning is assigned to the single view 'concrete product view'. Since we do not expect, that every feature can be assigned clearly to one single view, because the different reference areas are not absolutely independent, we also allow the assignment of a feature to two or more views. Such assignments are called *combined view* assignments. For example the feature "long" in a relative sense (i.e. length as a difference between workpiece and turning machine) is such a combined view feature, because it relates 'concrete product view' and 'concrete environment view' to one another.

Consistency and Redundancy Assessment. After the features have been assigned to the various single and combined views a consistency and redundancy assessment is performed (Tschaitschian, 1991). This assessment is first performed separately for each view. After this local consistency and redundancy assessment is established, the respective checks can be made at a more global level. These consistency and redundancy checks are less complex through the modularization of the knowledge base, since not every possible interaction between two arbitrary features has to be considered, but only the designated ones.

Formalization. Within the last two steps the so far elicited knowledge base is formalized. First, in a semiformalization, the expert has to define his features in terms of more simple expressions. Each feature is presented with its views and the expert has to fill in his explanations in a template (see lower part of Figure 4). He is only allowed to use terms of the respective views, since the feature belongs to this part of the knowledge base. These explanations are then used to give a formal definition of the features, and the problem classes are consequently defined by the conjunction of the respective feature formalizations. The formalization is also structured by the different views, so that this task is similarly modularized to the consistency and redundancy assessment.

The choice of a sufficient knowledge representation language is important and has to suffer the requirements given by the procedure. A first attempt has been made by using a KL-ONE like representation system, but unfortunately it failed, since it was too inefficient, and not powerful enough to define the features in a sufficient manner (see Reinartz, 1991).

Because the class definitions are based on expert judgements, the classes should be defined at the right level of generality (Rosch, 1978): They should be general enough so that a large number of specific problems fall into the different classes and they should be specific enough to provide operational knowledge for production planning.

A detailed description of the example application to 60 cases named above and the formalization approaches in a KL-ONE like knowledge representation language are given in (Reinartz, 1991) and (Schmalhofer & Thoben, in press).

3.4 Case Oriented Knowledge Acquisition with COKAM+

With the tool COKAM+ (see Schmidt, 1992) information about the complex machining operations is interactively extracted from a text and subsequently enhanced by the expert's elaborations. The extracted information is then mapped to a model of mechanical engineering actions (domain model) and in addition categorized according to the views which are derived from the model of expertise. The so collected knowledge thus provides an explanation of each step in the production plan and specifies the conditions which are required for its application and the resulting consequences.

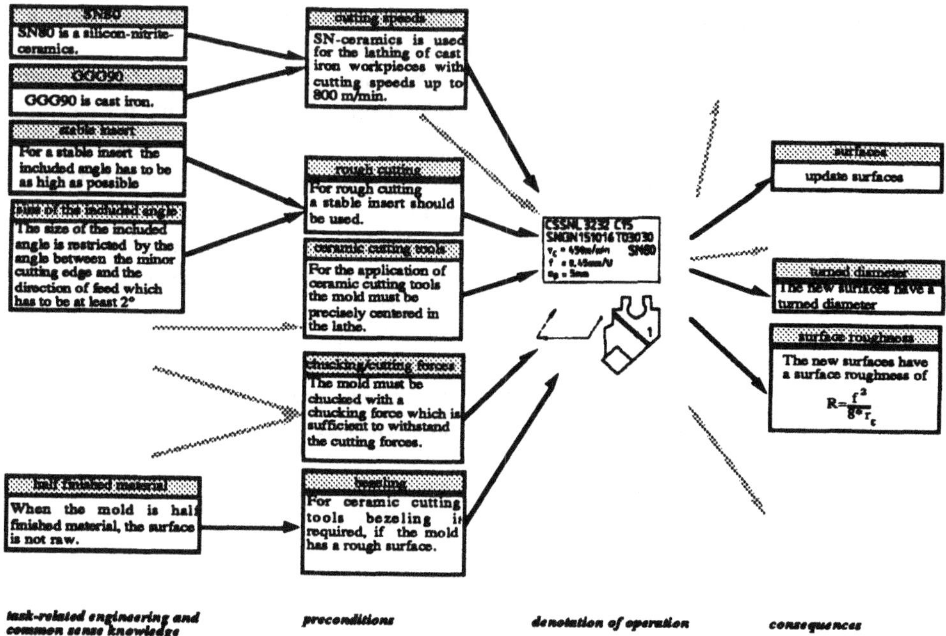

Figure 5: Documentation of the preconditions and consequences of operators with COKAM+ (after Schmidt, 1992)

Figure 5 shows an example from Schmidt (1992) which demonstrates how an operation is explained in terms of its preconditions and consequences. The particular operation (denotation of operation), that is explained here, is the first cut of the workplan that was shown in Figure 1. As can be seen from the first precondition node ("cutting speeds"), one of the general preconditions of this operation requires SN-ceramics to be used with a cutting speed lower than 800m/min. The nodes of the task-related engineering and common sense knowledge, that are linked to the first precondition node explain that the specific materials (SN80 and GGG90) fall into the required categories of SN ceramics and cast iron. The consequence nodes inform how for example the surface roughness resulting from the operation is determined. From such precondition and consequence descriptions STRIPS-like ADD and DELETE lists can later on be derived for the formal knowledge base.

3.5 Skeletal Plan Generation with SP-GEN

The skeletal plan generation procedure (SP-GEN) (Schmalhofer, Bergmann, Kühn & Schmidt, 1991) is based on explanation-based generalization as described by (Mitchell, Keller & Kedar-Cabelli, 1986). The domain and common sense knowledge acquired with COKAM+ is thereby used as the domain theory and the hierarchy of manufacturing classes is employed to specify operationality criteria. Depending upon the selected manufacturing class and the respective operationality criteria, a more or less general skeletal plan will be obtained from a given case. The problem classes elicited by CECoS are defined so that a useful skeletal plan will exist for each problem class.

A skeletal plan is constructed in SP-GEN in four phases:

1. In the first phase the execution of the source plan is simulated and explanations for the effects of the individual operations are constructed.
2. In the second phase the generalization of these explanations is performed with respect to a criterion of operationality, that specifies the vocabulary for defining abstract operators for the skeletal plan.
3. In the third phase, a dependency analysis of the resulting operator effects unveils the substantial interactions of the concrete plan.
4. In the fourth phase the concept descriptions for the abstract operators of the skeletal plan are formed by collecting and normalizing the important constraints for each operation that were indicated by the dependencies.

In summary, with the developed knowledge acquisition tools different types of information can thus be intelligently documented: its relevance and sufficiency is assessed, redundancies and contradictions are eliminated and knowledge is thereby verified.

4 Domain and Task-Specific Hypertext as the Intelligent Documentation

The development of an intelligent documentation of the real world knowledge which is relevant for some application such as production planning in mechanical engineering is an important stepping stone for constructing cooperative knowledge based systems.

Since the presented knowledge acquisition method integrates several information sources using different knowledge acquisition tools, and since knowledge is elicited with respect to a model of expertise, there is a need to structure and combine the resulting documents in a sophisticated manner. We propose to build a hypertext with the coordinated knowledge acquisition tools CECoS and COKAM+ to obtain intelligent documents. Therefore we also may integrate hypertext facilities in the knowledge acquisition method.

In the following we present an example of a possible hypertext, which can be built with CECoS and COKAM+. Further benefits for knowledge-based systems through incorporation of hypertext structures are given in the second part of this chapter.

Figure 6 shows the structure of the hypertext in which data is stored in a network of nodes connected by links. Each case is an instance of a problem class. The problem classes are hierarchically structured, where each class is defined by several features and each feature belongs to a certain category. The hypertext provides access to the classes of the hierarchy, their feature descriptions and all concrete cases which belong to a class. It also includes the visualization of the cases. Through the categorization of the features according to the model of expertise, it is possible to access features with respect to a certain view. For example the feature "long workpiece", which belongs to the 'concrete product view' (a single view), is used to define a terminal class in the problem hierarchy. These proposed hypertext facilities might be of interest in knowledge retrieval under specific aspects.

Analogous to a case each operator, which is part of a production plan, is an instance of an operator class. The hierarchically structured operator classes have dual definitions. The mechanical engineering (ME) descriptions refer to the CNC machine instructions which perform an operation of a certain type. Parallel to this definition, each operator class is also defined in terms of STRIPS-like preconditions and consequences which have been elicited with COKAM+. Abstract and refine relations (also from COKAM+) connect abstract and concrete operator descriptions. The CNC machine instructions, the STRIPS-like operator definitions and the abstract and refine relations, are also categorized according to the identified views.

Obviously the different hierarchical structures and the various task-related links, which make up the domain- and task-specific hypertext allow a better access to the information needed for production planning. The task-specific hypertext links provide an easy access to the information which is relevant for performing the task. For example, if a sequence of machining operations is needed which manufactures a certain type of workpiece, access to an operation sequence or even CNC machine instructions can easily be found via the problem class, into which the manufacturing problem falls. Similarly, an access to segments of CNC instructions may be found through the defined operator classes. The CNC-programs as well as macros are thus explained in terms of a model of expertise and stored accordingly, so that they can be easily accessed for reuse (Redmiles, 1990).

The dependencies which exist among the different information items with respect to the task that is to be performed are explicitly represented by the links of the hypertext, so that the important constraints for achieving the goals of a task are made explicit. What belongs together in a task is also stored closely together.

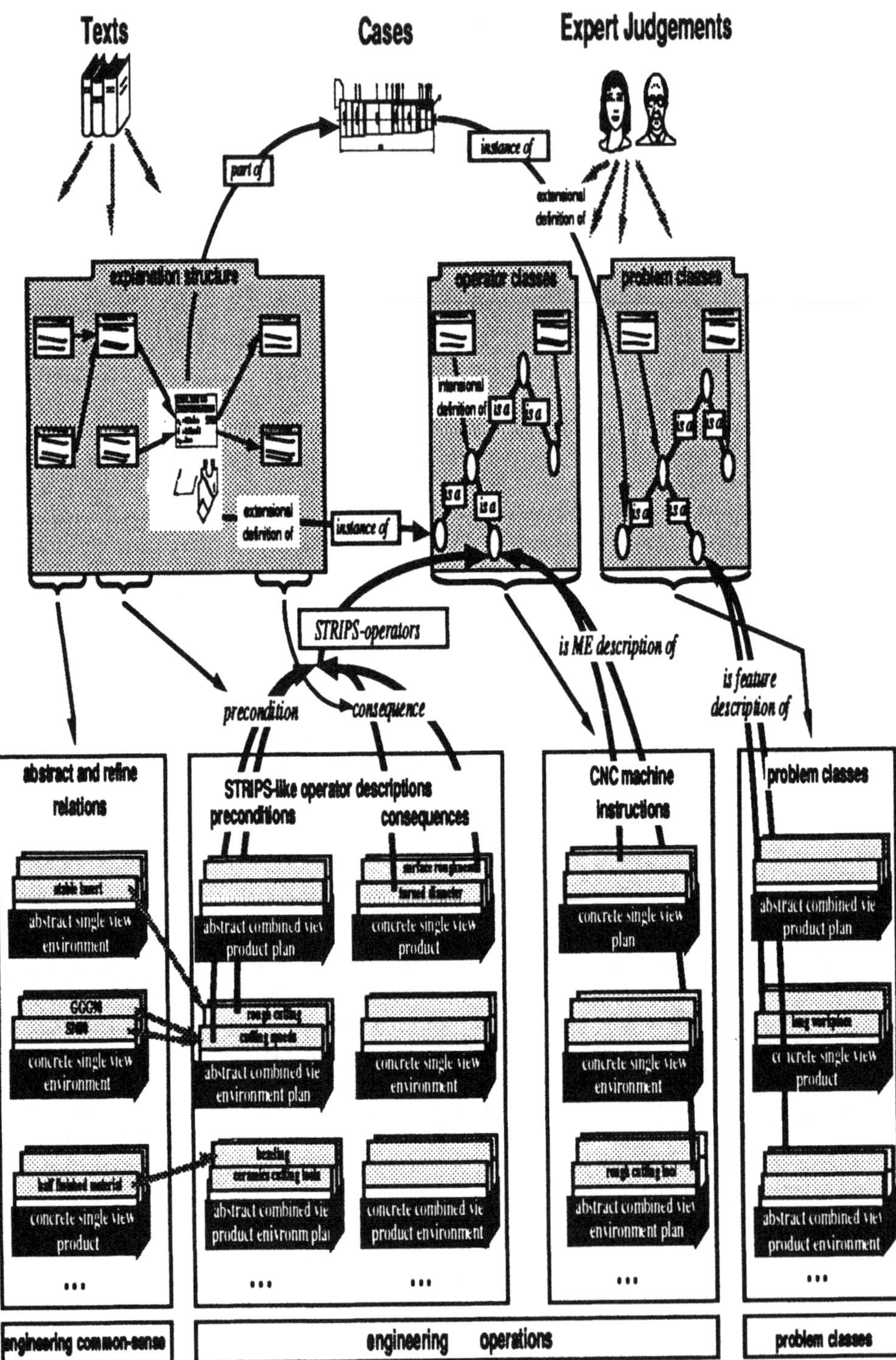

Figure 6: Intelligent documentation of relevant information sources as a domain- and task-specific hypertext

The hypertext also integrates all the available task-relevant information that was previously separately stored. By cross checking the information from different sources redundancies and contradictions are eliminated and the relevance and sufficiency of the stored information has been assessed. This yields an early knowledge verification. The proposed hypertext facilitates the integration of knowledge from several information sources and different acquisition tools and is thus a more intelligent documentation of the information, available in the field.

Hypertext provides powerful means for intelligently storing the elicitation history of knowledge units. For example, each knowledge unit in the formal knowledge base is linked to its semiformal and informal predecessors. In addition each unit is related to the model of expertise and the domain model, as well as to the respective class. Thus it is easy to follow the formalization process of a knowledge unit and to investigate knowledge units according to a common view or to a common task within production planning. It is even possible to retrieve knowledge units with respect to both of these aspects. Furthermore the context in which a knowledge unit has been elicited can be presented (e.g. the case including the concrete CNC program, a graphical presentation, the initial and final states, etc.). So hypertext techniques allow a powerful interface between informal and formal knowledge bases.

The hypertext structure also provides a good facility to generate high level explanations. Thus the user may look up an explanation for each operator generated by the expert system. The operator relies on several preconditions which have been successfully tested by the system, and has some consequences which are suitable to accomplish an intermediate production state. The preconditions and consequences can be explained to the user informally and on different levels of generality through the hypertext structure by following the links from the formal to the informal knowledge.

Since hypertexts provide browsing possibilities, the flexibility for extensions and other advantages, the proposed documentation is already useful in the conventional setting. The human problem solver is supported in finding an appropriate previous case for modification planning, respective CNC-programs and information can be more easily shared between different task categories, thus contributing to the goal of computer-integrated manufacturing.

The hypertext is also structured in accordance with the processes which are performed for constructing a manufacturing plan. It therefore forms an intermediate stage for building a respective knowledge-based system (Schmalhofer, Kühn & Schmidt, 1991). After the information, which is stored in the different nodes of the hypertext, is transferred into formal representations, the skeletal plan generation procedure SP-GEN can be used to develop a prototypical knowledge base. By striking a balance between the past and future developments, the barriers for innovation can thus be lowered.

5 Conclusion

The domain- and task-specific hypertext, which is built with CECoS and COKAM+ yields direct benefits for the human problem solving activities in the current conventional setting. The hypertext is structured according to a model of expertise, which reflects the

human problem solving strategies at a general level and which can, in addition, be employed for the top-down design of a knowledge-based system.
Therefore, the proposed intelligent documentation strikes a beneficial balance between the already existing conventional procedures, into which large investments have been made over long time periods and the necessity for introducing innovation via cooperative knowledge-based systems. Since intelligent documentation provides direct benefits and since it is an intermediate state for constructing knowledge based systems, it lowers the barrier for introducing innovation in complex real world domains.

The current conceptual developments of intelligent documentation in form of a domain-specific hypertext were elaborated on the basis of two previous implementations. Although the structures which were constructed by the previous implementations of the knowledge acquisition tools CECoS (Bergmann & Schmalhofer, 1991), COKAM+ (Schmidt & Schmalhofer, 1990) and SP-GEN (Schmalhofer, Bergmann, Kühn & Schmidt, 1991) bear a clear resemblancc to thc hypertext links shown in Figure 6, the previous versions of CECoS and COKAM+ were independently implemented. The practical experience with the actual implementations supplied essential insights for the development of the new concepts. This paper thus provides the conceptual frame for a coordinated implementation with an extended functionality that yields a domain- and task specific hypertext.

Acknowledgements

This research was funded as part of the ARC-TEC project by grant ITW 8902 C4 from BMFT (German ministry for research and technology). We would like to thank Ralph Bergmann, Otto Kühn, Ralf Legleitner and Gabriele Schmidt for their contributions to this work. Discussions on some issues of this paper with Phillip Hanschke, Andreas Lemke, Michel Manago and David Redmiles are much appreciated.

References

Anderson, J.R. (1990). *The adaptive character of thought*. Hillsdale, NJ: Lawrence Erlbaum.

Bergmann, R. & Schmalhofer, F. (1991). CECoS: A case experience combination system for knowledge acquisition for expert systems. *Behavior Research Methods, Instruments, & Computers*, 23, 142-148.

Breuker, J. & Wielinga, B. (1989). Models of expertise in knowledge acquisition. In Guida, G. & Tasso, C. (Eds.), *Topics in expert system design, methodologies and tools* (pp. 265 - 295). Amsterdam, Netherlands: North Holland.

Chase, W.G. & Ericcson, K.A. (1982). Skill and working memory. In Bower, G.H. (Ed.), *The psychology of learning and motivation* . New York: Academic Press.

Chi, M., Feltovich, P., & Glaser, R. (1981). Categorization and representation of physics problems by experts and novices. *Cognitive Science*, 5, 121-152.

Chien, S.A. (1989). Using and refining simplifications: Explanation-based learning of plans in intractable domains. In *Proceedings of the Eleventh International Joint Conference on Artificial Intelligence* (pp. 590-595). Palo Alto, CA: Morgan Kaufmann.

Egan, D.E. & Schwartz, B.J. (1979). Chunking in recall of symbolic drawings. *Memory and Cognition*, **7**, 149-158.

Fischer, G., Lemke, A., & Mastaglio, T. (1990). Using critics to enpower users. In Chew, J.C. & Whiteside, J. (Eds.), *Human Factors in Computing Systems (CHI '90 Conference Proceedings)* (pp. 337-347). Reading, MA: Addison-Wesley.

Friedland, P.E. & Iwasaki, Y. (1985). The concept and implementation of skeletal plans. *Journal of Automated Reasoning*, **1**, 161-208.

de Groot, A.D. (1966). Perception and memory versus thought: Some old ideas and recent findings. In Kleinmuntz, B. (Ed.), *Problem solving*. New York: Wiley.

Hammond, K. (1989). *Case-based planning*. London: Academic Press.

Hoffmann, J. & Zießler, C. (1983). Objektidentifikation in künstlichen Begriffshierarchien. *Zeitschrift für Psychologie*, **194**, 135-167.

Kühn, O. & Schmalhofer, F. (1992). Hierarchical skeletal plan refinement: Task and inference structures. In Bauer, C. & Karbach, W. (Eds.), *Proceedings of the 2nd KADS User Meeting* (pp. 201-210). München: Siemens AG.

Mitchell, T.M., Keller, R.M., & Kedar-Cabelli, S.T. (1986). Explanation-based generalization: A unifying view. *Machine Learning*, **1**, 47-80.

Redmiles, D.F. (1990). Explanation to support software reuse. In *Proceedings of the AAAI '90 Workshop on Explanation* .

Reinartz, T. (1991). *Definition von Problemklassen im Maschinenbau als eine Begriffsbildungsaufgabe* (DFKI-Document No. D-91-18). Kaiserslautern, Germany: German Research Center for Artificial Intelligence.

Reiser, B.J., Friedmann, P., Gevins, J., Kimberg, D.Y., Ranney, M., & Romero, A. (1988). A graphical programming language interface for an intelligent Lisp tutor. In Soloway, E., Frye, D., & Sheppard, S.B. (Eds.), *Human Factors in Computing Systems (CHI'88 Conference Proceedings)* (pp. 39-44). ACM Press.

Rosch, E. (1978). Principles of categorization. In Rosch, E. & Lloyd, B. (Eds.), *Cognition and categorization* . Hillsdale, NJ: Lawrence Erlbaum.

Schmalhofer, F., Bergmann, R., Kühn, O., & Schmidt, G. (1991). Using integrated knowledge acquisition to prepare sophisticated expert plans for their re-use in novel situations. In Christaller, T. (Ed.), *Proceedings of the 15th German Workshop on Artificial Intelligence* (pp. 62-73). Berlin: Springer-Verlag.

Schmalhofer, F., Kühn, O., & Schmidt, G. (1991). Integrated knowledge acquisition from text, previously solved cases, and expert memories. *Applied Artificial Intelligence*, **5**, 311-337.

Schmalhofer, F. & Thoben, J. (in press). The model-based construction of a case oriented expert system. In Schmalhofer, F., Strube, G., & Wetter, T. (Eds.), *Contemporary knowledge engineering and cognition*. Heidelberg: Springer-Verlag.

Schmidt, G. (1992). *Knowledge acquisition from text in a complex domain*. Paper to be presented at the Fifth International Conference on Industrial & Engineering Applications of Artificial Intelligence and Expert Systems in Paderborn, Germany.

Schmidt, G., Legleitner, R., & Schmalhofer, F. (1990). *Lautes Denken bei der Erstellung der Schnittaufteilung, der Werkzeugauswahl und Festlegung der Maschineneinstelldaten* (Interner Bericht des ARC-TEC Projektes). Kaiserslautern, Germany: German Research Center for Artificial Intelligence.

Schmidt, G. & Schmalhofer, F. (1990). Case-oriented knowledge acquisition from texts. In Wielinga, B., Boose, J., Gaines, B., Schreiber, G., & van Someren, M. (Eds.), *Current trends in knowledge acquisition (EKAW '90)* (pp. 302-312). Amsterdam: IOS Press.

Schmidt, G. & Wetter, T. (1989). Towards knowledge acquisition in natural language dialogue. In Boose, J.H., Gaines, B.R., & Ganascia, J.G. (Eds.), *Proceedings of the Third European Workshop on Knowledge Acquisition for Knowledge-Based Systems (EKAW '89)* (pp. 239-252). Paris, France.

Spur, G. (1979). *Produktionstechnik im Wandel*. München: Carl Hanser Verlag.

Thoben, J., Schmalhofer, F., & Reinartz, T. (1991). *Wiederholungs- Varianten- und Neuplanung bei der Fertigung rotationssymmetrischer Drehteile* (DFKI-Document No. D-91-16). Kaiserslautern, Germany: German Research Center for Artificial Intelligence.

Tschaitschian, B. (1991). *Eine integrative Wissenserhebung und -analyse mit CECoS: Konzepte und prototypische Implementierung*, Studienarbeit im Fachbereich Informatik, University of Kaiserslautern, Germany.

Wachsmuth, I. & Meyer-Fujara, J. (1990). *Addressing the retrieval problem in large knowledge bases* (Reportreihe Modularisierung wissensbasierter Systeme No. 3). Bielefeld, Germany: University of Bielefeld.

Yetim, F. (1991). Eine Hypertext-Komponente zu einem Expertensystem: Benutzerfragen für Erklärungsdialoge. In Maurer, H. (Ed.), *Hypertext/Hypermedia '91* (pp. 286-298). Berlin: Springer-Verlag.

eQuality: An Application of DDUCKS to Process Management

Jeffrey M. Bradshaw, Peter Holm, Oscar Kipersztok & Thomas Nguyen

Computer Science, Research and Technology, Boeing Computer Services
P.O. Box 24346, M/S 7L-64, Seattle, Washington 98124 USA (206) 865-3422;
jbrad@atc.boeing.com

Abstract. Process management is a method for improving Boeing's business processes, however many aspects have been difficult to implement. *eQuality* is a software system based on a framework called DDUCKS that is being designed to support the process management life cycle. We take a knowledge acquisition approach to the development of the tool, emphasizing the importance of mediating and intermediate knowledge representations. Sharing and reuse of tools, models, and representations is facilitated through a layered architecture. *eQuality's* process documentation capability includes a number of views, that can be used either in *sketchpad* or *model* mode. Using the views, an integrated business enterprise model may be developed. Analysis and simulation tools supporting process improvement are implemented with attribute, function, and task editors that make use of a user scripting language and extensible function library. A *virtual project notebook* is used to organize project information and help facilitate group meetings.

1 Process Management at The Boeing Company

The Boeing Company is undergoing fundamental changes in the way it manages its business processes. There are many catalysts for these changes, springing from both internal and external sources — for example, the Boeing Process and System Strategy, the need for concurrent product definition on the new 777 plane, cost management initiatives, CALS, and customer demand for low cost and high quality. Boeing CEO Frank Shrontz [72] has made continuous quality improvement the company's number one objective, affirming that it constitutes "the cornerstone of our business strategy to be the world's leading aerospace company."

In 1988, the company undertook a study of traditional aviation design and manufacturing processes. As a result of the study, the Corporate Computing Board developed a new process requiring *concurrent* design, build, and support activities. While concurrent design, build, and support efforts require significant advances in technology (e.g., 100% 3D CAD digital product definition and preassembly), an equally important challenge is to make the necessary cultural and organizational changes. In the past, processes and organizations remained unchanged when automated support tools were developed. However, new computing applications could do little of themselves to reduce problems of error and rework. Now we are required to document and streamline business, engineering, and manufacturing processes before we consider automating them. This is the only way to avoid automating wasteful practices or implementing obsolete design requirements [47].

Process management is a rubric that encompasses the several methodologies adopted by Boeing for improving business, engineering, and manufacturing processes. To implement process management, the company has formed many process improvement teams, each charged with understanding and streamlining a particular aspect of the business. The teams typically go through the following steps:

- Identify and *document* existing key cross-departmental processes using integrated models of the activities, the items flowing through the activities, and related entities such as organizations and resources.
- Establish points of measurement, then determine how to *improve* the process by minimizing defects, reducing cycle time, and eliminating unnecessary activities.
- Support the *execution* of processes, and monitor performance as part of continuous improvement.

We distinguish *process management* from *process implementation* methodologies and tools. Process management is targeted toward planned, repeatable, but modifiable business processes, regardless of whether automation is being considered. Process implementation methodologies, on the other hand, focus on solving a particular instance of a problem (e.g., creating a specific piece of software, ordering a part, manufacturing a given number of widgets before a particular deadline). They are geared toward successful completion of a unique, one-shot process. Our effort is currently oriented toward supporting process improvement teams; links to implementation methodologies and tools may be addressed in future stages of the project.

In 1989, we surveyed several process improvement teams to determine their current practices and needs. Our findings are summarized in Figure 1, which depicts process management as it is typically implemented. Most teams rely on sticky notes for the early stages of process documentation. Teams track issues and comments manually using large flip charts attached to the walls of the meeting room. Once there is consensus on the a description of the current process, a person who is expert in the use of drawing or CASE software creates a diagram of it. Relatively few teams make it past the process documentation phase. When they do try to measure the process, they use separate analysis and charting programs that are not integrated with the process diagramming tools. Sometimes they must key in information more than once in order to exchange data between different programs.

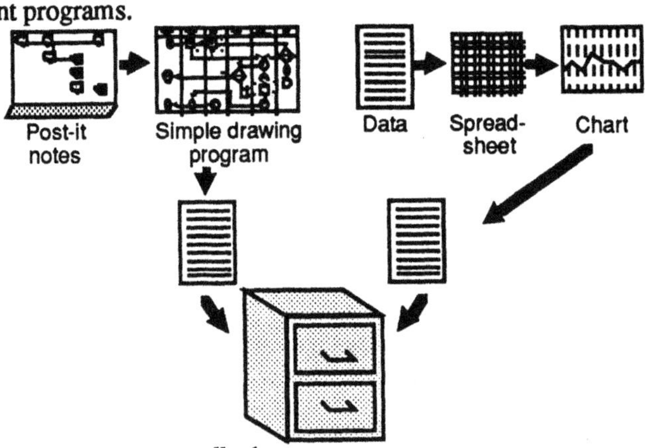

Figure 1. Process management as usually done

To address these problems, we needed to integrate the functions of an automated process management system (Figure 2). To manage the complexity of enterprise-wide business processes, we need more than thorough documentation—we must have process improvement tools to help us discover how our work can be simplified and streamlined; we must have work-flow execution tools operating on 'live' process models to support our performance of tasks and to facilitate measurement as part of continuous improvement.

To access, share, and reuse models within different tools or for different applications, we need means to translate between them without loss of meaning. A number of standard languages, protocols, and interchange formats are emerging [e.g., 17, 66]. The Semantic Unification Meta-Model (SUMM) is an effort being undertaken by the PDES Dictionary / Methodology Committee [29] to define a formal semantics for such modeling languages. An interface between process management tools and model unification capability based on standards such as the SUMM specification will provide means for data exchange with commercial software (e.g., Excelerator™, IDEF-based tools), internal Boeing tools (e.g., Boeing Flow), and repository management systems. The availability of automated interchange capability will also reduce barriers to active collaboration and sharing between research groups, in the spirit of previous manual efforts such as [60].

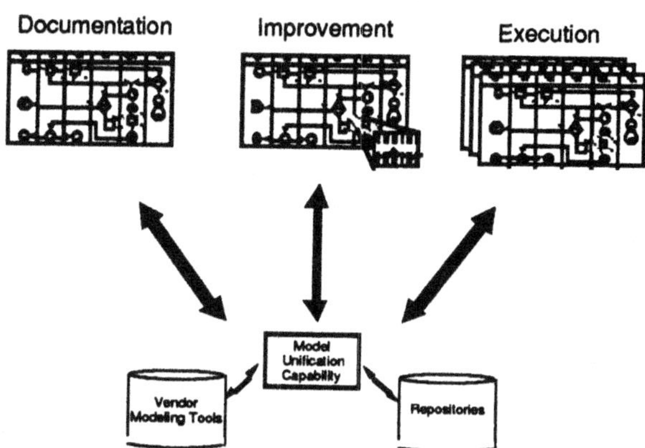

Figure 2. Automated process management support

Section two will present in general terms how a knowledge acquisition approach can be applied to the development of automated tools for process management. We will discuss the role and importance of mediating representations, a modeling framework for process management, and the architecture of the DDUCKS environment. Section three specifically describes *eQuality*, an application of DDUCKS to problems in process documentation, process improvement, and process execution. Section four presents our conclusions.

2 A Knowledge Acquisition Approach for Process Management

Our approach to process management support systems springs from our many years of work in knowledge acquisition for knowledge-based systems. Over the years, many of our views on knowledge acquisition have changed. We used to think of knowledge acquisition as something that occurred mainly in the early stages of system development. Now we have come to realize that knowledge acquisition tools can assist in formulation, validation, verification, and maintenance throughout the *lifetime* of a knowledge-based system. Thus, it might be said that researchers are attempting to do for knowledge engineering what

CASE is attempting to do for traditional software engineering [10, 30, 63]. Indeed, as the scope of application of knowledge acquisition work has broadened, lessons learned from the development of traditional knowledge-based systems have been applied to hybrid systems that combine conventional and knowledge-based components [e.g., 8. 14, 15, 321. Gaines [31] has suggested the term *knowledge support systems* for knowledge acquisition tools capable of targeting wider applications such as information retrieval, education, personal development, group decision support, and design rationale support. We think that the knowledge acquisition perspective has much to offer for many kinds of problems.

In sections 2.1 and 2.2, we describe some aspects of the knowledge acquisition perspective that have had an influence on *eQuality*. In particular we discuss knowledge acquisition as a modeling activity, and examine the role of mediating representations in the process of model formulation and refinement. Section 2.3 presents the system architecture and explains how it provides for reusability of tools, models, and representations.

2.1 Knowledge Acquisition as a Modeling Activity

Recent work in knowledge acquisition has emphasized that the creation of knowledge bases is a constructive modeling process, and not simply a matter of "expertise transfer" or "knowledge capture" [26]. For this reason, use of the term *conceptual modeling* has begun to replace the term *knowledge acquisition* to describe many of the activities in this field.

From a constructivist perspective, a model is not a 'picture' of the problem, but rather a device for the attainment or formulation of knowledge about it [27, 50]. Often, the most important outcome of a knowledge acquisition project is not the resulting knowledge-based system, but rather the insights gained through the process of articulating, structuring, and critically evaluating the underlying model [64]. From this, we infer that the value of the knowledge acquisition effort may derive not simply from a final 'correct' representation of the problem, but additionally from our success in framing the activity as a self-correcting enterprise that can subject any part of the model to critical scrutiny, including our background assumptions [79]. From this standpoint, the crucial question for knowledge engineers is not "How do we know the model is correct?" (every model is an incorrect oversimplification); but rather "How useful is the model (and the modeling process) in facilitating our understanding of the domain?"

Our understanding of models and the modeling process entails a life cycle perspective on knowledge acquisition. Modeling does not culminate at some arbitrary point in development, but rather extends throughout the life of the system. It follows that modeling tools must support the gradual evolution of the model through numerous cycles of refinement.

Each phase of development activity imposes its own requirements and difficulties. Serious problems of modeling can often be traced directly to the inadequacies of the particular knowledge representations used at a given stage of development. Many tools are limited in both their repertoire of modeling representations and their support for evolution and transformation of representations. The ideal conceptual modeling tool would support a smooth transition of the model from an easily communicated, relatively unconstrained statement of the problem to an unambiguous specification of design. A number of changes in representation may be required to accompany successive stages in model construction: from mental models to increasingly refined conceptual models via elicitation and analysis techniques, and eventually, from these highly elaborated models to an operational knowledge base via formalization and implementation procedures [38].

Unfortunately, the emphasis given to rapid prototyping in traditional accounts of knowledge acquisition, along with the faulty notion that 'the production of working code is the most important result of work done', often leads to the premature encoding of knowledge in an implementation formalism associated with a specific performance environment [10]. The unfortunate result is that no independent description of the model will exist other than the rule base itself and possibly some glossaries in the help information of the system [49].

The problems of premature encoding of knowledge in implementation-driven representations have spurred efforts to develop other representations that more adequately support the early stages of conceptual modeling. We call these *mediating representations.*

2.2 Mediating and Intermediate Representations

Mediating representations (e.g., repertory grids, network diagrams) are designed to reduce the problem of representation mismatch, the disparity between a person's natural description of the problem and its representation in some computable medium [43]. They provide a bridge between verbal data and typical knowledge representation schemes such as production rules [12, 49]. Work on mediating representations for conceptual modeling parallels work on visual programming languages for software engineers [e.g., 40].

The term *mediating representation* has various interpretations in the literature, however we take it to "convey the sense of... coming to understand through the representation" [49, p. 184]. A crucial feature is that mediating representations should be "easily readable by those who were not involved in the original development programme..." (21, p. 34). This is essential, since executable knowledge bases are seldom organized for direct use by humans, but instead for the convenience of the reasoning mechanisms of the performance environment. The design of a mediating representation, on the other hand, should be optimized for human understanding rather than machine efficiency.

Work on mediating representations aims to improve the modeling process by developing and improving representational devices available to the expert and knowledge engineer. Several automated conceptual modeling tools have incorporated effective mediating representations [13]. These tools to adopt one of two approaches. Either they contain interfaces that bear a close resemblance in appearance and procedure to the original manual task—for example, cancer-therapy protocol forms in OPAL [65] and engineering notebooks in vmacs [55], or they rely on some easily-learned, generic knowledge representation form—for example, repertory grids or directed graphs [7, 23, 28, 37, 52].

Over time the semantic gap between modeling systems and performance systems has widened dramatically. A distinguishing characteristic of some of the newer tools is the degree to which they promote the use of multiple perspectives on the same information. They also exemplify the push toward informal textual, graphical, and multimedia forms of knowledge representation [9, 23, 34, 35]. As new mediating representations have increased the richness, complexity, and subtlety of the knowledge elicited by automated conceptual modeling tools, a requirement has emerged for *intermediate representations*. Intermediate representations can integrate the diverse perspectives presented by the mediating representations. They help bridge the gulf between human participants and the implementation formalism required by the performance environment. In addition, intermediate representations facilitate the integration of conceptual modeling and performance systems, allowing rapid feedback throughout the process of system development [e.g., 36, 71, 59].

Figure 3 depicts a three-schemata approach to knowledge representation [27]. *Mediating representations* serve as external schemata, the *intermediate representation* corresponds to the conceptual schema, and the knowledge base or database implements an internal schema. The external schemata are optimized for communication, the conceptual schema for semantic completeness, and the internal schema for performance. Obvious similarities will be seen between our suggested architecture for conceptual modeling tools and the proposed ANSI-SPARC three-schema model for data management. The definitions for the three schemata given by van Griethuysen and King (77) provide a good summary of this perspective:

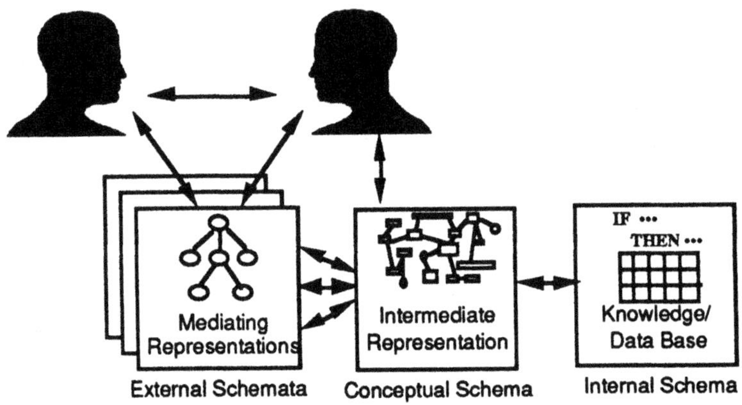

Figure 3. Three-schemata architecture

> "The... *conceptual schema* controls what is described in the information base. The conceptual schema controls the semantic meaning of all representations, that is, defines the set of checking, generating, and deducing procedures of the information at the conceptual level in the information system.
>
> The *external schemata* describe how the users wish to have the information represented. The external processor interfaces directly with the users and coordinates their information exchange.
>
> The *internal schema* describes the internal physical representation of the information... The mapping between the external schemata and the internal schema must preserve meaning as defined by the conceptual schema."

This approach allows views containing mediating representations to be coupled to the underlying intermediate representation so that any changes made to one view may be immediately reflected in all related views. Knowledge analysis and performance tools may be similarly designed to exploit the integration of information at the intermediate level.

2.3 An Architecture for Reusability of Tools, Models, and Representations

Because building conceptual modeling tools is labor intensive, their development can usually be justified only if they can be easily applied to more than a single application. Conceptual modeling tool developers interested in deriving the most benefit from their tools may look for areas consisting of several problems that can each be characterized by a general task model [6, 53]. Conceptual modeling tools can then be created that both fit the general task model and are tailorable to several specific problems.

Many conceptual modeling tools derive their power from relying on a well defined problem-solving model that establishes and controls the sequences of actions required to perform some task [6, 43, 51, 53]. For example, SALT [61] is based on a method for design called "propose-and-revise", while MOLE [25] uses a method of heuristic classification called "cover-and-differentiate". More recently, researchers have developed approaches that allow the knowledge engineer to *configure* systems from one or more problem-solving mechanisms [13, 62, 66, 69]. The problem-solving mechanisms define the kinds of knowledge applicable within each step, thereby making explicit the different roles knowledge plays. Having defined these roles, developers can design modeling tools appropriate to each kind of knowledge.

Musen [65] was one of the first to present an explicit, general approach to creating tailorable conceptual modeling tools. Conceptual modeling tools are tailored using a meta-level tool to edit a domain-independent conceptual model. The meta-level tool, PROTEGE, provides a system to generate knowledge editors tailored for various classes of treatment plans. Physician experts can then use the knowledge editors created by PROTEGE to develop knowledge bases (e.g., OPAL) that encode specific treatment plans in their medical specialty; the resulting systems (e.g., ONCOCIN) could then be used in turn by attending physicians to obtain therapy recommendations for a particular patient. PROTEGE-II generalizes the PROTEGE architecture to allow for alternate problem solving methods and interface styles [68, 69].

Besides the reuse of task models, a number of researchers have emphasized the importance of defining libraries of ontologies, with the goal of increasing knowledge base reusability [45, 57, 66, 73]. Alexander, Freiling, Shulman, Rehfuss, and Messick [4] introduced ontological analysis as a conceptual modeling technique for the preliminary analysis of a problem-solving domain (see also 3, 81]. This kind of analysis results in a rich conceptual model of static, dynamic, and epistemic aspects of the problem. The model can be extended by designers and users of the system and applied to problem-solving. Well-designed conceptual models can also be shared or reused by different tools and applications.

Our objective is to increase reusability by generalizing Musen's approach. We have implemented an "open architecture" integrating environment that allows for a high degree of connectivity among hardware and software components. This environment is called DDUCKS (Decision and Design Utilities for Comprehensive Knowledge Support; 14,

15]1. It is useful to think of DDUCKS in terms of four "layers" of functionality: workbench, shell, application, and consultation (Figure 4)[2]. Starting with any layer in the system, a user can produce a set of tools, models, ontologies, and representations that can be used to assist in configuration of a more specialized system at the layer below.

The DDUCKS workbench consists of five major elements:

- methodology-independent problem-solving task models (e.g., heuristic classification, constraint satisfaction);
- generic interaction paradigms (see section 3.1 below; e.g., graph view, matrix view, various widgets);
- a methodology-independent ontology (a specification of the abstract conceptual schema; e.g., generic object types such as entity, relationship);
- application-configuration process models (i.e., model of how to configurc the workbench for a particular application such as process management, decision support, or design);
- a standard library of inference types and functions (e.g., mathematical and logical mechanisms that implement problem-solving, analysis, or simulation procedures).

An instance of a shell (e.g., *Axotl II)*, created by using the conceptual modeling facilities generated by the workbench, may contain:

- methodology-specific problem-solving task models (e.g., maximization of expected utility across decision alternatives, hierarchical constraint satisfaction using extended AND-OR graphs, process optimization through event-based simulation)
- methodology-specific mediating representations created out of the combination of generic interaction paradigms with a particular semantic and possibly computational interpretation of the elements (e.g., process views, influence diagrams, repertory grids);
- a methodology-specific ontology (a specification of the schema itself; e.g., activities, performers; decision and chance nodes; elements and constructs);
- methodology-specific model-building process models (i.e., knowledge about how to acquire application-specific knowledge within the context of a methodology);
- methodology-specific extensions to the inference and function library.

---

[1] Either the first or second *D* in *DDUCKS* is silent, depending on whether one using the tool in a decision or design context.

[2] The four layers are simply a convenient abstraction that seem to apply to a number of applications. In reality, application configuration and tailoring is a continuous rather than discrete process which admits an unlimited number of "layers".

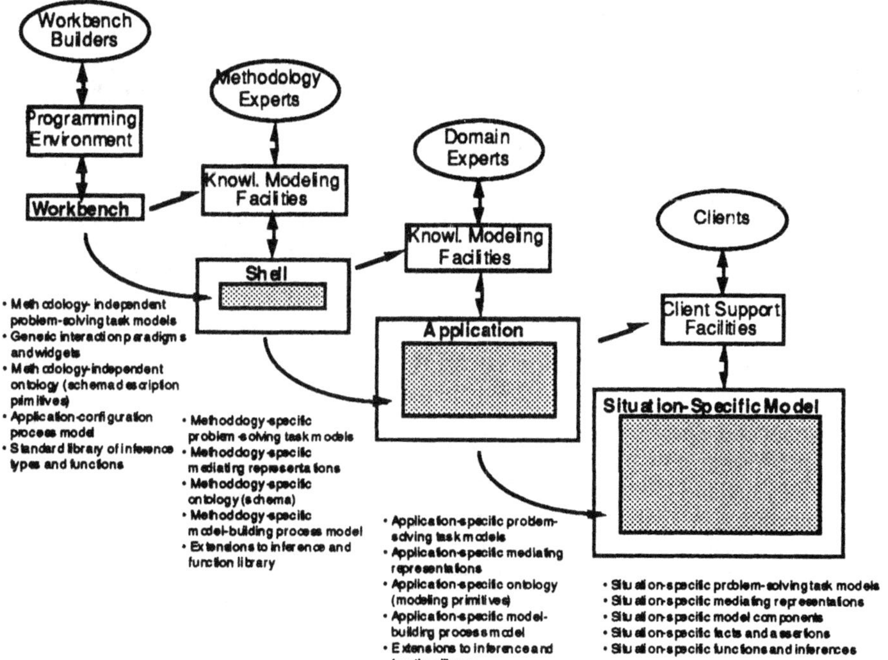

Figure 4. Four layers of functionality facilitate reusability (inspired by figure from Musen, 1989)

An instance of an application (e.g., *eQuality)*, created by using the conceptual modeling facilities generated by the shell, may contain:

- application-specific problem-solving task models;
- application-specific mediating representations (e.g., form-filling interfaces tailored to R&D investment decision makers, engineering process modelers, or space station designers that may be used in place of influence diagrams, generic process views, or grids);
- an application-specific ontology (extensions to the schema that become the modeling primitives for the application; e.g., go/no-go investment decision nodes, technical risk chance nodes; airplane design-build activities; alternatives and criteria);
- application-specific model-building process models (i.e., knowledge about how to conduct a consultation with clients such as R&D investment decision makers, airplane design-build process improvement team members, or space station designers);
- application-specific extensions to the inference and function library.

An instance of a consultation, created by using the consultation facilities generated by the application, may contain:

- situation-specific problem-solving task models (e.g., a model for a particular business, design, or decision-making process).
- situation-specific mediating representations (e.g., text and graphical annotation of views on the model);

- situation-specific model components (e.g., decision and chance nodes for a particular project decision model; activity and entity instances for a particular enterprise model; alternatives and criteria for a particular design decision);
- Situation-specific facts and assertions (e.g., particular information about a situation);
- situation-specific functions and inferences.

The complete situation-specific model represents the unique characteristics of a particular problem and comprises all the information mentioned above. This model is formulated, evaluated, and analyzed during the consultation to produce recommendations for action or for further model refinement.

3 *eQuality:* An Application of DDUCKS to Process Management

eQuality (enhanced *Quality*) is an application ofDDUCKS designed to support the enterprise integration and process improvement through the application of advanced modeling, analysis, and simulation tools. Process management methodologies provide a way to specify design activities and products as part of an *enterprise model*. The enterprise model captures the activities, resources, and organizational context of design from the process owner's point of view. It can also represent models of the structure of the products of design, for analysis and simulation purposes. Figure 5 depicts the components of *eQuality* as a set of project organization and meeting tools and six functional modules.

In the following three sections, we will describe the process documentation, process improvement, and project organization capabilities of *eQuality*.

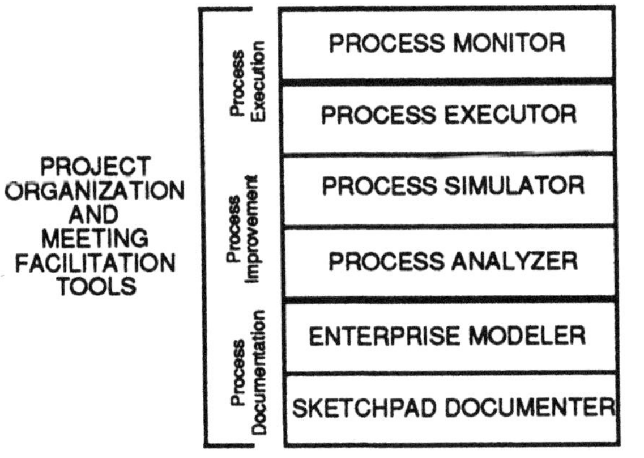

Figure 5. Six functional modules and a set of project organization and meeting tools support documentation, improvement, and execution phases of the life cycle

3.1 Process Documentation

Figure 6 is a view of knowledge representation in DDUCKS . The intermediate representation in DDUCKS (i.e., the conceptual model) consists of entities, relationships, and situations as the primary concepts, and domains, properties, and constraints as secondary concepts. We are using an enhanced version of CODE version 4 as the underlying semantic representation language [58, 74, 75]. We have derived our general taxonomy for conceptual modeling from Tauzovich and Skuce, with extensions supporting inferencing, analysis, and simulation.

CODE provides a rich, paradigm for the definition of knowledge level concepts. A collection of integrated tools support the important and frequently overlooked aspects of conceptual, ontological, and terminological analysis. Our extensions to the representation allow the system to share several features of Sowa's [76] conceptual graphs, and Gaines' [33] KRS, which interpret taxonomic and entity-relationship structures in terms of typed formal logics. A first order logic system and a simple natural language system, allow various types of syntactic and semantic checks to be performed, if desired. A comprehensive lexicon allows references to concepts to be automatically maintained and quickly accessed Default facilities for analysis and inferencing over conceptual structures can be augmented by users by means of an integrated scripting and query language.

User-interface management systems (UIMS) are becoming an essential part of interactive tool development and end-user tailoring [48]. We are extending the capabilities of a Smalltalk-80-based direct-manipulation user-interface builder to build a DDUCKS UIMS, called *Geoducks*[3] [56]*Geoducks* relies on the Smalltalk-80 MVC (model-view-controller) concept for managing different perspectives on data ([2, 42, 54]. The MVC approach provides an effective way to factor out the data in an underlying model from the data in dependent views, so that new views can easily be added to an existing model. A sophisticated dependency mechanism assures that changes to the model made within one view are immediately reflected in all related views. Class hierarchy mechanisms in Smalltalk-80 allow generic views of a certain sort to be easily specialized for different purposes. This, in conjunction with additional capability in *Geoducks*, has allowed us to define many different views on similar aspects of the model, as well as several similar views on different aspects of the model.

The six views surrounding the intermediate representation correspond to the generic user-interface interaction paradigms that are implemented as abstract "pluggable" view classes (Krasner & Pope, 1988; Adams, 1988a, b). These views are generic in the sense that they define the graphical form for the representation, but the form has no underlying semantics. Within *eQuality*, various configurations of these interaction paradigms can be called up in *sketchpad mode* to record free-form graphical and textual information. For example, individuals and groups can capture back-of-the-envelope drawings, agendas, issues, action items, requirements, and other information pertinent to their task. While not part of the formal model, users can link elements created in sketchpad mode to elements in other views in hypertext fashion.

---

[3] Pronounced "gooey-ducks".

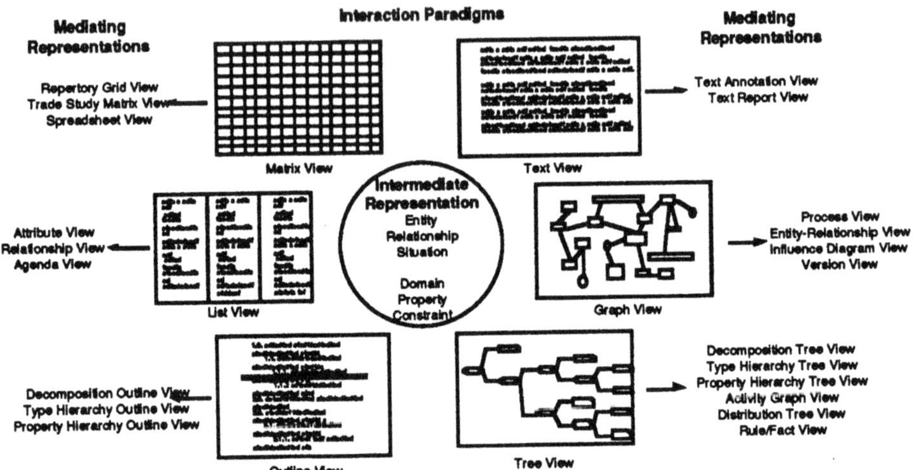

Figure 6. The intermediate representation in DDUCKS, surrounded by examples of generic interaction paradigms, and mediating representations.

By combining one or more of these generic interaction paradigms with a semantics defined in the intermediate representation and (for some representations) the problem-solving method, methodology-specific or application-specific mediating representations are defined. Mappings are defined between graphical actions in the model views and operations on logical entities, relationships, and properties in the intermediate representation. For example, influence diagrams combine a graph view with the concepts of decision, chance, and value nodes and the problem-solving method of maximization of expected utility across decision alternatives. Trade study matrices (a methodology-specific kind of repertory grid) are built out of a matrix view, the concepts of alternatives, criteria, and ratings, and a heuristic classification problem-solving method. Process views combine a graph view with the a formal definition of activities and relationships between them. Type definition views allow the users to extend the built-in ontology. Configured with semantic information, these mediating representations can operate in*model mode*, portraying different perspectives on the formal conceptual model in the intermediate representation. By virtue of the Smalltalk-80 model-view-controller paradigm, consistency is continuously maintained for all model views portraying the same version of the conceptual model.

3.2 Process Improvement

In parallel with development of process documentation tools, we are building analysis and simulation capability supporting process improvement. Simple drawing tools typically available to process improvement teams provide no support for analysis and simulation. Traditional analysis and simulation tools support alternatives analysis and richer models, but require a significant amount of training and data entry to achieve realistic results. *eQuality* is unique in that it addresses the needs of individuals who know a lot about their domain, but do not know very much about formal modeling. People do not have to worry about the simulation when they are creating various diagrams. However when they are ready, the system can use the information contained in the diagrams to support analysis and simulation.

Analysis tools within *eQuality* support the identification of bottlenecks, cost drivers, and the restructuring of processes to exploit concurrency. In addition to formal analysis, built-in knowledge-based system tools can provide support for heuristic analysis. Users can implement analysis metrics such as cycle time, defects per unit of output, and financial parameters using attribute and function editors that make use of a simple scripting language and extensible function library. Using MANIAC, we have developed an initial 'hot link' capability with Microsoft Excel™ that will increase the power and flexibility of the analysis tools.

Discrete-event simulation tools build on the analysis capabilities to provide insight on the dynamic behavior of the enterprise. Users can define active monitors during a running simulation to display results. The monitors selectively respond to changes in the model and dynamically display the results in an appropriate way. For example, a textual event monitor would print out a textual message that described a simulation event, while a graphical monitor such as a histogram or bar gauge might plot the number of occurrences of an event or the value of a parameter.

3.3 Process Execution

An eventual goal is to couple the streamlined enterprise models to the enterprise itself, supplying the semantic transformations that map the models to the enterprise and incorporating feedback from the enterprise concerning the actual execution of the models. We envision integrated process management technology that will someday enable us to move from the current situation where process documentation, if it exists at all, is represented on paper in three-ring binders and control room wall charts; to the near term where models of important processes can be available online in a form amenable to analysis and simulation; to the vision where 'live' process models are woven into the fabric of the way we perform out business. Enterprise models will never be kept up to date properly when they can only be maintained by modeling experts. Enterprise models will never be consistent with the way processes are actually performed until the model actually becomes executable.

We are currently prototyping future possibilities for process execution. To support this, a future release of *eQuality* could produce a form of the enterprise model that can be fed into planning, scheduling, and project management software and linked to relevant data and applications. Process instances could be created each time a process is executed, with status maintained in a repository. Process participants could receive knowledge-based help in carrying out their tasks as the process is executed. An intelligent agent could monitor the activity of the process, notifying process participants of exception conditions and helping to route data associated with the task. Decision analysis capability could help process participants deal with decisions involving high stakes, difficult tradeoffs, or critical uncertainties or risks. Data collected by monitors operating during the execution of the process could be fed back into *eQuality* and used as the basis for further process improvement.

3.4 Project Organization and Meeting Facilitation Tools

Creating a description of an enterprise typically involves the collection, organization, and refinement of a large body of documentation that may include reports, transcripts, glossaries, photographs, diagrams and various representations of formal models. Process improvement team members draw from this evolving corpus as they construct an enterprise model. Effective documentation is more useful during operation of the process before than during the process improvement phase [9]. If they are effectively designed and kept up-to-date, the sketchpad documentation and the enterprise model may later be reused for operations, diagnosis, maintenance and as the basis for improving similar processes in the future. However, the documentation currently produced by process improvement teams is often shallow, scattered, obsolete, incomplete, contradictory, or unintelligible, making maintenance and reuse of the knowledge difficult.

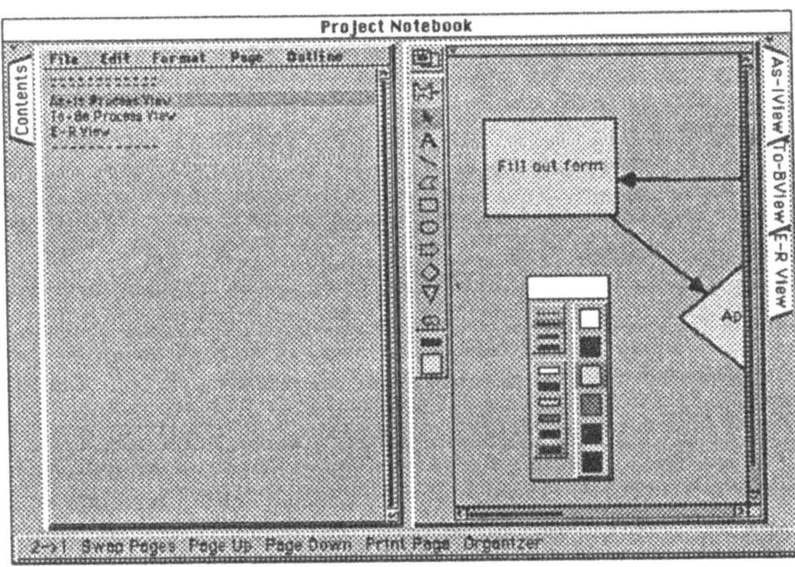

Figure 7. Screen snapshot of the project notebook facility

The volume and diversity of information that can be represented in *eQuality* drives a requirement for ways to manage, organize, and link that information. A *project notebook* facility helps team members collect and organize the diverse materials associated with a particular process improvement project (Figure 7). It also helps manage changes between different versions and views of the model as it evolves. The project notebook can assist in planning and modeling activities throughout the life of the project. Using project notebook *templates*, groups can tailor the contents of the boiler plate project notebook to be consistent with their own preferences for accessing, viewing, and using the information. For example, a process improvement team's blank notebook can come pre-configured with information about organizational standards (e.g., default set of concept types and relationships, standard icons and terms for concepts, reporting forms) and procedures (e.g., required steps in a project plan), just as a real notebook could be pre-loaded with labeled dividers and forms. In addition to its obvious use in managing information about the enterprise model and views, the project notebook supports the team as a simple computer-supported meeting facilitation tool and as a form of group memory.

3.5 Project Status

eQuality was originally implemented within a version of a Boeing-produced shell called *Axotl* [11, 14, 15] *Axotl* was developed on the Apple Macintosh and runs on all platforms that support ParcPlace Smalltalk-80 (e.g., Sun3 and SPARCstations, Apollo workstations, Hewlett-Packard series 300 and 400 systems, IBM '386 compatibles, IBM RS/6000, DECstations). From March to December 1991, a version of *eQuality*, containing sketchpad tools, project organization tools, limited enterprise modeling capability, and a set of prototypical analysis and simulation tools was evaluated at several sites within Boeing. Applications included finance, concurrent engineering, manufacturing, corporate internal audit, continuous quality improvement, and information system requirements analysis. Customers at these evaluation sites have used the software in each of their unique settings, and have provided valuable comments to guide future development directions. Based on results of the evaluation, we designed and developed a completely new version of the *Axotl II* shell as a host for general release of *eQuality* within The Boeing Company. The first general Boeing release of the documentation capability was made in April 1992. Development and evaluation of analysis and simulation capability will follow.

As part of a Boeing project called DIS (Design of Information Systems; Benda, 1991), we explored how knowledge acquisition and decision support tools can work cooperatively with one another and with commercial applications such as spreadsheets, databases, or hypermedia software. We described how such integrated tools could be used for applications such as group decision support in a computer-supported meeting environment [8]. We have developed a facility called MANIAC (MANager for InterApplication Communication) that supports intelligent communication and cooperation between applications. Plans for coordination among applications are modeled and executed using integrated planner capabilities in *Axotl*, while MANIAC provides the infrastructure for the actual message passing. Originally implemented as a driver in the 6.x version of the Macintosh operating system, MANIAC has been updated to take advantage of new interapplication communication protocols in version 7.0 (Apple events or Mac DDE for Microsoft applications). An interface to TCP/IP has been built so that we will eventually be able to transparent support for heterogeneous platforms in a networked environment.

4 Conclusions

We attribute much of the initial success of *eQuality* to the knowledge acquisition outlook. In focusing on process management rather than the development of a traditional knowledge-based system, we have seen even more acutely the need for modeling tool developers to attend to the 'acquirability' and reusability aspects of design. We conclude with the words of David Parnas on traditional software specification, which apply equally well to knowledge acquisition:

> "The word 'formal' has been commandeered by a bunch of people who feel that it isn't formal if human beings can read it… I have fallen into the same trap. I could write something and I could read it but my students couldn't. And they could write something and they could read it but I couldn't. And, not only that, but neither of us *wanted* to read it. … Therefore I have worked on new ways to write specifications so that people could read it… You can't imagine how overjoyed I was when a pilot told me we had made a mistake with the A7 [avionics software specified in an earlier project] — not because we made a mistake but because the pilot could tell us." [67]

It is our hope that a continued discussion and work on extending knowledge acquisition concepts and tools to additional areas of application will contribute to better communication and shared understanding between participants in system development.

Acknowledgements

We express our appreciation to Mike Anderson, Miroslav Benda, Kathleen Bradshaw, Beverly Clark, Jim Fulton, Cindy Holm, Earl Hunt, William Jones, Sharon Kipersztok, Cathy Kitto, Joe Koszarek, Tim Lethbridge, Allen Matsumoto, Steve Poltrock, Peter Russo, Bob Schneble, Doug Schuler, Kish Sharma, Dave Shema, Bruce Wilson, and Jack Woolley for their contributions and support. We also thank members of Boeing organizations who provided extensive feedback and suggestions on *eQuality* prototypes. This work has benefitted from discussions with John Boose, Guy Boy, Ken Ford, Brian Gaines, Mildred Shaw, and Doug Skuce, as well as numerous colleagues in the knowledge acquisition community. Stan Covington developed and helped conceptualize the first *eQuality* prototype. *Axotl II*, *eQuality*, and DDUCKS have been developed at the Boeing Computer Services Computer Science organization.

References

1. Adams, S.S. (1988b). MetaMethods: Active values. *HOOPLA!*, 1(1),.3-6.
2. Adams, S.S. (1988b). MetaMethods: The MVC paradigm. *HOOPLA!*, 1(4), July, 5-6, 13-21.
3. Akkermans, H., Van Harmelen, F., Schreiber, G. & Wielinga, B. (1992). A formalization of knowledge-level models for knowledge acquisition. In K. Ford & J. Bradshaw (Eds.), special knowledge acquisition issue of the *International Journal of Intelligent Systems*, in press. Also to appear in K. Ford & J.M. Bradshaw (Eds.), *Knowledge Acquisition as a Modeling Activity*. New York: John Wiley, volume in preparation.
4. Alexander, J.H., Freiling, M.J., Shulman, S.J., Rehfuss, S. & Messick, S.L. (1988). Ontological analysis: An ongoing experiment. In J.H. Boose & B.R. Gaines (Eds.), *Knowledge Acquisition Tools for Expert Systems*. London: Academic Press.
5. Bcnda, M. (1991). Design of information systems: Towards an engineering discipline. Boeing Computer Services Technical Report. Seattle, WA: Boeing Computer Services, Computer Science Organization.
6. Boose, J.H. (1989). A survey of knowledge acquisition techniques and tools. *Knowledge Acquisition Journal*, 1, 3-37.
7. Boose, J.H. & Bradshaw, J.M. (1987). Expertise transfer and complex problems: Using *Aquinas* as a knowledge-acquisition workbench for knowledge-based systems. *International Journal of Man-Machine Studies*, 26, 3-28. Also in J. Boose and B. Gaines (Eds.), *Knowledge Acquisition Tools for Expert Systems*. London: Academic Press, pp. 39-64.
8. Boose, J.H., Bradshaw, J.M., Koszarek, J.L. & Shema, D.B. (1992). Better group decisions: Using knowledge acquisition techniques to build richer decision models. *Proceedings of the 1992 Hawaii International Conference on Systems Sciences*, January.
9. Boy, G.A. (1991). Indexing hypertext documents in context. *Proceedings of the Third ACM Conference on Hypertext*, San Antonio, TX, December 15-18.
10. Bradshaw, J. M. & Boose, J.H. (1989). Knowledge acquisition as CASE for knowledge-based systems. Presentation at the *Third International Workshop on Computer-Aided Software Engineering* (CASE-89), London, July.

11. Bradshaw, J. M. & Boose, J.H. (1990). Decision analysis techniques for knowledge acquisition: Combining information and preferences using *Aquinas* and *Axotl*. *International Journal of Man-Machine Studies*, 32(2): 121-186. Also in J.H. Boose and B.R. Gaines (Eds.), *Progress in Knowledge Acquisition for Knowledge-Based Systems*. London: Academic Press.
12. Bradshaw, J.M. & Boose, J.H. (1992). Mediating representations for knowledge acquisition. Manuscript submitted to the *AAAI 1992 Reasoning with Diagrammatic Representations Session of the Spring Symposium*, Stanford, CA, March.
13. Bradshaw, J.M., Ford, K.M., Adams-Webber, J.R. & Boose, J.H. (1992). Beyond the repertory grid: New approaches to constructivist knowledge acquisition tool development. In K. Ford & J. Bradshaw (Eds.), special knowledge acquisition issue of the *International Journal of Intelligent Systems*, in preparation. Also to appear in K. Ford & J.M. Bradshaw (Eds.), *Knowledge Acquisition as a Modeling Activity*. New York: John Wiley, volume in preparation.
14. Bradshaw, J.M., Covington, S.P., Russo, P.J. & Boose, J.H. (1990). Knowledge acquisition for intelligent decision systems: Integrating *Aquinas* and *Axotl* in *DDUCKS*. In M. Henrion, R. Shachter, L.N. Kanal, & J. Lemmer, *Uncertainty in Artificial Intelligence 5*, Amsterdam: Elsevier, 1990.
15. Bradshaw, J. M., Covington, S. P., Russo, P. J., and Boose, J. H. (1991). Knowledge acquisition techniques for decision analysis using *Axotl* and *Aquinas*, *Knowledge Acquisition Journal*, 3(1), 49-77.
16. Bradshaw, J.M., Ford, K.M. & Adams-Webber, J. (1991). Knowledge representation for knowledge acquisition: A three-schemata approach. *Proceedings of the Sixth Banff Knowledge Acquisition Workshop*, Banff, Canada, October.
17. Burkhart, R., Dickson, S., Hanna, J., Perez, S., Sarris, T., Singh, M., Sowa, J. & Sundberg, C. (1991). IRDS Conceptual Schema Working Paper, October 18.
18. Clancey, W.J. (1990). Implications of the system-model-operator metaphor for knowledge acquisition. In H. Motoda, R. Mizoguchi, J. Boose, & B. Gaines (Eds.) Knowledge Acquisition for Knowledge Based Systems. Amsterdam: IOS Press.
19. Covington, S.P. & Bradshaw, J.M. (1989). *eQuality* Needs and Alternatives Survey. Seattle, WA: Boeing Computer Services, Computer Science Organization.
20. Daniels, R.M., Dennis, A.R., Hayes, G., Nunamaker, J.F. & Valacich, J. (1991). Enterprise Analyzer: Electronic support for group requirements elicitation. *IEEE* , 43-52.
21. Diaper, D. (1989). Designing expert systems—from Dan to Beersheba. In D. Diaper (Ed.) *Knowledge Elicitation: Principles, Techniques and Applications*. New York: John Wiley.
22. Edwards, J. (1991). *Ptech Overview Presentation*. Westborough, MA: Associative Design Technology.
23. Eisenstadt, M., Domingue, J., Rajan, T. & Motta, E. (1990). Visual knowledge engineering. *IEEE Transactions on Software Engineering*, 16(10), October, 1164-1177.
24. Eliot, L.B. (1991). Playing the top 20. *AI Expert*, 6(7), 11-12.
25. Eshelman, L. (1988). MOLE: A knowledge acquisition tool for cover-and-differentiate systems. In S. Marcus (ed.), *Automating Knowledge Acquisition for Expert Systems*. Boston, Massachusetts: Kluwer Academic Publishers.
26. Ford, K. & Bradshaw, J.M. (Eds.), *Knowledge Acquisition as a Modeling Activity*. New York: John Wiley, volume in preparation.
27. Ford, K., Bradshaw, J.M. , Adams-Webber, J.R. & Agnew, N. (1992). Knowledge acquisition as a constructivist modeling activity. In K. Ford & J. Bradshaw (Eds.), special knowledge acquisition issue of the *International Journal of Intelligent Systems*,

in preparation. Also to appear in K. Ford & J.M. Bradshaw (Eds.), *Knowledge Acquisition as a Modeling Activity*. New York: John Wiley, volume in preparation.

28. Ford, K.M., Stahl, H., Adams-Webber, J.R., Cañas, A.J.., Novak, J. & Jones, J.C. (1991). ICONKAT: An integrated constructivist knowledge acquisition tool. *Knowledge Acquisition Journal*, 3(2), 215-236.
29. Fulton, J.A., Zimmerman, J., Eirich, P., Burkhart, R., Lake, G.F., Law, M.H., Speyer, B. & Tyler, J. (1991). The Semantic Unification Meta-Model: Technical Approach. Report of the Dictionary/Methodology Committee of the IGES/PDES Organization, ISO TC184/SC4. Draft 0.4, September 25, 1991.
30. Gaines, B.R. (1988). Software engineering for knowledge-based systems. *Proceedings of the Second International Workshop on Computer-Aided Software Engineering*.
31. Gaines, B. R. (1989). Design requirements for knowledge support systems, *Proceedings of the Fourth Knowledge Acquisition for Knowledge-Based Systems Workshop*, Banff, October, pp. 12.1-20.
32. Gaines, B. R. (1990a). Knowledge acquisition based on an open-architecture knowledge representation server, *Proceedings of the AAAI-90 Workshop on Knowledge Acquisition: Practical Tools and Techniques*, Boston, July.
33. Gaines, B.R. (1991) Empirical investigation of knowledge representation servers: Design issues and applications experience with KRS. AAAI Spring Symposium: Implemented Knowledge Representation and Reasoning Systems. pp. 87-101. Stanford (March)—also SIGART Bulletin 2(3) 45-56.
34. Gaines, B.R. (1990b). An architecture for integrated knowledge acquisition systems. *Proceedings of the Fifth AAAI-Sponsored Knowledge Acquisition for Knowledge-Based Systems Workshop*, Banff, Canada, November.
35. Gaines, B.R. & Boose, J.H. (1991). Standards requirements, sources, and feasibility in knowledge acquisition.*Working notes of the AAAI Workshop on Standards in Expert Systems*. Anaheim, CA: July 14.
36. Gaines, B.R. & Rappaport, A.T. (1989). The automatic generation of classes, objects and rules at the interface between knowledge acquisition tools and expert system shells. IJCAI-89 Workshop on Knowledge Acquisition: Practical Tools and Techniques, Detroit, Michigan, August 1989.
37. Gaines, B.R. & Shaw, M.L.G. (1986). Interactive elicitation of knowledge from experts. Future Computing Systems, 1(2).
38. Gaines, B.R., Shaw, M.L.G. & Woodward, J.B. (1992). Modeling as a framework for knowledge acquisition methodologies and tools. In K. Ford & J. Bradshaw (Eds.), special knowledge acquisition issue of the *International Journal of Intelligent Systems*, in preparation. Also to appear in K. Ford & J.M. Bradshaw (Eds.), *Knowledge Acquisition as a Modeling Activity*. New York: John Wiley, volume in preparation.
39. Genesereth, M. R. & Fikes, R. (1991). Knowledge Interchange Format Version 2.2 Reference Manual. Logic Group Report, Logic-90-4. Stanford, CA: Stanford University Department of Computer Science, March.
40. Gilnert, E.P. (1990). (Ed.) *Visual Programming Environments: Paradigms and Systems*. Los Alamitos, California: IEEE Computer Society Press.
41. Goldberg, A.T. (1986). Knowledge-based programming: A survey of program design and construction techniques. *IEEE Trans. Software Eng.*, 12, 752-768.
42. Goldberg, A. (1990). Information models, views, and controllers. *Dr. Dobb's Journal*, July, 1-4.
43. Gruber, T.R. (1989). *The Acquisition of Strategic Knowledge*. New York: Academic Press.

44. Gruber, T.R. (1990). Justification-based knowledge acquisition. In H. Motoda, R. Mizoguchi, J. Boose, & B. Gaines (Eds.) *Knowledge Acquisition for Knowledge Based Systems*. Amsterdam: IOS Press.
45. Gruber, T.R. (1991a). The role of common ontology in achieving sharable, reusable knowledge bases. Stanford Knowledge Systems Laboratory Report No. KSL 91-10, February. To appear in J.A. Allen, R. Fikes, and E. Sandewall (Eds.), *Principles of Knowledge Representation and Reasoning: Proceedings of the Second International Conference*. San Mateo, CA: Morgan Kaufmann.
46. Gruber, T. (1991b). Ontolingua: A mechanism to support portable ontologies. Stanford Knowledge Systems Laboratory Technical Report KSL 91-66. Stanford, CA: Stanford University Department of Computer Science.
47. Hammer, M. (1990). Reengineering work: Don't automate, obliterate. *Harvard Business Review*, July-August, 104-112.
48. Hix, D. (1990). Generations of user-interface management systems. *IEEE Software*, September, 77-87.
49. Johnson, N. E. (1989). Mediating representations in knowledge elicitation. In D. Diaper (Ed.) *Knowledge Elicitation: Principles, Techniques and Applications*. New York: John Wiley.
50. Kaplan, A. (1963). *The Conduct of Inquiry*. New York: Harper and Row.
51. Karbach, W., Linster, M. & Voss, A. (1990). A confrontation of models of problem solving. *Knowledge Acquisition Journal*, in press.
52. Kelly, G. A. (1955). *The Psychology of Personal Constructs*. 2 volumes. New York: Norton.
53. Klinker, G. (1989). A framework for knowledge acquisition. *Proceedings of the Third Annual European Knowledge Acquisition Workshop*, Paris, France, July.
54. Krasner, G.E. & Pope, S.T. (1988). A cookbook for using the model-view-controller user interface paradigm in Smalltalk-80. *Journal of Object-Oriented Programming*, August-September, 26-49.
55. Lakin, F. (1990). Visual languages for cooperation: A performing medium approach to systems for cooperative work. In J. Galegher, R.E. Kraut, & C. Egido (Eds.), *Intellectual Teamwork: Social and Technological Foundations of Cooperative Work*. Hillsdale, N.J.: L. Erlbaum.
56. Laland, A., Novotny, R., Enzer, S. & Bortz, J. (1991). *The TIGRE Programming Environment*. Santa Cruz, CA: TIGRE Object Systems.
57. Lenat, D.B. & Guha, R.V. (1990). *Building Large Knowledge-based Systems*. Reading, MA: Addison-Wesley.
58. Lethbridge, T.C. (1991). Creative knowledge acquisition: An analysis. *Proceedings of the 1991 Banff Knowledge Acquisition for Knowledge-Based Systems Workshop*, Banff, Canada, October.
59. Linster, M. & Gaines, B.R. (1990). Supporting acquisition and performance in a hypermedia environment. Presentation at *Terminology and Knowledge Engineering Workshop*, Oct.
60. Linster, M. & Musen, M. (1991). Use of KADS to create a conceptual model of the ONCOCIN task. *Proceedings of the Sixth AAAI Knowledge Acquisition for Knowledge-based Systems Workshop*, Banff, Canada, October.
61. Marcus, S. (1988). SALT: A knowledge acquisition language for propose-and-revise systems. In S. Marcus (ed.), *Automating Knowledge Acquisition for Expert Systems*. Boston, Massachusetts: Kluwer Academic Publishers.
62. Marques, D., Klinker, G., Dallemagne, G., Gautier, P., McDermott, J. & Tung, D. (1991). More data on usable and reusable programming constructs. *Proceedings of the*

Sixth Banff Knowledge Acquisition for Knowledge-Based Systems Workshop. Banff, Canada, October 6-11.

63. McDermott, J., Dallemagne, G., Klinker, G., Marques, D. & Tung, D. (1990). Explorations in how to make application programming easier. In H. Motoda, R. Mizoguchi, J. Boose, & B. Gaines (Eds.) *Knowledge Acquisition for Knowledge Based Systems*. Amsterdam: IOS Press.
64. Moore, E.A. & Agogino, A.M. (1987). INFORM: An architecture for expert-directed knowledge acquisition. *International Journal of Man-Machine Studies*, 26, 213-230.
65. Musen, M. A. (1989). *Automated Generation of Model-Based Knowledge-Acquisition Tools*. San Mateo, CA: Morgan Kaufmann.
66. Neches, R. , Fikes, R., Finin, T., Gruber, T., Patil, R., Senator, T. & Swartout, W.R. (1991). Enabling technology for knowledge sharing.*AI Magazine*, Fall, 36-55.
67. Parnas, D. (1991). The use of formal methods for computer system documentation. Quoted in *Software Maintenance News*, 9(5), May, 29.
68. Puerta, A., Egar, J., Tu, S. & Musen, M. (1991). A multiple-method knowledge-acquisition shell for the automatic generation of knowledge-acquisition tools. Stanford Knowledge Systems Laboratory Report KSL-91-24. *Proceedings of the Sixth Banff Knowledge Acquisition for Knowledge-Based Systems Workshop*, Banff, Canada, 6-11.
69. Puerta, A., Egar, J., Tu, S. & Musen, M. (1992). Modeling tasks with mechanisms. In K. Ford & J. Bradshaw (Eds.), special knowledge acquisition issue of the *International Journal of Intelligent Systems*, in preparation. Also to appear in K. Ford & J.M. Bradshaw (Eds.), *Knowledge Acquisition as a Modeling Activity*. New York: John Wiley, volume in preparation.
70. Rich, C. & Waters, R.C. (1987). Artificial intelligence and software engineering. In W. E. L. Grimson and R.S. Patil (Eds.) *AI in the 1980s and Beyond: An MIT Survey*. Cambridge, MA: The MIT Press.
71. Shema, D.B. & Boose, J.H. (1988). Refining problem-solving knowledge in repertory grids using a consultation mechanism. *International Journal of Man-Machine Studies*, 29, 447-460.
72. Shrontz, F. (1990). Continuous quality improvement. *Manager: A Publication of the Boeing Management Association*, 9(2), March-April, 4-5.
73. Skuce, D. (1991a). A review of 'Building large knowledge based systems' by D. Lenat and R. Guha. *Artificial Intelligence*, in press.
74. Skuce, D. (1991b). A frame-like knowledge acquisition integrating abstract data types and logic. In J. Sowa (Ed.), *Principles of Semantic Networks*. San Mateo, CA: Morgan Kaufmann.
75. Skuce, D. (1991c). A wide spectrum knowledge management system. *Knowledge Acquisition Journal*, in press.
76. Sowa, J.F. (1991). Toward the expressive power of natural language. In J. Sowa (Ed.), Principles of Semantic Networks. San Mateo, CA: Morgan Kaufmann.
77. van Griethusen, J.J. & King, M.H. (Eds.) (1985). Assessment guidelines for conceptual schema language proposals (ISO TC97/SC21/WG5-3), August.
78. Webster, D.E., (1988). Mapping the design information representation terrain. *IEEE Computer Magazine*, December, 8-23.
79. Weimer, W. (1979). *Notes on the Methodology of Scientific Research*. Hillsdale, New Jersey: Erlbaum.
80. Wiederhold, G., Finin, T. & Fritzson, R. (1991). KQML: Partial report on a proposed knowledge acquisition language for intelligent applications, September 6.
81. Wielinga, B.J., Schreiber, A.Th. & Breuker, J.A. (1991). KADS: A modeling approach to knowledge engineering. *Knowledge Acquisition* , in press.

Lecture Notes in Artificial Intelligence (LNAI)

Vol. 383: K. Furukawa, H. Tanaka, T. Fujisaki (Eds.), Logic Programming '88. Proceedings, 1988. IX, 251 pages. 1989.

Vol. 390: J.P. Martins, E.M. Morgado (Eds.), EPIA 89. Proceedings. 1989. XII, 400 pages. 1989.

Vol. 395: M. Schmidt-Schauß, Computational Aspects of an Order-Sorted Logic with Term Declarations. VIII, 171 pages. 1989.

Vol. 397: K.P. Jantke (Ed.), Analogical and Inductive Inference. Proceedings, 1989. IX, 338 pages. 1989.

Vol. 406: C.J. Barter, M.J. Brooks (Eds.), AI '88. Proceedings, 1988. VIII, 463 pages. 1990.

Vol. 418: K.H. Bläsius, U. Hedtstück, C.-R. Rollinger (Eds.), Sorts and Types in Artificial Intelligence. Proceedings, 1989. VIII, 307 pages. 1990.

Vol. 419: K. Weichselberger, S. Pöhlmann, A Methodology for Uncertainty in Knowledge-Based Systems. VIII, 132 pages. 1990.

Vol. 422: B. Nebel, Reasoning and Revision in Hybrid Representation Systems. XII, 270 pages. 1990.

Vol. 437: D. Kumar (Ed.), Current Trends in SNePS – Semantic Network Processing System. Proceedings, 1989. VII, 162 pages. 1990.

Vol. 444: S. Ramani, R. Chandrasekar, K.S.R. Anjaneyulu (Eds.), Knowledge Based Computer Systems. Proceedings, 1989. X, 546 pages. 1990.

Vol. 446: L. Plümer, Termination Proofs for Logic Programs. VIII, 142 pages. 1990.

Vol. 449: M.E. Stickel (Ed.), 10th International Conference on Automated Deduction. Proceedings, 1990. XVI, 688 pages. 1990.

Vol. 451: V. Mařík, O. Stepánková, Z. Zdráhal (Eds.), Artificial Intelligence in Higher Education. Proceedings, 1989. IX, 247 pages. 1990.

Vol. 459: R. Studer (Ed.), Natural Language and Logic. Proceedings, 1989. VII, 252 pages. 1990.

Vol. 462: G. Gottlob, W. Nejdl (Eds.), Expert Systems in Engineering. Proceedings, 1990. IX, 260 pages. 1990.

Vol. 465: A. Fuhrmann, M. Morreau (Eds.), The Logic of Theory Change. Proceedings, 1989. X, 334 pages. 1991.

Vol. 475: P. Schroeder-Heister (Ed.), Extensions of Logic Programming. Proceedings, 1989. VIII, 364 pages. 1991.

Vol. 476: M. Filgueiras, L. Damas, N. Moreira, A.P. Tomás (Eds.), Natural Language Processing. Proceedings, 1990. VII, 253 pages. 1991.

Vol. 478: J. van Eijck (Ed.), Logics in AI. Proceedings. 1990. IX, 562 pages. 1991.

Vol. 481: E. Lang, K.-U. Carstensen, G. Simmons, Modelling Spatial Knowledge on a Linguistic Basis. IX, 138 pages. 1991.

Vol. 482: Y. Kodratoff (Ed.), Machine Learning – EWSL-91. Proceedings, 1991. XI, 537 pages. 1991.

Vol. 513: N. M. Mattos, An Approach to Knowledge Base Management. IX, 247 pages. 1991.

Vol. 515: J. P. Martins, M. Reinfrank (Eds.), Truth Maintenance Systems. Proceedings, 1990. VII, 177 pages. 1991.

Vol. 517: K. Nökel, Temporally Distributed Symptoms in Technical Diagnosis. IX, 164 pages. 1991.

Vol. 518: J. G. Williams, Instantiation Theory. VIII, 133 pages. 1991.

Vol. 522: J. Hertzberg (Ed.), European Workshop on Planning. Proceedings, 1991. VII, 121 pages. 1991.

Vol. 535: P. Jorrand, J. Kelemen (Eds.), Fundamentals of Artificial Intelligence Research. Proceedings, 1991. VIII, 255 pages. 1991.

Vol. 541: P. Barahona, L. Moniz Pereira, A. Porto (Eds.), EPIA '91. Proceedings, 1991. VIII, 292 pages. 1991.

Vol. 542: Z. W. Ras, M. Zemankova (Eds.), Methodologies for Intelligent Systems. Proceedings, 1991. X, 644 pages. 1991.

Vol. 543: J. Dix, K. P. Jantke, P. H. Schmitt (Eds.), Nonmonotonic and Inductive Logic. Proceedings, 1990. X, 243 pages. 1991.

Vol. 546: O. Herzog, C.-R. Rollinger (Eds.), Text Understanding in LILOG. XI, 738 pages. 1991.

Vol. 549: E. Ardizzone, S. Gaglio, F. Sorbello (Eds.), Trends in Artificial Intelligence. Proceedings, 1991. XIV, 479 pages. 1991.

Vol. 565: J. D. Becker, I. Eisele, F. W. Mündemann (Eds.), Parallelism, Learning, Evolution. Proceedings, 1989. VIII, 525 pages. 1991.

Vol. 567: H. Boley, M. M. Richter (Eds.), Processing Declarative Kowledge. Proceedings, 1991. XII, 427 pages. 1991.

Vol. 568: H.-J. Bürckert, A Resolution Principle for a Logic with Restricted Quantifiers. X, 116 pages. 1991.

Vol. 587: R. Dale, E. Hovy, D. Rösner, O. Stock (Eds.), Aspects of Automated Natural Language Generation. Proceedings, 1992. VIII, 311 pages. 1992.

Vol. 590: B. Fronhöfer, G. Wrightson (Eds.), Parallelization in Inference Systems. Proceedings, 1990. VIII, 372 pages. 1992.

Vol. 592: A. Voronkov (Ed.), Logic Programming. Proceedings, 1991. IX, 514 pages. 1992.

Vol. 596: L.-H. Eriksson, L. Hallnäs, P. Schroeder-Heister (Eds.), Extensions of Logic Programming. Proceedings, 1991. VII, 369 pages. 1992.

Vol. 597: H. W. Guesgen, J. Hertzberg, A Perspective of Constraint-Based Reasoning. VIII, 123 pages. 1992.

Vol. 599: Th. Wetter, K.-D. Althoff, J. Boose, B. R. Gaines, M. Linster, F. Schmalhofer (Eds.), Current Developments in Knowledge Acquisition - EKAW '92. Proceedings. XIII, 444 pages. 1992.

Lecture Notes in Computer Science

Vol. 561: C. Ding, G. Xiao, W. Shan, The Stability Theory of Stream Ciphers. IX, 187 pages. 1991.

Vol. 562: R. Breu, Algebraic Specification Techniques in Object Oriented Programming Environments. XI, 228 pages. 1991.

Vol. 563: A. Karshmer, J. Nehmer (Eds.), Operating Systems of the 90s and Beyond. Proceedings, 1991. X, 285 pages. 1991.

Vol. 564: I. Herman, The Use of Projective Geometry in Computer Graphics. VIII, 146 pages. 1991.

Vol. 565: J. D. Becker, I. Eisele, F. W. Mündemann (Eds.), Parallelism, Learning, Evolution. Proceedings, 1989. VIII, 525 pages. 1991. (Subseries LNAI).

Vol. 566: C. Delobel, M. Kifer, Y. Masunaga (Eds.), Deductive and Object-Oriented Databases. Proceedings, 1991. XV, 581 pages. 1991.

Vol. 567: H. Boley, M. M. Richter (Eds.), Processing Declarative Kowledge. Proceedings, 1991. XII, 427 pages. 1991. (Subseries LNAI).

Vol. 568: H.-J. Bürckert, A Resolution Principle for a Logic with Restricted Quantifiers. X, 116 pages. 1991. (Subseries LNAI).

Vol. 569: A. Beaumont, G. Gupta (Eds.), Parallel Execution of Logic Programs. Proceedings, 1991. VII, 195 pages. 1991.

Vol. 570: R. Berghammer, G. Schmidt (Eds.), Graph-Theoretic Concepts in Computer Science. Proceedings, 1991. VIII, 253 pages. 1992.

Vol. 571: J. Vytopil (Ed.), Formal Techniques in Real-Time and Fault-Tolerant Systems. Proceedings, 1992. IX, 620 pages. 1991.

Vol. 572: K. U. Schulz (Ed.), Word Equations and Related Topics. Proceedings, 1990. VII, 256 pages. 1992.

Vol. 573: G. Cohen, S. N. Litsyn, A. Lobstein, G. Zémor (Eds.), Algebraic Coding. Proceedings, 1991. X, 158 pages. 1992.

Vol. 574: J. P. Banâtre, D. Le Métayer (Eds.), Research Directions in High-Level Parallel Programming Languages. Proceedings, 1991. VIII, 387 pages. 1992.

Vol. 575: K. G. Larsen, A. Skou (Eds.), Computer Aided Verification. Proceedings, 1991. X, 487 pages. 1992.

Vol. 576: J. Feigenbaum (Ed.), Advances in Cryptology - CRYPTO '91. Proceedings. X, 485 pages. 1992.

Vol. 577: A. Finkel, M. Jantzen (Eds.), STACS 92. Proceedings, 1992. XIV, 621 pages. 1992.

Vol. 578: Th. Beth, M. Frisch, G. J. Simmons (Eds.), Public-Key Cryptography: State of the Art and Future Directions. XI, 97 pages. 1992.

Vol. 579: S. Toueg, P. G. Spirakis, L. Kirousis (Eds.), Distributed Algorithms. Proceedings, 1991. X, 319 pages. 1992.

Vol. 580: A. Pirotte, C. Delobel, G. Gottlob (Eds.), Advances in Database Technology – EDBT '92. Proceedings. XII, 551 pages. 1992.

Vol. 581: J.-C. Raoult (Ed.), CAAP '92. Proceedings. VIII, 361 pages. 1992.

Vol. 582: B. Krieg-Brückner (Ed.), ESOP '92. Proceedings. VIII, 491 pages. 1992.

Vol. 583: I. Simon (Ed.), LATIN '92. Proceedings. IX, 545 pages. 1992.

Vol. 584: R. E. Zippel (Ed.), Computer Algebra and Parallelism. Proceedings, 1990. IX, 114 pages. 1992.

Vol. 585: F. Pichler, R. Moreno Díaz (Eds.), Computer Aided System Theory – EUROCAST '91. Proceedings. X, 761 pages. 1992.

Vol. 586: A. Cheese, Parallel Execution of Parlog. IX, 184 pages. 1992.

Vol. 587: R. Dale, E. Hovy, D. Rösner, O. Stock (Eds.), Aspects of Automated Natural Language Generation. Proceedings, 1992. VIII, 311 pages. 1992. (Subseries LNAI).

Vol. 588: G. Sandini (Ed.), Computer Vision – ECCV '92. Proceedings. XV, 909 pages. 1992.

Vol. 589: U. Banerjee, D. Gelernter, A. Nicolau, D. Padua (Eds.) Languages and Compilers for Parallel Computing. Proceedings 1991. IX, 419 pages. 1992.

Vol. 590: B. Fronhöfer, G. Wrightson (Eds.), Parallelization in Inference Systems. Proceedings, 1990. VIII, 372 pages. 1992 (Subseries LNAI).

Vol. 591: H. P. Zima (Ed.), Parallel Computation. Proceedings 1991. IX, 451 pages. 1992.

Vol. 592: A. Voronkov (Ed.), Logic Programming. Proceedings, 1991. IX, 514 pages. 1992. (Subseries LNAI).

Vol. 593: P. Loucopoulos (Ed.), Advanced Information Systems Engineering. Proceedings. XI, 650 pages. 1992.

Vol. 594: B. Monien, Th. Ottmann (Eds.), Data Structures an Efficient Algorithms. VIII, 389 pages. 1992.

Vol. 595: M. Levene, The Nested Universal Relation Databas Model. X, 177 pages. 1992.

Vol. 596: L.-H. Eriksson, L. Hallnäs, P. Schroeder-Heiste (Eds.), Extensions of Logic Programming. Proceedings, 199 VII, 369 pages. 1992. (Subseries LNAI).

Vol. 597: H. W. Guesgen, J. Hertzberg, A Perspective of Con straint-Based Reasoning. VIII, 123 pages. 1992. (Subserie LNAI).

Vol. 598: S. Brookes, M. Main, A. Melton, M. Mislove, I Schmidt (Eds.), Mathematical Foundations of Programmin Semantics. Proceedings, 1991. VIII, 506 pages. 1992.

Vol. 599: Th. Wetter, K.-D. Althoff, J. Boose, B. R. Gaines, M Linster, F. Schmalhofer (Eds.), Current Developments Knowledge Acquisition - EKAW '92. Proceedings. XIII, 44 pages. 1992. (Subseries LNAI).